DSGE MODELS IN MACROECONOMICS: ESTIMATION, EVALUATION, AND NEW DEVELOPMENTS

ADVANCES IN ECONOMETRICS

Series Editors: Thomas B. Fomby, R. Carter Hill, Ivan Jeliazkov, Juan Carlos Escanciano and Eric Hillebrand

Recent Volumes:

Volume 20A: Econometric Analysis of Financial and Economic Time Series – Edited by Dek Terrell and Thomas B. Fomby

Volume 20B: Econometric Analysis of Financial and Economic Time Series – Edited by Dek Terrell and Thomas B. Fomby

Volume 21: Modelling and Evaluating Treatment Effects in Econometrics – Edited by Daniel L. Millimet, Jeffrey A. Smith and Edward Vytlacil

Volume 22: Econometrics and Risk Management – Edited by Jean-Pierre Fouque, Thomas B. Fomby and Knut Solna

Volume 23: Bayesian Econometrics – Edited by Siddhartha Chib, Gary Koop, Bill Griffiths and Dek Terrell

Volume 24: Measurement Error: Consequences, Applications and Solutions – Edited by Jane Binner, David Edgerton and Thomas Elger

Volume 25: Nonparametric Econometric Methods – Edited by Qi Li and Jeffrey S. Racine

Volume 26: Maximum Simulated Likelihood Methods and Applications – Edited by William Greene and R. Carter Hill

Volume 27A: Missing Data Methods: Cross-Sectional Methods and Applications – Edited by David M. Drukker

Volume 27B: Missing Data Methods: Time-Series Methods and Applications – Edited by David M. Drukker

ADVANCES IN ECONOMETRICS   VOLUME 28

DSGE MODELS IN MACROECONOMICS: ESTIMATION, EVALUATION, AND NEW DEVELOPMENTS

EDITED BY

NATHAN BALKE
Southern Methodist University, TX, USA

FABIO CANOVA
Universitat Pompeu Fabra, Barcelona, Spain

FABIO MILANI
University of California – Irvine, CA, USA

MARK A. WYNNE
Federal Reserve Bank of Dallas, TX, USA

Emerald

United Kingdom – North America – Japan
India – Malaysia – China

Emerald Group Publishing Limited
Howard House, Wagon Lane, Bingley BD16 1WA, UK

First edition 2012

Copyright © 2012 Emerald Group Publishing Limited

Reprints and permission service
Contact: permissions@emeraldinsight.com

British Library Cataloguing in Publication Data
A catalogue record for this book is available from the British Library

ISBN: 978-1-78190-305-6
ISSN: 0731-9053 (Series)

ISOQAR certified
Management Systems,
awarded to Emerald for
adherence to Quality
and Environmental
standards ISO 9001:2008
and 14001:2004,
respectively

Certificate Number 1985
ISO 9001
ISO 14001

INVESTOR IN PEOPLE

CONTENTS

LIST OF CONTRIBUTORS   *vii*

INTRODUCTION   *ix*

PART I: MODELING AND ESTIMATION PRACTICE

THE MODELING OF EXPECTATIONS IN
EMPIRICAL DSGE MODELS: A SURVEY
Fabio Milani   *3*

OPTIMAL MONETARY POLICY IN AN ESTIMATED
LOCAL CURRENCY PRICING MODEL
Eiji Okano, Masataka Eguchi, Hiroshi Gunji and   *39*
Tomomi Miyazaki

NEWS, NON-INVERTIBILITY, AND
STRUCTURAL VARS
Eric R. Sims   *81*

BAYESIAN ESTIMATION OF NOEM MODELS:
IDENTIFICATION AND INFERENCE IN
SMALL SAMPLES
Enrique Martínez-García, Diego Vilán and   *137*
Mark A. Wynne

FITTING U.S. TREND INFLATION:
A ROLLING-WINDOW APPROACH
Efrem Castelnuovo   *201*

EXPECTATION FORMATION AND MONETARY
DSGE MODELS: BEYOND THE RATIONAL
EXPECTATIONS PARADIGM
Fabio Milani and Ashish Rajbhandari
                                                                                                            253

PART II: ECONOMETRIC METHODOLOGY

APPROXIMATION PROPERTIES OF LAPLACE-TYPE
ESTIMATORS
Anna Kormilitsina and Denis Nekipelov   *291*

FREQUENCY DOMAIN ANALYSIS OF MEDIUM
SCALE DSGE MODELS WITH APPLICATION TO
SMETS AND WOUTERS (2007)
Denis Tkachenko and Zhongjun Qu   *319*

ON THE ESTIMATION OF DYNAMIC STOCHASTIC
GENERAL EQUILIBRIUM MODELS: AN EMPIRICAL
LIKELIHOOD APPROACH
Sara Riscado   *387*

STRUCTURAL ESTIMATION OF THE
NEW-KEYNESIAN MODEL: A FORMAL TEST
OF BACKWARD- AND FORWARD-LOOKING
BEHAVIOR
Tae-Seok Jang   *421*

LIST OF CONTRIBUTORS

Efrem Castelnuovo   Department of Economics, University of
                             Padova, Padova, Italy

Masataka Eguchi   Faculty of Economics, Keio University,
                             Tokyo, Japan

Hiroshi Gunji   Faculty of Economics and the Institute
                             of Economic Research, Daito Bunka
                             University, Tokyo, Japan

Tae-Seok Jang   Department of Economics, University of
                             Kiel, Kiel, Germany

Anna Kormilitsina   Department of Economics, Southern
                             Methodist University, Dallas, TX, USA

Enrique Martínez-García   Research Department, Federal Reserve
                             Bank of Dallas, Dallas, TX, USA

Fabio Milani   Department of Economics, University of
                             California, Irvine, CA, USA

Tomomi Miyazaki   Faculty of Economics, Toyo University
                             and Institute of Economic Research,
                             Hitotsubashi University, Tokyo, Japan

Denis Nekipelov   Department of Economics, University of
                             California, Berkeley, CA, USA

Eiji Okano   Faculty of Economics, Chiba Keizai
                             University, Chiba, Japan

Zhongjun Qu   Department of Economics, Boston
                             University, Boston, MA, USA

Ashish Rajbhandari   Department of Economics, University of
                             California, Irvine, CA, USA

Sara Riscado   Department of Economics, Universidad
                           Carlos III de Madrid, Madrid, Spain

Eric R. Sims   Department of Economics, University of
                           Notre Dame, Notre Dame, IN, USA;
                           National Bureau of Economic Research,
                           Cambridge, MA, USA; and IFO
                           Institute, Munich, Germany

Denis Tkachenko   Department of Economics, National
                           University of Singapore, Singapore

Diego Vilán   Department of Economics, University of
                           Southern California, Los Angeles, CA,
                           USA

Mark A. Wynne   Research Department, Federal Reserve
                           Bank of Dallas, Dallas, TX, USA

INTRODUCTION

This volume of *Advances in Econometrics* is devoted to dynamic stochastic general equilibrium (DSGE) models, which have gained popularity in both academic and policy circles as a theoretically and methodologically coherent way of analyzing a variety of issues in empirical macroeconomics. The volume is divided into two parts. The first part covers important topics in DSGE modeling and estimation practice, including the modeling and role of expectations, the study of alternative pricing models, the problem of non-invertibility in structural VARs, the possible weak identification in new open economy macro models, and the modeling of trend inflation. The second part is devoted to innovations in econometric methodology. The papers in this section advance new techniques for addressing key theoretical and inferential problems and include discussion and applications of Laplace-type, frequency domain, empirical likelihood, and method of moments estimators.

The volume begins with the article "The Modeling of Expectations in Empirical DSGE Models: A Survey" by Fabio Milani that examines how the literature is moving beyond the rational expectations hypothesis in macroeconomics. Whereas some of the methods employ mere refinements of the information structure but maintain rational expectations, others provide more significant departures from that benchmark. The article discusses the expectation formation process in a variety of structural macroeconomic models, both those assuming rational expectations and extensions that incorporate sunspots, news, sticky information, learning, heuristics, and subjective expectations.

In "Optimal Monetary Policy in an Estimated Local Currency Pricing Model" Eiji Okano, Masataka Eguchi, Hiroshi Gunji, and Tomomi Miyazaki develop two-county DSGE models with local currency pricing and producer currency pricing to analyze fluctuations in inflation and the nominal exchange rate under optimal monetary policy. The models are applied to Japanese and US data and are estimated by Bayesian techniques, revealing that local currency pricing is strongly supported by the data relative to producer currency pricing. The estimates also show that stabilizing consumer price index inflation minimizes welfare costs and is consistent with stabilizing the nominal exchange rate.

The article "News, Non-Invertibility, and Structural VARs" by Eric R. Sims discusses the problem of non-invertibility, which arises when the VAR model implied by the state space representation of a linearized DSGE model fails to perfectly reveal the state variables of that model. This disparity between the VAR innovations and the deep shocks may potentially invalidate structural impulse response analysis. The paper shows, however, that even with non-invertibility, structural VARs may perform reliably. A simulation study based on a medium scale DSGE model with news shocks reveals that structural VAR methods perform well in practice and produce impulse responses that closely correspond to the theoretical responses from the DSGE model and can discriminate among certain underlying specifications. The missing state variable problem underlying the non-invertibility is significantly decreased or even eliminated by conditioning on additional information.

In "Bayesian Estimation of NOEM Models: Identification and Inference in Small Samples" Enrique Martínez-García, Diego Vilán, and Mark A. Wynne provide a detailed examination of the problem of identification and inference in new open economy macro models, given their importance for analyzing monetary policy in open-economy environments. The paper shows that parameter estimation in fully specified models might be hindered by the relatively small sample sizes of typical macroeconomic time series and the possibility of weak structural identification. The paper concludes that models should be tested on simulated data to isolate parameters that may be weakly identified and that the implementation strategy should be carefully documented, as it can have significant impact on the strength of identification of key quantities of interest.

In the article "Fitting U.S. Trend Inflation: A Rolling-Window Approach," Efrem Castelnuovo investigates the role of trend inflation shocks for macroeconomic dynamics in the United States. The paper examines two DSGE models of the business cycle. The inflation target is modeled as a persistent stochastic process and identification of trend inflation shocks is achieved through a recently proposed measure of trend inflation. The paper finds that trend inflation shocks contribute substantially to the volatility of inflation and the policy rate, with the size of that contribution peaking between the mid-1970s and mid-1980s.

Departing from the rational expectations hypothesis in their article "Expectation Formation and Monetary DSGE Models: Beyond the Rational Expectations Paradigm," Fabio Milani and Ashish Rajbhandari study a new Keynesian monetary DSGE model under a variety of alternative expectational assumptions. The article demonstrates that the empirical results are very sensitive to the modeling and that the posterior estimates of the structural parameters and structural disturbances can differ significantly when expectational assumptions are modified. The implication is that the modeling of expectations has important effects on the empirical relevance of the model. The results reveal that the model performs worst under rational expectations, the introduction of news improves the fit, but the best-fitting specifications are those that involve learning. Expectations also have large effects on forecasting – survey expectations, news, and learning tend to improve short-run forecast accuracy, whereas rational expectations dominate over longer horizons.

The second part of the volume begins with the article "Approximation Properties of Laplace-Type Estimators" by Anna Kormilitsina and Denis Nekipelov. Laplace-type estimators deliver a simulation-based alternative to classical extremum estimation and have recently gained popularity in applied research. The article shows that despite the desirable asymptotic properties of Laplace-type estimators, convergence to the extremum of the objective function is not necessarily guaranteed in small samples. The paper, therefore, presents a simple test to verify such convergence. The methods are illustrated by examining a popular macroeconomic DSGE model.

A frequency domain perspective on parameter identification, estimation, and model diagnostics is presented in "Frequency Domain Analysis of Medium Scale DSGE Models with Application to Smets and Wouters (2007)" by Denis Tkachenko and Zhongjun Qu. The authors derive a non-identification curve, which helps reveal the parameters that need to be fixed to obtain local identification. The authors also compare estimates at different frequencies to find markedly different parameter values and impulse responses. Further spectrum comparisons suggest that business cycle frequency methods deliver better estimates of the features that the model is intended to capture. The results suggest that the frequency domain approach, with its ability to handle subsets of frequencies, constitutes a flexible framework for studying medium scale DSGE models.

An empirical likelihood approach to the estimation of DSGE models is employed in the article "On the Estimation of Dynamic Stochastic General Equilibrium Models: An Empirical Likelihood Approach" by Sara Riscado, who argues that moment-based estimators can be a valid alternative to maximum likelihood in this context. Because the empirical likelihood estimator only requires knowledge about the moments of the data generating process, it can easily be exploited in economies that are formulated through a set of moment conditions. The techniques are illustrated in a standard real business cycle model with a constant risk aversion, indivisible labor, and normal technological shocks.

The volume concludes with a paper by Tae-Seok Jang entitled "Structural Estimation of the New-Keynesian Model: A Formal Test of Backward- and Forward-Looking Behavior," which examines the sources of persistence in inflation and output in a structural new-Keynesian model. The paper proposes a formal test of backward- and forward-looking behavior captured through alternative specification of the Phillips and IS curves. Method of moments and maximum likelihood estimators are employed in estimation. The validity of moment conditions and the finite sample properties of estimators are investigated in Monte Carlo experiments and an application to US data is presented.

A research conference for contributors was held on November 4–6, 2012, on the campus of Southern Methodist University in Dallas, Texas. Generous financial support from the Department of Economics at Southern Methodist University, the Federal Reserve Bank of Dallas, and Emerald Publishing Limited is gratefully acknowledged. The views expressed in the articles comprising this volume are those of the authors and do not necessarily represent the views of the aforementioned sponsoring institutions. The volume was edited by four highly regarded macroeconomists – Nathan Balke, Fabio Canova, Fabio Milani, and Mark A. Wynne – whose hard work was instrumental in producing this volume.

Juan Carlos Escanciano
Thomas B. Fomby
R. Carter Hill
Eric Hillebrand
Ivan Jeliazkov
Series Editors

PART I
MODELING AND ESTIMATION PRACTICE

THE MODELING OF EXPECTATIONS IN EMPIRICAL DSGE MODELS: A SURVEY

Fabio Milani

ABSTRACT

This paper surveys the treatment of expectations in estimated Dynamic Stochastic General Equilibrium (DSGE) macroeconomic models.

A recent notable development in the empirical macroeconomics literature has been the rapid growth of papers that build structural models, which include a number of frictions and shocks, and which are confronted with the data using sophisticated full-information econometric approaches, often using Bayesian methods.

A widespread assumption in these estimated models, as in most of the macroeconomic literature in general, is that economic agents' expectations are formed according to the Rational Expectations Hypothesis (REH). Various alternative ways to model the formation of expectations have, however, emerged: some are simple refinements that maintain the REH, but change the information structure along different dimensions, while others imply more significant departures from rational expectations.

I review here the modeling of the expectation formation process and discuss related econometric issues in current structural macroeconomic

DSGE Models in Macroeconomics: Estimation, Evaluation, and New Developments
Advances in Econometrics, Volume 28, 3–38
ISSN: 0731-9053/doi:10.1108/S0731-9053(2012)0000028004

models. The discussion includes benchmark models assuming rational expectations, extensions based on allowing for sunspots, news, sticky information, as well as models that abandon the REH to use learning, heuristics, or subjective expectations.

Keywords: Expectations formation; DSGE models; rational expectations; adaptive learning; survey expectations; New Bayesian Macroeconometrics

JEL classification: C52; D84; E32; E50; E60

INTRODUCTION

How expectations are formed is a central issue in economics. Consumers, for example, need to form expectations about future income, taxes, interest rates, inflation, when taking their consumption and saving decisions, firms need to form expectations about future relative and aggregate prices, future demand conditions and sales, future marginal costs, and so forth, when deciding the current prices of their products and current levels of investment to maximize expected discounted profits, and policymakers need to forecast future inflation and output to set policies and maximize societal welfare. Most other economic decisions are affected in similar ways by expectations about the future.

The importance of expectations for individual decisions translates into a key role of the state of aggregate expectations for outcomes at the macroeconomic level as well. The dynamics of the main variables of interest to macroeconomists, such as output, aggregate consumption, investment, inflation, wages, stock prices, and so forth, depend on expected future values of the same aggregate variables and of other related variables.

Economists have long recognized the special role of expectations and attempted to formally model the expectations formation process. In the earlier stages of economic modeling, expectations were often assumed to be formed in a naïve or static fashion, as simply equal to the past values of the variables to be forecasted (e.g., Kaldor, 1938; Marshall, 1890, in the cobweb model). Subsequent research introduced "adaptive expectations" (first in Fisher, 1911, 1930, then in the seminal works by Cagan, 1956 and Friedman, 1957): expectations depend on previous period's expectations plus an error-correction term, and they can be equivalently written as a distributed lag of past observations, with exponentially declining weights.

Since the work of Lucas (1976) and Sargent and Wallace (1975), however, which expanded on earlier work by Muth (1961), the dominant assumption in macroeconomics and a true building block of macroeconomic theory has been the Rational Expectations Hypothesis (REH). Rational agents in the model form expectations that correspond to the same mathematical conditional expectation implied by the model that the researcher is using. Therefore, expectations are model consistent: agents in the model form expectations that happen to correspond to the true expectations generated by the model itself. In the most typical applications, economic agents are assumed to know the form and solution of the model, they know the parameters describing preferences, technology, constraints, and policy behavior, they know the distributions of exogenous shocks and the relevant parameters describing those distributions. The only source of uncertainty for agents is given by the realizations of the random exogenous shocks, which are unforecastable in advance (agents, instead, have access to the full history of the shocks).

Since Lucas, Sargent, and Wallace's so-called rational expectations revolution, macroeconomic models have almost universally employed the rational expectations assumption.

The quantitative properties of these models have been for a long time evaluated using calibration to match a number of moments and stylized business cycle facts (e.g., Kydland & Prescott, 1982). More empirically oriented work, using techniques more rooted in statistical theory, instead, often reverted to models that imposed only a limited amount of restrictions compared to rational expectations models with stringent cross-equation restrictions (e.g., Vector Autoregression [VAR] studies), or entirely backward-looking non-micro-founded models in which expectations did not play direct roles (e.g., Rudebusch & Svensson, 1999), but which were able to fit macroeconomic time series well.

A technique that revealed useful to estimate equations exploiting the REH was GMM. Hansen (1982) and Hansen and Singleton (1982) show how GMM allows the estimation of nonlinear Rational Expectations (RE) models, using moment conditions derived from the model's Euler equations. Several influential papers use GMM to estimate single equations describing the optimality condition for consumption (e.g., Hall, 1978; Hansen & Singleton, 1983), the evolution of inflation (Galí & Gertler, 1999), or the evolution of U.S. monetary policy over the postwar period (Clarida, Galí & Gertler, 2000). These limited-information estimation approaches exploit only a subset of the restrictions and structure imposed by the REH.

Only more recently, however, the estimation of fully structural models under rational expectations has become common and the relative literature has flourished. The models are usually estimated using full-information methods rather than equation by equation, the rational expectations cross-equation restrictions are thus exploited to full extent, and the estimation is likelihood based. Various papers estimate the models using classical approaches and maximum likelihood estimation (e.g., Ireland, 2004), but the majority of the empirical literature focused on the estimation of structural models now adopts a Bayesian perspective and it exploits MCMC techniques (e.g., Del Negro & Schorfheide, 2011; Fernandez-Villaverde, Guerron, & Rubio-Ramirez, 2010, provide recent reviews).

In this survey, I will review the modeling of the expectations formation process in the latter generation of microfounded macroeconomic models that are taken to the data using full-information methods. I will start with the dominant approach in the literature based on the REH. I will then review the refinements related to the modeling of expectations that have been introduced in the literature, and which conserve the benchmark assumption of rational expectations. The survey then moves on to consider the literatures that deviate from the REH. The deviation may be "small," as under a large part of the adaptive learning literature, or more drastic (e.g., by assuming heuristics).

Moreover, a new direction that seems to have become more frequent in the recent literature is the use of direct expectations data from surveys which, although having being often used to test the REH, hadn't really been exploited in the estimation of structural general equilibrium models until recently.

The main focus of this survey is, therefore, on the conventional and alternative modeling of expectations in dynamic macroeconomic models based on a general equilibrium environment. The survey is interested in empirical work, and specifically in the empirical work that focuses on the estimation of Dynamic Stochastic General Equilibrium (DSGE) models. Theoretical research based on alternative models of expectations is, therefore, with only few exceptions, not mentioned in the survey. Empirical research that has expectations as the main focus, but which is not based on structural DSGE models is also generally excluded from the scopes of the survey. The interests of the author, space, and time constraints in the preparation of the survey for this volume necessarily make it a selective and incomplete survey: given the breadth of the topic and the deep interest that economists have always shown toward the role of expectations, many relevant papers, literatures, modeling approaches, and so forth had to be omitted. The readership of this journal is varied and not necessarily focused on macroeconomics. This survey is, therefore, meant to be accessible to practitioners and readers outside the empirical macroeconomic literature.

The paper is organized as follows. The second section presents a benchmark current-generation DSGE model, which mainly serves to highlight the role of expectations in a state-of-the-art macro setting. The third section turns to the discussion on how expectations are modeled and typically inserted in such DSGE models. The initial focus is on the conventional assumption of rational expectations. The fourth section discusses the estimation of rational expectations DSGE models with particular reference to the context of the New Bayesian Macroeconometrics literature. I discuss advantages and problems with the REH in the fifth section, and move to present refinements, which, however, still maintain the rational expectations environment, in the sixth section. The seventh section discusses departures from rational expectations, with emphasis on models with adaptive learning, which represent the main alternative in the literature. The eighth section presents recent developments, which exploit observed data on expectations in the estimation of models with or without rational expectations. The ninth section concludes.

A PROTOTYPICAL DSGE MODEL

I briefly present a benchmark DSGE model that is used in its many variations in a large part of the current empirical macroeconomic literature. The model is based on Smets and Wouters (2007), who extend the model used in Christiano, Eichenbaum, and Evans (2005), and is reported here (in its loglinearized form) mostly to show the large role that various expectations play on the dynamics of the economy:[1]

$$y_t = c_y c_t + i_y i_t + u_y u_t + \varepsilon_t^g \tag{1}$$

$$c_t = c_1 c_{t-1} + (1 - c_1) E_t c_{t+1} + c_2 (l_t - E_t l_{t+1}) - c_3 (r_t - E_t \pi_{t+1} + \varepsilon_t^b) \tag{2}$$

$$i_t = i_1 i_{t-1} + (1 - i_1) E_t i_{t+1} + i_2 q_t + \varepsilon_t^i \tag{3}$$

$$q_t = q_1 E_t q_{t+1} + (1 - q_1) E_t r_{t+1}^k - (r_t - E_t \pi_{t+1} + \varepsilon_t^b) \tag{4}$$

$$y_t = \Phi_p (\alpha k_t^s + (1 - \alpha) l_t + \varepsilon_t^a) \tag{5}$$

$$k_t^s = k_{t-1} + u_t \tag{6}$$

$$u_t = u_1 r_t^k \tag{7}$$

$$k_t = k_1 k_{t-1} + (1 - k_1)i_t + k_2 \varepsilon_t^i \tag{8}$$

$$\mu_t^p = \alpha(k_t^s - l_t) + \varepsilon_t^a - w_t \tag{9}$$

$$\pi_t = \pi_1 \pi_{t-1} + \pi_2 E_t \pi_{t+1} - \pi_3 \mu_t^p + \varepsilon_t^p \tag{10}$$

$$r_t^k = -(k_t - l_t) + w_t \tag{11}$$

$$\mu_t^w = w_t - \left(\sigma_{;l} l_t + \frac{1}{1 - h/\gamma} \left(c_t - \frac{h}{\gamma} c_{t-1} \right) \right) \tag{12}$$

$$w_t = w_1 w_{t-1} + (1 - w_1) E_t(w_{t+1} + \pi_{t+1}) - w_2 \pi_t + w_3 \pi_{t-1} - w_4 \mu_t^w + \varepsilon_t^w \tag{13}$$

$$r_t = \rho_r r_{t-1} + (1 - \rho_r)[\chi_\pi \pi_t + \chi_y(y_t - y_t^*)] + \chi_{\Delta y}(\Delta y_t - \Delta y_t^*) + \varepsilon_t^r \tag{14}$$

The main building blocks on which the above model is based consist of a basic real business cycle (RBC) model, in which investment decisions, capital accumulation, households' labor supply decisions on how many hours to work, and shocks to total factor productivity play an important role, and of a stylized New Keynesian model, which allows for imperfect competition, nominal rigidities such as price and wage stickiness, and which assumes an interest-rate rule for monetary policy. The model is a successful combination of the two approaches, which is further extended to include features as variable capital utilization, habit formation in consumption, indexation in price and wage setting, and a variety of additional disturbances that help the model in fitting the data.

Eq. (1) gives the economy's aggregate resource constraint. Output y_t is absorbed by consumption c_t, by investment i_t, and by the resources used to vary the capacity utilization rate u_t. The model assumes that government spending is exogenous and captured by the disturbance ε_t^g.

Eq. (2) represents the Euler equation for consumption, where the contemporaneous value for consumption depends on expectations about future consumption, on lagged consumption, on current and expected hours of work l_t, and on the ex-ante real interest rate $(r_t - E_t \pi_{t+1})$. The term ε_t^b indicates a risk-premium shock (an exogenous shock that affects yields on bonds), which is sometimes substituted in the literature by a preference or discount-factor shock, which enters in similar ways (although with switched sign) in the Euler equation.

Eqs. (3) and (4) characterize the dynamics of investment. Current investment is influenced by expectations about future investment, by lagged investment, and by the value of capital stock q_t, which is itself driven by expectations about its future one-period-ahead value, by expectations about the rental rate on capital $E_t r_{t+1}^k$, and by the ex-ante real interest rate. The disturbances ε_t^i and ε_t^b affect the behavior of investment. The first denotes investment-specific technological change, while the second is the same risk-premium shock that also enters the consumption Euler equation and, hence, helps in fitting the comovement of the investment and consumption series.

Eq. (5) is a Cobb–Douglas production function: output is produced using capital services k_t^s and labor hours. Neutral technological progress enters the expression as the exogenous shock ε_t^a. The coefficient Φ_p captures fixed costs in production. Eq. (6) accounts for the possibility to vary the rate of capacity utilization: capital services are a function of the capital utilization rate u_t and of the lagged capital stock k_{t-1}. The degree of capital utilization itself varies as a function of the rental rate of capital, as evidenced by Eq. (7). From Eq. (11), the rental rate of capital is a function of the capital to labor ratio and of the real wage. Capital, net of depreciation, is accumulated according to Eq. (8).

Eqs. (9), (10), (12), and (13) summarize the equilibrium in the goods and labor markets. Inflation π_t is determined as a function of lagged inflation, expected inflation, and the price mark-up μ_t^p, which is equal to the difference between the marginal product of labor ($\alpha(k_t^s - l_t) + \varepsilon_t^a$) and the real wage w_t. The real wage depends on lagged and expected future real wages, on past, current, and expected inflation, and on the wage mark-up μ_t^w, which equals the difference between the real wage and the marginal rate of substitution between consumption and leisure. Inflation and wage dynamics are also affected by the exogenous price and wage markup shocks ε_t^p and ε_t^w (which are obtained by assuming a time-varying elasticity of substitution among differentiated goods).

Finally, Eq. (14) describes a Taylor rule: the monetary authority sets the interest rate r_t in response to changes in inflation and the output gap, defined as the difference between actual output and the level of output that would be achieved in the same economy, but under flexible prices. The policy rate also responds to the growth in the output gap. The term ε_t^r captures random deviations from the systematic policy rule.

The coefficients in the model are mostly composite functions of the "deep" preference and technology parameters, such as the degree of habits in consumption, the elasticities of intertemporal substitution and of labor supply, the Calvo price rigidity coefficients, and so forth.

The model governs the dynamics of 14 endogenous variables. The sources of uncertainty are given by Eq. (7) random shocks: to government spending, risk-premium, investment-specific and neutral technology, price and wage markup, and monetary policy. All exogenous shocks, often with the exception of the monetary policy shock, which is usually assumed to be *i.i.d.*, are assumed to follow AR(1) or ARMA(1,1) processes in the literature.

Seven expectation terms directly enter the model: expectations about future consumption $E_t c_{t+1}$, hours of work $E_t l_{t+1}$, inflation $E_t \pi_{t+1}$, investment $E_t i_{t+1}$, value of capital $E_t q_{t+1}$, rental rate of capital $E_t r^k_{t+1}$, and wages $E_t w_{t+1}$. The expectations are typically modeled as being formed according to the REH. The notation E_t in the model denotes model-consistent rational expectations, that is, the mathematical conditional expectation based on time-t information set and derived from the model (1) to (14) itself.

THE MODELING OF EXPECTATIONS

The quasi totality of papers in the empirical macroeconomics literature that is based on structural general equilibrium models shares one assumption: that expectations by households, firms, policymakers, entrepreneurs, etc., are formed according to REH.

The informational assumptions implicit in the REH – at least in the form in which it is typically used in estimated DSGE models – are quite strong: agents in the economy are assumed to know the values of all the parameters, the correct structural form of the model, the distribution of the shocks, their mean, autocorrelation, and standard deviation, and so forth. The only source of uncertainty for agents remains given by the future realizations of the shocks.[2] It should be mentioned that rational expectation frameworks can be, and have been, extended to limit the amount of knowledge that is attributed to agents. But in those cases, the degree of rationality and capacity to process information that agents are assumed to have may even increase. If agents are assumed to lack knowledge about some of the parameters or about some of the state variables in the system, they are allowed to learn them optimally in a Bayesian fashion. Sometimes, the fully rational learning solution gives rise to behavior that, some argue, is not entirely realistic (e.g., optimal learning in an environment in which the parameters of the economy are not fully known, may imply "experimentation," meaning that it is optimal for decision makers to sometimes take stark decisions only with the scope to speed up their learning process).

Moreover, in the model presented above, but also in more stylized models, expectations of different agents – consumers, firms, and policymakers – matter.

In more complicated environments, such as models that incorporate financial and credit frictions, expectations by entrepreneurs, financial intermediaries, and so forth, would also have to be considered. Under the strong form of the REH outlined above, the expectations of all the different actors are assumed to coincide. Obviously, this might not be true in reality. Mankiw, Reis, and Wolfers (2003) document substantial differences in the inflation forecasts by households and professional forecasters (which exist both within and between groups) and suggest "disagreement," measured by the cross-sectional variation of forecasts at each point in time, as a variable that may matter to understand business cycle dynamics. Policymakers also routinely monitor the expectations of different economic actors: the Swedish Riksbank, for example, publishes in its Monetary Policy Report inflation and other forecasts by households, companies, and money market players. Nontrivial differences emerge among their forecasts as well.[3]

When the interest on rational expectations models started to turn to their consequences for econometric practice, it became common to estimate single equations, typically Euler equations derived from economic agents' optimization, even in nonlinear form, by GMM (e.g., Hansen & Singleton, 1982). The GMM approach allowed researchers to avoid making distributional assumptions about the error terms. Moreover, since estimations were based on a limited information approach, misspecification in parts of the economic system other than the equation being considered, was prevented from contaminating the estimates for the main parameters of interest. On the other hand, limited-information approaches are known to be inefficient compared to full-information counterparts and they refrain from exploiting all the existing cross-equation restrictions that rational expectations imply. Various works (e.g., Lindé, 2005, in the case of the estimation of New Keynesian Phillips curves) also show that limited-information methods may lead to imprecise and biased estimates and are outperformed by full-information approaches when the equations of interest are characterized by both backward-looking and forward-looking behavior.

In recent years, system estimation by full-information methods has become predominant in the empirical macroeconomic literature. The model's equilibrium conditions are often loglinearized as in Eqs. (1)–(14), although estimation approaches based on higher-order approximations or using nonlinear models are possible (the analyses are more complicated, but these cases have been considered in An & Schorfheide, 2007; Fernandez-Villaverde & Rubio-Ramirez, 2007, for example).

Under the benchmark assumption of rational expectations, the model presented in Eqs. (1)–(14), along with the processes for the shocks, or any other model of choice, can be rewritten in state-space form as:

$$\Gamma_0 \xi_t = \Gamma_1 \xi_{t-1} + \Psi \varepsilon_t + \Pi \eta_t \tag{15}$$

where

$$\xi_t = [\Gamma_t, \Xi_t, \varepsilon_t, \tilde{\Gamma}_{t-1}]' \tag{16}$$

$$\Gamma_t = [y_t, c_t, i_t, q_t, l_t, k_t^s, u_t, k_t, \mu_t^p, \pi_t, r_t^k, \mu_t^w, w_t, r_t]' \tag{17}$$

$$\Xi_t = [E_t c_{t+1}, E_t i_{t+1}, E_t q_{t+1}, E_t l_{t+1}, E_t \pi_{t+1}, E_t r_{t+1}^k, E_t w_{t+1}]' \tag{18}$$

$$\varepsilon_t = [\varepsilon_t^g, \varepsilon_t^b, \varepsilon_t^i, \varepsilon_t^a, \varepsilon_t^p, \varepsilon_t^w, \varepsilon_t^r]' \tag{19}$$

$$\tilde{\Gamma}_t = [y_t, c_t, i_t, w_t]' \tag{20}$$

$$\varepsilon_t = [\varepsilon_t^g, \varepsilon_t^b, \varepsilon_t^i, \varepsilon_t^a, \varepsilon_t^p, \varepsilon_t^w, \varepsilon_t^r]' \tag{21}$$

$$\eta_t = [\eta_t^c, \eta_t^i, \eta_t^q, \eta_t^l, \eta_t^\pi, \eta_t^{rk}, \eta_t^w]' \tag{22}$$

where ξ_t denotes the state vector of the system, which includes the model endogenous variables collected in Γ_t, the expectation terms Ξ_t, the structural disturbances ε_t, and a subset of the endogenous variables in lagged terms (since these are typically needed to use growth rates of nonstationary variables in the estimation), and where ε_t includes i.i.d. innovations, and $\eta_t^c = c_t - E_{t-1} c_t$, $\eta_t^i = i_t - E_{t-1} i_t$, and so forth, denote the expectational errors, with the property that $E_t \eta_{t+1} = 0$ for all t's. All the disturbance terms that are not i.i.d. (e.g., shocks that follow an AR(1) process, such as the the technology shock, which evolves as $\varepsilon_t^a = \rho_a \varepsilon_{t-1}^a + \sigma_{;a} \varepsilon_t^a$) are typically included in the vector ε_t in Eq. (19) and they, are, therefore added in the state variable vector ξ_t, while the corresponding i.i.d. innovations (e.g., ε_t^a for the technology shock) or the shocks that are assumed as already i.i.d. in the model enter the vector ε_t in Eq. (21).

The model can then be solved using a variety of techniques (e.g., Blanchard & Kahn, 1980; Uhlig, 1999), for example following the approach by Sims (2000).

This approach is particularly attractive since it makes clear the interpretation of the expectational errors in terms of the structural shocks. Under rational expectations, in fact, the expectational errors are obtained as a function of the structural innovations and, hence, they can be solved out of the model, as made clear in Eq. (24) below. Sims' (2000) approach imposes restrictions on the growth rate of the variables in the vector ξ_t and it implies that a stable unique solution exists if there is a one-to-one mapping between the expectational errors and the structural shocks, which permit to remove the explosive components of ξ_t. The expectational errors are found from

$$\Psi^* \varepsilon_t + \Pi^* \eta_t = 0 \tag{23}$$

where Ψ^* and Π^* are transformed matrices with row vectors corresponding to the unstable eigenvalues in the system. Finally, if the equilibrium exists and is unique, the approach yields the rational expectations solution:

$$\xi_t = F\xi_{t-1} + G\varepsilon_t \tag{24}$$

where only the exogenous shocks ε_t remain as source of randomness in the economy; the elements in the matrices F and G are complicated nonlinear functions of the deep parameters in the original model.

EXPECTATIONS & THE "NEW (BAYESIAN) MACROECONOMETRICS"

The model solution in Eq. (24) can be easily taken to the data. Under the conventional assumption that the shocks are distributed as Normal, and given the linearity of the system, the RE solution can be paired to the observation equation $OBS_t = H_0 + H_1\xi_t$, and the likelihood function can be straightforwardly computed using the Kalman filter.[4]

While the model at this point could be estimated by classical methods, such as maximum likelihood, the dominant approach in the literature is to estimate the model using a Bayesian approach. Only relatively simple models could in fact be estimated by maximum likelihood, unless informative priors (in which case, one would employ a mixed approach by maximizing the posterior probability) or tight constraints on the parameter bounds are assumed.

Hence, the most popular approach in the literature has become the use of a Bayesian approach. The estimation works by generating draws from the posterior distribution, using MCMC (Markov chain Monte Carlo) methods, with the likelihood obtained at each draw through the Kalman filter. In the case of structural DSGE models, the MCMC procedure of choice is usually the random-walk Metropolis–Hastings (MH) algorithm.

A huge literature has appeared in the last ten years using exactly this approach. Various surveys of the literature are now available (e.g.,

An & Schorfheide, 2007; Del Negro & Schorfheide, 2011; Fernandez-Villaverde et al., 2010). Fernandez-Villaverde et al. (2010) propose the term "New Macroeconometrics" to define this recently developed literature. Given the Bayesian focus, this could also be labeled "New Bayesian Macroeconometrics."

In spite of any label, such evolution represents a clear shift from most of the previous macroeconomics literature, since now it is common and also expected to subject theoretical models to system-based estimation and to more stringent empirical tests.

PROBLEMS WITH THE RATIONAL
EXPECTATIONS HYPOTHESIS

The hypothesis of rational expectations carries a number of advantages. It is elegant and it leads to internally coherent theories: by construction, expectations by agents in the model are, on average, confirmed by the outcomes of the model. It solves obvious problems faced by previous static or adaptive expectation models: under those precursors, agents in the economy would make systematic forecast errors. Systematic forecast errors are instead prevented by the REH.

From a modeling point of view, rational expectations are particularly appealing because they remove all the parameters and degrees of freedom that may otherwise characterize the equations for expectations. Under the REH, modelers cannot arbitrarily vary expectations to fit different facts, since expectations are univocally determined by the model at hand.

But rational expectations have drawbacks too. It is well known that models with rational expectations, at least in their simplest form, typically fail to match the persistence of macroeconomic variables.[5] As a result, the models need to be extended to include, in addition to several highly autocorrelated exogenous shocks, various so-called "mechanical" sources of endogenous persistence.

Many have now become ubiquitous. First, the form of the households' utility function has changed. Households are assumed to derive utility not only from their current and future levels of consumption, but from the deviation of consumption from a stock of habits, either driven by the consumption level of their neighbors (through "catching up" or "keeping up" with the Joneses effects, both proxied by the level of aggregate consumption in the economy, although with different timing assumptions) or corresponding to their own consumption level in the previous period. The utility function is definitely plausible, but it still remains unclear whether microeconomic data are actually supportive of the existence of habit formation in consumption or not (e.g., Dynan, 2000, uses consumption data from the Panel Study of Income Dynamics and she fails to find evidence of habit formation at the individual level).

In addition, it is now standard to assume variable capital utilization and adjustment costs of investment or capital in the real side of the model. These modifications have a long history: variable capital utilization is necessary to obtain more realistic estimates of the Solow residual; investment adjustment costs are essential to match the sluggish response of investment to shocks; without those, the model responses would be highly unrealistic.

Other assumptions that are routinely added in the models concern indexation to past inflation in price and wage-setting decisions. Indexation implies that firms that are not allowed to reoptimize their prices or wage contracts in a given period, still change them to at least reflect increases in last period's aggregate inflation rate. These admittedly ad hoc indexation rules have been disproved many times: various studies have shown that they are inconsistent with the microeconomic evidence on price setting (e.g., Altissimo, Ehrmann, & Smets, 2006; Nakamura & Steinsson, 2008). It can certainly be argued that they are hardly structural and hence subject to the Lucas critique; nonetheless, they remain present in most macroeconomic models.

Another concern with estimated rational expectations models concerns the identification of structural parameters. Various papers (e.g., Beyer & Farmer, 2004; Canova & Sala, 2009) demonstrate that rational expectations models suffer from non-identification or weak identification of many crucial parameters. In the empirical DSGE literature, often the priors are not updated and end up overlapping with the posterior distributions for subset of parameters. It is well known that non-identification of some parameters does not create problems for the estimation of the model in a Bayesian context (Poirier, 1998). But a reading of the literature shows that this often happens for parameters as the Taylor rule response coefficients to inflation and output gap, which are key parameters for monetary business cycle models and also largely control the determinacy properties of the system equilibrium. Here, it is worth pointing out, however, that many identification problems may still remain under alternative approaches that deviate from rational expectations.

The main problem, however, with the REH would be if the modeling of expectations was grossly misspecified, not only at the individual, but also at the aggregate level, and if the main conclusions were widely sensitive to even small deviations from the benchmark rational expectations assumption.

Most tests in the literature are, in fact, implicitly joint tests of the model or theory at hand and of the associated REH. This is true for tests of the permanent income/life cycle hypothesis, tests of asset pricing equations, exchange rate models, Phillips curve specifications, and so forth. Misspecification in the modeling of expectations may lead to rejection of potentially valid theories and it may lead researchers to the use of models that would potentially be discarded under a different modeling of expectations (as an indicative example, nonrational expectations may allow standard theories to explain consumption and asset price behavior without recurring to new features as habit formation).

Amid recent trends in the literature toward progressively more sophisticated and comprehensive macroeconomic models, the rational expectations assumption is likely to become even stronger and its informational requirements even more stringent as the dimension and complexity of the models increase. In the three-equation New Keynesian model or in a basic RBC model à la Hansen (1985), the assumption of rational expectations may be a valid approximation. The model solution under rational expectations for the three-equation New Keynesian model, for example, resembles many VARs (with a similar set of variables) that have been estimated to identify the effects of monetary policy shocks and which are known to fit the data quite well. But in a medium-scale model à la Smets and Wouters, or its many extensions, agents under rational expectations are assumed to know a large number of coefficients, use a substantial number of state variables, and observe several disturbances, some of them not necessarily with simple interpretations, to form their expectations. Their implicit forecasting models, given by Eq. (24), in fact, easily contain more than a dozen regressors. The problem becomes even more serious in larger-scale models, and when the model includes additional variables, such as financial variables, as stock prices, exchange rates, and so forth, in which departures from rational expectations may be more pronounced. Misspecification in the formation of expectations anywhere in the large-scale model will unfortunately bias the rest of the coefficients.

Recently, structural rational expectations models have been also extended to include features such as regime switches in the coefficients at unknown times, time-varying structural coefficients, time-varying volatilities of the shocks, and so forth. Again maintaining the REH in those contexts may prove too stringent.

The paper by Milani and Rajbhandari (2012a), in this same issue, for example, highlights the sensitivity of the econometric properties of even a stylized benchmark New Keynesian model to the way expectations are modeled, with mechanisms ranging from rational expectations (with and without news) to non-fully rational learning and subjective expectations. The results seem to suggest, at a minimum, a need in the literature for more checks of the results' sensitivity to alternative expectation formation schemes.

Future changes in the literature concerning the REH may be even deeper. Woodford (2011), in a nontechnical interview on the methodology of macroeconomic theory, criticizes the postulate of rational expectations, based on internal consistency with the only existent model of the economy assumed by the researcher, and he goes on to predict that "The macro-economics of the future, I believe, will still make use of general-equilibrium models in which the behavior of households and firms is derived from considerations of intertemporal optimality, but in which the optimization is relative to the evolving beliefs of those actors about the future, which need not perfectly coincide with the predictions of the economist's model. ... But it will have to go beyond conventional late-twentieth-century methodology as well, by making the formation and revision of expectations an object of analysis in its own right, rather than treating this as something that should already be uniquely determined once the other elements of an economic model (specifications of preferences, technology, market structure, and government policies) have been settled."

REFINEMENTS OF RATIONAL EXPECTATION MODELS

We discuss here several extensions that maintain the REH intact, but that either assign a bigger role to fluctuations driven by expectational shifts (sunspots, news) or relax the informational assumptions to make the models more empirically realistic (imperfect knowledge, sticky information).

Sunspots

The empirical rational expectations DSGE literature typically imposes a dogmatic prior on the existence of multiple equilibria: the case of multiple equilibria receives a zero prior probability. Regions of indeterminacy are usually ruled out first by assuming priors on the parameters that ensure that, in the mixing, parameter draws only rarely imply the possibility of indeterminacy (e.g., by assuming a prior on the Taylor rule response coefficient toward inflation that assigns either zero or low probability to values below one). In addition, every time a MH draw includes a combination of parameters that implies indeterminacy, the draw is rejected, and the chain is asked to generate a new draw. This procedure corresponds to imposing a dogmatic zero-probability prior on indeterminacy regions.

The determinacy or indeterminacy of the equilibrium in the model presented in the second section largely depends on a version of the Taylor principle similar to the one obtained in more stylized three-equation New Keynesian models. When the Taylor principle is not satisfied, for example because the central bank fails to respond aggressively enough to variation in inflation, expectations become a function of an external source of fluctuations, unrelated to fundamentals, and labeled a "sunspot" in the literature. Sunspots induce self-fulfilling fluctuations in the economy.

We have seen before that if a solution exists and is unique, the expectational errors η_t can be expressed as a function of the structural shocks ε_t only. In the presence of indeterminacy, this is no longer true. In the full set of solutions, the expectational errors become a function of both the structural exogenous shocks (although with different coefficients) and of the sunspot shocks.

Lubik and Schorfheide (2003) show that linear rational expectations models can be written in the more general form in which multiple solutions may exist as

$$\Gamma_0 \xi_t = \Gamma_1 \xi_{t-1} + \Psi \varepsilon_t + \Pi \eta_t \tag{25}$$

$$\eta_t = A_1 \tilde{\eta}_t + A_2 \zeta_t \tag{26}$$

$$\tilde{\eta}_t = B_1 \varepsilon_t + B_2 \zeta_t \tag{27}$$

where A_1, A_2, B_1, B_2 are matrices of coefficients and, as discussed, expectational errors can now be solved as a function of fundamental and sunspot innovations:

$$\eta_t = C_1 \varepsilon_t + C_2 \zeta_t \tag{28}$$

Indeterminacy affects both the dependence of expectational errors on fundamental shocks (through C_1 being different from the corresponding matrix of coefficients under determinacy) and on nonfundamental sunspot shocks (which now have an effect on forecast errors).

As Lubik and Schorfheide (2004) show, the solution of the DSGE model under rational expectations can now be written as

$$\xi_t = F \xi_{t-1} + (G + \Delta) \varepsilon_t + \Lambda \zeta_t \tag{29}$$

Under determinacy, $\Delta = 0$ and $\Lambda = 0$. Indeterminacy, therefore, has two effects: it changes the propagation of structural shocks ε_t, which is no longer uniquely pinned down in the model, and it leads to self-fulfilling fluctuations in the state variables ξ_t driven by the sunspot shocks ζ_t.

The literature on indeterminacy and sunspots in macroeconomics has been predominantly theoretical (e.g., Benhabib & Farmer, 1999). The main interest was to show that multiple equilibria and sunspots significantly improve the endogenous propagation properties of business cycle models, which are severely lacking under determinacy.

But recently, a number of papers have hinted at the possibility that indeterminacy, typically caused by the monetary policymaker's failure to satisfy the Taylor principle in New Keynesian-style models, has been an empirically realistic feature of the U.S. economy, at least over portions of the post-World War II period. Clarida et al. (2000) use a limited-information single-equation estimation to find that Federal Reserve's policy did not respect the Taylor principle in the pre-Volcker (pre-1979) sample: such a monetary policy rule, if inserted in a structural New Keynesian model, would have been a source of macroeconomic instability due to indeterminacy and sunspot-driven fluctuations. Lubik and Schorfheide (2004) use a Bayesian estimation of the full system of equations in the New Keynesian model and they extend the typical likelihood-based estimation approaches used for DSGE models to allow for positive probabilities on regions of indeterminacy. Their paper represents a major step forward in the empirical literature, since it avoids imposing dogmatic priors on the probabilities of indeterminacy versus determinacy. Their empirical results end up being in line with Clarida et al.'s conclusions. The parameter estimates and posterior model probabilities indicate that the Fed moved from a monetary policy behavior that failed to satisfy the Taylor principle during the pre-1979 period to a more aggressive policy that satisfied the Taylor principle in the post-1982 period. The model achieves highest posterior probability under indeterminacy in the first subsample, while determinacy allows to fit the data better in the second subsample. Treadwell (2010) finds similar results using data for the remaining countries in the G-7 over the post-war sample. Hirose (2008) estimates a financial accelerator model on Japanese data and he also shows that indeterminacy and sunspots are supported by the data.

Overall, indeterminacy may allow rational expectations models to fit macro data without resorting to various frictions, since they do a good job in endogenously generating persistence. They are also useful in breaking down the tight link between forecast errors under rational expectations and

structural innovations, which may allow the model more degrees of freedom
to fit the data.

Given the continuing predominance in the literature of papers that
rule out the existence of indeterminacy, it is worth wondering whether
there are instances in which the empirical conclusions would change if
researchers departed from dogmatic priors on the probabilities of determinacy and indeterminacy. It seems that the evidence in medium-scale
models as Smets and Wouters (2007) is not particularly supportive toward
indeterminacy, but this may not be true in the more complicated models
that add a number of additional frictions, especially regarding banking
sectors or financial markets, as the evidence in Hirose (2008) appears to
suggest.

News

One recent important direction in the business cycle literature has been the
introduction of "news." Typically, the DSGE literature assumes that shocks
are entirely unanticipated by agents until they are realized and, therefore,
observed. The literature on news changes the information structure in the
models: agents can now receive news in some period t about future shocks
that will materialize only h periods ahead. Disturbances, therefore, include
both unanticipated and anticipated components. News can be fully realized
h periods later or they can fail to materialize, leading to revisions in
expectations. News models are particularly attractive since such downward
revisions in expectations may lead to volatility in the economy and create
recessions: RBC models that allow for news, therefore, do not necessarily
need volatile and often negative technology shocks to explain business cycles
and recessions.

Beaudry and Portier (2006), in a very influential paper, provide empirical
evidence from VAR models that an identified shock that does not affect
total factor productivity in the long run, but that is almost perfectly
correlated with the tfp shock (which does affect the economy in the long
run), is an important driver of business cycle fluctuations. Motivated by
their finding that this is a short-run shock, although correlated with long-
run tfp, they interpret it as "news" about future technology.

A major drawback of early models with news is that they fail to match
the comovement of the main business cycle variables in response to news
shocks. Jaimovich and Rebelo (2009) advance the theory on news shocks

by proposing a solution to the comovement problem: they show that a basic RBC model, if extended to include variable capital utilization, adjustment costs in investment, and a modified utility function with preferences that shut down the short-run wealth effect on labor supply, can match the business cycle comovement of output, consumption, investment, and hours, following a positive news shock about technology. The dynamics of business cycle models with news, issues in the literature, and proposed solutions, are clearly laid down in the survey by Lorenzoni (2011).

The previous works and a large part of the original literature on news focused on relatively stylized RBC models and almost exclusively on news about technology (Lorenzoni, 2009, is an exception considering news related to demand). But, more recently, news shocks have been inserted in larger scale DSGE models, under both flexible and sticky prices and wages, and with news that may refer to different types of shocks. Schmitt-Grohé and Uribe (2012) model news and insert it in a medium-scale DSGE model with flexible prices, but augmented to include habit formation in consumption, habit formation in leisure, investment adjustment costs, variable capacity utilization, and, in some specifications, preferences as in Jaimovich and Rebelo (2009). They allow permanent and transitory technology shocks, permanent and transitory investment-specific shocks, transitory government spending shocks, wage markup shocks, and preference shocks; each shock includes both an unanticipated and an anticipated (news) component.

In their model, each structural disturbance is assumed to evolve as:

$$\varepsilon_t = \rho \varepsilon_{t-1} + \varepsilon_t^0 + \varepsilon_{t-4}^4 + \varepsilon_{t-8}^8 \tag{30}$$

where ε_t^0 denotes a typical unanticipated innovation, while ε_{t-h}^h denotes news shocks that are known at time $t - h$ and materialize only h periods ahead. The horizon of news may clearly vary: they choose to focus only on news for four and eight quarters ahead in their paper, which should already include relevant anticipations at least for medium-term horizons (different horizon structures were also used in earlier versions of their work). An obvious way to select the relevant news horizons would be in terms of model fit: this is the approach followed in Fujiwara, Hirose, and Shintani (2011) and Milani and Treadwell (2012), who use Bayesian model comparison tools to verify the fit of a wide set of horizon combinations and to select "optimal," or best-fitting, horizons.

The state-space system significantly expands with the addition of news. For each disturbance, the corresponding portion of the state space can be written as:

$$
\begin{bmatrix} \varepsilon_t \\ \varepsilon_t^4 \\ \varepsilon_{t-1}^4 \\ \varepsilon_{t-2}^4 \\ \varepsilon_{t-3}^4 \\ \varepsilon_t^8 \\ \varepsilon_{t-1}^8 \\ \varepsilon_{t-2}^8 \\ \varepsilon_{t-3}^8 \\ \varepsilon_{t-4}^8 \\ \varepsilon_{t-5}^8 \\ \varepsilon_{t-6}^8 \\ \varepsilon_{t-7}^8 \end{bmatrix}
=
\begin{bmatrix}
\rho & 0 & 0 & 0 & 1 & 0 & 0 & 0 & 0 & 0 & 0 & 0 & 1 \\
0 & 0 & 0 & 0 & 0 & 0 & 0 & 0 & 0 & 0 & 0 & 0 & 0 \\
0 & 1 & 0 & 0 & 0 & 0 & 0 & 0 & 0 & 0 & 0 & 0 & 0 \\
0 & 0 & 1 & 0 & 0 & 0 & 0 & 0 & 0 & 0 & 0 & 0 & 0 \\
0 & 0 & 0 & 1 & 0 & 0 & 0 & 0 & 0 & 0 & 0 & 0 & 0 \\
0 & 0 & 0 & 0 & 0 & 0 & 0 & 0 & 0 & 0 & 0 & 0 & 0 \\
0 & 0 & 0 & 0 & 0 & 1 & 0 & 0 & 0 & 0 & 0 & 0 & 0 \\
0 & 0 & 0 & 0 & 0 & 0 & 1 & 0 & 0 & 0 & 0 & 0 & 0 \\
0 & 0 & 0 & 0 & 0 & 0 & 0 & 1 & 0 & 0 & 0 & 0 & 0 \\
0 & 0 & 0 & 0 & 0 & 0 & 0 & 0 & 1 & 0 & 0 & 0 & 0 \\
0 & 0 & 0 & 0 & 0 & 0 & 0 & 0 & 0 & 1 & 0 & 0 & 0 \\
0 & 0 & 0 & 0 & 0 & 0 & 0 & 0 & 0 & 0 & 1 & 0 & 0 \\
0 & 0 & 0 & 0 & 0 & 0 & 0 & 0 & 0 & 0 & 0 & 1 & 0
\end{bmatrix}
\begin{bmatrix} \varepsilon_{t-1} \\ \varepsilon_{t-1}^4 \\ \varepsilon_{t-2}^4 \\ \varepsilon_{t-3}^4 \\ \varepsilon_{t-4}^4 \\ \varepsilon_{t-1}^8 \\ \varepsilon_{t-2}^8 \\ \varepsilon_{t-3}^8 \\ \varepsilon_{t-4}^8 \\ \varepsilon_{t-5}^8 \\ \varepsilon_{t-6}^8 \\ \varepsilon_{t-7}^8 \\ \varepsilon_{t-8}^8 \end{bmatrix}
+
\begin{bmatrix}
\sigma_{;0} & 0 & 0 \\
0 & \sigma_{;4} & 0 \\
0 & 0 & 0 \\
0 & 0 & 0 \\
0 & 0 & 0 \\
0 & 0 & \sigma_{;8} \\
0 & 0 & 0 \\
0 & 0 & 0 \\
0 & 0 & 0 \\
0 & 0 & 0 \\
0 & 0 & 0 \\
0 & 0 & 0 \\
0 & 0 & 0
\end{bmatrix}
\begin{bmatrix} \tilde{\varepsilon}_t^0 \\ \tilde{\varepsilon}_t^4 \\ \tilde{\varepsilon}_t^8 \end{bmatrix}
$$

$$(31)$$

where $\tilde{\varepsilon}_t^h$ simply redefines the corresponding ε_t^h innovation, and the $\sigma_{;h}$ coefficients denote standard deviations.

Schmitt-Grohé and Uribe estimate the model using Bayesian methods. They also show a simulation exercise on artificial data to show that the standard deviation of news shocks are identified even under non-informative priors. News can therefore be disentangled from unanticipated shocks in the estimation. The identification of news, in particular, derives from the different impact that surprise and news shocks have on expectations of future macroeconomic variables, which need to be taken into account in most agents' optimization decisions. Unanticipated shocks are unforecastable and do not affect expectations. News, on the other hand, can be identified through their effect on future expectations. For example, expectations about future innovations can be expressed as:

$$
E_t \varepsilon_{t+h} = \begin{cases} \varepsilon_{t+h-4}^4 + \varepsilon_{t+h-8}^8 & 1 \leq h \leq 4 \\ \varepsilon_{t+h-8}^8 & 4 < h \leq 8 \\ 0 & h > 8 \end{cases}
\tag{32}
$$

The model can then be solved under rational expectations to find a solution as Eq. (24).

Schmitt-Grohé and Uribe find that a variety of news shocks combine to explain about half of output and other real variable fluctuations over the business cycle.

Similar approaches to introduce news are also followed in the paper by Fujiwara, Hirose, and Shintani (2011) and Khan and Tsoukalas (2011). The results in their cases are less supportive toward the so-called "news view" of the business cycle than those obtained in the previous paper. They both estimate medium-scale DSGE models with sticky prices, sticky wages (whereas Schmitt-Grohé and Uribe's paper focused on a flexible-price specification in the RBC tradition), à la Smets and Wouters (2007). It is certainly worth investigating in more detail in future research to what extent different model features affect the estimated impact of news shocks and the reasons behind the differences. Barsky and Sims (2009) are also more critical toward the news literature by finding that news shocks fail to explain most of the recent U.S. recessions, although using a VAR, rather than a fully fledged DSGE, model.

Various other papers have now studied the empirical role of news on macroeconomic outcomes. Milani and Treadwell (2012) allow for both unanticipated ("surprise") and anticipated ("news") components in monetary policy shocks, which are not considered in the other papers. News about monetary policy seems natural given the effort by policy makers to manage private-sector expectations, central banks' emphasis on policy announcements, transparency, and communication, and the effort by the private sector to anticipate future policy decisions. They find that news plays a larger role than monetary policy surprises on the variability of output and that the introduction of news changes the shape of impulse responses to monetary policy shocks: output is shown to respond less and more quickly to unanticipated policy shocks than typically found in the literature. The response to anticipated policy changes is, instead, larger and more persistent. Avdjiev (2011) illustrates how adding data on asset prices changes many of the empirical conclusions in estimated DSGE models with news-driven fluctuations. News shocks are now considered also in less traditional frameworks, moving away from news only about technology: Gomes and Mendicino (2011), for example, consider news related to the housing market and show that news accounts for a large fraction of house price variation.

The literature on introducing news in DSGE models is still young and rapidly expanding. A number of new papers are adding them in a variety of frameworks. The jury is still out on whether news represents a major source of economic fluctuations or not.

Limitations on Knowledge

The treatment of rational expectations has so far assumed full knowledge by economic agents. Although this is by far the most common case, the literature has recognized that limitations on the degree of knowledge can add elements of realism to the models, while remaining within the realm of rational expectations.

Among others, we point out the work by Schorfheide (2005), who allows for imperfect knowledge about the monetary authority's inflation target, by modeling agents that need to learn about its fluctuating value over time. While the model with perfect information still fits the data better, the limited information model better captures important episodes as the disinflation experience in the early 1980s.

Levine, Pearlman, Perendia, and Yang (2010) recognize that agents may not have full information about all the state variables in the system and about the disturbances hitting the economy. They build and estimate a model in which agents need to solve real-time filtering problems in order to infer the values of the state variables and shocks. Their approach breaks the asymmetry between information available to the econometrician, who uses only few observables in the estimation, and the economic agents in the model, who, typically, under rational expectations, dispose of much wider information sets. They show that the model with imperfect information creates endogenous realistic degrees of persistence, which allow it to fit the data well without standard mechanisms as habit formation and indexation.

Although more complicated, models in this spirit, which imply symmetric information between agents in the model and econometrician while retaining the REH, are clearly a promising avenue for future empirical research.

Sticky Information

Another popular alternative to extend the modeling of expectations, while keeping the benchmark REH, is through the assumption of sticky information. In the simplest specification, agents are assumed to update their information only with some probability λ in each period. On average, therefore, they update their information sets only once every $1/(1 - \lambda)$

periods. Mankiw and Reis (2002) introduce the sticky-information Phillips curve, based on the above-mentioned Calvo-style updating scheme for information. Reis, however, in a set of papers (e.g., 2006a, 2006b) provides deeper microfoundations for models with sticky information.

Turning to the empirical literature, several papers are interested in comparing models including inflation equations based on sticky prices with those based on sticky information. In particular, sticky-information alternatives are considered in the literature for their role in generating persistence in inflation that can match the persistence in actual data. In this survey, however, we are more interested in the empirical evidence regarding DSGE models, rather than that based on single equations.

Estimations of comprehensive DSGE models under sticky information exist, but they are few. Paustian and Pytlarczyk (2006), for example, estimate DSGE variants under Calvo price-setting and sticky information. They show that the standard model under Calvo strongly dominates the alternative. Trabandt (2007) finds that the two models do equally well, while Korenok's (2008) results also favor the sticky-price model. Overall, the results from the literature comparing New Keynesian Phillips curves obtained under sticky prices with the sticky-information Phillips curve are mixed, with the balance tipping in favor of sticky-price models.

Only few papers estimate full general equilibrium models that incorporate sticky information in all the relevant decisions in the model economy. The first papers to do this are those by Mankiw and Reis (2007) and Reis (2009a, 2009b), who consider a benchmark neoclassical model with flexible prices and introduce inattention regarding the consumption/saving, price setting, and wage setting decisions. There aren't, instead, many comparisons between DSGE models under pervasive sticky information and alternative models. From an empirical point of view, it is possible that a more satisfactory specification is likely to include both sticky prices and sticky information and maybe some of the frictions considered in Smets and Wouters (2007).

DEPARTURES FROM RATIONAL EXPECTATIONS: ADAPTIVE LEARNING

Agents under rational expectations have no incentives to revise their beliefs, since they already have full knowledge about the structure of the economy. A large literature on adaptive learning has asked whether agents would converge to the same equilibrium that exists under rational expectations if agents started with a more limited degree of knowledge and were allowed to learn over time using historical time series observations on the variables of interest. Agents would behave as econometricians by using available data and running simple regressions to form their beliefs, update their estimates, and obtain forecasts about the values of the aggregate variables that they need to solve their current optimization problems. Comprehensive introductions to adaptive learning models and literature are offered in Evans and Honkapohja (1999, 2001).

For almost three decades, the learning literature has mostly focused on the convergence properties of economic systems under learning to the rational expectations equilibrium, on evaluating the plausibility of the REH, and on providing a selection device to choose among multiple equilibria. More rarely, the studies focused on the role of learning during the transition period, for example, in response to changes in policy or during particular economic times (e.g., Marcet & Nicolini, 2003, stress the importance of departures from rational expectations and learning to generate hyperinflations in a Cagan-type monetary model).

More recently, an increasing number of papers has started studying at more depths the empirical role of transitional dynamics due to learning behavior and the effects of learning on business cycle models. Using simulation evidence, Williams (2004) tests the effects of adaptive learning in benchmark RBC and New Keynesian models and compares the implied moments with those obtained under rational expectations. He shows that while learning has small effects in an RBC setting, the effects are larger in the New Keynesian model.

Estimated general equilibrium models under learning have also become more common in recent years. Milani (2007) estimates a benchmark New Keynesian model extended to include "mechanical" sources of persistence as habit formation in private expenditures and indexation to past inflation in price setting. The paper shows that when the conventional assumption of rational expectations is relaxed to assume learning by economic agents, the estimated degrees of habit formation and indexation that are necessary to fit the data fall from values close to one to values close to zero. The results suggest that learning can induce realistic levels of persistence in the models, so that mechanical sources of persistence may be omitted. Moreover, the posterior model probabilities show that the model with learning fits the data better than the model with rational expectations does.

In the same spirit as the previously discussed work by Levine et al. (2010), also under learning, the informational differences between the researcher/econometrician estimating the model and the agents within the model are removed. While agents enjoy an informational advantage under rational expectations, under learning, they are assumed to have the same, more limited, knowledge that an econometrician working with the model would have: therefore, agents lack knowledge about the parameters of the model, they may lack knowledge about the current values of the shocks, and so forth. The deviation from rational expectations, however, is kept minimal. Agents still know the structural form of the model solution, that is, they use a correctly specified model that has the same regressors as the model solution under rational expectations. Therefore, expectations, while not fully rational, are typically interpreted as near-rational.

The model with near-rational expectations can be written in state space form as

$$A_0 \xi_t = A_1 \xi_{t-1} + A_2 \hat{E}_{t-1} \xi_{t+1} + D\varepsilon_t \qquad (33)$$

where $\xi_t = [\Gamma_t, \varepsilon_t, \tilde{\Gamma}_{t-1}]'$ using the same notation previously used for the rational expectations model. We assume here $t-1$ timing in the agents' information set when forming their expectations.

Under a model as (1)–(14), agents would estimate a linear model, which constitutes their Perceived Law of Motion (PLM)

$$\xi_t = a_t + b_t \xi_{t-1} + v_t \qquad (34)$$

where a_t and b_t are vectors and matrices of beliefs about the reduced-form coefficients. The beliefs are recursively updated following a constant-gain learning algorithm as

$$\hat{\phi}_t = \hat{\phi}_{t-1} + \bar{g} R_t^{-1} \chi_t (\xi_t - \chi_t' \hat{\phi}_{t-1}) \qquad (35)$$

$$R_t = R_{t-1} + \bar{g}(\chi_t \chi_t' - R_{t-1}) \qquad (36)$$

where $\chi_t \equiv \{1, \xi_{t-1}\}$, and $\hat{\phi}_t = [a_t', b_t']'$. Eq. (35) describes the updating of beliefs regarding the model solution coefficients, while Eq. (36) describes the updating of the variance–covariance matrix R_t of the associated regressors in χ_t. Beliefs at each point in time t are, therefore, equal to their value in the previous period plus an adjustment in the direction of the most recent forecast error. A key coefficient in models with learning is given by the constant-gain coefficient $\bar{g}$, which dictates the speed at which beliefs are revised in light of new information.

Using the available information and the updated beliefs, expectations are formed as

$$E_{t-1} \xi_{t+1} = (I + \hat{b}_{t-1}) \hat{a}_{t-1} + \hat{b}_{t-1}^2 \xi_{t-1} \qquad (37)$$

The resulting expectations can be substituted into the original model, yielding the Actual Law of Motion of the economy, or ALM, which, in state-space form, is given by:

$$\xi_t = A_t + F_t\xi_{t-1} + Gw_t \tag{38}$$

The model has similar form to the solution obtained under rational expectations, but the matrix of coefficients F_t is now time varying and the vector of intercepts is now allowed to be different from 0 (the value it would have under rational expectations) and it is also time varying.

In addition to the paper described above, a number of other papers show the usefulness of modeling learning in the formation of expectations to fit macroeconomic data. Milani (2006) follows Preston's (2005) approach by deriving a model with subjective expectations in which long-horizon forecasts about output, inflation, and interest rates matter. He shows that mechanical sources of persistence still become superfluous under learning.[6] Some of the empirical results that are typically found under the assumption of rational expectations may be sensitive the way expectations are modeled: Milani (2008a) shows that the evidence on the Federal Reserve's failure to satisfy the Taylor principle in the 1970s, which is found in Lubik and Schorfheide (2004), for example, doesn't carry through in models that allow for revisions in beliefs and learning. Along the same lines are the results in Milani (2009c): while many papers find evidence of large time variation in the exogenous inflation target that the Federal Reserve implicitly follows when the models are estimated under the assumption of rational expectations, the estimated time-varying target is much less variable and always close to 2.5% when knowledge about the economy is imperfect and beliefs are allowed to be updated over time. Primiceri (2006), Sargent, Williams, and Zha (2006), and Best (2010) model, instead, learning by the policymaker, rather than by the private sector, and show that evolving beliefs about the state of the economy helps explaining U.S. monetary policy decisions over the postwar sample.

The previous papers typically introduce learning in small-scale New Keynesian models. Slobodyan and Wouters (2012), instead, consider learning in medium-scale DSGE models à la Smets and Wouters. They show that learning improves the fit of the model compared with the benchmark case of rational expectations. Eusepi and Preston (2011) estimate a baseline RBC model under long-horizon expectations and learning. Again learning plays an important role, although possibly not as large as in monetary models of the business cycle. They show that the model is able to fit the data even assuming a technology shock that is 20–30% less volatile than it would need to be under rational expectations. This is important since the need for highly volatile technology shocks seems to be at odds with real-world evidence.

The empirical literature has usually assumed learning by agents with a constant gain. Old observations are discounted more heavily than more recent ones. Constant-gain learning is believed to work well in mimicking the behavior of forecasters that are worried about structural change in the parameters of the economy. The case of recursive-least-squares learning, where the gain is decreasing rather than constant, is standard in the theoretical literature, but less common in empirical work. One of the results emerging from the previous set of studies regards the evidence on the values of the gain that provide a better fit of the macro data. Most of the papers indicate that values around 0.02 (implying that observations in $t - 1, t - 2, \ldots, t - k$, are weighted as $(1 - 0.02), (1 - 0.02)^2, \ldots, (1 - 0.02)^k$), for quarterly data, are more realistic. The empirical estimates are thus consistent with those typically used in theoretical and calibrated studies.

An even better fit, however, may be obtained by allowing more flexible specifications of the gain, for example, by assuming that the gain is time varying and that its size adjusts endogenously to economic developments and past forecast errors (e.g., Milani, 2008c, following Marcet & Nicolini, 2003).

Finally, learning may be useful for situations in which it is important to capture time variations in the responses of the economy to shocks. Milani (2009b), for example, shows that evolving private-sector beliefs and learning can account for the empirical observation that oil price shocks seemed to cause large changes in output and inflation in the 1970s (in large part through self-fulfilling expectational effects), while shocks of similar magnitude generate only modest effects in the recent decade. The paper shows that an estimated general equilibrium model with an energy input and allowing for learning can rationalize the attenuation of the effects of oil price shocks, which is, instead, harder to capture through other explanations. Milani (2008b) also shows that the transmission of nonfundamental stock market shocks on the real economy has also varied over the sample as a result of different effects on beliefs.

From a theoretical point of view, Woodford (2010) studies the robust optimal monetary policy in the case of departures from model-consistent rational expectations. Given the uncertainty on the way private-sector expectations respond to policies and economic developments, these investigations should become more and more common.

While learning has proved useful both in theory and in the estimation of macroeconomic models, it is still an open question whether the assumed learning behavior is consistent with behavior at a more microeconomic level. Although some papers have started investigating the issue (e.g., Baranowski, 2011), more evidence on learning behavior on individual data is definitely needed.

More Drastic Departures from Rational Expectations

Models with adaptive learning assume deviations from rationality that remain on purpose limited. Other models assume deviations that are more drastic: for example, models that assume "heuristic" behavior in the formation of expectations. A recent paper by De Grauwe (2011) assumes heuristics by having agents who forecast by switching between two simple misspecified and biased rules: one that is consistently overly optimistic and the other that is overly pessimistic. De Grauwe inserts the forecasting rules in a New Keynesian model and he provides simulation evidence showing that heuristics leads to booms and busts driven by those waves of optimism and pessimism. Jang and Sacht (2012) estimate the model using moment-based methods.

These models are very recent and the corresponding literature still limited. I won't discuss them in larger detail in this survey.

EXPLOITING OBSERVED EXPECTATIONS FORM SURVEYS

One way to test whether the rational expectation hypothesis gives a valid approximation of the way forecasters in the economy form expectations is to look at the evidence from surveys. Direct data on subjective expectations from surveys have suscitated interest for a long time. The various uses of expectations in testing the REH are already discussed in Pesaran (1987) and in the Handbook chapter by Pesaran and Wheale (2006). Several studies use subjective expectations data to test the hypothesis of rational expectations, either in the aggregate, or at the individual level and using panel estimation (e.g., Keane & Runkle, 1990). Roberts (1997) and Adam and Padula (2011), among others, add subjective expectations to New Keynesian Phillips curves that are estimated using single equation methods. They show that subjective expectations may be a source of inflation persistence.

Observed expectations, however, have not been exploited very often in the context of fully fledged general equilibrium macroeconomic models, where rational expectations are typically assumed.

Recently, direct expectations from surveys have started being used more often in those contexts as well. Del Negro and Eusepi (2011) investigate whether a conventional DSGE model under rational expectations (with both perfect or imperfect information) is able to generate expected inflation series that match inflation forecasts from surveys. Aruoba and Schorfheide (2011) add survey inflation forecasts to their observables as additional information that can be used to infer the time-varying Fed's inflation target. Ormeno (2010) uses survey inflation expectations to discipline the estimation of models with learning of the type described in the previous section. Milani (2011, 2012) exploits a larger set of observed expectations to also estimate models with learning, but with the main interest of extracting expectation, or sentiment, shocks and analyze their contribution over the business cycle. Expectation/sentiment shocks are modeled by changing Eq. (37) to allow for excesses of unjustified optimism and pessimism in the formation of expectations, as

$$E_{t-1}\xi_{t+1} = (I + \hat{b}_{t-1})\hat{a}_{t-1} + \hat{b}_{t-1}^2 \xi_{t-1} + e_t \qquad (39)$$

where e_t defines the novel shocks. The papers conclude that sentiment shocks are a major driver of business cycle fluctuations, explaining up to half of the variability in output. The addition of a variety of expectations data is likely to be a promising and worthwhile area of future research for learning models.

Expectations data, however, can be used not only to discipline the estimation of models with learning or to check whether some of the implied expectation series under rational expectations are consistent with survey data, but also to discipline the estimation of rational expectation models. The information contained in expectations can allow researchers to better estimate not only expectations themselves, but also the structural shocks in the model, news, as well as structural parameters.

Steps in this direction are taken in Milani and Rajbhandari (2012b). They force rational expectations to be consistent with a large set of subjective expectations from surveys, spanning different forecasting horizons. In particular, that paper is interested in exploiting observed expectations to help in the extraction and identification of a variety of news shocks. Cole and Milani (2012) use a DSGE–VAR approach that includes observed data on expectations to investigate whether the hypothesis of rational expectations is severely misspecified in a monetary DSGE model and to find out where exactly such misspecification is more serious.

Survey expectations are being exploited more frequently in the evaluation of DSGE models. The use of observed expectations may allow researchers to retain the modeling advantages of rational expectations, while at the same time improving their empirical realism by requiring them to match the available expectations series as closely as possible. We regard this line of research as particularly promising.

Finally, we would like to mention that the use of survey expectations may be used to accommodate the existence of heterogeneous expectations in the model. This survey has sidestepped, as most of the literature, the possibility of heterogeneous expectations. Heterogeneity, uncertainty, and disagreement in the formation of expectations may, however, turn out being of primary importance for understanding aggregate fluctuations.[7]

CONCLUSIONS

REH has served as a building block for theoretical and empirical macroeconomic research for the last forty years. It has been widely successful.

Rational expectations DSGE models are now routinely developed and confronted with data in academic and policymaking institutions across the world. While empirical setbacks of rational expectations models have been numerous, the current generation of structural DSGE models, joining the better elements of RBC and New Keynesian approaches, has been particularly effective in matching macro data.

This survey, however, has also pointed out various empirical problems related to the REH, and it has presented an overview of some of the most popular extensions and alternatives in the literature. Given the pervasive uncertainty surrounding the formation of expectations, it is probably necessary that the macroeconomic literature starts to consistently check the sensitivity of the empirical conclusions that are obtained under rational expectations to even minimal departures from the benchmark REH.

A recent direction seems to move toward allowing expectations and shocks to expectations to directly cause business cycle fluctuations: the corresponding models emphasize expectations-driven business cycles, sometimes driven by psychological factors, which were already discussed by classic economists of the past as Pigou (1927), Keynes (1936), and Haberler (1937).

Finally, the survey has manifested the wish that even in the cases in which the REH is preserved, model-consistent expectations should be required to conform as closely as possible to the corresponding expectations series from surveys or other sources.

NOTES

1. The reader is referred to their papers for additional details on the models and full derivations from microfoundations.

2. Admittedly, I am considering here a rather strong form of the REH, which seems to be the form that is predominant in the empirical DSGE literature. A weaker form of the REH would simply posit that economic agents in the models optimally use all the available information when forming their expectations. In that case, the informational assumptions can be weakened at will, while keeping the sensible feature that agents process the information optimally. In this survey, the benchmark case of rational expectations is assumed to be the one under the strong form. Only recently, the DSGE literature has made progress in estimating empirically realistic environments in which agents optimally use the available information, under various degrees of information limitations; some examples will be discussed later. Many of the alternatives that will be discussed later in the survey are actually consistent with the weaker form of the REH; under adaptive learning, agents's behavior may not be fully optimal, but it is generally intended to be a good approximation of optimal behavior (e.g., Cogley & Sargent, 2008).

3. Additional evidence that expectations from surveys are heterogeneous is provided in Branch (2004, 2007).

4. The vector H_0 typically contains steady-state parameters, while H_1 is a selection matrix relating the observable series to the corresponding variables in the structural model.

5. For example, the basic RBC model fails to match the serial correlation of macroeconomic variables at business cycle frequencies unless an exogenous technology shock with autocorrelation in the 0.8–0.99 range is assumed. It is well known that the model lacks strong internal propagation mechanisms and the variables largely inherit the properties of the exogenous shock. In the benchmark New Keynesian model, the lack of persistence is evident by noticing that the variables respond instantly and adjust very quickly to shocks, such as a monetary policy shock. It is worth pointing out, however, that these model failures may be due to the REH, but also to other modeling features (optimizing behavior, utility function specifications, etc.) that are unrelated to expectations. As it's often the case, it is hard to separate the respective contributions of each element.

6. Milani (2009a) verifies whether the results are similar on Euro area data, finding more evidence of intrinsic persistence than in the United States.

7. A simple way to introduce heterogeneous expectations is to assume that different fractions of agents form expectations that correspond to either rational, naïve, or near-rational through learning. Levine et al. (2010) provide an example by

studying a model with an estimated fraction of agents that are allowed to form adaptive, rather than rational, expectations.

ACKNOWLEDGMENT

I would like to thank the editors of this journal, Tom Fomby, Carter Hill, and Ivan Jeliazkov, for giving me the opportunity of writing this survey, and an anonymous referee for comments.

REFERENCES

Adam, K., & Padula, M. (2011). Inflation dynamics and subjective expectations in the United States. *Economic Inquiry*, *49*(1), 13–25.
Altissimo, F., Ehrmann, M., & Smets, F. (2006). *Inflation persistence and price-setting behaviour in the euro area – A summary of the IPN evidence*. Occasional Paper Series 46, European Central Bank.
An, S., & Schorfheide, F. (2007). Bayesian analysis of DSGE models. *Econometric Reviews*, *26*(2/4), 113–172.
Aruoba, B., & Schorfheide, F. (2011). Sticky prices versus monetary frictions: An estimation of policy trade-offs. *American Economic Journal: Macroeconomics*, *3*(1), 60–90.
Avdjiev, S. (2011). *News driven business cycles and data on asset prices in estimated DSGE models*. BIS Working Papers No. 358. Basel, Switzerland.
Baranowski, R. (2011). *An empirical analysis of adaptive learning among individual professional forecasters*. Mimeo, UC Irvine.
Barsky, R. B., & Sims, E. R. (2009). *News shocks*. NBER Working Papers 15312. Cambridge, MA.
Beaudry, P., & Portier, F. (2006). Stock prices, news, and economic fluctuations. *American Economic Review*, *96*(4), 1293–1307.
Benhabib, J., & Farmer, R. E. A. (1999). Indeterminacy and sunspots in macroeconomics. In J. B. Taylor & M. Woodford (Eds.), *Handbook of macroeconomics* (1st ed., Vol. 1, Chap. 6, pp. 387–448). Amsterdam: Elsevier.
Best, G. (2010). *Policy preferences and policymakers' beliefs: The great inflation*. Mimeo, California State University, Fullerton, CA.
Beyer, A., & Farmer, R. E. A. (2004). *On the indeterminacy of New-Keynesian economics*. Working Paper Series 323. European Central Bank.
Blanchard, O. J., & Kahn, C. M. (1980). The solution of linear difference models under rational expectations. *Econometrica*, *48*(5), 1305–1311.
Branch, W. A. (2004). The theory of rationally heterogeneous expectations: Evidence from survey data on inflation expectations. *Economic Journal*, *114*(497), 592–621.
Branch, W. A. (2007). Sticky information and model uncertainty in survey data on inflation expectations. *Journal of Economic Dynamics and Control*, *31*, 245–276.
Cagan, P. (1956). The monetary dynamics of hyperinflation. In M. Friedman (Ed.), *Studies in the quantity theory of money*. Chicago, IL: University of Chicago Press.

Canova, F., & Sala, L. (2009). Back to square one: Identification issues in DSGE models. *Journal of Monetary Economics, 56*(4), 431–449.

Christiano, L. J., Eichenbaum, M., & Evans, C. L. (2005). Nominal rigidities and the dynamic effects of a shock to monetary policy. *Journal of Political Economy, 113*, 1–45.

Clarida, R., Galí, J., & Gertler, M. (2000). Monetary policy rules and macroeconomic stability: Evidence and some theory. *The Quarterly Journal of Economics, 115*(1), 147–180.

Cogley, T., & Sargent, T. J. (2008). Anticipated utility and rational expectations as approximations of Bayesian decision making. *International Economic Review, 49*(1), 185–221.

Cole, S., & Milani, F. (2012). *How well do new Keynesian models capture the interaction between expectations and macroeconomic variables: A DSGE-VAR approach.* Mimeo. UC Irvine.

De Grauwe, P. (2011). Animal spirits and monetary policy. *Economic Theory, 47*(2), 423–457.

Del Negro, M., & Eusepi, S. (2011). Fitting observed inflation expectations. *Journal of Economic Dynamics and Control, 35*(12), 2105–2131.

Del Negro, M., & Schorfheide, F. (2011). Bayesian macroeconometrics. In J. Geweke, G. Koop & H. van Dijk (Eds.), *The oxford handbook of Bayesian econometrics.* Oxford: Oxford University Press.

Dynan, K. E. (2000). Habit formation in consumer preferences: Evidence from panel data. *American Economic Review, 90*(3), 391–406.

Eusepi, S., & Preston, B. (2011). Expectations, learning, and business cycle fluctuations. *American Economic Review, 101*(6), 2844–2872.

Evans, G. W., & Honkapohja, S. (1999). Learning dynamics. In J. B. Taylor & M. Woodford (Eds.), *Handbook of Macroeconomics* (1st ed., Vol. 1, Chap. 7, pp. 449–542). Amsterdam: Elsevier.

Evans, G. W., & Honkapohja, S. (2001). *Learning and expectations in economics.* Princeton, NJ: Princeton University Press.

Fernández-Villaverde, J., Guerron, P., & Rubio-Ramírez, J. (2010). The new macroeconometrics: A Bayesian approach. In A. O'Hagan & M. West (Eds.), *Handbook of applied Bayesian analysis.* Oxford: Oxford University Press.

Fernández-Villaverde, J., & Rubio-Ramírez, J. (2007). Estimating macroeconomic models: A likelihood approach. *Review of Economic Studies, 74*(4), 1059–1087.

Fisher, I. (1911). The purchasing power of money, its determination and relation to credit, interest and crises. New York, NY: Macmillan. (Assisted by Harry G. Brown.)

Fisher, I. (1930). *The theory of interest.* New York, NY: Macmillan.

Friedman, M. (1957). *A theory of the consumption function.* Princeton, NJ: Princeton University Press.

Fujiwara, I., Hirose, Y., & Shintani, M. (2011). Can news be a major source of aggregate fluctuations? A Bayesian DSGE approach. *Journal of Money, Credit and Banking, 43*(1), 1–29.

Gali, J., & Gertler, M. (1999). Inflation dynamics: A structural econometric analysis. *Journal of Monetary Economics, 44*(2), 195–222.

Gomes, S., & Mendicino, C. (2011). *Housing market dynamics: Any news?* Working Papers w201121. Banco de Portugal.

Haberler, G. (1937). *Prosperity and depression: A theoretical analysis of cyclical movements.* Geneva: League of Nations.

Hall, R. E. (1978). Stochastic implications of the life cycle-permanent income hypothesis. *Journal of Political Economy, 86*(6), 971–987.

Hansen, G. D. (1985). Indivisible labor and the business cycle. *Journal of Monetary Economics*, *16*(3), 309–327.

Hansen, L. P. (1982). Large sample properties of generalized method of moments estimators. *Econometrica*, *50*(4), 1029–1054.

Hansen, L. P., & Singleton, K. J. (1982). Generalized instrumental variables estimation of nonlinear rational expectations models. *Econometrica*, *50*, 1269–1286.

Hansen, L. P., & Singleton, K. J. (1983). Stochastic consumption, risk aversion, and the temporal behavior of asset returns. *Journal of Political Economy*, *91*(2), 249–265.

Hirose, Y. (2008). Equilibrium indeterminacy and asset price fluctuation in Japan: A Bayesian investigation. *Journal of Money, Credit, and Banking*, *40*(5), 967–999.

Ireland, P. N. (2004). A method for taking models to the data. *Journal of Economic Dynamics and Control*, *28*(6), 1205–1226.

Jaimovich, N., & Rebelo, S. (2009). Can news about the future drive the business cycle? *American Economic Review*, *99*(4), 1097–1118.

Jang, T.-S., & Sacht, S. (2012). *Identification of animal spirits in a bounded rationality model: An application to the Euro area*. Mimeo. University of Kiel, Kiel.

Kaldor, N. (1938). The cobweb theorem. *Quarterly Journal of Economics*, *52*(2), 255–280.

Keane, M., & Runkle, D. E. (1990). Testing the rationality of price forecasts: New evidence from panel data. *American Economic Review*, *80*(4), 714–735.

Keynes, J. M. (1936). *The general theory of employment, interest and money*. London: Macmillan.

Khan, H. U., & Tsoukalas, J. (2011). The quantitative importance of news shocks in estimated DSGE models. *Journal of Money, Credit and Banking* (forthcoming).

Korenok, O. (2008). Empirical comparison of sticky price and sticky information models. *Journal of Macroeconomics*, *30*(3), 906–927.

Kydland, F., & Prescott, E. C. (1982). Time to build and aggregate fluctuations. *Econometrica*, *50*(6), 1345–1370.

Levine, P., Pearlman, J., Perendia, G., & Yang, B. (2010). *Endogenous persistence in an estimated DSGE model under imperfect information*. CDMA Working Paper Series 1002. St Andrews, Scotland, UK.

Lindé, J. (2005). Estimating new-Keynesian Phillips curves: A full information maximum likelihood approach. *Journal of Monetary Economics*, *52*(6), 1135–1149.

Lorenzoni, G. (2009). A theory of demand shocks. *American Economic Review*, *99*(5), 2050–2084.

Lorenzoni, G. (2011). News and aggregate demand shocks. *Annual Review of Economics*, *3*, 537–557.

Lubik, T. A., & Schorfheide, F. (2003). Computing sunspot equilibria in linear rational expectations models. *Journal of Economic Dynamics and Control*, *28*(2), 273–285.

Lubik, T. A., & Schorfheide, F. (2004). Testing for indeterminacy: An application to U.S. monetary policy. *American Economic Review*, *94*(1), 190–217.

Lucas, R. E. (1976). Econometric policy evaluation: A critique. *Carnegie-Rochester Conference Series on Public Policy*, *1*(1), 19–46.

Mankiw, G. N., & Reis, R. (2002). Sticky information versus sticky prices: A proposal to replace the new Keynesian Phillips curve. *The Quarterly Journal of Economics*, *117*(4), 1295–1328.

Mankiw, G. N., & Reis, R. (2007). Sticky information in general equilibrium. *Journal of the European Economic Association*, *5*(2-3), 603–613.

Mankiw, G. N., Reis, R., & Wolfers, J. (2003). *Disagreement about inflation expectations.* NBER Working Papers 9796. National Bureau of Economic Research, Cambridge, MA.

Marcet, A., & Nicolini, J. P. (2003). Recurrent hyperinflations and learning. *American Economic Review, 93*(5), 1476–1498.

Marshall, A. (1890). *Principles of economics.* London: Mcmillan.

Milani, F. (2006). A Bayesian DSGE model with infinite-horizon learning: Do "mechanical" sources of persistence become superfluous? *International Journal of Central Banking, 2*(3), 87–106.

Milani, F. (2007). Expectations, learning and macroeconomic persistence. *Journal of Monetary Economics, 54*(7), 2065–2082.

Milani, F. (2008a). Learning, monetary policy rules, and macroeconomic stability. *Journal of Economic Dynamics and Control, 32*(10), 3148–3165.

Milani, F. (2008b). *Learning about the interdependence between the macroeconomy and the stock market.* Mimeo. UC Irvine.

Milani, F. (2008c). *Learning and time-varying macroeconomic volatility.* Mimeo. UC Irvine.

Milani, F. (2009a). Adaptive learning and macroeconomic inertia in the Euro area. *Journal of Common Market Studies, 47*(3), 579–599.

Milani, F. (2009b). Expectations, learning, and the changing relationship between oil prices and the macroeconomy. *Energy Economics, 31*(6), 827–837.

Milani, F. (2009c). *Learning and the evolution of the fed's inflation target.* Mimeo. UC Irvine.

Milani, F. (2011). Expectation shocks and learning as drivers of the business cycle. *Economic Journal, 121*(552), 379–401.

Milani, F. (2012). *Sentiment and the U.S. business cycle.* Mimeo. UC Irvine.

Milani, F., & Rajbhandari, A. (2012a). Expectation formation and monetary DSGE models: Beyond the rational expectations paradigm. *Advances in Econometrics, 28* (this volume).

Milani, F., & Rajbhandari, A. (2012b). *Observed expectations, news shocks, and the business cycle.* Mimeo, UC Irvine.

Milani, F., & Treadwell, J. (2012). The effects of monetary policy "News" and "Surprises". *Journal of Money, Credit and Banking, 44*(8), 1667–1691.

Muth, J. A. (1961). Rational expectations and the theory of price movements. *Econometrica, 29*(6), 315–335.

Nakamura, E., & Steinsson, J. (2008). Five facts about prices: A reevaluation of menu cost models. *The Quarterly Journal of Economics, 123*(4), 1415–1464.

Ormeno, A. (2010). *Disciplining expectations: Using survey data in learning models.* Mimeo. Universitat Pompeu Fabra.

Paustian, M., & Pytlarczyk, E. (2006). *Sticky contracts or sticky information? Evidence from an estimated Euro area DSGE model.* Mimeo. Bank of England.

Pesaran, M. H. (1987). *The limits to rational expectations.* Oxford: Blackwell Publishing.

Pesaran, M. H., & Weale, M. (2006). *Survey expectations. Handbook of economic forecasting.* Amsterdam: Elsevier.

Pigou, A. C. (1927). *Industrial fluctuations.* London: Macmillan.

Poirier, D. (1998). Revising beliefs in nonidentified models. *Econometric Theory, 14*(4), 483–509.

Preston, B. (2005). Learning about monetary policy rules when long-horizon expectations matter. *International Journal of Central Banking, 1*(2), 81–126.

Primiceri, G. (2006). Why inflation rose and fell: Policymakers' beliefs and U.S. postwar stabilization policy. *Quarterly Journal of Economics, 121*(3), 867–901.

Reis, R. (2006a). Inattentive consumers. *Journal of Monetary Economics, 53*, 1761–1800.

Reis, R. (2006b). Inattentive producers. *Review of Economic Studies, 73*(3), 793–821.

Reis, R. (2009a). Optimal monetary policy rules in an estimated sticky-information model. *American Economic Journal: Macroeconomics, 1*(2), 1–28.

Reis, R. (2009b, Chapter 8). A sticky-information general equilibrium model for policy analysis. In K. Schmidt-Hebbel, C. Walsh & N. Loayza (Eds.), *Monetary policy under uncertainty and learning* (Vol. 13, 1st ed., Ch. 8, pp. 227–283). Santiago, Chile: Central Bank of Chile.

Roberts, J. M. (1997). Is inflation sticky? *Journal of Monetary Economics, 39*(2), 173–196.

Rudebusch, G., & Svensson, L. E. O. (1999). Policy rules for inflation targeting. In *Monetary policy rules* (pp. 203–262). National Bureau of Economic Research. (NBER Chapters.)

Sargent, T., & Wallace, N. (1975). 'Rational' expectations, the optimal monetary instrument, and the optimal money supply rule. *Journal of Political Economy, 83*(2), 241–254.

Sargent, T. J., Williams, N., & Zha, T. (2006). Shocks and government beliefs: The rise and fall of American inflation. *American Economic Review, 96*(4), 1193–1224.

Schmitt-Grohé, S., & Uribe, M. (2012). What's news in business cycles? *Econometrica* (forthcoming).

Schorfheide, F. (2005). Learning and monetary policy shifts. *Review of Economic Dynamics, 8*(2), 392–419.

Sims, C. A. (2000). Solving linear rational expectations models. *Computational Economics, 20*, 1–20.

Slobodyan, S., & Wouters, R. (2012). Learning in a medium-scale DSGE model with expectations based on small forecasting models. *American Economic Journal: Macroeconomics, 4*(2), 65–101.

Smets, F., & Wouters, R. (2007). Shocks and frictions in US business cycles: A Bayesian DSGE approach. *American Economic Review, 97*(3), 586–606.

Trabandt, M. (2007). *Sticky information vs. Sticky prices: A horse race in a DSGE framework.* Working Paper Series 209. Sveriges Riksbank.

Treadwell, J. (2010). *Monetary policy indeterminacy across the G7 and the great inflation.* Mimeo. UC Irvine.

Uhlig, H. (1999). A toolkit for analysing nonlinear dynamic stochastic models easily. In R. Marimon & A. Scott (Eds.), *Computational methods for the study of dynamic economies* (pp. 30–61). Oxford: Oxford University Press.

Williams, N. (2004). *Adaptive learning and business cycles.* Mimeo. University of Wisconsin, Madison, WI.

Woodford, M. (2010). Robustly optimal monetary policy with near-rational expectations. *American Economic Review, 100*(1), 274–303.

Woodford, M. (2011). *A response to John Kay.* New York, NY: Institute for New Economic Thinking.

OPTIMAL MONETARY POLICY IN AN ESTIMATED LOCAL CURRENCY PRICING MODEL

Eiji Okano, Masataka Eguchi, Hiroshi Gunji and Tomomi Miyazaki

ABSTRACT

We analyze fluctuations in inflation and the nominal exchange rate under optimal monetary policy with local currency pricing by developing two-country DSGE local currency pricing and producer currency pricing models. We estimate our models using Bayesian techniques with Japanese and US data, and calculate impulse response functions. Our estimation results show that local currency pricing is strongly supported against producer currency pricing. From the estimated parameters, we show that completely stabilizing consumer price index inflation is optimal from the viewpoint of minimizing welfare costs and that completely stabilizing consumer price index inflation is consistent with completely stabilizing the nominal exchange rate.

Keywords: Local currency pricing; optimal monetary policy; CPI inflation; fixed exchange rate; Bayesian estimation

JEL classification: E52; E62; F41

DSGE Models in Macroeconomics: Estimation, Evaluation, and New Developments
Advances in Econometrics, Volume 28, 39–79
Copyright © 2012 by Emerald Group Publishing Limited
All rights of reproduction in any form reserved
ISSN: 0731-9053/doi:10.1108/S0731-9053(2012)0000028005

INTRODUCTION

What kind of inflation rate should be stabilized from the viewpoint of minimizing welfare costs? Which exchange rate regime should be chosen from that viewpoint? These are important questions when discussing optimal monetary policy in an open economy. Current Chapter shows that consumer price index (CPI) inflation should be stabilized if we assume that prices are set in the consumers' currency (denoted local currency pricing, LCP). In addition, we show that stabilizing the CPI inflation rate is not inconsistent with a fixed exchange rate under LCP. Our finding contrasts with previous papers discussing optimal monetary policy using dynamic stochastic general equilibrium (DSGE) models because those papers show that the producer price index (PPI) inflation rate should be stabilized from that viewpoint even if an open economy is assumed.[1] Galí and Monacelli (2005) show that optimal monetary policy in a small open economy is consistent with PPI inflation targeting.[2] Although not mentioned explicitly, they assume that prices are set in the producers' currency (denoted producer currency pricing, PCP). They compare three policy regimes, PPI inflation-based and CPI inflation-based Taylor rules and a fixed exchange rate regime, and show that of these three regimes a PPI inflation-based Taylor rule produces macroeconomic volatility closest to that brought about by optimal monetary policy. In addition, their policy implications suggest that the optimal monetary policy outcome is not fundamentally different from the closed economy outcome. While they do not highlight firms' price-setting behavior, Galí and Monacelli (2005) imply that PPI inflation targeting is optimal under PCP. Developing a two-country model, Benigno and Benigno (2006) show implicitly that stabilizing PPI inflation minimizes welfare costs under PCP.

Reflecting on LCP, which cannot be ignored because of supporting empirical evidence, some studies in the new open economy macroeconomics (NOEM) literature and DSGE literature focus on LCP to discuss monetary policy. Introducing importers adopting LCP into Galí and Monacelli's (2005) model, Monacelli (2005) shows that the law of one price (LOOP) gap resembles a cost-push shock to the New Keynesian Philips Curve (NKPC) and implies that inflation–output gap tradeoffs cannot be dissolved by optimal monetary policy, although Galí and Monacelli (2005) suggest that those tradeoffs can be dissolved. Because of the appearance of a LOOP gap in the NKPC, he emphasizes that optimal monetary policy stabilizes the LOOP gap.[3] Devereux, Lane, and Xu (2006) show that CPI price stability maximizes households' utility, rather than nontradable goods price stability and a fixed exchange rate regime, in a model in which external shocks affect an emerging market via changes in interest rates and the terms of trade (TOT) by introducing financial frictions, a nontraded goods sector and importers adopting LCP. Devereux and Engel (2003) show that a fixed exchange rate regime minimizes welfare costs with their two-country model with LCP firms. While Devereux et al. (2006) consider a targeted inflation rate, Devereux and Engel (2003) consider a fixed exchange rate regime. In addition, only Devereux and Engel (2003) discuss optimal monetary policy explicitly. Hence, the type of inflation rate that should be stabilized from the viewpoint of minimizing welfare costs and the relationship between the exchange rate regime and optimal monetary policy is ambiguous.[4] Focusing on policy tradeoffs between stabilization of the prices of domestically produced goods and stabilization of the prices of imported goods, Corsetti, Dedola, and Leduc (2007) show that CPI stabilization is optimal from the viewpoint of maximizing households' utility. Their LCP model is quite sophisticated, because they introduce both upstream and downstream firms to generate policy tradeoffs between stabilization of the prices of domestically produced goods and stabilization of the prices of imported goods. They compare various policy regimes and show that strict CPI inflation targeting is close to optimal monetary policy in its effect on the volatility of the CPI inflation rate and real GDP. This result suggests that CPI stabilization is optimal from the viewpoint of minimizing welfare costs under LCP. However, they imply that complete stabilization in the nominal exchange rate is not consistent with complete CPI stabilization.[5] In addition, they do not clarify the relationship between inflation and the output gap.

To identify the type of inflation rate that should be stabilized under LCP and to clarify the relationship between the optimal targeted inflation rate and the exchange rate regime, we develop an LCP model that assumes a two-country setting at first. In addition, to clarify what affects differences in the policy implications of LCP, we also develop a two-country model with PCP, following studies such as Galí and Monacelli (2005) and Benigno and Benigno (2006). We estimate both models with a plausible interest rate feedback rule adopting Bayesian techniques as in Smets and Wouters (2003), Adjemian, Darracq-Paries, and Smets (2008) and Rabanal and Tuesta (2006) using Japanese and US data, and compare the plausibility of the two models. Well-microfounded loss functions under both LCP and PCP are derived from a second-order Taylor expanded utility function following Woodford (2003) and Galí (2008). We derive optimality conditions for central banks that minimize microfounded loss functions and simulate the LCP and PCP models with estimated posterior parameters.

Our estimation results for the PCP and LCP models are consistent with previous papers. Following Kass and Raftery (1995) and Jeffreys (1961) by comparing the LCP and PCP models, we find that the LCP model is more plausible than the PCP model. This finding is consistent with Engel and Rogers (1996), Goldberg and Knetter (1997), and Frankel, Parseley, and Wei (2004), who show that LCP is dominant.[6]

Our most important result is that optimal monetary policy under LCP produces no fluctuations in the CPI inflation rate. The PPI inflation rate is not stabilized under LCP. Roughly speaking, optimal monetary policy under LCP is CPI inflation targeting. This result is quite different from the result in Galí and Monacelli (2005). Our result is confirmed by the IRFs, volatility in the CPI inflation and the loss function stemming from a second-order approximated utility function. Interestingly, the quadratic terms of CPI inflation appear in our loss function and replace the quadratic terms of PPI inflation under LCP, although the quadratic terms of PPI inflation appear in our loss function under PCP as in Galí and Monacelli (2005) and Benigno and Benigno (2006).

Why do our policy implications differ from those of Galí and Monacelli (2005)? The existence of cost-push shocks in the NKPC implies that there are inflation–output gap tradeoffs. The NKPC based on PPI inflation under PCP, which is derived by Galí and Monacelli (2005), only consists of terms related to inflation and an output gap. Hence, stabilizing PPI inflation eliminates inflation–output gap tradeoffs simultaneously. The NKPC based on PPI inflation under LCP, however, includes terms related to changes in the nominal exchange rate. These terms operate as cost-push shocks. Hence, stabilizing PPI inflation does not eliminate inflation–output gap tradeoffs simultaneously under LCP. Under PCP, domestic inflation, namely PPI inflation, in terms of domestic currency is not affected by changes in the nominal exchange rate because domestic firms choose the optimal price in terms of the producers' currency. Hence, choosing zero PPI inflation produces a zero output gap or a fully stabilized output gap through the NKPC under PCP. Under LCP, however, firms choose the optimal price in terms of the consumers' currency. CPI inflation in terms of the consumers' currency is not affected by changes in the nominal exchange rate although PPI inflation in terms of the producers' currency is affected by changes in the nominal exchange rate, under LCP. In fact, our CPI-based NKPC under LCP does not include terms related to changes in the nominal exchange rate. Choosing zero CPI inflation produces a zero output gap or a fully stabilized output gap through the NKPC under LCP. Hence, optimal monetary policy under LCP induces no fluctuations in the CPI inflation rate.

Our result that there are no fluctuations in the nominal exchange rate under LCP is consistent with Devereux and Engel (2003). Another result, that there are no fluctuations in CPI inflation under LCP, is consistent with Corsetti et al. (2007). Summarizing our results, optimal monetary policy under LCP is not only consistent with CPI inflation targeting but also consistent with a fixed exchange rate. Hence, it can be said that we reconcile with Devereux and Engel (2003), who show that a fixed exchange rate regime is optimal, and with Corsetti et al. (2007), who show that CPI stabilization is optimal and there is a strong stabilization tradeoff between the nominal exchange rate and CPI inflation.

The rest of this chapter is organized as follows. The second section derives the LCP and PCP models. The third section estimates the LCP and PCP models using Bayesian techniques. The fourth section analyzes optimal monetary policy by deriving welfare costs and FONCs for central banks, and simulates the models. The fifth section concludes the chapter.

THE MODEL

We construct a two-country model belonging to the class of DSGE models with nominal rigidities and imperfect competition, basically following Galí and Monacelli (2005) and Monacelli (2005). We extend Galí and Monacelli's (2005) small open economy model to develop a two-country economy model following Obstfeld and Rogoff (2000a), although we assume all goods are tradable. The economy consists of two symmetric countries, H and F. Country H produces an array of differentiated goods indexed by the interval $h \in [0, 1]$, while country F produces an array of differentiated goods indexed by $f \in [1, 2]$. In addition, we derive two models; one of them adopts LCP, while the other adopts PCP.

Note that we define $v_t \equiv \ln(\frac{V_t}{V})$ if there are no provisions, where V_t denotes an arbitrary variable and V denotes the steady state value of V_t.

LCP Model

Under LCP, the LOOP does not necessarily hold because firms can choose the prices at which to sell goods in countries H and F separately. Thus, $P_t(h) = \mathscr{E}_t P_t^*(h)$ and $P_t(f) = \mathscr{E}_t P_t^*(f)$, hence $P_{H,t} = \mathscr{E}_t P_{H,t}^*$ and $P_{F,t} = \mathscr{E}_t P_{F,t}^*$ do not necessarily hold where $P_t(h)$ and $P_t(f)$ denote the price of a generic good produced in country H in terms of country H's currency,

$P_{H,t} \equiv [\int_0^1 P_t(h)^{1-\varepsilon} dh]^{\frac{1}{1-\varepsilon}}$ and $P_{F,t} \equiv [\int_1^2 P_t(f)^{1-\varepsilon} dh]^{\frac{1}{1-\varepsilon}}$ denote indices of the prices of generic goods produced in countries H and F, respectively, $\mathscr{E}_t$ denotes the nominal exchange rate and $\varepsilon > 1$ denotes the elasticity of substitution across goods.[7] Note that quantities and prices particular to country F are denoted by asterisks, while quantities and prices without asterisks are those in country H.

Households

The preferences of the representative household in country H are given by:

$$\mathscr{U} \equiv E_0 \sum_{t=0}^{\infty} \beta^t U_t \tag{1}$$

where $U_t \equiv \frac{1}{1-\sigma} C_t^{1-\sigma} - \frac{1}{1+\varphi} N_t^{1+\varphi}$ denotes the period utility, E_t denotes the expectation, conditional on the information set at period t, $\beta \in (0,1)$ denotes the subjective discount factor, C_t denotes consumption, $N_t \equiv \int_0^1 N_t(h) dh$ denotes hours of work, σ denotes the degree of relative risk aversion and φ denotes the inverse of the labor supply elasticity. The preferences of the representative household in country F are defined analogously.

More precisely, private consumption is a composite index defined by:

$$C_t \equiv \left[\left(\frac{1}{2}\right)^{\frac{1}{\eta}} C_{H,t}^{\frac{\eta-1}{\eta}} + \left(\frac{1}{2}\right)^{\frac{1}{\eta}} C_{F,t}^{\frac{\eta-1}{\eta}} \right]^{\frac{\eta}{\eta-1}} \tag{2}$$

where $C_{H,t} \equiv [\int_0^1 C_t(h)^{\frac{\varepsilon-1}{\varepsilon}} dh]^{\frac{\varepsilon}{\varepsilon-1}}$ and $C_{F,t} \equiv [\int_1^2 C_t(f)^{\frac{\varepsilon-1}{\varepsilon}} df]^{\frac{\varepsilon}{\varepsilon-1}}$ denote Dixit–Stiglitz-type indices of goods produced in countries H and F, respectively, and $\eta > 0$ denotes the elasticity of substitution between goods produced in countries H and F. Note that C_t^* is defined analogously to Eq. (2).

Total consumption expenditure by households in country H is given by $P_{H,t} C_{H,t} + P_{F,t} C_{F,t} = P_t C_t$. A sequence of budget constraints in country H is given by:

$$B_t + W_t N_t - T_t \geq P_t C_t + E_t(Q_{t,t+1} B_{t+1}) \tag{3}$$

where $Q_{t,t+1}$ denotes the stochastic discount factor, B_t denotes the nominal payoff of the bond portfolio purchased by households, W_t denotes the nominal wage, and T_t denotes lump-sum taxes. The budget constraint in country F is given analogously. Furthermore:

$$P_t \equiv \left(\frac{1}{2} P_{H,t}^{1-\eta} + \frac{1}{2} P_{F,t}^{1-\eta} \right)^{\frac{1}{1-\eta}} \tag{4}$$

denotes the CPI. P_t^* is defined analogously to this equation. Log-linearizing this equality yields $p_t = \frac{1}{2}p_{H,t} + \frac{1}{2}p_{F,t}$, which implies the following:

$$\pi_t = \frac{1}{2}\pi_{H,t} + \frac{1}{2}\pi_{F,t} \tag{5}$$

where $\pi_t \equiv p_t - p_{t-1}$ denotes CPI inflation with $\pi_{H,t} = p_{H,t} - p_{H,t-1}$ and $\pi_{F,t} = p_{F,t} - p_{F,t-1}$.

The optimal allocation of any given expenditure within each category of goods implies the demand functions as follows:

$$C_t(h) = \left(\frac{P_t(h)}{P_{H,t}}\right)^{-\varepsilon} C_{H,t}; \quad C_t(f) = \left(\frac{P_t(f)}{P_{F,t}}\right)^{-\varepsilon} C_{F,t}$$

$$C_t^*(h) = \left(\frac{P_t^*(h)}{P_{H,t}^*}\right)^{-\varepsilon} C_{H,t}^*; \quad C_t^*(f) = \left(\frac{P_t^*(f)}{P_{F,t}^*}\right)^{-\varepsilon} C_{F,t}^* \tag{6}$$

The optimal allocation of expenditures between domestic and foreign goods is given by:

$$C_{H,t} = \frac{1}{2}\left(\frac{P_{H,t}}{P_t}\right)^{-\eta} C_t; \quad C_{F,t} = \frac{1}{2}\left(\frac{P_{F,t}}{P_t}\right)^{-\eta} C_t$$

$$C_{H,t}^* = \frac{1}{2}\left(\frac{P_{H,t}^*}{P_t^*}\right)^{-\eta} C_t^*; \quad C_{F,t}^* = \frac{1}{2}\left(\frac{P_{F,t}^*}{P_t^*}\right)^{-\eta} C_t^* \tag{7}$$

The representative household maximizes Eq. (1) subject to Eq. (3). The optimality conditions are given by:

$$R_t \beta E_t \left(\frac{C_{t+1}^{-\sigma} P_t}{C_t^{-\sigma} P_{t+1}}\right) = 1 \tag{8}$$

which is a conventional Euler equation and

$$C_t^\sigma N_t^\varphi = \frac{W_t}{P_t} \tag{9}$$

which is a standard intratemporal optimality condition where $R_t \equiv 1 + r_t$ satisfying $R_t^{-1} = E_t(Q_{t,t+1})$ denotes the gross nominal return on a riskless one-period discount bond paying off one unit of the common currency (in short, the gross nominal interest rate), and r_t denotes the net nominal interest rate. Eq. (8) is an intertemporal optimality condition, namely the Euler equation, and Eq. (9) is an intratemporal optimality condition. Optimality conditions in country F are given analogously.

Log-linearizing Eq. (8), we obtain:

$$c_t = E_t c_{t+1} - \frac{1}{\sigma} \hat{r}_t + \frac{1}{\sigma} E_t \pi_{t+1} \tag{10}$$

with $\hat{r}_t \equiv \ln\left(\frac{R_t}{R}\right)$.

There is an uncovered interest rate parity (UIP) relationship for the gross nominal interest rate between countries H and F as follows:

$$R_t = R_t^* E_t \left(\frac{\mathscr{E}_{t+1}}{\mathscr{E}_t} \right)$$

with $R_t^* \equiv 1 + r_t^*$. Log-linearizing the UIP, we have the following familiar expression:

$$E_t(\Delta e_{t+1}) = \hat{r}_t - \hat{r}_t^*$$

with $\Delta v_t \equiv v_t - v_{t-1}$ and $e_t \equiv \ln(\frac{\mathscr{E}_t}{\mathscr{E}})$.

Combining Eq. (8) and UIP and iterating with an initial condition, we have the following optimal risk-sharing condition:

$$C_t^\sigma = \vartheta (C_t^*)^\sigma \mathscr{Q}_t$$

with $\mathscr{Q}_t \equiv \frac{\mathscr{E}_t P_t^*}{P_t}$ denoting the real exchange rate and ϑ denoting a constant depending on the initial value. Log-linearizing this equality, we have:

$$c_t = c_t^* + \frac{1}{\sigma} q_t \tag{11}$$

Our setting is definitely different from Betts and Devereux (2000), who introduce pricing-to-market behavior that is consistent with LCP in our definition into the Redux model developed by Obstfeld and Rogoff (1995). Although Betts and Devereux (2000) and this chapter allow violations of the LOOP, purchasing power parity (PPP) holds in this chapter ex post, although PPP does not necessarily hold in their chapter. While we assume an international risk-sharing condition as shown in Eq. (11), Betts and Devereux (2000) introduce restrictions in asset availability, which inhibits international optimal risk sharing.[8] Because of their setting, Eq. (11) is no longer applied, hence PPP is not necessarily applied. In addition, this implies that violation of PPP does not stem from LCP. We further discuss the relationship between the LOOP and PPP under LCP in section "Firms" under "LCP Model."

Market Clearing

The market for goods in country H satisfies the market clearing condition when domestic demand equals domestic supply, as follows:

$$Y_t(h) = C_t(h) + C_t^*(h) \tag{12}$$

where $Y_t(h)$ denotes the output of good h. The market clearing condition in country F is analogous. Substituting Eq. (6) into Eq. (12) yields:

$$Y_t(h) = \frac{1}{2}\left(\frac{P_t(h)}{P_{H,t}}\right)^{-\varepsilon}\left(\frac{P_{H,t}}{P_t}\right)^{-\eta}C_t + \frac{1}{2}\left(\frac{P_t^*(h)}{P_{H,t}^*}\right)^{-\varepsilon}\left(\frac{P_{H,t}^*}{P_t^*}\right)^{-\eta}C_t^* \tag{13}$$

Let $Y_t \equiv [\int_0^1 Y_t(h)^{\frac{\varepsilon-1}{\varepsilon}}dh]^{\frac{\varepsilon}{\varepsilon-1}}$ represent the index of aggregate output in country H. Under LCP, we obtain:

$$
\begin{aligned}
Y_t &= \frac{1}{2}\left(\frac{P_{H,t}}{P_t}\right)^{-\eta}C_t + \frac{1}{2}\left(\frac{P_{H,t}^*}{P_t^*}\right)^{-\eta}C_t^* \\
&= \frac{1}{2}\left(\frac{P_{H,t}}{P_t}\right)^{-\eta}C_t\left[1 + \left(\frac{P_{H,t}}{P_t}\right)^{\eta}\left(\frac{P_{H,t}^*}{P_t^*}\right)^{-\eta}\mathcal{Q}_t^{-\frac{1}{\sigma}}\right]
\end{aligned} \tag{14}
$$

by combining Eq. (13) and the Dixit–Stiglitz aggregators for output and prices, where we substitute the optimal risk sharing condition into the first equality in Eq. (14) to derive the second line in Eq. (14).

We define TOT as follows:

$$\mathcal{S}_t \equiv \frac{P_{F,t}}{\mathcal{E}_t P_{H,t}^*} \tag{15}$$

where $\mathcal{S}_t$ is the foreign TOT. The numerator is the export price of goods produced in country F in terms of country H's currency and the denominator is the export price of goods produced in country H in terms of country H's currency. Log-linearizing Eq. (15), we have:

$$s_t = p_{F,t} - e_t - p_{H,t}^* \tag{16}$$

where $s_t \equiv \ln \mathcal{S}_t$.

By log-linearizing Eq. (14), we have:

$$y_t = c_t + \frac{\eta}{2}s_t + \frac{1}{2}\left(\eta - \frac{1}{\sigma}\right)q_t$$

which is log-linearized market clearing in country H under LCP. There is a difference between this equality and Eq. (42) because the logarithmic real exchange rate q_t appears in this equality. However, this equality is equivalent to Eq. (42) because PPP holds, which implies that $q_t = 0$, although we assume LCP.

Combining log-linearized market clearing in country H and its counterpart in country F, we have:

$$s_t = \frac{1}{\eta}(y_t - y_t^*) - q_t$$

which clarifies the relationship between the TOT and relative output under LCP. As mentioned, $q_t = 0$ holds, although we assume LCP. Hence, this equality is equivalent to Eq. (41).

Firms
Each producer uses a linear technology to produce a differentiated good as follows:

$$Y_t(h) = A_t N_t(h) \tag{17}$$

where A_t denotes stochastic productivity in country H. Firms in country F have a technology analogous to that of firms in country H. The percentage deviation of productivity from its steady state value in countries H and F follows AR(1) processes $a_t = \rho a_{t-1} + \xi_t$ and $a_t^* = \rho a_{t-1}^* + \xi_t^*$ with ξ_t and ξ_t^* being i.i.d. shocks.

Using Dixit–Stiglitz aggregators, Eq. (17) can be rewritten as:

$$N_t = \frac{Y_t D_t}{A_t} \tag{18}$$

with $D_t \equiv \int_0^1 \frac{Y_t(h)}{Y_t} dh$. Because d_t is $o(\|\xi\|^2)$, a first-order approximation of this equality is given by:

$$y_t = a_t + n_t \tag{19}$$

which is consistent with Galí and Monacelli's (2005) log-linearized production function.

Following many DSGE studies including Galí and Monacelli (2005), we assume that firms set prices using Calvo–Yun-style price-setting behavior. Hence, $1 - \theta$ firms set new prices in each period, with an individual firm's probability of re-optimizing in any given period being independent of the time elapsed since it last set its prices. Each producer produces a single differentiated good and prices its good to reflect the elasticity of substitution across goods produced given the CPI. This is because each firm plays an active part in the monopolistically competitive market. In addition, we assume that firms have the ability to engage in price discrimination by setting a domestic price in terms of domestic currency for domestic sales that differs from the price that it sets for exports. This is LCP behavior. Under Calvo–Yun-style price-setting behavior and LCP behavior in a monopolistically competitive market, the maximization problems faced by producers in country H are as follows:

$$\max_{\tilde{P}_{H,t}, \tilde{P}^*_{H,t}} \sum_{k=0}^{\infty} \theta^k E_t \left\{ Q_{t,t+k} \left[\tilde{P}_{H,t} \left(\frac{\tilde{P}_{H,t}}{P_{H,t+k}} \right)^{-\varepsilon} C_{H,t+k} + \mathscr{E}_{t+k} \tilde{P}^*_{H,t} \left(\frac{\tilde{P}^*_{H,t}}{P^*_{H,t+k}} \right)^{-\varepsilon} C^*_{H,t+k} \right. \right.$$

$$\left. \left. - MC^n_{t+k} \left(\left(\frac{\tilde{P}_{H,t}}{P_{H,t+k}} \right)^{-\varepsilon} C_{H,t+k} + \left(\frac{\tilde{P}^*_{H,t}}{P^*_{H,t+k}} \right)^{-\varepsilon} C^*_{H,t+k} \right) \right] \right\} \qquad (20)$$

where $\tilde{P}_{H,t}$ and $\tilde{P}^*_{H,t}$ are the prices chosen by firms when they have an opportunity to change the prices of goods produced and sold in country H and goods produced in country H and sold in country F, respectively, $MC^n_t \equiv P_{P,t} MC_t$ denotes nominal marginal costs in country H, and $MC_t \equiv \frac{(1-\tau)W_t}{A_t P_{P,t}}$ and $P_{P,t}$ denotes the PPI in country H, which is defined as follows:

$$P_{P,t} \equiv \frac{P_{H,t} C_{H,t} + \mathscr{E}_t P^*_{H,t} C^*_{H,t}}{C_{H,t} + C^*_{H,t}}$$

which can be rewritten as $P_{P,t} = P_{H,t}$ when the LOOP holds. The PPI in country F is defined analogously. By log-linearizing this equality, we have $p_{P,t} = \frac{1}{2} p_{H,t} + \frac{1}{2}(e_t + p^*_{H,t})$, which implies the following:

$$\pi_{P,t} = \frac{1}{2} \pi_{H,t} + \frac{1}{2} \left(\Delta e_t + \pi^*_{H,t} \right) \qquad (21)$$

where $\pi_{P,t}$ denotes the PPI inflation rate in country H, $\pi_{H,t} \equiv p_{H,t} - p_{H,t-1}$ denotes the inflation rate of goods both produced and sold in country H, $\pi^*_{H,t} \equiv p^*_{H,t} - p^*_{H,t-1}$ denotes the inflation rate of goods produced in country H and sold in country F, respectively and $\pi_{P_t} = \pi_{H,t}$ holds when the LOOP holds.

Note that the maximization problems that producers in country F face are analogous to Eq. (20). Because of nominal rigidities, Eq. (20) looks complicated. When there are no nominal rigidities, namely $\theta \rightarrow 0$, Eq. (20) is equivalent to:

$$\max_{P_{H,t}, P^*_{H,t}} P_{H,t} C_{H,t} + \mathscr{E}_t P^*_{H,t} C^*_{H,t} - MC^n_t (C_{H,t} + C^*_{H,t})$$

which implies that each firm sets its price in terms of the local currency in which each firm's good is sold and pays costs to produce in terms of the producer's currency. Under LCP, we have multiple FONCs because firms can choose $\tilde{P}_{H,t}$ and $\tilde{P}^*_{H,t}$ separately. The FONCs for Eq. (20) are as follows:

$$\mathrm{E}_t\left[\sum_{k=0}^{\infty}\theta^k Q_{t,t+k}(\tilde{P}_{H,t}-\zeta MC^n_{t+k})\left(\frac{\tilde{P}_{H,t}}{P_{H,t+k}}\right)^{-\varepsilon}C_{H,t+k}\right]=0$$

$$\mathrm{E}_t\left[\sum_{k=0}^{\infty}\theta^k Q_{t,t+k}(\tilde{P}^*_{H,t}\mathscr{E}_{t+k}-\zeta MC^n_{t+k})\left(\frac{\tilde{P}^*_{H,t}}{P^*_{H,t+k}}\right)^{-\varepsilon}C^*_{H,t+k}\right]=0$$

which can be log-linearized as follows:

$$\tilde{p}_{H,t}=(1-\beta\theta)\sum_{k=0}^{\infty}(\beta\theta)^k\mathrm{E}_t(mc^n_{t+k})$$

$$\tilde{p}^*_{H,t}=(1-\beta\theta)\sum_{k=0}^{\infty}(\beta\theta)^k\mathrm{E}_t(mc^n_{t+k}-e_{t+k}) \tag{22}$$

with $\zeta\equiv\frac{\theta}{\theta-1}$ denoting a constant markup where we use the fact that $Q_{t,t+k}=\beta^k(\frac{C_{t+k}}{C_t})^{-\sigma}\frac{P_t}{P_{t+k}}$. FONCs for firms imply that firms set the price as a markup over a weighted average of expected future marginal costs. In particular, the first equality in Eq. (22) corresponds to the one derived by Galí and Monacelli (2005). The second equality in Eq. (22) is not a familiar expression, although it implies that firms set the price as a markup over a weighted average of expected future nominal marginal costs. The second equality in Eq. (22) is the log-linearized FONC for firms that produce goods in country H and sell them in country F. Those firms set the price in terms of country F's currency as a markup over a weighted average of expected future nominal marginal costs in terms of country F's currency. Next, we examine Eq. (22) after first discussing some identities including the relative prices peculiar to LCP behavior.

Under LCP, the LOOP does not necessarily hold because of Eqs. (20) and (22), which imply that firms set the prices of their goods in terms of the local currency, namely LCP. Because of this, there is a LOOP gap, which measures the degree of pass-through. Now, we discuss the LOOP gap and the real exchange rate in the context of our model. Following Monacelli (2005), we define the LOOP gap as follows:

$$\Psi_{H,t}\equiv\frac{\mathscr{E}_t P^*_{H,t}}{P_{H,t}};\quad \Psi_{F,t}\equiv\frac{\mathscr{E}_t P^*_{F,t}}{P_{F,t}}$$

where $\Psi_{H,t}$ and $\Psi_{F,t}$ denote the LOOP gap for goods produced in countries H and F, respectively. When the LOOP holds, we have $\Psi_{H,t} = \Psi_{F,t} = 1$.

Combining Eq. (7), the optimal risk-sharing condition and the definition of the TOT yields:

$$\Psi_{H,t} = \Psi_{F,t}^{-1} \mathscr{S}_t^{-1} \left(\frac{\mathscr{E}_t P_{F,t}^*}{P_{H,t}} \right) \mathscr{Q}_t^{-\frac{1}{\sigma\eta}}$$

which implies that the LOOP gap is a function of the TOT, the real exchange rate and the relative price of goods consumed domestically. Because $\mathscr{S}_t^{-1} \left(\frac{\mathscr{E}_t P_{F,t}^*}{P_{H,t}} \right) = \Psi_{H,t} \Psi_{F,t}$, that equality can be rewritten as follows:

$$\mathscr{Q}_t = 1$$

which implies that PPP holds, although the LOOP does not hold.[9] The log-linearized version of this equality is as follows:

$$q_t = 0 \tag{23}$$

In addition, substituting Eq. (23) into Eq. (11), we have $c_t = c_t^*$, which implies that the marginal utilities of consumption in the two countries are equal. In fact, households in both countries consume the same goods, although there is price discrimination. As mentioned, the LOOP does not necessarily hold, although Eq. (23) implies that the PPP is definitely applied. This sounds inconsistent at a glance. However, although the price of one good violates the LOOP, PPP holds when another good violates the LOOP inversely. In fact, substituting $\mathscr{Q}_t = 1$ into that equality, we have $\Psi_{H,t} = \Psi_{F,t}^{-1}$ and the log-linearized version of this as follows:

$$\psi_{H,t} = -\psi_{F,t}$$

which implies that gains from price discrimination correspond to losses from price discrimination.

The log-linearized market clearing conditions in countries H and F clarify the relationship between the nominal exchange rate, price level and TOT. Substituting the log-linearized definition of the CPI into the log-linearized market clearing conditions yields:

$$\begin{aligned} e_t &= p_t - p_t^* \\ &= p_{P,t} - p_{P,t}^* + s_t \\ &= p_{P,t} - p_{P,t}^* + \frac{1}{\eta}(y_t - y_t^*) \end{aligned} \tag{24}$$

where we use the log-linearized definition of PPI to derive the second line and Eq. (41) to derive the third line. Eq. (24) implies that the output differential between both countries affects the nominal exchange rate.

In turn, we examine Eq. (22), the log-linearized FONCs for firms under LCP. Using the definition of the LOOP gap, Eq. (22) can be rewritten as follows:

$$\tilde{p}_{H,t} = p_{H,t-1} + \sum_{k=0}^{\infty}(\beta\theta)^k E_t(\pi_{H,t+k}) + \frac{1-\beta\theta}{2}\sum_{k=0}^{\infty}(\beta\theta)^k E_t(\psi_{H,t+k})$$

$$+ (1-\beta\theta)\sum_{k=0}^{\infty}(\beta\theta)^k E_t(mc_{t+k})$$

$$\tilde{p}_{H,t}^* = p_{H,t-1}^* + \sum_{k=0}^{\infty}(\beta\theta)^k E_t(\pi_{H,t+k}^*) - \frac{1-\beta\theta}{2}\sum_{k=0}^{\infty}(\beta\theta)^k E_t(\psi_{H,t+k})$$

$$+ (1-\beta\theta)\sum_{k=0}^{\infty}(\beta\theta)^k E_t(mc_{t+k}) \tag{25}$$

As mentioned, firms set the price as a markup over a weighted average of future marginal cost. In our LCP setting, those firms' sales are not measured by the PPI, because it is the weighted average of the prices of goods selling in both country H and country F. However, real marginal cost is measured by the PPI, as shown in the definition of nominal marginal cost. That is, those firms obtain sales of $P_{H,t}$ and pay total costs of $P_{P,t}$ and the gap is $p_{P,t} - p_{H,t} = \frac{1}{2}\psi_{H,t}$, which implies that the gap corresponds to the LOOP gap in country H. Although the firms selling goods in country H have no currency disparity in sales and payments, LCP behavior generates the LOOP gap. Thus, a weighted average of the expected future LOOP gap in country H appears in the first equality in Eq. (25).

The price-setting behavior of the firms selling goods in country F generates the LOOP gap, as does the behavior of firms that sell goods in country H. These exporters obtain their revenue from the sale of goods exported in terms of country F's currency and pay total costs in terms of country H's currency. Their sales are measured in terms of country H's currency. Hence, their sales in terms of country F's currency are multiplied by the nominal exchange rate. They pay total costs measured by the PPI, as do the firms selling goods in country H. The gap is calculated by $p_{P,t} - (p_{H,t}^* + e_t) = -\frac{1}{2}\psi_{H,t}$. Thus, a weighted average of the expected future LOOP gap in country H appears in the second equality in Eq. (25), although the sign is contrary to the first equality. A similar mechanism works in firms in country F, not only for selling goods domestically but also for exporters. Although our LCP setting is different from Monacelli (2005), who assumes a small open economy and importers, our LCP setting clearly generates the LOOP gap, and this setting affects the nature of the NKPC and the amount of social welfare stemming from a second-order approximated utility function.

Marginal Cost and Natural Rate of Output
Substituting Eq. (9) into the definition of marginal cost, we obtain:

$$MC_t = (1 - \tau)\frac{C_t^\sigma N_t^\varphi}{A_t}\left(\frac{P_{P,t}}{P_t}\right)^{-1} \tag{26}$$

which is log-linearized as follows:

$$mc_t = \sigma c_t + \varphi n_t + \frac{1}{2}s_t - a_t \tag{27}$$

which is consistent with Galí and Monacelli's (2005) log-linearized marginal cost.

Under the flexible price equilibrium, $MC_t = \frac{1}{\iota}$, implying that the real marginal cost is constant and corresponds to the inverse of a constant markup. Using this fact and combining Eqs. (14), (18), and (26), we have the natural rate of output under LCP in country H as follows:

$$\bar{Y}_t = \frac{1}{2}\left\{\frac{P_{P,t}}{P_t}\frac{\zeta-1}{1-\tau}A_t^{1+\varphi}\left(\frac{P_{H,t}}{P_t}\right)^{-\eta\sigma}\left[1 + \left(\frac{P_{H,t}}{P_t}\right)^\eta\left(\frac{P_{H,t}^*}{P_t^*}\right)^{-\eta}\mathcal{Q}_t^{-\frac{1}{\sigma}}\right]^\sigma\right\}^{\frac{1}{\varphi+\sigma}}D_t^{-\frac{\varphi}{\varphi+\sigma}}$$

where $\bar{Y}_t$ denotes the natural rate of output in country H, which implies that the natural rate of output is a function not only of productivity but also of relative prices because of the open economy setting.

Before log-linearizing this equality, we define the output gap in country H x_t as the percentage deviation of output in country H y_t from its natural level $\bar{y}_t$. This relationship can be written as:

$$x_t \equiv y_t - \bar{y}_t \tag{28}$$

which is consistent with Galí and Monacelli's (2005) definition. The output gap in country F is defined analogously to Eq. (28).

Next, we log-linearize that equality. The log-linearized natural rate of output under LCP is given by:

$$\bar{y}_t = \frac{\omega_1\omega_2}{\omega_3}a_t - \frac{(\sigma\eta-1)\omega_2}{\omega_3}a_t^* \tag{29}$$

where $\omega_1 \equiv \eta(\sigma + 2\varphi) + 1$, $\omega_2 \equiv 2\eta(1 + \varphi)$ and $\omega_3 \equiv \omega_1^2 - (\sigma\eta - 1)^2$. Whereas Galí and Monacelli (2005) regard foreign output as exogenous because of their small open economy setting, foreign output, namely output in country F, is endogenous in our two-country setting. Thus, productivity in country F replaces foreign output in Eq. (29).

Next, we consider Eq. (27), which shows the percentage deviation of marginal cost from its steady state value. Substituting Eqs. (19) and (28) into Eq. (27) yields:

$$mc_t = \frac{\omega_1}{2\eta}x_t + \frac{\sigma\eta - 1}{2\eta}x_t^* \qquad (30)$$

which implies that real marginal cost in country H is the sum of the output gap in the two countries.

The Demand and Supply Sides
Substituting log-linearized market clearing and Eqs. (28) and (29) into Eq. (10) yields the New Keynesian IS Curve (NKIS) as follows:

$$x_t = E_t(x_{t+1}) - \frac{2\eta}{\sigma_\alpha}\hat{r}_t + \frac{2\eta}{\sigma_\alpha}E_t(\pi_{P,t+1}) + \frac{\sigma\eta - 1}{\sigma_\alpha}E_t(\Delta x_{t+1}^*) + \frac{2\eta}{\sigma_\alpha}\bar{r}_t \qquad (31)$$

where $\bar{r}_t \equiv -\sigma_\alpha((1 - \rho)(1 + \varphi)\omega_4)/(\omega_3)a_t - \sigma_\alpha((1 - \rho)(\sigma\eta - 1)(1 + \varphi)\omega_5)/(\omega_3)a_t^*$ denotes the natural rate of interest in country H with $\sigma_\alpha \equiv \sigma\eta + 1$, $\omega_4 \equiv \omega_1 - (\sigma\eta - 1)^2/\sigma_\alpha$ and $\omega_5 \equiv (\omega_1/\sigma_\alpha) - 1$. The NKIS in country F, which is analogous to Eq. (31), can be derived using the counterparts of Eqs. (10), (28), and (29).

Eq. (31) looks like an ordinary NKIS in the DSGE literature at a glance, however, because of LCP, Eq. (31) has some distinguishing features. Substituting Eq. (21) into Eq. (31), NKIS under LCP can be rewritten as follows:

$$\begin{aligned}
x_t = {} & E_t(x_{t+1}) - \frac{2\eta}{\sigma_\alpha}\hat{r}_t + \frac{\eta}{\sigma_\alpha}E_t(\pi_{H,t+1}) + \frac{\eta}{\sigma_\alpha}E_t(\pi_{H,t+1}^*) + \frac{\eta}{\sigma_\alpha}E_t(\Delta e_{t+1}) \\
& + \frac{\sigma\eta - 1}{\sigma_\alpha}E_t(\Delta x_{t+1}^*) + \frac{2\eta}{\sigma_\alpha}r_t \\
= {} & E_t(x_{t+1}) - \frac{\eta}{\sigma_\alpha}\hat{r}_t - \frac{\eta}{\sigma_\alpha}\hat{r}_t^* + \frac{\eta}{\sigma_\alpha}E_t(\pi_{H,t+1}) + \frac{\eta}{\sigma_\alpha}E_t(\pi_{H,t+1}^*) \\
& + \frac{\sigma\eta - 1}{\sigma_\alpha}E_t(\Delta x_{t+1}^*) + \frac{2\eta}{\sigma_\alpha}\bar{r}_t \qquad (32)
\end{aligned}$$

where we use log-linearized UIP to derive the second line. As shown in the first line, changes in the expected nominal exchange rate affect the NKIS.

The second line shows that not only the domestic nominal interest rate but also the foreign nominal interest rate appears in the NKIS.

Substituting the log-linearized Calvo's pricing rule and Eq. (30) into Eq. (25), we have equalities that determine the dynamics of inflation as follows:

$$\pi_{H,t} = \beta E_t(\pi_{H,t+1}) + \frac{\lambda}{2}\psi_{H,t} + \frac{\lambda\omega_1}{2\eta}x_t + \frac{\lambda(\sigma\eta - 1)}{2\eta}x_t^*$$

$$\pi_{H,t}^* = \beta E_t(\pi_{H,t+1}^*) - \frac{\lambda}{2}\psi_{H,t} + \frac{\lambda\omega_1}{2\eta}x_t + \frac{\lambda(\sigma\eta - 1)}{2\eta}x_t^* \qquad (33)$$

with $\lambda \equiv ((1 - \beta\theta)(1 - \theta))/\theta$. The first equality is the inflation dynamics for goods sold domestically and the second equality is the inflation dynamics for goods exported. Because Eq. (33) is derived from Eq. (25), the FONCs for firms in country H, the third and fourth terms on the RHS that stem from the real marginal cost in country H, are consistent between the equalities. The signs of the second terms on the RHS are opposite in the two equalities. The reason is that the losses from price discrimination are compensated by the gains from price discrimination, and vice versa. The counterpart of Eq. (33) is derived from the counterpart of Eq. (25).

Substituting Eq. (33) into Eq. (21), we have the NKPC in country H as follows:

$$\pi_{P,t} = \beta E_t(\pi_{P,t+1}) + \frac{\lambda\omega_1}{2\eta}x_t + \frac{\lambda(\sigma\eta - 1)}{2\eta}x_t^* - \frac{\beta}{2}E_t(\Delta e_{t+1}) + \frac{1}{2}\Delta e_t$$

and substituting the counterpart of Eq. (33) into Eq. (21) yields the counterpart of this equality in country F. This NKPC features the appearance of changes in the nominal exchange rate. Gali and Monacelli (2005) mention that full stabilization of domestic prices coincides with full stabilization of the output gap, namely $x_t = \pi_{H,t} = 0$ for all t. In our model, their domestic prices correspond to the PPI and they assume fully exogenous foreign output, which implies that the percentage deviation of marginal cost from its steady state value is not affected by the percentage deviation of foreign output from its steady state value. That is, they claim that full stabilization of PPI implies that output is at its natural rate if we ignore the foreign output gap or assume $\sigma\eta = 1$ in this equality. Even if we ignore the foreign output gap or assume $\sigma\eta = 1$ in this equality, full stabilization of PPI does not necessarily imply that output is at its natural rate because of changes in the nominal exchange rate, as shown in the fourth and fifth terms on the RHS. Changes in the nominal exchange rate act as cost-push shocks under LCP. Thus, full stabilization of PPI no longer implies that output is at its natural rate if we ignore the foreign output gap or assume $\sigma\eta = 1$. Substituting Eqs. (24), (29), and (28) into that equality, we can eliminate changes in the nominal exchange rate and obtain:

$$\pi_{P,t} = \beta E_t(\pi_{P,t+1}) + \beta E_t(\pi^*_{P,t+1}) - \frac{\beta}{\eta}E_t(x_{t+1}) + \frac{\beta}{\eta}E_t(x^*_{t+1}) + \kappa_\varpi x_t$$

$$- \kappa_\varsigma x^*_t - \pi^*_{P,t} - \frac{1}{\eta}x_{t-1} + \frac{1}{\eta}x^*_{t-1} + \omega_6 a_t - \omega_6 a_{t-1} - \omega_6 a^*_t + \omega_6 a^*_{t-1},$$

(34)

with $\kappa_\varpi \equiv (1 + \beta + \lambda\omega_1)/\eta$, $\kappa_\varsigma \equiv (1 + \beta - \lambda(\sigma\eta - 1))/\eta$, $\omega_6 \equiv (\omega_2\varpi_3(\sigma + \phi))/\omega_3$ and $\varpi_3 \equiv 1 + \beta(1 - \rho)$. Exogenous shocks appear in Eq. (34), which shows that exogenous productivity affects PPI inflation.

Monacelli (2005) derives a CPI-based NKPC. Following Monacelli (2005), we derive a CPI-based NKPC. Substituting the first equality in Eq. (33) and its counterpart in country F into Eq. (5) yields:

$$\pi_t = \beta E_t(\pi_{t+1}) + \frac{\kappa_\alpha}{2}x_t + \frac{\kappa_\alpha}{2}x^*_t$$

(35)

with $\kappa_\alpha \equiv \lambda(\sigma + \varphi)$. As mentioned by Galí and Monacelli (2005), κ_α is consistent with the slope coefficient for a standard closed economy NKPC. Full stabilization of CPI inflation rather than PPI inflation implies that output is at its natural rate when the nominal interest rate in both countries absorbs the effects of changes in productivity in NKISs. Galí and Monacelli (2005) demonstrate that a full stabilization of PPI inflation implies that output is at its natural level and there is no output gap in their non-LCP setting in a small open economy, as mentioned. However, our CPI-based NKPC Eq. (35) implies that full stabilization of CPI inflation implies that output is at its natural level and there is no output gap in our LCP setting in a two-country model.

Why do our policy implications differ from those of Galí and Monacelli (2005)? The existence of cost-push shocks in the NKPC implies that there are inflation–output gap tradeoffs. The NKPC based on PPI inflation under PCP, which is derived by Galí and Monacelli (2005), only consists of terms related to inflation and an output gap. Hence, stabilizing PPI inflation eliminates inflation–output gap tradeoffs simultaneously. The NKPC based on PPI inflation under LCP, however, includes terms related to changes in the nominal exchange rate. These terms operate as cost-push shocks. Hence, stabilizing PPI inflation does not eliminate inflation–output gap tradeoffs simultaneously under LCP. Under PCP, domestic inflation, namely PPI inflation, in terms of domestic currency, is not affected by changes in the nominal exchange rate because domestic firms choose the optimal price in terms of the producers' currency. Hence, choosing zero PPI inflation produces a zero output gap or a fully stabilized output gap through the NKPC under PCP. Under LCP, however, firms choose the optimal price in terms of the consumers' currency. CPI inflation in terms of the consumers' currency is not affected by changes in the nominal exchange rate although PPI inflation in terms of the producers' currency is affected by changes in the nominal exchange rate, under LCP. In fact, our CPI-based NKPC under LCP in Eq. (35) does not include terms related to changes in the nominal exchange rate. Choosing zero CPI inflation produces a zero output gap or a fully stabilized output gap through the NKPC under LCP. Hence, optimal monetary policy under LCP induces no fluctuations in the CPI inflation rate. This can be understood alternatively and intuitively by comparing Eqs. (5) and (21). To derive Eq. (34), we use Eq. (21) implying that PPI inflation is affected by changes in the nominal exchange rate, while we use Eq. (5) to derive Eq. (35).

In addition, Eq. (35) contrasts with the CPI-based NKPC in Monacelli (2005). In his LCP setting, importers purchase foreign goods in terms of foreign currency while they sell foreign goods in terms of domestic currency. Because importers maximize their profits, the LOOP gap appears in the CPI-based NKPC in Monacelli (2005). Our LCP setting is quite different from Monacelli's (2005) setting. Goods markets are fully partitioned, so there are no importers and each producer prices their goods in terms of consumers' currency. As mentioned in section "Firms" under "LCP Model," the LOOP gap does not appear in Eq. (35), in contrast with Monacelli (2005).

PCP Model

Under PCP, the LOOP holds, which is given by $P_t(h) = \mathscr{E}_t P_t^*(h)$ and $P_t(f) = \mathscr{E}_t P_t^*(f)$, hence:

$$P_{H,t} = \mathscr{E}_t P_{H,t}^*; \quad P_{F,t} = \mathscr{E}_t P_{F,t}^* \tag{36}$$

and

$$p_{H,t} = e_t + p_{H,t}^*; \quad p_{F,t} = e_t + p_{F,t}^* \tag{37}$$

hold.

Households
The preferences of the representative household, the private consumption index, the optimal allocation of any given expenditure within each category

of goods and the optimal allocation of expenditures between domestic and foreign goods are given by Eqs. (1), (2), (6), and (7), as in the LCP model. Because households face the same optimization problem, the intertemporal and intratemporal optimality conditions are given by Eqs. (8) and (9). UIP holds in the PCP model, hence the optimal risk-sharing condition holds in the PCP model. The log-linearized definition of the CPI, the intertemporal optimality condition and the risk-sharing condition are given by Eqs. (5), (10), and (11).

Market Clearing
The market clearing condition is given by Eq. (12) as in the LCP model. Substituting Eqs. (6) and (7) into Eq. (12), we obtain Eq. (13). Because of the LOOP, Eq. (13) can be rewritten as:

$$Y_t(h) = \left(\frac{P_t(h)}{P_{H,t}}\right)^{-\varepsilon}\left(\frac{P_{H,t}}{P_t}\right)^{-\eta}C_t$$

by using Eq. (36). Substituting the Dixit–Stiglitz aggregator of output into this equality yields:

$$Y_t = \left(\frac{P_{H,t}}{P_t}\right)^{-\eta}C_t \qquad (38)$$

which is a demand function consistent with that of Benigno and Benigno (2006).[10]

The definition of the TOT is given by Eq. (15). Substituting Eq. (36) into Eq. (15) yields:

$$\mathscr{S}_t = \frac{P_{F,t}}{P_{H,t}} \qquad (39)$$

which is only applicable to the PCP model because Eq. (36) is not applicable to the LCP model.

Log-linearizing Eq. (39), we have:

$$s_t = p_{F,t} - p_{H,t} \qquad (40)$$

Eq. (40) is only applicable to the PCP model because Eq. (37) does not hold under LCP, as is true for Eq. (39).

Substituting Eq. (37) into log-linearized Eq. (14), we have:

$$s_t = \frac{1}{\eta}(y_t - y_t^*) \qquad (41)$$

which clarifies the relationship between the TOT and relative output under PCP. Galí and Monacelli (2005) and Benigno and Benigno (2006), who assume PCP, derive the same equality.

Log-linearizing Eq. (38) yields:

$$y_t = \frac{\eta}{2} s_t + c_t \tag{42}$$

where we use Eq. (37). As mentioned, Eq. (42) is the final form of log-linearized market clearing under LCP in country H. The difference in price-setting behavior between LCP and PCP does not affect market clearing.

Firms
Firms' technology is given by Eq. (17), which can be rewritten as Eq. (18). Thus, log-linearized technology is given by Eq. (19) as in the LCP model.

We assume Calvo–Yun-style price-setting behavior as in the LCP model. However, the maximization problem faced by firms under PCP is quite simple. Because of $\tilde{P}_{H,t} = \mathcal{E}_t \tilde{P}^*_{H,t}$ and Eq. (36), Eq. (20) can be rewritten as:

$$\max_{\tilde{P}_{H,t}} \sum_{k=0}^{\infty} \theta^k E_t \left\{ Q_{t,t+k} \left[(\tilde{P}_{H,t} - MC^n_{t+k}) \left(\frac{\tilde{P}_{H,t}}{P_{H,t+k}} \right)^{-\varepsilon} (C_{H,t+k} + C^*_{H,t+k}) \right] \right\} \tag{43}$$

which is common in studies assuming Calvo pricing. Substituting Eq. (36) into the definition of the PPI, we have $P_{P,t} = P_{H,t}$, and substituting Eq. (37) into Eq. (21) yields:

$$\pi_{P,t} = \pi_{H,t} \tag{44}$$

The FONC of Eq. (43) is given by:

$$E_t \left[\sum_{k=0}^{\infty} \theta^k Q_{t,t+k} (\tilde{P}_{H,t} - \zeta MC^n_{t+k}) \left(\frac{\tilde{P}_{H,t}}{P_{H,t+k}} \right)^{-\varepsilon} (C_{H,t+k} + C^*_{H,t+k}) \right] = 0$$

which is a familiar expression in studies assuming PCP. Log-linearizing this equality, we have:

$$\tilde{p}_{H,t} = (1 - \beta\theta) \sum_{k=0}^{\infty} (\beta\theta)^k E_t(mc^n_{t+k})$$

which corresponds to the first equality in Eq. (22). The terms related to the LOOP gap disappear, because the LOOP holds in the PCP model. This equality can be rewritten as follows:

$$\tilde{p}_{H,t} = p_{H,t-1} + \sum_{k=0}^{\infty} (\beta\theta)^k E_t(\pi_{H,t+k}) + (1 - \beta\theta) \sum_{k=0}^{\infty} (\beta\theta)^k E_t(mc_{t+k}) \tag{45}$$

which corresponds to one derived by Galí and Monacelli (2005). Because of the LOOP, the LOOP gap disappears in Eq. (45), although the LOOP gap appears in the first equality in Eq. (25).

Marginal Cost and Natural Rate of Output
Substituting Eq. (9) into the definition of marginal cost, we obtain Eq. (26) and its log-linearized equality Eq. (27). However, the natural rate of output under PCP appears to be quite different from that under LCP. Combining not only Eqs. (14), (18), and (26) but also $P_{P,t} = P_{H,t}$, we have:

$$\bar{Y}_t = \left[\frac{\zeta^{-1}}{1-\tau} A_t^{1+\varphi} \left(\frac{P_{H,t}}{P_t} \right)^{-(\sigma\eta-1)} \right]^{\frac{1}{\sigma+\varphi}} D_t^{-\frac{\varphi}{\sigma+\varphi}}$$

which can be log-linearized as follows:

$$\bar{y}_t = \frac{\omega_1 \omega_2}{\omega_3} a_t - \frac{(\sigma\eta - 1)\omega_2}{\omega_3} a_t^*$$

This equality is consistent with the log-linearized natural rate of output under LCP in Eq. (29), although the natural rate of output is quite different between PCP and LCP before log-linearizing. This implies that differences in price-setting behavior do not affect the natural rate of output.

The natural rate of output under PCP is consistent with the one under LCP, implying the same relationship between marginal cost and the output gap. In fact, substituting Eqs. (19), (27), (28), and (41) into Eq. (42) yields:

$$mc_t = \frac{\omega_1}{2\eta} x_t + \frac{\sigma\eta - 1}{2\eta} x_t^*$$

which is consistent with Eq. (30). The difference between the PCP and LCP models is in the price-setting behavior. Because the marginal cost has no relationship with the price-setting behavior, Eq. (30) holds under both PCP and LCP. Note that Galí and Monacelli (2005) show that real marginal cost has a relationship only with the domestic output gap, and their result is different from Eq. (30). This difference stems from our two-country setting. As mentioned, foreign output is not exogenous in our setting, and productivity in country F appears in Eq. (29), while foreign output appears in their expression in terms of the percentage deviation from its steady state value. In their setting, foreign output rather than foreign productivity affects the domestic natural rate of output. The foreign output gap no longer affects the domestic output gap, which is determined by the percentage deviation of domestic real marginal cost from its steady state value. Because the percentage deviation of domestic real marginal cost from its steady state value corresponds to its deviation from its flexible price equilibrium value, the foreign output gap disappears in Galí and Monacelli (2005). In fact, we have $mc_t = \frac{\omega_1}{2\eta} x_t$ if we regard output in country F as exogenous.

The Demand and Supply Sides
Substituting Eqs. (21), (23), (41), and (42) into Eq. (10) yields NKIS as follows:

$$x_t = E_t(x_{t+1}) - \frac{2\eta}{\sigma_\alpha}\hat{r}_t + \frac{2\eta}{\sigma_\alpha}E_t(\pi_{P,t+1}) + \frac{\sigma\eta - 1}{\sigma_\alpha}E_t(\Delta x^*_{t+1}) + \frac{2\eta}{\sigma_\alpha}\bar{r}_t \qquad (46)$$

which is consistent with NKIS under LCP in Eq. (31). While the LOOP does not hold in the LCP model, it holds in the PCP model. Hence, NKISs are not the same in both models, although they are similar. Substituting Eq. (44) into Eq. (46), we have:

$$x_t = E_t(x_{t+1}) - \frac{2\eta}{\sigma_\alpha}\hat{r}_t + \frac{2\eta}{\sigma_\alpha}E_t(\pi_{H,t+1}) + \frac{\sigma\eta - 1}{\sigma_\alpha}E_t(\Delta x^*_{t+1}) + \frac{2\eta}{\sigma_\alpha}\bar{r}_t$$

which is applicable only to the PCP model, and $\pi_{H,t}$ replaces $\pi_{P,t}$ in this equality. Because the LOOP holds in the PCP model, changes in neither the expected nominal exchange rate nor the foreign nominal interest rate appear in NKIS under PCP.

By rearranging Eq. (45), we have NKPC in country H under PCP as follows:

$$\pi_{P,t} = \beta E_t(\pi_{P,t+1}) + \frac{\lambda\omega_1}{2\eta}x_t + \frac{\lambda(\sigma\eta - 1)}{2\eta}x^*_t \qquad (47)$$

which is the two-country version of NKPC derived by Galí and Monacelli (2005). While the foreign output gap appears in Eq. (47), it does not appear in the NKPC derived by Galí and Monacelli (2005), who assume a small open economy where foreign variables are exogenous. Because our model is a two-country model where the foreign variables are endogenous, the foreign output gap appears in our NKPC under PCP. In fact, if we regard output in country F as exogenous, we have:

$$\pi_{P,t} = \beta E_t(\pi_{P,t+1}) + \frac{\lambda\omega_1}{2\eta}x_t$$

which is similar to the NKPC derived by Galí and Monacelli (2005), and can be derived alternatively if $\sigma\eta = 1$ in our two-country model under PCP because the foreign output gap disappears in such a case. Galí and Monacelli (2005) show that full stabilization of PPI implies that $x_t = \pi_{H,t} = 0$, which is plausible if the output gap in country F disappears in Eq. (47). Because of our two-country setting, the foreign output gap does not disappear as long as we do not assume $\sigma\eta = 1$. Hence, full stabilization of PPI does not necessarily imply $x_t = \pi_{H,t} = 0$ in our two-country setting.

ESTIMATION

In this section, we estimate the LCP and PCP models with an interest rate feedback rule using a Bayesian technique for Japanese and US data.

Interest Rate Feedback Rule

To estimate the LCP and PCP models, both models are closed by the following interest rate feedback rule:

$$\hat{r}_t = \varrho\hat{r}_{t-1} + (1 - \varrho)(\phi\pi_t + \phi_x x_t) + m_t \tag{48}$$

$$\hat{r}_t^* = \varrho^*\hat{r}_{t-1}^* + (1 - \varrho^*)(\phi^*\pi_t^* + \phi_x^* x_t^*) + m_t^* \tag{49}$$

where m_t and m_t^* denote policy shifters in countries H and F, respectively, and we use monetary policy shifters that follow AR(1) processes $m_t = \rho_m m_{t-1} + \zeta_t$ and $m_t^* = \rho_m^* m_{t-1}^* + \zeta_t^*$ with ζ_t and ζ_t^* being i.i.d. shocks.

Bayesian Estimation

There are many methods for estimating DSGE models. Since the seminal paper of Kydland and Prescott (1982), many studies have applied calibration methods, in which the parameters are set to be consistent with the model in the steady state. On the other hand, some researchers use the moments of their model to estimate the deep parameters. One of the most popular of these methods is the generalized method of moments (GMM). Furthermore, maximum likelihood (ML) estimation has often been used, for example, Sargent (1989) and Ireland (2004). ML estimation is a full-information analysis, because researchers need not only the information of their model but also that of the stochastic process. Bayesian estimation is also a full-information analysis. Instead of ML estimation, it takes into account information about the parameters known to researchers prior to estimation. Recently, most researchers have used Bayesian methods, that is, Smets and Wouters (2003) and Rabanal and Tuesta (2006). In this section, we estimate our models using Bayesian methods.

Following Rabanal and Tuesta (2006), we set the discount factor β equal to 0.995 so as to be consistent with the nominal rate of interest, 2% per year in the steady state. To estimate the other parameters, we assume their prior distribution as follows. The parameter of relative risk aversion, σ, the elasticity of substitution between goods produced, η, the elasticity of labor supply, φ, the reaction coefficients to CPI inflation, ϕ and ϕ^*, and the reaction coefficients to the output gap, ϕ_x and ϕ_x^*, are all assumed to follow a normal distribution. The parameter of price stickiness, θ, the interest rate inertia parameter in the interest rate feedback rules, ϱ and ϱ^*, and the coefficients of the AR(1) processes, ρ, ρ^*, ρ_m, and ρ_m^*, are all assumed to be distributed as a beta distribution. The standard deviations of ξ, ξ^*, ζ and ζ^* are assumed to follow an inverse gamma distribution. For the parameter of the first prior, we follow Obstfeld and Rogoff's (2000b) estimation results, we follow Benigno and Benigno's (2006) setting based on Obstfeld and Rogoff's (2000b) estimation results for the parameter of the second prior and we follow Galí and Monacelli's (2005) setting or Smets and Wouters' (2003) setting for the others. These assumptions are shown in Table 1.

We estimate the parameters using a Markov-chain Monte Carlo (MCMC) method with these priors. The likelihood function of the observed data series is evaluated by a Kalman filter. The posterior distribution of the parameters is obtained through the Metropolis–Hastings algorithm. For the posterior distribution, 200,000 draws are created using the Metropolis–Hastings algorithm, and the first half of these draws is discarded.

Data

We estimate our models using Japan as country H and the United States as country F. The data on real GDP, interest rates on government bonds, and the CPI are from International Financial Statistics (IFS) provided by the IMF. We use quarterly observations for the period 1980:Q1 to 2008:Q4. The data on the labor force are from the OECD Economic Outlook database.

To obtain the real per capita GDP gap series, we divide real GDP by the labor force and apply the HP filter. As suggested by Hodrick and Prescott (1997) for quarterly data, we set the smoothing parameter to be 1,600. We divide the annual interest rate by four to get the quarterly interest rate. The

Table 1. Prior Distributions of Parameters.

Parameter	Distribution	Mean	SD
σ	Normal	3	1
η	Normal	4.5	1
φ	Normal	3	1
θ	Beta	0.75	0.05
ϱ	Beta	0.8	0.1
ϱ^*	Beta	0.8	0.1
ϕ	Normal	1.7	0.1
ϕ^*	Normal	1.7	0.1
ϕ_x	Normal	0.125	0.05
ϕ_x^*	Normal	0.125	0.05
ρ	Beta	0.85	0.1
ρ^*	Beta	0.85	0.1
ρ_m	Beta	0.85	0.1
ρ_m^*	Beta	0.85	0.1
σ_ξ	Inv. Gamma	0.4	2
σ_ξ^*	Inv. Gamma	0.4	2
σ_ζ	Inv. Gamma	0.1	2
σ_ζ^*	Inv. Gamma	0.1	2

first difference of the logarithmic CPI is used as the CPI inflation rate. All series, except for interest rates, are seasonally adjusted using X12-ARIMA.

Results

Table 2 reports the posterior means and 90% credible intervals for the parameters in both the LCP and PCP models. The mean of the relative risk aversion parameter σ is estimated to be 4.440 in the LCP model and 2.518 in the PCP model, respectively (the third row in Table 2). The value of σ in the PCP model is similar to some studies, such as 2.045 in Levin, Onatski, Williams, and Williams (2005) and 2.041 in Iiboshi, Nishiyama, and Watanabe (2006). The estimates of the parameter for the inverse of the labor supply elasticity φ are 2.389 in the LCP model and 5.737 in the PCP model (the fifth row in Table 2). The estimate of φ in the LCP model is close to those in Smets and Wouters (2003), Iiboshi et al. (2006) and Sugo and Ueda (2008), who estimate this parameter within the range 2.149–2.503. η is estimated to be 4.526 in the LCP model and 8.174 in the PCP model (the fourth row in Table 2). The estimate of η in the LCP model is close to

Table 2. Posterior Distributions of Parameters.

Parameter	LCP Model		PCP Model	
	Mean	90% Interval	Mean	90% Interval
σ	4.440	[3.159, 5.688]	2.518	[1.759, 3.260]
η	4.526	[2.923, 6.148]	8.174	[6.939, 9.485]
φ	2.389	[0.820, 3.875]	5.737	[4.525, 6.941]
θ	0.910	[0.888, 0.931]	0.909	[0.891, 0.926]
ϱ	0.647	[0.523, 0.775]	0.321	[0.209, 0.430]
ϱ^*	0.539	[0.406, 0.658]	0.339	[0.238, 0.440]
ϕ	1.264	[1.064, 1.410]	1.582	[1.409, 1.760]
ϕ^*	1.673	[1.507, 1.823]	1.574	[1.396, 1.750]
ϕ_x	0.257	[0.189, 0.323]	0.212	[0.138, 0.284]
ϕ_x^*	0.087	[0.041, 0.135]	0.170	[0.097, 0.241]
ρ	0.714	[0.556, 0.888]	0.440	[0.358, 0.528]
ρ^*	0.662	[0.581, 0.741]	0.735	[0.674, 0.794]
ρ_m	0.845	[0.748, 0.956]	0.994	[0.989, 1.000]
ρ_m^*	0.998	[0.996, 0.999]	0.993	[0.988, 0.999]
σ_ξ	0.352	[0.091, 0.681]	1.264	[1.083, 1.456]
σ_ξ^*	4.719	[1.568, 7.985]	0.687	[0.541, 0.843]
σ_ζ	0.069	[0.041, 0.095]	0.214	[0.139, 0.289]
σ_ζ^*	0.201	[0.135, 0.271]	0.213	[0.139, 0.286]

Obstfeld and Rogoff (2000b), who estimate it to be 4.5. The price-stickiness parameter θ is estimated to be 0.910 in the LCP model and 0.909 in the PCP model. These results imply that prices are constant for about 11.11 quarters. The estimates of the price-stickiness parameter are close to the 0.875 for Japan reported in Sugo and Ueda (2008) and the 0.873 for the United States in Adjemian et al. (2008). Therefore, our estimated results for θ are plausible.

Regarding interest rate feedback rules, the coefficients of the inflation rate in country H ϕ are 1.264 in the LCP Model and 1.582 in the PCP Model (the ninth row in Table 2). These results are similar to those in some Japanese studies that estimate interest rate feedback rules such as Kimura and Tanemura (2000), Kamada and Muto (2000) and Fujiwara, Hara, Hirakata, Kimura, and Watanabe (2007), who estimate the value to range from 1.33 to 1.60 using Japanese data. For F ϕ^*, the coefficients of the inflation rate are estimated as 1.673 in the LCP model and 1.574 in the PCP model (the 10th row in Table 2). These results are close to the results of Mehra and Sawhney (2010), who estimate the coefficients of the inflation rate to be 1.5 in the

United States. The coefficients of the output gap in country H ϕ_x are 0.257 in the LCP model and 0.212 in the PCP model, which are larger than those in Sugo and Ueda (2008), who report this coefficient to be 0.11 (the 11th row in Table 2). In country F, ϕ_x^* is 0.087 in the LCP model and 0.170 in the PCP model, which are larger than those in some studies for the United States such as Smets and Wouters (2003) and Levin et al. (2005) (the 12th row in Table 2). The results for interest rate inertia in country H ϱ are 0.647 in the LCP model and 0.321 in the PCP model, which are less than those reported in Sugo and Ueda (2008), who estimate the inertia parameter to be 0.842 in Japan (the seventh row in Table 2). The interest rate inertia parameter in country F ϱ^* is 0.539 in the LCP model and 0.339 in the PCP model, which are smaller than those of the United States, which are 0.956 in Smets and Wouters (2003) and 0.832 in Levin et al. (2005) (the eighth row in Table 2). The fact that our parameters are smaller than those in previous studies may be attributed to the difference in the sample periods. The coefficients of the AR(1) processes for productivity ρ and ρ^* are estimated to be between 0.440 and 0.735 in the LCP and PCP models, respectively (the 13th and 14th rows in Table 2). These results do not contradict the result in Galí and Monacelli (2005), who report an AR(1) coefficient for productivity of 0.66.

Some estimation results are similar between the PCP model and the LCP model. However, three deep parameters, σ, φ and η, are obviously different between the two models. While the result of σ in the PCP model is similar to that of previous studies, the results for the other two deep parameters φ and η in the LCP model are close to previous studies. Incidentally, in the LCP model, the AR(1) coefficient of productivity in country H ρ and that in country F ρ^* are similar to the results shown in Galí and Monacelli (2005). Furthermore, because the interest rate inertia parameters ϱ and ϱ^* of the LCP model are larger than those of the PCP model, it can be said that the estimates of ϱ and ϱ^* in the LCP model, but not in the PCP model, somewhat reflect the results of Sugo and Ueda (2008), who mention that monetary policy has significant inertia. The LCP model may be plausible from the viewpoint of the estimation results. We further discuss whether the LCP or PCP models are plausible in the next subsection.

Model Comparison

In the previous section, we estimated the LCP and PCP models. Next, we formally compare these models using Bayes factors. Denoting M_{LCP} and

M_{PCP} as the LCP and PCP models, respectively, and D as the data, the posterior odds ratio for M_{LCP} against M_{PCP} is:

$$\frac{P(M_{LCP}|D)}{P(M_{PCP}|D)} = \frac{P(M_{LCP})}{P(M_{PCP})}\frac{P(D|M_{LCP})}{P(D|M_{PCP})}$$

The second term on the right-hand side of this equation is called the Bayes factor. As we do not have any information on which model is plausible, we set the priors $P(M_{LCP})$ and $P(M_{PCP})$ equal to 0.5. In this case, the first term on the right-hand side is unity, so that the posterior odds ratio is equal to the Bayes factor.

Following Kass and Raftery (1995), we use three indices: the Bayes factor B, $2\ln B$ and $\log_{10} B$. Kass and Raftery (1995) suggest that according to their values, B and $2\ln B$ are considered to be (i) not worth more than a bare mention, (ii) positive, (iii) strong, and (iv) very strong. Furthermore, the criteria of Jeffreys (1961) are (i) not worth more than a bare mention, (ii) substantial, (iii) strong, and (iv) decisive. We estimate the marginal likelihood using the Laplace approximation and the modified harmonic mean.

The estimated Bayes factors are shown in Table 3, all of which have large values. It suggests that the evidence in favor of M_{LCP} is "very strong" ($B > 150$). The results of $2\ln B$ are also the same as those for B, that is, $2\ln B$ of greater than 10 means "very strong." Furthermore, the values of $\log_{10} B$ being greater than two are interpreted as "decisive." Therefore, the LCP model is strongly supported against the PCP model from the data, and this finding is consistent with Engel and Rogers (1996), Goldberg and Knetter (1997), and Frankel et al. (2004), who show that the LCP model is dominant.

Table 3. Model Comparison with Bayes Factors.

Index	Laplace Approximation	Modified Harmonic Mean
$\ln P(D|M_{LCP})$	-556.80	-556.98
$\ln P(D|M_{PCP})$	-575.65	-575.13
B	1.52×10^8	7.63×10^7
$2\ln(B)$	37.68	36.30
$\log_{10}(B)$	8.18	7.88

OPTIMAL MONETARY POLICY UNDER LCP AND PCP

In this section, we discuss the properties of optimal monetary policy in the LCP and PCP models. We derive microfounded period loss functions to obtain optimality conditions for the central banks. We simulate the LCP and the PCP models with optimality conditions, which replace the interest rate feedback rule, to obtain impulse response functions, and discuss the properties of optimal monetary policy in the LCP and PCP models.

Welfare Costs

We assume that each country has a central bank, and that these central banks conduct optimal monetary policy. Central banks minimize welfare costs. Welfare costs consist of the period loss function, which is derived from the welfare criteria. Following Woodford (2003) and Galí (2008), we have a second-order approximated utility function as follows:

$$\mathcal{W}^W_{LCP} = -\mathcal{L}^W_{LCP} + \text{t.i.p.} + o(\|\xi\|^3); \quad \mathcal{W}^W_{PCP} = -\mathcal{L}^W_{PCP} + \text{t.i.p.} + o(\|\xi\|^3)$$

(50)

where $\mathcal{L}^W_{LCP} \equiv \mathrm{E}_0 \sum_{t=0}^{\infty} \beta^t L^W_{LCP,t}$ and $\mathcal{L}^W_{PCP} \equiv \mathrm{E}_0 \sum_{t=0}^{\infty} \beta^t L^W_{PCP,t}$ denote the loss function in LCP and PCP models, respectively, $\mathcal{W}^W_{LCP} = \frac{1}{2}(\mathcal{W}_{LCP} + \mathcal{W}^*_{LCP})$ and $\mathcal{W}^W_{PCP} = \frac{1}{2}(\mathcal{W}_{PCP} + \mathcal{W}^*_{PCP})$ denote the average welfare criteria in the LCP and PCP models, respectively, W^W_{LCP} and W^W_{PCP} denote the welfare criteria in country H in the LCP and PCP models, respectively, with $\mathcal{W} \equiv \sum_{t=0}^{\infty} \mathrm{E}_0(\mathcal{W}_t)$ and $\mathcal{W}_t \equiv \frac{U_t - U}{U_C C}$. Furthermore:

$$L^W_{LCP,t} \equiv \frac{1}{2}\left[\frac{\varepsilon}{2\lambda}\pi_t^2 + \frac{\varepsilon}{2\lambda}(\pi_t^*)^2 + (\sigma + \varphi)(x_t^W)^2 + \frac{(1 + \phi)\eta^2}{4}z_t^2\right]$$

(51)

$$L^W_{PCP} \equiv \frac{1}{2}\left[\frac{\varepsilon}{2\lambda}\pi_{P,t}^2 + \frac{\varepsilon}{2\lambda}(\pi_{P,t}^*)^2 + (\sigma + \varphi)(x_t^W)^2 + \frac{(1 + \phi)\eta^2}{4}z_t^2\right]$$

(52)

are period loss functions in countries H and F, respectively, $z_t \equiv s_t - \bar{s}_t$ being the deviation of the TOT from its efficient level, $\bar{s}_t \equiv \frac{1+\varphi\eta}{\eta^2(1+\varphi)}\bar{y}_t^R$ being the efficient level of TOT. Note that we define $v_t^W \equiv \frac{1}{2}(v_t + v_t^*)$ and $v_t^R \equiv v_t - v_t^*$.

Eqs. (51) and (52) imply that the role of central banks is minimizing fluctuations in the deviation of the TOT from its efficient level z_t and the average output gap x_t^W in the LCP and PCP models. On stabilizing inflation, the role of central banks is different between the LCP and PCP models. The quadratic terms of the CPI inflation rate appears and replaces the quadratic terms of PPI inflation in our loss function under LCP in Eq. (51), although the quadratic terms of PPI inflation appear in our loss function under PCP in Eq. (52), as in Galí and Monacelli (2005) and Benigno and Benigno (2006). These facts imply that the role of central banks is minimizing fluctuations in the LCP model, while in the PCP model their role is minimizing fluctuations in PPI inflation.

FONCs for Central Banks

We next briefly discuss the FONCs for the central banks. We assume that the central bank in each country conducts cooperatively optimal monetary policy with commitment. Under LCP, central banks minimize Eq. (51) and the FONCs for them are given by:

$$\pi_t^W = -\frac{1}{\varepsilon}(x_t^W - x_{t-1}^W) \tag{53}$$

$$z_t = 0 \tag{54}$$

Because of commitment, lagged variables appear in the FONCs. Eqs. (53) and (54) determine the equilibrium path of the output gap, CPI inflation and the deviations of the TOT from its efficient level in the LCP model along with the structural model. Eq. (53) implies that there are no tradeoffs between the output gap and inflation in an economy consisting of two countries under optimal monetary policy. This implication is consistent with the outcome under the assumption of a closed economy. Eq. (54) implies that full stabilization of the deviation in the TOT from its efficient level is optimal regardless of preferences such as the elasticity of substitution between goods produced in countries H and F η and the relative risk aversion σ.

    Under PCP, central banks minimize Eq. (52), and the FONCs for them are given by:

$$\pi_t^W = -\frac{1}{\varepsilon}(x_t^W - x_{t-1}^W)$$

$$\pi_{P,t}^R = -\frac{(1+\varphi)\eta^2}{\varepsilon(1+\eta\varphi)}(z_t - z_{t-1}) \tag{55}$$

One of the FONCs is consistent with Eq. (53), and Eqs. (53) and (55) determine the equilibrium path of the output gap, PPI inflation and the deviation of the TOT from its efficient level in the PCP model along with the structural model. Because one of the FONCs is consistent with Eq. (53), there are no tradeoffs between the output gap and inflation in the economy that consists of two countries under optimal monetary policy. Eq. (55) does not show clear implications of the tradeoffs between the output gap and inflation. However, under the special case, the implications of Eq. (55) are clear. By substituting $\eta = 1$ into Eq. (55), we have:

$$\pi_{P,t}^R = -\frac{1}{\varepsilon}(x_t^R - x_{t-1}^R)$$

which implies that inflation–output-gap tradeoffs are fully dissolved in each country under optimal monetary policy when the elasticity of substitution between goods produced in countries H and F is unity.

Simulation

In this section, we simulate optimal monetary policy in the LCP and PCP models. The optimality conditions for the central banks, Eqs. (53), (54) and (55), replace the interest rate feedback rules Eqs. (48) and (49) in the LCP and PCP models. Fig. 1 shows the impulse responses to a one-standard-deviation increase in the productivity shock in country H, ξ_t, in the LCP model under the parameters estimated in section "Results" under "Estimation." Fig. 2 shows those in the PCP model. Note that the elasticity of substitution across goods ε is calibrated to 11 following Ferrero's (2009) calibrated parameter value, because the elasticity of substitution across goods only appears in the optimality condition and cannot be estimated because this elasticity does not appear in the estimated LCP and PCP models. Figs. 1 and 2 depict posterior means (solid lines) and pointwise 90% posterior probability intervals (dotted lines) for the impulse responses to one-standard-deviation shocks in the percentage deviation from the steady state. Macroeconomic volatilities that are evaluated at the posterior mean parameters are shown in Table 4.[11]

Under PCP, the PPI inflation rate in countries H and F is more stabilized than the CPI inflation rate in countries H and F (panels 3–6 in Fig. 2). This result is consistent with Galí and Monacelli (2005), who imply that PPI inflation targeting produces a zero output gap. This result can be understood by paying attention to Eq. (47). Although this setting does not correspond to our estimation result, we have NKPC in the

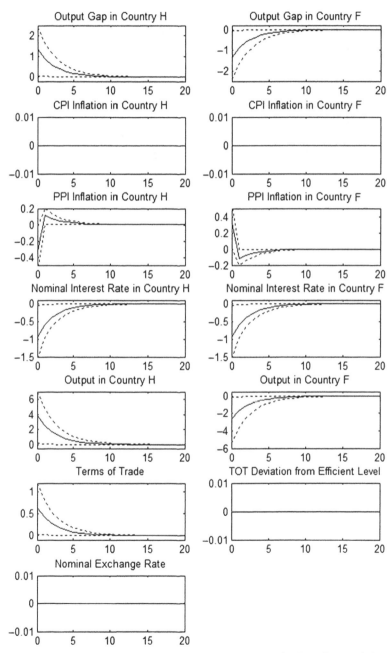

Fig. 1.   IRFs to Productivity Shocks in Country *H* in the LCP Model.

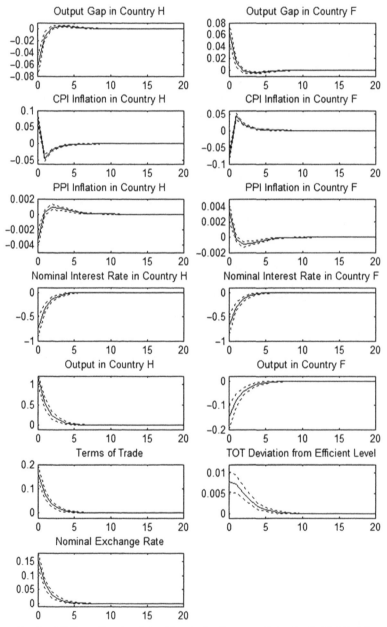

Fig. 2.   IRFs to Productivity Shocks in Country *H* in the PCP Model.

Table 4. Macroeconomic Volatility to a One-SD Increase in Productivity.

Shocks	LCP Model		PCP Model	
	ξ_t	ξ_t^*	ξ_t	ξ_t^*
x_t^W	0.00000	0.00000	0.00000	0.00000
π_t^W	0.00000	0.00000	0.00000	0.00000
x_t	0.00091	0.01340	0.00066	0.00036
x_t^*	0.00091	0.01340	0.00066	0.00036
$\pi_{P,t}$	0.00045	0.00586	3.65E-05	2.01E-05
$\pi_{P,t}^*$	0.00045	0.00586	3.65E-05	2.01E-05
π_t	0.00000	0.00000	0.00092	0.00050
π_t^*	0.00000	0.00000	0.00092	0.00050
$\hat{r}_t$	0.00162	0.02177	0.00833	0.00200
$\hat{r}_t^*$	0.00162	0.02177	0.00753	0.00217
y_t	0.00399	0.01604	0.01326	0.00097
y_t^*	0.00131	0.04604	0.00176	0.00725
s_t	0.00121	0.01435	0.00185	0.00101
z_t	0.00000	0.00000	0.00013	6.89E-05
e_t	0.00000	0.00000	0.00175	0.00096

PCP model under a special case by substituting $\sigma = \eta = 1$ into Eq. (47) as follows:

$$\pi_{P,t} = \beta E_t(\pi_{P,t+1}) + \frac{\lambda \omega_1}{2\eta} x_t$$

This NKPC implies that stabilizing PPI inflation stabilizes the output gap simultaneously, and is consistent with the one derived by Galí and Monacelli (2005), although the slope of our NKPC is slightly different from theirs because we assume a two-country economy. Because the special case $\sigma = \eta = 1$ does not correspond to our posterior result, the PPI inflation rate is not completely stabilized and fluctuates slightly, and the volatilities in the PPI inflation rate in countries H and F are 3.65E-05 and 2.01E-05 to changes in productivity in countries H and F, respectively (the seventh and eighth rows in Table 4).[12] Needless to say, the nominal exchange rate fluctuates in the PCP model (the 17th row in Table 4 and panel 13 in Fig. 2). This fact implies that a flexible exchange rate regime is the optimal regime under PCP.

Under LCP, CPI inflation rather than PPI inflation is completely stabilized, and this result is different from Galí and Monacelli (2005) (the ninth and 10th rows in Table 4 and panels 3 and 4 in Fig. 1). This can be understood by examining Eq. (35), which can be rewritten as:

$$\pi_t = \beta E_t(\pi_{t+1}) + \kappa_\alpha x_t^W$$

This equality implies that CPI inflation is zero when the average output gap is stabilized. In fact, the volatility of the average output gap x_t^W is zero, as shown in the third row in Table 4. In addition, the fifth and sixth rows in Table 4 and panels 1 and 2 in Fig. 1 show that volatilities and fluctuations in the output gap in countries H and F are symmetric. This suggests that the average output gap is zero because $x_t^W = \frac{1}{2}(x_t + x_t^*)$. Interestingly, the nominal exchange rate is completely stabilized under LCP, as shown in the 17th row in Table 4 and the 13th panel in Fig. 1. As mentioned in section "Firms" under "LCP Model," PPP always holds, even if LCP is assumed. Hence, $e_t + p_t^* = p_t$ holds. Perfect stabilization in CPI inflation implies $p_t = p_t^* = 0$, which is consistent with $e_t = 0$. Thus, under LCP, there are neither changes in CPI inflation nor in the nominal exchange rate. This is consistent with Devereux and Engel (2003), who develop an NOEM model assuming LCP and showing that a fixed exchange rate is an optimal regime from the viewpoint of maximizing welfare. Our result that there are no fluctuations in the nominal exchange rate stems from stabilizing the CPI inflation rate. Perfect stabilization in CPI inflation is consistent with perfect stabilization in the CPI level.[13] Thus, it can be said that our result is consistent with Corsetti et al. (2007), who show that CPI stabilization is optimal. We now reconcile Devereux and Engel's (2003) main finding with Corsetti et al.'s (2007) main finding, although Corsetti et al. (2007) point out that there is a strong tradeoff in stabilization between the nominal exchange rate and the CPI. Perfect stabilization in CPI inflation is not inconsistent with perfect stabilization in the nominal exchange rate.

CONCLUSION

We analyzed optimal monetary policy in an LCP model by comparing it with a PCP model, and produced two main findings, as follows. Optimal monetary policy under LCP produces no fluctuations in the CPI inflation rate. Roughly speaking, optimal monetary policy under LCP is CPI inflation targeting. This result is quite different from the result in Galí and Monacelli (2005) who show that stabilizing in the PPI inflation is optimal. We also showed that there are no fluctuations in the nominal exchange rate under LCP. Roughly speaking, optimal monetary policy under LCP is consistent with a fixed exchange rate regime, as showed by Devereux and Engel (2003). We reconciled our results with Devereux and Engel (2003), and derived policy implications that are consistent with Woodford's (2001) motivation.

Our policy implication for LCP is important, because our estimation results based on Japanese and US data strongly support the LCP model. Regarding our empirical and theoretical results, it can be said that central banks, not only in Japan and the United States, but also in other countries where LCP is dominant, should pursue monetary policy that stabilizes the CPI inflation rate from the viewpoint of minimizing welfare costs.

Our finding sheds light on Mussa's puzzle, which focuses on the comovement of the nominal exchange rate and real exchange rate, as in Betts and Devereux (2000). Because complete stabilization in the CPI inflation rate coincides with complete stabilization in the nominal exchange rate under LCP, one of the answers to Mussa's puzzle may be optimal monetary policy under LCP. Solving Mussa's puzzle along with the result in this chapter remains an objective for future research.

NOTES

1. In many DSGE studies, there is no distinction between the definitions of PPI inflation, domestic inflation and GDP inflation.
2. Galí and Monacelli (2005) term the Taylor rule which includes PPI inflation a domestic inflation-based Taylor rule rather than a PPI inflation-based Taylor rule. However, their definition of domestic inflation is consistent with our definition of PPI inflation.
3. Note that Monacelli (2005) does not analyze optimal monetary policy explicitly.
4. In fact, Devereux and Engel (2003) do not discuss fluctuations in the inflation rate under a fixed exchange rate that minimize welfare costs under the LCP, and Devereux et al. (2006) imply that there is a tradeoff between CPI stabilization and nominal exchange rate stabilization.
5. In fact, they state that complete CPI stabilization may not be desirable.
6. Engel and Rogers (1996), Goldberg and Knetter (1997) and Frankel et al. (2004) report a high degree of stability in import prices in the local currency.
7. By citing Betts and Devereux (2000), Mark (2001) explains LCP clearly.
8. Although they develop a two-country model that consists of a home and a foreign country, internationally tradable assets are denominated in the home country's currency.
9. This equality implies that the marginal utility of consumption in country H is identical to that in country F. Hence, the UIP can be derived by simply combining

Eq. (8) and its counterpart in country F, although we describe that we assume the UIP in section "Households" under "LCP Model."

10. We do not include government expenditure. Thus, government expenditure does not appear in the equalities, although it appears in Benigno and Benigno (2006).

11. As shown in the optimality conditions in Eqs. (53), (54), and (55), the LCP and PCP models are not affected by ζ_t and ζ_t^*. Only ξ_t and ξ_t^* affect the LCP and PCP models under optimal monetary policy.

12. In the special case, balanced trade is attained and the foreign output gap does not affect domestic inflation under PCP. However, in the general case $\sigma < 1$ and $\eta \neq 1$, which is consistent with our estimation result, the foreign output gap affects domestic inflation, as shown in Eq. (47). Hence, a tradeoff between PPI inflation and the output gap cannot be completely dissolved even if optimal monetary policy is conducted. See Benigno and Benigno (2006) for details.

13. We assume a zero inflation deterministic steady state.

ACKNOWLEDGMENT

We would like to thank Andrea Ferrero, Carter Hill, Chikafumi Nakamura, Efrem Castelnuovo, Eiji Ogawa, Fabio Milani, Tom Fomby, Ivan Jeliazkov, Martin Fukac, Tae-Sok Jang, Mark A. Wynne, an anonymous referee, and seminar and conference participants at Hitotsubashi University, National Graduate Institute for Policy Studies, Southern Methodist University and Vanderbilt University. All errors are our own. This research is financially assisted by the Zengin Foundation for Studies on Economics and Finance.

REFERENCES

Adjemian, S., Darracq-Paries, M., & Smets, F. (2008). *A quantitative perspective on optimal monetary policy cooperation between the US and the Euro area*. ECB Working Paper No. 884.

Benigno, P., & Benigno, G. (2006). Designing targeting rules for international monetary policy cooperation. *Journal of Monetary Economics, 53*, 473–506.

Betts, C., & Devereux, M. B. (2000). Exchange rate dynamics in a model of pricing-to-market. *Journal of International Economics, 50*, 215–244.

Corsetti, G., Dedola, L., & Leduc, S. (2007). Optimal monetary policy and the sources of local-currency price stability. In *International dimensions of monetary policy*. Chicago, IL: University of Chicago Press.

Devereux, M. B., & Engel, C. (2003). Monetary policy in the open economy revisited: Price setting and exchange rate flexibility. *Review of Economic Studies, 70*, 765–784.

Devereux, M. B., Lane, P. R., & Xu, J. (2006). Exchange rates and monetary policy in emerging market economies. *Economic Journal, 116*, 478–506.

Engel, C., & Rogers, J. H. (1996). How wide is the border? *American Economic Review, 86*, 1112–1125.

Ferrero, A. (2009). Fiscal and monetary rules for a currency union. *Journal of International Economics, 77,* 1–10.

Frankel, J., Parseley, D., & Wei, S.-J. (2004). *Slow pass-through around the world: A new import for developing countries?* Mimeo. Harvard University.

Fujiwara, I., Hara, N., Hirakata, N., Kimura, T., & Watanabe, S. (2007). Japanese monetary policy during the collapse of the bubble economy. *Monetary and Economic Studies, 25,* 89–128.

Galí, J. (2008). *Monetary policy, inflation and the business cycle.* Princeton, NJ: Princeton University Press.

Galí, J., & Monacelli, T. (2005). Monetary policy and exchange rate volatility in a small open economy. *Review of Economic Studies, 72,* 707–734.

Goldberg, P. K., & Knetter, M. M. (1997). Goods prices and exchange rates: What have we learned? *Journal of Economic Literature, 35,* 1243–1272.

Hodrick, R. J., & Prescott, E. C. (1997). Post-war U.S. business cycles: An empirical investigation. *Journal of Money, Credit and Banking, 29,* 1–16.

Iiboshi, H., Nishiyama, S.-I. and Watanabe, T. (2006). *An estimated dynamic stochastic general equilibrium model of the Japanese economy: A Bayesian analysis.* Mimeo.

Ireland, P. N. (2004). A method for taking models to the data. *Journal of Economic Dynamics and Control, 28,* 1205–1226.

Jeffreys, H. (1961). *Theory of probability* (3rd ed.). Oxford, UK: Oxford University Press.

Kamada, K., & Muto, I. (2000). Analysis of Japanese financial policies using forward-looking models [Fuowa-do Rukkingu Moderu ni Yoru Wagakuni Kinyu Seisaku no Bunseki]. *Monetary and Economic Studies [Kin'yu Kenkyu], 19,* 103–144 (in Japanese).

Kass, R. E., & Raftery, A. E. (1995). Bayes factors. *Journal of the American Statistical Association, 90*(430), 773–795.

Kimura, T., & Tanemura, T. (2000). Financial policy rules and macroeconomic stability [Kinyu Seisaku Ru-ru to Makuro Keizai no Anteisei]. *Monetary and Economic Studies [Kin'yu Kenkyu], 19,* 101–159 (in Japanese).

Kydland, F., & Prescott, E. (1982). Time to build and aggregate fluctuations. *Econometrica, 50,* 1345–1370.

Levin, A. T., Onatski, A., Williams, J., & Williams, N. M. (2005). Monetary policy under uncertainty in micro-founded macroeconometric models. *NBER Macroeconomics Annual, 20,* 229–287.

Mark, N. (2001). *International macroeconomics and finance.* Oxford, UK: Blackwell.

Mehra, Y. P., & Sawhney, B. (2010). Inflation measure, Taylor rules, and the Greenspan–Bernanke years. *Economic Quarterly, 96,* 123–151.

Monacelli, T. (2005). Monetary policy in a low pass-through environment. *Journal of Money, Credit and Banking, 37,* 1047–1066.

Obstfeld, M., & Rogoff, K. (1995). Exchange rate dynamics redux. *Journal of Political Economy, 103,* 624–660.

Obstfeld, M., & Rogoff, K. (2000a). New directions for stochastic open economy models. *Journal of International Economics, 50,* 117–153.

Obstfeld, M., & Rogoff, K. (2000b). The six major puzzles in international finance: Is there a common cause? *NBER Macroeconomics Annual, 15,* 339–412.

Rabanal, P., & Tuesta, V. (2006). *Euro-dollar real exchange rate dynamics in an estimated two-country model: What is important and what is not.* CEPR Discussion Paper, No. 5957.

Sargent, T. (1989). Two models of measurements and the investment accelerator. *Journal of Political Economy, 97*, 251–287.

Smets, F., & Wouters, R. (2003). An estimated dynamic stochastic general equilibrium model of the Euro area. *Journal of the European Economic Association, 1*, 1123–1175.

Sugo, T., & Ueda, K. (2008). Estimating a dynamic stochastic general equilibrium model for Japan. *Journal of the Japanese and International Economies, 22*, 476–502.

Woodford, M. (2001). *Inflation stabilization and welfare.* NBER Working Paper, No. 8071.

Woodford, M. (2003). *Interest and prices.* Princeton, NJ: Princeton University Press.

APPENDIX

Details of the Data

Output Gap: We first obtain the quarterly, seasonally adjusted series of real GDP from IFS provided by the International Monetary Fund (IMF) and the labor force from the OECD Economic Outlook database provided by the OECD. The sample period is 1980:Q2 to 2008:Q4. Second, we divide real GDP by the labor force to obtain real per capita GDP. Finally, we apply the HP filter to real per capita GDP to obtain potential real per capita GDP. Thus we obtain the real per capita GDP gap. As suggested by Hodrick and Prescott (1997) for quarterly data, we set the smoothing parameter equal to 1,600.

Inflation Rates: To calculate the inflation rate, we first obtain consumer prices for all items from the IFS, based on 2005 prices. The sample period is 1980:Q1 to 2008:Q4. This is one period longer than the other variables, because we calculate the inflation rate as the growth rate of the CPI, so we need the 1980:Q1 CPI figure to calculate the 1980:Q2 inflation rate. We then use X12-ARIMA to obtain the seasonally adjusted series. The inflation rate is the first difference of the logarithmic CPI.

Interest Rates: For both countries, we use the annual percentage interest rate on government bonds, from the IFS. To obtain the quarterly interest rate, we divide this figure by four.

NEWS, NON-INVERTIBILITY, AND STRUCTURAL VARS[☆]

Eric R. Sims

ABSTRACT

A state space representation of a linearized DSGE model implies a VAR in terms of observable variables. The model is said be non-invertible if there exists no linear rotation of the VAR innovations which can recover the economic shocks. Non-invertibility arises when the observed variables fail to perfectly reveal the state variables of the model. The imperfect observation of the state drives a wedge between the VAR innovations and the deep shocks, potentially invalidating conclusions drawn from structural impulse response analysis in the VAR. The principal contribution of this chapter is to show that non-invertibility should not be thought of as an "either/or" proposition – even when a model has a non-invertibility, the wedge between VAR innovations and economic shocks may be small, and structural VARs may nonetheless perform reliably. As an increasingly popular example, so-called "news shocks" generate foresight about changes in future fundamentals – such as productivity, taxes, or government spending – and lead to an unassailable missing state variable problem and hence non-invertible VAR representations.

[☆]This is a revised version of a chapter that previously circulated under the title "Non-Invertibilities and Structural VARs." I am grateful to Robert Barsky as well as two anonymous referees for helpful comments.

DSGE Models in Macroeconomics: Estimation, Evaluation, and New Developments
Advances in Econometrics, Volume 28, 81–135
Copyright © 2012 by Emerald Group Publishing Limited
All rights of reproduction in any form reserved
ISSN: 0731-9053/doi:10.1108/S0731-9053(2012)0000028006

Simulation evidence from a medium scale DSGE model augmented with news shocks about future productivity reveals that structural VAR methods often perform well in practice, in spite of a known non-invertibility. Impulse responses obtained from VARs closely correspond to the theoretical responses from the model, and the estimated VAR responses are successful in discriminating between alternative, nested specifications of the underlying DSGE model. Since the non-invertibility problem is, at its core, one of missing information, conditioning on more information, for example through factor augmented VARs, is shown to either ameliorate or eliminate invertibility problems altogether.

Keywords: Structural VAR; non-invertibility; non-fundamentalness; news shocks; factor models

JEL classification: E00; E17; C32

INTRODUCTION

Structural VARs (SVARs) are frequently used, either formally or informally, as a tool to construct, refine, and parameterize dynamic stochastic general equilibrium (DSGE) models.[1] The validity of this practice hinges upon whether or not SVARs can reliably uncover relevant objects of interest from fully specified DSGE models, such as the impulse responses to structural shocks. There are numerous problems that can arise when analyzing vector autoregressions (VARs) estimated on relatively short data sets; among these are issues due to downward biased autoregressive coefficients in finite samples and the so-called lag truncation bias.[2] Another, potentially more severe, problem is that there may exist no direct mapping between the innovations in the observable variables included in a VAR and the structural shocks of the underlying DSGE model.

While VARs are often touted for their flexibility and lack of imposed structure, and indeed are often pejoratively referred to as "atheoretic," there nevertheless exists a tight connection between fully specified DSGE models and VARs. The equilibrium of a log-linearized DSGE model can usually be expressed in terms of a state space system. The state space of the model implies a VAR in terms of the observed variables. The model is said to be invertible if there exists, in population, a linear rotation of the VAR innovations which recovers the deep structural shocks of the underlying DSGE model. If no such mapping exists, the model is said to be non-invertible.

The so-called "non-invertibility" (or sometimes "non-fundamental") problem has been known to exist for some time but has only recently received much attention.[3] At its core, it means that innovations from a VAR on a set of observable variables may not, even in population, be used to exactly uncover the structural shocks of a fully specified DSGE model. The non-invertibility problem is fundamentally one of missing information. As shown in the second section, it arises when the observed variables do not span the full state space of the underlying DSGE model. When this happens, the population innovations of a VAR on observed variables are a combination of the true structural shocks from the underlying DSGE model and what amounts to measurement error from forecasting the state conditional on the observables. The mixing of the structural shocks with this measurement error potentially confounds any analysis based on the rotations of the reduced form VAR innovations, which is the core of the structural VAR methodology.

A principal objective of this chapter is to argue and show that non-invertibility should not be thought of as an "either/or" proposition. There may exist situations in which a model has a non-invertible VAR representation but where structural VARs nevertheless perform reliably. I make these arguments on the basis of analysis of a conventional, medium scale DSGE model with a number of real and nominal frictions. A non-invertibility is hard-wired into the model by augmenting it with a particular kind of shock that generates foresight about changes in future productivity – a so called "news shock."

There has recently been renewed interest in the economic effects of "news shocks" about changes in future fundamentals – although in this chapter I consider news about productivity, other papers have explored news about taxes and government spending changes. Much of this literature is empirical and makes use of structural VAR techniques. For example, Beaudry and Portier (2006) and Barsky and Sims (2011) study the role of news about future productivity, while Mountford and Uhlig (2009) and Forni and Gambetti (2011) focus on anticipated changes in government spending, all within the context of structural VARs. Leeper, Walker, and Yang (2011) show, however, that foresight about changes in future state variables very likely leads to non-invertible VAR representations. The intuition is fairly straightforward. News shocks – which are, by construction, unobservable to an econometrician – are also state variables, as agents in the underlying economy must keep track of lagged values of these shocks when making current decisions. Hence, foresight leads to an unassailable missing state variable problem. The non-observation of the state may drive a wedge between VAR innovations and economic shocks, and potentially invalidates any conclusions drawn from structural VARs. Given the growing popularity of the news literature, an important contribution of this chapter is to investigate the quantitative relevance of non-invertibility for analysis based on SVARs.

The third section lays out a DSGE model that serves as a laboratory for investigating the significance of non-invertibility for VARs. The model features two sources of "real rigidity" – internal habit formation in consumption and investment adjustment costs – and one source of "nominal rigidity" – price stickiness according to the staggered contracts in Calvo (1983). Under specific parameter restrictions it nests simpler models – for example, setting all three parameters governing the degree of frictions to zero yields the canonical real business cycle (RBC) model, while setting the habit formation and investment adjustment cost parameters to zero but keeping price stickiness gives rise to a textbook sticky price model with capital. To keep things simple, the baseline model features only two stochastic disturbances – a conventional surprise productivity shock and the news shock about future productivity.

Using the "poor man's invertibility condition" derived in Fernandez-Villaverde et al. (2007), in the fourth section I analytically show that the presence of news shocks, as long as there is more than one period of anticipation, generates non-invertible VAR representations when TFP growth and any other variable of the model are observed.[4] I then conduct a battery of Monte Carlo exercises in which I examine the performance of apparently well-specified SVARs. Although the model has a number of frictions, the relatively simple shock structure lends itself to estimating a small VAR system and using a conventional recursive identifying assumption. In particular, I estimate two variable VARs featuring TFP growth and output on data simulated from the model. I rotate the statistical innovations into structural shocks using a Choleski decomposition of the innovation variance-covariance matrix with TFP growth ordered first. This recursive ordering conforms with the theoretical implications of the model – the innovation in TFP growth is identified with the conventional surprise technology shock, while the innovation in output orthogonalized with respect to TFP growth is identified with the news shock. While this is a particularly simple example, it is nevertheless instructive and is not without precedent in the literature. For example, Beaudry and Portier (2006) identify news shocks with stock price innovations orthogonalized with respect to TFP growth.[5]

In spite of the presence of a known non-invertibility, SVARs applied to model simulated data perform well in recovering the impulse responses to the model's two shocks. The estimated responses to both kinds of technology shocks are qualitatively in line with the predictions of the model. Though there are biases in the estimated responses, these are typically quantitatively small and are mostly at long forecast horizons. The short horizon responses, in contrast, are estimated quite precisely. The different nested parameterizations of the model make very different predictions about the behavior of output in response to both news and surprise technology shocks. For example, in the RBC model output falls in response to good news about future productivity and rises by more than productivity after a surprise technology shock. In contrast, in the fully parameterized model output rises after good news and rises after a surprise positive technology shock, but by substantially less than productivity. The estimated VARs do a very good job at picking up these features in the simulations. This means that the VARs can be an effective tool at discriminating between different nested versions of a model.

The simplicity of the assumed shock structure in the DSGE model lends itself to estimating two variable VARs with a recursive restriction. This is nice in that it allows one to cleanly focus in on the role of non-invertibility, but it is rather unrealistic and therefore may lack wider appeal. In the fifth section I consider a number of robustness checks in richer model environments. In particular, I consider situations in which TFP is not observed by the econometrician, in which there are additional "demand shocks," and in which an econometrician mistakenly introduces other sources of bias into the estimated VAR. Among other things, these modifications of the model structure invalidate the simple recursive identifying assumption that is used throughout the fourth section. Using long run restrictions, shape/sign restrictions, and combinations of short run, long run, and shape restrictions I conduct additional Monte Carlo exercises on VAR systems featuring between two and four variables. In all cases the identified VAR impulse responses are good approximations to the true model impulse responses to both news and surprise technology shocks.

In summary, the simulation results of the fourth and fifth sections suggest that VARs can be an effective tool for empirical researchers even if a model is technically non-invertible. While this finding may prove comforting to some, it is nevertheless not possible to draw sweeping conclusions about the perniciousness of non-invertibility more generally. If one wants to use a VAR in a situation in which non-invertibility may arise, the onus is on that researcher to convince his or her readers that invertibility is not a major problem in that particular context. I therefore consider in the sixth section what steps a researcher can take to ameliorate or eliminate problems stemming from non-invertibility while remaining within the flexible limited information framework that VARs provide. Non-invertibility is fundamentally a problem of missing information; hence, adding more information is the most straightforward way to deal with it.

In the sixth section I consider conditioning on additional "information variables." These information variables are noisy signals about future productivity, but are otherwise not central to the solution of the model. If the signals are precise enough – or if one conditions on enough information variables – then the missing states are essentially revealed, and the invertibility problem vanishes. I show that adding these variables to the VAR systems considered in the fouth section works to reduce the small biases in the estimated impulse responses to both news and surprise technology shocks. One quickly runs into a sort of "curse of dimensionality" problem, however, as conditioning on many information variables quickly consumes degrees of freedom. I therefore consider compressing the information variables using principal components and estimate factor-augmented VARs. The impulse responses obtained from the factor augmented VARs are essentially unbiased at all horizons. These results suggests that factor-augmented VARs, which are coming into increasing popularity, are an effective tool for researchers interested in using VAR techniques but who are nevertheless concerned about the potential for biases stemming from non-invertibility. Recent papers such as Giannone and Reichlin (2006), Forni, Giannone, Lippi, and Reichlin (2009), and Forni, Gambetti, and Sala (2011) have also advocated for the use of factor-augmented VARs to overcome problems due to non-invertibility, the last paper specifically in the context of news shocks. Factor-augmented VAR methods have appeal in that they are straightforward to implement, while maintaining the relative lack of structure that full information techniques require.[6]

The remainder of the chapter is organized as follows. The second section reviews the mapping between DSGE models and VARs, discusses reasons why invertibility may fail, and derives a simple condition to check whether a system is non-invertible. The third section lays out a DSGE model with both real and nominal frictions and a hard-wired non-invertibility because of the presence of foresight about productivity. The fourth section conducts a number of Monte Carlo exercises for different, nested versions of the model to examine the performance of SVARs. The fifth section conducts additional Monte Carlo exercises in richer environments in which a simple recursive identification is not available. The sixth section considers conditioning on more information as a way to overcome invertibility issues. The final section offers concluding thoughts.

THE MAPPING BETWEEN DSGE MODELS AND VARS

A log-linearized DSGE models yields a state-space representation of the following form:

$$s_t = A s_{t-1} + B \varepsilon_t \tag{1}$$

$$x_t = C s_{t-1} + D \varepsilon_t \tag{2}$$

s_t is $k \times 1$ vector of state variables, x_t is a $n \times 1$ vector of observed variables, and ε_t is a $m \times 1$ vector of structural shocks. The variance–covariance matrix of these shocks is diagonal and given by Σ_ε. A, B, C, and D are matrixes of conformable size whose elements are functions of the deep parameters of the model. So as to facilitate a comparison with standard assumptions in the structural VAR literature, I restrict attention to the case in which $n = m$, so that there are the same number of observed variables as shocks. D is thus square and hence invertible.

One can solve for ε_t from (2) as:

$$\varepsilon_t = D^{-1}(x_t - C s_{t-1})$$

Plugging this into (1) yields:

$$s_t = (A - BD^{-1}C) s_{t-1} + BD^{-1} x_t$$

Solving backwards, one obtains:

$$s_t = (A - BD^{-1}C)^{t-1} s_0 + \sum_{j=0}^{t-1} (A - BD^{-1}C)^{j-1} BD^{-1} x_{t-j} \tag{3}$$

If $\lim_{t \to \infty} (A - BD^{-1}C)^{t-1} = 0$, then the history of observables perfectly reveals the current state. This requires that the eigenvalues of $(A - BD^{-1}C)$ all be strictly less than one in modulus. If this condition is satisfied, (3) can be plugged into (2) to yield a VAR in observables in which the VAR innovations correspond to the structural shocks:

$$x_t = C \sum_{j=0}^{t-1} (A - BD^{-1}C)^{j-1} BD^{-1} x_{t-1-j} + D \varepsilon_t \tag{4}$$

The condition that the eigenvalues of $(A - BD^{-1}C)$ all be strictly less than unity is the "poor man's invertibility" condition given in Fernandez-Villaverde et al. (2007). It is a sufficient condition for a VAR on observables to have innovations that map directly back into structural shocks in population. When satisfied, a finite order VAR(p) on x_t will yield a good approximation to Eq. (4), and conventional estimation and identification strategies will allow one to uncover the model's impulse responses to structural shocks.

When this condition for invertibility is not satisfied the state space system nevertheless yields a VAR representation in the observables, though the VAR innovations no longer correspond to the structural shocks. The crux of the problem when the invertibility condition is not met is that the observables do not perfectly reveal the state vector. To see this, use the Kalman filter to form a forecast of the current state, $\hat{s}_t$, given observables and a lagged forecast:

$$\hat{s}_t = (A - KC)\hat{s}_{t-1} + Kx_t \tag{5}$$

Here K is the Kalman gain. It is the matrix that minimizes the forecast error variance of the filter, that is, $\Sigma_s = E(s_t - \hat{s}_t)(s_t - \hat{s}_t)'$. K and Σ_s are the joint solutions to the following two equations:

$$\Sigma_s = (A - KC)\Sigma_s(A - KC)' + B\Sigma_\varepsilon B' + KD\Sigma_\varepsilon D'K' - B\Sigma_\varepsilon D'K' - KD\Sigma_\varepsilon B' \tag{6}$$

$$K = (A\Sigma_s C' + B\Sigma_\varepsilon D')(C\Sigma_s C' + D\Sigma_\varepsilon D')^{-1} \tag{7}$$

Given values of K and Σ_s, add and subtract $C\hat{s}_{t-1}$ from the right hand side of Eq. (2) to obtain:

$$x_t = C\hat{s}_{t-1} + u_t \tag{8}$$

$$u_t = C(s_{t-1} - \hat{s}_{t-1}) + D\varepsilon_t \tag{9}$$

Lagging Eq. (5) one period and recursively substituting into Eq. (8), one obtains an infinite order VAR representation in the observables:

$$x_t = (A - KC)^{t-1}\hat{s}_0 + C\sum_{j=0}^{t-1}(A - KC)^j Kx_{t-1-j} + u_t \tag{10}$$

Under weak conditions, Hansen and Sargent (2007) show that $(A - KC)$ is a stable matrix, so that the $(A - KC)^{t-1}\hat{s}_0$ term disappears in the limit and the infinite sum on the lagged observables converges in mean square.

The innovations in this VAR representation are comprised of two orthogonal components: the true structural shocks and the error in forecasting the state. The innovation variance is given by:

$$\Sigma_u = C\Sigma_s C' + D\Sigma_\varepsilon D' \tag{11}$$

Fernandez-Villaverde et al. (2007) show that the eigenvalues of $(A - BD^{-1}C)$ being less than unity in modulus implies that $\Sigma_s = 0$. When $\Sigma_s = 0$, then $\Sigma_u = D\Sigma_\varepsilon D'$, and it is straightforward to show that Eq. (10) reduces to Eq. (4). If the "poor man's invertibility" condition is not satisfied, then $\Sigma_s \neq 0$, and the innovation variance from the VAR is strictly larger than the innovation variance in the structural model. This discussion unveils a critical point – the failure of invertibility is part and parcel a failure of the observables to reveal the state vector. Non-invertibility is fundamentally an issue of missing information.

This discussion also reveals that non-invertibility is not necessarily an "either/or" proposition. Eq. (11) makes clear that the extent to which a failure of invertibility might "matter" quantitatively is how large Σ_s – that is, how hidden the state is. This has a number of implications. First, even if the condition for invertibility fails, Σ_s may nevertheless be "small," meaning that $\Sigma_u \approx D\Sigma_\varepsilon D'$. Put differently, the VAR innovations may very closely map into the structural shocks even if a given system is technically non-invertible. Second, what observable variables are included in a VAR might matter – some observables may do a better job of forecasting the missing states, hence leading to smaller Σ_s and a closer mapping between VAR innovations and structural shocks. Finally, adding more observable variables should always work to lower Σ_s, and thus ameliorate problems due to non-invertibility. This means that estimating larger dimensional VARs may generally be advantageous relative to the small systems that are frequently estimated in the literature. It also potentially speaks to the benefits of estimating factor augmented models, which can efficiently condition on large information sets. I return to this issue in the sixth section below.

A DSGE MODEL

For the purposes of examining quantitatively how important non-invertibility may be to applied researchers, I consider a standard DSGE model with a particular kind of shock that is known to lead to an invertibility problem. The model is DSGE model with both nominal and real frictions.

On the real side, there is habit formation in consumption, convex investment adjustment costs, and imperfect competition. On the nominal side there is price rigidity. A nice feature of the model is that, under certain parameter restrictions, it reverts to a simple neoclassical growth model with variable labor supply. The shock that generates the non-invertibility, for reasons to be discussed below, is a "news shock" about anticipated technological change.

The next subsections describe the decision problems of the various actors in the model as well as results concerning aggregation and the definition of equilibrium.

Households

There is a representative household that consumes a final good, makes decisions to accumulate capital, supplies labor, holds riskless one period nominal bonds issued by a government, and holds nominal money balances. Imposing standard functional forms, its decision problem can be written:

$$\max_{c_t,n_t,I_t,k_{t+1},M_{t+1},B_{t+1}} E_0 \sum_{t=0}^{\infty} \beta^t \left(\ln(c_t - \gamma c_{t-1}) - \theta \frac{n_t^{1+\xi}}{1+\xi} + \chi \frac{\left(\frac{M_{t+1}}{p_t}\right)^{1-v}}{1-v} \right)$$

s.t.

$$c_t + I_t + \frac{B_{t+1} - B_t}{p_t} + \frac{M_{t+1} - M_t}{p_t} \leq w_t n_t + R_t k_t + i_{t-1}\frac{B_t}{p_t} + \frac{\Pi_t}{p_t} + \frac{T_t}{p_t}$$

$$k_{t+1} = \left(1 - \frac{\tau}{2}\left(\frac{I_t}{I_{t-1}} - \Delta_I\right)^2\right)I_t + (1-\delta)k_t$$

γ governs the degree of internal habit formation in consumption, ξ is the inverse Frisch labor supply elasticity, and v will determine the elasticity of the demand for real balances with respect to the nominal interest rate, i_t. p_t is the price of goods in terms of money. w_t and R_t are the real factor prices for labor and capital, respectively. B_t and M_t are the dollar amounts of bonds and money with which the household enters the period. I_t is investment in physical capital, Π_t is nominal profits distributed lump sum from firms, and T_t is nominal lump sum tax/transfers from the government. τ is a parameter governing the cost of adjusting investment, with Δ_I the (gross) balanced growth path growth rate of investment.

The first order conditions for an interior solution to the household problem are:

$$\lambda_t = \frac{1}{c_t - \gamma c_{t-1}} - \beta \gamma E_t \frac{1}{c_{t+1} - \gamma c_t} \tag{12}$$

$$\theta n_t^\xi = \lambda_t w_t \tag{13}$$

$$\lambda_t = \beta E_t \lambda_{t+1} (1 + i_t) \frac{p_t}{p_{t+1}} \tag{14}$$

$$\mu_t = \beta E_t (\lambda_{t+1} R_{t+1} + (1 - \delta) \mu_{t+1}) \tag{15}$$

$$\chi \left(\frac{M_{t+1}}{p_t} \right)^{-\nu} = \left(\frac{i_t}{1 + i_t} \right) \lambda_t \tag{16}$$

$$\lambda_t = \mu_t \left(1 - \frac{\tau}{2} \left(\frac{I_t}{I_{t-1}} - \Delta_I \right)^2 - \tau \left(\frac{I_t}{I_{t-1}} - \Delta_I \right) \left(\frac{I_t}{I_{t-1}} \right) \right)$$
$$+ \beta \tau E_t \mu_{t+1} \left(\frac{I_{t+1}}{I_t} - \Delta_I \right) \left(\frac{I_{t+1}}{I_t} \right)^2 \tag{17}$$

λ_t is the current value Lagrange multiplier on the flow budget constraint and μ_t is the multiplier on the accumulation equation. Eq. (12) defines the marginal utility of consumption, Eq. (13) is a labor supply condition, Eq. (14) is the Euler equation for bonds, and Eq. (15) is the Euler equation for capital. Eq. (16) implicitly defines the demand for real balances. Eq. (17) is the first order condition with respect to investment. When there are no adjustment costs, $\lambda_t = \mu_t$, and Eqs. (14)–(15) define the usual approximate arbitrage condition between the real interest rate on bonds and the return on capital.

Production

Production is split up into two subsectors. The final goods sector is competitive and aggregates a continuum of intermediate goods, $y_{j,t}$, $j \in (0, 1)$. The production technology for the final good is a CES aggregate of the intermediate goods, with $\varepsilon > 1$ the elasticity of substitution:

$$y_t = \left(\int_0^1 y_{j,t}^{\frac{\varepsilon-1}{\varepsilon}} dj \right)^{\frac{\varepsilon}{\varepsilon-1}}$$

Profit maximization yields a demand curve for each intermediate and an aggregate price index:

$$y_{j,t} = \left(\frac{p_{j,t}}{p_t}\right)^{-\varepsilon} y_t \tag{18}$$

$$p_t = \left(\int_0^1 p_{j,t}^{1-\varepsilon} dj\right)^{\frac{1}{1-\varepsilon}} \tag{19}$$

Intermediate goods firms are price-takers in factor markets and produce output according to a standard Cobb-Douglas production function:

$$y_{j,t} = a_t k_{j,t}^\alpha n_{j,t}^{1-\alpha} \tag{20}$$

a_t is a technology shifter that is common across firms. Because firms have pricing power (as long as $\varepsilon < \infty$), it is helpful to break the firm problem into two parts. In the first stage firms choose inputs to minimize total cost subject to producing as much as is demanded at a given price:

$$\min_{n_{j,t}, k_{j,t}} w_t n_{j,t} + R_t k_{j,t}$$

s.t.

$$a_t k_{j,t}^\alpha n_{j,t}^{1-\alpha} \geq \frac{1}{p_t}\left(\frac{p_{j,t}}{p_t}\right)^{-\varepsilon} y_t$$

The first order conditions are:

$$w_t = mc_{j,t}(1-\alpha)a_t\left(\frac{k_{j,t}}{n_{j,t}}\right)^\alpha \tag{21}$$

$$R_t = mc_{j,t}\alpha a_t\left(\frac{k_{j,t}}{n_{j,t}}\right)^{\alpha-1} \tag{22}$$

$mc_{j,t}$, the multiplier on the production constraint, and has the interpretation of real marginal cost. Because all intermediate firms face the same factor prices, it is straightforward to show that real marginal cost will be the same across firms and that all firms will hire capital and labor in the same ratio.

It is assumed that firms face exogenous price stickiness in setting their prices. This makes the pricing problem dynamic. Following Calvo (1983) and much of the subsequent literature, let $1 - \varphi$ be the probability that a firm is allowed to adjust its price in any period. This probability is independent of where the firm's price is or when it last adjusted. When setting its price, the firm seeks to maximizes the expected present discounted value of future profits, where profits are discounted by both the stochastic discount factor measured in utils, $\Lambda_{t+s} = \beta^s \lambda_{t+s}$, and the probability that a price chosen today is still in effect in the future, φ^s. The problem of a firm with the ability to update in date t is:

$$\max_{p_{j,t}} E_t \sum_{s=0}^{\infty} (\varphi\beta)^s \Lambda_{t+s} \left(\frac{p_{j,t}}{p_{t+s}} \left(\frac{p_{j,t}}{p_{t+s}} \right)^{-\varepsilon} y_t - mc_t \left(\frac{p_{j,t}}{p_{t+s}} \right)^{-\varepsilon} y_t \right)$$

The solution is an optimal reset price, $p_t^{\#}$, satisfying:

$$p_t^{\#} = \frac{\varepsilon}{\varepsilon - 1} \frac{\sum\limits_{s=0}^{\infty} (\varphi\beta)^s (mc_{t+s} p_{t+s}^{\varepsilon} y_{t+s})}{\sum\limits_{s=0}^{\infty} (\varphi\beta)^s (p_{t+s}^{\varepsilon-1} y_{t+s})}$$

Note that $p_t^{\#}$ does not depend on j, and is hence the same for all updating price-setters. This follows from the fact that marginal cost, mc_t, is the same for all firms. The optimal reset price is essentially a markup over marginal cost. If $\varphi = 0$, so that prices are flexible, this formula reduces to the standard fixed markup over marginal cost, with the markup given by $\varepsilon/(\varepsilon - 1)$.

Government

The sole role of the government is to set nominal interest rates according to a Taylor rule. The government then prints a sufficient amount of nominal money, M_{t+1}, so that the money market clears at the desired interest rate. Any seignorage revenue is remitted to households lump sum via T_t. The Taylor rule is:

$$i_t = \rho i_{t-1} + (1 - \rho)\psi_{\pi}(\pi_t - \pi^*) + (1 - \rho)\psi_y \left(\frac{y_t}{y_{t-1}} - \Delta_y \right) \quad (23)$$

$0 \leqslant \rho \leqslant 1$ is an interest rate smoothing parameter, π^* is an exogenous inflation target, and ψ_{π} and ψ_y are response coefficients to inflation and the output "growth gap," where Δ_y is the balanced growth path (gross) growth rate of output. I abstract from a monetary shock and restrict attention to parameter values that yield a determinate rational expectations equilibrium.

Remittance of seignorage revenue requires that:

$$T_t = M_{t+1} - M_t \quad (24)$$

Exogenous Process

For simplicity there is only one exogenous stochastic variable in the model – the level of technology, a_t. It is assumed to follow a random walk with drift subject to two stochastic disturbances:

$$\ln a_t = g_a + \ln a_{t-1} + \varepsilon_t + u_{t-q} \qquad (25)$$
$$\varepsilon_t \sim N(0, \sigma_e)$$
$$u_t \sim N(0, \sigma_u)$$

ε_t is a standard technology shock. u_t is a "news shock" in the sense that agents in the economy see it in period t, but it has no effect on the level of technology until period $t+q$, where $q \geqslant 1$. For reasons to be spelled out below, the presence of news shocks like this can easily lead to the non-invertibility problem. The two kinds of technology shocks are assumed to be distributed independently. This assumption is less restrictive than it may seem – it would be straightforward to allow the shocks to be correlated and then partition them into orthogonal components.

Aggregation and Equilibrium

The notion of equilibrium is standard – it is a set of prices and quantities consistent with the first order conditions of households and firms holding and the budget constraints binding with equality. Market-clearing requires that total capital and labor demand equal that supplied by households:

$$\int_0^1 n_{j,t} dj = n_t$$
$$\int_0^1 k_{j,t} dj = k_t$$

Aggregate inflation evolves according to:

$$1 + \pi_t = ((1 - \varphi)(1 + \pi_t^{\#})^{1-\varepsilon} + \varphi)^{\frac{1}{1-\varepsilon}} \qquad (26)$$

Here $1 + \pi_t^{\#} = p_t^{\#}/p_{t-1}$. Aggregation of the intermediate firm production functions yields:

$$y_t = \frac{a_t k_t^{\alpha} n_t^{1-\alpha}}{v_t} \qquad (27)$$

v_t is a deadweight loss due to price dispersion:

$$v_t = \int_0^1 \left(\frac{p_{j,t}}{p_t}\right)^{-\varepsilon} dj$$

It can be written recursively as:

$$v_t = (1 - \varphi)\left(\frac{1 + \pi_t^{\#}}{1 + \pi_t}\right)^{-\varepsilon} + \varphi(1 + \pi_t)^{\varepsilon} v_{t-1} \tag{28}$$

Aggregate bond market-clearing ($B_t = 0$) and the combination of the government and household budget constraints yields the standard aggregate accounting identity:

$$y_t = c_t + I_t \tag{29}$$

After normalizing variables to account for balanced growth owing to the unit root in technology, the model is solved via log-linearizing about the normalized steady state using standard techniques. The normalizations are as follows:

$$\hat{a}_t = \frac{a_t}{a_{t-1}}, \quad \hat{c}_t = \frac{c_t}{a_t^{\frac{1}{1-\alpha}}}, \quad \hat{y}_t = \frac{y_t}{a_t^{\frac{1}{1-\alpha}}}, \quad \hat{I}_t = \frac{c_t}{a_t^{\frac{1}{1-\alpha}}}, \quad \hat{k}_t = \frac{k_t}{a_{t-1}^{\frac{1}{1-\alpha}}}$$

Most other variables of the model, including hours, are stationary by construction. In logs, these normalizations imply cointegrating relationships that can be brought to the data. The solution of the transformed model gives rise to a state space system of the form in equations Eqs. (1)–(2).

Different parameterizations of the model nest popular, simpler models. When $\tau = 0$, $\gamma = 0$, $\varphi = 0$, and $\varepsilon = \infty$ the model reverts to a standard competitive RBC model. I will refer to this model as the "RBC model." $\varepsilon < \infty$ gives rise an RBC model with imperfect competition; this leads to a steady state distortion (due to price being greater than marginal cost), but has no first order effects on the equilibrium dynamics, and is therefore not of much interest in its own right. $\varphi > 0$ but $\tau = 0$ and $\gamma = 0$ is a standard "sticky price model." I will refer to the general specification of the model as the "full model."

Why Do News Shocks Give Rise to Non-Invertibility?

A non-invertibility means that a VAR estimated on observable variables will fail to perfectly recover a model's underlying structural shocks, even with an infinite sample size. As noted in the second section, the problem occurs when the included observable variables fail to perfectly reveal the state vector. When this is the case, the innovations from a VAR in observables are a combination of the structural shocks and errors in forecasting the state.

In many circumstances a researcher concerned about non-invertibility can simply include the relevant state variables in the list of observables and estimate a VAR with those variables included. This is not feasible in a model with news shocks, because the presence of news shocks introduces an unassailable missing state variable problem. When there are anticipation effects, with $q \geqslant 1$, u_t becomes both a shock and a state variable. This is because agents at time t must keep track of realizations of $u_{t-1}, \ldots, u_{t-q-1}$ when making choices at time t; because these shocks have not yet affected a_t, even if a_t is observed the full state is hidden. This poses a potentially serious problem, since the entire structural VAR enterprise is about identifying shocks, not conditioning on them.

In order to see this point clearly, it is helpful to introduce additional state variables which keep track of lagged news shocks. There will be q additional states for q periods of anticipation. Define these as $z_{i,t}$ for $i = 1, \ldots q$. Doing so allows one to write a process for technology that satisfies the Markov property:

$$\ln a_t = g_a + \ln a_{t-1} + \varepsilon_t + z_{1,t-1} \tag{30}$$

$$z_{1,t} = z_{2,t-1} \tag{31}$$

$$z_{2,t} = z_{3,t-1} \tag{32}$$

$$\vdots$$

$$z_{q,t} = u_t \tag{33}$$

The agents in the economy must keep track of the zs; given that these are just equal to the news shock at various lags, the econometrician cannot directly condition on the zs. Hence, the state vector cannot, in general, be observed based on a history of observables, and the conditions for invertibility are likely to fail.

Some authors, most notably Blanchard, L'Hullier, and Lorenzoni (2011), have studied environments in which agents observe noisy signals about the underlying state of the economy and must solve a signal extraction problem. In a sense, the agents in the economy presented in this section also observe noisy signals about the future state of the economy, though the problem is considerably simpler. While the news shock does generate perfect foresight about future z, it does not lead to perfect foresight about the level of future $\ln a_t$. This is because of the presence of the surprise technology shock, ε_t. Agents could observe a positive news shock today, u_t, that does not materialize into higher $\ln a_{t+q}$ because of a low realization of ε at any of the dates in between, $t+1, \ldots, t+q$. On average, of course, the news shock is realized because the expected realizations of the surprise technology shocks are all zero, and this average response is what is reflected in an impulse response function, either one computed directly from the model or identified from a VAR. A feasible modification of the problem, though not considered here, would be to allow agents to observe only a noisy measure of u_t, which would then translate into a noisy forecast of future z and an even noisier forecast of future $\ln a$ relative to the specification described above. This setup would necessitate solving a signal extraction problem in which the agents in the economy effectively choose how much attention to pay to the signal of u_t, with agents reacting less the noisier is the signal. This kind of setup poses no special problems as pertains estimating a VAR, though it does require that special attention be paid to how one defines and interprets an impulse response.[7]

VARS WITH NON-INVERTIBILITY: MONTE CARLO RESULTS

In this section I conduct several Monte Carlo experiments. The objective is to examine how well an apparently correctly specified structural VAR performs on model simulated data when there is a known non-invertibility. Can a VAR come close to replicating the structural model's theoretical impulse responses to shocks when there is a non-invertibility? Can estimated VAR impulse responses be used to differentiate between competing models? This section seeks to provide some answers to these questions.

Consider the model described in the previous section (under any of the nested parameter configurations). The model has two stochastic shocks – the conventional surprise technology shock and the news shock. Suppose that a researcher observes TFP growth, $\ln \hat{a}_t = \ln a_t - \ln a_{t-1}$, and another variable, say output, $\ln \hat{y}_t$.[8] Recall that because of the normalization, observed output is: $\ln y_t - \frac{1}{1-\alpha} \ln a_t$, so this imposes the cointegrating relationship of the structural model.[9] Suppose a researcher estimates a VAR(p) on the system $x_t = [\ln \hat{a}_t \ \ln \hat{y}_t]$ (abstracting from the constant term):

$$x_t = A_1 x_{t-1} + \cdots + A_p x_{t-p} + u_t, \quad E(u_t u_t') = \Sigma_u \tag{34}$$

Where u_t is a vector of innovations with variance-covariance matrix Σ_u, which in general is not diagonal. It is assumed there exists a mapping between orthogonal shocks, e_t, and the reduced form innovations given by: $u_t = A_0^{-1} e_t$, where A_0^{-1} is the "impact matrix". After normalizing the variance of each orthogonal shock to unity, one sees that $\Sigma_u = A_0^{-1} A_0^{-1}{}'$. With n variables in the system, one needs to impose $n(n-1)/2$ restrictions to uniquely recover A_0^{-1}.

In the proposed VAR system, a recursive orthogonalization of the innovations, with $\ln \hat{a}_t$ "ordered" first, is apparently consistent with the implications of the model. This amounts to A_0^{-1} being identified as the Choleski decomposition of the estimated variance-covariance matrix of residuals. Surprise movements in TFP growth would be identified with the surprise technology shock, while surprise movements in output (or any other variable) orthogonalized with respect TFP innovations would be identified with the news shock. This kind of empirical strategy is precisely what is often employed in the empirical literature. Beaudry and Portier (2006), for example, estimate a two variable with VAR with TFP and stock prices, identifying stock price movements uncorrelated with TFP innovations as news shocks.

For each of the nested parameter configurations (RBC, sticky price, and the full model), I conduct the following Monte Carlo experiments. For the finite sample experiment, I create 500 different data sets with 200 observations each. 200 observations is about the size of most postwar US data sets. On each simulated data set, I estimate a VAR with 8 lags, and orthogonalize the innovations such that TFP growth is ordered first. For each simulation I compute impulse responses to news and surprise technology shocks, and then compare the distribution of estimated response to the true responses from the model. For the large sample experiment, I create one data set with 100,000 observations, estimate a VAR with 8 lags with TFP growth ordered first, and compare the responses to the true model responses.[10]

These experiments require selecting parameter values for the model. Several parameters are fixed at levels across the different nested specifications. The unit of time is taken to be a quarter. The growth rate of TFP, g_a, is set to 0.0025. This means that TFP grows by about 1% at an annual frequency. The Cobb-Douglas share parameter, α, is fixed at 1/3. With average productivity growth of 1%, output and its components will grow at 1.5% on average, which is broadly consistent with the post-war US per capita data. The subjective discount factor, β, is 0.99, while the inflation target is set to $\pi^* = 0.005$, or 2% at an annual frequency. This implies an average annualized nominal interest rate of $i = 5.6\%$. The depreciation rate on capital is set to $\delta = 0.02$. The parameter ξ, which is the inverse Frisch labor supply elasticity, is fixed at one. There is substantial disagreement on the value of this parameter in the literature; many macro models need a high elasticity while most micro studies point to a low elasticity. The central estimate in Kimball and Shapiro (2010) is unity, which strikes a middle ground between the micro and macro literatures. The scaling parameter on the disutility of labor, θ, is always fixed such that steady state hours are $1/3$ of the normalized time endowment of one. Because of the presence of the Taylor rule and separability in preferences, the parameters governing the utility from holding real balances, χ and v, need not be calibrated. The standard deviations of the two shocks are fixed at $\sigma_\varepsilon = 0.01$ and $\sigma_u = 0.005$. These shock magnitudes are not chosen with any particular moments in mind, but they do imply that surprise technology shocks drive more of the unconditional variance of TFP growth than do news shocks (80% vs. 20%). This kind of calibration is necessary to produce data with similar co-movement among output and its components that is observed in actual data.[11] As we will see below, the surprise technology shock being more important than news shocks tends to exacerbate any problems due to non-invertibility, and can therefore be considered relatively conservative. Finally, the time lag between the revelation of news and its affect on productivity, q, is set to 3. This means that there are three quarters of anticipation.

The other parameters of the model govern the degree of frictions, and therefore the magnitudes of the departure from the simple real business cycle RBC framework. When prices are sticky, φ is set to 0.7. This implies that the average duration between prices changes is between three and four quarters, which is broadly consistent with micro estimates (e.g., Bils & Klenow, 2004) and a number of macro estimates. The parameters of the Taylor rule are set to $\rho = 0.8$, $\psi_\pi = 1.5$, and $\psi_y = 0.5$. These are in line with standard calibrations and estimates within the literature. For real frictions, the habit formation parameter is set to $\gamma = 0.7$ and the investment adjustment cost parameter is $\tau = 2.5$. These are the central estimates in Christiano et al. (2005). Table 1 summarizes the parameter values for the different cases.

Full Model

In the fully parameterized model with both real and nominal frictions, the state vector is:[12]

$$s_t = [\ln \hat{y}_t \quad \ln \hat{k}_t \quad i_t \quad \ln v_t \quad z_{1,t} \quad z_{2,t} \quad z_{3,t} \quad \ln \hat{I}_t \quad \ln \hat{c}_t]'$$

Table 1. Parameters.

Full Model	RBC Model	Sticky Price Model
$\beta = 0.99$	$\gamma = 0$	$\gamma = 0$
$\delta = 0.02$	$\tau = 0$	$\tau = 0$
$g_a = 0.0025$	$\varphi = 0$	
$\pi^* = 0.005$		
$\alpha = \frac{1}{3}$		
$\zeta = 1$		
$\sigma_e = 0.01$		
$\sigma_u = 0.005$		
$\theta \Rightarrow n^* = \frac{1}{3}$		
$\gamma = 0.7$		
$\tau = 2.5$		
$\varphi = 0.7$		
$\epsilon = 11$		
$\rho = 0.8$		
$\psi_\pi = 1.5$		
$\psi_y = 1.5$		

Notes: The left column, labeled "Full Model," lists the parameter values used in the fully parameterized specification. The remaining columns list the parameter restrictions relative to the full model.

With three periods of anticipation there are three additional state variables – $z_{1,t}$, $z_{2,t}$, and $z_{3,t}$. TFP growth and normalized output are observed. Denote the vectors of observables as $x_t = [\ln \hat{a}_t \ln \hat{y}_t]'$. The shock vector is $\varepsilon_t = [\varepsilon_t u_t]$. After solving the model at the parameter values given in Table 1, the "poor man's invertibility condition" of Fernandez-Villaverde, Rubio-Ramirez, Sargent, and Watson (2007), and discussed in the second section, can easily be checked. In section A.1 the numeric values of the A, B, C, and D matrixes are shown, as are the eigenvalues of the matrix $M = (A - BD^{-1}C)$. The maximum modulus of the eigenvalues of M is 1.32. Hence, the invertibility condition fails.

Fig. 1 plots impulse response obtained from Monte Carlo simulations of the "full model." The solid lines are the theoretical responses in the model of the log levels of output and TFP to both news and surprise technology shocks.[13] The left panel plots responses from the finite sample simulations; the right panel shows results for the large sample simulation. In the finite sample panel, the dashed lines are the mean responses to the two shocks averaged over 500 different simulations of the model with 200 observations each. The shaded gray regions represent the middle 68% of the distribution

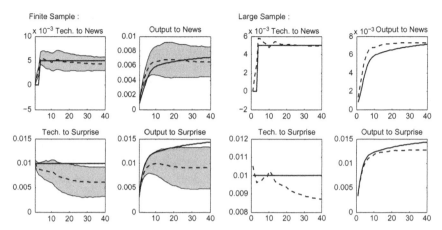

Fig. 1. Monte Carlo Results in Full Model.

Notes: The solid lines are the theoretical impulse responses to news and surprise technology shocks in the "Full Model" using the parameterization as described in the text. For the Monte Carlo exercises the VARs feature ln $\hat{a}_t$ and ln $\hat{y}_t$ and are estimated with $p = 8$ lags. In the left panel, labeled "Finite Sample," the dashed lines are the mean responses averaged across 500 simulations of data sets with 200 observations each, while the shaded gray regions depict the middle 68% of the distribution of estimated responses across the 500 simulations. In the right panel, labeled "Large Sample," the dashed lines are the estimated impulse responses from the estimation on one sample with 100,000 observations.

of estimated responses across the 500 simulations. In the large sample panel, the dashed lines are the points estimates of the impulse responses obtained from one estimation of the VAR on a single data set with 100,000 observations. All VARs are estimated with $p = 8$ lags, and the innovations are orthogonalized with TFP growth ordered first.

A quick visual inspection reveals that, on average, the structural VAR does a good job of capturing the qualitative dynamics of the impulse responses to both kinds of technology shocks. Turning first to the finite sample results, the estimated responses to the news shock are essentially unbiased at horizons up to forty quarters – the average estimated responses roughly lie atop the true model responses. Further, the distributions of estimated responses are fairly tight and are centered around the true responses. The results are somewhat worse for the responses to the surprise technology shock, with some downward bias in the estimated responses, particularly at longer forecast horizons. Nevertheless, the impulse responses at short forecast horizons are estimated quite well, and the longer horizon dynamics are qualitatively in line with the true model dynamics.

The right panel plots responses obtained in the "large sample" exercise. The dashed lines are very close to the true model responses at all horizons for both shocks. That they do not lie exactly on top of the true model responses is a direct consequence of the non-invertibility resulting because of the presence of foresight – non-invertibility means that, even in an infinitely large sample, a VAR cannot exactly recover the true impulse responses of the underlying model. What this exercise reveals is that the large sample bias is relatively small, and, for all practice purposes, likely of little importance. In either finite or large samples, the VAR does a very good job at recovering the model's dynamics in response to both shocks.

Table 2 provides some quantitative evidence on the quality of fit of the estimated VARs. It shows the average absolute deviations of the impulse responses estimated in the simulations relative to the true model responses, at forecast horizons from impact to 40 quarters. For the large sample panel the numbers are simply the average deviation over 40 quarters of the estimated responses on one data set with 100,000 observations relative to the model responses; for the small sample panel the numbers are based on the deviation of the average estimated response across simulations. The

Table 2.   Mean Absolute Deviations: VAR Monte Carlo Exercises.

	Tech. to News	Output to News	Tech. to Surprise	Output to Surprise	Average
Large Sample					
Full	0.0266	0.0698	0.0693	0.0871	0.0632
RBC	0.0676	0.1006	0.0366	0.0596	0.0661
Sticky Price	0.1062	0.1402	0.0403	0.0619	0.0872
Small Sample					
Full	0.0466	0.0522	0.2833	0.3545	0.1841
RBC	0.0974	0.1339	0.2595	0.3375	0.2071
Sticky Price	0.2031	0.2662	0.1278	0.1524	0.1874

Notes: These numbers represent the average absolute deviations of the estimated impulse responses relative to the true responses in the models over the first 40 horizons, times 100, for the various different Monte Carlo exercises. In the "Large Sample" block the numbers are based on one sample with 100,000 observations relative to the true model responses. In the "Small Sample" block the numbers are based on the difference between the average estimated responses across 500 simulations relative to the true model responses. The final column, labeled "Average," shows the average of the mean absolute deviations of all four impulse responses.

numbers in the table are multiplied by 100, so they have the interpretation of average percentage point deviations. The average absolute deviations in the case of the news shock in the large simulation of the full model are 0.026 percentage points and 0.07 percentage points, for the TFP and output responses, respectively. These numbers are very small. For example, the TFP response after three quarters is 0.5%. On average the estimated response thus lies between 0.47% and 0.53%. The large sample biases in response to the surprise technology shock are somewhat larger, but nevertheless small. As one would expect, the finite sample biases tend to be larger, but are again small and likely of little practical concern.

RBC Model

The RBC model is a special case of the full model with the parameter restrictions $\varphi = \gamma = \tau = 0$. This turns out to substantially simplify the model, significantly reducing the state space. The state vector for this model is:

$$s_t = [\ln \hat{k}_t \ z_{1,t} \ z_{2,t} \ z_{3,t}]'$$

Section A.2 shows the values of the parameters of the state space system when TFP growth and normalized output are observed by an econometrician. As in the full model case, the invertibility condition fails – the maximum modulus of the eigenvalues of $M = (A - BD^{-1}C)$ is 1.0572.

Fig. 2 shows results for both the finite and large sample Monte Carlo exercises for the RBC model. One interesting thing to note is that the theoretical impulse responses of output to both news and surprise technology shocks differ a great deal relative to the full model with both real and nominal frictions. In particular, in the RBC model output declines on impact in response to good news about productivity growth, while it rises by more than productivity in response to the surprise technology shock. These features are captured very well by the estimated VARs – in both finite and large samples, the impact effects in response to both kinds of technology shocks are estimated quite well. Examining Table 2, the biases in the estimated responses to the news shock are somewhat larger relative to the full model here; the reverse is true in response to the surprise technology shock. In both cases, the large sample biases, while present, are very small. In short, the VAR seems to do a good job.

In spite of its simplicity, an advantage of the RBC model is that it is very easy to see why the presence of news shocks leads to the invertibility problem.

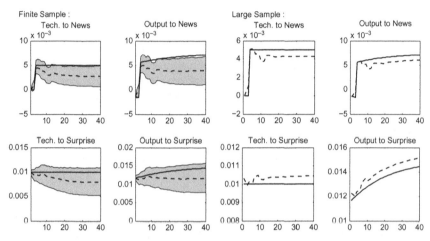

Fig. 2.   Monte Carlo Results in RBC Model.

Notes: The solid lines are the theoretical impulse responses to news and surprise technology shocks in the "RBC Model" using the parameterization as described in the text. For the Monte Carlo exercises the VARs feature ln $\hat{a}_t$ and ln $\hat{y}_t$ and are estimated with $p = 8$ lags. In the left panel, labeled "Finite Sample," the dashed lines are the mean responses averaged across 500 simulations of data sets with 200 observations each, while the shaded gray regions depict the middle 68% of the distribution of estimated responses across the 500 simulations. In the right panel, labeled "Large Sample," the dashed lines are the estimated impulse responses from the estimation on one sample with 100,000 observations.

Suppose that there were only one shock in the model, the surprise technology shock, ε_t. In this case, the state space of the model would simply be the transformed capital stock, ln $\hat{k}_t$. Hence, the matrixes A and B would just be scalars. Referring to section A.2, they would take on values $A = 0.9554$ and $B = -1.4331$. The matrixes of the observer equation, with output observed, would also be scalars, equal to $C = 0.2210$ and $D = -0.3315$. Then $M = (A - BD^{-1}C) = 0.9554 - (-1.4331 \times 0.2210/ - 0.3315)$, which is equal to 0. Hence, the invertibility condition is satisfied. This means that a univariate autoregression of ln $\hat{y}_t$ will correctly (in a large enough sample with enough lags) recover the impulse response to a technology shock as well as the time series of technology shocks.[14] In contrast, it is straightforward to show that if there are only news shocks and no surprise shocks, a univariate autoregression in either output or TFP growth is non-invertible. It is the presence of anticipation effects that drives the non-invertibility.

Sticky Price Model

The sticky price model imposes that $\gamma = \tau = 0$, so that the only friction relative to a simple RBC model is price stickiness. The state vector for this model is:

$$s_t = [\ln \hat{y}_t \ \ln \hat{k}_t \ i_t \ \ln v_t \ z_{1,t} \ z_{2,t} \ z_{3,t}]'$$

The maximum modulus of the eigenvalues of $M = (A - BD^{-1}C)$ is 1.2397, indicating a failure of the condition for invertibility. Fig. 3 shows results from the Monte Carlo simulations. The model impulse responses to the news shock are quite similar to the RBC counterparts, whereas the response to the surprise technology shock are rather different, with output significantly undershooting on impact. In both finite and large samples these effects are captured quite well in the estimated VARs. In finite samples there

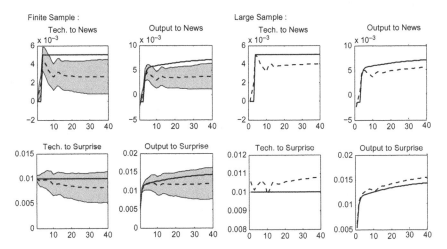

Fig. 3. Monte Carlo Results in Sticky Price Model.

Notes: The solid lines are the theoretical impulse responses to news and surprise technology shocks in the "Sticky Price Model" using the parameterization as described in the text. For the Monte Carlo exercises the VARs feature $\ln \hat{a}_t$ and $\ln \hat{y}_t$ and are estimated with $p = 8$ lags. In the left panel, labeled "Finite Sample," the dashed lines are the mean responses averaged across 500 simulations of data sets with 200 observations each, while the shaded gray regions depict the middle 68% of the distribution of estimated responses across the 500 simulations. In the right panel, labeled "Large Sample," the dashed lines are the estimated impulse responses from the estimation on one sample with 100,000 observations.

is some downward bias at longer horizons in response to both shocks, but qualitatively the estimated responses line up well with the model's. The large sample results continue to exhibit some bias but this is again relatively small.

Using SVARs to Conduct Model Comparisons

One of the main uses of structural VARs is to employ a common restriction that holds across different, potentially non-nested, models and to compare the qualitative pattern of impulse responses in the VAR to predictions from the different models. For example, many models predict that technology shocks should be the sole source of the unit root in labor productivity. But these models differ in terms of their predictions about the effects of technology shocks on other variables in the short run – RBC models with few real frictions, for example, typically predict that hours should increase following technological improvement, whereas some sticky price models with insufficiently accomodative monetary policy predict the opposite. As a leading example, Gali (1999) identifies technology shocks in a VAR setting and shows that productivity improvements lead to an immediate hours decline, leading him to conclude that sticky price, New Keynesian models are more promising than RBC models.[15]

The different nested versions of the model presented above also make very different predictions about the responses of output and hours to both news and surprise technology shocks. In the RBC model, for example, output declines on impact in response to good news (so that hours decline as well), while output rises by more than TFP on impact following a surprise shock (so that hours increase). The full model has the exact opposite prediction: hours and output increase on impact following good news, while hours decline on impact in response to a surprise technology shock. In the sticky price model hours decline on impact in response to both shocks, so that output falls following good news and rises, but by less than TFP, after the surprise technology shock.

Can estimated VARs do a good job of differentiating between these different models? The Monte Carlo results discussed above and graphically depicted in Figs. 1 through 3 show a clear answer: yes. The small biases that are present are mostly at longer forecast horizons. In either small or large samples, the impact effects of both news and surprise technology shocks are estimated both accurately and precisely. For example, in the RBC and sticky price model simulations, the estimated output response declines immediately and only rises when TFP improves, just as in the models. In the full model, output is estimated to rise on impact following a news shock and is estimated to rise by less than productivity after a surprise shock, again just as in the data. In short, a researcher hoping to use the impulse responses from an estimated VAR to qualitatively differentiate between these different models would likely be quite successful.

Non-Invertibility and the Relative Importance of Shocks

In the simulation results up to this point, the relative importance of the two stochastic shocks has been held fixed. While this may seem innocuous, the relative importance of the two kinds of shocks turns out to matter somewhat for the performance of the VARs.

Fig. 4 plots impulse responses obtained for the large sample Monte Carlo exercise for the full model under two different parameterizations of the standard deviation of the surprise technology shock: $\sigma_\varepsilon = 0.01$ (which is the benchmark value) and $\sigma_\varepsilon = 0.001$. The standard deviation of the news shock is fixed at its benchmark value, $\sigma_u = 0.005$. The solid line depicts the true model responses to the news shock, while the dashed and dotted lines, respectively, represent the responses obtained in sample sizes of 100,000 under the two different parameterizations of the magnitude of the surprise shock. In either case the estimation of the responses to the news shock is good, but it is visually apparent that the fit is significantly better when the news shock is relatively more important – that is, when the standard deviation of the surprise technology shock is small. Quantitatively, the average absolute deviation of the TFP response to the news shock is 0.026 percentage points in the large shock case and 0.008 percentage points in the small shock case. For the response of output, these differences are 0.07 percentage points and 0.01, respectively. In short, there is a large improvement in fit for the responses to the news shock when the surprise shock is less important in relative terms.

That the fit of the VARs improves as the news shock becomes relatively more important is easiest to understand by referencing back to Eq. (11): $\Sigma_u = C\Sigma_s C' + D\Sigma_\varepsilon D'$. The variance of the forecast of the state conditional on observables, Σ_s, drives a wedge between the VAR innovations, u_t, and the deep economic shocks, ε_t. The missing state variables that account for the non-invertibility are lagged values of news shocks: $u_{t-1}, \ldots, u_{t-q}$. It stands to reason that, as the relative importance of ε_t shocks declines, the observed variables will do a better job of revealing lagged values of the news shock.

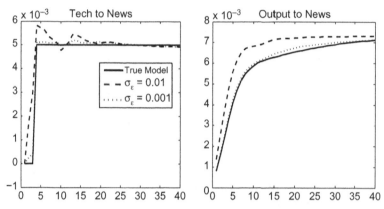

Fig. 4. Monte Carlo Results: Large vs. Small Surprise Shocks.

Notes: The solid lines are the theoretical impulse responses to a news shock in the "Full Model" using the parameterization as described in the text. The dashed and dotted lines represent the estimated responses from a large sample Monte Carlo exercise using two different values for the standard deviation of surprise technology shocks: $\sigma_\varepsilon = 0.01$ (dashed line, which also corresponds to the baseline used in previous figures) and $\sigma_\varepsilon = 0.001$ (dotted line). 100,000 observations are simulated from the "Full Model" and then a VAR is estimated on a system featuring TFP growth and normalized output, with the news shock identified as the orthogonalized output innovation. The VAR uses $p = 8$ lags.

Fig. 5 plots the Euclidian norm of Σ_s (a measure of the "size" of the variance in forecasting the state) as a function of the relative magnitude of the standard deviations of the two shocks. For this exercise, σ_u is held fixed at 0.005 and σ_ε is varied. One observes that, as $\sigma_u/\sigma_\varepsilon$ gets large, Σ_s goes to zero and the wedge disappears. Feve and Jidoud (2011) make the same point analytically in a simpler environment with news shocks about productivity. Perhaps surprisingly, the fit of the estimated VARs is not much worse than the benchmark when news shocks are relatively unimportant, though the fit does improve fairly significantly as news shocks become relatively more important.

The Role of the Anticipation Lag

Up to this point the "anticipation lag" between when agents observe a news shock and when it affects technology has been fixed at $q = 3$. This choice is

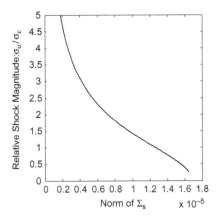

Fig. 5. Theoretical Wedge and Varying Shock Magnitudes.
Notes: This figure plots the Euclidian norm of Σ_s, the variance-covariance matrix of period t optimal forecast of the state, as a function of the relative shock magnitudes between surprise, ε_t, and news shocks, u_t. This is done in the context of the "Full Model" conditional on observing TFP growth and normalized output. The vertical axis plots the ratio of the the standard deviation of u_t divided by the standard deviation of ε_t against the determinant of Σ_s, which is obtained numerically from solving the Ricatti Eqs. (6)–(7).

arbitrary though it conforms with much of the theoretical work on news shocks. Nevertheless, the quality of the results varies in an interesting and instructive way with the anticipation lag. The manner in which the results vary reinforces the notion that non-invertibility is fundamentally a problem of informational insufficiency.

First, consider the case in which $q = 1$, so that there is only one period of anticipation. Section A.5 presents the numerical values of the state space matrixes for the "full model" when $q = 1$ and shows that the eigenvalues of $(A - BD^{-1}C)$ are all strictly less than unity in modulus. In other words, the model with one period of anticipation gives rise to an invertible VAR representation in output and technology. This means that an estimated VAR in these variables on a long enough sample with enough lags will exactly recover the impulse responses to both news and surprise technology shocks. Kurmann and Otrok (2011) similarly find an invertible VAR representation based on a Smets and Wouters (2007) type model with one period anticipated growth shocks. The intuition for this is reasonably straightforward – with only one period of anticipation, there is only one additional state, $z_{1,t} = u_t$. The innovation in output (or other variables from the model) orthogonalized with respect to current technology growth reveals that missing state. With multiple periods of anticipation the innovation in the second variable in the system cannot perfectly reveal q missing states if $q > 1$. Hence, for news shocks to generate non-invertibility there must be more than one period of anticipation.

Moving beyond the case of $q = 1$, since non-invertibility is fundamentally the result of informational deficiency, it stands to reason that the more missing state variables there are, the worse will be the performance of VARs. Since the anticipation lag increases the state vector one for one, one should expect that VARs perform more poorly as the anticipation lag increases.

Table 3 shows summary statistics for Monte Carlo exercises using data generated from the full model with different anticipation lags. To focus in on the bias due to non-invertibility, these statistics are based on estimating a VAR in technology growth and output on one data set of 100,000 observations (i.e., the "large sample" exercise). The structure of the table is similar to Table 2 – it shows the average absolute deviation of the responses of each variable to the two identified shocks over a forty period forecast horizon. The final column shows the average of the average deviations, which serves as a crude metric for the overall bias of the VAR impulse responses relative to the model responses. As the final column indicates, the average fit declines as q, the anticipation lag, increases. The intuition for this is straightforward – the bigger is q, the more missing state variables there are, and therefore the bigger is the wedge between the VAR innovations and shocks. Though there are biases in the estimated responses to the surprise

Table 3.   Mean Absolute Deviations: Different Anticipation Lags.

	Tech. to News	Output to News	Tech. to Surprise	Output to Surprise	Average
Anticipation Lag					
$q = 2$	0.0330	0.0273	0.0389	0.0454	0.0362
$q = 8$	0.0996	0.1495	0.0459	0.0544	0.0874
$q = 16$	0.1942	0.3300	0.0485	0.0679	0.1601

Notes: These numbers represent the average absolute deviations of the estimated impulse responses relative to the true responses in the models over the first 40 horizons, times 100, for different news anticipation lags in the full model specification in a two variable VAR in $\ln \hat{a}_t$ and $\ln \hat{y}_t$. The final column, labeled "Average," shows the average of the mean absolute deviations of all four presented impulse responses.

technology shock, these are fairly similar for different q. The biases in the estimated responses to news shocks, in contrast, rise with q. For extremely long anticipation lags (e.g., $q = 16$), the VAR biases are quite large.[16] The average absolute deviation of the estimated output response over forty forecast horizons, for example, is 0.33%. This is quite large when considering that the long run response of output to a news shock as calibrated is 0.75%.

These findings have some implications for the existing empirical literature on new shocks. Beaudry and Portier (2006), for example, present impulse responses to a news shock which have no discernable effect on TFP for a period of four or five years. The Monte Carlo exercise with $q = 16$ suggests that, if the true response to a news shock had a delay of that long, there would be little hope of a structural VAR recovering the impulse responses correctly.[17] This makes interpreting the Beaudry and Portier (2006) impulse responses as responses to news problematic. The impulse responses identified in Barsky and Sims (2011), in contrast, affect measured TFP within a few quarters (and show quite different impact effects on hours and output). If the true news process affects productivity quickly then there is a much better chance that these impulse responses are accurate representations of the true responses from an economic model.

ROBUSTNESS

The Monte Carlo exercises to this point have been conducted in a relatively simple environment. In particular, I have restricted attention to a two variable system in which a recursive identification lines up with the implications of news and surprise technology shocks in the economic model. This has been done with the goal of cleanly focusing in on the role of non-invertibility as a source of bias in impulse responses obtained from estimated VARs. Nevertheless, one might be interested in how non-invertibilities matter in more realistic environments with which researchers typically have to grapple – for example, in situations in which exogenous TFP is not observed, in which there are more than two shocks, or when the VAR is subject to some other kind of specification bias. This section considers several extensions to more realistic environments and confirms that the same basic results from the earlier Monte Carlo analyses obtain.

Though much of the empirical work on news shocks which uses VARs assumes that "true technology" is well-measured by a suitably constructed total factor productivity (TFP) series, in practice this assumption may be problematic.[18] I therefore consider cases in which TFP is unobserved by the econometrician. Separately identifying surprise technology shocks from news shocks is generally accomplished with a short run recursive assumption as implemented throughout the fourth section; without a measure of TFP, however, recursive zero restrictions are generally not available. As such, I begin by assuming that there is no surprise technology shock – the only source of movements in $\ln a_t$ in the model are news shocks. In terms of the process for technology, this can be accomplished by setting the variance of ε_t to zero. So as to avoid stochastic singularity and be able to estimate a VAR with more than one variable, I augment the model with a "demand" shock to the monetary policy rule, replacing Eq. (23) with:

$$i_t = \rho i_{t-1} + (1-\rho)\psi_\pi(\pi_t - \pi^*) + (1-\rho)\psi_y\left(\frac{y_t}{y_{t-1}} - \Delta_y\right) + v_{i,t}, \quad v_{i,t} \sim N(0, \sigma_v)$$

$$(35)$$

For the purposes of the Monte Carlo exercise I simulate data from the full model with the modified shock process using the baseline parameterization for news (i.e., $q = 3$ and $\sigma_u = 0.005$) and set the standard deviation of the policy shock to $\sigma = 0.0015$, or 15 basis points. I conduct the "small sample" exercise of the previous section – I draw shocks and generate 500 samples with 200 observations of data each. I estimate a VAR in output growth and the consumption–output ratio: $x_t = [\Delta \ln y_t, \ln c_t - \ln y_t]$.[19] I use a long run restriction to separate out the technology news shock from the monetary policy shock, imposing that only the news shock may have a permanent effect on the level of output in the long run. This restriction is consistent with the implications of the underlying model.[20]

Fig. 6 summarizes the Monte Carlo results. The solid lines show theoretical impulse responses of the levels of output and consumption to a news shock (upper row) and the monetary policy shock (lower row). The dashed lines are the average estimated response over the 500 simulations, and the shaded gray regions the middle 68% of the distribution of estimated responses. Qualitatively the estimated VAR does a very good job at replicating the model's dynamics to both shocks. The estimated responses to the news shock are essentially unbiased on impact and for several horizons thereafter; these responses are slightly downward biased at longer horizons but the magnitude of the bias is not large. The estimated responses to the policy shock are also quite good, on both a qualitative and quantitative dimension. In short, the VAR with the long run restriction does a good job at capturing the dynamic responses to both the news shock and the policy shock, even when TFP is unobserved.

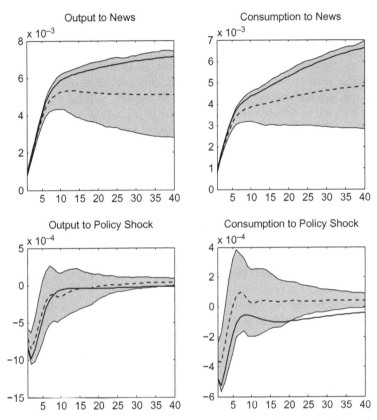

Fig. 6. Monte Carlo Results: Two Variable Model, TFP Unobserved, LR Restriction. *Notes:* The solid lines are the theoretical impulse responses to a news shock about productivity and to a monetary policy shock in the full specification of the model in which (i) there is no surprise technology shock and (ii) the standard deviation of monetary policy shocks is set to 0.15 basis points. For the Monte Carlo exercise the estimated VAR features $\Delta \ln y_t$ and $\ln c_t - \ln y_t$ and is estimated with $p = 8$ lags. The shocks are identified using a long run restriction such that the news shock is the sole source of the unit root in output. The dashed lines are the mean responses to each shock averaged across 500 simulations of data with 200 observations each, while the shaded gray regions depict the middle 68% of the distribution of estimated responses across the 500 simulations.

Next I consider the more challenging case in which there are both news and surprise technology shocks (for this exercise there is no monetary policy shock), but continue to assume that the econometrician cannot observe TFP. I continue to generate 500 data sets from the full model with 200

observations each. For this exercise I consider estimating a two variable
VAR in the growth rate of average labor productivity and labor hours,
$x_t = [\Delta(\ln y_t - \ln n_t) \ln n_t]$.[21]

The challenging aspect of this system is that "conventional" VAR
identifying restrictions are not available. Since both shocks permanently
affect the nonstationary variables of the model, a long run restriction
cannot be used to differentiate between the two kinds of technology shocks.
And since TFP is not observed, and all other variables react on impact to
both kinds of technology shocks, short run zero restrictions are not
available either. I therefore employ a modified sign/shape restriction to
separately identify the news and surprise technology shocks. In particular,
I identify the news shock as the orthogonal shock which generates an
impulse response of labor productivity with the greatest difference between
the response at a horizon of 40 quarters from the impact response. Even
though average labor productivity reacts immediately to news shocks
because of movements in hours, this restriction gets at the idea that the news
shock should have a much bigger longer run effect on average productivity
than on impact.

Before discussing the Monte Carlo results I briefly discuss the mechanics
of this particular restriction. In the VAR system Eq. (34) the reduced form
innovations are a function of the structural shocks: $u_t = A_0^{-1} e_t$. For a
particular A_0^{-1} satisfying $A_0^{-1} A_0^{-1'} = \Sigma_u$, call it $\tilde{A}_0^{-1}$, the entire space of
permissible impact matrixes can be represented by $\tilde{A}_0^{-1} \tilde{D}$, where $\tilde{D}$ is an
orthonormal matrix, for example, $\tilde{D}\tilde{D}' = I$. The sign/shape restriction
methodology consists of (i) starting with an arbitrary $\tilde{A}_0^{-1}$, say a Choleski
decomposition and, (ii) searching over the space of orthonormal matrixes,
$\tilde{D}$, for an impact matrix, $\tilde{A}_0^{-1} \tilde{D}$ that satisfies the sign/shape restriction. Step
(i) ensures that the resulting impact matrix satisfies $A_0^{-1} A_0^{-1'} = \Sigma_u$. In many
applications step (ii) results in a *set* of candidate impulse vectors – that is,
there is not point identification, but rather set identification (see, e.g., Faust,
1998, and Uhlig, 2005). Because my restriction is not simply qualitative
(e.g., a monetary tightening lowers both output and prices), but can rather
be quantified in terms of the difference between the impulse response of
labor productivity at horizon 40 relative to impact, my restriction achieves
point identification.

Fig. 7 summarizes the results from the sign/shape restriction exercise,
where again the dashed line represents the average estimated response across
the 500 simulations, the solid line the true model response, and the shaded
gray region the middle 68% of the distribution of estimated responses. The
VAR does a very good job at capturing the model's responses to the two

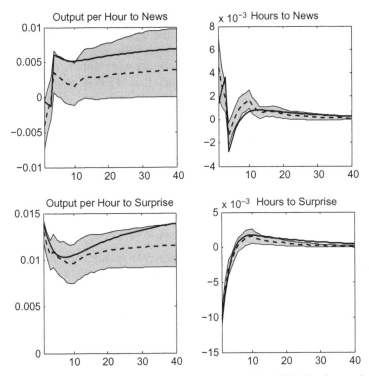

Fig. 7. Monte Carlo Results: Two Variable Model, TFP Unobserved, Sign Restriction.

Notes: The solid lines are the theoretical impulse responses to a news shock about productivity and to a surprise technology shock in the full model. For the Monte Carlo exercise the estimated VAR features the growth rate of average labor productivity, $\Delta(\ln y_t - \ln n_t)$ and log hours worked, $\ln n_t$, and is estimated with $p = 8$ lags. The shocks are identified with a shape restriction: in particular, the news shock is identified as the shock that results in an impulse response with the largest difference between the level response of average productivity at a 40 period horizon relative to the impact response. The dashed lines are the mean responses to each shock averaged across 500 simulations of data with 200 observations each, while the shaded gray regions depict the middle 68% of the distribution of estimated responses across the 500 simulations.

technology shocks. In response to the news shock hours rise slightly on impact and remain high until the level of technology improves three periods later, after which time they sharply decline. The response of labor productivity mirrors the movements in hours – it initially falls and then sharply rebounds when technology actually improves, and continues to rise thereafter. The impulse responses from the sign restricted VAR do a good job at capturing these features. The results for the surprise technology shocks are even better – here the biases are very small. In spite of the non-invertibility and in spite of the fact that TFP is not observed, the VAR does a very good job at capturing the dynamic response to both technology shocks.

As a final robustness exercise I consider the realistic modification of the underlying DSGE model in which there are more than two shocks. In addition to both kinds of technology shocks (news and surprise), I assume that there are two "demand shocks" – a monetary policy shock as in Eq. (35), and a preference shock that shifts the disutility of labor. The preference shock obeys a stationary AR(1):

$$\ln \theta_t = (1 - \rho_\theta)\theta^* + \rho_\theta \ln \theta_{t-1} + \varepsilon_{\theta_t} \tag{36}$$

Here $\rho_\theta \in (0, 1)$ and θ^* is chosen to generate steady state labor hours of one-third. For the Monte Carlo exercises the parameterization is the same as in the benchmark, with the volatility of the monetary policy shock of 15 basis points and the volatility of the preference shock of 1%, with $\rho_\theta = 0.9$. As earlier, I generate 500 data sets with 200 observations each.

I conduct two separate Monte Carlo exercises on data generated from the four shock system. For simplicity I assume that the researcher can observe TFP, though the results using average labor productivity and sign restrictions are similar. In one case I assume that a researcher estimates a four variable VAR in TFP growth, output and consumption normalized relative to the level of TFP (which imposes the model based cointegrating relationships), and hours worked: $x_t = [\ln \hat{a}_t \ \ln \hat{y}_t \ \ln \hat{c}_t \ \ln n_t]$. In the other case I assume that the researcher estimates a three variable VAR in TFP growth, normalized output, and hours: $x_t = [\ln \hat{a}_t \ \ln \hat{y}_t \ \ln n_t]$. The second specification introduces another bias in addition to non-invertibility, since there are four economic shocks but the estimated VAR model includes only three variables.

With four shocks, even though TFP is observed, a recursive identification is inconsistent with the predictions of the model. This is because the innovation in any of the other three variables orthogonalized with respect to the TFP innovation will be driven by both the news shock and the two demand shocks. As such, I implement a combined short run/long run identification. I use two long run restrictions to separate out the two technology shocks from the two demand shocks, and use a short run zero restriction to identify the surprise technology shock from the news shock. In particular, the restrictions are (i) only the two technology shocks have a long run impact on ln a_t, and (ii) the news shock has no immediate impact on ln a_t.[22] These restrictions are sufficient to uniquely identify the two technology shocks, but do not identify the other shocks. The same restrictions can be used in either the three or the four variable VAR systems.

Figs. 8 and 9 show the Monte Carlo results; Fig. 8 for the four variable system and Fig. 9 for the mis-specified three variable system. Focusing first on the four variable system, one sees that the estimated responses to the news shock align quite closely with the true model responses, particularly at shorter forecast horizons. The transitional dynamics to the new steady state are also estimated quite well, with only evidence of some small bias in the output response at longer forecast horizons. Focusing on the responses to

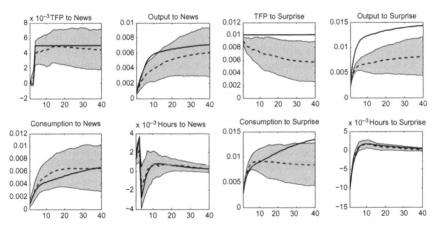

Fig. 8. Monte Carlo Results: Four Variable Model, LR and SR Restrictions.

Notes: The solid lines are the theoretical impulse responses to a news shock about productivity and to a surprise technology shock in the full model with four shocks: a news shock, a surprise technology shock, a monetary policy shock, and a labor supply preference shock. For the Monte Carlo exercise the estimated VAR features ln $\hat{a}_t$, ln $\hat{y}_t$, ln $\hat{c}_t$, and ln n_t, total hours worked, and is estimated with $p = 8$ lags. The news and surprise technology shocks are identified with a combined short run and long run restriction: the long run restriction says that these two shocks are the sole source of the unit root in observed TFP, and the short run restriction says that news shock does not affect TFP on impact. The remaining two shocks are left unidentified. The dashed lines are the mean responses to each shock averaged across 500 simulations of data with 200 observations each, while the shaded gray regions depict the middle 68% of the distribution of estimated responses across the 500 simulations.

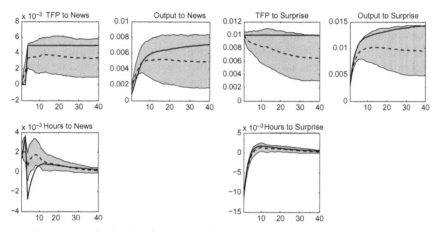

Fig. 9.   Monte Carlo Results: Three Variable Model (Four Shocks), LR and SR Restrictions.

Notes: The solid lines are the theoretical impulse responses to a news shock about productivity and to a surprise technology shock in the full model with four shocks: a news shock, a surprise technology shock, a monetary policy shock, and a labor supply preference shock. For the Monte Carlo exercise the estimated VAR features $\ln \hat{a}_t$, $\ln \hat{y}_t$, and $\ln n_t$, total hours worked, and is estimated with $p = 8$ lags. The model is misspecified in the sense that there are four shocks in the data generating process but only three variables are included in the VAR. The news and surprise technology shocks are identified with a combined short run and long run restriction: the long run restriction says that these two shocks are the sole source of the unit root in observed TFP, and the short run restriction says that news shock does not affect TFP on impact. The dashed lines are the mean responses to each shock averaged across 500 simulations of data with 200 observations each, while the shaded gray regions depict the middle 68% of the distribution of estimated responses across the 500 simulations.

the surprise technology shock, there is some more evidence of bias in the responses, particularly at longer forecast horizons. It should be noted, however, that VAR impulse responses are quite good on impact and at short horizons, and the hours response is estimated very well over all horizons.

Fig. 9 summarizes the Monte Carlo results for the three variable system. The identification is the same as in the four variable system. As noted, in addition to the non-invertibility due to news, an additional bias is introduced due to the fact that the VAR is estimated with three variables, whereas there are four shocks in the model. The estimated impulse responses to both kinds of technology shocks nevertheless remain quite good. Qualitatively the estimated responses to the news shock are in line with the responses from the model. Relative to the four variable VAR, however, the three variable system does not do as good of a job at capturing the large drop in hours when productivity improves, and the longer horizon biases in the output and TFP responses are somewhat larger. The quality of the estimated responses to the surprise technology actually appears somewhat better than in the three variable system. In terms of mean biases this is illusory, as the distribution of estimated responses is quite a bit wider in the three variable system. Nevertheless, the VAR does a good job at qualitatively matching the dynamic responses to the surprise technology shock, and the estimated hours response is quite good.

There are a number of different permutations on these Monte Carlo exercises one could consider for the four shock model. One is mentioned above, and that is assuming that the econometrician cannot observe TFP. In that case, one can estimate either a three or four variable model, replacing TFP with average labor productivity. The long run restrictions used to separate out the two technology shocks from the two demand shocks are the same, and one can replace the zero recursive restriction to identify the news shock with the sign/shape restriction implemented above in the two variable example. These results turn out to be quite similar in terms of how closely the estimated responses align with the model responses. I also considered including different observables in the VAR system; here, too, the results are fairly similar. Finally, I considered alternative parameterizations of non-technology shocks. As shown in section "Non-Invertibility and the Relative Importance of Shocks," the relative magnitudes of the news and surprise technology shocks impact the bias in the estimated responses to the news shock. The relative magnitudes of the unidentified shocks can also matter for the quality of fit of the identified responses (where in these exercises the unidentified shocks are the demand shocks). It turns out that the biases of the identified responses grow with the relative magnitude of the non-identified shocks, as suggested by Canova and Paustian (2011). However, even when increasing the magnitudes of these shocks by a lot – say, a factor of three – the estimated responses to the two identified technology shocks remain qualitatively quite good with relatively small biases, particularly at short horizons.

ADDING INFORMATION

The Monte Carlo results of the previous two sections demonstrate that conventional VAR techniques may perform quite well, even in the face of a known non-invertibility. While these results may prove comforting to some, particularly those interested in the economic effects of news shocks about productivity, it is nevertheless not possible to use them to draw sweeping conclusions about the reliability of VAR techniques when the set of observables has a non-invertible VAR representation. Short of imposing the extra structure that full information techniques require, what can a researcher concerned about biases resulting from a potential non-invertibility do?

As the title of this section suggests, adding information to the set of observed variables is the most straightforward route to go. Non-invertible representations arise when the observables fail to perfectly forecast the state vector of the DSGE model serving as the data generating process. Adding additional variables to the set of observables can only improve the forecast of the state, and thus reduce the magnitude of the wedge between VAR innovations and deep shocks.

In the context of the DSGE model considered so far, it is not possible to condition on more observables – one can only condition on as many observables as there are shocks when estimating the VAR. So as to circumvent this stochastic singularity issue, suppose that an econometrician observes a set of "information variables." These are variables that convey information about the underlying state of the model, but are not otherwise part of the solution of the model. For example, these information variables could be stock prices, survey measures of consumer or business confidence, bond spreads, etc. In particular, I assume that these information variables are noisy signals about the news shock at time t – in other words, they are potentially useful in forecasting future productivity conditional on current observed productivity. Let there be Q of these variables, each obeying:

$$s_{i,t} = u_t + v_{i,t}, \quad i = 1, \ldots, Q \tag{37}$$

The error term $v_{i,t}$ represents the noise in each signal. These are i.i.d. across i, with mean zero and are drawn from a normal distribution with fixed variance. It is clear that, for Q sufficiently large, conditioning on lags of $s_{i,t}$ in a VAR will perfectly reveal the missing states, since the $s_{i,t}$ will average out to the u_t by application of a law of large numbers. This is a particularly simple informational structure, but could easily be extended on a number of different dimensions – for example, there could be persistence in the signals, the signals could respond to other economic shocks, the noise innovations in the signals could be correlated with one another or across time, etc. The broader point is that conditioning on more information will reduce the variance in the forecast of the state vector, and therefore ought to improve the performance of estimated VARs.

To see this point clearly, Fig. 10 shows some Monte Carlo results when incorporating these information series as additional variables in an otherwise standard VAR. Because it arguably has the worst overall fit in the simulations of the fourth section, I consider the frictionless RBC model as the data generating process. So as to fix ideas, I focus here on the "large

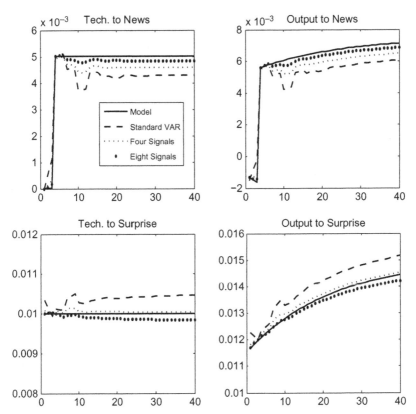

Fig. 10. Adding Information to the VAR: RBC Model.
Notes: The solid lines are the impulse responses to both news and surprise technology shocks in the RBC model. For the Monte Carlo simulations, 100,000 observations are simulated from the model, with additional noisy "information variables" about future productivity included in a VAR featuring $\ln \hat{a}_t$ and $\ln \hat{y}_t$, identified using a recursive restriction with TFP growth ordered first and output ordered second. The dashed, small dotted, and wide dotted lines show the estimated responses with no signals included in the VAR, with four signals, and with eight signals, respectively.

sample" exercise of simulating one data set with 100,000 observations. The standard deviation of the signals is set to 0.005. The solid line shows the true model responses to both shocks, while the dashed lines are the estimated responses from the conventional two variable, recursively identified VAR estimated on ln $\hat{a}_t$ and ln $\hat{y}_t$. The thin dotted line shows the estimated responses from that same VAR augmented with four independent signals, while the thick dotted line shows the responses estimated when the VAR includes eight independent signals.[23] The identifying restrictions are the same as above – the surprise shock is associated with the innovation in TFP growth ordered first, while the news shock is identified with the innovation in output ordered second. It is visually apparent that the fit improves as more of the information variables are added: the biases are smaller in the VAR with four signals than in the conventional two variable VAR, while the biases in the VAR with eight signals are smaller than the VAR with four signals. Extending this exercise to more information variables continues this pattern: the more information variables on which one conditions, the smaller are the large sample biases in the estimated impulse responses.[24] Table 4 shows the mean absolute deviations of the estimated impulse responses of output and TFP to both news and surprise technology shocks over a forty quarter forecast horizons. The final column shows the average of the mean deviations as a measure of overall fit. The pattern is quite evident – as more information variables are added, the average of the average absolute deviations becomes smaller.

The above large sample exercise of simply adding more variables to the VAR is informative, but may not be of much practical interest when estimating VAR systems on relatively short sample sizes. Adding more than a couple of additional series in a sample of, say, 200, with more than a year's worth of lags quickly becomes prohibitive. With different motivations and in different contexts, a number of researchers have made use of factor analytic methods.[25] These methods make use of principal components to compress large sets of data into a small number of common components. This effectively allows one to condition on a large amount of information without consuming too many degrees of freedom.

As an alternative to estimating a VAR system with many additional variables, consider estimating the following factor augmented VAR: $x_t = [\ln \hat{a}_t \ \ln \hat{y}_t \ F_t]'$, where F_t is the first principal component of Q information variables. Isolating just the first principal component in this context makes sense as the information variables only have one common component – the news shock. With enough information variables, conditioning on the common component will be equivalent to conditioning on

Table 4. Mean Absolute Deviations: Adding Information.

	Tech. to News	Output to News	Tech. to Surprise	Output to Surprise	Average
Number of Signals					
Standard VAR ($s = 0$)	0.0634	0.0932	0.0298	0.0511	0.0594
$s = 1$	0.0613	0.0924	0.0272	0.0454	0.0566
$s = 2$	0.0500	0.0758	0.0160	0.0288	0.0426
$s = 4$	0.0369	0.0562	0.0056	0.0130	0.0279
$s = 8$	0.0206	0.0317	0.0074	0.0078	0.0169
Factor VAR	0.0068	0.0102	0.0159	0.0200	0.0132

Notes: These numbers represent the average absolute deviations of the estimated impulse responses relative to the true responses in the models over the first 40 horizons, times 100, for different numbers of additional information variables included in a two variable VAR in ln $\hat{a}_t$ and ln $\hat{y}_t$. The final column, labeled "Average" shows the average of the mean absolute deviations of all four presented impulse responses.

current and lagged news shocks, and hence any biases due to non-invertibility ought to disappear, since the missing state variables will effectively be revealed.

Fig. 11 shows impulse responses obtained from both finite and large sample Monte Carlo exercises making use of the first principal component of $Q = 30$ factors (the number 30 is arbitrary; the important point is that it be "large"). I again take the frictionless RBC model as the data generating process. The standard deviation of the noise innovations in the information variables is again set to 0.005. The estimation procedure takes place in two steps. In the first step, the first principal component of the Q information series is obtained, F_t. In the second step, a conventional unrestricted VAR is estimated with ln $\hat{a}_t$, ln $\hat{y}_t$, and F_t. The identifying restrictions are as above – the surprise technology shock is identified with the innovation in TFP growth, while the news shock is identified as the output innovation ordered second. No interpretation is given to the innovation in F_t ordered last.

Turning first to the large sample results, one observes that the large sample biases have essentially disappeared. The estimated impulse responses virtually lie atop the true model responses at all horizons. That any biases remain is mainly a function of Q being finite – conditioning on sufficiently more variables in the first stage would cause any remaining biases to vanish entirely. The last row of Table 4 shows average mean absolute deviations of the responses estimated in the large sample exercise from the true model

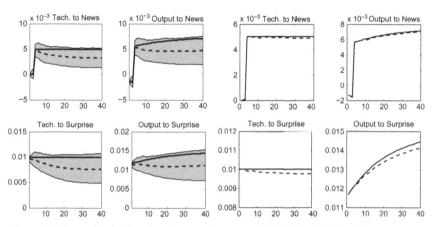

Fig. 11. Monte Carlo Results: Factor Augmented VAR (RBC Model).

Notes: The solid lines are the theoretical responses to news and surprise technology shocks in the RBC model. For the Monte Carlo exercises the estimated VARs include $\ln \hat{a}_t$, $\ln \hat{y}_t$, and the first principal component of thirty noisy signals about future productivity. The VARs are estimated with $p = 8$ lags. In the left panel, labeled "Finite Sample," the dashed lines are the mean responses averaged across 500 simulations of data sets with 200 observations each, while the shaded gray regions depict the middle 68 percent of the distribution of estimated responses across the 500 simulations. In the right panel, labeled "Large Sample," the dashed lines are the estimated impulse responses from the estimation on one sample with 100,000 observations.

counterparts and reveals that the factor augmented VAR represents an improvement over both the two variable system and the systems augmented with smaller numbers of information variables. The results are also substantially better in finite samples in comparison with the simple two variable VAR – comparing the finite sample results in Fig. 11 with Fig. 2, there is a clear improvement. Here there remains some downward bias in the responses at longer horizons, but this is primarily due to finite sample bias in autoregressive coefficients, and is largely unrelated to non-invertibility. The estimated responses are essentially unbiased on impact and for a number of quarters thereafter. Similar results obtain for simulations from the other version of the model with frictions.

These simulations results suggest that a sensible way of dealing with a potential non-invertibility is to estimate a factor-augmented VAR, with the series used to construct the factors explicitly chosen with the goal in mind of forecasting unobserved states. Indeed, this is consistent with the recommendations in Giannone and Reichlin (2006), Forni et al. (2009), and Forni et al. (2011). Since non-invertibility is fundamentally a missing information problem, factor methods, which allow an econometrician to condition on a very large data set, are an appropriate, flexible, and simple way to deal with the issue, short of resorting to full information methods.

CONCLUDING THOUGHTS

Fernandez-Villaverde et al. (2007) recommend that researchers estimate the structural parameters of detailed models using full information techniques. If one believes in a particular DSGE specification, then this is sound advice – from an efficiency perspective one would never want to recover impulse responses from a VAR if one strongly believed in the underlying DSGE model. The advantage of VARs and similar limited information techniques is that they do not impose as much structure as full information methods, and are therefore less subject to specification bias and can be used to make cross-model comparisons. However, the mapping between DSGE models and VARs is not always clean. The so-called non-invertibility problem arises when the VAR on a set of observables cannot be mapped back into the structural form of an economic model. This means that analysis based on VARs may not prove very useful in building and refining fully specified DSGE models.

This chapter has focused on the issue of non-invertibility within the context of a particular shock structure known to create problems – so-called "news shocks" which generate foresight about exogenous changes in future productivity. In so doing, it has emphasized that invertibility is not an "either/or" proposition – a particular model may be technically non-invertible but the resulting biases in estimated impulse responses may nonetheless be small. Non-invertibility is best understood as a problem of missing information – therefore, the most straightforward way to deal with it while remaining within the scope of limited information methods is to condition on more information. In particular, estimating VARs which condition on more information – either through adding additional variables informative about the missing states directly or through factor augmented VARs – works to eliminate the biases due to non-invertibility. These methods are relatively straightforward to implement and do not require imposing the structure that full information estimation methods require.

NOTES

1. There is a long list of chapters in this literature, and any selection of chapters will invariably be incomplete. Nevertheless, a sampling of chapters that employ VARs as tools to construct, refine, or estimate the parameters of DSGE models includes Gali (1999), Christiano, Eichenbaum, and Evans (2005), Fisher (2006), Sims and Zha (2006), Altig, Christiano, Eichenbaum, and Lindé (2011), Barsky and Sims (2012), and Sims (2011).

2. For a discussion of how downward-biased AR coefficients can affect identification (see Faust & Leeper, 1997). For a discussion of the lag-truncation bias – which means that most DSGE models imply VAR(∞) models, while researchers in practice estimate finite order models – see Chari, Kehoe, and McGrattan (2008).

3. For early treatments of this issue, see Quah (1990), Hansen and Sargent (1991), Hansen, Roberds, and Sargent (1991), and Lippi and Riechlin (1994). A well-known recent treatment of this problem is found in Fernandez-Villaverde, Rubio-Ramirez, Sargent, and Watson (2007).

4. As is common in the literature, I restrict attention to the "square case" in which the number of observables equals the number of shocks.

5. There is a debate within the literature over how to best identify news shocks within SVAR settings. See, for example, the discussion in Barsky and Sims (2011). So as to focus on the role of non-invertibility, I restrict attention here to a simple case in which a recursive identification is valid.

6. Dupor and Han (2011) develop a four step procedure to partially identify impulse responses when non-invertibility is feared present. Their approach cannot always eliminate a non-invertibility problem, whereas conditioning on a very large information set can.

7. Blanchard et al. (2011) look at whether a VAR identified with long run restrictions can separately identify "news" (a true signal about permanent productivity) from "noise" (a signal about productivity that is false ex-post). The answer is no, but this is because a long run restriction on an impulse response function is an ex-ante restriction, and the agents in the model only learn that the signal is false ex-post. These authors refer to the problem resulting from this signal extraction problem as a non-invertibility, but this is a bit of a mischaracterization. Since the agents in their economy cannot separate out the true component of a signal from the false component ex-ante, neither can an econometrician estimating a VAR. If, rather than trying to identify IRFs to the "deeper" shocks that the agents cannot separate out, the econometrician seeks only to identify the impulse response to an innovation in the signal, then there may be no invertibility problem. Non-invertibility problems as stressed in most of the recent literature, and in the present chapter, ask whether an econometrician can identify shocks observed by agents. The exercise in Blanchard et al. (2011) tasks the econometrician with identifying shocks that agents cannot observe, which can only be (partially) accomplished with full information methods.

8. For the remainder of this section I focus on the case in which output is observed. The results are essentially the same conditioning on other observed variables.

9. Alternatives would be to estimate a VAR in levels, $X_t = [\ln a_t \ \ln y_t]$, or a vector error correction model (VECM). These are all asymptotically equivalent. The Monte Carlo results below turn out to be very similar in all cases.

10. The choice of 8 lags is somewhat arbitrary. As shown in the second section, the mapping from model to data yields a VAR(∞). Finite data samples require finite lag lengths, with $p < \infty$. This introduces an additional source of bias, the so-called "lag truncation bias" emphasized, for example, in Chari et al. (2008). In practice $p = 8$ lags appears to provide a sufficiently good approximation to the VAR(∞), so that estimating with 8 lags isolates the bias due to non-invertibility. The results discussed below are qualitatively the same, though a little worse, with fewer than 8 lags (e.g., the popular $p = 4$ specification with a year's worth of lags).

11. Jaimovich and Rebelo (2009) provides a nice intuitive introduction for why news shocks tend to generate counterfactual co-movement among output and its components in many standard macro models.

12. Note that the level of technology does not *directly* show up in the state space. It is, however, *implicitly* part of the state in terms of the normalized variables, for example, $\ln \hat{y}_t = \ln y_t - (1/1 - \alpha) \ln a_t$.

13. The log levels are obtained by (i) cumulating the response of the growth rate of TFP to the shock and (ii) adding $1/1 - \alpha$ times the cumulated log level TFP response to the response of normalized output.

14. This statement requires some clarification; the impulse response estimated from the autoregression would correctly recover the impulse response of the *normalized* variable $\ln \hat{y}_t = \ln y_t - (1/1 - \alpha) \ln a_t$. The innovations in the autoregression correspond to the technology shocks after normalizing the variance of these shocks to some value (typically 1 in the applied literature).

15. It should be pointed out that Gali's (1999) results are disputed within the literature, and the sign of the hours response to a permanent technology shock appears to depend on whether hours enter the VAR in first differences or levels. The purpose of the present chapter is not to dissect those results, but rather to use that chapter as a motivating example for how VARs are used to make model comparisons.

16. These exercises are conducted with a fixed lag length, $p = 8$, as the anticipation lag, q, varies. It bears pointing out that one needs at least as many lags in the VAR as the anticipation lag to have any hope of capturing the dynamics implied by the model. In that sense the "cards are stacked" against the specification with $q = 16$. Nevertheless, allowing for a much longer lag structure preserves the basic pattern evident in the table. I maintain $p = 8$ to (i) maintain congruity with Table 2 and (ii) to be consistent with empirical work using VARs, which almost never uses more than two years worth of lags.

17. It is worth pointing out that magnitude of the biases depends on the interaction of the discount factor, β, with the anticipation lag. For example, the quality of the Monte Carlo results is essentially the same for a quarterly calibration with $q = 4$ and $\beta = 0.99$, and an annual calibration with $q = 1$ and $\beta = 0.96$.

18. In practice there is some debate about how to best measure TFP. The measure produced by Basu, Fernald, and Kimball (2006) uses some simple theoretical restrictions to attempt to control for factor hoarding and thus produces a measure of TFP which is immune to criticisms that it largely measures unobserved factor variation due to demand shocks.

19. This specification imposes the model generated cointegrating relationship, which is necessary to use a long run restriction. A consumption-output VAR is also estimated in Cochrane (1994), which in many ways is an important antecedent to the more recent literature on news shocks.

20. The long run restriction is implemented as in Gali (1999). The long run response of the cumulated sums of the variables in the VAR to the two orthogonal shocks is given by the matrix $C_0 = (I - \sum_{j=1}^{p} A_j)^{-1} A_0^{-1}$. Letting the policy shock occupy position 2, the restriction imposes that A_0^{-1} satisfy $A_0^{-1} A_0^{-1'} = \Sigma_u$ and be such that the long run response of the level of output to the second shock be zero, for example, that the (1,2) element of C_0 be zero.

21. In practice the variables in the VAR do not matter much. I consider a different system here than in the previous exercise mainly for breadth of coverage, but also because the average productivity growth-hours VAR is popular in the literature, for example, Gali (1999).

22. Using similar notation to above, the long run responses of the cumulated sums of the variables in the VAR are given by: $C_0 = (I - \sum_{j=1}^{p} A_j)^{-1} A_0^{-1}$. With TFP growth in the first position in the system and the surprise and news shocks indexed by 1 and 2, the two long run restrictions impose that the (1,3) and (1,4) elements of C_0 be zero. The short run restriction that news not immediately effect TFP requires that the (1,2) element of A_0^{-1} be 0.

23. To be clear, the estimated VARs are then: $X_t = [\ln \hat{a}_t \ \ln \hat{y}_t \ s_{1,t} \ldots s_{r,t}]'$, for $r = 4$ or $r = 8$.

24. It is worth pointing out that the standard deviation of the noise innovations, σ_v, does have an effect on these conclusions. If the signals are very precise, then one does not need to add many signals to the VAR for the large sample biases to vanish. In contrast, noisier signals necessitate including more information variables in order to reduce the large sample biases.

25. For applications in macroeconomics, see, for example Bernanke, Boivin, and Eliasz (2005) and Stock and Watson (2005).

REFERENCES

Altig, D., Christiano, L., Eichenbuam, M., & Lindé, J. (2011). Firm-specific capital, nominal rigidities, and the business cycle. *Review of Economic Dynamics*, *14*(2), 225–247.

Barsky, R., & Sims, E. (2011). News shocks and business cycles. *Journal of Monetary Economics*, *58*(3), 273–289.

Barsky, R., & Sims, E. (2012). Information, animal spirits, and the meaning of innovations in consumer confidence. *American Economic Review*, *102*(4), 1343–1377.

Basu, S., Fernald, J., & Kimball, M. (2006). Are technology improvements contractionary? *American Economic Review*, *96*(5), 1418–1448.

Beaudry, P., & Portier, F. (2006). Stock prices, news, and economic fluctuations. *American Economic Review*, *96*(4), 1293–1307.

Bernanke, B., Boivin, J., & Eliasz, P. (2005). Measuring the effects of monetary policy: A factor-augmented vector autoregressive (FAVAR) approach. *Quarterly Journal of Economics*, *120*(1), 387–422.

Bils, M., & Klenow, P. J. (2004). Some evidence on the importance of sticky prices. *Journal of Political Economy, 112*(5), 947–985.

Blanchard, O., L'Hullier, J.-P., & Lorenzoni, G. (2011). *News, noise, and fluctuations: An empirical exploration.* Unpublished manuscript. Massachusetts Institute of Technology, Cambridge, MA.

Calvo, G. (1983). Staggered prices in a utility maximizing framework. *Journal of Monetary Economics, 12*(3), 383–398.

Canova, F., & Paustian, M. (2011). Business cycle measurement with some theory. *Journal of Monetary Economics, 58*(4), 345–361.

Chari, V. V., Kehoe, P., & McGrattan, E. (2008). Are structural VARs with long-run restrictions useful in developing business cycle theory? *Journal of Monetary Economics, 55*(8), 1337–1352.

Christiano, L., Eichenbuam, M., & Evans, C. (2005). Nominal rigidities and the dynamic effects of a shock to monetary policy. *Journal of Political Economy, 113*(1), 1–45.

Cochrane, J. (1994). Permanent and transitory components of GNP and stock prices. *Quarterly Journal of Economics, 109*(1), 241–265.

Dupor, W., & Han, J. (2011). *Handling non-invertibility: Theory and applications.* Unpublished manuscript. Ohio State University, Columbus, OH.

Faust, J. (1998). On the robustness of identified VAR conclusions about money. *Carnegie-Rochester Conference Series on Public Policy, 49,* 207–244.

Faust, J., & Leeper, E. (1997). When do long-run identifying restrictions give reliable results? *Journal of Business & Economic Statistics, 15*(3), 345–353.

Fernandez-Villerde, J., Rubio-Ramirez, J., Sargent, T., & Watson, M. (2007). ABCs (and Ds) of understaning VARs. *American Economic Review, 97*(3), 1021–1026.

Feve, P., & Jidoud, A. (2011). *Identifying news shocks from SVARs.* Unpublished manuscript. Toulouse School of Economics, Toulouse.

Fisher, J. (2006). The dynamic effects of neutral and investment-specific technology shocks. *Journal of Political Economy, 114*(3), 413–451.

Forni, M., & Gambetti, L. (2011). *Fiscal foresight and the effects of government spending.* Unpublished manuscript. Universitat Autonoma de Barcelona, Barcelona.

Forni, M., Gambetti, L., & Sala, L. (2011). *No news in business cycles.* Unpublished manuscript. Universitat Autonoma de Barcelona, Barcelona.

Forni, M., Giannone, D., Lippi, M., & Reichlin, L. (2009). Opening the black box: Structural factor models with large cross sections. *Econometric Theory, 25*(5), 1319–1347.

Gali, J. (1999). Technology, employment, and the business cycle: Do technology shocks explain aggregate fluctuations? *American Economic Review, 89*(1), 249–271.

Giannone, D., & Reichlin, L. (2006). Does information help recovering structural shocks from past observations? *Journal of the European Economic Association, 4*(2-3), 455–465.

Hansen, L., Roberds, W., & Sargent, T. (1991). Time series implications of present value budget balance and of martingale models of consumption and taxes. In L. P. Hansen, J. Heaton, A. Marcet, W. Roberds & T. J. Sargent (Eds.), *Rational expectations econometrics* (pp. 121–163). Boulder, CO: Westview Press.

Hansen, L., & Sargent, T. (1991). Two difficulties in interpreting vector autoregressions. In L. P. Hansen, J. Heaton, A. Marcet, W. Roberds & T. J. Sargent (Eds.), *Rational expectations econometrics* (pp. 77–120). Boulder, CO: Westview Press.

Hansen, L., & Sargent, T. (2007). *Recursive linear models of dynamic economies.* Unpublished manuscript. New York University, New York, NY.

Jaimovich, N., & Rebelo, S. (2009). Can news about the future drive business cycles? *American Economic Review*, *99*(4), 1097–1118.

Kimball, M., & Shapiro, M. D. (2010). *Labor supply: Are income and substitution effects both large or both small?* Unpublished manuscript. University of Michigan, Ann Arbor, MI.

Kurmann, A., & Otrok, C. (2011). *News shocks and the term structure of interest rates: A challenge for DSGE models.* Unpublished manuscript. University of Missouri, Columbia, MO.

Leeper, E., Walker, T., & Yang, S.-C. (2011). *Foresight and information flows.* Unpublished manuscript. Indiana University, Bloomington, IN.

Lippi, M., & Reichlin, L. (1994). The dynamic effects of aggregate demand and supply disturbances: Comment. *American Economic Review*, *83*(3), 644–652.

Mountford, A., & Uhlig, H. (2009). What are the effects of fiscal policy shocks? *Journal of Applied Econometrics*, *24*(6), 960–992.

Quah, D. (1990). Permanent and transitory movements in labor income: An explanation for 'Excess Smoothness' in consumption. *Journal of Political Economy*, *98*(3), 449–475.

Sims, C., & Zha, T. (2006). Does monetary policy generate recessions? *Macroeconomic Dynamics*, *10*(2), 231–272.

Sims, E. (2011). *Permanent and transitory technology shocks and the behavior of hours: A challenge for DSGE models.* Unpublished manuscript. University of Notre Dame, Notre Dame, IN.

Smets, F., & Wouters, R. (2007). Shocks and frictions in US business cycles: A bayesian DSGE approach. *American Economic Review*, *97*(3), 586–606.

Stock, J., & Watson, M. (2005). *Implications of dynamic factor models for VAR analysis.* Unpublished manuscript. Princeton University, Princeton, NJ.

Uhlig, H. (2005). What are the effects of monetary policy on output? Results from an agnostic identification procedure. *Journal of Monetary Economics*, *52*(2), 381–419.

APPENDIX: STATE SPACE REPRESENTATION OF THE VARIOUS MODELS

This appendix provides details on the parameters of the state space representations of the various nested models.

A.1 The Full Model

The state vector is:

$$s_t = [\ln \hat{y}_t \ \ln \hat{k}_t \ i_t \ \ln v_t \ z_{1,t} \ z_{2,t} \ z_{3,t} \ \ln \hat{I}_t \ \ln \hat{c}_t]'$$

The vector of observables is:

$$x_t = [\ln \hat{a}_t \ \ln \hat{y}_t]'$$

These variables represent logarithmic deviations from their normalized steady state values. The shock vector is $\varepsilon_t = [\varepsilon_t \ u_t]'$. The parameters of the state space representation are:

$$A = \begin{bmatrix}
0.0552 & 0.0746 & -0.4402 & -0.0909 & -1.1461 & 0.3006 & 0.2305 & 0.1544 & 0.4798 \\
0.0034 & 0.9723 & -0.0267 & -0.0049 & -1.4857 & 0.0111 & 0.0070 & 0.0185 & -0.0037 \\
-0.0603 & -0.0278 & 0.4806 & 0.0424 & -0.0452 & 0.0096 & 0.0407 & 0.0307 & 0.0875 \\
0.0175 & -0.0179 & -0.1398 & 0.7656 & -0.0410 & -0.0105 & 0.0089 & 0.0077 & 0.0200 \\
0.0000 & 0.0000 & 0.0000 & 0.0000 & 0.0000 & 1.0000 & 0.0000 & 0.0000 & 0.0000 \\
0.0000 & 0.0000 & 0.0000 & 0.0000 & 0.0000 & 0.0000 & 1.0000 & 0.0000 & 0.0000 \\
0.0000 & 0.0000 & 0.0000 & 0.0000 & 0.0000 & 0.0000 & 0.0000 & 0.0000 & 0.0000 \\
0.1417 & -0.1717 & -1.1291 & -0.2051 & -0.8958 & 0.4691 & 0.2960 & 0.7831 & -0.1558 \\
0.0319 & 0.1411 & -0.2543 & -0.0600 & -1.2136 & 0.2552 & 0.2129 & -0.0153 & 0.6513
\end{bmatrix}$$

$$B = \begin{bmatrix}
-1.1461 & 0.1603 \\
-1.4857 & 0.0029 \\
-0.0452 & 0.0551 \\
-0.0410 & 0.0198 \\
0.0000 & 0.0000 \\
0.0000 & 0.0000 \\
0.0000 & 1.0000 \\
-0.8958 & 0.1206 \\
-1.2136 & 0.1711
\end{bmatrix}$$

$$C = \begin{bmatrix} 0.0000 & 0.0000 & 0.0000 & 0.0000 & 1.0000 & 0.0000 & 0.0000 & 0.0000 & 0.0000 \\ 0.0552 & 0.0746 & -0.4402 & -0.0909 & -1.1461 & 0.3006 & 0.2305 & 0.1544 & 0.4798 \end{bmatrix}$$

$$D = \begin{bmatrix} 1.0000 & 0.0000 \\ -1.1461 & 0.1603 \end{bmatrix}$$

The modulus of the eigenvalues of the matrix $M = (A - BD^{-1}C)$ are:

$$\Lambda = (1.3208 \quad 1.3208 \quad 0.5781 \quad 0.9471 \quad 0.7239 \quad 0.8057 \quad 0.0000 \quad 0.0000 \quad 0.0000)$$

There are two eigenvalues with modulus outside the unit circle. Hence, the "poor man's invertibility condition" is not satisfied.

A.2 The RBC Model

The state vector is:

$$s_t = [\ln \hat{k}_t \ z_{1,t} \ z_{2,t} \ z_{3,t}]'$$

The vector of observables is the same as above.
The parameters of the state space representation are:

$$A = \begin{bmatrix} 0.9554 & -1.4331 & -0.0745 & -0.0704 \\ 0.0000 & 0.0000 & 1.0000 & 0.0000 \\ 0.0000 & 0.0000 & 0.0000 & 1.0000 \\ 0.0000 & 0.0000 & 0.0000 & 0.0000 \end{bmatrix}$$

$$B = \begin{bmatrix} -1.4331 & -0.0666 \\ 0.0000 & 0.0000 \\ 0.0000 & 0.0000 \\ 0.0000 & 1.0000 \end{bmatrix}$$

$$C = \begin{bmatrix} 0.0000 & 1.0000 & 0.0000 & 0.0000 \\ 0.2210 & -0.3315 & -0.2903 & -0.2745 \end{bmatrix}$$

$$D = \begin{bmatrix} 1.0000 & 0.0000 \\ -0.3315 & -0.2597 \end{bmatrix}$$

The modulus of the eigenvalues of the matrixes $M = (A - BD^{-1}C)$ are:

$$\Lambda = (0.8987 \quad 1.0572 \quad 1.0572 \quad 0.0000)$$

Again, the conditions required for invertibility are not met.

A.3 The Sticky Price Model

The state vector is:

$$s_t = [\ln \hat{y}_t \ \ln \hat{k}_t \ i_t \ v_t \ z_{1,t} \ z_{2,t} \ z_{3,t}]'$$

The vector of observables is as above. The parameters of the state space representation are:

$$A = \begin{bmatrix} 1.1043 & -0.4590 & -8.8015 & -0.2184 & -0.9680 & -0.4384 & -0.3754 \\ 0.1192 & 0.8796 & -0.9498 & -0.0143 & -1.4982 & -0.1024 & -0.0921 \\ 0.0996 & -0.1080 & -0.7942 & 0.0036 & 0.0125 & -0.0737 & -0.0590 \\ 0.0453 & -0.0314 & -0.3611 & 0.7524 & -0.0208 & -0.0151 & -0.0108 \\ 0.0000 & 0.0000 & 0.0000 & 0.0000 & 0.0000 & 1.0000 & 0.0000 \\ 0.0000 & 0.0000 & 0.0000 & 0.0000 & 0.0000 & 0.0000 & 1.0000 \\ 0.0000 & 0.0000 & 0.0000 & 0.0000 & 0.0000 & 0.0000 & 0.0000 \end{bmatrix}$$

$$B = \begin{bmatrix} -0.9680 & -0.3095 \\ -1.4982 & -0.0818 \\ 0.0125 & -0.0455 \\ -0.0208 & -0.0073 \\ 0.0000 & 0.0000 \\ 0.0000 & 0.0000 \\ 0.0000 & 1.0000 \end{bmatrix}$$

$$C = \begin{bmatrix} 0.0000 & 0.0000 & 0.0000 & 0.0000 & 1.0000 & 0.0000 & 0.0000 \\ 1.1043 & -0.4590 & -8.8015 & -0.2184 & -0.9680 & -0.4384 & -0.3754 \end{bmatrix}$$

$$D = \begin{bmatrix} 1.0000 & 0.0000 \\ -0.9680 & -0.3095 \end{bmatrix}$$

he modulus of the eigenvalues of the matrixes $M = (A - BD^{-1}C)$ are:

$$\Lambda = (1.2397 \ 1.2397 \ 0.8087 \ 0.8087 \ 0.7638 \ 0.0000 \ 0.0000)$$

The conditions for invertibility are not satisfied.

A.4 The Full Model with One Period Anticipation

The full model with one period of anticipation is similar to that presented in A.1 but the state space can be reduced because of one period of anticipation. In particular, the process for technology can be written:

$$\ln a_t = g_a + \ln a_{t-1} + \varepsilon_t + z_{1,t-1}$$
$$z_{1,t} = u_{t-1}$$

For this specification the state vector is:

$$s_t = [\ln \hat{y}_t \;\; \ln \hat{k}_t \;\; i_t \;\; \ln v_t \;\; z_{1,t} \;\; \ln \hat{I}_t \;\; \ln \hat{c}_t]'$$

The vector of observables is again TFP growth and normalized output, $\ln \hat{a}_t$ and $\ln \hat{y}_t$, and the shock vector is $\varepsilon_t = [\varepsilon_t \;\; u_t]'$. The parameters of the state space representation are:

$$A = \begin{bmatrix}
0.0552 & 0.0746 & -0.4402 & -0.0909 & -1.1461 & 0.1544 & 0.4798 \\
0.0034 & 0.9723 & -0.0267 & -0.0049 & -1.4857 & 0.0185 & -0.0037 \\
-0.0603 & -0.0278 & 0.4806 & 0.0424 & -0.0452 & 0.0307 & 0.0875 \\
0.0175 & -0.0179 & -0.1398 & 0.7656 & -0.0410 & 0.0077 & 0.0200 \\
0.0000 & -0.0000 & -0.0000 & -0.0000 & 0.0000 & 0.0000 & 0.0000 \\
0.1417 & -0.1717 & -1.1291 & -0.2051 & -0.8958 & 0.7831 & -0.1558 \\
0.0319 & 0.1411 & -0.2543 & -0.0600 & -1.2136 & -0.0153 & 0.6513
\end{bmatrix}$$

$$B = \begin{bmatrix}
-1.1461 & 0.3006 \\
-1.4857 & 0.0111 \\
-0.0452 & 0.0096 \\
-0.0410 & -0.0105 \\
0.0000 & 1.0000 \\
-0.8958 & 0.4691 \\
-1.2136 & 0.2552
\end{bmatrix}$$

$$C = \begin{bmatrix}
-0.0000 & -0.0000 & -0.0000 & 0.0000 & 1.0000 & 0.0000 & 0.0000 \\
0.0319 & 0.1411 & -0.2543 & -0.0600 & -1.2136 & -0.0153 & 0.6513
\end{bmatrix}$$

$$D = \begin{bmatrix} 1.0000 & -0.0000 \\ -1.2136 & 0.2552 \end{bmatrix}$$

The modulus of the eigenvalues of the matrixes $M = (A - BD^{-1}C)$ are:

$$\Lambda = (0.5381\ 0.9411\ 0.8043\ 0.7294\ 0.0000\ 0.0000\ 0.0000)$$

Since the maximum modulus of the eigenvalues lies inside of the unit circle, the conditions for invertibility are satisfied with only one period of anticipation.

BAYESIAN ESTIMATION OF NOEM MODELS: IDENTIFICATION AND INFERENCE IN SMALL SAMPLES

Enrique Martínez-García, Diego Vilán and Mark A. Wynne

ABSTRACT

Open-Economy models are central to the discussion of the trade-offs monetary policy faces in an increasingly more globalized world (e.g., Marínez-García & Wynne, 2010), but bringing them to the data is not without its challenges. Controlling for misspecification bias, we trace the problem of uncertainty surrounding structural parameter estimation in the context of a fully specified New Open Economy Macro (NOEM) model partly to sample size. We suggest that standard macroeconomic time series with a coverage of less than forty years may not be informative enough for some parameters of interest to be recovered with precision. We also illustrate how uncertainty also arises from weak structural identification, irrespective of the sample size. This remains a concern for empirical research and we recommend estimation with simulated observations before using actual data as a way of detecting structural parameters that are prone to weak identification. We also recommend careful evaluation and documentation of the implementation strategy

DSGE Models in Macroeconomics: Estimation, Evaluation, and New Developments
Advances in Econometrics, Volume 28, 137–199
ISSN: 0731-9053/doi:10.1108/S0731-9053(2012)0000028007

*(specially in the selection of observables) as it can have significant effects
on the strength of identification of key model parameters.*

Keywords: Global slack hypothesis; new open economy
macroeconomics; Phillips curve; Bayesian estimation

JEL classification: C11; C13; F41

INTRODUCTION

Dynamic stochastic general equilibrium (DSGE) models are micro-founded,
multivariate representations of the data-generating process (DGP) underlying some macro time series. DSGE modelling has become widely used
in macroeconomics and international macro partly due to the well-known
shortcomings of reduced-form and partial equilibrium approaches – shortcomings ranging from lack of structural interpretability to missing out on
important cross-equation restrictions that can result in misleading empirical
inferences. However, the quantitative evaluation and assessment of DSGE
models (open-economy or otherwise) requires that we take a stand on the
appropriate method to do so. The international macro literature has relied
extensively on calibration techniques, although econometric tools and
Bayesian estimation in particular have become increasingly more common
(see, e.g., Lubik & Schorfheide, 2006).

The proponents of the statistical toolkit argue that econometric methods
can be quite effective in "letting the data speak for itself." The aim of this
chapter is to review the challenges that may hinder the use of structural
estimation with open-economy DSGE models. Most of our discussion,
though, applies equally to closed-economy DSGE models since the estimation shares the same problems of model misspecification, data availability
and weak structural identification.

Model misspecification is thought to be pervasive in open-economy
models and remains a point of contention between those who favor calibration and those who prefer estimation (see, e.g., Canova, 1994). Estimating a
misspecified or underspecified model can lead to biased structural estimates,
an issue that is well-understood in the estimation of open-economy DSGE
models given that the current class of models imposes strong restrictions
on actual time series data that are hard to reconcile with the evidence. In this
chapter we focus on the less-often-discussed challenges of implementation in

small samples and weak identification in the structural estimation of a DSGE model, even when researchers are *confident* about their model's accurate characterization of the DGP underlying the observed data. To ensure that misspecification error does not affect our findings, we calibrate a variant of the two-country model of Martínez-García and Wynne (2010) as our laboratory economy and work with simulated data.[1]

The structural estimation of international macro models is complicated by the fact that some economically relevant concepts such as the output gap are model dependent and unobservable. The Bayesian treatment of unobserved endogenous variables (like the output gap) and structural parameters as jointly distributed means that estimates of each reflect uncertainty about the others. Another key advantage of Bayesian estimation over other likelihood-based approaches such as maximum likelihood estimation is that prior distributions can be used to incorporate additional relevant information that is not contained in the estimation sample of observed macro time series. We focus our empirical investigation on standard Bayesian estimation techniques partly because of those perceived advantages and partly because a significant share of the empirical international macro literature uses them.[2]

Lubik and Schorfheide (2006), among others, advocate a structural evaluation of the role of openness with Bayesian estimation techniques and raise awareness of model misspecification and identification problems. Unlike them, we work with simulated data from the fully specified, small-scale model of Martínez-García and Wynne (2010) rather than with actual data so that we can preclude misspecification bias in our estimation. With controlled experiments using simulated data we can more clearly isolate the effect of structural identification from that of misspecification. We can also derive more precise empirical inferences using Bayesian techniques on the international transmission of shocks and explore the sensitivity of the estimates to data selection and sample size.

As a result, the chapter provides a practitioners' perspective on the complexities of estimating open-economy models, exploiting the cross-equation restrictions of the model to make the problem of weak structural identification in international macro more transparent. Our work is closely related to that of An and Schorfheide (2007) who provide a thorough review of Bayesian methods using a small-scale (closed-economy) New Keynesian model as their DGP and work also with simulated data. They also have an extensive discussion of the issue of structural identification, which is complementary to ours. We share the interest in the development of empirically viable New Open Economy Macro (NOEM) models with Lubik and Schorfheide (2006). While they document the inability of a richer NOEM model to explain exchange rate movements in the data, we place the emphasis on understanding the first-order effects of the international transmission of shocks and the role of openness in the dynamics of cyclical inflation for which our model is more suitable. Our investigation here is also closely influenced by Ríos-Rull, Schorfheide, Fuentes-Albero, Kryshko, and Santaeulàlia-Llopis (2011) which emphasizes the importance of substance – the significance and economic content of the empirical inferences we make – over the techniques that researchers use.

The chapter is structured as follows. The second section outlines the variant of the NOEM model developed by Martínez-García (2008) and Martínez-García and Wynne (2010) as well as its calibration. This model serves as the DGP for the simulated data that we use in our empirical investigation. More details about its building blocks can be found in the appendix. The third section discusses the solution and estimation methodology, and illustrates the problem with identification of structural parameters. The fourth section reports our results regarding the role of sample size and variable selection and provides further evidence of weak identification even after controlling for sample size and misspecification. Finally, the fifth section concludes by putting our empirical evaluation exercise into perspective.

BENCHMARK TWO-COUNTRY MODEL

We work with the two-country DSGE model with complete asset markets and nominal rigidities of Martínez-García and Wynne (2010), subject to country-specific productivity and monetary shocks. The framework, which is a variant of the standard workhorse NOEM model of Clarida et al. (2002), is our benchmark specification for the analysis of the international transmission of shocks. Its building blocks are summarized in the appendix, but a more detailed derivation can be found in Martínez-García (2008).

For tractability, we abstract from capital and durable goods (see, e.g., Chari, Kehoe, & McGrattan, 2002; Engel & Wang, 2011; Martínez-García & Søndergaard, 2013) and adopt a cashless economy (see, e.g., Woodford, 2003). Pass-through is complete and the law of one price holds at the variety level (even under price stickiness) by assuming that prices are set always in the producer's own currency.[3]

The model features two standard distortions in the goods markets – monopolistic competition in production and price-setting subject to

Calvo (1983) contracts. Monopolistic competition in final goods markets introduces a distortion in the allocation of resources (labor) within a country, but we correct for that by introducing an optimal labor subsidy for firms fully funded with non-distortionary, lump-sum taxes raised from the local households.[4] Price stickiness is the key friction as it breaks monetary neutrality in the short-run – establishing an open-economy Phillips curve relationship between domestic inflation and global slack that monetary policy can exploit. Absent nominal rigidities (under flexible prices), monetary policy has no real effects neither in the long-run (steady state) nor the short-run (dynamics). This friction is fundamental to explain the dynamics of the model, and also crucial to identify the international propagation mechanism. Understanding this channel for monetary non-neutrality and the real effects that come with it is of great importance to determine the scope and trade-offs of monetary policy in an open economy.

The First-Order Dynamics of the Model

We summarize the log-linearized equilibrium conditions of the model in Tables 1 and 2. We denote $\hat{z}_t \equiv \ln(\frac{Z_t}{Z})$ the deviation of a given variable in logs from its steady state. We define a vector of endogenous variables, $\hat{Y}_t$, and a vector of exogenous variables, $\hat{X}_t$. We split the vector of endogenous variables into a vector of core variables, $\hat{Y}_t^c$, and a vector of noncore variables, $\hat{Y}_t^n$. In our model, the endogenous core variables $\hat{\pi}_t$ and $\hat{\pi}_t^*$ denote Home and Foreign inflation (quarter-over-quarter changes in the consumption-based price index) respectively, $\hat{x}_t$ and $\hat{x}_t^*$ define the Home and Foreign output gaps (deviations of output from its frictionless level), while $\hat{i}_t$ and $\hat{i}_t^*$ are the Home and Foreign one-period nominal interest rates set by the policy-makers. The noncore variables of the model include aggregate Home and Foreign output, $\hat{y}_t$ and $\hat{y}_t^*$, aggregate Home and Foreign consumption, $\hat{c}_t$ and $\hat{c}_t^*$, aggregate Home and Foreign employment, $\hat{l}_t$ and $\hat{l}_t^*$, and Home and Foreign real wages, $\hat{w}_t - \hat{p}_t$ and $\hat{w}_t^* - \hat{p}_t^*$. We also derive expressions for the terms of trade, $\hat{tot}_t$, the real exchange rate, $\hat{rs}_t$, real exports and real imports, $\hat{exp}_t$ and $\hat{imp}_t$, and the real trade balance, $\hat{tb}_t$.

The vector of exogenous variable $\hat{X}_t$ includes two types of country-specific, exogenous shocks in the model: Home and Foreign productivity shocks, $\hat{a}_t$ and $\hat{a}_t^*$, and Home and Foreign monetary shocks to the Taylor rule, $\hat{m}_t$ and $\hat{m}_t^*$. We model the productivity shocks and the monetary shocks as two VAR(1) stochastic processes, but we only incorporate cross-country

Table 1. New Open Economy Macro (NOEM) Model: Core Equations.

<hr>

Home Economy

Phillips curve	$\hat{\pi}_t \approx \beta\mathbb{E}_t(\hat{\pi}_{t+1}) + \left(\dfrac{(1-\alpha)(1-\beta\alpha)}{\alpha}\right)[(\xi\phi + \Theta\gamma)\hat{x}_t + ((1-\xi)\phi + (1-\Theta)\gamma)\hat{x}_t^*]$
Output gap	$\gamma(2\xi-1)(\mathbb{E}_t[\hat{x}_{t+1}] - \hat{x}_t) \approx ((2\xi-1)+\Gamma)[\hat{r}_t - \hat{\bar{r}}_t] - \Gamma[\hat{r}_t^* - \hat{\bar{r}}_t^*]$
Monetary policy	$\hat{i}_t \approx [\psi_\pi\hat{\pi}_t + \psi_x\hat{x}_t] + \hat{m}_t$
Fisher equation	$\hat{r}_t \equiv \hat{i}_t - \mathbb{E}_t[\hat{\pi}_{t+1}]$
Natural interest rate	$\hat{\bar{r}}_t \approx \gamma[\Theta(\mathbb{E}_t[\hat{\bar{y}}_{t+1}] - \hat{\bar{y}}_t) + (1-\Theta)(\mathbb{E}_t[\hat{\bar{y}}_{t+1}^*] - \hat{\bar{y}}_t^*)]$
Potential output	$\hat{\bar{y}}_t \approx \left(\dfrac{1+\phi}{\gamma+\phi}\right)[\Lambda\hat{a}_t + (1-\Lambda)\hat{a}_t^*]$

<hr>

Foreign Economy

Phillips curve	$\hat{\pi}_t^* \approx \beta\mathbb{E}_t(\hat{\pi}_{t+1}^*) + \left(\dfrac{(1-\alpha)(1-\beta\alpha)}{\alpha}\right)[((1-\xi)\phi + (1-\Theta)\gamma)\hat{x}_t + (\xi\phi + \Theta\gamma)\hat{x}_t^*]$
Output gap	$\gamma(2\xi-1)(\mathbb{E}_t[\hat{x}_{t+1}^*] - \hat{x}_t^*) \approx -\Gamma[\hat{r}_t - \hat{\bar{r}}_t] + ((2\xi-1)+\Gamma)[\hat{r}_t^* - \hat{\bar{r}}_t^*]$
Monetary policy	$\hat{i}_t^* \approx [\psi_\pi\hat{\pi}_t^* + \psi_x\hat{x}_t^*] + \hat{m}_t^*$
Fisher equation	$\hat{r}_t^* \equiv \hat{i}_t^* - \mathbb{E}_t[\hat{\pi}_{t+1}^*]$
Natural rate	$\hat{r}_t^* \approx \gamma[(1-\Theta)(\mathbb{E}_t[\hat{\bar{y}}_{t+1}] - \hat{\bar{y}}_t) + \Theta(\mathbb{E}_t[\hat{\bar{y}}_{t+1}^*] - \hat{\bar{y}}_t^*)]$
Potential output	$\hat{\bar{y}}_t^* \approx \left(\dfrac{1+\phi}{\gamma+\phi}\right)[(1-\Lambda)\hat{a}_t + \Lambda\hat{a}_t^*]$

<hr>

Exogenous, Country-Specific Shocks

Productivity shock
$$\begin{pmatrix} \hat{a}_t \\ \hat{a}_t^* \end{pmatrix} \approx \begin{pmatrix} \delta_a & \delta_{a,a*} \\ \delta_{a,a*} & \delta_a \end{pmatrix}\begin{pmatrix} \hat{a}_{t-1} \\ \hat{a}_{t-1}^* \end{pmatrix} + \begin{pmatrix} \hat{\varepsilon}_t^a \\ \hat{\varepsilon}_t^{a*} \end{pmatrix}$$

$$\begin{pmatrix} \hat{\varepsilon}_t^a \\ \hat{\varepsilon}_t^{a*} \end{pmatrix} \sim N\left(\begin{pmatrix} 0 \\ 0 \end{pmatrix}, \begin{pmatrix} \sigma_a^2 & \rho_{a,a*}\sigma_a^2 \\ \rho_{a,a*}\sigma_a^2 & \sigma_a^2 \end{pmatrix}\right)$$

Monetary shock
$$\begin{pmatrix} \hat{m}_t \\ \hat{m}_t^* \end{pmatrix} \approx \begin{pmatrix} \delta_m & 0 \\ 0 & \delta_m \end{pmatrix}\begin{pmatrix} \hat{m}_{t-1} \\ \hat{m}_{t-1}^* \end{pmatrix} + \begin{pmatrix} \hat{\varepsilon}_t^m \\ \hat{\varepsilon}_t^{m*} \end{pmatrix}$$

$$\begin{pmatrix} \hat{\varepsilon}_t^m \\ \hat{\varepsilon}_t^{m*} \end{pmatrix} \sim N\left(\begin{pmatrix} 0 \\ 0 \end{pmatrix}, \begin{pmatrix} \sigma_m^2 & \rho_{m,m*}\sigma_m^2 \\ \rho_{m,m*}\sigma_m^2 & \sigma_m^2 \end{pmatrix}\right)$$

<hr>

Composite Parameters

$$\Theta \equiv \xi\left[\frac{\sigma\gamma - (\sigma\gamma-1)(2\xi-1)}{\sigma\gamma - (\sigma\gamma-1)(2\xi-1)^2}\right]$$

$$\Lambda \equiv 1 + (\sigma\gamma-1)\left[\frac{\gamma(1-\xi)(2\xi)}{\phi(\sigma\gamma - (\sigma\gamma-1)(2\xi-1)^2) + \gamma}\right]$$

$$\Gamma \equiv (1-\xi)[\sigma\gamma + (\sigma\gamma-1)(2\xi-1)]$$

Table 2. New Open Economy Macro (NOEM) Model: Noncore Equations.

Home Economy	
Output	$\hat{y}_t = \hat{\bar{y}}_t + \hat{x}_t$
Consumption	$\hat{c}_t \approx \Theta\hat{y}_t + (1 - \Theta)\hat{y}_t^*$
Employment	$\hat{l}_t \approx \hat{y}_t - \hat{a}_t$
Real wages	$(\hat{w}_t - \hat{p}_t) \approx \gamma\hat{c}_t + \phi\hat{l}_t \approx (\phi + \gamma\Theta)\hat{y}_t + \gamma(1 - \Theta)\hat{y}_t^* - \phi\hat{a}_t$

Foreign Economy	
Output	$\hat{y}_t^* = \hat{\bar{y}}_t^* + \hat{x}_t^*$
Consumption	$\hat{c}_t^* \approx (1 - \Theta)\hat{y}_t + \Theta\hat{y}_t^*$
Employment	$\hat{l}_t^* \approx \hat{y}_t^* - \hat{a}_t^*$
Real wages	$(\hat{w}_t^* - \hat{p}_t^*) \approx \gamma\hat{c}_t^* + \phi\hat{l}_t^* \approx \gamma(1 - \Theta)\hat{y}_t + (\phi + \gamma\Theta)\hat{y}_t^* - \phi\hat{a}_t^*$

International Relative Prices and Trade	
Real exchange rate	$\widehat{rs}_t \approx (2\xi - 1)\widehat{tot}_t$
Terms of trade	$\widehat{tot}_t \approx \left[\dfrac{\gamma}{\sigma\gamma - (\sigma\gamma - 1)(2\xi - 1)^2}\right](\hat{y}_t - \hat{y}_t^*)$
Home real exports	$\widehat{exp}_t \approx \Xi\hat{y}_t + (1 - \Xi)\hat{y}_t^*$
Home real imports	$\widehat{imp}_t \approx -(1 - \Xi)\hat{y}_t - \Xi\hat{y}_t^*$
Home real trade balance	$\widehat{tb}_t \equiv \hat{y}_t - \hat{c}_t = (1 - \xi)(\widehat{exp}_t - \widehat{imp}_t) \approx (1 - \Theta)(\hat{y}_t - \hat{y}_t^*)$

Composite Parameters	
	$\Theta \equiv \xi\left[\dfrac{\sigma\gamma - (\sigma\gamma - 1)(2\xi - 1)}{\sigma\gamma - (\sigma\gamma - 1)(2\xi - 1)^2}\right]$
	$\Xi \equiv \left[\dfrac{\sigma\gamma + (\sigma\gamma - 1)(2\xi - 1)(1 - \xi)}{\sigma\gamma - (\sigma\gamma - 1)(2\xi - 1)^2}\right]$

spillovers in the stochastic process for productivity shocks as can be seen in Table 1. Productivity innovations and monetary innovations can be correlated across countries, but not with each other.

Table 3 describes the full dynamics of the economy in a frictionless environment under flexible prices and perfect competition. We refer to the frictionless equilibrium allocation as the potential of the economy. We denote $\hat{\bar{z}}_t \equiv \ln(\frac{\bar{Z}_t}{\bar{Z}})$ the deviation of an endogenous variable in logs from its

Table 3.   Flexible Price (RBC) Model: Core and Noncore Equations.

Home Economy	
Inflation	$\mathbb{E}_t[\hat{\bar{\pi}}_{t+1}] \approx \psi_\pi \hat{\bar{\pi}}_t + \hat{m}_t - \hat{\bar{r}}_t$
Output (potential)	$\hat{\bar{y}}_t \approx \left(\frac{1+\phi}{\gamma+\phi}\right)[\Lambda \hat{a}_t + (1-\Lambda)\hat{a}_t^*]$
Monetary policy	$\hat{\bar{i}}_t \approx \psi_\pi \hat{\bar{\pi}}_t + \hat{m}_t$
Fisher equation	$\hat{\bar{r}}_t \equiv \hat{\bar{i}}_t - \mathbb{E}_t[\hat{\bar{\pi}}_{t+1}]$
Natural interest rate	$\hat{\bar{r}}_t \approx \gamma[\Theta(\mathbb{E}_t[\hat{\bar{y}}_{t+1}] - \hat{\bar{y}}_t) + (1-\Theta)(\mathbb{E}_t[\hat{\bar{y}}_{t+1}^*] - \hat{\bar{y}}_t^*)]$
Consumption	$\hat{\bar{c}}_t \approx \Theta \hat{\bar{y}}_t + (1-\Theta)\hat{\bar{y}}_t^*$
Employment	$\hat{\bar{l}}_t \approx \hat{\bar{y}}_t - \hat{a}_t$
Real wages	$(\hat{\bar{w}}_t - \hat{\bar{p}}_t) \approx \gamma \hat{\bar{c}}_t + \phi \hat{\bar{l}}_t \approx (\phi + \gamma\Theta)\hat{\bar{y}}_t + \gamma(1-\Theta)\hat{\bar{y}}_t^* - \phi \hat{a}_t$

Foreign Economy	
Inflation	$\mathbb{E}_t[\hat{\bar{\pi}}_{t+1}^*] \approx \psi_\pi \hat{\bar{\pi}}_t^* + \hat{m}_t^* - \hat{\bar{r}}_t^*$
Output (potential)	$\hat{\bar{y}}_t^* \approx \left(\frac{1+\phi}{\gamma+\phi}\right)[(1-\Lambda)\hat{a}_t + \Lambda \hat{a}_t^*]$
Monetary policy	$\hat{\bar{i}}_t^* \approx \psi_\pi \hat{\bar{\pi}}_t^* + \hat{m}_t^*$
Fisher equation	$\hat{\bar{r}}_t^* \equiv \hat{\bar{i}}_t^* - \mathbb{E}_t[\hat{\bar{\pi}}_{t+1}^*]$
Natural interest rate	$\hat{\bar{r}}_t^* \approx \gamma[(1-\Theta)(\mathbb{E}_t[\hat{\bar{y}}_{t+1}] - \hat{\bar{y}}_t) + \Theta(\mathbb{E}_t[\hat{\bar{y}}_{t+1}^*] - \hat{\bar{y}}_t^*)]$
Consumption	$\hat{\bar{c}}_t^* \approx (1-\Theta)\hat{\bar{y}}_t + \Theta \hat{\bar{y}}_t^*$
Employment	$\hat{\bar{l}}_t^* \approx \hat{\bar{y}}_t^* - \hat{a}_t^*$
Real wages	$(\hat{\bar{w}}_t^* - \hat{\bar{p}}_t^*) \approx \gamma \hat{\bar{c}}_t^* + \phi \hat{\bar{l}}_t^* \approx \gamma(1-\Theta)\hat{\bar{y}}_t + (\phi + \gamma\Theta)\hat{\bar{y}}_t^* - \phi \hat{a}_t^*$

International Relative Prices and Trade	
Real exchange rate	$\widehat{\bar{rs}}_t \approx (2\xi - 1)\widehat{\bar{tot}}_t$
Terms of trade	$\widehat{\bar{tot}}_t \approx \left[\dfrac{\gamma}{\sigma\gamma - (\sigma\gamma - 1)(2\xi - 1)^2}\right](\hat{\bar{y}}_t - \hat{\bar{y}}_t^*)$
Home real exports	$\widehat{\bar{exp}}_t \approx \Xi \hat{\bar{y}}_t + (1-\Xi)\hat{\bar{y}}_t^*$
Home real imports	$\widehat{\bar{imp}}_t \approx -(1-\Xi)\hat{\bar{y}}_t - \Xi \hat{\bar{y}}_t^*$
Home real trade balance	$\widehat{\bar{tb}}_t \equiv \hat{\bar{y}}_t - \hat{\bar{c}}_t = (1-\xi)(\widehat{\bar{exp}}_t - \widehat{\bar{imp}}_t) \approx (1-\Theta)(\hat{\bar{y}}_t - \hat{\bar{y}}_t^*)$

Table 3. (*Continued*)

Exogenous, Country-Specific Shocks	
Productivity shock	$\begin{pmatrix} \hat{a}_t \\ \hat{a}_t^* \end{pmatrix} \approx \begin{pmatrix} \delta_a & \delta_{a,a^*} \\ \delta_{a,a^*} & \delta_a \end{pmatrix} \begin{pmatrix} \hat{a}_{t-1} \\ \hat{a}_{t-1}^* \end{pmatrix} + \begin{pmatrix} \hat{\varepsilon}_t^a \\ \hat{\varepsilon}_t^{a*} \end{pmatrix}$
	$\begin{pmatrix} \hat{\varepsilon}_t^a \\ \hat{\varepsilon}_t^{a*} \end{pmatrix} \sim N\left(\begin{pmatrix} 0 \\ 0 \end{pmatrix}, \begin{pmatrix} \sigma_a^2 & \rho_{a,a^*}\sigma_a^2 \\ \rho_{a,a^*}\sigma_a^2 & \sigma_a^2 r \end{pmatrix} \right)$
Monetary shock	$\begin{pmatrix} \hat{m}_t \\ \hat{m}_t^* \end{pmatrix} \approx \begin{pmatrix} \delta_m & 0 \\ 0 & \delta_m \end{pmatrix} \begin{pmatrix} \hat{m}_{t-1} \\ \hat{m}_{t-1}^* \end{pmatrix} + \begin{pmatrix} \hat{\varepsilon}_t^m \\ \hat{\varepsilon}_t^{m*} \end{pmatrix}$
	$\begin{pmatrix} \hat{\varepsilon}_t^m \\ \hat{\varepsilon}_t^{m*} \end{pmatrix} \sim N\left(\begin{pmatrix} 0 \\ 0 \end{pmatrix}, \begin{pmatrix} \sigma_m^2 & \rho_{m,m^*}\sigma_m^2 \\ \rho_{m,m^*}\sigma_m^2 & \sigma_m^2 \end{pmatrix} \right)$

Composite Parameters
$\Theta \equiv \xi \left[\dfrac{\sigma\gamma - (\sigma\gamma - 1)(2\xi - 1)}{\sigma\gamma - (\sigma\gamma - 1)(2\xi - 1)^2} \right]$
$\Lambda \equiv 1 + (\sigma\gamma - 1)\left[\dfrac{\gamma(1 - \xi)(2\xi)}{\phi(\sigma\gamma - (\sigma\gamma - 1)(2\xi - 1)^2) + \gamma} \right]$
$\Xi \equiv \left[\dfrac{\sigma\gamma + (\sigma\gamma - 1)(2\xi - 1)(1 - \xi)}{\sigma\gamma - (\sigma\gamma - 1)(2\xi - 1)^2} \right]$

steady state value in this setting. The exogenous monetary and productivity shocks are invariant to the model specification – the frictionless model and the benchmark NOEM model are subject to the same realization of these shocks. It follows from the characterization of the dynamics of the frictionless model that neither the monetary policy rule nor monetary shocks have an impact on any real variables (i.e., on (potential) output, consumption, employment, real wages, and the (natural) real interest rates).

Productivity shocks enter into the NOEM dynamics described in Tables 1 and 2 only through their impact on the dynamics of the natural real rates $\tilde{r}_t$ and $\tilde{r}_t^*$ and potential output $\tilde{y}_t$ and $\tilde{y}_t^*$ of the frictionless equilibrium. The natural rates can be expressed as a function of expected changes in Home and Foreign potential output, reflecting the fact that real rates respond to expected *changes* in real economic activity – as measured by potential output growth – rather than to the overall level of economic activity. In turn, we characterize potential output for each country, $\tilde{y}_t$ and $\tilde{y}_t^*$, as a function of the Home and Foreign productivity shocks. The natural rates in each country are affected by the dynamics of productivity in both countries due to openness to trade. However, these rates do not necessarily equalize across countries in spite of the symmetry of the model because Home-product bias in consumption implies different consumption baskets for the Home and Foreign countries and prevents consumption demand from equalizing between them in response to country-specific shocks.[5]

The core structure of the model described in Tables 1, 2 and 3 incorporates an open-economy Phillips curve. This equilibrium condition fleshes out the *global slack hypothesis* – that is, the idea that in a world open to trade under short-run monetary non-neutrality arising from nominal rigidities, the relevant trade-off for monetary policy is between local inflation and global (rather than local) slack. Martínez-García and Wynne (2010) provide some further discussion of the open-economy Phillips curve. The deterministic, zero-inflation steady state of the model presented in Table 4 is identical for the NOEM and frictionless models, reflecting the fact that monetary neutrality still holds in the long-run. Monetary policy has no direct impact on real variables in steady state, so long-run neutrality is preserved even though nominal rigidities in the NOEM model introduce a trade-off between local inflation and global output gap in the short-run dynamics.

The open-economy IS equation ties the evolution of the output gaps – deviations of actual output from their frictionless potential – to both Home and Foreign demand through the real interest rates in both countries. Nominal rigidities introduce an intertemporal wedge between the actual real interest rate (the opportunity cost of consumption today versus consumption tomorrow) and the natural (real) rates of interest that would prevail in a frictionless equilibrium. Demand responds to deviations of each country's real interest rate from its natural (real) rate as that shifts consumption across time. The fact that Home-product bias precludes in general the possibility of consumption and interest rate equalization across countries means that we cannot summarize demand shifts in terms of a world real interest rate in deviations from a world natural rate alone.

The Home and Foreign monetary policy rules complete the specification of the core model. Monetary policy is modelled with a Taylor (1993)-type rule that aims at domestic stabilization (even in a fully integrated world) by reacting to local conditions as determined by each country's inflation and output gap.[6] To be consistent with the simple rule laid out in Taylor (1993), we assume that the persistence in policy rates can be thought of as *extrinsic* or exogenous inertia in the policy-making process (and out of the policy-makers control). *Extrinsic* persistence could result from imperfections such

Table 4. New Open Economy Macro (NOEM) and Flexible Price
(RBC) Models: Steady State.

	Home Economy

Output $\quad\quad\quad\quad\quad \bar{Y} = \bar{Y}(h) = \bar{C}$

Consumption $\quad\quad \bar{C} = \left(\dfrac{1}{\kappa}\right)^{\frac{1}{\gamma+\phi}} (A)^{\frac{1+\phi}{\gamma+\phi}}$

$\quad\quad\quad\quad\quad\quad \bar{C}(h) = 2\bar{C}^H, \quad \bar{C}(f) = 2\bar{C}^F, \bar{C}^H = \xi\bar{C}, \quad \bar{C}^F = (1-\xi)\bar{C}^*$

Employment $\quad\quad \bar{L} = \bar{L}(h) = \dfrac{\bar{Y}}{A}$

Real wages $\quad\quad \dfrac{\bar{W}}{\bar{P}} = A$

Prices $\quad\quad\quad\quad \bar{P} = \bar{P}^H = \bar{\bar{P}}(h)$

Interest rates $\quad\quad 1 + \bar{i} = 1 + \bar{r} = \dfrac{1}{\beta}$

	Foreign Economy

Output $\quad\quad\quad\quad\quad \bar{Y}^* = \bar{Y}^*(f) = \bar{C}^*$

Consumption $\quad\quad \bar{C}^* = \bar{C}$

$\quad\quad\quad\quad\quad\quad \bar{C}^*(h) = 2\bar{C}^{H*}, \quad \bar{C}^*(f) = 2\bar{C}^{F*}, \quad \bar{C}^{H*} = (1-\xi)\bar{C}^*, \quad \bar{C}^{F*} = \xi\bar{C}^*$

Employment $\quad\quad \bar{L}^* = \bar{L}^*(f) = \dfrac{\bar{Y}^*}{A}$

Real wages $\quad\quad \dfrac{\bar{W}^*}{\bar{P}^*} = A$

Prices $\quad\quad\quad\quad \bar{P}^* = \bar{P}^{F*} = \bar{\bar{P}}^*(f)$

Interest rates $\quad\quad 1 + \bar{i}^* = 1 + \bar{r}^* = \dfrac{1}{\beta}$

	International Relative Prices and Trade

Real exchange rate $\quad\quad \overline{RS} \equiv \dfrac{\overline{SP^*}}{\bar{P}} = 1$

Terms of trade $\quad\quad \overline{ToT} \equiv \dfrac{\bar{P}^F}{\overline{SP^{H*}}} = \dfrac{\bar{P}^F}{\bar{P}^H} = \dfrac{\bar{P}^{F*}}{\bar{P}^{H*}} = 1$

Home real exports $\quad\quad \overline{EXP} = \bar{C}^{H*} = (1-\xi)\bar{C}^* = (1-\xi)\bar{C}$

Home real imports $\quad\quad \overline{IMP} = \bar{C}^F = (1-\xi)\bar{C}$

Home real trade balance $\quad \overline{TB} = \overline{EXP} - \overline{IMP} = 0$

as the slow acquisition of information relevant for policy-making or from lags in decision-making that we do not model explicitly. In contrast, *intrinsic* or endogenous inertia results from policy-makers intentionally smoothing out their policy response to changing economic conditions (see, e.g., Rudebusch, 2002, 2006, for further discussion).

Calibrating Structural Parameters

Even with the reduction of the parameter space that comes from the adoption of an optimal labor subsidy and the assumption that the deep structural parameters governing tastes, technologies and shocks are essentially symmetric in the two countries, the long-run (steady state) and short-run (dynamics) of the model still depend on a large number of parameters – 18 in total.[7] 15 of those parameters affect the dynamics of the model, while up to 7 parameters enter in the determination of the steady state. We further divide the set of 18 model parameters into a group of 9 shock parameters that characterize the exogenous shock processes and 9 structural parameters that describe the endogenous propagation mechanism. Out of the 9 shock parameters, 7 affect the dynamics while the remaining 2 (the unconditional means of the shocks) do not. Out of the 9 structural parameters, 8 affect the endogenous propagation of the shocks and the other one solely appears in the deterministic steady state.

We list the 15 parameters of the model that affect its short-run dynamics in Table 5, as this information is relevant both to calibrate the model and to elicit consistent priors. Those 15 model parameters need to be calibrated first in order to simulate data. We assess the problem of weak identification under the Bayesian estimation method attempting to recover the calibrated model parameters by estimating the model with simulated data. Here we provide a succinct description of the sources used to calibrate those structural parameters.

Parameters Related to the Steady State (Long-Run)
Typically, long-run historical averages of the relevant macroeconomic time-series are used to calibrate parameters that affect the steady state of the model. Given our specification, there are at most 7 parameters that enter into the steady state: the intertemporal discount factor, β, the inverse of the intertemporal elasticity of substitution, γ, the inverse of the Frisch elasticity of labor supply, ϕ, the labor disutility scaling factor, κ, the share of locally produced goods, ξ, the unconditional mean of the productivity shock, A,

Table 5. Structural and Shock Parameters: Calibration and Prior Distributions.

Calibration		Prior Distributions				
Structural Parameters	Calibrated Value	Structural Parameters	Domain	Density	Mean	Std. Dev.
Nonpolicy parameters		*Nonpolicy parameters*				
β	0.99	β	–	Fixed	0.99	–
γ	5	γ	$\mathbb{R}^+$	Gamma	5	5
ϕ	5	ϕ	$\mathbb{R}^+$	Gamma	5	5
σ	1.5	σ	$\mathbb{R}^+$	Gamma	1.5	1
ξ	0.94	$2\xi-1$	$(0,1)$	Beta	0.88	0.01
α	0.74	α	$(0,1)$	Beta	0.75	0.07
Policy parameters		*Policy parameters*				
ψ_π	1.24	$\psi_\pi-1$	$\mathbb{R}^+$	InvGamma	0.24	2
ψ_x	0.33	ψ_x	$\mathbb{R}^+$	InvGamma	0.33	2
Shock Parameters		Shock Parameters				
δ_a	0.97	δ_a	–	Fixed	0.97	–
δ_{a,a^*}	0.025	$\dfrac{1}{2}+\dfrac{1}{2}\dfrac{\delta_{a,a^*}}{0.03}$	$(0,1)$	Beta	0.91667	0.05
σ_a	0.73	σ_a	$\mathbb{R}^+$	InvGamma	0.73	3
ρ_{a,a^*}	0.29	ρ_{a,a^*}	$(0,1)$	Beta	0.29	0.18
δ_m	0.92	δ_m	$(0,1)$	Beta	0.92	0.02
σ_m	0.36	σ_m	$\mathbb{R}^+$	InvGamma	0.36	5
ρ_{m,m^*}	0.5	ρ_{m,m^*}	$(0,1)$	Beta	0.5	0.22
		Nonstructural, shock parameter				
		σ_v	$\mathbb{R}^+$	InvGamma	0.10	1

Notes: The share of locally produced goods ξ and the spillovers between Home and Foreign productivity shocks δ_{a,a^*} are transformed to adjust their range to the domain of the Beta distribution. In order to satisfy the Taylor principle, we also transform the sensitivity of monetary policy to deviations from the inflation target ψ_π to adjust its range (set above one) to the domain of the Gamma distribution. While the constraints on the shock parameters ensure the shock processes are well-behaved and stationary, existence and uniqueness requires the policy parameter ψ_π to be slightly above 1 for very low values of the policy parameter ψ_x and slightly below 1 otherwise. Hence, restricting the policy parameter ψ_π to satisfy the Taylor principle in this open economy model is neither necessary nor sufficient to ensure determinacy but is a conventional practice that we merely follow here.

Para (v) and Para (s) refer to the pair of parameters that characterize each prior distribution. For the Normal distribution, the mean is $\mu = v$ and the variance is $\sigma^2 = s^2$. For the Beta distribution, the mean is $\mu = v/(v + s)$ and the variance is $\sigma^2 = vs/((v + s)^2(v + s + 1))$. For the Gamma distribution, the mean is $\mu = vs$ and the variance is $\sigma^2 = vs^2$. For the Uniform distribution, the upper and lower bound of the support are v and s respectively, while the mean is $\mu = (v + s)/2$ and the variance is $\sigma^2 = (v-s)^2/12$. For the Inverse Gamma distribution, the mean is $\mu = s/(v-1)$ and the variance is $\sigma^2 = s^2/((v-1)^2(v-2))$.

and the unconditional mean of the monetary shock, M. At most 4 of those 7 parameters can be matched to long-run historical averages simultaneously based on the steady state relationships described in Table 4.

The parameters M, A and κ do not affect the dynamics of the NOEM model or the dynamics of its flexible price (frictionless) counterpart. Therefore, without loss of generality, we simply normalize $A = M = \kappa = 1$ and obtain a steady state in which output, consumption and employment (in levels) for the Home and Foreign countries are all equal to one. Under the normalization of A and κ, the preference parameters γ and ϕ cannot be pinned down by steady state relationships. However, the intertemporal discount factor, β, and the share of locally produced goods in the consumption basket, ξ, are two preference parameters that can be matched to historical macroeconomic time series based on steady state relationships.

We set the intertemporal discount factor β at 0.99 to attain an average yearly interest rate of 4% (i.e., we choose β to imply that $(\frac{1}{\beta})^4 = 1.041$). We set the share of locally produced goods in the consumption basket ξ at 0.94 in order to obtain an average import share of 6% for the United States. These choices are taken from Chari et al. (2002), who rely on United States and European data for their calibration.

Parameters Related to the Model Dynamics (Short-Run)
Given our model, there are 6 structural (nonpolicy) parameters and 2 policy parameters that affect the dynamics of the NOEM model. The structural (nonpolicy) parameters include the intertemporal discount factor, β, the inverse of the intertemporal elasticity of substitution, γ, the inverse of the Frisch elasticity of labor supply, ϕ, the elasticity of substitution between Home and Foreign bundles, σ, the share of locally produced goods, ξ, and the Calvo price stickiness parameter, α. The policy parameters include the sensitivity of the monetary policy rule to deviations from the inflation target, ψ_π, and from the potential output target, ψ_x.

The calibration of these (policy and nonpolicy) structural parameters can be done in many different ways, leading to a wide range of plausible parameter values. Typically, it is recommended not to base the calibration of the key endogenous propagation parameters on time series macro data that is central to the question being investigated in order to avoid a *circularity* problem. It is also not recommended to use parameter estimates that are derived under theoretical constraints or economic relationships that are not compatible with (or easily mapped into) the structure of the model being explored to avoid biasing the calibration. We revisit some of the most conventional calibration strategies and the dispersion of the suggested parameterizations in the context of calibrating our NOEM model:

Frisch elasticity of labor supply: The Frisch elasticity of labor supply, $\frac{1}{\phi}$, is commonly identified in the literature on the basis of micro-level data. Pencavel (1986) reports that the typical point estimate of the labor supply elasticity for men is 0.2, with a range of estimates going from 0 to 0.45. Other surveys on the empirical micro literature include Card (1994) and Browning, Hansen, and Heckman (1999) and more recently Keane (2010). Most micro studies consistently indicate that the Frisch elasticity of labor supply lies below 1. Macro-estimates can also be used in order to pin down the Frisch elasticity of labor supply, but there exists a disconnect between the macro and the micro evidence. For example, Rotemberg and Woodford (1998b) and Rotemberg and Woodford (1998a) argue that the inverse of the Frisch elasticity ϕ needs to be as low as $\frac{1}{9.5} = 0.10526$ to match the relatively weak observed response of real wages to monetary disturbances and other macro features of the labor market. Based on the micro evidence, we set the Frisch elasticity of labor supply $\frac{1}{\phi}$ at 0.2 to match the number reported by Pencavel (1986).[8]

Elasticity of intertemporal substitution: The elasticity of intertemporal substitution, $\frac{1}{\gamma}$, is often identified on the basis of macro-level data. Still, the empirical macro literature provides a wide range of possible values for this parameter. On the one hand, Hall (1988) and Yogo (2004) – estimating the inverse of the elasticity of intertemporal substitution γ from the co-movement of aggregate consumption with real yields – argue that its value is likely above 5. On the other hand, most business cycle models – including many international business cycle models – typically assume a much lower value for the inverse elasticity γ (see, e.g., Lucas's, 1990, warning that "even $\gamma = 2$ seems high"). We set γ equal to 5, as in Chari et al. (2002) and Martínez-García and Søndergaard (2013), in order to approximate the volatility of the real exchange rate relative to output.

Elasticity of intratemporal substitution between Home and Foreign goods: The elasticity of intratemporal substitution between Home and Foreign goods, σ, is commonly identified on the basis of macro-level data. Based on empirical estimates of trade models, it is generally noted that plausible values of the U.S. elasticity of intratemporal substitution lie between 1 and 2. We follow Backus, Kehoe, and Kydland (1994) and Chari et al. (2002) setting the elasticity σ to be equal to 1.5.

Frequency of price adjustments: The Calvo parameter, α, is often identified using micro-level data. However, the empirical micro literature provides a wide range of possible values for α. Bils and Klenow (2004) suggested that the median frequency of price changes implies a duration of only 4.3 months based on evidence from the U.S. CPI. Klenow and Kryvtsov (2008) and Nakamura and Steinsson (2008) report a range of 7–10 months based on U.S. CPI data, while prices in the Euro-Area CPI appear to change even less frequently according to Dhyne et al. (2006). The evidence surveyed by Taylor (1999) and more recently the micro price studies reviewed by Klenow and Malin (2010) are consistent with the view that prices change on average closer to once a year (after excluding most short-lived price changes). The convention prevalent in most of the NOEM literature is that prices remain unchanged for an average of four quarters implying that $\alpha = 0.75$ (see, e.g., Chari et al., 2002; Martínez-García & Søndergaard, 2013, among others). We adopt the standard value of 0.75 for the degree of price stickiness α to be consistent with the NOEM literature.

Policy parameters: We assume that the Taylor rule is inertial of the *extrinsic* type, as the original rule proposed in Taylor (1993) did not include *intrinsic* inertia. The parameters of the Taylor rule are often estimated jointly with the monetary shock process to fit the data. We adopt the policy parameters estimated for the U.S. in equation 18 of Rudebusch (2002) together with his estimates of the AR(1) parameters for the monetary policy shock–assuming the policy rule is identical in both countries. Hence, we set ψ_π at 1.24 and ψ_x at 0.33 which are fairly close to the values of 1.5 and 0.5 respectively proposed by Taylor (1993).

Parameters Related to the Exogenous Shock Processes
Typically, the identification of the parameters associated with the exogenous shock processes involves two steps. The first step consists in deriving – whenever possible – a time series for the realization of the shocks. To do so we have to map the data as closely as possible to the model using a few key equilibrium conditions and perhaps some previously calibrated structural parameters (e.g., the production function and the capital share are needed to derive a measure of the Solow residual from data on output, the stock of capital and hours worked). The second step generally involves estimating a pre-specified stochastic process on the time series realization derived in the first step.

In our model, there are just two country-specific shocks that we have to consider: productivity shocks and monetary shocks. The two key equations needed to infer a realization of these shocks are the aggregate production function and the monetary policy rule. Under the assumption of linear-in-labor technologies, we can map the labor productivity of these countries into the productivity shocks of the model (that is, $\hat{a}_t$ and $\hat{a}_t^*$). In this case, no structural parameters are needed to infer a realization of the productivity shocks.[9]

For the parameterization of the VAR(1) productivity shock process, we follow Heathcote and Perri (2002) who use real GDP and employment data from 1973 to 1998 to obtain a realization of the productivity shock for the U.S. and a foreign aggregate that bundles together 15 European countries, Canada and Japan. Their approach is similar to the one we would require in this model (although they adjust the labor data with a labor share set at 0.64). Based on their estimates, we set δ_a (the persistence parameter) at 0.97 and $\delta_{a,a*}$ (the cross-country spill-over parameter) at 0.025. The volatility σ_a is set at 0.73 and the correlation between domestic and foreign innovations $\rho_{a,a*}$ at 0.29. Monetary and productivity innovations are assumed to be uncorrelated with each other, and we rule out by construction the presence of spillovers between monetary and productivity shocks.

The calibration of the monetary policy shock is a bit less straightforward than that of the productivity shock, so we use the joint estimates of the Taylor rule and the monetary shock process from Rudebusch (2002). For the VAR(1) monetary shock process, we set δ_m at 0.92 and σ_m at 0.36 for the persistence and volatility in both countries. We complete the description of the dynamics by choosing the correlation between Home and Foreign monetary innovations $\rho_{m,m*}$ to be 0.5 as in Chari et al. (2002).

METHODOLOGY: SOLUTION AND ESTIMATION

We use the log-linear approximation of the workhorse NOEM model described in Tables 1, 2, and 3 as our DGP and collect all the model parameters in the vector

$$\lambda = (\beta, \kappa, \gamma, \phi, \sigma, \xi, \alpha, \psi_\pi, \psi_x, A, \delta_a, \delta_{a,a*}, \sigma_a, \rho_{a,a*}, M, \delta_m, \sigma_m, \rho_{m,m*}; \theta, \varphi)$$

The dynamics of the core endogenous variables can be cast in the form of a canonical linear rational expectations (LRE) difference system, that is,[10]

$$A_0(\lambda)\mathbb{E}_t[\hat{Y}_{t+1}^c] = A_1(\lambda)\hat{Y}_t^c + B(\lambda)\hat{X}_t \qquad (1)$$

where the matrices $A_0(\lambda)$, $A_1(\lambda)$, and $B(\lambda)$ are in terms of a subset of the model parameters λ. We represent the driving process for the exogenous shocks as,

$$\hat{X}_t = \rho\hat{X}_{t-1} + \hat{\varepsilon}_t, \quad \mathbb{E}_t[\hat{\varepsilon}_t\hat{\varepsilon}_t^T] = \Omega \qquad (2)$$

where ρ governs the dynamics and Ω the variances-covariances in terms of a subset of the model parameters λ. The driving process includes the monetary shocks and the natural rates from the frictionless model described in Table 3 – the productivity shocks are subsumed into the natural rates. As shown in Table 2, the log-linearized conditions for the noncore endogenous variables can be expressed as a linear transformation of the endogenous core variables and the exogenous shocks, that is,

$$\hat{Y}_t^n = C_0(\lambda)\hat{Y}_t^c + C_1(\lambda)\hat{X}_t \tag{3}$$

where the matrices $C_0(\lambda)$ and $C_1(\lambda)$ are expressed in terms of a subset of the model parameters λ.

Model Solution. The log-linear approximation method used by Martínez-García and Wynne (2010) is quite popular in the literature because of its tractability. It transforms an otherwise nonlinear DSGE model into an LRE system of equations which we know how to solve easily and estimate. However, the choice of a solution method is not without consequence as it imposes practical limitations on the empirical work. We make note of some of those concerns here:

a. Log-linear and linear approximations are a case of the first-order perturbation method. Perturbation methods are meant to approximate smooth policy functions only locally. While in many cases a first-order local approximation suffices to explore the model, this is not always advisable. For example, the risk-premium generally drops out from a consumption-based asset pricing equation after a first-order approximation, so a higher-order approximation would be needed to capture asset price movements. There are a number of global approximation schemes that can be tried to solve the model, but they are rarely used in estimation due to time-constraints and the complexity of the solution methods.

  One source of misspecification comes from the approximation error that we introduce when using a log-linearized model. We bypass this problem by adopting the canonical model fitted into Eqs. (1)–(3) as the true DGP. Nonlinear solution and estimation methods are becoming increasingly more important for proper structural identification, in part to minimize this approximation error. We refer the interested reader to Aruoba, Fernández-Villaverde, and Rubio-Ramírez (2004) for alternative solution methods, and An and Schorfheide (2007) for a review of perturbation methods in the context of Bayesian estimation.

b. The existence and uniqueness of a local solution to the LRE system in Eqs. (1)–(2) generally depends on the region of the parameter space: either a local solution exists and is unique (determinacy), there are multiple stable solutions (indeterminacy), or there are no stable solutions. Blanchard and Kahn (1980) discuss the conditions that ensure local existence and uniqueness whenever $A_0(\lambda)$ in Eq. (1) is nonsingular, and King and Watson (1998) offer an extension whenever $A_0(\lambda)$ is permitted to be singular. We solve the LRE model based on the generalized Schur decomposition method (see, e.g., Villemot, 2011), as implemented by the software package Dynare. The selection of priors is generally truncated at the boundary of the determinacy region or, as we do here, puts a very small probability mass on parameter values that imply indeterminacy or nonexistence a priori and discards all draws from outside the determinacy region in the estimation. Lubik and Schorfheide (2004) are among the few exceptions where a DSGE model is estimated through Bayesian techniques without restricting the parameter space to the determinacy region.

Truncation of the prior distribution is not without its pitfalls – in particular, because the size of the determinacy region of the parameter space could be sensitive to modelling assumptions. For instance, Galí (2008) illustrates with the closed-economy workhorse New Keynesian model how the determinacy region generally shrinks whenever monetary policy responds to expected rather than current inflation and output gaps. Under the standard monetary policy rule, policy-makers must respond with enough "strength" to deviations of inflation from its target to prevent the emergence of multiple equilibria (often referred to as the Taylor principle). Under a forward-looking interest rate rule, policy-makers must preclude the possibility of "overreacting" as well. We bypass this issue because the determinacy region is invariant in all our experiments.

c. If a stable local solution to the LRE system in Eqs. (1)–(2) exists and is unique, then the transition equation that describes it takes the following reduced form,

$$\hat{Y}_t^c = D_0(\lambda)\hat{Y}_{t-1}^c + D_1(\lambda)\hat{X}_t \tag{4}$$

where the matrix $D_0(\lambda)$ characterizes the impact of lagged core endogenous variables and $D_1(\lambda)$ determines the influence of current and lagged exogenous shocks. The matrices $D_0(\lambda)$ and $D_1(\lambda)$ are expressed in terms of a subset of the structural parameters λ. The relationship between the reduced-form solution of a linearized DSGE model and a corresponding finite VAR representation is extensively covered in Ravenna (2007) and Fernández-Villaverde, Rubio-Ramírez, Sargent, and Watson (2007), while the Bayesian econometrics of the DSGE-VAR analysis are reviewed by An and Schorfheide (2007).

Misspecification bias could arise from the invalid or incorrect specification of the cross-equation restrictions of the model, and manifest itself attaining a worse fit and out-of-sample performance than a competing unrestricted VAR. The same argument can be extended to comparisons across DSGE models too. It is worth pointing out that in the presence of weak structural identification it may be possible to find a selection of priors for the estimation of a misspecified model that approximates the fit of the unrestricted VAR by muting the invalid cross-equation restrictions. However, that would result in misleading inferences about the structural parameters and the model itself. In our investigation, we rule out this form of misspecification as well because we estimate the exact same benchmark LRE system that is used as the DGP for the simulated data.

d. For Bayesian estimation, even under the best circumstances, the transition equation in Eq. (4) may need to be supplemented with a system of observation/measurement equations,

$$\hat{Y}_t^{obs} = F(\lambda)\hat{Y}_t^c + \hat{v}_t \tag{5}$$

$$\hat{v}_t = \rho_v \hat{v}_{t-1} + \hat{\varepsilon}_t^v, \quad \mathbb{E}_t[\hat{\varepsilon}_t^v \hat{\varepsilon}_t^{vT}] = V \tag{6}$$

where $\hat{v}_t$ is a measurement error vector and the matrix $F(\lambda)$ is expressed in terms of a subset of the model parameters λ. We treat the autocorrelation matrix ρ_v and the variance–covariance matrix V for the measurement error shock as separate from the vector of model parameters λ, and we abstract from measurement error in the benchmark estimation.

Measurement equations may be needed because not all core variables described by Eq. (4) are actually observable. Given that domestic and foreign output gaps are unobservable, the set of observable variables included in the observation Eq. (5) may have to be augmented – specially if we take into account that the other two core variables in each country (inflation and the nominal interest rate) are both nominal and the output gap is the only core variable that is real. In principle, the observable vector $\hat{Y}_t^{obs}$ may include both core and noncore variables, but the selection is not a trivial matter as we illustrate in this chapter.

All observable variables are expressed in deviations from steady state, so the issue of pre-filtering (de-meaning) the data or estimating the long-run steady state jointly has to be addressed. This is one of the aspects of implementation that we investigate in this chapter which affects the set-up of the observation equation in Eq. (5).[11] Nonetheless, the most crucial issue in international macroeconomics which determines Eq. (5) remains that of data availability. The lack of consistent, time series data is a severe limitation that restricts the choice of observable variables in practice more often than theoretical considerations do.

Data Simulation. We simulate the calibrated model described in the previous section over 11,000 periods, and drop the first 1,000 observations of each series to preclude any effect of the initial conditions on the simulation. We keep a long sample with the remaining 10,000 periods of the simulation, but also select one shorter subsample of 160 observations to illustrate the importance of sample size. We use Bayesian estimation methods on the long and short samples to investigate the ability of these techniques to recover the *true* parameters. The short subsample corresponds to 40 years of quarterly data and is meant to capture a fairly long, but plausible length for international macro time series data. The long sample of 10,000 periods (2,500 years of quarterly data) allows us to point out the estimation gains that can be attained as the sample size for estimation becomes arbitrarily large.

Fig. 1 describes the simulated data by plotting Home and Foreign output, Home and Foreign inflation, terms of trade and the trade balance for the short subsample. Fig. 1 also includes scatter plots for Home and Foreign inflation with respect to Home output, for Home and Foreign inflation with respect to Foreign output, and for Home and Foreign inflation with respect to terms of trade for the short sample.

We contrast the estimation results with the short sample of 160 observations against the results with the longer sample of 10,000 observations to show the practical limitations of small-sample inference. As noted by Evans (1996) in his survey of economic anomalies associated with the "peso problem," this issue arises when the realized moments of the observables within sample differ significantly from those of the *true* joint distribution – implied by the DGP process underlying the data – leading to distorted econometric inferences. The "peso problem" can be confounded in the data with misspecification of the DGP process or weak structural identification, but that is something we can take care of when working with simulated data as we choose the sample size and model specification.

In this chapter, the shape of the distribution is presumed to be known to the researcher since we take the *true* DGP process as given. However, the distribution itself is a function of the model parameters that need to be recovered and identified from simulated data – and the researcher in our experiments does not know the *true* parameter values. Hence, if the sample

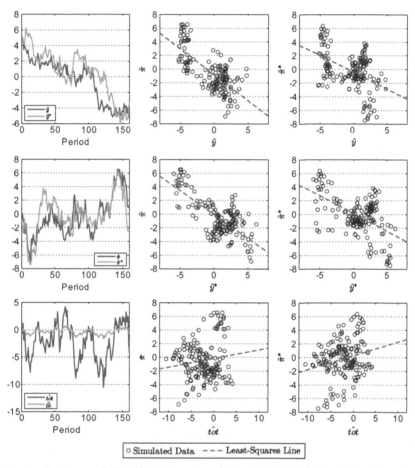

Fig. 1. Features of the Short Sample of Simulated Data Used for Bayesian Estimation

Note: The model is simulated over 10,000 periods with code written for Dynare version 4.2.2 and Matlab version 7.13.0.564. We select a subsample of 160 periods for estimation purposes. The first column in this figure illustrates the realization of the subsample including domestic and foreign output in the top panel, domestic and foreign inflation in the middle panel, and the terms of trade and trade balance in the bottom panel. This figure also illustrates the linear relationship observed in the data between domestic inflation (second column) and foreign inflation (third column) with respect to domestic output (top panel), foreign output (middle panel), and terms of trade (bottom panel). The dashed line is the least-squares line that summarizes the type of relationship that we find between the data in each scatter plot. The code for the simulation is available upon request from the authors.

moments computed with the available macro time series do not coincide with the population moments (the theoretical moments) that could be indicative of a latent "peso problem" within sample that can affect our estimates.

The empirical inference problem that comes from small samples arises because the data sample is insufficient to precisely recover the unobserved *true* model parameters and, therefore, biased parameter estimates emerge in an attempt to fit an observed empirical distribution that differs from the *true* one. This problem can seriously distort the model comparison, policy analysis and forecasting for which these estimated DSGE models are so often used. That is so even when the DGP process is actually known without any uncertainty and only the model parameters are unobserved. However, we aim to control for that with the long sample of 10,000 periods since the empirical distribution ought to approximate the *true* distribution in the limit as the sample size becomes sufficiently large.

In Table 6, we summarize how the features of these time series data (the long and short samples) compare against the theoretical moments implied by the NOEM model.[12] It is interesting to note how the divergence between the sample moments and the theoretical moments can be very large for samples of 40 years of quarterly data (160 observations) and even be significant for a sample of 10,000 observations, especially for Home and Foreign output. In spite of the inherent symmetry of the model, the sample moments in some cases can differ a lot between the Home and Foreign countries. The mean and the volatility of the series seem to be quite far off from their population counterparts, and even persistence at long lags seems to differ. Looking at the skewness and kurtosis of the long- and short-sample series using the Jarque–Bera statistic also gives us a different reading about the normality of the observed data depending on whether we look at the long sample or at the short sample, although it is already known that the Jarque–Bera statistic is less reliable in small samples. All this evidence suggests that with a conventional sample size of no more than 160 observations our empirical inferences with simulated data can be prone to the "peso problem."

Estimation Method. The LRE system in Eqs. (1)–(2) has to be solved before the model can actually be estimated, but the choices we make on how to solve the model are to a great extent conditioned by our estimation techniques. The appeal of linear and log-linear methods, for instance, is predicated on the literature's drive for tractability and applicability of standard econometric techniques in the analysis of DSGE models. In this sense, the model solution described in Eq. (4) together with the driving

Table 6.   Description of Model Simulation: Data Moments.

	Home Output			Foreign Output		
	Short Sample	Long Sample	Theoretical	Short Sample	Long Sample	Theoretical
Mean	−0.4618	−0.7159	0.0000	0.6325	−0.6896	0.0000
Std. Dev.	2.6963	4.1997	3.6940	2.9712	4.2035	3.6940
Skewness	−0.3915	−0.3585	–	0.5831	−0.2753	–
Kurtosis	1.8653	2.9229	–	2.6060	2.6252	–
Jarque–Bera	12.67***	216.67***	–	10.10**	184.90***	–
Autocorrel.(1)	0.9607	0.9923	0.9902	0.9698	0.9922	0.9902
Autocorrel.(5)	0.8520	0.9649	0.9538	0.8415	0.9645	0.9538

	Home Inflation			Foreign Inflation		
	Short Sample	Long Sample	Theoretical	Short Sample	Long Sample	Theoretical
Mean	−0.4655	0.0711	0.0000	−0.2018	−0.1439	0.0000
Std. Dev.	2.8420	2.4776	2.3635	2.8305	2.4951	2.3635
Skewness	0.6257	0.0421	–	−0.2435	0.1011	–
Kurtosis	3.0720	2.8357	–	3.3601	2.9873	–
Jarque–Bera	10.48**	14.20***	–	2.45	17.12***	–
Autocorrel.(1)	0.9451	0.9291	0.9221	0.9421	0.9305	0.9221
Autocorrel.(5)	0.7475	0.6909	0.6678	0.7021	0.7096	0.6678

	Terms of Trade			Trade Balance		
	Short Sample	Long Sample	Theoretical	Short Sample	Long Sample	Theoretical
Mean	−2.2184	−0.0533	0.0000	−0.3519	−0.0084	0.0000
Std. Dev.	3.1865	4.5123	4.5140	0.5055	0.7158	0.7161
Skewness	−0.2217	−0.1672	–	−0.2217	−0.1672	–
Kurtosis	2.3206	3.0565	–	2.3206	3.0565	–
Jarque–Bera	4.39*	47.92***	–	4.39*	47.92***	–
Autocorrel.(1)	0.8835	0.9424	0.9442	0.8835	0.9424	0.9442
Autocorrel.(5)	0.4823	0.7499	0.7508	0.4823	0.7499	0.7508

This table reports a number of moments for the series of Home and Foreign output, Home and Foreign inflation, terms of trade and the trade balance. We calculate those moments for the short sample of 160 observations and for the full-length sample of 10,000 observations. Moreover, we also include the corresponding theoretical moments for these series. All statistics are computed after each series is simulated under the calibration described in Table 5. We use Matlab 7.13.0.564 and Dynare v4.2.4 for the stochastic simulation.

process of the model in Eq. (2) and the measurement equations in Eqs. (5)–(6) constitute a linear system of equations that fits naturally into a state-space representation. This makes it possible to use the standard Kalman filter and to apply econometric techniques based on the likelihood function such as Bayesian estimation. For a discussion of the complexity of Bayesian estimation with nonlinear solution methods (higher-order perturbation methods) we refer to An and Schorfheide (2007).

Let us denote the prior density $p(\lambda)$, the likelihood function by $\mathscr{L}(\lambda \mid \hat{Y}^{obs})$ and the posterior distribution as $p(\lambda \mid \hat{Y}^{obs}) \propto \mathscr{L}(\lambda \mid \hat{Y}^{obs})p(\lambda)$. The estimation of a linear or log-linear state-space model solution proceeds as follows: for a given draw, the LRE is solved to obtain the reduced-form solution as noted earlier. If a unique stable solution exists as in Eq. (4), then the Kalman filter is used to evaluate the likelihood function $\mathscr{L}(\lambda \mid \hat{Y}^{obs})$ with the linear state-space system given by Eqs. (4), (2), and (5) and also to infer the posterior. Otherwise, $\mathscr{L}(\lambda \mid \hat{Y}^{obs})p(\lambda)$ is set to zero. A Metropolis–Hastings (MH) algorithm – one of the algorithms of the Markov Chain Monte Carlo (MCMC) class – is used to generate draws from the posterior distribution of the model parameters λ. Under general regularity conditions, the posterior distribution of λ is asymptotically normal.

This Monte Carlo-based algorithm generates Markov chains with a stationary distribution that approximate a Gaussian posterior distribution around the mode with a scaled version of the asymptotic covariance matrix. This allows us to efficiently represent the posterior distribution around the mode. We maximize the posterior density kernel with a Newton-type optimization routine. We implement the algorithm with the software package Dynare, using a routine that initializes the MH algorithm from a point in the parameter space with a high posterior density value (not necessarily the posterior mode).[13] For further reference on MCMC algorithms, we suggest Robert and Casella (1999).

Two observations are pertinent at this point in regards to our choice of the Bayesian estimation method:

a. The stochastic singularity in Bayesian econometrics refers to the fact that estimation cannot be implemented on an LRE model that generates a rank-deficient covariance matrix for the observable variables. In this chapter we pursue the standard approach to handle this singularity and set the number of observables used for the estimation to be equal to the number of structural shocks in the model (Home and Foreign monetary shocks, Home and Foreign natural rates). This limits the amount of time series data that can be incorporated into the estimation (and the information available for identification), but otherwise does not restrict the composition of the vector of observables $\hat{Y}^{obs}$. One strand of the literature has resorted to modifying the model by adding so-called measurement error or other nonstructural shocks in order to expand the set of observables. In this chapter we assess the effect that the selection of observables and the inclusion of nonstructural shocks may have on identification.

b. As Guerrón-Quintana (2010) illustrates, the log-likelihood function of the DSGE model depends on the selection of observables. We find that the specification of the measurement equation and the selection of observables can have a direct effect on the estimation because some observables might be more informative than others and also because the structural parameters enter directly into the matrix $F(\lambda)$ in the measurement Eq. (5). Therefore, the choice of observable variables $\hat{Y}^{obs}$ may complicate or facilitate the identification of the structural parameters of interest in the model depending on how they appear in $F(\lambda)$. In this chapter we pay close attention to the selection of variables for these reasons.

Structural Identification: An Illustration

The problem of structural identification in a LRE model is best illustrated with a simple example from our benchmark model. Let us define the world aggregate variables $\hat{z}_t^W$ as $\hat{z}_t^W \equiv \frac{1}{2}\hat{z}_t + \frac{1}{2}\hat{z}_t^*$. Then, we can write the dynamics of the world economy as if it were a closed-economy based on the following pair of equations,

$$\hat{\pi}_t^W \approx \beta \mathbb{E}_t[\hat{\pi}_{t+1}^W] + \Phi(\phi + \gamma)\hat{x}_t^W \tag{7}$$

$$\gamma(\mathbb{E}_t[\hat{x}_{t+1}^W] - \hat{x}_t^W) \approx (\hat{i}_t^W - \mathbb{E}_t[\hat{\pi}_{t+1}^W]) - \hat{r}_t^W \tag{8}$$

where we define the composite parameter $\Phi \equiv ((1-\alpha)(1-\beta\alpha)/\alpha)$ for the slope of the Phillips curve. We complete the description of the world economy with an expanded specification of the monetary policy rule that allows the nominal interest rate to respond to the output gap as well as to output growth, that is,

$$\hat{i}_t^W \approx [\psi_\pi \hat{\pi}_t^W + \psi_x \hat{x}_t^W + \psi_{\Delta y}(\hat{y}_t^W - \hat{y}_{t-1}^W)] + \hat{m}_t^W \tag{9}$$

where $\hat{y}_t^W = \hat{\bar{y}}_t^W + \hat{x}_t^W$ and $\hat{\bar{y}}_t^W$ refers to the world potential output. Combining Eqs. (7) and (8) with Eq. (9) we can describe the world LRE model under this expanded policy rule as,

$$
\begin{pmatrix} \hat{x}_t^W \\ \hat{\pi}_t^W \end{pmatrix} \approx \Psi \begin{bmatrix} \gamma & 1 - \beta\psi_\pi \\ \Phi\gamma(\gamma + \phi) & \Phi(\gamma + \phi) + \beta(\gamma + \psi_x + \psi_{\Delta y}) \end{bmatrix} \begin{pmatrix} \mathbb{E}_t[\hat{x}_{t+1}^W] \\ \mathbb{E}_t[\hat{\pi}_{t+1}^W] \end{pmatrix} + \cdots
$$

$$
\Psi \begin{bmatrix} \psi_{\Delta y} & 0 \\ \Phi(\phi + \gamma)\psi_{\Delta y} & 0 \end{bmatrix} \begin{pmatrix} \hat{x}_{t-1}^W \\ \hat{\pi}_{t-1}^W \end{pmatrix} + \cdots
$$

$$
\Psi \begin{bmatrix} 1 \\ \Phi(\phi + \gamma) \end{bmatrix} \left(\hat{\bar{r}}_t^W - \psi_{\Delta y}\left(\hat{\bar{y}}_t^W - \hat{\bar{y}}_{t-1}^W\right) - \hat{m}_t^W \right) \tag{10}
$$

with $\Psi \equiv 1/(\gamma + \psi_x + \psi_{\Delta y} + \Phi(\phi + \gamma)\psi_\pi)$. This system of expectational difference equations includes a backward-looking component only if monetary policy responds actively to output growth (i.e., when $\psi_{\Delta y} > 0$), but not in our benchmark policy specification (i.e., when $\psi_{\Delta y} = 0$).

Notice that the degree of openness ξ does not enter into the world system described here, and neither does the intratemporal elasticity of substitution between Home and Foreign consumption bundles σ. Therefore, neither the composition of the consumption baskets nor the propagation of shocks through international risk-sharing affect the world allocation. The only parameters that affect the world dynamics and can be identified from this system of equations are the Calvo parameter α, the intertemporal discount factor β, the inverse of the intertemporal elasticity of substitution γ, the inverse of the Frisch elasticity of labor supply ϕ, and the policy parameters ψ_π, ψ_x and $\psi_{\Delta y}$.

Here we examine the response of the world economy to a monetary shock *alone* and consider world inflation $\hat{\pi}_t^W$ to be the relevant observable variable. Since world potential output $\hat{\bar{y}}_t^W$ and the world natural rate of interest $\hat{\bar{r}}_t^W$ are not affected by the monetary shocks anyway, we set them to zero at all times. To close the description of the world economic system, we derive the world forcing process for monetary shocks $\hat{m}_t^W$ as follows,

$$
\hat{m}_t^W = \delta_m \hat{m}_{t-1}^W + \hat{\varepsilon}_t^{mW}
$$

$$
\hat{\varepsilon}_t^{mW} \sim N(0, \sigma_{mW}^2), \quad \sigma_{mW}^2 \equiv \sigma_m^2 \left(\frac{1 + \rho_{m,m*}}{2} \right) \tag{11}
$$

Let us further assume that monetary shocks are perfectly correlated across countries (i.e., $\rho_{m,m*} = 1$) such that the variance of the world monetary shocks equals the variance of the country shocks (i.e., $\sigma_{mW}^2 = \sigma_m^2$). It is possible to show that if all country-specific shocks are perfectly correlated, then the world aggregates suffice to fully describe the dynamics of our benchmark model as it would be the case that $\hat{\pi}_t^W \approx \hat{\pi}_t \approx \hat{\pi}_t^*$ and $\hat{x}_t^W \approx \hat{x}_t \approx \hat{x}_t^*$.

Weak structural identification may arise from the lack of informative content of the time series available for estimation. Naturally, the closer each country is to behaving like the world economy, the less information content we would expect from country time series on which to pin down the model parameters. The proper identification of ζ and σ is crucial to help us understand the real effects of monetary shocks and their international transmission, but it is not possible from the world system described in Eqs. (10) and (11). With the full, two-country model their exact identification may still be hindered especially in small samples if it turns out that there is little cross-country dispersion on the observables (country inflation rates) to help us with the identification.

In the model, we can trace the problem partly to the cross-country correlation of shocks – the more strongly correlated shocks are, the less informative the country-specific observables are. In other words, observable variables might be more or less informative for identification purposes depending on the region of the parameter space where the *true* parameters lie. In principle, however, it may be possible to compensate for the low information content of a given observable series with a longer time series sample – if one is available – before having to replace it with another observable.

Weak structural identification can also arise from the nonlinear way in which the vector of model parameters λ enters into the reduced-form solution of the model in Eqs. (4), (5) and (6) – whenever multiple combinations of parameters can ultimately lead to the same joint distribution for the observables. This is a serious impediment to identifying the Calvo parameter α independently in most variants of the New Keynesian model, so it is customary to estimate instead a composite parameter such as Φ. But the problem is potentially more severe and pervasive than it is conventionally acknowledged.

Let us consider model $\mathscr{M}_1$ as given by the world LRE system in Eq. (10) where the monetary policy is that of our benchmark specification (i.e., $\psi_x > 0$ and $\psi_{\Delta y} = 0$) and the unobserved monetary shock process in Eq. (11) is serially correlated with $0 < \delta_m < 1$. Alternatively, consider model $\mathscr{M}_2$ as given by the world LRE system in Eq. (10) where the monetary policy follows a different rule that responds to output growth instead of the output gap (i.e., $\psi_x = 0$ and $\psi_{\Delta y} > 0$) and the unobserved monetary shock process in Eq. (11) is serially uncorrelated with $\delta_m = 0$. For both specifications, the law of motion for the vector of core endogenous variables $(\hat{x}_t^W, \hat{\pi}_t^W)$ that describes the model solution can be expressed as,

$$\hat{x}_t^W = \frac{1}{\chi_0} \hat{\pi}_t^W \tag{12}$$

$$\hat{\pi}_t^W = \chi_1 \hat{\pi}_{t-1}^W + \eta_t^W, \quad \eta_t^W \sim N(0,1) \tag{13}$$

which corresponds to a simplified autoregressive representation of the general solution postulated in Eq. (4). In order for this conjecture to be consistent with the model in Eqs. (10) and (11) we also assume that the volatility of the world monetary shock is defined generically as $\sigma_{mW}^2 = \sigma_m^2 = (\Phi(\gamma + \phi)\Upsilon)^{-2}$ where the composite parameter $\Upsilon \equiv (1/(1 - \beta\chi_1)(\gamma(1 - \chi_1) + \psi_x + \psi_{\Delta y}) + \Phi(\gamma + \phi)(\psi_\pi - \chi_1))$ is model-specific and depends on what each model imposes on the policy parameters ψ_x and $\psi_{\Delta y}$ as well as on the solution each model implies for the reduced-form coefficient χ_1. In general, we can say that the LRE models $\mathcal{M}_1$ and $\mathcal{M}_2$ differ in their specification of the policy rule, but also on the persistence and volatility of the world monetary shock.

Taking this conjecture as a given for model $\mathcal{M}_1$, we can verify by the method of undetermined coefficients that,

$$\chi_0 \equiv \frac{\Phi(\phi + \gamma)}{1 - \beta\chi_1} > 0 \tag{14}$$

$$\chi_1 \equiv \delta_m \in (0,1)$$
$$\eta_t^W = -\Phi(\gamma + \phi)\Upsilon\hat{\varepsilon}_t^{mW}$$
$$\text{where } \Upsilon \equiv \left(\frac{1}{(1 - \beta\delta_m)(\gamma(1 - \delta_m) + \psi_x) + \Phi(\gamma + \phi)(\psi_\pi - \delta_m)} \right) \tag{15}$$

and $\mathbb{V}[\eta_t^W] = 1$. Similarly, we take the same conjecture to model $\mathcal{M}_2$, and using again the method of undetermined coefficients we obtain,

$$\chi_0 = \frac{\Phi(\phi + \gamma)}{1 - \beta\chi_1} > 0 \quad \text{if } \chi_1 \in (-1,1) \tag{16}$$

$$(\chi_1)^3 - \left(\frac{\gamma(1+\beta) + \beta\psi_{\Delta y} + \Phi(\gamma+\phi)}{\gamma\beta}\right)(\chi_1)^2 + \cdots$$

$$\left(\frac{\gamma + (1+\beta)\psi_{\Delta y} + \Phi(\gamma+\phi)\psi_\pi}{\gamma\beta}\right)\chi_1 - \left(\frac{\psi_{\Delta y}}{\gamma\beta}\right) = 0$$

$$\eta_t^W = -\Phi(\gamma+\phi)\Upsilon\hat{\varepsilon}_t^{mW}$$

$$\text{where } \Upsilon \equiv \left(\frac{1}{(1-\beta\chi_1)(\gamma(1-\chi_1)+\psi_{\Delta y}) + \Phi(\gamma+\phi)(\psi_\pi - \chi_1)}\right) \quad (17)$$

and again $\mathbb{V}[\eta_t^W] = 1$. The exact solution to model $\mathcal{M}_2$ involves a cubic equation on χ_1, but whenever a well-defined and unique real solution exists it will take the same form as the solution to model $\mathcal{M}_1$. The bottom line of this illustration is that the LRE models $\mathcal{M}_1$ and $\mathcal{M}_2$ are observationally equivalent and, therefore, generate the exact same joint probability distribution for the observable series (inflation). For a similar point, see also An and Schorfheide (2007).

Model comparison and identification become difficult in a situation like this one and depend on the modelling choices that the researcher makes (rather than the data). Notice that we have added productivity shocks to our benchmark model because they are viewed as a key driver of business cycles, but that modelling choice has the potential to introduce differences between models $\mathcal{M}_1$ and $\mathcal{M}_2$ that we can exploit to tell them apart. We have also ruled out ex ante the extended form of the monetary policy rule in Eq. (9) which rules out model $\mathcal{M}_2$ as a possible DGP for the data and bypasses the problem illustrated here even when monetary shocks are the sole drivers of business cycles. The problem, of course, comes because those modelling choices are not always "easy to justify."

From the solution of both models we know that we are only estimating the composite parameter χ_1. In model $\mathcal{M}_1$ we cannot identify any other structural parameter other than δ_m, while in model $\mathcal{M}_2$ we cannot separately identify the parameters $(\beta, \gamma, \alpha, \gamma, \phi, \psi_\pi, \psi_{\Delta y})$. Conditional on a given model, if one parameter cannot be identified in the sense described here, then identification will not improve with sample size. Consider model $\mathcal{M}_1$ where δ_m is the identified structural parameter and $\bar{\lambda} = (\beta, \gamma, \alpha, \gamma, \phi, \psi_\pi, \psi_{\Delta y})$ is the vector of model parameters that we cannot identify. The likelihood function becomes $\mathscr{L}(\delta_m, \bar{\lambda} \mid \hat{\pi}^W) = \tilde{\mathscr{L}}(\delta_m \mid \hat{\pi}^W)$ and the posterior distribution can be decoupled exploiting Bayes theorem as,

$$p(\delta_m, \bar{\lambda} \mid \hat{\pi}^W) = p(\delta_m \mid \hat{\pi}^W)p(\bar{\lambda} \mid \delta_m)$$

Thus, since the prior distribution of $p(\bar{\lambda} \mid \delta_m)$ does not change with the observed data, it introduces curvature in the posterior distribution and could end up masking the errors of identification in the structural parameters that actually affect the model solution. A comparison between different priors and the resulting posterior can often provide valuable guidance on structural parameters of interest that may be difficult to identify.

However, we must be mindful that detecting identification problems in larger DSGE models such as those so popular in central banking for policy analysis is much more complicated given that the mapping from the vector of model parameters λ into the state–space representation that determines the joint probability distribution of the observable variables $\hat{Y}^{obs}$ is highly nonlinear and can rarely be solved for analytically.

BAYESIAN ESTIMATION: SOME FINDINGS

The data that we use in all our estimations is obtained from simulating the NOEM model under the benchmark calibration summarized in Table 5. We incorporate all relevant empirical evidence reviewed in subsection "Calibrating Structural Parameters" in our selection of priors, matching the prior mean to correspond to the calibrated parameter values. We use other moments of the prior distribution to assign a likelihood to the range of plausible values found in the literature. In this sense, we explicitly recognize that some parameters are more difficult to pin down than others. Then, we assess the strength of the identification strategy implemented through Bayesian estimation techniques controlling for sample size and abstracting from model misspecification.

In the next two subsections, first, we give a brief overview of the assumptions we make about prior distributions for the structural parameters of the model and we explain how the available data sources influence our choices, and, second, we design a number of experiments intended to illustrate how the strength of identification may depend on features that are out of the researchers control (for instance, the sample size or data availability) or may result from the choices the researcher makes in attempting to bring the model 'closer' to the data (e.g., the selection of observables or the inclusion of nonstructural shocks to expand the set of observables).

In all of our experiments, we emphasize the importance of the sample size in accounting for parameter uncertainty – suggesting that 40 years worth of quarterly data, which is considered a *long* time series in international macro, may not be "long enough" to resolve the uncertainty surrounding some identifiable parameters even when estimating a barebones open-economy macro model.[14]

Eliciting Priors

Our priors on the relevant model parameters are summarized in Table 5. We maintain these prior distributions invariant in all our subsequent estimations, taking them as given.[15] We only consider prior densities of the Beta, Gamma, Inverse Gamma, Normal, and Uniform distributions as well as the degenerate distribution that puts mass one on a single value. In a few cases, we rely on linear transformations of a model parameter to ensure the range of values that the prior distribution of the parameter can take is consistent with theory. We also impose on all cases that the prior mean must be equal to the true value of the parameter in our calibration to be consistent with our own views about the data sources used to parameterize the model. We choose the prior distribution as well as the dispersion to reflect the degree of ex ante uncertainty that exists regarding those parameter values.

Since we match the prior mean to the *true* parameter value used to calibrate and simulate the model, the aim of the estimation is to investigate whether the Bayesian techniques applied to observable macro time series can contribute to reduce the dispersion (or uncertainty) surrounding the true value of these parameters and summarized in our choice of priors. In other words, can we expect Bayesian techniques to help us reveal additional information that is not already incorporated in the priors? If so, what is the effect of sample size on the tightness of the posteriors that we obtain and the precision of our identification of the parameters of interest?

Structural Parameters

As is sometimes done, we use a degenerate prior for the intertemporal discount factor β and fix it at 0.99. For the share of locally produced goods in the consumption basket, ξ, we linearly transform the parameter to $2\xi - 1$ and choose a tight Beta distribution as the prior for the transformed parameter. We center this prior around 0.88 (which corresponds to the calibrated value of 0.94 for ξ) and impose a small standard deviation of 0.01. This specification emphasizes that with the historically low import share observed for the United States, one should not expect ex ante the parameter $(1 - \xi)$ in the model – which defines the degree of trade openness – to be too large.

We adopt the Gamma distribution centered around 5 for the inverse of the intertemporal elasticity of substitution, γ, and the inverse of the Frisch elasticity of labor supply, ϕ. We impose a wide standard deviation of 5 for both in order to encompass the wide range of values considered as plausible for these parameters in the literature. We adopt the Gamma distribution centered around 1.5 for the intratemporal elasticity of substitution between Home and Foreign bundles, σ, with a wide standard deviation of 1 to recognize the importance of this parameter for the international transmission of shocks and to capture the uncertainty surrounding its *true* value.

We adopt the Beta distribution centered around 0.75 for the Calvo parameter, α, with standard deviation 0.07.[16] The Calvo parameter α indicates the fraction of firms that are not able to reoptimize in any given period. We favor a Beta prior that puts little mass on values of the parameter range above 0.9 (which imply expected durations of more than ten quarters) and below 0.5 (which imply expected durations of less than two quarters). The parameter for the policy response to deviations from the inflation target, ψ_π, is linearly transformed in order to be consistent with the domain of the Inverse Gamma distribution and to rule out violations of the Taylor principle (requiring interest rates to respond more than one-for-one to inflation). Although satisfying the Taylor principle doesn't guarantee existence and uniqueness, it reduces the region of the parameter space where that would not be the case to a minimal expression. Hence, we estimate $\psi_\pi - 1$ with a prior centered at 0.24 (which implies a prior mean of 1.24 for ψ_π) and a prior standard deviation of 2. Similarly, we select an Inverse Gamma distribution for the parameter that defines the policy response to fluctuations of the output gap, ψ_x, with a prior mean of 0.33 and standard deviation of 2.

Parameters of the Shock Processes
The prior distributions for the partial autocorrelations of both productivity and monetary shocks are restricted to lie within the interval $(0,1)$ to rule out negative values for δ_a and δ_m which seem unsupported by the data. For simplicity, we adopt a degenerate distribution for the persistence of the productivity shock δ_a to match its calibrated value of 0.97, as there is broad agreement that the Solow residuals are pretty persistent. Adopting a degenerate prior for δ_a, in turn, allows us more flexibility to impose a diffuse prior on the key spillover parameter $\delta_{a,a*}$ and still guarantee the stationarity of the stochastic process for productivity.

It follows from the choice of δ_a that in order for the VAR(1) process that describes the productivity shocks to remain stationary we need $\delta_{a,a*}$ to be between -0.03 and 0.03. We linearly transform the spillover parameter into $\frac{1}{2} + \frac{1}{2}\frac{\delta_{a,a^*}}{0.03}$ so that its range can be defined over the (0,1)-interval and select the Beta distribution for our prior. We center the prior around 0.91667 (which corresponds to 0.025 for δ_{a,a^*}) and set its standard deviation at 0.05.

Having imposed *extrinsic* inertia on the monetary policy rule, we select a Beta distribution for the first-order autocorrelation of the monetary shocks, δ_m, restricting its parameter space to the interval (0,1). The prior is centered around 0.92 with a prior standard deviation equal to 0.02. The prior means of the productivity shock and monetary shock volatilities, σ_a and σ_m, are set at their calibrated values of 0.73 and 0.36, respectively. We select an Inverse Gamma distribution to represent the prior of both volatility parameters, with a large standard deviation of 5 for each – leaving it open for the data to determine the contribution of each shock to explain endogenous volatility.

We restrict the range of the parameter space for the cross-country correlation of innovations, ρ_{a,a^*} and ρ_{m,m^*}, to lie in the (0,1)-interval. We choose rather diffuse Beta priors for these cross-country correlations. We center ρ_{a,a^*} at the calibrated value of 0.29 with a standard deviation of 0.18, and ρ_{m,m^*} at the calibrated value of 0.5 with a standard deviation of 0.22. In choosing this specification, we are indicating that our understanding of the proper value for these correlations is not very precise.

In some of our estimation exercises, we also incorporate a measurement error term modelled as a pure white noise. This is a nonstructural shock added to the specification of the estimated model for the purpose of increasing the set of observable variables that we consider in the estimation. The shock process for measurement error is characterized with only one parameter, the volatility term σ_ν. The prior mean is set at a low value of 0.10, as we expect this *ad hoc* measurement error shock to have only a "small" contribution to business cycles. We select an Inverse Gamma as the prior distribution, and impose a standard deviation of 1.

Bayesian Estimation

The model is estimated with a short sample of 160 observations generated from our benchmark calibrated NOEM model, and with a long sample of 10,000 observations. A sample of 160 observations is equivalent to 40 years of quarterly macro data, which is typically a longer time span than most estimated open-economy macro models can cover due to data limitations and other coverage problems, due to the maintained assumption of an invariant monetary policy regime over the entire period, etc. The long sample of 10,000 periods is used as a reference to assess the precision of the estimation in small samples, as indicated earlier. In all our experiments we take the model-implied DGP as given and rule out the possibility of model misspecification. We also keep the priors invariant.

In order to avoid stochastic singularity in Bayesian estimation, we have the same number of observable variables as structural shocks in our model. Since we have monetary and productivity shocks that are country-specific, that means we have four structural shocks and – accordingly – we should have four observable variables. Given the model's emphasis on the international transmission of monetary policy and on monetary non-neutrality, it seems appropriate to include both real and nominal variables in the set of observables that we estimate in order to help us explore empirically the trade-offs that the "global slack hypothesis" postulates. In this sense, the observable variables in our benchmark estimation are Home and Foreign output as well as Home and Foreign inflation.

The NOEM framework described in Table 1 suggests that the trade-off between nominal and real variables can be articulated in terms of inflation and the output gaps (more specifically, between local inflation and a combination of Home and Foreign output gaps). Since output gaps are not directly measured in the data, for estimation purposes we choose to complete the core model with a pair of measurement equations that relate actual observed output to the output gaps (from Table 2) and with a model to describe the dynamics of potential output (from Table 3). Hence, we incorporate a pair of equations that describe current observable output as the sum of potential output and the output gap of each country and also a pair of equations defining the potential output of both economies as a function of the unobserved productivity shocks. In doing so, we jointly estimate a model for potential output together with the fully fledged NOEM model.

Having established this benchmark, now we investigate the sensitivity of Bayesian inference to the implementation strategy that an applied researcher will follow in regards to: (a) the decision of whether to prefilter the data or not before estimating the model, (b) the choice of observable variables for the estimation, and (c) the choice of whether to include nonstructural shocks in the estimation to extend the set of observables. In this section, we shall revise all three aspects of the implementation in the context of investigating the model of Martínez-García and Wynne (2010) with Bayesian techniques.

Pre-filtering the Data
Our benchmark estimation reveals a number of model parameters for which the posterior distribution is dominated by the prior distribution (see Fig. 2). Here, we distinguish between the power of the Bayesian method to recover the *true* structural parameter and the information gain that is attained

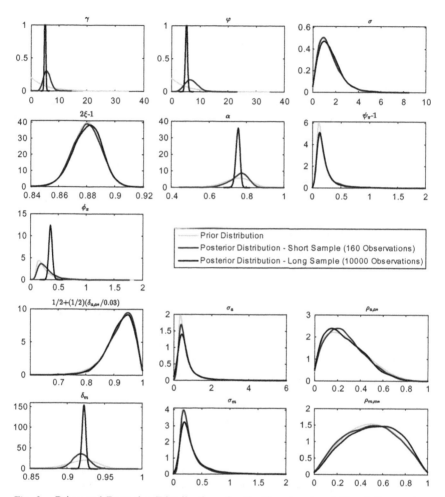

Fig. 2. Prior and Posterior Distributions for the Structural and Shock Parameters of the Model.

Note: The code is written for Matlab version 7.13.0.564. This figure plots the prior distributions of all 13 structural (policy and nonpolicy) and shock parameters that do not receive a degenerate prior distribution. It also includes the posterior distribution estimated from a short sample of 160 observations and the long sample of 10,000 observations. The estimation is done under the benchmark implementation based on four observables: Home and Foreign output, Home and Foreign inflation. The code for this figure is available upon request from the authors.

through estimation relative to what our prior beliefs were. The fact that all priors are centered around their *true* parameter values facilitates the point identification irrespective of whether the posterior and prior differ, but Bayesian estimation becomes less useful in practice as a tool for economic analysis whenever posteriors and priors are very "close" to each other as a result of weak identification. That overlap may be indicative that the observable series have revealed very little information that is new about the parameters which we did not know already before estimating the model, but this does not necessarily mean that the parameter is weakly identified. Alternatively, the overlap between priors and posteriors can occur because our priors already incorporated all relevant information there is in those observable series about the parameter.

The structural (policy and nonpolicy) parameters that show fairly similar prior and posterior distributions in our benchmark estimation are σ (which affects international risk-sharing through terms of trade fluctuations), ξ (which defines the degree of trade openness), and ψ_π (which describes the policy response to inflation). In turn, the posterior distributions change significantly for γ and ϕ (which affect the slope of the Phillips curve), α (which indicates the degree of price stickiness), and ψ_x (which describes the policy response to the output gap). For the shock parameters, however, only the persistence parameter of the monetary shocks, δ_m, appears to change as we update our priors with the information extracted from the realization of the observables.

In most instances, we observe that Bayesian estimation is able to recover most of the *true* parameters, even with a short sample of 160 observations. However, the presence of small sample inference problems (akin to the "Peso problem" discussed earlier) is vividly illustrated with our estimation results. We see how the posterior mean estimated for ϕ with the short sample is 40% higher than the *true* parameter. This is not trivial, as ϕ enters into the determination of the slope of the Phillips curve (Table 1) and affects the perceived trade-offs that monetary policy is facing. The issues arising with small samples can also be illustrated with the precision of our estimation results. Generally, the set of parameters for which the posterior distribution differs from the prior distribution conforms with the principle that posterior dispersion is smaller than prior dispersion around the mean and declines with the sample size. This is most noticeable in the comparison between the posterior distribution derived from the 160-observation sample and the 10,000-observation sample in Fig. 2, or in the confidence intervals reported and summarized in the first block of Table 7.

Table 7.   Structural and Shock Parameters: Posterior Distributions.

		No Pre-Filtering			
	True	Short Sample		Long Sample	
		Mean	90%-CI	Mean	90%-CI
Structural parameters					
β	0.99	0.99	–	0.99	–
γ	5	5.7636	[3.6611, 7.8426]	5.0315	[4.6493, 5.4286]
ϕ	5	7.0027	[3.3510, 10.4756]	5.1702	[4.5748, 5.7889]
σ	1.5	1.4601	[0.1216, 2.7907]	1.5236	[0.1044, 2.8228]
$2\xi-1$	0.88	0.8799	[0.8638, 0.8968]	0.8803	[0.8638, 0.8969]
α	0.75	0.7587	[0.6775, 0.8374]	0.7544	[0.7366, 0.7728]
$\psi_\pi - 1$	0.24	0.2255	[0.0514, 0.4309]	0.2229	[0.0528, 0.4090]
ψ_x	0.33	0.2865	[0.0936, 0.4857]	0.3637	[0.3088, 0.4150]
Shock parameters					
δ_a	0.97	0.97	–	0.97	–
$\frac{1}{2} + \frac{1}{2}\frac{\delta_{a,a^*}}{0.03}$	0.91667	0.9209	[0.8567, 0.9919]	0.9181	[0.8526, 0.9918]
σ_a	0.73	0.6833	[0.1643, 1.2897]	0.7975	[0.1587, 1.4242]
ρ_{a,a^*}	0.29	0.2774	[0.0080, 0.5217]	0.2686	[0.0087, 0.5079]
δ_m	0.92	0.9187	[0.9008, 0.9364]	0.9228	[0.9187, 0.9270]
σ_m	0.36	0.2905	[0.0876, 0.5254]	0.3494	[0.0801, 0.6541]
ρ_{m,m^*}	0.50	0.4938	[0.1297, 0.8593]	0.5181	[0.1555, 0.8744]
		Pre-Filtering			
	True	Short Sample		Long Sample	
		Mean	90%-CI	Mean	90%-CI
Structural parameters					
β	0.99	0.99	–	0.99	–
γ	5	5.8585	[3.7275, 7.8711]	5.0179	[4.5949, 5.4134]
ϕ	5	7.0490	[3.6452, 10.4458]	5.1455	[4.5288, 5.7959]
σ	1.5	1.5074	[0.1228, 2.8900]	1.2656	[0.1465, 2.3279]
$2\xi-1$	0.88	0.8800	[0.8637, 0.8970]	0.8798	[0.8611, 0.8959]
α	0.75	0.7594	[0.6828, 0.8386]	0.7534	[0.7349, 0.7722]
$\psi_\pi - 1$	0.24	0.1925	[0.0571, 0.3394]	0.2297	[0.0540, 0.4357]
ψ_x	0.33	0.2866	[0.0934, 0.5016]	0.3604	[0.3061, 0.4120]
Shock parameters					
δ_a	0.97	0.97	–	0.97	–
$\frac{1}{2} + \frac{1}{2}\frac{\delta_{a,a^*}}{0.03}$	0.91667	0.9157	[0.8433, 0.9872]	0.9123	[0.8375, 0.9897]

Table 7. (*Continued*)

	True	Pre-Filtering			
		Short Sample		Long Sample	
		Mean	90%-CI	Mean	90%-CI
σ_a	0.73	0.7148	[0.1684, 1.3085]	0.8411	[0.1561, 1.9273]
ρ_{a,a^*}	0.29	0.2872	[0.0103, 0.5536]	0.3022	[0.0323, 0.5515]
δ_m	0.92	0.9181	[0.8996, 0.9373]	0.9224	[0.9183, 0.9265]
σ_m	0.36	0.3286	[0.0799, 0.6182]	0.3291	[0.0820, 0.5883]
ρ_{m,m^*}	0.50	0.4974	[0.1325, 0.8561]	0.4615	[0.0989, 0.8332]

This table reports the point estimates and 90 percent confidence intervals for all the model parameters (except the three parameters that we normalize in steady state). The first block reports the estimates without pre-filtering (de-meaning) the data, while the second block shows the estimates on pre-filtered (de-meaned) data. We estimate the NOEM model for the short sample of 160 observations and for the full-length sample of 10,000 observations. All estimations use simulated data on Home and Foreign output and Home and Foreign inflation as observables, under the calibration described in Table 5. We use Matlab 7.13.0.564 and Dynare v4.2.4 for the stochastic simulation and estimation.

The NOEM model we are investigating here does not incorporate deterministic or stochastic time trends explicitly. Hence, the question of pre-filtering in our model can be stated in terms of whether to demean or not to demean the data for estimation purposes. Three parameters are fundamental in that regard: the parameters κ, A and M. These three parameters enter into the determination of the steady state, but they do not affect the short-run dynamics of the model. That was the primary reason why we chose to normalize them in the first place. These three parameters, however, have a direct effect on the steady state level of output in each country – as can be seen from Table 4 – and Home and Foreign output are among our benchmark observable variables.

Looking at the population (theoretical) and sample means – in particular for the short sample of 160 periods – for Home and Foreign output reported in Table 6 it would be possible to dispute whether the data has been simulated with or without normalizing the steady state. If we suspect the parameters κ, A and M have not been normalized, then a case can be made for pre-filtering (demeaning) the data prior to estimation. Since the parameters that determine the steady state level of output do not affect the short-run dynamics, pre-filtering the data rather than augmenting the measurement equations with the steady state for Home and Foreign output

to estimate those three parameters jointly with the rest of the model should
not bias our empirical inferences.

Here, we know that the simulated data comes from a model where the
steady state output is normalized but estimate the model after demeaning
the data as an applied researcher unaware of that fact would do. Our results
with demeaned data reported in the second block of Table 7 suggest that this
particular form of pre-filtering does little to alter the results or the precision
of the estimation as implied by the posterior distributions of the model
parameters – even for the short-sample of 160 quarters. Detrending the data
may be a much less innocuous form of pre-filtering, which does not arise in
our benchmark model.[17]

Selection of Observables
In order to avoid stochastic singularity in Bayesian estimation, we must
have at least as many shocks (structural or otherwise) in the model as we
have observed variables. Therefore, some of the key practical decisions that
researchers have to make in using Bayesian estimation involve deciding:
how many shocks to include and, most importantly, which observables
among all the available macro time series ought to be incorporated in the
estimation. Here we consider a model characterized by only four structural
shocks – which means that we need four observable variables – and
experiment with the selection of alternative sets of four macro time series. In
our benchmark implementation, we make inferences based on Home and
Foreign output, as well as Home and Foreign inflation, and report the
results in Table 7.

Now we reevaluate the model estimation findings when we replace
Foreign output with either the terms of trade or the trade balance, while
keeping the number of observables fixed at four. We summarize the results
in Table 8, with the findings using terms of trade reported in the first block
and the findings using the trade balance reported in the second block.

Looking at the estimation results for the long sample of 10,000
observations including the terms of trade among the observables instead
of Foreign output, the most significant change we observe is in the
estimation of the parameter σ. The increased precision of the estimate can be
observed in the evidence reported for the short sample of 160 periods, as the
confidence intervals become tighter whenever the terms of trade are included
among the observables. The parameter σ plays an important role in allowing
international risk-sharing through fluctuations of the terms of trade. Hence,
adding the terms of trade to the set of observables that we use has the
advantage of helping us reveal further information about this parameter

Table 8. Structural and Shock Parameters: Posterior Distributions.

Home Output, Terms of Trade, Home Inflation, and Foreign Inflation

	True	Short Sample		Long Sample	
		Mean	90%-CI	Mean	90%-CI
Structural parameters					
β	0.99	0.99	–	0.99	–
γ	5	5.8654	[3.5917, 8.3601]	5.1565	[4.7377, 5.5614]
ϕ	5	6.9422	[3.1429, 10.3996]	5.2618	[4.6554, 5.8752]
σ	1.5	1.5137	[1.2656, 1.7916]	1.4919	[1.4411, 1.5449]
$2\xi-1$	0.88	0.8807	[0.8639, 0.8967]	0.8804	[0.8634, 0.8965]
α	0.75	0.7612	[0.6812, 0.8389]	0.7577	[0.7402, 0.7758]
$\psi_\pi-1$	0.24	0.2059	[0.0568, 0.3869]	0.2101	[0.0574, 0.3989]
ψ_x	0.33	0.2819	[0.0874, 0.4811]	0.3595	[0.3096, 0.4099]
Shock parameters					
δ_a	0.97	0.97	–	0.97	–
$\frac{1}{2}+\frac{1}{2}\frac{\delta_{a,a*}}{0.03}$	0.91667	0.9187	[0.8451, 0.9931]	0.9210	[0.8522, 0.9902]
σ_a	0.73	0.6235	[0.1743, 1.1660]	0.6574	[0.1748, 1.1769]
$\rho_{a,a*}$	0.29	0.2917	[0.0083, 0.5675]	0.2484	[0.0097, 0.5381]
δ_m	0.92	0.9199	[0.9011, 0.9385]	0.9232	[0.9191, 0.9272]
σ_m	0.36	0.3348	[0.0822, 0.6094]	0.3113	[0.0848, 0.5727]
$\rho_{m,m*}$	0.50	0.4944	[0.1433, 0.8434]	0.4951	[0.1299, 0.8512]

Home Output, Trade Balance, Home Inflation, and Foreign Inflation

	True	Short Sample		Long Sample	
		Mean	90%-CI	Mean	90%-CI
Structural parameters					
β	0.99	0.99	–	0.99	–
γ	5	5.8647	[3.7001, 7.9597]	5.0335	[4.6607, 5.4311]
ϕ	5	7.1927	[3.4306, 10.6495]	5.1749	[4.5558, 5.7518]
σ	1.5	1.4735	[0.1136, 2.8629]	1.4833	[0.0984, 2.8185]
$2\xi-1$	0.88	0.8800	[0.8632, 0.8964]	0.8793	[0.8622, 0.8957]
α	0.75	0.7624	[0.6832, 0.8423]	0.7546	[0.7375, 0.7730]
$\psi_\pi-1$	0.24	0.2350	[0.0556, 0.4169]	0.2204	[0.0572, 0.3985]
ψ_x	0.33	0.3142	[0.0888, 0.5436]	0.3627	[0.3057, 0.4115]
Shock parameters					
δ_a	0.97	0.97	–	0.97	–
$\frac{1}{2}+\frac{1}{2}\frac{\delta_{a,a*}}{0.03}$	0.91667	0.9158	[0.8431, 0.9899]	0.9161	[0.8435, 0.9910]

Table 8. (*Continued*)

Home Output, Trade Balance, Home Inflation, and Foreign Inflation

| | True | Short Sample | | Long Sample | |
		Mean	90%-CI	Mean	90%-CI
σ_a	0.73	0.6824	[0.1631, 1.3100]	0.7260	[0.1716, 1.3612]
ρ_{a,a^*}	0.29	0.2679	[0.0078, 0.5261]	0.2995	[0.0115, 0.5888]
δ_m	0.92	0.9200	[0.9017, 0.9386]	0.9227	[0.9184, 0.9266]
σ_m	0.36	0.3081	[0.0879, 0.5707]	0.3180	[0.0840, 0.6133]
ρ_{m,m^*}	0.50	0.5027	[0.1448, 0.8618]	0.5216	[0.1672, 0.8870]

This table reports the point estimates and 90 percent confidence intervals for all the model parameters (except the three parameters that we normalize in steady state). The first block reports the estimates obtained using Home output, terms of trade, Home inflation and Foreign inflation as observables. The second block shows the estimates based on Home output, trade balance, Home inflation and Foreign inflation as the observables. We estimate the NOEM model for the short sample of 160 observations and for the full-length sample of 10,000 observations. All estimations use simulated data under the calibration described in Table 5. We use Matlab 7.13.0.564 and Dynare v4.2.4 for the stochastic simulation and estimation.

that we could not uncover using the set of observables in our benchmark implementation. This is the most significant difference that we detect, but it indicates that the estimation results and what we learn from the estimation of the model depends on our data selection – an issue already highlighted, among others, by Guerrón-Quintana (2010).

The empirical results of our estimation for the case in which Foreign output is replaced by the trade balance do not change that much from our benchmark. The information content brought by the trade series is less relevant, as we do not see a significant gain in the precision of our estimates of the parameter σ relative to the benchmark implementation – not even for the full length sample of 10,000 periods. The lesson we derive from these very simple exercises is that researchers must be mindful of these issues in the selection of observables for Bayesian estimation.

It is not obvious how to establish general guidelines on selecting observables that can be applied on every occasion. Common sense suggests that researchers may want to investigate the features of the model carefully as understanding its mechanics and implications could help in the selection of observables by pointing towards the data that can reveal the most useful information about the key structural parameters. Having said that, in practice the data selection may be already significantly limited simply due to data availability constraints and other data-related concerns that prevent us from using the series that are most relevant for our question. For example, in international macro, the quality and availability of time series data for emerging economies or the sample length of the data available and its quality are always a major handicap.

Inclusion of Nonstructural Shocks
We often see applications of the Bayesian estimation method where the set of observables is *conveniently* expanded with the addition of nonstructural shocks. Partly the goal of doing that is to increase the information set that the Bayesian procedure can use to help refine the estimates by pulling in more data. One common practice is to increase the set of observables with the addition of measurement error shocks into the estimated model, which arguably can also help capture the likely errors in the measurement of some of the variables themselves. The specification of those measurement error shocks, however, is often rather ad hoc, and little motivation is given for the exogenous processes ascribed to them. While this may be capturing important features of the data that is appropriate to take into account and serves to expand the set of observables, it might also introduce a form of misspecification bias in the estimation.

Here the simulated data observed is without measurement error, but we take the role of a researcher that does not know that. We introduce a random measurement error on either Foreign output or the terms of trade (assuming that foreign series might be more prone to mismeasurement). We model the measurement error as white noise with low volatility in hopes of keeping the distortion (or misspecification) from biasing our findings significantly, while taking advantage of the additional informational content of one more observable variable. In this case, we consider as our observables Home and Foreign output, Home and Foreign inflation, and the terms of trade.

The evidence is reported and summarized in Table 9, where the first block reports the estimation under the assumption that the error appears in the measurement of Foreign output while the second block assumes that it appears in the measurement of terms of trade. The most interesting finding is that we can obtain greater precision in the estimates of the parameter σ from the inclusion of terms of trade among the set of observables, but only if the nonstructural measurement error shock is added to the terms of trade equation and not to the Foreign output equation. This is a significant finding because it clearly indicates that the addition of ad hoc nonstructural shocks does not guarantee that more information will ultimately result into better estimates for the parameters we are interested in. In other words,

Table 9.   Structural and Shock Parameters: Posterior Distributions.

		Nonstructural, Measurement Error on Foreign Output			
	True	Short Sample		Long Sample	
		Mean	90%-CI	Mean	90%-CI
Structural parameters					
β	0.99	0.99	–	0.99	–
γ	5	5.8157	[3.6438, 7.8787]	5.1791	[4.7803, 5.5706]
ϕ	5	6.6937	[3.2634, 10.0788]	5.1439	[4.5296, 5.7134]
σ	1.5	1.5367	[0.1122, 2.9909]	1.6150	[0.1473, 3.0138]
$2\xi-1$	0.88	0.8792	[0.8618, 0.8950]	0.8805	[0.8652, 0.8966]
α	0.75	0.7540	[0.6795, 0.8395]	0.7552	[0.7378, 0.7732]
$\psi_\pi-1$	0.24	0.2062	[0.0535, 0.3856]	0.2204	[0.0567, 0.4278]
ψ_x	0.33	0.2930	[0.0920, 0.5107]	0.3594	[0.3068, 0.4113]
Shock parameters					
δ_a	0.97	0.97	–	0.97	–
$\frac{1}{2}+\frac{1}{2}\frac{\delta_{a,a^*}}{0.03}$	0.91667	0.9113	[0.8323, 0.9902]	0.9105	[0.8347, 0.9903]
σ_a	0.73	0.7176	[0.1745, 1.2618]	0.6579	[0.1770, 1.2617]
ρ_{a,a^*}	0.29	0.2920	[0.0068, 0.5525]	0.2652	[0.0073, 0.5067]
δ_m	0.92	0.9189	[0.8988, 0.9361]	0.9228	[0.9187, 0.9267]
σ_m	0.36	0.3278	[0.0829, 0.5997]	0.3121	[0.0799, 0.5813]
ρ_{m,m^*}	0.50	0.4897	[0.1243, 0.8400]	0.4947	[0.1438, 0.8464]
σ_v	0.10	0.1081	[0.0220, 0.2293]	0.1215	[0.0223, 0.1981]

		Nonstructural, Measurement Error on Terms of Trade			
	True	Short Sample		Long Sample	
		Mean	90%-CI	Mean	90%-CI
Structural parameters					
β	0.99	0.99	–	0.99	–
γ	5	5.6391	[4.0870, 7.4937]	5.0363	[4.6390, 5.4032]
ϕ	5	6.7938	[4.0923, 9.7174]	5.1833	[4.5541, 5.7415]
σ	1.5	1.5577	[1.3953, 1.7533]	1.5035	[1.4505, 1.5545]
$2\xi-1$	0.88	0.8846	[0.8711, 0.8979]	0.8749	[0.8616, 0.8884]
α	0.75	0.7614	[0.6959, 0.8261]	0.7550	[0.7381, 0.7717]
$\psi_\pi-1$	0.24	0.2141	[0.0573, 0.3980]	0.1990	[0.0568, 0.3564]
ψ_x	0.33	0.2739	[0.0893, 0.4483]	0.3632	[0.3106, 0.4171]
Shock parameters					
δ_a	0.97	0.97	–	0.97	–
$\frac{1}{2}+\frac{1}{2}\frac{\delta_{a,a^*}}{0.03}$	0.91667	0.8923	[0.7929, 0.9836]	0.9162	[0.8524, 0.9595]

Table 9. (*Continued*)

	True	Short Sample		Long Sample	
		Mean	90%-CI	Mean	90%-CI
σ_a	0.73	0.6972	[0.1729, 1.3435]	0.7117	[0.1574, 1.2953]
ρ_{a,a^*}	0.29	0.2741	[0.0207, 0.5306]	0.2296	[0.0076, 0.4101]
δ_m	0.92	0.9187	[0.9016, 0.9351]	0.9229	[0.9192, 0.9270]
σ_m	0.36	0.3261	[0.0794, 0.6178]	0.3121	[0.0825, 0.6143]
ρ_{m,m^*}	0.50	0.6386	[0.3232, 0.9610]	0.5657	[0.2539, 0.8408]
σ_v	0.10	0.0855	[0.0224, 0.1562]	0.0911	[0.0227, 0.1767]

Nonstructural, Measurement Error on Terms of Trade

This table reports the point estimates and 90 percent confidence intervals for all the model parameters (except the three parameters that we normalize in steady state). The first block reports the estimates including a nonstructural measurement error on Foreign output, while the second block shows the estimates based on the inclusion of a nonstructural measurement error on the terms of trade. All measurement errors are modelled as pure white noise. We estimate the NOEM model for the short sample of 160 observations and for the full-length sample of 10,000 observations. All estimations use simulated data on Home and Foreign output, Home and Foreign inflation and terms of trade as observables, under the calibration described in Table 5. We use Matlab 7.13.0.564 and Dynare v4.2.4 for the stochastic simulation and estimation.

adding more observable series does not guarantee a resolution to our identification problems.

We can also point out that misspecification bias can be significant whenever we incorporate shocks arbitrarily in our estimated model (solely for the purpose of expanding the number of observables), especially in short samples. This may also occur depending on where we *locate* those measurement error shocks. We see, for instance, that the estimates of the correlation between Home and Foreign monetary innovations ρ_{m,m^*} in the short sample of 160 observations vary by 30% depending on whether we have measurement errors placed in the estimated model either on the foreign output equation or on the terms of trade equation.

Setting up guidelines to deal with measurement errors is not a trivial matter. Our exercise suggests that adding ad hoc shocks to the model solely for the sake of increasing the number of observables that we can use in our estimation can be counterproductive as it introduces misspecification bias in the estimation. It seems much more robust to add measurement errors whenever we have actual evidence that some data may be measured with error. That would help us determine the structure of the stochastic process that those nonstructural shocks follow as well as the proper measurement equations that would be affected by their presence. In any case, although adding measurement error shocks increases the number of observable variables that we can use for Bayesian estimation, that does not necessarily mean – as we have seen here – that we will end up with more information revealed through the posterior distributions of the key parameters of the model.

Bayesian IRFs and Structural Shocks

As we have discussed extensively, the recovery of the structural parameters – especially given our prior selection – through the implementation of conventional Bayesian techniques does not necessarily guarantee that the information revealed by the macro time series data is giving us greater economic insight about the model. Another way in which we can assess the economic insight gained through Bayesian estimation other than with posterior distributions is by looking at the Bayesian impulse response functions (IRFs) estimated from the model. IRFs can yield important insights about the misspecification and identification of the model, as emphasized by An and Schorfheide (2007). In particular, they can provide a different perspective on the uncertainty surrounding the Bayesian estimation and that is what we aim to highlight here.

Figs. 3(A) and 3(B) compare the mean trajectory of the Bayesian IRFs in response to Home and Foreign monetary shocks under our benchmark implementation (based on Home and Foreign output as well as Home and Foreign inflation) as the observables against the theoretical IRFs of the calibrated NOEM model. The figures also include confidence intervals to illustrate the precision attained with the estimation. All mean IRFs and confidence intervals are reported for both the long and the short samples for contrast.

The derivation of the IRFs depends on the proper identification of the structural shocks in the context of the estimation. Therefore, the ability of the Bayesian techniques to recover the structural shocks is intimately connected to its ability to replicate the IRFs of the *true* DGP. In Fig. 4, we illustrate both the *true* innovations to the structural shocks as well as the discrepancy that we find between the *true* innovations and the smoothed shock innovations recovered from the Bayesian estimation for the short sample of 160 observations. The evidence would suggest that the implied Bayesian IRFs are not distorted by the inference of the structural shock innovations, even in small samples.

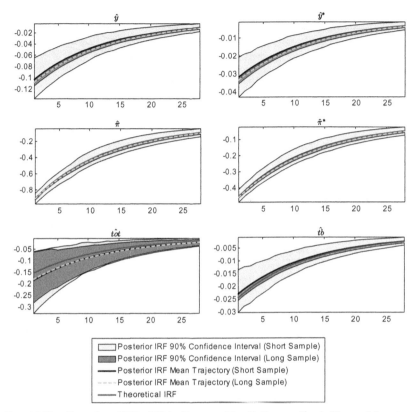

Fig. 3(A). Bayesian IRFs With Respect To Orthogonalized Home Monetary Shock Innovations.

Note: The code is written for Matlab version 7.13.0.564. This figure plots the Bayesian impulse response functions (IRFs) for Home output, Foreign output, Home inflation, Foreign inflation, terms of trade and the trade balance in response to Home monetary shock innovations. The Bayesian IRFs are estimated from a short sample of 160 observations and the long sample of 10,000 observations. The estimation is done under the benchmark implementation based on four observables: Home and Foreign output, Home and Foreign inflation. The code for this figure is available upon request from the authors.

We conclude from our estimation exercise that the posterior mean trajectory is often fairly well-aligned with the corresponding theoretical IRFs, even when the estimation is based on a short sample. However, we find that the precision with which the model estimation can recover the true

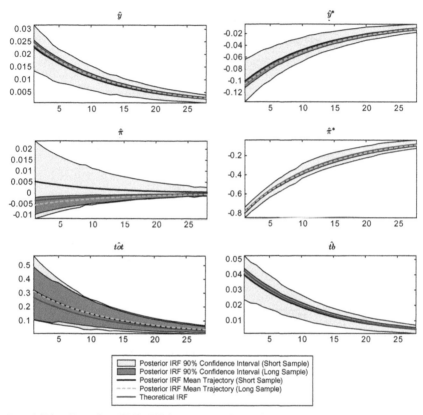

Fig. 3(B). Bayesian IRFs With Respect To Orthogonalized Foreign Monetary Shock Innovations.

Note: The code is written for Matlab version 7.13.0.564. This figure plots the Bayesian impulse response functions (IRFs) for Home output, Foreign output, Home inflation, Foreign inflation, terms of trade and the trade balance in response to Foreign monetary shock innovations. The Bayesian IRFs are estimated from a short sample of 160 observations and the long sample of 10,000 observations. The estimation is done under the benchmark implementation based on four observables: Home and Foreign output, Home and Foreign inflation. The code for this figure is available upon request from the authors.

IRFs depends on the nature of the shock and also on the endogenous variable that is being shocked. Here we only report the trajectories of the Bayesian IRFs in response to monetary shocks as understanding the international transmission of monetary shocks is a crucial purpose of the NOEM model. We refer the interested reader to the working paper

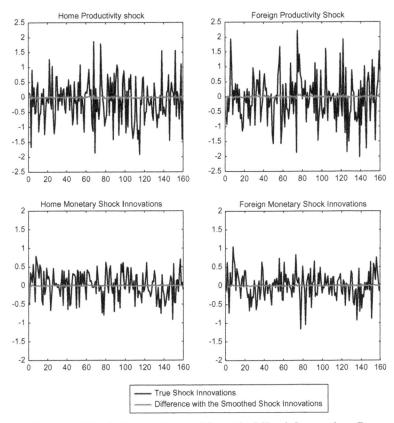

Fig. 4. Structural Shocks Innovations and Smoothed Shock Innovations Recovered Through Bayesian Estimation.
Note: The code is written for Matlab version 7.13.0.564. This figure plots the realization of the structural shock innovations for Home productivity, Foreign productivity, Home monetary shock and Foreign monetary shock corresponding to the short sample of 160 observations. The figure also illustrates the difference between the structural shock innovations and the recovered smoothed shock innovations from the Bayesian estimation of the short sample of 160 observations. The estimation is done under the benchmark implementation based on four observables: Home and Foreign output, Home and Foreign inflation. The code for this figure is available upon request from the authors.

version in Martínez-García et al. (2012) for an illustration of the Bayesian IRFs in response to productivity shocks.

We observe from the Bayesian IRFs in Fig. 3(A) and 3(B) that the uncertainty surrounding the response to monetary shocks in a short sample can be quite large, and the same can be said for the productivity shocks not reported here. In some instances, such as the response of Home inflation to Foreign monetary shocks, we can even get the wrong *sign* about the international transmission of shocks if we look at the average trajectory of the estimated Bayesian IRF – thinking that a contractionary (positive) Foreign monetary shock raises Home inflation when it does not, as can be seen in Fig. 3(B). Naturally, we also observe that the tightness of the confidence interval around most of the estimated IRFs increases as we increase the sample size – even though, admittedly, a long sample size is something that remains a luxury for international macroeconomists.

"Peso problems" and the uncertainty associated with the weak information content of the data affecting some of our estimates may be resolved by increasing the information available with a "long enough" sample, but weak identification cannot necessarily be compensated with more observations. Figs. 3(A) and 3(B) illustrate how the uncertainty surrounding the response of terms of trade to monetary shocks (whether Home or Foreign) barely changes when we compare the Bayesian IRFs estimated with the short and long samples. It is interesting to point out that consistent with our earlier discussion on the information content of terms of trade, we observe that in our benchmark implementation the estimation of the response of terms of trade to all structural shocks (also for productivity shocks as shown in the working paper version in Martínez-García et al., 2012) remains significantly wider than that of other macro variables even with a very long sample of 10,000 observations.

Hence, while the Bayesian IRFs do not tell us where the structural identification problem lies *exactly*, the problem surely manifests itself in the uncertainty surrounding this salient feature of the international data. In other words, wide confidence intervals around the estimated Bayesian IRFs can also be a warning sign – like the overlap between prior and posterior distributions is – of possible weak identification, but can be the result of empirical inference problems in short samples as well.

CONCLUDING REMARKS

In this chapter we have evaluated some of the challenges that researchers are faced with when attempting a structural evaluation of an open-economy macro model. Working with the simplest possible specification of a two-country model that generates a short-run relationship between global slack and domestic inflation we explore the problems associated with parameter identification and empirical inference in samples of the size typically available to international macroeconomists. We find that – even controlling for model misspecification – weak identification of key structural parameters is an issue that cannot be easily resolved or circumvented when applying Bayesian techniques.

Using a conventional calibration of the benchmark NOEM model of Martínez-García and Wynne (2010), we generate artificial data which we then use to explore the ability of Bayesian estimation techniques to recover the *true* parameter values of the DGP and to infer new information about the parameters themselves beyond what we incorporated into the priors. We find in our estimation with simulated data in controlled experiments that structural identification is sensitive to the choice of observables, the addition of nonstructural shocks and other modelling choices that researchers often make without much discussion. We also show that misspecification can arise when introducing ad hoc shocks into the estimating model and that the identification of some parameters of interest could be improved by carefully selecting/adding observables. As a practical suggestion to deal with these identification concerns in more complex model environments, we propose "testing" the model – as a preliminary step in Bayesian estimation – with simulated data to detect how sensitive the estimation could be to our intended implementation strategy.

NOTES

1. Building on recent developments in the New Open Economy Macro (NOEM) literature (see, e.g., Clarida, Galí, & Gertler, 2002), Martínez-García (2008) and Martínez-García and Wynne (2010) develop a tractable structural framework that articulates a relationship between global slack and the cyclical component of local inflation (the *global slack hypothesis*). The model illustrates that the international transmission of shocks through trade depends on features of the economy such as the monetary policy of the trading partners, the elasticity of substitution between domestic and imported goods or the slope of the Phillips curve. This workhorse, small-scale model is fully described with three equations per country and constitutes the basis for the current class of medium- to large-scale NOEM models that have become so prevalent in academic and policy analysis.

2. While classical methods are beyond the scope of this chapter, Canova (2007) is a useful reference as it covers both classical and Bayesian methods for the analysis and evaluation of DSGE models.

3. For details on the role of international price-setting in the misallocation of demand across countries and the design of optimal monetary policy, see also Engel (2009).

4. Monopolistic competition introduces a mark-up over marginal costs that is a function of the elasticity of substitution across varieties within a country, θ. The mark-up is the only place where the parameter θ shows up in the model up to a first-order approximation, so the optimal labor subsidy φ which neutralizes the mark-up distortion also makes the pair (φ, θ) irrelevant for the characterization of the steady state and the dynamics of the model.

5. That is the case except in a knife-edge situation where both Home and Foreign households' share of domestic and imported goods coincides with the share of locally produced goods which is $\frac{1}{2}$ in the model.

6. The frictionless allocation can be approximated if monetary policy-makers in both countries aggressively target local inflation to ensure that $\hat{\pi}_t = 0$ and $\hat{\pi}_t^* = 0$ for all t. That would be a limiting case of the Taylor rule posited here where the response to inflation deviations becomes arbitrarily large. The Taylor rule specification is consistent with other institutional arrangements too. For example, depending on the parameterization of the responses to inflation and the output gap, it would be consistent with a policy framework where the central bank operates under a dual mandate (the Fed) or under a single mandate on price stability (the ECB).

7. In fact, the model has two more structural parameters: the elasticity of substitution across varieties within a country, θ, and the labor subsidy, φ. We do not count them here because by choosing an optimal labor subsidy $\varphi = \frac{1}{\theta}$, both drop from the steady state as well as the first-order dynamics.

8. Ríos-Rull et al. (2011), emphasize the heterogeneity in the micro data measurements used to parameterize ϕ. For instance, the survey of Pencavel (1986) refers exclusively to the labor supply of men and does not distinguish between the intensive and extensive margins on employment. Depending on the question and model at hand, this micro evidence may not be the most appropriate.

9. In a richer model with capital and labor as inputs in a Cobb–Douglas production function and with competitive factor markets, the capital share in the production function can be determined through the steady state relationships (see, e.g., the discussion in Ríos-Rull et al., 2011).

10. The core of the model refers to a (minimal) set of equations that uniquely determines the path of a core subset of endogenous variables by their initial conditions and the path of the exogenous shocks specified.

11. The model does not incorporate growth explicitly, but most of these macroeconomic time series trend upwards in the data. Therefore, the calibration/ estimation strategy would have to be adapted in the presence of (deterministic or stochastic) time trends. See An and Schorfheide (2007) and also Ferroni (2011) for a recent discussion on pre-filtering the data versus estimating the trend jointly with the rest of the model.

12. Mean refers to the average of the series. Standard deviation (std. dev.) is a measure of dispersion of the series. Skewness is a measure of asymmetry of the distribution of the series around its mean. Zero skewness (such as for the normal distribution) means the distribution is symmetric; positive skewness means that the distribution has a long right tail; and negative skewness means that the distribution has a long left tail. Kurtosis measures the peakedness of the distribution of the series. The kurtosis of 3 is characteristic of the normal distribution. A distribution is

leptokurtic (higher, narrower peak around the mean and fatter tails than the normal) if the kurtosis is above 3, and is platykurtic (lower, wider peak around the mean and thinner tails than the normal) if the kurtosis is below 3. Autocorrelation is a measure of the cross-correlation or similarity of the series at different lags of time separation between the observations. The autocorrelations reported are those of the one-period lag and the five-period lag. The Jarque–Bera is a goodness-of-fit test statistic to assess whether the skewness and kurtosis of the series are consistent with those of the normal distribution. Under the null hypothesis (that the distribution has the skewness and kurtosis of the normal), the Jarque–Bera statistic is distributed as a χ^2 with 2 degrees of freedom. For the Jarque-Bera statistic, no stars indicate that the null of normality is rejected at a level higher than 10 percent. The stars indicate that: *Rejects the null at the 10 percent level. **Rejects the null at the 5 percent level. *** Rejects the null at the 1 percent level.

13. The proliferation of software to automate the solution of DSGE models and do Bayesian estimation (e.g., Dynare) has significantly reduced the costs of implementing Bayesian econometrics. We use Dynare in our chapter in part to illustrate that, but also to encourage researchers to consider the circumstances and questions for which these techniques might truly be useful.

14. We only show the results for one short sample of 160 periods and the long sample of 10,000 here. For details on two other short samples that we investigated, we refer the interested reader to the working paper version in Martínez-García et al. (2012).

15. While we acknowledge that there is no unique way of eliciting priors and that other researchers may reach different conclusions on the selection of priors by emphasizing other sources of information not covered here or by weighting differently the ones we have mentioned before, we want to take the role of priors seriously as reflecting our ex ante views and beliefs about these parameters. We also want to tie our hands to facilitate comparisons across different experiments, and preclude the priors themselves from becoming a source of additional degrees of freedom that can be used to *fine-tune* the estimation at the "discretion" of the researcher.

16. The parameters β and α tend to be hard to identify simultaneously through the Phillips curve relationship. The Calvo parameter α is regarded as more uncertain than the parameter β, and of greater interest to researchers because it is directly connected to the nominal friction of the model (the degree of nominal rigidity). Hence, we follow the practice of imposing a degenerate prior on β which is meant (at least in part) to facilitate a more precise estimation of the Calvo parameter α.

17. For a recent discussion on pre-filtering the data versus estimating the trend jointly with the rest of the model, see Ferroni (2011).

ACKNOWLEDGMENT

We would like to thank Nathan Balke, María Teresa Martínez-García, the editor, two anonymous referees, and participants in the 10th annual

Advances in Econometrics conference for helpful suggestions. An extended version of this chapter is available as Federal Reserve Bank of Dallas Globalization and Monetary Policy Institute Working Paper No. 105. All remaining errors are ours alone. The views expressed in this chapter are those of the authors and do not necessarily reflect the views of the Federal Reserve Bank of Dallas, or the Federal Reserve System.

REFERENCES

An, S., & Schorfheide, F. (2007). Bayesian analysis of DSGE models. *Econometric Reviews*, *26*(2/4), 113–172.

Aruoba, S. B., Fernández-Villaverde, J., & Rubio-Ramírez, J. F. (2004). Comparing solution methods for dynamic equilibrium economies. *Journal of Economic Dynamics and Control*, *30*(12), 2477–2508.

Backus, D. K., Kehoe, P. J., & Kydland, F. E. (1994). Dynamics of the trade balance and the terms of trade: The J-curve? *American Economic Review*, *84*(1), 84–103.

Bils, M., & Klenow, P. J. (2004). Some evidence on the importance of sticky prices. *Journal of Political Economy*, *112*(5), 947–985.

Blanchard, O. J., & Kahn, C. M. (1980). The solution of linear difference models under rational expectations. *Econometrica*, *48*(5), 1305–13011.

Browning, M., Hansen, L. P., & Heckman, J. J. (1999, Chapter 8). Micro data and general equilibrium models. In J. B. Taylor & M. Woodford (Eds.), *Handbook of macroeconomics* (Vol. I, pp. 543–633). Amsterdam, Netherlands: Elsevier Science B.V.

Calvo, G. A. (1983). Staggered prices in a utility-maximizing framework. *Journal of Monetary Economics*, *12*(3), 383–398.

Canova, F. (1994). Statistical inference in calibrated models. *Journal of Applied Econometrics*, *9*(Suppl.), S123–S144.

Canova, F. (2007). *Methods for applied macroeconomic research*. Princeton, NJ: Princeton University Press.

Card, D. (1994). Intertemporal labor supply: An assessment. In C. Sims (Ed.), *Advances in econometrics* (pp. 49–78). Cambridge, UK: Cambridge University Press.

Chari, V. V., Kehoe, P. J., & McGrattan, E. R. (2002). Can sticky price models generate volatile and persistent real exchange rates? *Review of Economic Studies*, *69*(3), 533–563.

Clarida, R., Galí, J., & Gertler, M. (2002). A simple framework for international monetary policy analysis. *Journal of Monetary Economics*, *49*(5), 879–904.

Dhyne, E., Álvarez, L. J., Le Bihan, H., Veronese, G., Dias, D., Hoffmann, J., … Vilmunen, J. (2006). Price changes in the euro area and the united states: Some facts from individual consumer price data. *Journal of Economic Perspectives*, *20*(2), 171–192.

Engel, C. (2009, April). *Currency misalignments and optimal monetary policy: A reexamination*. NBER Working Paper no. 14829. National Bureau of Economic Research, Cambridge, MA.

Engel, C., & Wang, J. (2011). International trade in durable goods: Understanding volatility, cyclicality, and elasticities. *Journal of International Economics*, *83*(1), 37–52.

Evans, M. D. (1996, Chapter 21). Peso problems: Their theoretical and empirical implications. In G. S. Maddala & C. R. Rao (Eds.), *Handbook of statistics: Statistical methods in finance* (Vol. 14, pp. 613–646). Amsterdam, Netherlands: Elsevier Science B.V.

Fernández-Villaverde, J., Rubio-Ramírez, J. F., Sargent, T., & Watson, M. (2007). A, B, C, (and D)'s for understanding VARs. *American Economic Review, 97*, 1021–1026.

Ferroni, F. (2011). Trend agnostic one-step estimation of DSGE models. *B.E. Journal of Macroeconomics Advances, 11*(1), 25.

Galí, J. (2008). *Monetary Policy, inflation, and the business cycle: An introduction to the New Keynesian framework.* Princeton, NJ: Princeton University Press.

Guerrón-Quintana, P. A. (2010). What you match does matter: The effects of data on DSGE estimation. *Journal of Applied Econometrics, 25*(5), 774–804.

Hall, R. E. (1988). Intertemporal substitution in consumption. *Journal of Political Economy, 96*(2), 339–357.

Heathcote, J., & Perri, F. (2002). Financial autarky and international business cycles. *Journal of Monetary Economics, 49*(3), 601–627.

Keane, M. P. (2010). *Labor supply and taxes: A survey.* Working Paper No. 160. School of Finance and Economics, University of Technology Sydney, Sydney.

King, R. G., & Watson, M. W. (1998). The solution of singular linear difference systems under rational expectations. *International Economic Review, 39*(4), 1015–1026.

Klenow, P. J., & Kryvtsov, O. (2008). State-dependent or time-dependent pricing: Does it matter for recent U.S. inflation? *Quarterly Journal of Economics, 123*(3), 863–904.

Klenow, P. J., & Malin, B. A. (2010, Chapter 6). Microeconomic evidence on price-setting. In B. M. Friedman & M. Woodford (Eds.), *Handbook of monetary economics* (Vol. 3, pp. 231–284). Amsterdam, Netherlands: Elsevier Science B.V.

Lubik, T. A., & Schorfheide, F. (2004). Testing for indeterminacy: An application to U.S. monetary policy. *American Economic Review, 94*(1), 190–217.

Lubik, T. A., & Schorfheide, F. (2006). A Bayesian look at new open economy macro-economics. In M. Gertler & K. Rogoff (Eds.), *NBER Macroeconomics Annual 2005* (pp. 313–366). Cambridge, MA: MIT Press.

Lucas, R. E. (1990). Supply-side economics: An analytical review. *Oxford Economic Papers, 42*(2), 293–316.

Martínez-García, E. (2008). *Globalization and monetary policy: An introduction.* Globalization and Monetary Policy Institute Working Paper No. 11, Federal Reserve Bank of Dallas, Dallas, TX.

Martínez-García, E., & Søndergaard, J. (forthcoming, 2013). Investment and real exchange rates in sticky price models. *Macroeconomic Dynamics, 17*(2).

Martínez-García, E., Vilán, D., & Wynne, M. A. (2012). *Bayesian estimation of NOEM models: Identification and inference in small samples.* Globalization and Monetary Policy Institute Working Paper No. 105, Federal Reserve Bank of Dallas, Dallas, TX.

Martínez-García, E., & Wynne, M. A. (2010). *The global slack hypothesis.* Federal Reserve Bank of Dallas Staff Papers, 10, Dallas, TX.

Nakamura, E., & Steinsson, J. (2008). Five facts about prices: A reevaluation of menu cost models. *Quarterly Journal of Economics, 123*(4), 1415–1464.

Pencavel, J. (1986, Chapter 1). Labor supply of men: A survey. In O. Ashenfelter & R. Layard (Eds.), *Handbook of labor economics* (Vol. I, pp. 3–102). Amsterdam, Netherlands: Elsevier Science B.V.

Ravenna, F. (2007). Vector autorregressions and reduced form representations of DSGE models. *Journal of Monetary Economics, 54*, 2048–2064.

Robert, C., & Casella, G. (1999). *Monte Carlo statistical methods*. New York, NY: Springer Verlag.

Rotemberg, J. J., & Woodford, M. (1998a). Interest rate rules in an estimated sticky price model. In J. B. Taylor (Ed.), *Monetary policy rules*. Chicago, IL: University of Chicago Press.

Rotemberg, J. J., & Woodford, M. (1998b). An optimization-based econometric model for the evaluation of monetary policy. In B. S. Bernanke & J. J. Rotemberg (Eds.), *NBER Macroeconomics Annual 1997* (Vol. 12, pp. 297–346). Cambridge, MA: MIT University Press.

Rudebusch, G. D. (2002). Term structure evidence on interest rate smoothing and monetary policy inertia. *Journal of Monetary Economics, 49*(6), 1161–1187.

Rudebusch, G. D. (2006). Monetary policy inertia: Fact or fiction? *International Journal of Central Banking, 2*(4), 85–135.

Ríos-Rull, J.-V., Schorfheide, F., Fuentes-Albero, C., Kryshko, M., & Santaeulàlia-Llopis, R. (2011). *Methods versus substance: Measuring the effects of technology shocks on hours*. Mimeo, University of Pennsylvania, PA.

Taylor, J. B. (1993). Discretion versus policy rules in practice. *Carnegie-Rochester Conference Series on Public Policy, 39*, 195–214.

Taylor, J. B. (1999, Chapter 15). Staggered price and wage setting in macroeconomics. In J. B. Taylor & M. Woodford (Eds.), *Handbook of macroeconomics* (Vol. 1B, pp. 1009–1050). Amsterdam, Netherlands: Elsevier Science B.V.

Villemot, S. (2011, April). *Solving rational expectations models at first order: What Dynare does*. Dynare Working Paper Series no. 2, CEPREMAP. Paris, France.

Woodford, M. (2003). *Interest and prices: Foundations of a theory of monetary policy*. Princeton, NJ: Princeton University Press.

Woodford, M. (2010, Chapter 1). Globalization and monetary control. In J. Galí & M. J. Gertler (Eds.), *International dimensions of monetary policy, NBER Conference Report* (pp. 13–77). Chicago, IL: University of Chicago Press.

Yogo, M. (2004). Estimating the elasticity of intertemporal substitution when instruments are weak. *Review of Economics and Statistics, 86*(3), 797–810.

APPENDIX

Building Blocks of the Model

The model is a simplified version of the two-country framework of Martínez-García and Wynne (2010): (a) with equal population size in both countries in terms of the households' share in each country and the fraction of total varieties that each country produces (i.e., $\frac{1}{2}$ is located in each country); and (b) with identical local-product bias in each country's consumption basket (i.e., $(1 - \xi)$ is the share of imported goods for both countries). In contrast, Clarida et al. (2002) and Woodford (2010) – among others – make the assumption that both countries have the same share of Home and Foreign goods in their consumption baskets (ensuring that PPP holds whenever the law of one price holds unlike what happens in this model).

Households
The lifetime utility for a representative household in the Home country is additively separable in consumption, C_t, and labor, L_t, that is,

$$\sum_{\tau=0}^{+\infty} \beta^\tau \mathbb{E}_t \left[\frac{1}{1-\gamma}(C_{t+\tau})^{1-\gamma} - \frac{\kappa}{1+\phi}(L_{t+\tau})^{1+\phi} \right] \qquad (A.1)$$

where $0 < \beta < 1$ is the subjective intertemporal discount factor, $\gamma > 0$ is the inverse of the intertemporal elasticity of substitution, and $\phi > 0$ is the inverse of the Frisch elasticity of labor supply. The scaling factor $\kappa > 0$ determines the steady state labor. The Home household maximizes its lifetime utility subject to the sequence of budget constraints,

$$P_t C_t + \int_{\omega_{t+1} \in \Omega} Q_t(\omega_{t+1}) B_t(\omega_{t+1}) \leqslant B_{t-1}(\omega_t) + W_t L_t + Pr_t - T_t \qquad (A.2)$$

where W_t is the nominal wage in the Home country, P_t is the Home consumption price index (CPI), T_t is a nominal lump-sum tax (or transfer) from the Home government, and Pr_t are (per-period) nominal profits from all firms producing the Home varieties. The budget includes a portfolio of one-period Arrow–Debreu securities (contingent bonds) internationally traded and in zero net supply, $B_t(\omega_{t+1})$. For simplicity, these contingent bonds are quoted in the unit of account of the Home country. The Home price of the contingent bonds is denoted $Q_t(\omega_{t+1})$, while the Foreign price is $Q_t^*(\omega_{t+1}) = \frac{1}{S_t}Q_t(\omega_{t+1})$ and S_t is the nominal exchange rate. Similarly, for the representative household in the Foreign country.

Access to a full set of internationally traded, one-period Arrow–Debreu securities completes the local and international asset markets recursively. Under complete asset markets, households can perfectly share risks domestically and internationally. Hence, the intertemporal marginal rate of substitution is equalized across countries in every state of nature,

$$\beta\left(\frac{C_{t+1}}{C_t}\right)^{-\gamma}\frac{P_t}{P_{t+1}} = \beta\left(\frac{C_{t+1}^*}{C_t^*}\right)^{-\gamma}\frac{P_t^*S_t}{P_{t+1}^*S_{t+1}} \tag{A.3}$$

where P_t^* is the Foreign CPI and C_t^* stands for Foreign consumption. We define the real exchange rate as $RS_t \equiv \frac{S_tP_t^*}{P_t}$, so by backward recursion the *perfect international risk-sharing condition* in Eq. (A.3) becomes,

$$RS_t = \upsilon\left(\frac{C_t^*}{C_t}\right)^{-\gamma} \tag{A.4}$$

where $\upsilon \equiv \frac{S_0P_0^*}{P_0}\left(\frac{C_0^*}{C_0}\right)^{\gamma}$ is a constant that depends on initial conditions. If the initial conditions correspond to the symmetric steady state, then the constant υ is equal to one. We can also price a redundant one-period, uncontingent nominal bond with the price of the contingent Arrow–Debreu securities and obtain a standard pair of stochastic Euler equations for both countries,

$$\frac{1}{1+i_t} = \beta\mathbb{E}_t\left[\left(\frac{C_{t+1}}{C_t}\right)^{-\gamma}\frac{P_t}{P_{t+1}}\right] \tag{A.5}$$

$$\frac{1}{1+i_t^*} = \beta\mathbb{E}_t\left[\left(\frac{C_{t+1}^*}{C_t^*}\right)^{-\gamma}\frac{P_t^*}{P_{t+1}^*}\right] \tag{A.6}$$

where i_t is the riskless, nominal interest rate in the Home country and i_t^* is its Foreign country counterpart. The households' optimization problem also results in a pair of labor supply equations,

$$\frac{W_t}{P_t} = \kappa(C_t)^{\gamma}(L_t)^{\phi} \tag{A.7}$$

$$\frac{W_t^*}{P_t^*} = \kappa(C_t^*)^{\gamma}(L_t^*)^{\phi} \tag{A.8}$$

plus the appropriate no-Ponzi games, transversality conditions and the budget constraint of both representative households.

C_t is a CES aggregator of Home and Foreign goods for the representative Home country household defined as,

$$C_t = \left[(\xi)^{\frac{1}{\sigma}}(C_t^H)^{\frac{\sigma-1}{\sigma}} + (1 - \xi)^{\frac{1}{\sigma}}(C_t^F)^{\frac{\sigma-1}{\sigma}} \right] \tag{A.9}$$

where $\sigma > 0$ is the elasticity of substitution between the Home-produced consumption bundle C_t^H and the Foreign-produced consumption bundle C_t^F. Analogous preferences are assumed for the Foreign country representative household, except that C_t^* is defined as a CES aggregator of Home and Foreign goods in the following terms,

$$C_t^* = \left[(1 - \xi)^{\frac{1}{\sigma}}(C_t^{H*})^{\frac{\sigma-1}{\sigma}} + (\xi)^{\frac{1}{\sigma}}(C_t^{F*})^{\frac{\sigma-1}{\sigma}} \right] \tag{A.10}$$

The share of Home-produced goods in the Home consumption basket and Foreign-produced goods in the Foreign basket must satisfy that $\frac{1}{2} \leqslant \xi < 1$.

The subindexes C_t^H and C_t^{H*} indicate respectively Home and Foreign consumption of the bundle of differentiated varieties produced in the Home country. Similarly, C_t^F and C_t^{F*} denote Home and Foreign consumption of the bundle of differentiated varieties produced in the Foreign country. These subindexes are defined as follows,

$$C_t^H = \left[\left(\frac{1}{2}\right)^{-\frac{1}{\theta}} \int_0^{\frac{1}{2}} C_t(h)^{\frac{\theta-1}{\theta}} dh \right]^{\frac{\theta}{\theta-1}}, \quad C_t^F = \left[\left(\frac{1}{2}\right)^{-\frac{1}{\theta}} \int_{\frac{1}{2}}^1 C_t(f)^{\frac{\theta-1}{\theta}} df \right]^{\frac{\theta}{\theta-1}} \tag{A.11}$$

$$C_t^{H*} = \left[\left(\frac{1}{2}\right)^{-\frac{1}{\theta}} \int_0^{\frac{1}{2}} C_t^*(h)^{\frac{\theta-1}{\theta}} dh \right]^{\frac{\theta}{\theta-1}}, \quad C_t^{F*} = \left[\left(\frac{1}{2}\right)^{-\frac{1}{\theta}} \int_{\frac{1}{2}}^1 C_t^*(f)^{\frac{\theta-1}{\theta}} df \right]^{\frac{\theta}{\theta-1}} \tag{A.12}$$

where $\theta > 1$ is the elasticity of substitution across differentiated varieties within a country. Similarly, total output and labor are expressed as,

$$\frac{1}{2} Y_t = \left[\left(\frac{1}{2}\right)^{-\frac{1}{\theta}} \int_0^{\frac{1}{2}} Y_t(h)^{\frac{\theta-1}{\theta}} dh \right]^{\frac{\theta}{\theta-1}}, \quad \frac{1}{2} Y_t^* = \left[\left(\frac{1}{2}\right)^{-\frac{1}{\theta}} \int_{\frac{1}{2}}^1 Y_t^*(f)^{\frac{\theta-1}{\theta}} df \right]^{\frac{\theta}{\theta-1}} \tag{A.13}$$

$$\frac{1}{2}L_t = \left[\left(\frac{1}{2}\right)^{-\frac{1}{\theta}} \int_0^{\frac{1}{2}} L_t(h)^{\frac{\theta-1}{\theta}} dh\right]^{\frac{\theta}{\theta-1}}, \quad \frac{1}{2}L_t^* = \left[\left(\frac{1}{2}\right)^{-\frac{1}{\theta}} \int_{\frac{1}{2}}^1 L_t^*(f)^{\frac{\theta-1}{\theta}} df\right]^{\frac{\theta}{\theta-1}} \quad \text{(A.14)}$$

where Y_t and Y_t^* denote the total output per-household produced by firms in the Home and Foreign countries respectively, while L_t and L_t^* refer to the per-household total labor employed. The CPIs that correspond to this specification of consumption preferences are,

$$P_t = \left[\xi(P_t^H)^{1-\sigma} + (1-\xi)(P_t^F)^{1-\sigma}\right]^{\frac{1}{1-\sigma}} \quad \text{(A.15)}$$

$$P_t^* = \left[(1-\xi)(P_t^{H*})^{1-\sigma} + \xi(P_t^{F*})^{1-\sigma}\right]^{\frac{1}{1-\sigma}} \quad \text{(A.16)}$$

and,

$$P_t^H = \left[2\int_0^{\frac{1}{2}} P_t(h)^{1-\theta} dh\right]^{\frac{1}{1-\theta}}, \quad P_t^F = \left[2\int_{\frac{1}{2}}^1 P_t(f)^{1-\theta} df\right]^{\frac{1}{1-\theta}} \quad \text{(A.17)}$$

$$P_t^{H*} = \left[2\int_0^{\frac{1}{2}} P_t^*(h)^{1-\theta} dh\right]^{\frac{1}{1-\theta}}, \quad P_t^{F*} = \left[2\int_{\frac{1}{2}}^1 P_t^*(f)^{1-\theta} df\right]^{\frac{1}{1-\theta}} \quad \text{(A.18)}$$

where P_t^H and P_t^F are the price subindexes for the Home-produced and Foreign-produced bundles of varieties in the Home market. The Home and Foreign price of the Home-produced variety h is given by $P_t(h)$ and $P_t^*(h)$, respectively. Similarly for the subindexes P_t^{H*} and P_t^{F*} in the Foreign market and for the prices $P_t(f)$ and $P_t^*(f)$ of the Foreign-produced variety f.

Firms
Each firm supplies the Home and Foreign markets with its own differentiated variety under monopolistic competition. We assume producer currency pricing (PCP), so firms set Home and Foreign prices invoicing local sales and exports in their local currency. The PCP assumption implies that the law of one price (LOOP) holds at the variety level (i.e. $P_t(h) = S_t P_t^*(h)$ and $P_t(f) = S_t P_t^*(f)$), so it follows that $P_t^H = S_t P_t^{H*}$ and $P_t^F = S_t P_t^{F*}$. However, the assumption of Home-product bias in consumption leads to deviations from purchasing power parity (PPP) in the model whenever $\xi \neq \frac{1}{2}$. For this reason, $P_t \neq S_t P_t^*$ and so the real exchange rate deviates from one (i.e., $RS_t \equiv \frac{S_t P_t^*}{P_t} \neq 1$).

Given households' preferences, we can derive the demand for any Home variety h and for any Foreign variety f as,

$$Y_t(h) = \frac{1}{2}C_t(h) + \frac{1}{2}C_t^*(h) = \left(\frac{P_t(h)}{P_t^H}\right)^{-\theta} \times \cdots$$

$$\left\{\left(\frac{P_t^H}{P_t}\right)^{-\sigma}\left[\xi C_t + (1-\xi)\left(\frac{1}{RS_t}\right)^{-\sigma}C_t^*\right]\right\}, \quad \text{if } h \in \left[0,\frac{1}{2}\right] \quad (A.19)$$

$$Y_t^*(f) = \frac{1}{2}C_t(f) + \frac{1}{2}C_t^*(f) = \left(\frac{P_t(f)}{P_t^F}\right)^{-\theta} \times \cdots$$

$$\left\{\left(\frac{P_t^F}{P_t}\right)^{-\sigma}\left[(1-\xi)C_t + \xi\left(\frac{1}{RS_t}\right)^{-\sigma}C_t^*\right]\right\}, \quad \text{if } f \in \left(\frac{1}{2},1\right] \quad (A.20)$$

Firms maximize profits subject to a partial adjustment rule à la Calvo (1983) on nominal prices at the variety level. In each period, every firm receives with probability $0<\alpha<1$ a signal to maintain their prices and with probability $1-\alpha$ a signal to reoptimize. The fraction of reoptimizing Home firms in any given period chooses a price $\tilde{P}_t(h)$ optimally to maximize the expected discounted value of their profits, that is,

$$\sum_{\tau=0}^{+\infty} \mathbb{E}_t\left\{(\alpha\beta)^\tau \left(\frac{C_{t+\tau}}{C_t}\right)^{-\gamma} \frac{P_t}{P_{t+\tau}}[\tilde{Y}_{t,t+\tau}(h)(\tilde{P}_t(h) - (1-\varphi)MC_{t+\tau})]\right\} \quad (A.21)$$

subject to the constraint of always satisfying demand given by (A.19) at the chosen price $\tilde{P}_t(h)$ for as long as those prices remain unchanged. $\tilde{Y}_{t,t+\tau}(h)$ indicates the total consumption demand of variety h at time $t+\tau$ whenever the prevailing prices are unchanged since time t, i.e. whenever $P_{t+\tau}(h) = \tilde{P}_t(h)$. Local governments raise lump-sum taxes from households in order to subsidize labor employment. We introduce the labor subsidy φ as proportional to the nominal marginal cost and time-invariant. Firms produce their own varieties subject to a linear-in-labor technology. Moreover, we impose competitive local labor markets and homogeneity of the labor input (although labor is immobile across countries) ensuring that wages equalize within a country. Hence, the (before-subsidy) nominal marginal cost is given by,

$$MC_t \equiv \left(\frac{W_t}{A_t}\right), \quad MC_t^* \equiv \left(\frac{W_t^*}{A_t^*}\right) \quad (A.22)$$

where MC_t and MC_t^* are the Home and Foreign (before-subsidy) nominal marginal costs respectively. Home and Foreign nominal wages are denoted by W_t and W_t^*, while Home and Foreign productivity shocks are A_t and A_t^*. Similarly, we describe the problem of the re-optimizing Foreign firms and define the optimal price $\tilde{P}_t^*(f)$ and the corresponding demand schedule $\tilde{Y}_{t,t+\tau}^*(f)$.

The optimal pricing rule of the re-optimizing Home firms at time t is given by,

$$\tilde{P}_t(h) = \left(\frac{\theta}{\theta-1}(1-\varphi)\right) \frac{\sum_{\tau=0}^{+\infty}(\alpha\beta)^\tau \mathbb{E}_t\left[\left(\frac{C_{t+\tau}^{-\gamma}}{P_{t+\tau}}\right)\tilde{Y}_{t,t+\tau}(h)MC_{t+\tau}\right]}{\sum_{\tau=0}^{+\infty}(\alpha\beta)^\tau \mathbb{E}_t\left[\left(\frac{C_{t+\tau}^{-\gamma}}{P_{t+\tau}}\right)\tilde{Y}_{t,t+\tau}(h)\right]} \qquad (A.23)$$

and the optimal pricing rule of the reoptimizing Foreign firms is,

$$\tilde{P}_t^*(f) = \left(\frac{\theta}{\theta-1}(1-\varphi)\right) \frac{\sum_{\tau=0}^{+\infty}(\alpha\beta)^\tau \mathbb{E}_t\left[\left(\frac{C_{t+\tau}^{*-\gamma}}{P_{t+\tau}^*}\right)\tilde{Y}_{t,t+\tau}^*(f)MC_{t+\tau}^*\right]}{\sum_{\tau=0}^{+\infty}(\alpha\beta)^\tau \mathbb{E}_t\left[\left(\frac{C_{t+\tau}^{*-\gamma}}{P_{t+\tau}^*}\right)\tilde{Y}_{t,t+\tau}^*(f)\right]} \qquad (A.24)$$

Monopolistic competition in production introduces a mark-up between prices and marginal costs, $\frac{\theta}{\theta-1}$, which is a function of the elasticity of substitution across varieties within a country $\theta>1$. We choose an optimal labor subsidy $\varphi = \frac{1}{\theta}$ in both countries to neutralize this mark-up wedge. Given the inherent symmetry of the Calvo-type pricing scheme, the price subindexes P_t^H and P_t^{F*} evolve according to the following pair of equations,

$$(P_t^H)^{1-\theta} = \alpha(P_{t-1}^H)^{1-\theta} + (1-\alpha)(\tilde{P}_t(h))^{1-\theta} = (S_t P_t^{H*})^{1-\theta} \qquad (A.25)$$

$$(P_t^{F*})^{1-\theta} = \alpha(P_{t-1}^{F*})^{1-\theta} + (1-\alpha)(\tilde{P}_t^*(f))^{1-\theta} = \left(\frac{P_t^F}{S_t}\right)^{1-\theta} \qquad (A.26)$$

The price subindexes, P_t^{H*} and P_t^F, follow from the LOOP condition.

Monetary Policy

We model monetary policy in the Home and Foreign countries according to Taylor (1993)-type rules on the short-term nominal interest rates, i_t and i_t^*, that is,

$$1 + i_t = (1 + \bar{i}) \frac{M_t}{M} \left[\left(\frac{\Pi_t}{\bar{\Pi}} \right)^{\psi_\pi} \left(\frac{Y_t}{\bar{Y}_t} \right)^{\psi_x} \right] \tag{A.27}$$

$$1 + i_t^* = (1 + \bar{i}^*) \frac{M_t^*}{M^*} \left[\left(\frac{\Pi_t^*}{\bar{\Pi}^*} \right)^{\psi_\pi} \left(\frac{Y_t^*}{\bar{Y}_t^*} \right)^{\psi_x} \right] \tag{A.28}$$

where M_t and M_t^* are the Home and Foreign monetary policy shocks, and $\psi_\pi > 1$ and $\psi_x > 0$ represent the sensitivity of the monetary policy rule to movements in inflation and the output gap respectively. $\Pi_t \equiv P_t/P_{t-1}$ and $\Pi_t^* \equiv P_t^*/P_{t-1}^*$ are the (gross) CPI inflation rates, while $\bar{\Pi}$ and $\bar{\Pi}^*$ are the corresponding steady state inflation rates, $\bar{i}$ and $\bar{i}^*$ are the steady state Home and Foreign nominal interest rates, and $M = M^*$ is the unconditional mean of the Home and Foreign monetary shocks. Y_t and Y_t^* define the per-household output levels, while $\bar{Y}_t$ and $\bar{Y}_t^*$ are the potential per-household output levels that monetary policy tracks – potential output being defined as the output level that would prevail if all frictions could be eliminated, that is, in a frictionless economy with competitive firms and flexible prices. The ratios $Y_t/\bar{Y}_t$ and $Y_t^*/\bar{Y}_t^*$ define the output gap in levels for the Home and Foreign country. This index of monetary policy takes the form of the standard rule postulated by Taylor (1993) once it is log-linearized.

FITTING U.S. TREND INFLATION: A ROLLING-WINDOW APPROACH

Efrem Castelnuovo

ABSTRACT

The role of trend inflation shocks for the U.S. macroeconomic dynamics is investigated by estimating two DSGE models of the business cycle. Policymakers are assumed to be concerned with a time-varying inflation target, which is modeled as a persistent and stochastic process. The identification of trend inflation shocks (as opposed to a number of alternative innovations) is achieved by exploiting the measure of trend inflation recently proposed by Aruoba and Schorfheide (2011). Our main findings point to a substantial contribution of trend inflation shocks for the volatility of inflation and the policy rate. Such contribution is found to be time dependent and highest during the mid-1970s to mid-1980s.

Keywords: Trend inflation shocks; new-Keynesian DSGE models; rolling-window approach; great moderation

JEL classification: E31; E32; E52

DSGE Models in Macroeconomics: Estimation, Evaluation, and New Developments
Advances in Econometrics, Volume 28, 201–252
ISSN: 0731-9053/doi:10.1108/S0731-9053(2012)0000028008

INTRODUCTION

This chapter investigates the following questions: (i) Are shocks to trend inflation relevant to describing the U.S. macroeconomic dynamics? (ii) Which distortions arise if trend inflation shocks are not modeled? (iii) Has the relevance of trend inflation shocks varied over time? (iv) What is the relative importance of such shocks with respect to more conventional, temporary monetary policy shocks?

We answer these questions by estimating two different Dynamic Stochastic General Equilibrium (DSGE) models of the business cycle that are commonly employed in the monetary macroeconomic literature. The first one is a small-scale new-Keynesian model featuring a few nominal and real frictions. The presence of nominal rigidities gives monetary policy shocks the power to influence the real side of the economy on top of inflation and the policy rates. A version of this model is extensively analyzed in Woodford (2003). The second model is a version of the medium-scale framework popularized by Christiano, Eichenbaum, and Evans (2005) and taken to the U.S. data by Smets and Wouters (2007). This model features a number of nominal and real frictions in the attempt to offer a richer representation of the shocks affecting the U.S. economy and the transmission mechanisms regulating their impact on the macroeconomic dynamics. We modify these two frameworks by formalizing a time-varying inflation target, otherwise labeled "trend inflation," which we model as a persistent process whose variance is jointly estimated with the rest of our models' parameters. In this way, shocks to trend inflation concur in determining the volatility of our variables of interest.

Our empirical exercise aims at assessing to what extent trend inflation shocks participated to the formation of the great inflation in the 1970s and the great moderation in the post-1984 period. Hence, the contribution of this chapter to the existing literature is twofold. First, we include an exogenous measure of trend inflation in the set of observables employed to estimate our DSGE models. Second, we perform rolling-window estimations, which allow us to compare the evolution of the model parameters, the volatilities of the shocks over time, and the contribution of trend inflation shocks in determining the U.S. macroeconomic dynamics (in particular, the volatilities of inflation, output, and the policy rate).

Two different interpretations may be assigned to the evolution of the low-frequency component of inflation. The first one refers to such movements as changes in the inflation target pursued by the Federal Reserve over time. According to this interpretation, the upward trending inflation rate occurred in the 1970s may be interpreted as "[...] due to a systematic tendency for Federal Reserve policy to translate the short-run price pressures set off by adverse supply shocks into more persistent changes in the inflation rate itself - part of an effort by policymakers to avoid at least some of the contractionary impact those shocks would otherwise have had on the real economy." (Ireland, 2007, p. 1853). Given that, by assumption, agents possess full information on the structure of the economy and compute their expectations rationally, this is our preferred interpretation of trend inflation in this chapter. The second interpretation relates to a learning process by the Federal Reserve, which got to understand the inflation-output volatility trade-off in place while observing the reaction of the U.S. economic environment to its policy moves. This interpretation suggests that the "[...] changing beliefs about the output-inflation trade-off generated a pro-nounced low-frequency, hump-shaped pattern in inflation" (Cogley, Primiceri, & Sargent, 2010, p. 57). Following Ireland (2007) and a number of subsequent contributions, we model trend inflation as an exogenous, autoregressive process taking care of the evolution of the Federal Reserve's inflation target.[1] Hence, we formalize neither the decisional process by the Federal Reserve to vary its target over time nor the learning process possibly inducing the evolution of such target. Hence, our contribution provides a quantitative assessment on the relevance of the shocks hitting the low-frequency component of inflation, and leaves some related modeling challenges to future research.

    Our results read as follows. First and foremost, a substantial participation of trend inflation shocks to the volatilities of inflation and the policy rate is detected. An investigation involving the sample 1965–2005 suggests that trend inflation shocks are the main determinant of the volatility of inflation and the federal funds rate, and are relatively more important than standard monetary policy shocks. Second, such shocks explain a negligible portion of the volatility of the U.S. output. Third, the omission of trend inflation shocks leads to an overestimation of the role of supply shocks in determining the dynamics of inflation and the federal funds rate. In particular, the estimated contribution of wage mark-up shocks turns out to be doubled. Fourth, there are evident instabilities in the estimated volatility of trend inflation shocks as well as the other structural shocks modeled in our analysis. Fifth, the contribution of trend inflation shocks to inflation and the policy rate dynamics is found to be time-varying. Sixth, even when allowing for parameter instability in our estimated frameworks, trend inflation shocks emerge as extremely important to explain the evolution of the nominal side of the U.S. economy. In particular, their share is large when the mid-1970s to mid-1980s are considered. Finally, the relative importance of trend inflation shocks in explaining the dynamics of the nominal (real) side of the economy is larger (smaller) than that of standard, temporary policy shocks.

Movements in trend inflation have already been identified as one of the possible drivers of the post-WWII U.S. macroeconomic environment.[2] According to Cogley et al. (2010), trend inflation is the single most important factor behind the U.S. inflation dynamics. Evidence in favor of a drop in the persistence of the inflation gap correlated with a fall in trend inflation is provided by Cogley and Sbordone (2008). Coibion and Gorodnichenko (2011a) couple a small-scale DSGE model with a policy rule featuring a time-varying inflation target, and show that the reduction in trend inflation occurred since the mid-1980s has importantly contributed to lead the U.S. economy to the Great Moderation phase.[3]

Our chapter makes further steps in the assessment of the relevance of trend inflation as for post-WWII U.S. inflation dynamics. In particular, we conduct rolling-window estimations of a small-scale DSGE model featuring trend inflation and temporary policy shocks with post-WWII U.S. data. To do so, we employ a set of macroeconomic indicators, among which the empirical proxy for trend inflation recently proposed by Aruoba and Schorfheide (2011).[4] This is, in our opinion, a crucial departure from the existing literature. Several reasons justify the use of an "observable" measure of trend inflation. First, trend inflation is often interpreted as the inflation target pursued by the Federal Reserve.[5] Hence, it is typically modeled as a latent process entering a simple policy rule. This is problematic from an econometric standpoint, in that two persistent latent processes (the trend inflation process and the monetary policy shock process) enter the (log-linearized) policy rule jointly. Then, it becomes difficult to disentangle the effects of these two shocks on the endogenous variables of interest. The employment of a measure of trend inflation, on top of a set of 'standard' macroeconomic indicators (among which we include the federal funds rate), allows us to circumvent this identification issue and sharpen our estimates on the effects of trend inflation against other shocks. Second, as shown by Castelnuovo et al. (2012), there is a huge amount of heterogeneity as for the estimates of trend inflation in the literature. Such heterogeneity is likely to be due to differences in cross-equation restrictions, assumptions on expectation formation, observables used in the estimation, and a variety of other factors. The employment of a proxy for trend inflation computed "externally" to our DSGE models makes trend inflation robust to model misspecification. Third, different sample choices may give rise to different estimates of trend inflation for the very same point in time due to, for example, sampling uncertainty. This is clearly an unfortunate side-effect of estimations conducted without proxies for trend inflation, above all when attempting to assess its role over time. The employment of an 'observable' for trend inflation help us tackling these issues.

We proceed as follows. First, we estimate our DSGE models over the post-WWII sample 1965–2005.[6] Conditional on the estimated framework, we compute the variance decomposition of the observables employed in our Bayesian estimation. This allows us to assess the relative role of trend inflation shocks, standard transitory monetary policy shocks, and other identified structural innovations. As anticipated, however, our exercise is designed to detect the possibly *time-varying* role played by trend inflation shocks in affecting the post-WWII U.S. macroeconomic dynamics. One may think of the turbulent 1970s as being a very different environment for policymakers when contrasted with the "great moderation" phase. We tackle this issue by running rolling-window estimations of our DSGE model with Bayesian techniques, a strategy already followed (in models featuring no trend inflation) by Canova (2009), Giacomini and Rossi (2010), Cantore, Ferroni, and Léon-Ledesma (2011), Canova and Ferroni (2012), and Castelnuovo (2012a). This strategy enables us to detect instabilities in possibly all structural parameters of our framework by relying on standard techniques suited to estimate linear frameworks.

Different approaches to model instabilities in the structural parameters are available to econometricians. Modern monetary DSGE models of the business cycle that features time-varying coefficients and stochastic volatilities have been estimated by Fernández-Villaverde and Rubio-Ramírez (2007, 2008) and Fernández-Villaverde, Guerrón-Quintana, and Rubio-Ramírez (2010). Time-varying volatilities are assumed to follow an AR(1) process in log-terms to ensure the positivity of such volatilities. This leads to a mix of *levels* (of the structural shocks) and *logs* (of the volatilities of the structural shocks) that creates a nonlinear structure. A second-order approximation of the policy functions is therefore needed to capture such relevant nonlinearities and estimate the parameters of interest. This has two consequences. First, rational expectations are solved by appealing to perturbation methods (that are superior to alternatives, see Fernández-Villaverde and Rubio-Ramírez (2010) and the references therein). Second, once the model is solved for rational expectations, the likelihood function is evaluated by appealing to particle filtering. This methodology is extremely powerful and econometrically clean. However, given its computations costs, it forces the econometrician to stick to a limited number of time-varying parameters. This is unfortunate, because given the likely covariance of the structural parameters of interest, fixing a subset of parameters while leaving the complementary subset free to change is likely to induce biases in the simulated density (see Canova & Ferroni, 2012, for a discussion). In contrast, rolling-window estimations allow to trace instabilities in (possibly) *all* structural parameters in a convenient manner, so enabling us to overcome this issue.

Another alternative to handle parameter instability is represented by regime-switching, which has recently been adopted to estimate DSGE frameworks by a number of authors (Bianchi, 2011; Liu, Waggoner, & Zha, 2011). This technique is obviously extremely powerful, in that it enables to identify different phases characterizing the economic environment (e.g., "tranquil" times as opposed to "turbulent" periods). As a matter of fact, however, it forces the data to "pick and choose" among a necessarily limited number of states, that is, to "discretize" the economy. Differently, rolling-windows, in principle, just "let the data speak" as for the relevant "state" among the possible infinite ones per each given window, so offering a natural generalization of the regime-switching approach.

Wrapping up, we see the rolling-window methodology as complementary to the time-varying coefficients/stochastic-volatility and the regime-switching approaches. Of course, there is no free lunch. The cost is that of abstracting from the role that time-varying parameters may play in influencing agents' expectations, that is, with our rolling-window approach we are forced to assume that agents have neither memory of the past windows nor are able to exploit past and current information on parameters' drifts to form expectations on the future evolution of the economy. Moreover, rolling-window estimation is adequate as an initial step in detecting instabilities in the structural parameters of their framework. They, however, do not represent a generalization of the alternatives we discusses earlier such as regime-switching coefficients or smoothly time-varying coefficients and volatilities. In light of the results presented in this chapter, we see the application of more sophisticated techniques to detect structural instabilities in a DSGE framework as the natural following step, which we leave to future research.

The chapter closest to ours are probably Ireland (2007) and Cogley et al. (2010) as for the small-scale model application, and Sbordone et al. (2010) and Del Negro and Eusepi (2011) as regards the application with the Smets and Wouters' (2007) model. Ireland (2007) builds up a small-scale DSGE model in which firms may index their prices to trend inflation, which is interpreted as the inflation target pursued by the Federal Reserve. He finds that trend inflation is responsible for the bulk of the volatility of inflation and the policy rate in the sample under scrutiny. Ireland's (2007) analysis assumes the structure of the U.S. economy not to feature any instability over the post-WWII sample. Cogley et al. (2010) relax this assumption by engaging in a subsample analysis focusing on the pre- vs. post-Volcker periods. They document a fall in the inflation gap persistence and volatility, which is shown to be related to the reduction in the variance of trend inflation shocks during the great moderation. Shordone et al. (2010) estimate a medium-scale model à la Smets and Wouters (2007) conditional on the great moderation sample. Their evidence supports the relevance of trend inflation shocks as for the volatility of the nominal side of the economy. Del Negro and Eusepi (2011) estimate a variety of medium-scale models by employing Survey of Professional Forecaster's short-term inflation expectations measures on top of a standard set of macroeconomic indicators. In particular, they deal with a medium-scale model à la Smets and Wouters (2007) that features a fix inflation target; the same-medium scale model but with a time-varying inflation target; and an imperfect information model in which agents infer the time-varying target from the observation of the federal funds rate as in Erceg and Levin (2003). Their empirical exercise points to the empirical superiority of the perfect information model with the time-varying trend inflation. As in this chapters, we assume trend inflation to follow an autoregressive process whose variance is estimated jointly with the rest of the parameters of interest. We also find support for the role of trend inflation shocks as drivers of the U.S. inflation and policy rate in the United States. We add on these literature by showing that the contribution of such shocks in determining the volatility of the nominal side of the economy has followed an "inverted U-shape," with the highest value, at least as for inflation, recorded in the mid-1980s. Moreover, we show that models omitting trend inflation shocks overestimate the contribution of supply shocks in determining inflation and the federal funds rate. In particular, the shocks to the wage mark-up are those that get inflated the most in presence of this form of model misspecification.

This chapter develops as follows. The second section presents a helicopter tour over the literature dealing with the estimation of the trend inflation process. The third section presents our small-scale model, its estimates, and the variance decomposition analysis performed with such framework. The fourth section develops our rolling-window investigation conditional on the small-scale model presented in the third section. The fifth section moves to the analysis based on the Smets and Wouters (2007) model, and presents our full-sample and rolling-window estimates. The sixth section concludes. An Appendix including some details on the Bayesian estimation of our

DSGE models as well as the description of the Smets and Wouters (2007) framework is also provided.

TREND INFLATION ESTIMATES:
A HELICOPTER TOUR

Fig. 1 displays a number of trend inflation estimates in the literature. It focuses on a selection of contributions in the literature, that is, Kozicki and

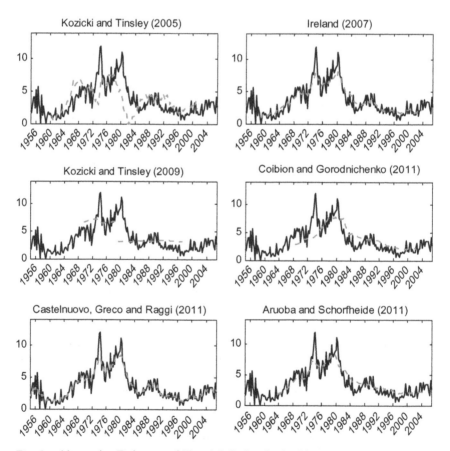

Fig. 1. Alternative Estimates of Trend Inflation in the Literature. Trend Inflation Estimates: A Comparison.
Notes: Solid blue lines: GDP deflator quarterly inflation; red dashed lines: Trend inflation estimates, different contributions. Sources of other contributions' estimates reported in the text.

Tinsley (2005), Ireland (2007), Kozicki and Tinsley (2009), Coibion and Gorodnichenko (2011a, 2011b), and Aruoba and Schorfheide (2011), and Castelnuovo et al. (2012).[7] To offer a sense of how such estimates may relate to a measure of inflation, we contrast them with the U.S. GDP deflator inflation rate.[8]

Panel [1,1] displays Kozicki and Tinsley's (2005) estimate of trend inflation. Kozicki and Tinsley (2005) employ a VAR model featuring variations in the Fed's inflation target that are imperfectly perceived by the private sector, which is unable to perfectly distinguish between permanent target shocks and transitory policy shocks and learn over this difference as more information enter its information set. The changes of the inflation target partly reflect the Fed's response to supply shocks hitting the U.S. economy over the post-WWII period. Kozicki and Tinsley's (2005) estimated target moves from values smaller than 2% in the early 1960s to values close to 8% at the end of the 1970s. Their trend inflation measure takes somewhat higher values than ours in the late 1960s and early 1970s. Interestingly, their estimated inflation target drops to zero during the Volcker disinflation, then it gradually returns to around 4% from the mid-1980s to the mid-1990s, and slightly lowers later on.

Ireland (2007) estimates a microfounded DSGE model of the business cycle with perfect information enjoyed by all agents of the economic system. The trend inflation process is modeled as a random walk.[9] His estimate of the inflation target is quite similar to the one proposed by Stock and Watson (2007), who work with reduced-form models for the U.S. inflation rate that allow for trend inflation and time-varying volatility of the stochastic components they consider, and it is statistically consistent with the one proposed by Cogley and Sbordone (2008), once the uncertainty surrounding the latter is taken into account. Panel [1,2] superimposes Ireland's (2007) estimate of the Federal Reserve's target to actual inflation. Ireland's (2007) trend inflation estimate 'filters' the U.S. inflation rate and captures its low-frequency component. He obtains his estimate by working with a microfounded DSGE model that features firms that, when not reoptimizing their prices, just set them conditional on a convex combination involving past and trend inflation. As in our chapter, the central bank is assumed to react to a measure of the inflation gap conditional on a time-varying inflation target.

A different picture emerges from Kozicki and Tinsley's (2009) contribution. They estimate a policy rule with time-varying coefficients using real-time Greenbook data and imposing a set of restrictions consistent with intermediate money supply targeting. The resulting trend inflation is estimated to lie between 6.1% and 7.2% in the period 1970–1980, then dramatically falls to about 3% in the 1980s and 1990s, a phase in which no intermediate money supply targeting is implemented.[10] Panel [2,1] shows a dramatic difference between their target and, say, Ireland's (2007). Such difference may be due, among other reasons, to the fact that they account for some restrictions implied by money supply targeting.

Coibion and Gorodnichenko (2011) propose an estimate of trend inflation conditional on a Taylor rule featuring time-varying coefficients and estimated with real-time Greenbook data. Such rule features a time-varying intercept, which they interpret as being a combination of time-dependent objects such as trend inflation, the equilibrium real interest rate, and the target growth rates for the output growth and the output gap. Some assumptions on the evolution of the last three objects enable Coibion and Gorodnichenko (2011) to recover the evolution of the trend inflation process. Their estimated target, displayed in Panel [2,2], turns out to be smoother than ours, with an empirical standard deviation reading 1.76 vs. the larger 1.92 associated to Ireland's (2007) estimate (conditional on Coibion and Gorodnichenko's sample). However, a similar pattern emerges, in that both measures clearly follow the upward inflation trend of the 1970s, the Volcker disinflation occurred in the early 1980s, and the somewhat gradual stabilization of inflation realized in the 1990s. Notably, the correlation between these two measures of trend inflation reads 0.84.

Panel [3,2] focuses on the estimate obtained by Castelnuovo et al. (2012). They work with a very flexible Taylor rule that features possibly time-varying policy coefficients, trend inflation, and heteroskedastic shocks. They find clear evidence in favor of such model of the U.S. policy conduct when contrasted with a constrained version of it featuring no time-varying inflation target. Interestingly, their trend inflation estimate, which is obtained with a single-equation approach allowing for policy time-dependence along the previously mentioned dimensions, is extremely similar to Ireland's (2007), whose estimation is obtained with a microfounded DSGE model featuring absence of any time-dependent object.

Finally, a different approach to compute trend inflation is followed by Aruoba and Schorfheide (2011). They combine three different measures of inflation – quarterly GDP inflation filtered through a one-sided band pass filter, 1-year- and 10-year-ahead inflation expectations from the Survey of Professional Forecasters – by using a small state-space model. Then, they extract the common factor via the Kalman filter. Panel [3,3] plots Aruoba and Schorfheide's (2011) estimate. Such measure turns out to be quite similar to those proposed by Ireland (2007) and Castelnuovo et al. (2012).

This is interesting, in light of the fact that Aruoba and Schorfheide's estimate involves measures of expectations that are not considered in the other two investigations.

Fig. 1 points to the heterogeneity of estimates present in the literature. In summary, Ireland's (2007), Castelnuovo et al. (2011) and Aruoba and Schorfheide's (2011) propose extremely similar estimates (despite of the strikingly different methodologies, samples, and data employed). Coibion and Gorodnichenko's (2011) estimate is fairly similar to those obtained by these three papers. Kozicki and Tinsley (2005) offer a somewhat different picture, in that their trend inflation estimate suggest realizations like the dramatic drop to zero in the early 1980s, which are absent in the remaining estimate under scrutiny. Finally, Kozicki and Tinsley's (2009) suggest a quite stable trend inflation estimate that features a clear "break in mean" at the end of the 1970s. In drawing these comparisons, one must keep in mind that differences may be due to a variety of reasons, including differences in selected samples, data transformation (e.g., the quarterly inflation rate used in our exercise and in Ireland, 2007, as opposed to the four-quarter inflation rate employed by Kozicki & Tinsley, 2005), structure imposed to the data (e.g., simple rules as in our case, Kozicki & Tinsley, 2005 and Coibion & Gorodnichenko, 2011, structural vector autoregressions as in Kozicki & Tinsley, 2005, state-space representations as in Aruoba & Schorfheide, 2011, DSGE frameworks as in Ireland, 2007), vintage of the data ("real-time" vs. "revised" data).

In our DSGE model-based analysis, we will focus on Aruoba and Schorfheide's (2011) estimate on trend inflation for various reasons. First, it is a model-free measure of trend inflation. DSGE models are typically misspecified along some dimensions (Del Negro, Schorfheide, Smets, & Wouters, 2007). Clearly, model misspecification may lead to a potentially distorted estimate of the trend inflation process. From this standpoint, it is "safer" to rely on externally combined observables when feeding the measurement equations of our DSGE models with a measure of trend inflation. Second, expectations over future inflation are likely to be quite informative on the trend inflation process, in that rational agents should form their expectations over future inflation by appealing, first and foremost, to their predictions on the low-frequency component of inflation. Third, as already stressed in the Introduction, the role of innovations to the policy rate *per se* vs. innovations to the inflation target is hard to identify unless an empirical proxy of trend inflation is employed.

We now turn to our structural analysis.

A STRUCTURAL ANALYSIS WITH A SMALL-SCALE
DSGE MODEL

The small-scale framework we work with reads as follows:

$$\pi_t = \beta(1 + \alpha\beta)^{-1}E_t\pi_{t+1} + \alpha(1 + \alpha\beta)^{-1}\pi_{t-1} + \kappa x_t + \varepsilon_t^{\pi} \qquad (1)$$

$$x_t = \gamma E_t x_{t+1} + (1 - \gamma)x_{t-1} - \sigma^{-1}(R_t - E_t\pi_{t+1}) + \varepsilon_t^{x} \qquad (2)$$

$$R_t = (1 - \varphi_R)(\pi_t^{*} + \varphi_{\pi}(\pi_t - \pi_t^{*}) + \varphi_x x_t) + \varphi_R R_{t-1} + \varepsilon_t^{R} \qquad (3)$$

$$\pi_t^{*} = \rho_{*}\pi_{t-1}^{*} + v_t^{*} \qquad (4)$$

$$\varepsilon_t^{k} = \rho_k \varepsilon_{t-1}^{k} + v_t^{k}, k \in \{\pi, x, R\} \qquad (5)$$

$$v_t^{j} \sim i.i.d.N(0, \sigma_j^2), j \in \{\pi, *, x, R\} \qquad (6)$$

Eq. (1) is an expectational new-Keynesian Phillips curve (NKPC) in which π_t stands for the inflation rate, β represents the discount factor, x_t identifies the output gap, whose impact on current inflation is influenced by the slope-parameter κ, α identifies indexation to past inflation, and ε_t^{π} may be interpreted as a 'cost-push shock'; γ is the weight of the forward-looking component in the intertemporal IS curve (2); σ^{-1} stands for households' intertemporal elasticity of substitution; ε_t^{x} is a stochastic component that works as a 'demand' shock; φ_{π}, φ_y, and φ_R are the policy parameters capturing the systematic monetary part of the monetary policy conduct, which is here represented by a standard Taylor rule (3); the monetary policy shock ε_t^{R} allows for a stochastic evolution of the policy rate.

The evolution of the inflation target – formalized by Eq. (4) – is dictated by the autoregressive parameter ρ_{*} as well as the volatility σ_{*} of its innovation ε_t^{*}. This process is typically assumed to be a random walk or a very-persistent variance-stationary process capturing the low-frequency component of the inflation rate, which are likely to be sensible approximations of the time-varying target set by monetary-policy authorities (see, Aruoba & Schorfheide, 2011; Coibion & Gorodnichenko, 2011a; Cogley et al., 2010; Ireland, 2007, among others). The autoregressive processes (5) are intended to account for the possible persistence of the shocks affecting the economic environment. Such shocks are loaded by the mutually independent martingale-differences (6), which close the model.[11] Since the seminar contribution by Clarida, Galí, and Gertler (2000), this model has been extensively employed to scrutinize the drivers of the U.S. macroeconomic dynamics.

The version of the model we consider omits to account for the role played by price dispersion as for the structure of the NKPC in a world in which steady-state trend inflation (in net terms) is allowed to take a strictly positive value. However, a recent paper by Ascari, Castelnuovo, and Rossi (2011) shows that such role is, from an empirical standpoint, likely to be negligible.

Model Estimation

We estimate the model (1)–(6) with Bayesian methods. Bayesian methods have been shown to perform relatively better than alternatives like classical maximum likelihood or GMM as for DSGE models like those employed in this chapter (Canova & Sala, 2009). Readers interested into in depth-discussions on the pros and cons of using Bayesian techniques versus other estimation methods are referred to An and Schorfheide (2007) and Fernández-Villaverde (2010).

Data and Priors

We work with quarterly U.S. data. We employ four observables, which we demean prior to estimation. The output gap is computed as log-deviation of the real GDP with respect to the potential output estimated by the Congressional Budget Office. The inflation rate is the quarterly growth rate of the GDP deflator. For the short-term nominal interest rate we consider the effective federal funds rate expressed in quarterly terms (averages of monthly values). The source of these data is the Federal Reserve Bank of St. Louis' website. As discussed in the introduction, we also employ the measure of trend inflation elaborated by Aruoba and Schorfheide (2011). From the private sector's standpoint, such measure can be interpreted as an anchor for long-term inflation expectations. Aruoba and Schorfheide's trend inflation estimate is based on three different measures of inflation expectations, that is, the GDP deflation inflation filtered by a one-sided Band-Pass filter, the one-year ahead inflation expectations provided by the Survey of Professional Forecasters, and the 10-year ahead inflation expectations coming from the same source. Such measures are combined by the employment of a small state-space model with which the common factor is extracted via the Kalman filter.[12] We work with the sample 1965:I-2005:IV.[13]

The priors employed in our estimation are indicated in Table 1. Some parameters are hardly identified in our model, then we calibrate them as it is

Table 1. Bayesian Estimates of the Small-Scale DSGE Model. 1965:I-2005:IV U.S. Data.

Param.	Interpretation	Priors Baseline Set	Post. Means [5h,95th] (1)	Post. Means [5h,95th] (2)	Post. Means [5h,95th] (3)	Priors Alternative set (4)	Post.Means [5h,95th] (4)
β	Discount factor	Calibr.	0.99 [-]	0.99 [-]	0.99 [-]	Calibr.	0.99 [-]
κ	NKPC, slope	$\mathcal{N}(0.1, 0.015)$	0.11 [0.09,0.13]	0.09 [0.07,0.12]	0.11 [0.09,0.13]	$\mathcal{N}(0.1, 0.015)$	0.01 [0.01,0.01]
α	Price indexation	$\mathscr{B}(0.5, 0.2)$	0.09 [0.02,0.15]	0.08 [0.01,0.15]	0.04 [0.01,0.08]	**B(0.75, 0.15)**	0.69 [0.58,0.82]
γ	IS, forw. look. degree	$\mathscr{B}(0.5, 0.2)$	0.71 [0.66,0.76]	0.78 [0.69,0.86]	0.70 [0.64,0.76]	$\mathscr{B}(0.5, 0.2)$	0.46 [0.39,0.53]
σ	Inverse of the IES	$\mathcal{N}(3, 1)$	5.45 [4.44,6.51]	5.10 [3.91,6.30]	5.49 [4.30,5.70]	$\mathcal{N}(3, 1)$	5.46 [4.18,6.64]
φ_π	T. Rule, inflation	$\mathcal{N}(1.5, 0.3)$	2.22 [1.95,2.51]	2.22 [1.90,2.55]	2.16 [1.78,2.55]	$\mathcal{N}(1.5, 0.3)$	1.80 [1.43,2.15]
φ_x	T. Rule, output gap	$\mathscr{G}(0.3, 0.2)$	0.03 [0.01,0.05]	0.20 [0.10,0.30]	0.04 [0.01,0.07]	$\mathscr{G}(0.3, 0.2)$	0.28 [0.18,0.40]
φ_R	T. Rule, inertia	$\mathscr{B}(0.5, 0.285)$	0.73 [0.68,0.78]	0.75 [0.70,0.81]	0.73 [0.66,0.80]	$\mathscr{B}(0.5, 0.285)$	0.83 [0.79,0.88]
ρ_π	AR coeff. cost-push shock	$\mathscr{B}(0.75, 0.15)$	0.98 [0.97,0.99]	0.98 [0.96,0.99]	0.98 [0.97,0.99]	**B(0.25, 0.15)**	0.06 [0.01,0.11]
ρ_x	AR coeff. demand shock	$\mathscr{B}(0.5, 0.2)$	0.70 [0.60,0.80]	0.76 [0.68,0.85]	0.68 [0.58,0.78]	$\mathscr{B}(0.5, 0.2)$	0.39 [0.24,0.57]

		Prior	(1)	(2)	(3)	Prior	(4)
ρ_R	AR coeff. mon. pol. shock	B(0.5, 0.2)	0.39 [0.25,0.49]	0.21 [0.07,0.33]	0.32 [0.17,0.46]	B(0.5, 0.2)	0.25 [0.12,0.40]
ρ_*	AR coeff. trend infl. shock	Calibr.	0.995 [-]	0.995 [-]	0.995 [-]	Calibr.	0.995 [-]
σ_π	Std. dev. cost-push shock	IG(0.2, 0.1)	0.14 [0.12,0.16]	0.09 [0.06,0.12]	0.13 [0.11,0.16]	IG(0.2, 0.1)	0.17 [0.16,0.19]
σ_x	Std. dev. demand shock	IG(0.2, 0.1)	0.16 [0.11,0.22]	0.16 [0.11,0.22]	0.15 [0.11,0.20]	IG(0.2, 0.1)	0.36 [0.25,0.44]
σ_R	Std. dev. mon. pol. shock	IG(0.2, 0.1)	0.29 [0.27,0.31]	0.25 [0.22,0.28]	0.28 [0.24,0.31]	IG(0.2, 0.1)	0.25 [0.22,0.27]
σ_*	Std. dev. trend infl. shock	IG(0.2, 0.1)	0.05 [0.04,0.06]	0.11 [0.06,0.15]	0.05 [0.04,0.06]	IG(0.2, 0.1)	0.05 [0.04,0.06]
$log(ML)$			−13.05				−20.68

Notes: Prior densities: Figures indicate the (mean, st.dev.) of each prior distribution. Posterior densities: Figures reported indicate the posterior mean and the [5th,95th] percentile of the estimated densities. Scenarios. (1): Baseline; (2): Estimation with trend inflation as an unobservable factor (no proxy in the measurement equation); (3): Estimation with trend inflation proxied by a one-sided Band-Pass filter applied to GDP deflator inflation; (4): Estimation with a set of alternative priors (higher prior mean on price indexation, lower prior mean on autoregressive parameter of the cost-push shock. Log-Marginal Likelihoods reported when comparable to the Baseline scenario. Details on the estimation procedure provided in the text.

customary in this literature. The discount factor is fixed to 0.99, a value quite common in this literature. The persistence of the trend inflation model is also calibrated. This is a choice done to avoid having troubles in converging to the ergodic posterior density of our model, troubles that might arise in dealing with this close-to-unit root trend inflation observable. Following Cogley et al. (2010), we set ρ_* to 0.995. This value implies a bounded value for the trend inflation variance in population and, at the same time, it allows us to capture the extremely high persistence of the trend inflation process. An alternative would be to allow for a unit-root in trend inflation. However, Cogley et al. (2010) show that a unit root in trend inflation is likely to induce a very low predictability of the inflation gap by models like the ours. This would be at odds with the fact documented by Cogley et al. (2010), who employ VARs with time-varying coefficients and stochastic volatility to model the post-WWII U.S. data and find that such predictability has been high before the advent of Paul Volcker as Federal Reserve's chairman.

As for the estimated parameters, we employ standard priors. In particular, we assume a fairly conservative value for the slope of the NKPC, an aggressive reaction to the inflation gap by the Federal Reserve, and a high persistence of the cost-push shock. We are fairly agnostic as for the remaining parameters, whose a priori domain is suggested by economic considerations.

Notice that, in conducting our Bayesian estimations, we exclude parametrizations consistent with the absence of an equilibrium or multiple equilibria under rational expectations. The latter case is often advocated when describing the U.S. monetary policy conduct during the 1970s (for the seminal paper in this area, see Clarida et al., 2000). Likelihood-based estimations of DSGE models with multiple equilibria, however, require the econometrician to choose a single equilibria out of the many, a choice that is not irrelevant as for the moments implied by the model (Castelnuovo, 2012b).[14] Therefore, our analysis focuses on parametrizations implying a unique equilibrium under rational expectations.

Posteriors

We verify a smooth convergence towards the posterior density by the graphical analysis elaborated by Brooks and Gelman (1998). A visual inspection of the posterior density confirms the absence of bimodalities and plateaus.[15] The outcome of our Bayesian estimation is reported in Table 1. All parameters assume very conventional values. The slope of the Phillips curve takes a posterior-mean value equal to 0.11, quite in line with the calibration suggested by Ireland (2004). Price indexation is very low, a finding not surprising in light of the very high persistence of the cost-push shock autoregressive process. The weight of the forward-looking component is estimated to be larger than that of past output but clearly smaller than one, a result offering support to the hypothesis of habit formation in consumption elaborated by Furher (2000). The intertemporal elasticity of substitution takes a value in line with a variety of estimates in the literature (Benati & Surico, 2008, 2009). Monetary policy is estimated to exert an aggressive reaction against inflation fluctuations (in deviations with respect to trend inflation), a very mild reaction to the output gap, and a reasonable amount of persistence. Shocks are estimated to be persistent. As for our shocks' standard deviations, that of trend inflation is quite precisely estimated.

Are our posterior densities heavily influenced by our choice of employing Aruoba and Schorfheide's (2011) estimate of the Federal Reserve's inflation target? To answer this question, we re-estimated the model without such a proxy, therefore treating trend inflation as an unobservable latent factor. Table 1 (column identified by "(2)") reports our posterior densities. The main change with respect to the baseline scenario regards the standard deviation of the trend inflation process, which turns out to be doubled with respect to the baseline scenario "(1)." The remaining structural parameters are in general just mildly affected by the omission of the empirical proxy by Aruoba and Schorfheide's (2011). The two parameters affected the most are policymakers' reaction to the output gap, which substantially increases, and the persistence of the cost-push shock, which is basically halved with respect to the baseline case.

Turning to Aruoba and Schorfheide's (2011) proxy again, one may want to dig deeper in order to understand what the role played by short- and long-term inflation expectations is. Aruoba and Schorfheide's estimate of trend inflation is obtained by combining three different measures of inflation expectations, that is, a low-frequency representation of GDP deflator inflation extracted via a one-sided version of the Band-Pass filter, a 1-year ahead inflation expectation measure, and a 10-year ahead inflation expectation measure. The latter two indicators are from the Survey of Professional Forecasters, which is currently managed by the Federal Reserve Bank of Philadelphia.[16] Survey-based measures may be contaminated by measurement errors. Moreover, they can be misleading indicators of the Federal Reserve's inflation target if expectations are not formed in a fully-rational fashion, or if agents do not have a full knowledge of the structural model in place. To take this "measurement error" issue into account, we reestimate the model with a measure of trend inflation exclusively based on the Band-Pass filter as computed by Aruoba and Schorfheide (2011). Table 1 reports our posterior means (see column "(3)"). As a matter of fact, one can hardly notice any variations with respect to the baseline case. The only parameter that seems to be affected by the change in the proxy for trend inflation is price indexation, whose posterior mean turns out to be lower. However, the 90% credible sets suggest that one should be very cautious before claiming a strong effect of the change in our proxy on the estimated value of such parameter. A possible interpretation of this result is that the Band-Pass filtered inflation rate is a good proxy of Aruoba and Schorfheide's (2011) measure of trend inflation. This is hardly surprising, given the correlation between these two measures.[17]

The high degree of persistence of the cost-push shock ε_t^π is due to the high degree of persistence of the inflation rate. In contrast, the degree of price indexation α is estimated to be negligible. However, one may suspect the existence of an alternative mode characterized by a "high indexation-low cost-push shock persistence," which could emerge conditional on a different set of priors. We investigate this issue by running an alternative estimation conditional on two different a-priori parameter densities, that is, $\alpha \sim B(0.75, 0.15)$ and $\rho_\pi \sim B(0.25, 0.15)$. The remaining priors are kept as in our "baseline" case.

Table 1 (column "(4)") collects the outcome of this estimation. Several comments are in order. First, the choice of the priors drive the result as for price indexation and the persistence of the cost-push shock. In particular, the former (posterior mean) reads 0.69, while the latter 0.06. Therefore, different priors may very well "turn the world upside down" as for these two parameters, which are key to describe the dynamics of the U.S. inflation. Second, the choice of different priors as for these two parameters has got evident implications as far as most of the remaining parameters are concerned. In particular, the slope of the NKPC gets "squeezed" toward zero; the degree of forward-lookingness in the IS curve and the persistence of the non policy demand shock turn out to be substantially lower; the policy reaction to inflation, while remaining aggressive, is estimated to be milder, while that to the output gap much more aggressive; the degree of policy gradualism is found to be higher, while the persistence of the policy shock more moderate; the volatility (standard deviation) of the non policy demand shock is also found to be larger. Third, and most importantly, the overall "fit" of the model is measured to be worse conditional on these alternative priors. In terms marginal likelihoods, computed by adopting the "modified harmonic mean" approach proposed by Geweke (1999), we found a difference (expressed in log-points) of about 7.5. This translates into a Bayes factor of about 1,808, which provides us with a "very strong" evidence in favor of the model with "low indexation and high cost-push shock persistence."[18] Therefore, in the rest of the chapter, we will concentrate on the "low indexation-high cost-push shock persistence" formulation of the model.

What is the role played by trend inflation shocks as opposed to other innovations in shaping our observables? We investigate this issue in the following section.

Variance Decomposition

We assess the role of trend inflation shocks by appealing to a standard variance decomposition exercise. Our computations (conditional on the model's posterior mode) will refer to two different horizons, that is, 8-step and ∞-step ahead. The former one is intended to assess the contribution of the structural shocks at "business cycle frequencies." Differently, the second one aims at pinning down the drivers of the U.S. macroeconomic "unconditional variances," which are of clear interest as for welfare evaluations (see, e.g., Woodford, 2003).

Table 2 – Panel A collects the contribution of the four structural shocks (cost-push, non policy demand, monetary policy, and trend inflation) as for the three variables of interest (output, inflation, the policy rate). The 8-step ahead decomposition assigns a dominant role of the cost-push shock as for the business cycle fluctuations of output, with a contribution over 90%. Inflation is explained by an ensemble of shocks, with the non policy demand shock providing the largest contribution (40%), the supply shock a quite substantial one (about 30%), the policy shock playing an important role (about 20%), and the trend inflation shock being the responsible of as much as 10% of the forecast error variance decomposition. The demand shock turns out to be a key-driver for the policy rate as well, whose volatility at business cycle frequencies is also importantly determined by the policy shock and the cost-push shock. Differently, the trend inflation shock plays a marginal role here.

Trend inflation shocks are shocks to the low-frequency component of inflation. One may therefore argue that different results may be obtained when focusing on the ∞-step ahead decomposition. Table 2 – Panel B offers support to this intuition. First, the role of trend inflation is estimated to be

Table 2. Variance Decomposition Implied by the Small-Scale DSGE
Model. 1965:I-2005:IV U.S. Data.

		Var/shocks	v^π	v^y	v^R	v^*
Panel A						
Trend	8−step ahead	x	92.11	5.77	2.10	0.02
inflation		π	28.21	39.53	21.74	10.52
shocks		R	20.54	42.46	32.85	4.15
Panel B						
	∞−step ahead	x	99.30	0.51	0.19	0.00
		π	44.12	12.19	6.71	36.99
		R	49.05	14.77	11.25	24.94
Panel C						
No trend	8−step ahead	x	87.29	10.29	2.42	
inflation		π	59.09	34.88	6.03	−
shocks		R	30.93	45.23	23.84	
Panel D						
	∞−step ahead	x	98.60	1.14	0.27	
		π	91.42	7.33	1.25	−
		R	83.51	11.36	5.13	

Notes: Figures conditional on the posterior mode values of the model. Panel A and B: Scenarios
with trend inflation shocks; Panel C and D: Scenarios without trend inflation shocks. Details on
the estimation procedure provided in the text.

large as for the volatility of inflation and the policy rate, with about 37% of
the former and 25% of the latter explained by changes in the Federal
Reserve's inflation target. Trend inflation shocks compete with "supply"
shocks in determining the volatility of these two variables, with the latter
shocks remaining the main drivers of inflation and the short-term policy
rate. The role of standard monetary policy shocks is marginal, even if they
explain about 11% of the sample variance of the policy rate. The
contribution of "demand" shocks is noticeable, with a share larger than
10% as for both variables. Interestingly, trend inflation shocks do not
contribute to explain the volatility of our empirical measure of the output
gap, which is almost entirely explained by supply shocks. This is far from
surprising, because shocks to the supply side of the economy (above all,

those hitting inflation first) are typically those responsible for the inflation-output volatility trade-off in this model.

What if an econometrician failed to model trend inflation shocks? Table 2 – panels C and D reports the figures obtained by estimating a restricted version of our model that features a fixed inflation target, that is, with "muted" trend inflation shocks. Interestingly, evident distortions affect the identification of the drivers of the U.S. economic environment. Conditional on the analysis at business cycle frequencies, one can detect a strong over estimation of the contribution of the demand shock as for the volatility of output. The participation of the cost-push shock to the forecast error of inflation gets doubled, while that of the policy rate turns out to be severely underestimated. Finally, the supply shock's participation as for the volatility of the policy rate is estimated to be around 50% larger. As far as our unconditional volatilities are concerned, the contribution of the supply shock to the volatilities of inflation and the federal funds rate turns out to be dramatically inflated, while the participation of demand and policy shocks gets slightly reduced. This exercise suggests that, conditional on the post-WWII U.S. sample, the omission of trend inflation may return estimated moments that are heavily distorted by model misspecification.

Our framework does not explicitly model variations in the natural level of the real interest rate, which is typically estimated to be very persistent. Therefore, the dynamics of such omitted factor could in principle bias our inflation target's estimated standard deviation upward and inflate its contribution as for the forecast error variance decomposition of inflation and the federal funds rate. To control for the effects of this model misspecification, we estimate our model by employing filtered measures of the federal funds rate that retains cyclical frequencies only. Such cyclical representation of the policy rate is obtained by subtracting Aruoba and Schorfheide's proxy of trend inflation from the federal funds rate series. We then estimate our model with such "purged" measure of the federal funds rate along with our observables for inflation, the inflation target, and the output gap. A variance-decomposition exercise points to a reduction of the contribution of trend inflation as for the volatility of inflation and the policy rate, with figures reading 25% as for the former and 17% as for the latter (figures referring to the ∞–*step* ahead decomposition). The remaining "explanatory power" is assigned to supply shocks, whose contribution to the variance of inflation (federal funds rate) goes up to 59% (57%). However, the main message of our benchmark exercise, that is, the large role played by trend inflation shocks in explaining the dynamics of the nominal side of the economy, remains qualitatively unaffected.

Is our variance decomposition analysis affected by the employment of Aruoba and Schorfheide's (2011) "observable" for the inflation target? Table 3 contrasts the variance decomposition of our baseline scenario (already collected in Table 2, and reproposed here for easing the reader) with that conditional on the model being estimated without any observable as for trend inflation. As for trend inflation shocks, the largest variation when not exploiting the proxy in the estimation phase regards the forecast error for inflation at business cycle frequencies (whose figures are collected in Panels A and C), which basically turns out to be twice as much as what recorder in the baseline scenario, which is, some 20%. As a matter of fact, however, the shock which gains the most in absolute terms is the supply shock, which goes up to 58% (from 28%). The identification of the drivers of the inflation rate at business cycle frequencies are importantly affected by

Table 3. Variance Decomposition Implied by the Small-Scale DSGE Model. 1965:I-2005:IV U.S. Data.

	Var/shocks		v^{π}	v^{y}	v^{R}	v^{*}
Panel A						
Trend inflation	*8−step ahead*	x	92.11	5.77	2.10	0.02
as 'observable'		π	28.21	39.53	21.74	10.52
		R	20.54	42.46	32.85	4.15
Panel B						
	$\infty−step\ ahead$	x	99.30	0.51	0.19	0.00
		π	44.12	12.19	6.71	36.99
		R	49.05	14.77	11.25	24.94
Panel C						
Trend inflation	*8−step ahead*	x	87.57	10.62	1.63	0.18
as latent factor		π	58.50	19.78	2.53	19.19
		R	34.41	42.96	14.76	7.87
Panel D						
	$\infty−step\ ahead$	x	98.02	1.66	0.25	0.07
		π	56.31	3.53	0.45	39.71
		R	57.32	9.50	2.92	30.26

Notes: Figures conditional on the posterior mode values of the model. Panel A and B: Scenarios with an observable for trend inflation; Panel C and D: Scenarios without an observable for trend inflation. Details on the estimation procedure provided in the text.

the choice of not employing the observable for the inflation target. The demand shock's contribution to inflation volatility is some 40% when the proxy is used in the estimation, and some 20% when it is not, while that of the monetary policy shock is about 20% when the target is "observable" versus a much more moderate 2.53% when it is not. This latter shock's contribution to the forecast error of the policy rate turns out to be halved when dropping Aruoba and Schorfheide's (2011) proxy from the list of observables employed in the estimation of our DSGE model.

Moving to the ∞–*step* ahead decomposition (Table 3, panels B and D), one can notice that, while being present, the differences between the scenario with versus without an observable for trend inflation are much milder. As for the variance decomposition of output, differences are in fact negligible. Moving to inflation's, we notice in particular a larger role assigned to supply shocks when trend inflation is not "observable" (from 44% to 56%), a substantial reduction in that of nonpolicy demand shocks (from 12% to 3.5%) and of policy shocks (from 6.71% to 0.45%). Finally, when considering the forecast error variance decomposition of the policy rate, we notice an increase in the participation of the supply shocks (the difference amounts to about 8%), a reduction in the contribution of demand and the policy shocks (some 5% and 8.3%, respectively), and an increase in that of the trend inflation shock of about 6%.

Our results on the ∞–*step* ahead forecast error variance decomposition turn out to be somewhat more robust to the omission of the observable for trend inflation with respect to analysis conducted at business cycle. Moreover, the unconditional forecast error variance decomposition is of clear interest from policy purposes due to its link with microfounded welfare indicators (for a discussion, see Woodford, 2003). Finally, it allows us to draw comparisons with some relevant contributions which dealt with trend inflation shocks (e.g., Cogley et al., 2010; Ireland, 2007). Therefore, the remainder of the chapter will focus on the ∞–*step* ahead forecast error variance decomposition.

So far, we have scrutinized a fixed sample of U.S. data, 1965:I-2005:IV. Obviously, one may wonder how stable the contribution of trend inflation is over time. In the attempt to investigate the role of trend inflation shocks further, Fig. 2 reports inflation and the federal funds rate as modeled by our DSGE framework (baseline scenario) along with their counterfactual counterparts computed by setting trend inflation shocks to zero at all times. Evidently, the relative contribution of trend inflation shocks to inflation and the policy rate is far from being stable. In particular, trend inflation shocks play a great role in explaining inflation and the policy rate during the

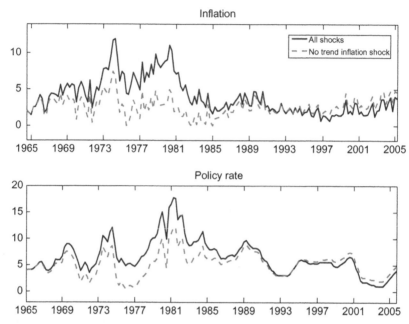

Fig. 2.   Variance Decomposition – Role of Trend Inflation Shocks.
Notes: Smoothed series, model calibrated with posterior mean.

great inflation phase of the 1970s. Differently, the role of variations in trend inflation is almost negligible during the great moderation. Clearly, this evidence calls for a deepening of the role of trend inflation over time, which requires the employment of a more flexible approach as for the estimation of our DSGE model. Our choice is to undertake a rolling-window investigation, which is developed in the following section.

ROLLING-WINDOW APPROACH

We then move to the investigation of the possible instabilities affecting this model's relationships by implementing a rolling-window approach. In particular, we start from the 1965:I-1979:IV window and estimate the model, then we move the first and last observation of the window by two years and repeat the estimation. We keep the size of the window fixed (at 60 observations, which is a 15-year window) to minimize the differences in the precision of our estimates due to the sample-size. Our last window covers 1991:I-2005:IV, that is, we consider fourteen different windows, which enable us to assess fourteen different posterior densities for all the parameters of interest.

The width of our window is fairly in line with the one chosen by previous contributions when estimating small- or medium-scale DSGE models with this technique. Canova (2009) works with a window-size of 80 observations (20 years) with a small-scale model with constant trend inflation. Castelnuovo (2012a) employs 60 observations (15 years) with a small-scale framework featuring real balances in the equilibrium equations of inflation and output as well as a positive reaction of the Federal Reserve to the growth rate of nominal money. Canova and Ferroni (2012) scrutinizes a medium-scale model à la Smets and Wouters (2007) by focusing on windows of 68 quarters (17 years). A similar choice is made by Giacomini and Rossi (2010), who stick to a 70-quarter window size. Cantore et al. (2011) choose a window-size of 60 observations (15 years) as a benchmark, but explores alternative sizes up to 90 quarters. Our choice of a window-size of 15 years appears to be reasonable in light of the number of parameters present in the models we aim at estimating. Much smaller sizes, between 16 and 39 observations, are actually suggested by Inoue, Rossi, and Jin (2011), who develop a methodology to select the size of the window in the forecasting context when multiple models are jointly evaluated. Our purpose is clearly different, in that we aim at providing an ex-post description of the data. To achieve our goal, our sample numerosity must be high enough to allow the data to influence the posterior density via their impact on the likelihood function.

Window-Specific Parameters

Fig. 3 plots some selected percentiles of the posterior densities of our structural parameters against the windows considered in our estimation. We notice some instability as for the slope of the Phillips curve, which drops when the mid-1980s and 1990s are considered. Some previous literature (e.g., Best, 2011; Primiceri, 2006) found the slope of the NKPC to be unstable mostly during the mid-1960s to the late 1970s. Our result lines up with the empirical evidence on the reduction of such a slope occurring in sync with the advent of the Great Moderation (see Carlstrom, Fuerst, & Paustian, 2009, for a discussion). We also find instabilities in the weight of expected output in the IS curve, as well as the persistence of the cost-push shock, again when the window 1988–1999 is taken into account. The inverse of the

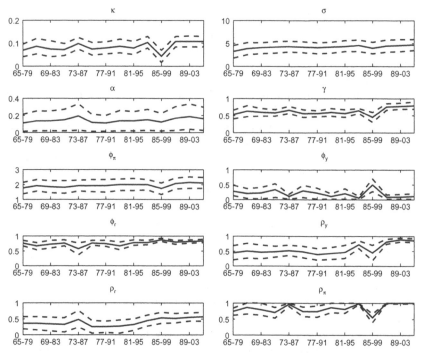

Fig. 3. Evolution of the Structural Parameters of Our Small-Scale DSGE Model.
Notes: Definitions of the structural parameters given in Table 1. Solid line: Posterior median. Dotted lines: 5th and 95th posterior percentiles. Evolution of the parameters constructed by employing fourteen rolling windows of 15-year constant length. Windows: [1965:I-1979:IV, 1967:I-1981:IV, . . . , 1991:I-2005:IV].

intertemporal elasticity of substitution and the systematic policy reaction to inflation grow over time. Also the degree of interest rate smoothing and the persistence of the monetary policy shock appear to increase over time. The reaction of the output gap features ups and downs. Overall, however, the credible sets of these parameters hardly display important differences when moving from a window to another.

Fig. 4 plots the evolution of the volatilities of our shocks. A number of considerations can be made. First, the volatility of supply and demand shocks display a downward (although nonmonotonic) trend. Second, the volatilities of our monetary policy shocks, i.e., the standard innovation to the policy rate and shocks to trend inflation, feature a hump-shaped volatility over our windows. Both volatilities increase over the first five windows, peak

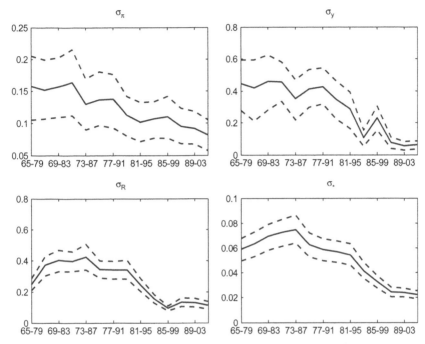

Fig. 4. Evolution of the Shocks' Standard Deviations of Our Small-Scale DSGE Model.

Notes: Definitions of the shocks' standard deviations given in Table 1. Solid line: Posterior median. Dotted lines: 5th and 95th posterior percentiles. Evolution of the shocks' standard deviations constructed by employing fourteen rolling windows of 15-year constant length. Windows: [1965:I-1979:IV, 1967:I-1981:IV, ..., 1991:I-2005:IV].

at 1973–1987, then slowly decrease as the observations of 1980s and 1990s become dominant in the windows under investigation. This result supports the findings in Justiniano and Primiceri (2008) and Fernández-Villaverde et al. (2010) on the relevance of modeling time-conditional variances of the structural shocks identified in DSGE models.

This picture is intriguing in light of the evolution of the volatility of actual inflation and the federal funds rate, which is depicted in Fig. 5. Clearly, this hump-shaped pattern is a feature of the U.S. data as for these two variables, as also documented by Canova (2009). Interestingly, the correlation between the volatility of the shocks affecting trend inflation and that of actual inflation (as measured by its sample standard deviation) is 0.64,

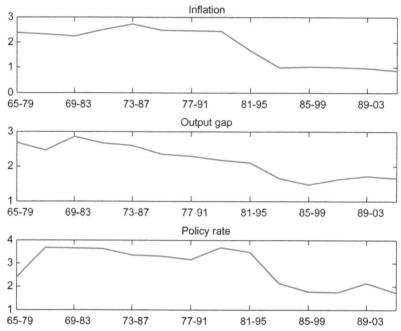

Fig. 5. Evolution of the Standard Deviations of Our Observables.
Notes: Sample moments computed by considering quarterly rates of inflation and the policy indicator. Evolution of the moments constructed by employing fourteen rolling windows of 15-year constant length. Windows: [1965:I-1979:IV, 1967:I-1981:IV, ..., 1991:I-2005:IV].

larger than the one involving the volatility of the policy rate and trend inflation shocks, which reads 0.53. Even larger the correlations between these observables' sample standard deviations and the volatility of the standard policy rate shock, which read 0.91 and 0.80 as for inflation and the policy rate, respectively.

Window-Specific Variance Decomposition

The presence of subsample instabilities as those documented in the previous section naturally calls to recompute the variance decomposition of our observables by accounting for the time-dependence of our estimated parameters. Fig. 6 collects the outcome of our exercise. Various considerations are in order. The relative contribution of trend inflation and cost-push

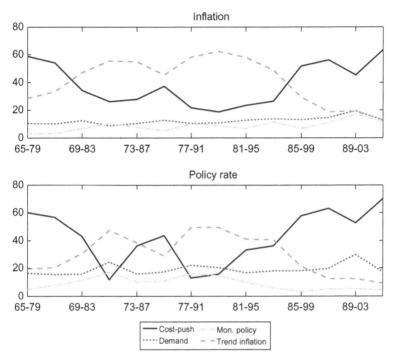

Fig. 6. Evolution of the Variance Decomposition Implied by the Estimated Small-Scale DSGE Model.
Notes: Window-specific variance decomposition computed by calibrating the small-scale model with its posterior mode values.

shocks is clearly time dependent. Trend inflation shocks explain about 28% of the volatility of inflation at the beginning of the sample. Then, these shocks' participation becomes larger, and hits its highest level in 1979–1993 with a share of about 62%. Subsequently, their contribution drastically declines and ends up being in line with that of the demand shock at the end of the sample, that is, 12%. This "inverted-U" relationship is negatively correlated with the contribution offered by the cost-push shock, which starts off at a level as high as 59%, then declines to about 19% in 1979–1993, and increases again in the last windows, with a contribution in 1991–2005 of about 63%. Differently, the contribution of demand and standard monetary policy shocks is quite stable over time, with the former being responsible for about 12% of the volatility of inflation and the latter about 8%.

The "inverted-U" contribution by trend inflation also applies as for
the volatility of the policy rate, with a participation of about 20% during
the period 1965–1979, around 49% in 1977–1991, and a decline in the
second part of the sample under investigation to its lowest figure – 9% – in
1991–2005. The behavior of the participation of the cost-push shock is more
complex, in that it records its highest values at the beginning and at the end
of the sample – 60% and 70%, respectively – and "oscillates" in the middle
of it, with the lowest value – 12% – in 1971–1989. Again, the contribution of
the remaining demand shocks is fairly constant over time, with a share
of about 19% attributable to the shock hitting the IS curve, and 9% to the
standard monetary policy shock.

Our results suggest that (i) the contribution of trend inflation shocks to
the volatility of the nominal side of the economy is substantial; (ii) such
contribution is time-varying; (iii) a description of the post-WWII U.S.
economy based on the "Volcker-appointment break" only, which would
call for an analysis contrasting the great inflation phase and the great
moderation period, would probably fail to capture the richness of the
evolution of the participation of the trend inflation shocks over time.

A LARGER-SCALE DSGE MODEL

Of course, a poor description of the processes that drive inflation and the
policy rate in the U.S. economy may in principle lead to an overestimation
of the role of trend inflation. As a matter of fact, virtually all central banks
and a large number of researchers have drifted their attention to the richer
medium-scale framework à la Smets and Wouters (2007) for some years
now. This model features a variety of nominal and real frictions as well as
a set of shocks that can be given a structural interpretation. We then
re-propose our analysis by considering an estimated version of the Smets
and Wouters' (2007) model, whose shocks can be given a structural
interpretation. We refer to Smets and Wouters (2007) and to our appendix
for a full description of the model.

Data and Priors

We first estimate Smets and Wouters' (2007) framework with Bayesian
techniques over the sample 1965:I-2005:IV. We use the seven observables
employed by Smets and Wouters (2007) (quarterly growth rates of GDP,

consumption, investments, and wages, all expressed in per-capita, real terms; log of hours; GDP deflator quarterly inflation; and federal funds rate) plus the measure of trend inflation developed by Aruoba and Schorfheide (2011). As done with the small-scale model, we consider a Taylor rule in which the policymakers react to a measure of the inflation gap (as opposed to raw inflation) determined by considering an exogenous process for trend inflation as the one described by Eq. (4).

The model features a deterministic growth rate driven by labor-augmenting technological progress, so that the data do not need to be detrended before estimation. Tables 3 and 4 document the priors we employed, which are the same as Smets and Wouters' (2007).

Posteriors

Our results are in line with most of the literature focusing on the estimation of DSGE models for the U.S. economy with great moderation data. In particular, we find a strong systematic policy reaction to inflation, a mild reaction to the model-consistent output gap, and a slightly stronger one to output growth. Monetary policy is conducted with a fair amount of gradualism. Our evidence points to a fairly large degree of habit formation in consumption, and lends support to the modeling of frictions in capital formation. The posterior means of the Calvo price and wage parameters are comparable with a large number of estimates obtained with macroeconomic U.S. data. Shocks to TFP, Government spending, price and wage mark-ups feature a high degree of correlation, also considering the MA(1) component of these last two shocks. Tables 3 and 4 collect some selected percentiles of our posterior densities.

Variance Decomposition: Full Sample Analysis ...

We appeal to the variance decomposition analysis to gauge the role of trend inflation vs. other shocks conditional on the estimated medium-scale framework à la Smets and Wouters (2007). Table 5 – Panel A collects the figures computed by considering our model with trend inflation vs. an alternative that features a fixed inflation target. Interestingly, the results obtained with our small-scale model (see previous section) are fully confirmed by the analysis with the richer Smets and Wouters' (2007) framework. Shocks to trend inflation are responsible for most of the volatility of inflation and

Table 4. Bayesian Estimates of the Smets and Wouters' (2007) DSGE
Model – Structural Parameters. 1984:I-2008:II U.S. Data.

Param.	Interpretation	Priors	Posterior Means [5h,95th]
ϕ	Capital adj. cost elasticity	$Normal(4, 1.5)$	5.72 [4.10,7.24]
σ_c	Risk aversion	$Normal(1.5, 0.375)$	1.23 [1.07,1.37]
h	Habit formation	$Beta(0.7, 0.1)$	0.73 [0.66,0.80]
ξ_w	Wage stickiness	$Beta(0.5, 0.1)$	0.65 [0.54,0.78]
σ_l	Elast. lab. supply	$Normal(2, 0.75)$	0.85 [0.05,1.65]
ξ_p	Price stickiness	$Beta(0.5, 0.1)$	0.67 [0.61,0.74]
ι_w	Wage indexation	$Beta(0.5, 0.15)$	0.58 [0.37,0.78]
ι_p	Price indexation	$Beta(0.5, 0.15)$	0.16 [0.07,0.27]
ψ	Capacity utiliz. elast.	$Beta(0.5, 0.15)$	0.57 [0.40,0.75]
$\Phi-1$	Fixed c. in prod. (share)	$Normal(0.25, 0.125)$	0.48 [0.37,0.60]
r_π	T. Rule, inflation	$Normal(1.5, 0.25)$	2.09 [1.79,2.41]
ρ	T. Rule, inertia	$Beta(0.75, 0.10)$	0.81 [0.77,0.85]
r_y	T. Rule, output gap	$Normal(0.125, 0.05)$	0.00 [-0.01,0.02]
$r_{\Delta y}$	T. Rule, output growth	$Normal(0.125, 0.05)$	0.20 [0.15,0.24]
π	St. state inflation rate	$Gamma(0.625, 0.10)$	0.61 [0.51,0.70]
$100(\beta^{-1}-1)$	St. state interest rate	$Gamma(0.25, 0.10)$	0.25 [0.09,0.40]
l	St. state hours worked	$Normal(0, 2)$	0.18 [-2.37,2.60]

Notes: Prior densities: Figures indicate the (mean,st.dev.) of each prior distribution. Posterior densities: Figures reported indicate the posterior mean and the [5th,95th] percentile of the estimated densities. Details on the estimation procedure provided in the text.

almost half the volatility of the policy rate. Such shocks are just negligible as for the dynamics of real variables. Again, when employing trend inflation to control for the effects of the (otherwise unmodeled) low-frequency component of the federal funds rate, we record a reduction of the contribution of trend inflation shocks as for the policy rate and inflation. However, such reduction is marginal as for the policy rate (45% explained by trend inflation shocks), and more marked, but far from overturning our main message, as for inflation (47% explained by our inflation target shocks).

Table 5.   Bayesian Estimates of the Smets and Wouters' (2007) DSGE model - Shock Processes. 1984:I-2008:II U.S. Data.

Param.	Interpretation	Priors	Posterior Means [5h,95th]
σ_a	TFP shock, st.dev.	$InvGamma(0.1, 2)$	0.50 [0.46,0.55]
σ_b	Risk-premium shock, st.dev.	$InvGamma(0.1, 2)$	0.24 [0.20,0.28]
σ_g	Gov. spending shock, st.dev.	$InvGamma(0.1, 2)$	0.55 [0.50,0.52]
σ_I	Invest.-specific tech. shock, st.dev.	$InvGamma(0.1, 2)$	0.44 [0.36,0.52]
σ_r	Mon. policy shock, st.dev.	$InvGamma(0.1, 2)$	0.24 [0.22,0.27]
σ_p	Price mark-up shock, st.dev.	$InvGamma(0.1, 2)$	0.14 [0.12,0.16]
σ_w	Wage mark-up shock, st.dev.	$InvGamma(0.1, 2)$	0.27 [0.23,0.31]
σ_*	Trend inflation shock, st. dev.	$InvGamma(0.1, 2)$	0.05 [0.04,0.06]
ρ_a	TFP shock, AR(1) coeff.	$Beta(0.5, 0.2)$	0.96 [0.95,0.98]
ρ_b	Risk-premium shock, AR(1) coeff.	$Beta(0.5, 0.2)$	0.25 [0.12,0.38]
ρ_g	Gov. sp. shock, AR(1) coeff.	$Beta(0.5, 0.2)$	0.95 [0.94,0.97]
ρ_I	Invest.-spec. tech. shock, AR(1) coeff.	$Beta(0.5, 0.2)$	0.69 [0.58,0.78]
ρ_r	Mon. pol. shock, AR(1) coeff.	$Beta(0.5, 0.2)$	0.17 [0.06,0.28]
ρ_p	Price mark-up shock., AR(1) coeff.	$Beta(0.5, 0.2)$	0.92 [0.87,0.98]
ρ_w	Wage mark-up shock, AR(1) coeff.	$Beta(0.5, 0.2)$	0.98 [0.97,0.99]
μ_p	Price mark-up shock, MA(1) coeff.	$Beta(0.5, 0.2)$	0.73 [0.61,0.86]
μ_w	Wage mark-up shock, MA(1) coeff.	$Beta(0.5, 0.2)$	0.85 [0.75,0.95]
ρ_{ga}	Gov.spending-TFP shocks, correlation	$Beta(0.5, 0.2)$	0.51 [0.37,0.65]

Notes: Prior densities: Figures indicate the (mean,st.dev.) of each prior distribution. Posterior densities: Figures reported indicate the posterior mean and the [5th,95th] percentile of the estimated densities. Details on the estimation procedure provided in the text.

When omitting trend inflation shocks (Table 5 – Panel B), other shocks's contribution gets inflated. In particular, the shocks to the price and wage mark-ups turn out to be substantially magnified by the omission of a trend inflation process in the model.

As we learnt with our previous analysis, however, the contribution of trend inflation shocks is likely to be time dependent. Therefore, we move to our rolling-window analysis and estimate the Smets and Wouters (2007) model over different windows.

... and Rolling-Window Investigation

Figs. 7 and 8 depict the evolution of our estimated structural parameters and shocks' volatilities. While some instabilities affecting the former ones may be detected, a clear time-dependence emerges when considering the variances of our structural shocks. All shocks tend to become less volatile when moving from the 1960s and 1970s to the great moderation, with the interesting exception of the innovations affecting the wage mark-up. As before, our monetary policy shocks display a hump-shaped evolution, which makes us hint that such shocks might importantly contribute to explain the evolution of the U.S. inflation and policy rate.

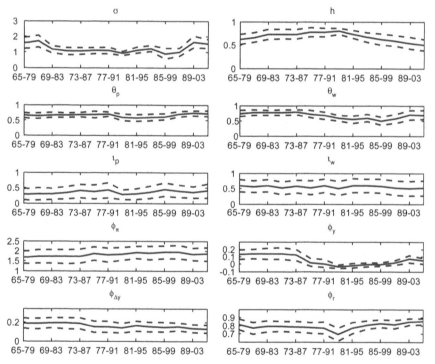

Fig. 7. Evolution of the Structural Parameters of the Smets and Wouters' (2007) DSGE Model.

Note: Definitions of the structural parameters given in Table 1. Solid line: Posterior median. Dotted lines: 5th and 95th posterior percentiles. Evolution of the parameters constructed by employing fourteen rolling windows of 15-year constant length. Windows: [1965:I-1979:IV, 1967:I-1981:IV, ..., 1991:I-2005:IV].

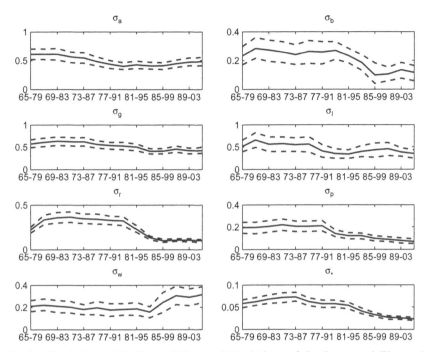

Fig. 8. Evolution of the Shocks' Standard Deviations of the Smets and Wouters' (2007) DSGE Model.

Notes: Definitions of the shocks' standard deviations given in Table 1. Solid line: Posterior median. Dotted lines: 5th and 95th posterior percentiles. Evolution of the shocks' standard deviations constructed by employing fourteen rolling windows of 15-year constant length. Windows: [1965:I-1979:IV, 1967:I-1981:IV, ..., 1991:I-2005:IV].

Fig. 9 shows the evolution of the contribution of ours shocks on the volatilities of our interest. The top panel, which focuses on inflation, is extremely similar to the one in Fig. 6. The contribution of trend inflation shocks is large and time-varying, with an "inverted-U" relationship qualitatively very similar and quantitatively even larger than the one suggested by the small scale model. "Supply" shocks, that is, TFP shocks and shocks to the mark-ups, play a substantial role, and tend to explain the largest share of inflation volatility towards the end of the sample. Again, we observe a fairly constant participation of "demand" shocks (here, Government spending, risk-premium, investment-specific technology shocks) and

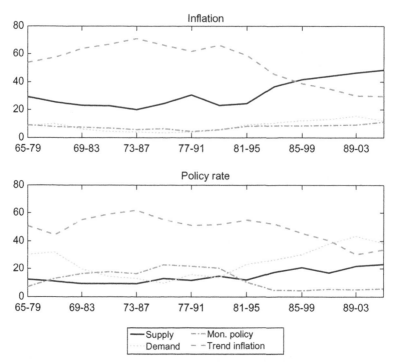

Fig. 9. Rolling-Window Variance Decomposition Implied by the Smets and Wouters (2007) Model.
Notes: Model calibration: Window-specific posterior mode. "Supply" and "Demand" shocks defined as in Smets and Wouters (2007), that is, supply shocks: TFP, price mark-up, and wage mark-up shocks; demand shocks: Investment-specific tech., Government spending, and risk-premium shocks. Version of the model with reaction to the output gap set to zero to ease the computation of the posterior mode (very similar results were obtained by relaxing this constraint).

standard monetary policy innovations, with the former explaining about 8% of the volatility of inflation, and the latter 7%.

Trend inflation shocks are estimated to be substantially relevant also as for the volatility of the policy rate. Again, the bell-shaped evolution of the contribution of such shocks is confirmed also by this medium-scale model, with a participation peaking at 49% as for the window 1979–1993. Differently with respect to the story told by the small-scale model, supply shocks play a role somewhat comparable to monetary policy shocks, with an evolution over time that appears to be complementary to that provided

Table 6. Variance Decomposition Implied by the Smets and Wouters' (2007) DSGE Model. 1965:I-2005:IV U.S. Data.

	Var/shocks	v^a	v^b	v^g	v^l	v^r	v^p	v^w	v^*
Panel A									
Trend	HRS	1.55	1.86	5.25	7.51	2.51	8.87	72.35	0.10
inflation	R	5.66	7.00	2.30	16.00	12.64	3.84	3.71	48.85
shocks	π	2.48	1.19	0.70	3.97	6.36	16.87	11.16	57.27
	γ_{GDP}	14.28	18.75	26.98	20.76	6.40	6.04	6.64	0.15
	γ_{CON}	6.19	56.58	0.45	0.83	11.59	5.21	18.89	0.28
	γ_{INV}	4.89	3.48	0.66	78.92	3.48	5.83	2.66	0.10
	γ_{WAG}	6.64	1.45	0.05	1.98	2.02	26.45	61.33	0.08
Panel B									
No trend	HRS	2.02	2.13	6.68	11.43	2.74	8.39	66.61	
inflation	R	8.60	6.34	3.94	26.78	12.54	6.98	34.82	
shocks	π	4.15	0.52	1.03	4.70	3.66	29.02	56.92	
	γ_{GDP}	16.07	18.40	26.63	22.12	5.35	5.45	5.98	−
	γ_{CON}	6.89	58.32	1.26	1.62	10.66	5.29	15.96	
	γ_{INV}	5.80	2.88	1.15	80.85	2.48	4.63	2.21	
	γ_{WAG}	5.80	0.39	0.08	2.20	0.81	27.08	63.64	

Notes: Figures conditional on the posterior mode values of the model. Details on the estimation procedure provided in the text.

by standard monetary policy innovations. Interestingly, here demand shocks play a larger role than suggested by the small-scale model, with a quantitatively important, time-dependent participation that follows a U-shaped pattern hitting its peak value of 43% in the window 1989–2003.[19]

Wrapping up, estimates conducted with the Smets and Wouters (2007) framework confirm our findings, the most important ones we reiterate here: (i) the contribution of trend inflation shocks to the volatility of the nominal side of the economy is substantial; (ii) such contribution is time-varying; (iii) a description of the post-WWII U.S. economy based on the "Volcker-appointment break," which would call of an analysis contrasting the great inflation phase and the great moderation period, would probably represent just a part of the richness of the evolution of the participation of the trend inflation shocks over time (Table 6).

CONCLUSIONS

This chapter investigated the role of shocks to trend inflation for the post-WWII U.S. economic environment. Two new-Keynesian models of the business cycle, a small-scale AD/AS model à la Woodford (2003) and a medium-scale framework à la Smets and Wouters (2007) were modified to account for the time-varying inflation target possibly pursued by the Federal Reserve during the period 1965–2005. A mapping between the model-consistent, latent trend inflation process and the trend inflation estimate recently proposed by Aruoba and Schorfheide (2011) was imposed in the estimation. Particular attention was posed to the time-dependence of the role of the shocks to trend inflation identified with our estimated frameworks. Such time dependence was assessed by appealing to a rolling-window approach, which enabled us to gauge the variations in the estimated parameters featured by our models.

Our main findings point to a substantial contribution of trend inflation shocks in determining the volatility of variables such as inflation and the policy rate. Such contribution is found to be larger than that assigned to standard monetary policy innovations. The relative importance of trend inflation shocks in highest when observations belonging to the 1980s dominate our investigated subsamples, and less relevant (but still very relevant) during the 1970s and especially the 1990s. In contrast, we find the dynamics of the real side of the U.S. economy to be hardly explained by trend inflation shocks.

While our assumption of an exogenous trend inflation process made it possible to appreciate its role from an empirical standpoint, it is clearly unsatisfactory when turning to using these models for policy purposes. A structural interpretation for the low-frequency component of inflation is clearly needed. Interesting research pointing to the role of that learning processes of the structure of the economy by the Fed may have played in shaping the low frequencies of the U.S. inflation process have been proposed by, among others, Cogley and Sargent (2005), Primiceri (2006), Sargent et al. (2006), and Carboni and Ellison (2009), and Milani (2009). Milani (2007) and Milani and Rajbhandari (2011) have shown that models that feature learning mechanisms turn out to be empirically superior than models endowed with standard rational expectation-formation as for the post-WWII U.S. macroeconomic data. Paving the "learning avenue" is likely to be a particularly exciting research agenda for the years to come.

Another worth-exploring route relates to the distinction between policy surprises and policy "news." On top of policy surprises, that is, unexpected departures from the Taylor rate, policy "news," which are expected policy moves by the Federal Reserve due to communications, announcements, and the like, are potentially powerful shocks in terms of impact on the economic environment, as suggested by some recent empirical investigations (Milani & Treadwell, 2012). Clearly, a distinction between news to the federal funds rate conditional on a fixed-inflation target versus news to the policy rate due to an expected variation in such target can be made.

Finally, our results are obtained via Bayesian estimations conditional on a time-domain approach. In two recent papers, Tkachenko and Qu (2011a, 2011b) study parameter identification, estimation, and inference in medium-scale DSGE models from a frequency-domain perspective. In a recent contribution, Sala (2011) conducts a similar effort. Such approach naturally leads them to focus on the business cycle frequencies of interest for DSGE model-builders. We see the investigation of the role of trend inflation shocks undertaken with the lenses offered by a frequency-domain approach as an intriguing effort for future research.

NOTES

1. See Castelnuovo (2012c) for an attempt to endogenize the Federal Reserve's inflation target on the basis of past inflation realizations.

2. Evidence in favor of trend inflation's variability is provided, among others, by Belaygorod and Dueker (2005), Cogley and Sargent (2005), Kozicki and Tinsley (2005), Ireland (2007), Stock and Watson (2007), Cogley and Sbordone (2008), Leigh (2008), Kozicki and Tinsley (2009), Sbordone, Tambalotti, Rao, and Walsh (2010), Castelnuovo (2010), Coibion and Gorodnichenko (2011a), Coibion and Gorodnichenko (2011b), Aruoba and Schorfheide (2011), Del Negro and Eusepi (2011), Castelnuovo, Greco, and Raggi (2012), Castelnuovo (2012c).

3. Further elaborations by Ascari, Branzoli, and Castelnuovo (2011) unveil an interaction involving trend inflation and wage indexation that turns out to be relevant in assessing policymakers' ability to anchor inflation expectations in the U.S. economic environment.

4. Aruoba and Schorfheide (2011) consider survey measures (1-year- and 10-year-ahead inflation expectations coming from the Survey of Professional Forecasters) and a low-frequency component of GDP deflator inflation extracted with a Band-Pass filter. The common factor extracted by combining such "observables" with a small state-space model is their empirical proxy for trend inflation.

5. Imperfect knowledge of the economic structure and the evolution of the perceived inflation-output volatility trade-off by the Federal Reserve is one of the possible ways to make the trend inflation process endogenous (in this chapter, it is assumed to be an exogenous process). Interesting efforts in this direction have already been undertaken by Cogley and Sargent (2005), Primiceri (2006), Sargent, Williams, and Zha (2006), Carboni and Ellison (2009), and Milani (2009).

6. The sample width is due to our willingness to use the original estimates of trend inflation by Aruoba and Schorfheide (2011).

7. The sources of these estimates read as follows. Kozicki and Tinsley (2005, 2009) and Ireland (2007): Original files provided by the authors. Coibion and Gordnichenko (2011): American Economic Review (website), their paper, zip file under "Additional Materials Download Data Set," "GreenBookForecasts for

AER.xlsx" file, Trend Inflation, Smoothed estimates. Monthly estimates converted to quarterly estimates by selecting the latest available observation within each quarter. Aruoba and Schorfheide (2011): American Economic Review (website), their paper, zip file under "Additional Materials – Download Data Set," "inflation-target.xls" file, "filtered f2" estimates. Castelnuovo et al. (2012): Files available upon request.

8. Note that just part of the authors whose estimates are analyzed in this Section work with GDP deflator inflation. Therefore, the difference between inflation and a given trend inflation estimate represents by no means an attempt to "judge" its "plausibility." Again, the presence of trend inflation is intended to offer a sense of the economic situation in place in different phases of the post-WWII U.S. economic history.

9. Ireland (2007) contrasts different processes of trend inflation, some of which allow for a systematic reaction to structural shocks hitting the economic system. The role of such shocks, however, turns out to be empirically negligible. Panel [1,2] shows the case labelled by Ireland (2007, Fig. 5, p. 1869) as "Federal Reserve's Target as Implied by the Constrained Model with an Exogenous Inflation Target."

10. Evidence in favor of a decline of the role of money growth as a driver of the (Hodrick–Prescott filtered) U.S. real GDP when moving from the 1970s to the great moderation is found by Castelnuovo (2012a).

11. As a matter of fact, the shocks to inflation ε_t^π and output ε_t^x are likely to be convolutions of "deep" innovations. For instance, the "cost-push" shock ε_t^π might very well capture price-mark up shocks, shocks to the possibly time-varying elasticity of substitution among goods, and other disturbances. The same holds as for the "nonpolicy demand shifter" ε_t^x, which does not allow us to discriminate among (say) investment-specific technology shocks, shocks to consumers' preferences, or fiscal shocks, and others. However, this chapter's ultimate goal is to pin down the relative role played by identified shocks such as shocks to trend inflation and monetary policy shocks in shaping the dynamics of the economy. Therefore, the "reduced form" nature of the inflation and output shocks does not prevent us in any manner from performing such an assessment.

12. Further details on the construction of this measure of trend inflation are provided in Aruoba and Schorfheide (2011, pp. 70–71).

13. Aruoba and Schorfheide (2011) employ the sample 1965:I-2005:I. In our rolling-window estimation, we will use windows of fixed-length (details are provided in the following section). Given the selection of our window-size as well as our set of initial observations (one per each window), we work with a slightly extended sample, that is, 1965:I-2005:IV. The last three "observations" of the inflation target we employ in our estimations are obtained by assuming a fixed target during the 2005. Given that such year clearly belongs to the Great Moderation sample, we believe this assumption to be quite plausible.

14. For a prior-free test of indeterminacy in the U.S. based on GMM techniques, see Castelnuovo and Fanelli (2011).

15. This part of the analysis, not documented here for the sake of brevity, is available upon request.

16. As for the 10-year ahead inflation expectations, the data for the period 1979–1991 are from the Livingston Survey and the Blue Chip Economic Indicators. All series on inflation expectations come from the Federal Reserve Bank of Philadelphia.

17. As documented by Aruoba and Schorfheide in their footnote 7 (2011, p. 71), by regressing their estimates of trend inflation on the measure computed via the Band-Pass filter (1-year ahead inflation expectations/10-year ahead inflation expectations), one obtains a coefficient equal to 0.57 (0.22/0.23).
18. According to Kass and Raftery (1995), a Bayes factor between 1 and 3 is "not worth more than a bare mention," between 3 and 20 suggests a "positive" evidence in favor of one of the two models, between 20 and 150 suggests a "strong" evidence against it, and larger than 150 "very strong" evidence.
19. The outcome of our rolling-window exercises are robust to moderate variations of the width of our windows.

ACKNOWLEDGMENTS

We thank Fabio Milani (editor) and an anonymous referee for detailed comments on a previous version of this chapter. Martin Fukač, Tae-Seok Jang, Ivan Jeliazkov, Mark A. Wynne, and participants at the "Advances in Econometrics: DSGE Models in Macroeconomics – Estimation, Evaluation, and New Developments" (Southern Methodist University, Dallas, November 4–6, 2011) provided us with useful feedback. We are also grateful to Olivier Coibion, Peter Ireland, and Sharon Kozicki for kindly providing us with datasets and computer codes to replicate some of the results documented in this paper. All remaining errors are ours.

REFERENCES

Adjemian, S., Bastani, H., Juillard, M., Mihoubi, F., Perendia, G., Ratto, M., & Villemot, S. (2011, April). *Dynare: Reference manual, version 4.* Dynare Working Paper No. 1. Available at http://www.dynare.org/wp-repo/dynarewp001.pdf
An, S., & Schorfheide, F. (2007). Bayesian analysis of DSGE models. *Econometric Reviews, 26,* 113–172.
Aruoba, S. B., & Schorfheide, F. (2011). Sticky prices versus monetary frictions: An estimation of policy trade-offs. *American Economic Journal: Macroeconomics, 3,* 60–90.
Ascari, G., Branzoli, N., & Castelnuovo, E. (2011). *Trend inflation, wage indexation and determinacy in the U.S.* Universities of Pavia, Wisconsin-Madison, and Padova.
Ascari, G., Castelnuovo, E., & Rossi, L. (2011). Calvo vs. Rotemberg in a Trend inflation world: An empirical investigation. *Journal of Economic Dynamics and Control, 35,* 1852–1867.
Belaygorod, A., & Dueker, M. (2005). Discrete monetary policy changes and changing inflation targets in estimated dynamic stochastic general equilibrium models. *Federal Reserve Bank of St. Louis Review, 87*(6), 719–733.
Benati, L., & Surico, P. (2008). Evolving U.S. Monetary policy and the decline of inflation predictability. *Journal of the European Economic Association, 6*(2/3), 634–646.

Benati, L., & Surico, P. (2009). VAR analysis and the great moderation. *American Economic Review*, *99*(4), 1636–1652.

Best, G. (2011). Policy preferences and policymakers. Beliefs: The great inflation, Missouri State University.

Bianchi, F. (2011). Regime switches, agents. Beliefs, and Post-World War II U.S. macro-economic dynamics. *Review of Economic Studies*.

Brooks, S., & Gelman, A. (1998). General methods for monitoring convergence of iterative simulations. *Journal of Computational and Graphical Statistics*, *7*(4), 434–455.

Calvo, G. (1983). Staggered prices in a utility-maximizing framework. *Journal of Monetary Economics*, *12*, 383–398.

Canova, F. (2009). What explains the great moderation in the US? A structural analysis. *Journal of the European Economic Association*, *7*(4), 697–721.

Canova, F., & Ferroni, F. (2012). The dynamics of US inflation: Can monetary policy explain the changes? *Journal of Econometrics*, *167*(1), 47–60.

Canova, F., & Sala, L. (2009). Back to square one: Identification issues in DSGE models. *Journal of Monetary Economics*, *56*(4), 431–449.

Cantore, C., Ferroni, F., & Léon-Ledesma, M. A. (2011). Interpreting the hours-technology time varying relationship. University of Surrey, Banque de France, and University of Kent. Mimeo.

Carboni, G., & Ellison, M. (2009). The great inflation and the greenbook. *Journal of Monetary Economics*, *56*(6), 831–841.

Carlstrom, C. T., Fuerst, T. S., & Paustian, M. (2009). Inflation persistence, monetary policy, and the great moderation. *Journal of Money, Credit and Banking*, *41*(4), 767–786.

Castelnuovo, E., Greco L., & Raggi, D. (forthcoming). Policy rules, regime switches, and trend inflation: An empirical investigation for the U.S. *Macroeconomic Dynamics*.

Castelnuovo, E. (2010). Trend inflation and macroeconomic volatilities in the post-WWI U.S. economy. *North American Journal of Economics and Finance*, *21*(1), 19–33.

Castelnuovo, E. (2012a). Estimating the evolution of money's role in the U.S. Monetary business cycle. *Journal of Money, Credit and Banking*, *44*(1), 23–52.

Castelnuovo, E. (2012b). Policy switch and the great moderation: The role of equilibrium selection. *Macroeconomic Dynamics*, *16*(3), 449–471.

Castelnuovo, E. (2012c). Testing the structural interpretation of the price puzzle with a cost channel model. *Oxford Bulletin of Economics and Statistics*, *74*(3), 425–452.

Castelnuovo, E., & Fanelli, L. (2011). *Monetary policy indeterminacy in the U.S.: Results from a classical test*. University of Bologna, Dip. di Scienze Economiche, Quaderno di Dipartimento Serie Ricerche Num. 8.

Christiano, L., Eichenbaum, M., & Evans, C. (2005). Nominal rigidities and the dynamic Effects of a shock to monetary policy. *Journal of Political Economy*, *113*(1), 1–45.

Clarida, R., Galí, J., & Gertler, M. (2000). Monetary policy rules and macroeconomic stability: Evidence and some theory. *Quarterly Journal of Economics*, *115*, 147–180.

Cogley, T., Primiceri, G. E., & Sargent, T. (2010). Inflation-gap persistence in the U.S.. *American Economic Journal: Macroeconomics*, *2*(1), 43–69.

Cogley, T., & Sargent, T. (2005). The conquest of U.S. inflation: Learning and robustness to model uncertainty. *Review of Economic Dynamics*, *8*, 528–563.

Cogley, T., & Sbordone, A. (2008). Trend inflation, indexation, and inflation persistence in the new Keynesian Phillips curve. *American Economic Review*, *98*(5), 2101–2126.

Coibion, O., & Gorodnichenko, Y. (forthcoming). Why are target interest rate changes so persistent? *American Economic Journal: Macroeconomics.*

Coibion, O., & Gorodnichenko, Y. (2011a). Monetary policy, trend inflation and the great moderation: An alternative interpretation. *American Economic Review, 101,* 341–370.

Del Negro, M., & Eusepi, S. (2011). Fitting observed inflation expectations. *Journal of Economic Dynamics and Control, 35*(12), 2105–2131.

Del Negro, M., Schorfheide, F., Smets, F., & Wouters, R. (2007). On the fit of new-Keynesian models. *Journal of Business and Economic Statistics, 25*(2), 124–162.

Erceg, C., & Levin, A. (2003). Imperfect credibility and inflation persistence. *Journal of Monetary Economics, 50*(4), 915–944.

Fernández-Villaverde, J. (2010). The econometrics of DSGE models. *SERIES: Journal of the Spanish Economic Association, 1,* 3–49.

Fernández-Villaverde, J., Guerrón-Quintana, P., & Rubio-Ramírez, J. F. (2010). *Fortune or virtue: Time-invariant volatilities versus parameter drifting in U.S. Data.* NBER Working Paper No. 15928.

Fernández-Villaverde, J., & Rubio-Ramírez, J. (2007). Estimating macroeconomic models: A likelihood approach. *Review of Economic Studies, 74,* 1059–1087.

Fernández-Villaverde, J., & Rubio-Ramírez, J. (2007). How structural are structural parameters? In D. Acemoglu, K. Rogoff & M. Woodford (Eds.), *NBER Macro-economics Annual* (Vol. 22, 83–137). University of Chicago Press.

Fernández-Villaverde, J., & Rubio-Ramírez, J. F. (2010). *Macroeconomics and volatility: Data, models, and estimation.* Mimeo. University of Pennsylvania and Duke University.

Furher, J. C. (2000). Habit formation in consumption and its implications for monetary-policy models. *American Economic Review, 90*(3), 367–390.

Geweke, J. (1999). Using simulation methods for Bayesian econometric models: Inference, development and communication. *Econometric Reviews, 18,* 1–73.

Giacomini, R., & Rossi, B. (2010). *Model comparisons in unstable environments.* Mimeo. UCL and Duke University.

Haario, H., Saksman, E., & Tamminen, J. (2001). An adaptive metropolis algorithm. *Bernoulli, 7*(2), 223–242.

Inoue, A., Rossi, B., & Jin, L. (2011). *Consistent model selection over rolling windows.* North Carolina State University and Duke University.

Ireland, P. (2004). Technology shocks in a new Keynesian model. *The Review of Economics and Statistics, 86*(4), 923–936.

Ireland, P. (2007). Changes in Federal Reserve's inflation target: Causes and consequences. *Journal of Money, Credit and Banking, 39*(8), 1851–1882.

Justiniano, A., & Primiceri, G. (2008). The time-varying volatility of macroeconomic fluctuations. *American Economic Review, 98*(3), 604–641.

Kass, R., & Raftery, A. (1995). Bayes factors. *Journal of the American Statistical Association, 90,* 773–795.

Kimball, M. (1995). The quantitative analytics of the basic Neomonetarist model. *Journal of Money, Credit and Banking, 27*(4), 1241–1277.

Kozicki, S., & Tinsley, P. (2005). Permanent and transitory policy shocks in an empirical macro model with asymmetric information. *Journal of Economic Dynamics and Control, 29,* 1985–2015.

Kozicki, S., & Tinsley, P. (2009). Perhaps the 1970s FOMC did what it said it did. *Journal of Monetary Economics, 56,* 842–855.

Leigh, D. (2008). Estimating the Federal Reserve's implicit inflation target: A state-space approach. *Journal of Economic Dynamics and Control, 32*, 2013–2030.

Liu, Z., Waggoner, D., & Zha, T. (2011). Sources of macroeconomic fluctuations: A regime-switching DSGE approach. *Quantitative Economics, 2*(2), 251–301.

Milani, F., & Treadwell, J. (forthcoming). The effects of monetary policy "news" and "surprises." *Journal of Money, Credit and Banking*.

Milani, F. (2007). Expectations, learning and macroeconomic persistence. *Journal of Monetary Economics, 54*(7), 2065–2082.

Milani, F. (2009). *Learning and the evolution of the fed's inflation target*. Mimeo. University of California at Irvine.

Milani, F., & Rajbhandari, A. (2011). Expectations formation and monetary DSGE models: Beyond the rational expectations paradigm. Paper presented at the "Advances in Econometrics: DSGE Models in Macroeconomics-Estimation, Evaluation, and New Development" conference, Southern Methodist University, Dallas, November 4–6, 2011.

Primiceri, G. (2006). Why inflation rose and fell: Policymakers, beliefs and U.S. postwar stabilization policy. *Quarterly Journal of Economics, 121*, 867–901.

Sala, L. (2011). *DSGE models in the frequency domain*. Mimeo. Bocconi University and IGIER.

Sargent, T., Williams, N., & Zha, T. (2006). Shocks and government beliefs: The rise and fall of American Inflation. *American Economic Review, 96*(4), 1193–1224.

Sbordone, A. M., Tambalotti, A., Rao, K., & Walsh, K. (2010). Policy analysis using DSGE Models: An Introduction. *Federal Reserve Bank of New York Policy Review, 16*(2), 23–43.

Smets, F., & Wouters, R. (2003). An estimated dynamic stochastic general equilibrium model of the Euro Area. *Journal of the European Economic Association, 1*, 1123–1175.

Smets, F., & Wouters, R. (2007). Shocks and frictions in US business cycle: A Bayesian DSGE approach. *American Economic Review, 97*(3), 586–606.

Stock, J. H., & Watson, M. W. (2007). Why has inflation become harder to forecast? *Journal of Money, Credit and Banking, 39*(1), 3–33.

Tkachenko, D., & Qu, Z. (2011a). Frequency domain analysis of medium scale DSGE models with application to Smets and Wouters (2007), paper presented at the "Advances in Econometrics: DSGE Models in Macroeconomics-Estimation, Evaluation, and New Development" conference, Southern Methodist University, Dallas, November 4–6, 2011.

Tkachenko, D., & Qu, Z. (2011b). *Identification and frequency domain QML estimation of linearized DSGE models. Quantitative Economics, 3*(1), 95–132.

Woodford, M. (2003). *Interest and prices: Foundations of a theory of monetary policy*. Princeton, NJ: Princeton University Press.

APPENDIX A

A.1   Bayesian Estimation

To perform our Bayesian estimations we employed *DYNARE*, a set of algorithms developed by Michel Juillard and collaborators (Adjemian, Bastani, Juillard, Mihoubi, Perendia, Ratto, & Villemot, 2011). *DYNARE* is freely available at the following URL: http://www.dynare.org/.

The simulation of the target distribution is basically based on two steps.

- First, we initialized the variance-covariance matrix of the proposal distribution and employed a standard random-walk Metropolis–Hastings for the first $t \leqslant t_0 = 20,000$ draws. To do so, we computed the posterior mode by the 'csminwel' algorithm developed by Chris Sims. The inverse of the Hessian of the target distribution evaluated at the posterior mode was used to define the variance-covariance matrix C_0 of the proposal distribution. The initial VCV matrix of the forecast errors in the Kalman filter was set to be equal to the unconditional variance of the state variables. We used the steady-state of the model to initialize the state vector in the Kalman filter.
- Second, we implemented the "Adaptive Metropolis" (AM) algorithm developed by Haario, Saksman, and Tamminen (2001) to simulate the target distribution. Harrio et al. (2011) show that their AM algorithm is more efficient than the standard Metropolis–Hastings algorithm. In a nutshell, such algorithm employs the history of the states (draws) so to "tune" the proposal distribution suitably. In particular, the previous draws are employed to regulate the VCV of the proposal density. We then exploited the history of the states sampled up to $t > t_0$ to continuously update the VCV matrix C_t of the proposal distribution. While not being a Markovian process, the AM algorithm is shown to possess the correct ergodic properties. For technicalities, see Harrio et al. (2001).

As for the small-scale three-equation DSGE model, we simulated two chains of 400,000 draws each, and discarded the first 90% as burn-in. To scale the variance-covariance matrix of the chain, we used a factor so to achieve an acceptance rate belonging to the (23%, 40%) range. The stationarity of the chains was assessed via the convergence checks proposed by Brooks and Gelman (1998). The region of acceptable parameter realizations was truncated so to obtain equilibrium uniqueness under rational expectations. When turning to the Smets and Wouters' (2007) model, we employed 100,000 draws of the Metropolis–Hastings to simulate the posterior density of such framework.

A.2   The Smets-Wouters (2007) Model

The Smets andWouters (2007) model is a Dynamic Stochastic General Equilibrium framework extremely popular in academic and institutional circles. The model features a number of shocks and frictions, which offer a quite rich representation of the economic environment and allow for a satisfactory in-sample fit of a set of macroeconomic data (Del Negro et al., 2007). Moreover, Smets and Wouters (2007) show that this model is quite competitive when contrasted with Bayesian-VARs as for forecasting exercises, in particular for the elaboration of medium-term predictions.

The Smets and Wouters (2007) model features sticky nominal price and wage settings that allow for backward-looking inflation indexation; habit formation in consumption; investment adjustment costs; variable capital utilization and fixed costs in production. The stochastic dynamics is driven by seven structural shocks, namely a total factor productivity shock, two shocks affecting the intertemporal margin (risk premium shocks and investment-specific technology shocks), two shocks affecting the intratemporal margin (wage and price mark-up shocks), and two policy shocks (exogenous spending and monetary policy shocks).

In a nutshell, the model features the following main ingredients. Households maximize a nonseparable utility function in consumption and labor over an infinite life horizon. Consumption appears in the utility function in quasi-difference form with respect to a time-varying external habit variable. Labor is differentiated by a union, so there is some monopoly power over wages, which results in explicit wage equation and allows for the introduction of sticky nominal wages à la Calvo (1983). Households rent capital services to firms and decide how much capital to accumulate given the capital adjustment costs they face. The utilization of the capital stock can be adjusted at increasing cost. Firms produce differentiated goods, decide on labor and capital inputs, and set prices conditional on the Calvo model. The Calvo model in both wage and price setting is augmented by the assumption that prices that are not reoptimized are partially indexed to past inflation rates. Prices are therefore set in function of current and expected marginal costs, but are also determined by the past inflation rate. The marginal costs depend on wages and the rental rate of capital. Similarly, wages depend on past and expected future wages and inflation. The model features, in both goods and labor markets, an aggregator that allows for a time-varying demand elasticity depending on the relative price as in Kimball (1995). This is important because the introduction of real rigidity allows us to estimate a more reasonable degree of price and wage stickiness.

The log-linearized version of the DSGE model around its steady-state growth path reads as follows:

$$y_t = c_y c_t + i_y i_t + z_y z_t + \varepsilon_t^g \tag{A.2.1}$$

$$c_t = c_1 c_{t-1} + (1 - c_1)E_t c_{t+1} + c_2(l_t - E_t l_{t+1}) - c_3(r_t - E_t \pi_{t+1} + \varepsilon_t^b) \tag{A.2.2}$$

$$i_t = i_1 i_{t-1} + (1 - i_1)E_t i_{t+1} + i_2 q_t + \varepsilon_t^i \tag{A.2.3}$$

$$q_t = q_1 E_t q_t + 1 + (1 - q_1)E_t r_{t+1}^k - (r_t - E_t \pi_{t+1} + \varepsilon_t^b) \tag{A.2.4}$$

$$y_t = \varphi_p(\alpha k_t^s + (1 - \alpha)l_t + \varepsilon_t^a) \tag{A.2.5}$$

$$k_t^s = k_{t-1} + z_t \tag{A.2.6}$$

$$k_t = z_1 r_t^k \tag{A.2.7}$$

$$k_t = k_1 k_{t-1} + (1 - k_1)i_t + k_2 \varepsilon_t^i \tag{A.2.8}$$

$$\mu_t^p = \alpha(k_t^s - l_t) + \varepsilon_t^a - w_t \tag{A.2.9}$$

$$\pi_t = \pi_1 \pi_{t-1} + \pi_2 E_t \pi_{t+1} - \pi_3 \mu_t^p + \varepsilon_t^p \tag{A.2.10}$$

$$r_t^k = -(k_t - l_t) + w_t \tag{A.2.11}$$

$$\mu_t^w = k_t - (\sigma_l l_t + (1 - \lambda/\gamma)^{-1}(c_t - \lambda/\gamma c_{t-1})) \tag{A.2.12}$$

$$w_t = w_1 w_{t-1} + w_2(E_t w_{t+1} + E_t \pi_{t+1}) - w_2 \pi_t + w_3 \pi_{t-1} - w_4 \mu_t^w + \varepsilon_t^w \tag{A.2.13}$$

$$\begin{aligned} r_t = {} & \rho r_{t-1} + (1 - \rho)(r_\pi + r_y(y_t - y_t^p)) \\ & + r_{\Delta y}[(y_t - y_t^p) - (y_{t-1} - y_{t-1}^p)] + \varepsilon_t^R \end{aligned} \tag{A.2.14}$$

$$\varepsilon_t^x = \rho_x \varepsilon_{t-1}^x + v_t^x, x = (b, i, a, R) \tag{A.2.15}$$

$$\varepsilon_t^g = \rho_g \varepsilon_{t-1}^g + v_t^g + \rho_{ga} v_t^a \tag{A.2.16}$$

$$\varepsilon_t^z = \rho_x \varepsilon_{t-1}^z + v_t^z - \chi_z v_{t-1}^z, z = (p, w) \tag{A.2.17}$$

$$v_t^j \sim N(0, \sigma_j^2) \tag{A.2.18}$$

where:

$$c_y = 1 - g_y - i_y \tag{A.2.19}$$

and g_y and i_y are the steady-state exogenous spending-output ratio and investment-output ratio, with:

$$i_y = (\gamma - 1 + \delta)k_y \tag{A.2.20}$$

where γ is the steady-state growth rate, δ is the depreciation rate of capital, k_y is the steady-state capital-output ratio; $z_y = R_*^y k_y$ is the steady-state rental rate of capital. Notice that Eq. (A.2.16), the one of the stochastic process of the government spending, allows for the productivity shock to affect it. This is so because exogenous spending, in this model, includes net exports, which may be affected by domestic productivity development.

As for the consumption Euler equation (A.2.2):

$$c_1 = \frac{\lambda}{\gamma}\left(1 + \frac{\lambda}{\gamma}\right) \tag{A.2.21}$$

$$c_2 = \frac{(\sigma_c - 1)\dfrac{W_*^h L_*}{C_*}}{\sigma_c\left(1 + \dfrac{\lambda}{\gamma}\right)} \tag{A.2.22}$$

$$c_3 = \frac{1 - \dfrac{\lambda}{\gamma}}{\left(1 + \dfrac{\lambda}{\gamma}\right)\sigma_c} \tag{A.2.23}$$

Current consumption is a function of past and expected future consumption, of expected growth in hours worked, of the ex ante real interest rate, and of a disturbance term ε_t^b. Under the assumption of no habits ($\lambda = 0$) and that of log-utility in consumption ($\sigma_c = 1$), $c_1 = c_2 = 0$, then the standard purely forward looking consumption equation is obtained. The disturbance term ε_t^b represents a wedge between the interest rate controlled by the central bank and the return on assets held by the households. A positive shock to this wedge increases the required return on assets held by the households. At the same time, it increases the cost of capital and it decreases the value of capital and investment (see below). This is basically a shock very similar to a net-worth shock. This disturbance is assumed to follow a standard AR(1) process.

The dynamics of investment is captured by the investment Euler equation (A.2.3), where:

$$i_1 = \frac{1}{1 + \beta\gamma^{1-\sigma_c}} \tag{A.2.24}$$

$$i_2 = \frac{1}{1 + \beta\gamma^{1-\sigma_c}\gamma^2\phi} \tag{A.2.25}$$

where ϕ is the steady-state elasticity of the capital adjustment cost function, and β is the discount factor applied by households. Notice that capital adjustment costs are a function of the change in investment, rather than its level. This choice is made to introduce additional dynamics in the investment equation, which is useful to capture the hump-shaped response of investment to various shocks. In this equation, the stochastic disturbance ε_t^i represents a shock to the investment-specific technology process, and is assumed to follow a standard first-order autoregressive process.

The value-of-capital arbitrage equation (A.2.4) suggests that the current value of the capital stock q_t depends positively on its expected future value (with weight $q_1 = \beta\gamma^{-\sigma_c}(1 - \delta)$), as well as the expected real rental rate on capital $E_t r_{t+1}^k$ and on the ex ante real interest rate and the risk premium disturbance.

Eq. (A.2.5) is the first one of the supply side block. It describes the aggregate production function, which maps output to capital (k_t^s) and labor services (l_t). The parameter α captures the share of capital in production, and the parameter φ_p is one plus the share of fixed costs in production, reflecting the presence of fixed costs in production.

Eq. (A.2.6) suggest that the newly installed capital becomes effective with a one-period delay, hence current capital services in production are a function of capital installed in the previous period k_t and the degree of capital utilization z_t. As stressed by Eq. (A.2.7), the degree of capital utilization is a positive function of the rental rate of capital, $z_t = z_1 r_t^k$, where $z_1 = (1 - \psi)/\psi$ and ψ is a positive function of the elasticity of the capital utilization adjustment cost function normalized to belong to the $[0,1]$ domain.

Eq. (A.2.8) describes the accumulation of installed capital k_t, featuring the convolutions:

$$k_1 = (1 - \delta)/\gamma \tag{A.2.26}$$

$$k_2 = \left[1 - \left(1 - \frac{\delta}{\gamma}\right)\right](1 + \beta\gamma^{1-\sigma_c})\gamma^2\phi \tag{A.2.27}$$

Installed capital is a function not only of the flow of investment but also of the relative efficiency of these investment expenditures as captured by the investment-specific technology disturbance ε_t^i, which follows an autoregressive, stationary process.

Eq. (A.2.9) relates to the monopolistic competitive goods market. Cost minimization by firms implies that the price mark-up μ_t^p, defined as the difference between the average price and the nominal marginal cost or the negative of the real marginal cost, is equal to the difference between the marginal product of labor and the real wage w_t, with the marginal product of labor being itself a positive function of the capital-labor ratio and total factor productivity.

Profit maximization by price-setting firms gives rise to the new-Keynesian Phillips curve, that is, Eq. (A.2.10), with the convolutions being:

$$\pi_1 = \frac{\iota_p}{1 + \beta\gamma^{1-\sigma_c}\iota_p} \tag{A.2.28}$$

$$\pi_2 = \frac{\beta\gamma^{1-\sigma_c}}{1 + \beta\gamma^{1-\sigma_c}\iota_p} \tag{A.2.29}$$

$$\pi_3 = \frac{1}{1 + \beta\gamma^{(1-\sigma_c)}\iota_p} \frac{(1 - \beta\gamma^{1-\sigma_c}\xi_p)(1 - \xi_p)}{\xi_p[(\varphi_p - 1)\varepsilon_p + 1]} \tag{A.2.30}$$

Notice that, in maximizing their profits, firm have to face price stickiness à la Calvo (1983). Firms that cannot reoptimize in a given period index their prices to past inflation as in Smets and Wouters (2003). In equilibrium, inflation π_t depends positively on past and expected future inflation, negatively on the current price mark-up, and positively on a price mark-up disturbance ε_t^p. The price mark-up disturbance is assumed to follow an ARMA(1,1) process. The inclusion of the MA term is to grab high-frequency fluctuations in inflation. When the degree of price indexation $\iota_p = 0$, $\pi_1 = 0$ and Eq. (A.2.10) collapses to the purely forward-looking, standard NKPC. The assumption that all prices are indexed to either lagged inflation or trend inflation ensures the verticality of the Phillips curve in the long run. The speed of adjustment to the desired mark-up depends, among others, on the degree of price stickiness ξ_p, the curvature of the Kimball goods market aggregator ε_p, and the steady-state mark up, which in equilibrium is itself related to the share of fixed costs in production ($\varphi_p - 1$) via a zero-profit condition. In particular, when all prices are flexible ($\xi_p = 0$) and the price mark-up shock is zero at all times, Eq. (A.2.10) reduces to the familiar condition that the price mark-up is constant, or equivalently that there are no fluctuations in the wedge between the marginal product of labor and the real wage. Cost minimization by firms also implies that the rental rate of capital is negatively related to the capital-labor ratio and positively to the real wage (both with unitary elasticity) (see Eq. (A.2.11)).

Similarly, in the monopolistically competitive labor market, the wage mark-up will be equal to the difference between the real wage and the marginal rate of substitution between working and consuming, an equivalence captured by Eq. (A.2.12), where σ is the elasticity of labor supply with respect to the real wage and λ is the habit parameter in consumption. Eq. (A.2.13) shows that real wages adjust only gradually to the desired wage mark-up due to nominal wage stickiness and partial indexation, the convolutions related to this equation being:

$$w_1 = \frac{1}{1 + \beta \gamma^{1-\sigma_c}} \tag{A.2.31}$$

$$w_2 = \frac{1 + \beta \gamma^{1-\sigma_c} l_w}{1 + \beta \gamma^{1-\sigma_c}} \tag{A.2.32}$$

$$w_3 = \frac{l_w}{1 + \beta \gamma^{1-\sigma_c}} \tag{A.2.33}$$

$$w_4 = \frac{l_w}{1 + \beta \gamma^{1-\sigma_c}} \frac{(1 - \beta \gamma^{(1-\sigma_c)} \xi_w)(1 - \xi_w)}{\xi_w[(\varphi_w - 1)\varepsilon_w + 1]} \tag{A.2.34}$$

Notice that if wages are perfectly flexible ($\xi_w = 0$), the real wage is a constant mark-up over the marginal rate os substitution between consumption and leisure. When wage indexation is zero ($l_w = 0$), real wages do not depend on lagged inflation. Notice that, symmetrically with respect to the pricing scheme analyzed earlier, also the wage-mark up disturbance follows an ARMA(1,1) process.

The model is closed by Eq. (A.2.14), which is a flexible Taylor rule postulating a systematic reaction by policymakers to current values of inflation, the output gap, and output growth. In particular, one of the objects policymakers react to is the output gap, defined as a difference between actual and potential output (in logs). Consistently with the DSGE model, potential output is defined as the level of output that would prevail under flexible prices and wages in the absence of the two mark-up shocks. Then, policymakers engineer movements in the short-run policy rate r_t, movements which happen gradually given the presence of interest rate smoothing ρ. Stochastic departures from the Taylor rate, that is, the rate that would realize in absence of any policy rate shocks, are triggered by a stochastic AR(1) process.

Finally, Eqs. (A.2.15)–(A.2.18) define the stochastic processes of the model, which features, as already pointed out, seven shocks (total factor productivity, investment specific technology, risk premium, exogenous spending, price mark-up, wage mark-up, and monetary policy).

Notice that the model features a deterministic growth rate driven by labor-augmenting technological progress, so that the data do not need to be detrended before estimation.

EXPECTATION FORMATION AND MONETARY DSGE MODELS: BEYOND THE RATIONAL EXPECTATIONS PARADIGM

Fabio Milani and Ashish Rajbhandari

ABSTRACT

Empirical work in macroeconomics almost universally relies on the hypothesis of rational expectations (RE).

This chapter departs from the literature by considering a variety of alternative expectations formation models. We study the econometric properties of a popular New Keynesian monetary DSGE model under different expectational assumptions: the benchmark case of RE, RE extended to allow for "news" about future shocks, near-RE and learning, and observed subjective expectations from surveys.

The results show that the econometric evaluation of the model is extremely sensitive to how expectations are modeled. The posterior distributions for the structural parameters significantly shift when the assumption of RE is modified. Estimates of the structural disturbances under different expectation processes are often dissimilar.

The modeling of expectations has important effects on the ability of the model to fit macroeconomic time series. The model achieves

DSGE Models in Macroeconomics: Estimation, Evaluation, and New Developments
Advances in Econometrics, Volume 28, 253–288
Copyright © 2012 by Emerald Group Publishing Limited
ISSN: 0731-9053/doi:10.1108/S0731-9053(2012)0000028009

its worse fit under RE. The introduction of news improves fit. The best-fitting specifications, however, are those that assume learning. Expectations also have large effects on forecasting. Survey expectations, news, and learning all work to improve the model's one-step-ahead forecasting accuracy. RE, however, dominate over longer horizons, such as one-year ahead or beyond.

Keywords: Expectation formation; RE; news shocks; adaptive learning; survey expectations; econometric evaluation of DSGE models

JEL classification: C52; D84; E32; E37; E50

INTRODUCTION

Expectations are central to most economic decisions by households, firms, and policymakers. Also at the aggregate level, the state of expectations represents a major influence on macroeconomic outcomes.

A building block of macroeconomic theory is the assumption that all expectations in the economy are formed according to the Rational Expectations (RE) Hypothesis. Empirical work in macroeconomics is almost universally conducted under the same hypothesis. As a result, the existing evidence on the properties of microfounded models, on the values of "deep" parameters, as well as most conclusions on the reaction of the economy to different shocks, on the transmission of policy changes, and so forth, critically hinge on the validity of RE as a reasonable approximation of how aggregate expectations are formed in practice.

Despite its prevalence in the profession, some economists are critical toward the RE hypothesis because it endows economic agents with an extreme knowledge and capacity to process information. An alternative approach in the literature, therefore, relaxes RE by assuming that agents have the same limited knowledge that a researcher estimating the model would have in real time. Agents can only observe data up to the period they live in and they use those observations to form beliefs and recursively learn about economic relationships.

Several papers have studied asymptotic convergence of systems with learning to the RE equilibrium (e.g., see Evans & Honkapohja, 2013, for an overview). Milani (2007, 2011) shows that learning dynamics during the transition period, instead, matters for the business cycle behavior of macroeconomic variables.

The main scope of this chapter is to provide a comprehensive assessment of how the modeling of expectations affects the properties and empirical performance of DSGE models used for monetary policy and business cycle analysis. Our setting is a baseline New Keynesian model, which has been extensively used in the monetary economics literature to study the interaction of output, inflation, and short-term interest rates.

In our analysis, we assume four different main modeling frameworks for expectations:

(1) Rational Expectations (benchmark).
(2) Rational Expectations, but allowing for "news" shocks.
(3) Near-Rational Expectations with Adaptive Learning (constant gain).
(4) Observed Survey Expectations.

Assumption (1) is the typical assumption in the literature. Agents know the structure of the model, the model parameters, and the distributions of the shocks. The source of uncertainty for agents is given by random unexpected shocks to aggregate demand, supply, and monetary policy decisions. Assumption (2) follows a recent growing strand of literature that stresses the role of "news" as driving forces of business cycles. Economic agents still have RE. But they receive news about future structural shocks. Shocks, therefore, have both an unanticipated component (as under the conventional case) and an anticipated component. Recent papers by Beaudry and Portier (2006), Jaimovich and Rebelo (2009), and Schmitt-Grohé and Uribe (2008) attribute to news about future technology shocks the bulk of economic fluctuations, while Milani and Treadwell (2012) single out a nonnegligible role for private-sector anticipations about future monetary policy decisions. News can represent either communications by policymakers or other authorities or, simply, beliefs by the private sector about future shocks, which may or may not materialize afterwards. Assumption (3) relaxes the RE assumption. Yet, the deviation is intended to be small: expectations are formed in a "near"-rational fashion. Economic agents use a model to form expectations that maintains the same structural form as the model solution under RE. But agents lack knowledge about the model coefficients (e.g., they do not know technology parameters as the Calvo price stickiness coefficient or parameters related to other consumers' preferences). They obtain estimates of the reduced-form coefficients by using available historical data and learning about them over time. The assumption that expectations are formed near-rationally as the outcome of a learning process has been studied extensively in recent decades in a variety of settings (e.g., Evans & Honkapohja, 2001, 2013). Finally, assumption (4) chooses to exploit available data on observed, subjective, expectations from surveys (we use here expectations data from the Survey of Professional Forecasters). Those expectations are assumed to be formed from a learning model similar to the one used in (3). Economic agents, however, can deviate from the point forecasts implied by their learning model: they may be overly optimistic – by forecasting, for example, a higher future output than implied by their learning model – or overly pessimistic. These waves of over-optimism and over-pessimism are defined as "expectation shocks" in the model (a similar interpretation is offered in Milani, 2011).

We study the implications of the different modeling assumptions regarding the formation of expectations on the empirical performance of the DSGE model. In particular, we investigate the impact the various expectation formation mechanisms have on:

- the posterior estimates for structural parameters;
- the estimation and characteristics of exogenous structural shocks;
- the in-sample fit of the model;
- the out-of-sample forecasting performance.

The main interest of this chapter does not really lie in running a horse-race among the competing models of expectations formation and picking a winner: the chapter, in fact, shows that the specifications that produce the best in-sample fit are not necessarily those that outperform the others in forecasting, and the models that do well in forecasting the short-run are different from those outperforming in the long-run. The main objective of this chapter, instead, lies mostly in gauging to what extent empirical conclusions and properties of even a simple benchmark economic model, such as the New Keynesian model, may be sensitive to assumptions about the formation of expectations. We believe that showing the uncertainty surrounding the formation of expectations and its effects on the empirical results is of interest on its own. We can speculate that the modeling of expectations will have even larger effects when one moves to larger set-ups, such as medium-scale models à la Smets and Wouters (2007). It is common in the literature to almost exclusively consider RE as the assumption of choice, without testing whether conclusions are robust to deviations from such hypothesis. Our scope is to show that uncertainty concerning the expectation formation mechanism should be taken seriously, since its impact on several conclusions may be substantial.

The empirical results reveal, in fact, that the modeling of expectations has large implications on the econometric properties of the model. The posterior estimates for the structural preference, technology, and policy parameters are quite sensitive to the specific way expectations are modeled. The properties of exogenous shocks also vary across specifications. For example, given the difficulty of models RE to endogenously generate persistence, the estimation points toward exogenous shocks that need to evolve as AR processes with autoregressive coefficients close to one. Alternative expectation formation mechanisms may solve in part the persistence problem. The serial correlation that is required to match the persistence of observed macroeconomic variables is smaller in the model with news, and even smaller when RE are replaced by either learning or survey expectations. The estimated structural shocks across model specifications display only limited correlation among each others.

The introduction of learning and survey expectations can lead to improvements in the model's in-sample ability to fit macroeconomic data. The conventional specification with RE ranks last in terms of model fit, judging by the models' marginal likelihoods.

The evidence regarding out-of-sample forecasting performance is more mixed. The results differ depending on the forecast horizon. For one-quarter-ahead forecasts, survey expectations dominate the alternatives, whereas RE perform less well. For longer-term forecasts, however, the rankings largely reverse: the model with RE easily outperforms the alternatives for horizons one and two-year ahead, while deviations from RE given by learning and survey measures significantly worsen the forecasting performance.

A BENCHMARK MONETARY DSGE MODEL

This section outlines the derivation of the model equations for a typical small-scale monetary DSGE model. The derivation is now standard in the New Keynesian literature (e.g., Woodford, 2003).

We present the version of the model with the more conventional and accepted microfoundations, i.e., one which is not modified to include the so-called "mechanical" sources of persistence (e.g., Milani, 2006) as indexation to past inflation by monopolistically competitive price setters and habit formation in consumers' preferences. The assumption of indexation has been repeatedly shown to be inconsistent with the microeconomic evidence on price setting (e.g., Nakamura & Steinsson, 2008). The evidence regarding habit formation is less clear-cut, but it seems hard to find supportive evidence using households' consumption data (e.g., Dynan, 2000).

Households

Each household maximizes the following discounted sum of future expected utility functions

$$\max_{C_t,L_t,B_t} E_0 \sum_{t=0}^{\infty} \beta^t \left[e^{\tilde{g}_t} \frac{C_t^{1-\sigma^{-1}}}{1-\sigma^{-1}} - \frac{L_t^{1+\chi}}{1+\chi} \right] \tag{1}$$

subject to the period budget constraint

$$C_t + \frac{B_t}{P_t} = W_t L_t + \frac{(1+R_{t-1})B_{t-1}}{P_t} + \frac{D_t}{P_t} - T_t \tag{2}$$

Each household derives utility from consumption C_t and disutility from hours of labor supplied L_t. The coefficient β denotes the discount factor, while σ and χ denote the elasticities of intertemporal substitution and the inverse of the elasticity of labor supply. The term $e^{\tilde{g}_t}$ denotes an aggregate taste shock. In the budget constraint Eq. (2), B_t denotes nominal bond holdings, P_t denotes the aggregate price level, W_t the real wage, R_t the nominal interest rate, D_t dividend distributions, and T_t net transfers or taxes.

The first-order conditions imply

$$e^{\tilde{g}_t} C_t^{-\frac{1}{\sigma}} = \lambda_t \tag{3}$$

$$\lambda_t = \beta(1+R_t)E_t\left[\lambda_{t+1}\left(P_t/P_{t+1}\right)\right] \tag{4}$$

$$L_t^{\chi} = \lambda_t W_t \tag{5}$$

From Eqs. (3) and (4), we can obtain the following Euler equation (after loglinearization around a zero-inflation steady state)

$$c_t = E_t c_{t+1} - \sigma(i_t - E_t \pi_{t+1} - \tilde{\rho} - E_t \Delta \tilde{g}_{t+1}) \tag{6}$$

where $\tilde{\rho} = -\log \beta$ is the discount rate, c_t now denotes consumption in log deviations from the steady state, i_t denotes the short-term nominal interest rate, π_t denotes the inflation rate, and $\tilde{g}_t = \log(e^{\tilde{g}_t})$.

It is possible to rewrite the Euler equation in terms of the output gap, which is the relevant variable for monetary policy, by using the resource constraint $c_t = y_t$ and the output gap definition $x_t = y_t - y_t^*$. We obtain:

$$x_t = E_t x_{t+1} - \sigma(i_t - E_t \pi_{t+1}) + g_t \tag{7}$$

where the redefined demand shock g_t includes previous preference shocks $\tilde{g}_t$ and potential output terms y_t^*.

Firms

Firms are assumed to operate under monopolistic competition. Prices are sticky à la Calvo: each firm re-optimizes its price in every period with probability $(1 - \alpha)$ and keep its price fixed to the previously set price with probability α.

Each firm maximizes the expected discounted sum of future profits to choose an optimal price p_t^*

$$\max_{p_t^*} E_t \left\{ \sum_{\tau=0}^{\infty} (\alpha\beta)^{\tau} \frac{\lambda_{t+\tau}}{\lambda_t} \left[p_t^* \left(\frac{p_t^*}{P_{t+\tau}} \right)^{-\theta} Y_{t+\tau} - W_{t+\tau} \left(\left(\frac{p_t^*}{P_{t+\tau}} \right)^{-\theta} \frac{Y_{t+\tau}}{A_{t+\tau}} \right)^{\frac{1}{\eta}} \right] \right\} \tag{8}$$

where we have used the expressions for the product's demand curve $y_t^i = (p_t^i/P_{t+\tau})^{-\theta} Y_{t+\tau}$ and the production function $y_t^i = A_t(L_t^i)^{\eta}$, and where P_t denotes the aggregate price level, A_t denotes aggregate technology, θ indicates the elasticity of substitution among differentiated products, and η accounts for potentially diminishing returns to scale in the production function. Log-linearization of the problem's first-order condition, along with several manipulations, leads to the familiar New Keynesian Phillips curve:

$$\pi_t = \beta E_t \pi_{t+1} + \kappa x_t + \mu_t \tag{9}$$

where $\kappa \equiv ((1 - \alpha)(1 - \alpha\beta)(\omega + \sigma^{-1}))/\alpha$, and μ_t denotes a cost-push supply shock. The cost-push shock is often simply appended to the model in the literature (as done here), but it can also be derived endogenously by assuming a time-varying elasticity of substitution among differentiated goods θ_t, instead.

Government and Monetary Policy

Government is assumed to have access to lump-sum taxation and Ricardian equivalence holds. In this environment, the details of fiscal policy do not influence the rest of the model.

The central bank is assumed independent from government and it sets the value of a short-term interest rate, which represents its policy instrument. Monetary policy decisions are assumed to be well approximated empirically by a Taylor rule, which is described in the next section.

Monetary DSGE Model

The aggregate economy is, therefore, summarized by the following prototypical New Keynesian model, which characterizes the joint dynamics of the output gap, inflation, and the interest rate:

$$x_t = \mathbb{E}_t x_{t+1} - \sigma(i_t - \mathbb{E}_t \pi_{t+1}) + g_t \tag{10}$$

$$\pi_t = \beta \mathbb{E}_t \pi_{t+1} + \kappa x_t + \mu_t \tag{11}$$

$$i_t = \rho i_{t-1} + (1 - \rho)\left[\chi_\pi \pi_t + \chi_x x_t + \chi_{\Delta\pi}\Delta\pi_t + \chi_{\Delta x}\Delta x_t\right] + v_t \tag{12}$$

Eq. (10) is the loglinearized consumer's Euler equation. The output gap x_t is a function of the expected one-period-ahead output gap $\mathbb{E}_t x_{t+1}$, of the ex ante real interest rate $(i_t - \mathbb{E}_t \pi_{t+1})$, and of the demand disturbance g_t, which accounts for exogenous shift in consumers' preferences. The coefficient σ denotes the elasticity of intertemporal substitution.

Eq. (11) is the New Keynesian Phillips curve. Current inflation is determined by expectations about future inflation $\mathbb{E}_t \pi_{t+1}$, by the current output gap x_t, and by the supply cost-push shock μ_t. The coefficient β denotes the discount factor, while κ is a composite coefficient, which moves closer to zero the higher the Calvo coefficient, and, therefore, the higher the degree of price stickiness in the economy.

Eq. (12) is a Taylor rule, which allows for inertia in the policy instrument. The monetary policymaker sets the policy instrument i_t in reaction to movements in current inflation and current output gap with coefficients χ_π and χ_x; as in Smets and Wouters (2003, 2007), changes in inflation and the output gap from $t - 1$ to t also enter the central bank's reaction function. The policy rate is adjusted only partially in every period toward its desired level; the coefficient ρ accounts for the degree of partial adjustment. Deviations from systematic monetary policy are captured by the term v_t, which denotes the monetary policy shock.

All disturbances g_t, μ_t, and v_t are assumed to follow AR(1) processes with AR coefficients ρ_g, ρ_μ, and ρ_v.

To make clear that we focus on alternative mechanisms of expectation formation, we replace E_t in the loglinearized equations with the generic operator $\mathbb{E}_t$, which hence defines the expectation terms in the model. Those can either correspond to the mathematical expectation operator E_t, which stands for RE, or they can instead denote subjective, nonnecessarily RE. The next section will present various alternative ways of modeling expectations.

THE FORMATION OF EXPECTATIONS

Expectations play a key role in the model. Households' consumption-saving and firms' price-setting decisions depend on expectations about future macroeconomic variables. While macroeconomic research typically assumes that such expectations are formed according to the RE hypothesis, here we evaluate the model under a variety of alternative expectation formation processes.

The Benchmark: Rational Expectations

The vast majority of DSGE models that are used to analyze the interaction between the dynamics of macroeconomic variables and monetary policy decisions use the RE hypothesis. Economic agents are assumed to form expectations that correspond to the mathematical expectation conditional on the correct model of the economy and on knowing the values of all model parameters, the distribution of the shocks, and so forth. The source of randomness for agents remains the realization of future exogenous disturbances.

Under RE, the model can be represented in state-space form as

$$\Gamma_0 \xi_t = \Gamma_1 \xi_{t-1} + \Psi w_t + \Pi \zeta_t \tag{13}$$

where $\xi_t = [x_t, \pi_t, i_t, E_t x_{t+1}, E_t \pi_{t+1}, g_t, \mu_t, v_t]'$, $w_t = [\varepsilon_t^g, \varepsilon_t^\mu, \varepsilon_t^v]'$, $\zeta_t = [\zeta_t^x, \zeta_t^\pi]'$, with $\zeta_t^x = x_t - E_{t-1} x_t$ and $\zeta_t^\pi = \pi_t - E_{t-1} \pi_t$ denoting the expectational errors.

The expectational errors are uniquely determined as a function of the structural innovations (assuming that the equilibrium exists and is unique). A major advantage of RE consists of removing any free parameter to characterize the formation of expectations. The cost of this approach, however, is that if expectations are not exactly formed in this way, the RE hypothesis introduces a potentially sizeable misspecification, which would affect conclusions about the dynamics of macroeconomic variables, as output and inflation, the effects of policy, and the drivers of business cycle fluctuations.

The model Eq. (13) can be solved as in Sims (2000) to find the solution

$$\xi_t = F\xi_{t-1} + Gw_t \tag{14}$$

which can be joined to the measurement equation $Obs_t = H\xi_t$, linking observables to the corresponding variables in the model (through the selection matrix H), to form a linear Gaussian state-space system, which can be estimated using classical or Bayesian likelihood-based methods.

Tweaking RE: Rational Expectations with News

A recent literature has emphasized the role of news, particularly regarding future technology shocks, as potential driving forces that can give rise to expectation-driven business cycles (e.g., Beaudry & Portier, 2006).

In this environment, we maintain the assumption of RE, but we extend it to include both anticipated ("news") and unanticipated components in the shocks. The disturbances g_t, μ_t, and v_t now evolve as:

$$g_t = \rho_g g_{t-1} + \varepsilon_t^g + \eta_{t-h}^{g,h} \tag{15}$$

$$\mu_t = \rho_\mu \mu_{t-1} + \varepsilon_t^\mu + \eta_{t-h}^{\mu,h} \tag{16}$$

$$v_t = \rho_v v_{t-1} + \varepsilon_t^v + \eta_{t-h}^{v,h} \tag{17}$$

where $\eta_{t-h}^{j,h}$ denotes news that becomes known in $t - h$ about shocks that will materialize h periods ahead.

A news component in the disturbances can be added in the state-space representation as follows[1] (we assume here news at horizon $h = 4$, and show only the modification due to the demand shock g_t, to save space):

$$
\begin{bmatrix} g_t \\ \eta_t^{g,4} \\ \eta_{t-1}^{g,4} \\ \eta_{t-2}^{g,4} \\ \eta_{t-3}^{g,4} \end{bmatrix}
=
\begin{bmatrix} \rho_g & 0 & 0 & 0 & 1 \\ 0 & 0 & 0 & 0 & 0 \\ 0 & 1 & 0 & 0 & 0 \\ 0 & 0 & 1 & 0 & 0 \\ 0 & 0 & 0 & 1 & 0 \end{bmatrix}
\begin{bmatrix} g_{t-1} \\ \eta_{t-1}^{g,4} \\ \eta_{t-2}^{g,4} \\ \eta_{t-3}^{g,4} \\ \eta_{t-4}^{g,4} \end{bmatrix}
+
\begin{bmatrix} \sigma_t^g & 0 \\ 0 & \sigma_t^{\eta_{g,4}} \\ 0 & 0 \\ 0 & 0 \\ 0 & 0 \end{bmatrix}
\begin{bmatrix} \varepsilon_t^g \\ \tilde{\eta}_t^{g,4} \end{bmatrix}
\tag{18}
$$

where $\tilde{\eta}_t^{g,4}$ simply redefines the news shock.

In the estimation, news shocks are identified through their impact on future expectations regarding structural disturbances, which will, in turn, affect agents' economic decisions. For example, assuming again, for simplicity, a news horizon $h = 4$, we would have

$$g_t = \rho_g g_{t-1} + \varepsilon_t^g + \eta_{t-4}^{g,4} \tag{19}$$

$$g_{t+1} = \rho_g \left(\rho_g g_{t-1} + \varepsilon_t^g + \eta_{t-4}^{g,4} \right) + \varepsilon_{t+1}^g + \eta_{t-3}^{g,4} \tag{20}$$

$$E_t g_{t+1} = \rho_g g_t + \eta_{t-3}^{g,4} = \rho_g^2 g_{t-1} + \rho_g \eta_{t-4}^{g,4} + \eta_{t-3}^{g,4} \tag{21}$$

$$E_t g_{t+2} = \rho_g^2 g_t + \eta_{t-2}^{g,4} = \rho_g^3 g_{t-1} + \rho_g^2 \eta_{t-4}^{g,4} + \rho_g \eta_{t-3}^{g,4} + \eta_{t-2}^{g,4} \tag{22}$$

$$E_t g_{t+3} = \rho_g^3 g_t + \eta_{t-1}^{g,4} = \rho_g^4 g_{t-1} + \rho_g^3 \eta_{t-4}^{g,4} + \rho_g^2 \eta_{t-3}^{g,4} + \rho_g \eta_{t-2}^{g,4} + \eta_{t-1}^{g,4} \tag{23}$$

$$E_t g_{t+4} = \rho_g^4 g_t + \eta_t^{g,4} = \rho_g^5 g_{t-1} + \rho_g^4 \eta_{t-4}^{g,4} + \rho_g^3 \eta_{t-3}^{g,4} + \rho_g^2 \eta_{t-2}^{g,4}$$
$$+ \rho_g \eta_{t-1}^{g,4} + \eta_t^{g,4} \tag{24}$$

$$E_t g_{t+5} = \rho_g^5 g_t = \rho_g^6 g_{t-1} + \rho_g^5 \eta_{t-4}^{g,4} + \rho_g^4 \eta_{t-3}^{g,4} + \rho_g^3 \eta_{t-2}^{g,4} + \rho_g^2 \eta_{t-1}^{g,4} + \rho_g \eta_t^{g,4} \tag{25}$$

etc.

which show how expectations at different horizons are affected by combinations of current and past news.

The estimation procedure, therefore, treats both the news and the unanticipated components in the shocks as unobserved, and, through the Kalman filter, it provides its best estimates of how they evolve over the sample.

An important decision in the estimation of model with news is the choice of the news horizon. Milani and Treadwell (2012) present a comprehensive analysis of the model fit under a variety of horizons. Here, we estimate the model under horizons equal to one quarter, $h = 1$, and to four quarters, $h = 4$. We have also estimated the model with horizon $h = 8$, with similar results. Longer horizons quickly become computationally intractable, given that news substantially expands the state space.

The addition of news changes the information structure in the model. Agents still form RE, but their information set is now expanded to include news and the stochastic processes of the shocks also change to include both expected and unexpected components. Hence, a comparison between the two models may not be entirely obvious. In the empirical section, we ask, however, whether these modifications are enough to change the estimates of structural parameters in the model and other model properties.

Beyond RE: Learning

The assumption of RE endows agents with a vast amount of knowledge about their economic environment. A number of papers relax the assumption of RE to assume, instead, adaptive learning by economic agents (e.g., Evans & Honkapohja, 2001). This literature still considers a relatively small deviation from RE. Agents use a model that has the same structural form as the solution under RE. But they are assumed to lack knowledge about some of the model coefficients (e.g., it can be assumed that agents do not know the value of the Calvo parameter). Hence, they do not know the values of the reduced-form coefficients and they try to learn them over time using historical time series.

Under learning, we assume that agents estimate the following Perceived Law of Motion (PLM)

$$\begin{bmatrix} x_t \\ \pi_t \\ i_t \end{bmatrix} = a_t + b_t \begin{bmatrix} x_{t-1} \\ \pi_{t-1} \\ i_{t-1} \end{bmatrix} + \varepsilon_t \tag{26}$$

The PLM corresponds to a VAR(1) estimated on the model's endogenous variables. The VAR has the same form as the minimum state variable solution of the system under RE, with the assumption, which we believe empirically realistic, that agents are unable to observe the exogenous disturbances. The coefficients in a_t and b_t are unknown to economic agents. The intercept terms in a_t have all values equal to zero under RE (since variables enter Eqs. (13)–(14) demeaned); this information, however, is not known to agents, who also need to learn about the values of the intercepts from historical data. Learning about a_t can be interpreted as learning about the steady states or about the trends of the variables. Given that the model that agents use remains very close to RE, this approach is usually defined as *near*-rational.

The learning approach implies that economic agents do not have better information than econometricians. Under RE, econometricians do not have knowledge about the model coefficients and about the realizations of innovations, while agents in the model have full knowledge. Under learning, instead, agents in the model are assumed to have a similar degree of knowledge as the econometrician estimating the model. Agents learn about coefficients in a_t and b_t using the available historical data up to each point t. They update their beliefs according to constant-gain learning as

$$\hat{\varphi}_t = \hat{\varphi}_{t-1} + \bar{g}R_t^{-1}\mathbf{X}_t(\mathbf{Y}_t - \hat{\varphi}_{t-1}'\mathbf{X}_t)' \tag{27}$$

$$R_t = R_{t-1} + \bar{g}(\mathbf{X}_t\mathbf{X}_t' - R_{t-1}) \tag{28}$$

where $\mathbf{Y}_t \equiv \{x_t, \pi_t, i_t\}'$, $\mathbf{X}_t' \equiv \{1, \mathbf{Y}_{t-1}'\}$, and $\hat{\varphi}_t' = (a_t, b_t)$. Eq. (27) describes the updating of beliefs regarding reduced-form coefficients, while Eq. (28) describes the updating of the associated precision matrix R_t. Agents' beliefs are, therefore, equal to their values in the previous period, plus an update in the direction of the most recent forecast error.

The constant-gain coefficient $\bar{g}$, which influences the extent to which agents react to new information in every period, is estimated along with the other structural parameters in the system. By varying one parameter, the constant gain, it is possible to approximate very heterogeneous learning processes.

Expectations are formed from the PLM (26), using the most recent beliefs, as obtained from Eq. (27) and Eq. (28):

$$\hat{E}_{t-1}\begin{pmatrix} x_{t+1} \\ \pi_{t+1} \\ i_{t+1} \end{pmatrix} = (I + b_{t-1})a_{t-1} + b_{t-1}^2 \begin{pmatrix} x_{t-1} \\ \pi_{t-1} \\ i_{t-1} \end{pmatrix} \tag{29}$$

To break the simultaneity between the formation of expectations and the reaction of the economy (i.e., with expectations being a function of time-t variables, but also time-t variables being a function of expectations formed at time t), it is typical in the adaptive learning literature to assume that agents, when forming expectations in t about variables in $t + 1$, can observe the values of the endogenous variables only up to $t - 1$. Therefore, we denote expectations formed under learning as $\hat{E}_{t-1}$. The timing, therefore, is as follows. Economic agents, at time t, run regressions from their PLM of variables in $t - 1$ on their lagged values in $t - 2$. They use the resulting beliefs and the variables they observe up to $t - 1$ to form expectations about variables in $t + 1$.

Expectations formed as in Eq. (29) can be substituted back into the original model Eqs. (10)–(12): the resulting system is referred to as the Actual Law of Motion (ALM) of the economy. The ALM can be written in state-space form as

$$\xi_t = A_t + F_t\xi_{t-1} + Gw_t \tag{30}$$

where the parameter vector A_t and the parameter matrix F_t are now time-varying due to agents' learning, and which can again be linked to the measurement equation $Obs_t = H\xi_t$ to evaluate the likelihood of the system.

Beyond RE: Observed Survey Expectations

A further departure from RE consists on exploiting observed expectations from surveys for $\mathbb{E}_t$ as variables to match in the estimation. The same strategy has been used in Milani (2011). The observed expectations are assumed to be, on average, the outcomes of a near-rational learning model. In every period, however, agents are allowed to form expectations that depart from the point forecasts implied by their near-rational learning models. They can exceed in optimism, for example, by forecasting higher levels of the output gap or lower levels of inflation than suggested by the learning model, or in pessimism.

In this case, both the PLM and the constant-gain learning formulas remain given by

$$
\begin{bmatrix} x_t \\ \pi_t \\ i_t \end{bmatrix} = a_t + b_t \begin{bmatrix} x_{t-1} \\ \pi_{t-1} \\ i_{t-1} \end{bmatrix} + \varepsilon_t \tag{31}
$$

and

$$
\hat{\varphi}_t = \hat{\varphi}_{t-1} + \bar{\mathbf{g}} R_t^{-1} \mathbf{X}_t (\mathbf{Y}_t - \hat{\varphi}_{t-1}' \mathbf{X}_t)' \tag{32}
$$

$$
R_t = R_{t-1} + \bar{\mathbf{g}}(\mathbf{X}_t \mathbf{X}_t' - R_{t-1}) \tag{33}
$$

as in the previous section.

Expectations, however, are now formed as:

$$
\tilde{E}_{t-1} \begin{pmatrix} x_t \\ \pi_t \\ i_t \end{pmatrix} = a_{t-1} + b_{t-1} \begin{pmatrix} x_{t-1} \\ \pi_{t-1} \\ i_{t-1} \end{pmatrix} + \begin{pmatrix} e_t^{x_0} \\ e_t^{\pi_0} \\ 0 \end{pmatrix} \tag{34}
$$

and

$$
\tilde{E}_{t-1} \begin{pmatrix} x_{t+1} \\ \pi_{t+1} \\ i_{t+1} \end{pmatrix} = a_{t-1} + b_{t-1} \tilde{E}_{t-1} \begin{pmatrix} x_t \\ \pi_t \\ i_t \end{pmatrix} + \begin{pmatrix} e_t^{x_1} \\ e_t^{\pi_1} \\ 0 \end{pmatrix} \tag{35}
$$

The variables e_t^z define the expectation shocks in the model. They are identified as the component of observed expectations that cannot be justified by the learning model. The expectation shocks can refer either to optimism and pessimism regarding future real activity ($e_t^{x_0}$ and $e_t^{x_1}$) or future inflationary pressures ($e_t^{\pi_1}$ and $e_t^{\pi_0}$), at different horizons. The expectation shocks are allowed to be serially correlated, and they evolve as AR(1) processes.

In the estimation, we will use one and two-period-ahead forecasts for output growth and inflation as additional observable variables that we need to match.

RATIONAL VERSUS NONRATIONAL EXPECTATIONS ECONOMETRICS

The macroeconometrics literature has recently seen a spurt of work focused on the estimation of structural models with the use of full-information techniques, either based on maximum likelihood or, more often, on Bayesian methods.

The quasi totality of such studies impose the assumption of RE. The assumption of RE is typically taken as given without much analysis of how the results would differ if expectations were to only minimally deviate from fully rational.

Here we present an econometric evaluation of a popular small-scale New Keynesian model and show how many of its properties are sensitive to the way expectations are modeled.

We estimate the same model under the different expectation formation mechanisms presented in sections "The Benchmark: Rational Expectations" to "Beyond RE: Observed Survey Expectations." In all cases, we use U.S. data with a sample that spans the period from 1968:IV to 2005:I (1968:IV is chosen as starting date, since the expectation data that we'll use are available from that date). We use data on output growth, calculated as the log quarterly difference of Real GDP, inflation, calculated as the quarter-to-quarter log difference in the GDP implicit price deflator, and the effective federal funds rate (transformed into a quarterly rate to be consistent with the inflation series). We assume a piecewise-linear trend in output, with a break in the slope in 1994 to capture a change in slope during the New Economy period.[2] We have considered estimation under a linear trend without the change in slope and the results were similar.

In the case described in section "Beyond RE: Observed Survey Expectations", in which expectations are proxied by survey expectations, we also use the expected one and two-period-ahead forecasts for output growth, and the expected one and two-period-ahead forecasts for inflation as additional observables that we try to match in the estimation. Given that we estimate models in which we try to infer agents' learning process, news, or excesses in optimism or pessimism over the sample, it is crucial to match as closely as possible the information set that economic subjects had available over the period. To this scope, in all cases, we use real time data in the estimation. Real time data on GDP growth and inflation are obtained from the Real Time Data Set made available by the Federal Reserve Bank of Philadelphia (for all series we use the vintage available at the time to forecasters as a description of the economy), while the effective federal funds rate, which is not revised, is obtained from FRED, the Federal Reserve Economic Database, hosted by the Federal Reserve Bank of St. Louis. For the *real-time* data, we use only the first vintage of each observation, rather than the last revised vintage as common in the literature. By using only the first vintage, we therefore refrain from modeling the process of revisions. An alternative, which would be possible to consider in our state-space framework, but which would significantly complicate the analysis, would be to assume that agents observe initial releases as well as different vintages (or final vintages) of the series and impose a model for the revisions.

Observed data on output growth and inflation expectations are obtained from the Survey of Professional Forecasters. These consist of forecasts for the variables one-quarter and two-quarters ahead, and we use the mean across forecasters (we abstract from issues related to the entry and exit of forecasters in the survey, which may potentially lead to some composition bias in the sample). More details on the data and transformations that were imposed on the variables are provided in the Data Appendix section.

For each specification, we estimate the following vector of common coefficients:

$$\Theta = \{\sigma, \alpha, \rho, \chi_\pi, \chi_x, \chi_{\Delta\pi}, \chi_{\Delta x}, \rho_g, \rho_\mu, \rho_v, \sigma_g, \sigma_\mu, \sigma_v\} \tag{36}$$

In the model with news, we also estimate the standard deviations of the news shocks: σ_{η_g}, σ_{η_μ}, σ_{η_v}; in the model with learning, we also estimate the constant gain coefficient $\bar{g}$ and, in one case, the vector of initial beliefs $\hat{\varphi}_{0|0}$; in the model with observed expectations, learning, and expectation shocks, we also estimate the constant gain coefficient, as well as the autoregressive and standard deviation coefficients $(\rho_{e_{x_1}}, \rho_{e_{x_0}}, \rho_{e_{\pi_1}}, \rho_{e_{\pi_0}}, \sigma_{e_{x_1}},$ $\sigma_{e_{x_0}}, \sigma_{e_{\pi_1}},$ and $\sigma_{e_{\pi_0}})$, which describe the dynamics of the expectation shocks.

We assume prior distributions that closely follow those used in recent studies that estimate comparable New Keynesian models. The prior distribution for σ, the intertemporal elasticity of substitution is a Gamma with mean 1 and standard deviation 0.5. The mean matches the values typically used in calibrated versions of general equilibrium models. The standard deviation is large enough to capture the uncertainty regarding the value of σ in the literature, given that estimates range from close to 0, particularly from microeconometric studies, to values substantially above 1, in structural macro estimations. We choose Beta distributions for the parameters that should have support between 0 and 1 from theory. The Calvo parameter has prior mean equal to 0.6 with standard deviation 0.05. This roughly matches the micro evidence on price setting, which suggests prices that remain on average fixed for 8–11 quarters (e.g., Nakamura & Steinsson, 2008): the prior mean is set at the low end of the estimates (but higher than the prior mean in Smets & Wouters, 2007, for example). The Beta priors for the autoregressive coefficients in the disturbance equations all have mean equal to 0.5 and standard deviation 0.15. These prior distributions remain rather uninformative. We assume Normal distributions for the reaction coefficients in the monetary policy rule, with prior mean equal to 1.5 for the reaction to inflation and to 0.125 for the reaction to the output gap. While the priors for the Taylor rule coefficients assign a nonzero probability to regions of the parameter space that do not satisfy the Taylor principle, they are the most typical choices in the DSGE literature (indeterminacy is, instead, typically ruled out by rejecting in the MCMC procedure each draw that does not satisfy the determinacy conditions, which corresponds to assigning a zero prior to indeterminacy). An alternative would be to use Gamma priors for the Taylor coefficients. We assume inverse Gamma priors for the standard deviations of the shocks. In the models with learning, we select a prior distribution with mean 0.025 and standard deviation 0.005 for the constant gain coefficient.

The models are estimated using Bayesian methods. Draws from the posterior distribution are generated using the Metropolis–Hastings algorithm. We use the Kalman filter to evaluate the likelihood of the system at each MCMC iteration. We run 200,000 draws, discarding the first quarter of draws as initial burn-in.

ECONOMETRIC EVALUATION

Expectation Formation and Parameter Estimates

The posterior estimates for the structural parameters under the different expectation formation alternatives are shown in Table 1.

Table 1. Prior Distributions and Posterior Estimates, Across
Expectation Formation Models.

	Prior Distributions			Posterior Distributions					
Params.	Distr.	Mean	SD	RE	News $(h=1)$	News $(h=4)$	Learning	Learning I.B.	Survey
σ	G	1	0.5	0.42 [0.25,0.62]	0.59 [0.33,0.98]	0.83 [0.51,1.18]	0.92 [0.50,1.33]	0.78 [0.47,1.11]	0.90 [0.54,1.29]
α	B	0.6	0.05	0.75 [0.68,0.81]	0.83 [0.79,0.88]	0.86 [0.81,0.90]	0.84 [0.81,0.88]	0.82 [0.77,0.86]	0.83 [0.79,0.87]
ρ	B	0.7	0.1	0.62 [0.50,0.73]	0.80 [0.73,0.85]	0.82 [0.77,0.86]	0.89 [0.85,0.93]	0.89 [0.84,0.93]	0.90 [0.85,0.93]
χ_π	N	1.5	0.125	1.66 [1.42,1.90]	1.78 [1.55,1.97]	1.73 [1.51,1.94]	1.42 [1.17,1.67]	1.43 [1.21,1.67]	1.44 [1.20,1.68]
χ_x	N	0.125	0.0625	0.01 [−0.03,0.05]	0.18 [0.07,0.30]	0.24 [0.16,0.33]	0.23 [0.12,0.35]	0.22 [0.11,0.33]	0.23 [0.11,0.35]
$\chi_{\Delta\pi}$	N	0.1	0.05				0.08 [−0.02,0.17]	0.08 [0,0.16]	0.09 [−0.01,0.17]
$\chi_{\Delta x}$	N	0.1	0.05				0.10 [0.02,0.20]	0.09 [0,0.19]	0.08 [−0.01,0.17]
ρ_g	B	0.5	0.15	0.83 [0.76,0.90]	0.73 [0.62,0.82]	0.72 [0.60,0.84]	0.52 [0.38,0.66]	0.55 [0.41,0.68]	0.51 [0.35,0.66]
ρ_μ	B	0.5	0.15	0.99 [0.98,0.99]	0.92 [0.79,0.99]	0.76 [0.60,0.88]	0.42 [0.23,0.63]	0.50 [0.31,0.69]	0.48 [0.32,0.64]
ρ_v	B	0.5	0.15	0.42 [0.30,0.53]	0.26 [0.14,0.40]	0.23 [0.11,0.34]	0.27 [0.14,0.41]	0.25 [0.12,0.41]	0.28 [0.15,0.43]
σ_g	IG	0.33	1	0.11 [0.07,0.19]	0.14 [0.08,0.22]	0.28 [0.20,0.38]	0.99 [0.86,1.13]	0.97 [0.86,1.08]	0.86 [0.76,0.96]
σ_μ	IG	0.33	1	0.42 [0.24,0.66]	0.12 [0.08,0.18]	0.11 [0.08],0.15	0.40 [0.34,0.45]	0.40 [0.35,0.45]	0.33 [0.30,0.37]
σ_v	IG	0.25	1	0.29 [0.23,0.36]	0.13 [0.08,0.21]	0.08 [0.06,0.11]	0.21 [0.18,0.23]	0.20 [0.18,0.23]	0.21 [0.18,0.23]
σ_η^g	IG	0.25	1				0.35 [0.16,0.60]	0.37 [0.17,0.55]	
σ_η^μ	IG	0.25	1				0.09 [0.06,0.16]	0.13 [0.08,0.21]	
σ_η^v	IG	0.25	1				0.17 [0.11,0.22]	0.21 [0.18,0.24]	
$\bar{g}$	B	0.025	0.005				0.023 [0.015,0.033]	0.018 [0.011,0.028]	0.025 [0.017,0.033]
$\rho_e^{x_1}$	B	0.5	0.15						0.56 [0.43,0.69]
$\rho_e^{\pi_1}$	B	0.5	0.15						0.48 [0.33,0.63]
$\rho_e^{x_0}$	B	0.5	0.15						0.41 [0.27,0.56]
$\rho_e^{\pi_1}$	B	0.5	0.15						0.65 [0.56,0.74]
$\sigma_e^{x_1}$	IG	0.33	1						0.95 [0.83,1.06]
$\sigma_e^{\pi_1}$	IG	0.33	1						0.16 [0.14,0.18]
$\sigma_e^{x_0}$	IG	0.33	1						0.20 [0.18,0.23]
$\sigma_e^{\pi_0}$	IG	0.33	1						0.21 [0.17,0.24]

Note: The numbers below the column head "Posterior Distributions" denote posterior mean;
the numbers in square brackets denote 95% posterior probability intervals.

Assumptions about the modeling of expectations largely influence the parameter estimates. It is apparent, for example, that there is large variation in the estimate of the intertemporal elasticity of substitution across specifications, with posterior means ranging from 0.42 to 0.92. Figs. 1–6 show the posterior distributions for a selection of the main parameters across models with different expectation formation assumptions.

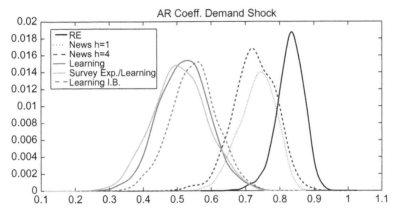

Fig. 1. Posterior Distributions: AR Coefficient for Demand Shock g_t.
Note: The figure shows posterior distributions in the estimated models across different expectation formation schemes.

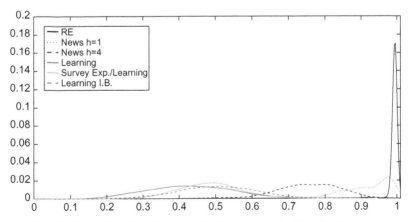

Fig. 2. Posterior Distributions: AR Coefficient for Supply Shock μ_t.

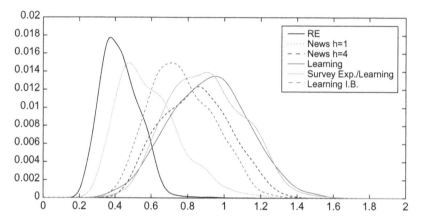

Fig. 3. Posterior Distributions: Intertemporal Elasticity of Substitution σ.

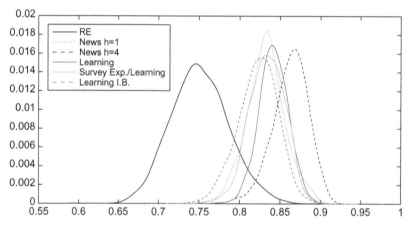

Fig. 4. Posterior Distributions: Calvo Price Stickiness α.

First, Figs. 1 and 2 clearly reveal the well known difficulty of the model under RE to endogenously generate levels of persistence that can match those in macroeconomic variables. The model requires extreme degrees of serial correlation in the exogenous shocks to match such persistence. The posterior distributions for the autoregressive coefficients for the demand and supply shocks g_t and μ_t fall very close to the upper bound of one. Extending the model to allow for news about future shocks improves the model's ability to capture persistence: the posterior distributions shift to the

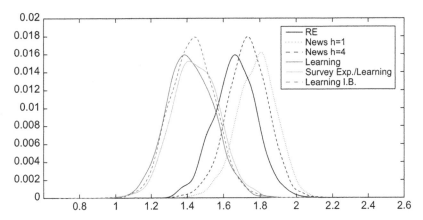

Fig. 5. Posterior Distributions: Monetary Policy Reaction Toward Inflation χ_π.

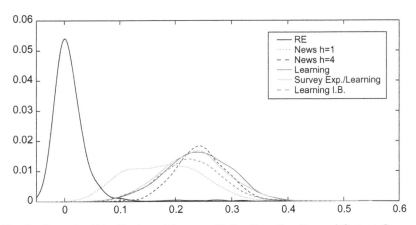

Fig. 6. Posterior Distributions: Monetary Policy Reaction Toward Output Gap χ_x.

left, with most probability mass for AR coefficients between 0.7 and 0.8. The use of either learning or survey expectations further improve the model in this direction: the updating of beliefs endogenously creates persistence, so that lower levels of serial correlation in the exogenous shocks are necessary (the posterior distributions concentrate around 0.4–0.5).

Turning to the preference, technology, and policy coefficients, we see that the values of the coefficients that are most consistent with the data seem to be sensitive to the modeling of how expectations are formed. Fig. 3 shows the posterior distributions for σ, the elasticity of intertemporal substitution. The best-fitting values are relatively low under RE, with mode around 0.3 and mean around 0.4. The incorporation of news, learning, or survey expectations affects the distributions, which shift to the right to assign larger probabilities to values closer to 1. Fig. 4 refers to the Calvo price stickiness parameter. The posterior distribution for α falls around 0.7–0.75 under RE, while the distributions move toward values around 0.85 for all other models. Figs. 5 and 6 show the distributions related to the monetary policy reaction coefficients toward inflation and the output gap. The reaction toward inflation appears smaller in estimated models under learning or survey expectations, while the reaction toward the output gap is estimated to be smaller under RE than under all other specifications. In most of the figures, the shifts are substantial, with posterior distributions that display small regions of overlap.

Our results here are not meant to show that one specification has to be preferred to the others. But, overall, the results provide, instead, substantial evidence that the estimates for structural parameters are far from robust to the use of alternative expectation formation mechanisms. This sensitivity to variations in the modeling of expectations is mostly ignored in the literature.

Expectation Formation and Structural Shocks

We have seen in the previous section that assumptions about expectations have important consequences on persistence and on the estimated degree of serial correlation in the structural shocks. Shocks need to be more persistent under RE than they are when news, learning, or subjective expectations are allowed for.

Table 2 reports the correlation of equivalent shocks across models estimated with different expectation formation schemes. Significant differences emerge among the shocks. The demand shock estimated under RE has correlation that ranges from 0.44 to 0.67 with estimated shocks in the same model, but with different expectational assumptions. The similarity between demand shocks obtained in models with news and in those with learning is also limited (the correlation is between 0.28 and 0.59). The results are along the same lines for the supply shock. There are some similarities between the shock series estimated under RE and under news, but large differences with the shocks obtained in models with learning. Models with learning and

Table 2. Estimated Structural Shocks: Correlation Across Expectation Formation Models.

	RE	News ($h=1$)	News ($h=4$)	Learning	Learning I.B.	Survey
Demand Shock g_t						
RE	1					
News ($h=1$)	0.67	1				
News ($h=4$)	0.59	0.92	1			
Learning	0.52	0.28	0.33	1		
Learning I.B.	0.58	0.35	0.38	0.99	1	
Survey	0.46	0.44	0.59	0.66	0.66	1
Supply Shock μ_t						
RE	1					
News ($h=1$)	0.81	1				
News ($h=4$)	0.76	0.98	1			
Learning	0.28	0.53	0.57	1		
Learning I.B.	0.31	0.53	0.56	0.99	1	
Survey	0.40	0.58	0.60	0.83	0.83	1
MP Shock v_t						
RE	1					
News ($h=1$)	0.88	1				
News ($h=4$)	0.80	0.99	1			
Learning	0.61	0.90	0.94	1		
Learning I.B.	0.67	0.93	0.96	0.99	1	
Survey	0.66	0.92	0.95	0.99	0.99	1

survey expectations give rise to supply shocks that are similar to one another. The correlations are closer, instead, for monetary policy shocks. In this case, the shocks obtained in models with news, learning, or survey expectations are very close to each other, while there are still differences between them and the implied series under RE.

As a word of caution, we would like to point out that comparing shocks across models may be difficult. For example, in the model with news, the shocks considered in the table contain both unanticipated and anticipated components, while in the other models the shock realizations are unknown to the private sector. Assumptions about the underlying stochastic processes, therefore, may somewhat differ across specifications. But it is fair to say that before assigning a clear structural interpretation to shocks, it should be shown that their dynamics are reasonably robust to different modeling assumptions, such as different sensible expectation formation mechanisms.

Expectation Formation and Model Fit

An obvious way to choose the most appropriate model of expectation formation is in terms of model fit. Table 3 reports the models' marginal likelihoods under the different expectation formation mechanisms, along with the corresponding Bayes factors, expressed by considering the model with RE as the null hypothesis.[3] Marginal likelihoods are a standard tool in Bayesian model comparison and have many desirable properties. For example, they automatically penalize models with additional parameters and increasing degrees of complexity (while the classical likelihood itself would only increase with complexity). Bayes factors are obtained in the table as ratios between the marginal likelihood of each model and the marginal likelihood of the benchmark model with RE (assuming equal model probabilities a priori).

The model with the conventional assumption of RE yields the lowest fit. Maintaining RE, but extending the expectation formation process to include news about future exogenous shocks leads to improvement in fit, in particular when news refer to a longer horizon ($h = 4$ rather than $h = 1$). The models with learning, however, dominate in terms of fit. The best-fitting model assumes learning by economic agents and it allows their initial beliefs to be estimated along with the remaining parameters in the model.

The marginal likelihood for the model that uses survey data on expectations is not comparable to the others, since the set of observables is different

Table 3.   Bayesian Model Comparison: Models' Log Marginal
Likelihoods and Bayes Factors.

	Marginal Likelihood	Bayes Factor
RE	310.39	1
News ($h = 1$)	309.81	1.79
News ($h = 4$)	296.83	7.7452×10^5
Learning	290.94	2.7992×10^8
Learning I.B.	**286.06**	3.6846×10^{10}
Survey Exp.	–	–

Note: The marginal likelihood for the model with survey expectations is not reported as not comparable with the others (given that the estimation uses a different set of observables). According to Jeffrey's (1961) scale of evidence, Bayes factors above values of 100 represent "decisive" evidence in favor of a model versus the other.

(here, it includes also observed expectations about output growth and inflation, in addition to realized output growth, inflation, and interest rates).

Jeffrey (1961) provides an interpretative scale to judge the strength of the evidence in favor of an alternative model with respect to the model in the null hypothesis. According to his scale, the Bayes factor values in Table 3 provide "decisive" evidence for all models, except the model with news with a one-period horizon, against the RE benchmark (Jeffrey indicates a value of the Bayes factor equal to 100 as cutoff, after which the evidence is considered decisive). If one had to calculate the Bayes factors of the models with learning even against the best model that maintains RE (i.e., the model with news at horizon equal to 4 periods), the Bayes factors would still reveal "decisive" evidence in favor of the learning models (Bayes factors 361.41 and 4.7572×10^4, depending on whether initial beliefs are also estimated or not).

Expectation Formation and DSGE Forecasting Performance

In addition to in-sample fit, we evaluate the out-of-sample forecasting performance of the model regarding future output growth, inflation, and interest rates across different expectational assumptions. To generate out-of-sample forecasts, we estimate recursively each model. We start from an initial sample that spans the period between 1968:IV and 1979:IV and generate one, four, and eight-period-ahead forecasts at the end of the sample. Then, we recursively add one year of observations, by reestimating the models for the period 1968:IV and 1980:IV, for the period 1968:IV and 1981:IV, and so forth, and each time generating the corresponding forecasts at the end of the sample.

As measure of forecasting performance we compute Root Mean Squared Errors (RMSE). We also evaluate the multivariate forecasting accuracy using the trace and the (log) determinant of the scaled forecast mean squared error matrix at each horizon h, $\Sigma_{MSE}(h)$:

$$\Sigma_{MSE}(h) = \frac{1}{N_f} \sum_{t=T}^{T+N_f-1} \bar{\varepsilon}_{t+h|t} \bar{\varepsilon}'_{t+h|t} \tag{37}$$

where N_f denotes the number of forecasts, $\bar{\varepsilon}_{t+h|t} = M^{-1/2} \varepsilon_{t+h|t}$, $\varepsilon_{t+h|t}$ is the vector of h-step-ahead forecast errors given information in t, and M denotes a scaling matrix, which is here assumed to be diagonal with variances of the variables being forecasted on the diagonal. The determinant is usually preferred as a measure of accuracy since model rankings are invariant to the choice of the scaling matrix. Here we present both criteria, since they can, in principle, provide different information: the trace is usually affected in larger part by forecast errors for the variables that are hardest to forecast, while the determinant is influenced to a larger extent by those that are easiest to forecast (e.g., Christoffel et al., 2011).

Fig. 7 displays the posterior distribution for the RMSEs relative to forecasts of output growth and inflation at one, four, and eight-period-ahead horizons, and across expectation formation models. Fig. 8 shows the posterior distributions for the log determinant and trace statistics.

The model with survey expectations dominates for forecasts at the one-period horizon for output growth. The models with news and with learning both improve upon the standard case of RE. RE models (in the cases with and without news) perform better for inflation forecasting: the RMSEs are smaller than those obtained under learning. Moreover, the model with RE performs extremely well over longer horizons.

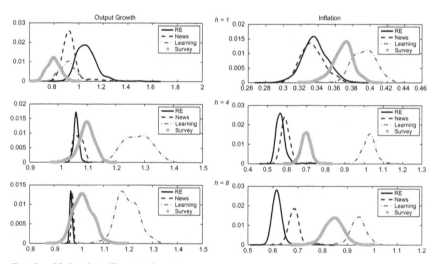

Fig. 7.   Univariate Forecasting Accuracy.
Note: The figure shows the posterior distribution of the RMSE for output growth and inflation forecasts. The top panels refer to one-quarter-ahead forecasts, the middle panels to four-quarter-ahead forecasts, the bottom panels to eight-quarter-ahead forecasts. Each panel displays the posterior distributions obtained for the model under different expectation formation schemes.

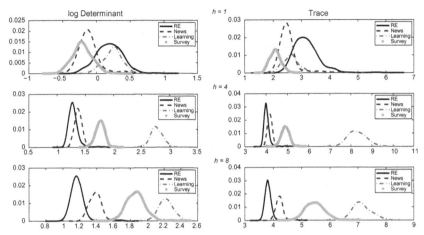

Fig. 8. Multivariate Forecasting Accuracy.
Note: The figure shows the posterior distributions of the log determinant (left) and of the trace of the forecast errors MSE matrix. The top panels refer to one-quarter-ahead forecasts, the middle panels to four-quarter-ahead forecasts, the bottom panels to eight-quarter-ahead forecasts. Each panel displays the posterior distributions obtained for the model under different expectation formation schemes.

The measures of multivariate forecast accuracy indicate that survey expectations carry information that allows the econometrician to improve the one-period-ahead forecasting performance of the model. The model with survey expectations ranks first, followed by the model with news and learning; the model with RE ranks last. In this case, therefore, the rankings based on in-sample model fit and out-of-sample forecasting performance are similar. Moving to longer forecasting horizons, however, leads to major reversals in the rankings. At the four- and eight- period horizons, the model with RE dominates all other alternatives. The model with RE extended to include news performs slightly worse and comes second in the ranking. The model with survey expectations and, particularly, the model with learning appear to perform rather poorly if evaluated in terms of their forecasting ability over long horizons.

While a number of papers have focused on assessing the forecasting success of DSGE models under RE, the evidence is scant under learning. A recent paper that, among other things, seeks to assess the forecasting ability of a model with learning is Slobodyan and Wouters (2009). That paper seems to reach a similar conclusion: learning helps in forecasting in the short run, but it is outperformed by RE over longer horizons.

Identifying the reasons why RE perform well in the long run requires additional work. Here, we point out that RE enjoy some advantages over the alternatives that may be fruitful in forecasting. For example, the learning models assume that agents do not have information regarding the steady states of the variables and that they attempt to learn them over time in the same way as they learn about other parameters (i.e., they learn about coefficients in the vector a_t in Eq. (26), which can be interpreted as steady-state coefficients). The steady-states are, instead, perfectly known at all times under RE. This assumption of full knowledge about the steady states may favor the model with RE over the medium to long run. Moreover, the model with RE assumes that agents dispose of information up to time t when forming expectations in $t + 1$ and that they observe the values and histories of the shocks in time t. Under learning, we assume that agents in t can observe only endogenous variables up to $t - 1$ and that they do not know the values of the shocks. This limited knowledge may again favor the model with RE.

Another feature that may be penalizing the learning models at longer horizons is the possibility that the agents' real-time PLMs at least in some periods and in some draws may become unstable. In the estimation, we don't impose stability or other constraints on agents' beliefs (letting them be exclusively driven by the data) and it's possible that in some situations the PLMs are characterized by complex (or unstable, although this doesn't happen in the full-sample estimation) eigenvalues. Instability would clearly worsen the forecasting performance, especially at longer horizons. A more in-depth investigation is beyond the scope of this chapter, but it will be interesting in future research to check to what extent adding some degree discipline to agents' beliefs would improve the long-run forecasting performance of learning models.

Finally, and more from a modeling perspective, the model with learning is imposed on the same loglinearized model equations that are obtained under RE; current macroeconomic variables depend exclusively on expectations up to $t + 1$. Preston (2005), however, shows that the derivation of the model under subjective expectations can lead to laws of motion that imply that current values of the variables depend on long-horizon expectations as well. A model with learning with long-horizon expectations has been estimated in Milani (2006). Maybe extending the learning model to allow for long-horizon expectations may improve its forecasting performance beyond the one-period-ahead horizons.

WHAT HAVE WE LEARNED?

The main scope of the chapter was to investigate whether estimates of structural parameters and the econometric properties of macroeconomic models were likely robust to some popular deviations from the benchmark hypothesis of RE.

The empirical results we found carry several messages. First, it is unrealistic to assume that conclusions that are obtained for DSGE model, even in small scale environments, are likely to be reasonably robust to even small deviations from the benchmark assumption of RE.

The previous section has shown that parameter estimates, estimates of the unobserved structural shocks, in-sample model fit, and out-of-sample forecasting performance are largely affected by the modeler's assumptions about how expectations are formed.

More work is, instead, needed to choose among the various models of expectations formation.

The RE hypothesis, which is used in the vast majority of theoretical and empirical work in macroeconomics, may worsen the fit of the model. The conventional model with RE, in fact, ranks last in model fit according to the marginal likelihoods. The model with learning fits the data substantially better than do the alternatives. If one is interested in forecasting one-quarter-ahead macroeconomic variables, the use of survey expectations is valuable. The model with survey expectations achieves the overall best out-of-sample forecasting performance in the very short run. But when the attention turns to slightly longer horizons (from one-year ahead and beyond), the model with RE strongly outperforms the alternatives.

These results may be taken to suggest that appropriate models of expectations formation may be adjusted depending on the purpose at hand. Researchers interested in modeling short-run economic dynamics may need to take economic agents' learning processes and less-than-fully RE into account, while researchers interested in economic adjustment in the medium to long-run may do well or better by maintaining the assumption of RE.

Our main point, however, is that, at a minimum, the chapter's results should suggest the need for modelers and econometricians to check the sensitivity of their results to alternative expectation formation processes.

CONCLUSIONS

Current macroeconomic theory is built on the assumption that economic agents form expectations according to the RE hypothesis. The conclusions that are derived from empirical work in macroeconomics also hinge on the validity of RE.

In this chapter, we have evaluated the consequences of relaxing the assumption of RE in a popular small-scale monetary DSGE model in the New Keynesian tradition. We have shown that the econometric properties of the model are extremely sensitive to the way expectations are modeled. The formation of expectations is a dimension in which the effects of misspecification and any analysis of sensitivity are largely lacking in the literature. The evidence presented in this chapter shows that the formation of expectations should be studied more critically in estimated DSGE models.

Limitations

Besides the various expectation models that we examined in this chapter, we recognize that there are other alternatives that have not been included. For example, it can be assumed that economic agents retain RE, but that their information is sticky or that they optimally choose to be at times inattentive to economic developments (Mankiw & Reis, 2007; Sims, 2010). Within learning models, there are various other ways in which agents could be assumed to learn, which may differ from the constant gain learning assumed in this chapter (e.g., recursive-least-squares learning, or learning with a time-varying endogenous gain, as in Milani, 2008). Finally, they may have imperfect information about some of the shocks or variables and they may solve signal extraction problems (e.g., Levine et al., 2010).

Moreover, we would like to point out several potential limitations regarding the perspective offered in this chapter.

First, we have employed a rather narrow interpretation of RE: here agents have full knowledge about the structure of the model, its parameters, the distributions of the shocks, and the history of endogenous variables and shocks up to each period in time. The definition of RE, however, may be broadened (and, indeed, it has often been broadened in the literature) to simply mean that agents will rationally use all the information that is available to them at each point in time: RE can, therefore, coexist with imperfect knowledge, such as imperfect information about some of the shocks (the literature has often considered imperfect information about a time-varying Fed's inflation target, for example), learning about some parameters (e.g., unknown, and possibly time-varying, coefficients in the Taylor rule), and so forth. In such cases, the information sets attributed to agents under RE and adaptive learning are brought closer together and separating the two may possibly become a much harder task. The main difference would still remain that in models with learning such as those used in this chapter, agents are not fully rational: given incomplete knowledge, they do not learn optimally given the assumed model of the economy, while they would optimally process the information under RE. Near-rational models with learning are meant to provide an approximation of optimal solutions that may be too difficult to compute by agents in situations in which the amount of knowledge is limited.

Second, the model that we have chosen as reference may be misspecified. In the chapter, we are implicitly always considering a "joint hypothesis": one regarding the form of the expectation formation mechanism and the other implicitly assuming that the structural model we use is an appropriate description of the data-generating process for the macroeconomic series we try to explain. If the structural model is misspecified, structural estimates may be biased, we may not be able to fully recover the structural shocks, and the biases may translate into different conclusions regarding the expectation-formation mechanism. At the same time, we believe that this is true in most cases in the literature. In the empirical DSGE literature, for example, it is typical to test the role of various frictions (e.g., by shutting down in turn habit formation, adjustment costs in investment, price or wage stickiness, etc.) or extensions to the baseline model (e.g., by adding a financial accelerator mechanism or search and matching in the labor market): tests of their importance are also implicitly joint test of such model features, but also of the expectation formation hypothesis. This chapter suggests that this practice may be problematic: assumptions about expectations may easily be as or more important than assumptions about other details in the model.

Third, the comparison across the four models with different expectation schemes may not always be straightforward, given differences in some of the auxiliary modeling assumptions. For example, under learning we have assumed that agents dispose of an information set including variables up to $t-1$, while under RE their information set includes variables up to t; in the benchmark RE model and in the models with learning, the shocks are entirely unanticipated by the private sector, while in the models with news, the shocks contain both unanticipated and anticipated components. It will be worthwhile testing the extent to which these differences matter.

Finally, a pervasive problem in the the DSGE literature lies in the choices regarding how to detrend real variables, in this case GDP, and how to construct measures of the output gap. Most papers typically proceed by either detrending the data before the estimation using a statistical procedure (linear or quadratic trend, Hodrick–Prescott filter, band-pass filter, and so forth), or using a model-consistent output gap, calculated as the deviation between actual output and the corresponding level of output that would obtain in the same exact economy, but under flexible prices. In this chapter, we have chosen to consider the simplest case of a linear trend (although with a break in slope), to keep the trend as consistent as possible across model specicifcations, and with the idea that this would be more likely to approximate the detrending procedure forecasters had in mind, at least over large portions of the sample, when forming their expectations. But it is well known that different detrending schemes and the use of statistical measures in place of the theoretically consistent output gap may have important effects on the results (e.g., Neiss & Nelson, 2003, 2005). A more detailed study of the interaction between detrending procedures, output gap measures, and expectation formation assumptions, is certainly warranted.

The aim of this chapter was to shed light on some of the empirical implications of alternative expectation formation schemes in a benchmark monetary business cycle model. But future research is needed to provide more definitive evidence on the best model of expectations formation and on the role of alternative expectational assumptions in more complicated models.

NOTES

1. News shocks are introduced in the same way in Schmitt-Grohé and Uribe (2008).

2. Therefore, in the estimation, we consider an empirical proxy for the output gap, rather than the welfare-relevant definition, i.e., the deviation of output from the level that would prevail in the same economy, but under flexible prices. We use a statistical proxy here (based on a linear trend), which we keep consistent across model specifications. The model-consistent theoretical output gap would, instead, differ across specifications and, it is likely, that different assumptions about expectations would also imply diverse output gap estimates. We don't pursue that avenue here. Regarding the chosen piecewise-linear trend, the literature often assumes a break in the trend slope in the 1970s. In earlier estimations, we have used a trend with breaks in the slope both in 1973 and in 1994, but dropped the break in the 1970s in subsequent estimations, given that our sample starts only few periods in advance and also because the change in the slope seemed less apparent and less sizeable in the

1970s than in 1994 in the real-time data set that we use (the estimated trend on revised data would likely differ).

3. The marginal likelihoods are calculated using Geweke's modified harmonic mean approximation.

ACKNOWLEDGEMENT

We would like to thank co-editor Mark Wynne and an anonymous referee for detailed comments and suggestions, which have definitely improved the chapter.

REFERENCES

Beaudry, P., & Portier, F. (2006). Stock prices, news, and economic fluctuations. *American Economic Review, 96*(4), 1293–1307.

Christoffel, K., Coenen, G., & Warne, A. (2010). *Forecasting with DSGE models.* Working Paper Series 1185, European Central Bank.

Dynan, K. E. (2000). Habit formation in consumer preferences: Evidence from panel data. *American Economic Review, 90*(3), 391–406.

Evans, G. W., & Honkapohja, S. (2001). *Learning and expectations in economics.* Princeton, NJ: Princeton University Press.

Evans, G. W., & Honkapohja, S. (2013). Learning as a rational foundation for macroeconomics and finance (with Seppo Honkapohja). In R. Frydman & E. S. Phelps (Eds.), *Rethinking expectations: The way forward for macroeconomics.* Princeton, NJ: Princeton University Press.

Jaimovich, N., & Rebelo, S. (2009). Can news about the future drive the business cycle? *American Economic Review, 99*(4), 1097–1118.

Jeffrey, H. (1961). *Theory of probability.* Oxford, UK: Oxford University Press.

Levine, P., Pearlman, J., Perendia, G., & Yang, B. (2010). *Endogenous persistence in an estimated DSGE model under imperfect information.* CDMA Working Paper Series 1002.

Mankiw, G. N., & Reis, R. (2007). Sticky information in general equilibrium. *Journal of the European Economic Association, 5*(2-3), 603–613.

Milani, F. (2006). A Bayesian DSGE model with infinite-horizon learning: Do "mechanical" sources of persistence become superfluous? *International Journal of Central Banking, 2*(3), 87–106.

Milani, F. (2007). Expectations, learning and macroeconomic persistence. *Journal of Monetary Economics, 54*(7), 2065–2082.

Milani, F. (2008). *Learning and time-varying macroeconomic volatility.* Mimeo, University of California, Irvine, CA.

Milani, F. (2011). Expectation shocks and learning as drivers of the business cycle. *Economic Journal, 121*(552), 379–401.

Milani, F., & Treadwell, J. (2012). The effects of monetary policy "news" and "surprises". *Journal of Money, Credit and Banking.*

Nakamura, E., & Steinsson, J. (2008). Five facts about prices: A reevaluation of menu cost models. *The Quarterly Journal of Economics, 123*(4), 1415–1464.

Neiss, K. S., & Nelson, E. (2003). The real-interest-rate gap as an inflation indicator. *Macroeconomic Dynamics*, 7(2), 239–262.

Neiss, K. S., & Nelson, E. (2005). Inflation dynamics, marginal cost, and the output gap: Evidence from three countries. *Journal of Money, Credit, and Banking*, 37(6), 1019–1045.

Preston, B. (2005). Learning about monetary policy rules when long-horizon expectations matter. *International Journal of Central Banking*, 1(2).

Schmitt-Grohe, S., & Uribe, M. (2008). *What's news in business cycles?* NBER Working Paper No. 14215.

Sims, C. A. (2000). Solving linear RE models. *Computational Economics*, 20, 1–20.

Sims, C. A. (2010). Rational inattention and monetary economics. In B. M. Friedman & M. Woodford (Eds.), *Handbook of monetary economics* (Vol. 3, pp. 155–181). Amsterdam: Elsevier.

Slobodyan, S., & Wouters, R. (2009). *Learning in an estimated medium-scale DSGE model*. CERGE-EI Working Papers wp396.

Smets, F., & Wouters, R. (2003). An estimated dynamic stochastic general equilibrium model of the euro area. *Journal of the European Economic Association*, 1(5), 1123–1175.

Smets, F., & Wouters, R. (2007). Shocks and frictions in US business cycles: A Bayesian DSGE approach. *American Economic Review*, 97(3), 586–606.

Woodford, M. (2003). *Interest and prices: Foundations of a theory of monetary policy*. Princeton, NJ: Princeton University Press.

DATA APPENDIX

We document here the observable variables that we use in the estimation, the transformations that were imposed on the series, and the corresponding variable in the model. The data are all for the United States and the sample is 1968:IV–2005:I.

x_t Real GDP: We use Real GDP (acronym: ROUTPUT), Billions of Real Dollars, Seasonally Adjusted, obtained from the Real Time Data Set for Macroeconomists hosted by the Federal Reserve Bank of Philadelphia. We compute quarterly output growth as $[\log(\text{Real GDP}_t) - \log(\text{Real GDP}_{t-1})] \times 100$ and link output growth to x_t in the model through the observation equation: $[\log(\text{Real GDP}_t) - \log(\text{Real GDP}_{t-1})] \times 100 = \Delta x_t + \gamma_t$, where γ_t capture the piecewise linear trend, i.e., $\gamma_t = \gamma_1$ before 1994 and $\gamma_t = \gamma_2$ after 1994.

π_t Inflation rate: To construct quarterly inflation, we use the Implicit Price Deflator series (acronym: P), index level, seasonally adjusted, obtained from the Real Time Data Set for Macroeconomists hosted by the Federal Reserve Bank of Philadelphia. The base year in the real-time vintages vary, therefore, we reexpress all observations using the same base year. Inflation is calculated as $[\log(P_t) - \log(P_{t-1})] \times 100$. The series is demeaned. The observation equation is simply: $[\log(P_t) - \log(P_{t-1})] \times 100 = \pi_t$.

i_t Nominal Interest rate: We use the Effective Federal Funds Rate (acronym: FEDFUNDS) from FRED, the Federal Reserve Database maintained by the Federal Reserve Bank of St. Louis. The Federal Funds rate is divided by four to express it in quarterly rates. The observable is matched to the variable i_t in the model as $FFR_t/4 = i_t$.

In the specification that uses observed expectations, the estimation adds to the previous set of observables the following:

$\hat{E}_{t-1}x_t$,

$\hat{E}_{t-1}x_{t+1}$ GDP growth forecasts (one-period-ahead and two-period-ahead): We use forecasts for real GDP (acronym: RGDP) obtained from the Survey of Professional Forecasters. We use mean responses across forecasters as our expectations measures.

We use columns four and five corresponding to forecasts RGDP2 and RGDP3 (one-quarter and two-quarter ahead).

Forecasts for the growth rates can be computed as $[\log(RGDP2_t) - \log(RGDP1_t)] \times 100$ and $[\log(RGDP3_t) - \log(RGDP2_t)] \times 100$, where RGDP1 represents the forecasters' estimate in t of real GDP in $t-1$. The forecasts are matched to the expectations in the model using the observation equations $[\log(RGDP2_t) - \log(RGDP1_t)] \times 100 = \hat{E}_{t-1}\Delta x_t + \hat{\gamma}_t$ and $[\log(RGDP3_t) - \log(RGDP2_t)] \times 100 = \hat{E}_{t-1}\Delta x_{t+1} + \hat{\gamma}_t$, where we allow the trend coefficients $\hat{\gamma}_t$ inferred by forecasters to differ from those in γ_t.

$\hat{E}_{t-1}\pi_t$, $\hat{E}_{t-1}\pi_{t+1}$ Inflation rate (one-period-ahead and two-period-ahead): We use forecasts for the GDP implicit price deflator (acronym: PGDP) obtained from the Survey of Professional Forecasters. We use mean responses across forecasters as our expectations measures. We use columns four and five corresponding to forecasts PGDP2 and PGDP3 (one-quarter and two-quarter ahead).

Forecasts for inflation rates are computed as $[\log(PGDP2_t) - \log(PGDP1_t)] \times 100$ and $[(PGDP3_t) - \log(PGDP2_t)] \times 100$, where PGDP1 represents the forecasters' estimate in t of the price level in $t-1$. The expected inflation series are demeaned before the estimation. The forecasts are matched to the expectations in the model using the observation equations $[\log(PGDP2_t) - \log(PGDP1_t)] \times 100 = \hat{E}_{t-1}\pi_t$ and $[\log(PGDP3_t) - \log(PGDP2_t)] \times 100 = \hat{E}_{t-1}\pi_{t+1}$.

PART II
ECONOMETRIC METHODOLOGY

APPROXIMATION PROPERTIES OF LAPLACE-TYPE ESTIMATORS

Anna Kormilitsina and Denis Nekipelov

ABSTRACT

The Laplace-type estimator (LTE) is a simulation-based alternative to the classical extremum estimator that has gained popularity in applied research. We show that even though the estimator has desirable asymptotic properties, in small samples the point estimate provided by LTE may not necessarily converge to the extremum of the sample objective function. Furthermore, we suggest a simple test to verify if the estimator converges. We illustrate these results by estimating a prototype dynamic stochastic general equilibrium model widely used in macroeconomics research.

Keywords: Laplace-type estimator; simulation-based estimation; extremum estimation

JEL classification: C01; C02; C12

INTRODUCTION

Because modern econometric models commonly used in applied research are highly nonlinear, estimation of model parameters involving the search

DSGE Models in Macroeconomics: Estimation, Evaluation, and New Developments
Advances in Econometrics, Volume 28, 291–318
ISSN: 0731-9053/doi:10.1108/S0731-9053(2012)0000028010

of a supremum of a statistical objective function is often extremely challenging. To facilitate parameter estimation, Chernozhukov and Hong (2003) suggest using the Laplace-type estimator (LTE), which allows one to replace the time-consuming search for the maximum with a stochastic algorithm. The LTE is a standard simulation procedure applied to classical estimation problems, which consists in formulating a quasi-likelihood function based on a pre-specified classical objective function. The quasi-likelihood is then combined with prior parameter distribution to obtain a quasi-posterior distribution of the parameters of interest. Available simulation algorithms (such as MCMC algorithms) can then be used to estimate the structural parameters by sampling from this nonstandard distribution. Chernozhukov and Hong (2003) demonstrate that under mild regularity conditions, the LTE is asymptotically efficient in the standard, "frequentist" sense. Therefore, parameter estimate and its covariance matrix can be computed as the corresponding moments of the stationary distribution. This finding led to an array of empirical work (see Auerbach & Gorodnichenko, 2012; Schmitt-Grohé & Uribe, 2011; Kormilitsina, 2011; Christiano, Trabandt, & Walentin, 2010; Coibion, 2010, among many others) that rely on the LTE in various empirical applications.

This chapter shows that in spite of the convenience and ease of use, there is a potential problem with practical application of the LTE. Even under conditions of Chernozhukov and Hong (2003), which guarantee that the LTE is valid asymptotically, the convergence point of the LTE can be arbitrarily different from the GMM or maximum likelihood estimator in smaller samples. The problem may occur even if the algorithm converges, so that MCMC draws stabilize over the course of iterations.

To provide intuition for our results, consider an example where $L(\theta)$ is the objective function of the parameter of interest θ, and $\{\theta_t\}_{t=1}^{\infty}$ is the set of draws from the posterior distribution generated as part of the LTE algorithm. Then at iteration t the estimate of the parameter of interest can be computed as a sample average $\hat{\theta}_t = \frac{1}{t}\sum_{i=1}^{t}\theta_t$. Under standard regularity conditions, the strong law of large numbers will hold, and $\hat{\theta}_t \xrightarrow{\text{a.s.}} \bar{\theta}$, where $\bar{\theta}$ is the expected value of the quasi-posterior distribution. The Central Limit Theorem adapted to stationary reversible Markov chains implies that

$$T_t = \sqrt{t}(\hat{\theta}_t - \bar{\theta}) \xrightarrow{d} \mathcal{N}(0, \Sigma_\theta)$$

In other words, the running estimate $\hat{\theta}_t$ will have a path-independent variance: the "approximate" variance of the parameter evaluated at iteration t of the MCMC generating algorithm will not be affected by the distance between $\hat{\theta}_t$ and the "settlement point" $\bar{\theta}$. If we define L_t as a scaled and normalized process for the objective function $L(\cdot)$ in the following way:[1]

$$L_t = \sqrt{t}(L(\hat{\theta}_t) - L(\bar{\theta}))$$

then its mean-value expansion is[2]

$$\sqrt{t}(L(\hat{\theta}_t) - L(\bar{\theta})) \sim \frac{\partial L(\bar{\theta})}{\partial \theta} T_t$$

from which it follows that[3]

$$L_t \xrightarrow{d} \frac{\partial L(\bar{\theta})}{\partial \theta} \mathcal{N}(0, \Sigma_\theta) \tag{1}$$

If $\hat{\theta}$ coincides with the extremum of the objective θ^*, then $\partial L(\bar{\theta})/\partial \theta = 0$, and Eq. (1) implies a degenerate limiting distribution for L_t. In other words, L_t will converge to 0 as $t \to \infty$. If, however $\bar{\theta} \neq \theta^*$, the limiting distribution of L_t will be normal, and as $t \to \infty$, L_t will not concentrate around 0. Therefore, the behavior of the normalized objective function L_t crucially depends on whether the mean of the quasi-posterior parameter distribution delivers supremum to the quasi-likelihood function.

We obtain our results by approximating the objective function with a continuous-time stochastic process. This strategy has become increasingly popular in the theoretical studies of sampling algorithms (see Gelfand & Mitter, 1993; Roberts & Tweedie, 1996; Roberts, Gelman, & Gilks, 1997; Roberts & Rosenthal, 2007). We then rely on the stability theory of continuous time stochastic dynamic systems to formulate the test of the null hypothesis that $\bar{\theta} = \theta^*$.

To illustrate the idea, we build and estimate a prototype dynamic stochastic general equilibrium (DSGE) model widely used in the macroeconomic literature (see Christiano, Eichenbaum, & Evans, 2005; Smets & Wouters, 2007; Altig, Christiano, Eichenbaum, & Lindé, 2011; Christiano, Ilut, Motto, & Rostagno, 2008; DiCecio, 2009, among many others). We show that even in this simple model, the LTE may not represent the maximum of the sample likelihood function, and this discrepancy can be more pronounced in smaller samples.

The remainder of this chapter is organized as follows. The second section derives the continuous time approximation for the process of normalized objective. In the third section, we show how the stability theory for stochastic processes can be applied to the analysis of the LTE and develop a test for convergence of the LTE to the maximum of the analyzed objective function. Then, the fourth section presents a quantitative exercise to accompany the theoretical results. Finally, the fifth section concludes.

DISTRIBUTION THEORY

We start by characterizing the limit processes of the scaled objective function in cases where the algorithm does and does not converge to the maximum of the corresponding objective function. We make a note that our results only concern with the convergence of the approximate maximum to the maximum of given objective function. In other words, we are not concerned with consistency of the resulting estimator, our only focus is the convergence of the stochastic approximation to the true maximum of the objective function. We make assumptions regarding the considered sample objective function. These assumptions are directly verifiable for each given objective function.

Assumption 1. Suppose that objective function $L(\cdot)$ satisfies the following assumptions:

(i) $L(\cdot)$ is a nonnegative function with the support in the compact set $\Theta \subset \mathbb{R}^p$
(ii) $L(\cdot)$ has a unique (attainable) global maximum at $\theta^* \in \Theta$.
(iii) $\int_\Theta \exp(-L(\theta)) \, d\theta < C < \infty$ for some constant C. Also for some $\gamma > 0$ the integral $\int_\Theta \|\theta\|^{2+\gamma} \exp(-L(\theta)) \, d\theta < \infty$.
(iv) For each point θ in the interior of Θ there exists $r > 0$ such that for all $\rho < r$ there exists a vector $D(\theta)$ and a matrix $H(\theta)$ which are both continuous in θ such that

$$\sup_{|\delta| \leqslant \rho} \left\| L(\theta + \delta) - L(\theta) - D(\theta)' \, \delta - \frac{1}{2} \delta' \, H(\theta) \, \delta \right\| = R(\theta, \rho)$$

such that $\lim_{|\delta| \to 0} \rho^{-4} \int_\Theta |R(\theta, \rho)|^2 \exp(-L(\theta)) \, d\theta = 0$. Moreover $D(\theta^*) = 0$.

Assumption 1 specifies the class of problems for which our methodology applies. First, we assume that the parameter space is compact and the maximum indeed exists in this set. Second, we assume that one can construct a probability distribution from the considered objective function. This probability distribution has to have finite first and second moment along with the $2 + \gamma$-moment. In this case, the Central Limit Theorem will apply to the sample of i.i.d. draws from the corresponding distribution. Finally, we assume that the expectation of the objective function with respect to the distribution generated by that objective function is "sufficiently smooth." The smoothness in our case reduces to the possibility of representing the objective function with a second-order polynomial such that the error of this representation approaches to zero in expectation.

Next we provide simple distribution results and then extend them to characterize the limiting process corresponding to the scaled objective function L_t.

Theorem 1. *Under conditions of Assumption 1 the following results hold for an i.i.d. sample $\{\theta_i\}_{i=1}^t$ from the distribution generated by the objective function $L(\cdot)$:*

(i) $\hat{\theta}_t \overset{p}{\longrightarrow} \bar{\theta} = (\int_\Theta \exp(-L(\theta)) \, d\theta)^{-1} \int_\Theta \theta \exp(-L(\theta)) \, d\theta$

(ii) $\sqrt{t}(\hat{\theta}_t - \bar{\theta}) \Rightarrow \mathcal{N}(0, \Sigma)$ *with some positive semi-definite matrix Σ.*

Proof. Provided Assumption 1 (iii), we can define $\bar{L} = (\int_\Theta \exp(-L(\theta)) \, d\theta)^{-1}$. Then $\bar{L} \exp(-L(\theta))$ will be a proper probability density function. Then we can apply Kolmogorov's strong LLN which leads to result (i).

Then also noting that Assumption 1 (iii) can be re-stated as $E[|\theta|^{2+\delta}] < \infty$ for a random variable θ sampled from the density $\bar{L} \exp(-L(\theta))$. Then we can apply the Lindeberg–Levy CLT which directly leads to result (ii). ∎

Next, consider the object $T_t = \sqrt{t}(\hat{\theta}_t - \bar{\theta})$. We can treat this object as a stochastic process indexed by t. As the behavior of this stochastic process is harder to characterize because it is in discrete time, we can consider its continuous-time approximations. To do that we can make a standard construction

$$T_{\tau,t} = \frac{1}{\sqrt{[t\tau]}} \sum_{i=1}^{[t\tau]} (\theta_i - \bar{\theta})$$

with $\tau \in [0, 1]$ and $[\cdot]$ denoting the integer part of the number. Also denote $\Sigma = \bar{L} \int (\theta - \bar{\theta})(\theta - \bar{\theta})' \exp(-L(\theta)) \, d\theta$.

Theorem 2. *Under conditions of Assumption 1*

$$\Sigma^{-1/2} T_{t,\tau} \Rightarrow \int_0^\tau dW(z)$$

where W is the p-dimensional Brownian motion with independent components.

Proof. Provided that the draws $\{\theta_i\}_{i=1}^{t}$ are i.i.d. with finite first and second moments, the process θ_t is a martingale difference sequence. Using the results in Stock (1994) we conclude that processes T_t and $T_{\tau,t}$ are close such that sup $\| T_{\tau,t} - T_t \| = o_p(1)$. Therefore, we can apply the Functional Central Limit Theorem to obtain the result of the theorem. ∎

Consider the process

$$L_{\tau,t} = \sqrt{[\tau\, t]}(L(\hat{\theta}_{[\tau\, t]}) - L(\bar{\theta}))$$

where $\tau \in [0, 1]$. These results are formalized in the following theorem, Theorem states that when $\hat{\theta}_t$ converges to point $\bar{\theta}$ that is not extremum, the scaled objective function will resemble the normal distribution. If $\bar{\theta} = \theta^*$, then the process will decay at the rate $1/\sqrt{t}$.

Theorem 3.

(i)   *Suppose that $\bar{\theta} \neq \theta^*$. Then*

$$L_{\tau,t} \Rightarrow D(\bar{\theta})'\Sigma^{1/2} W(\tau)$$

(ii) *Suppose that $\bar{\theta} = \theta^*$. Then*

$$[\tau\, t]L_{\tau,t} \Rightarrow \frac{1}{2} W(\tau)'\Sigma^{1/2'} H(\theta^*)'\Sigma^{1/2} W(\tau)$$

(iii) *Suppose that $\bar{\theta} = \theta^*$. Then*

$$\sqrt{t - [\tau\, t]}L_{\tau,t} \Rightarrow \frac{1}{2}\sqrt{\frac{1-\tau}{\tau}} W(\tau)'\Sigma^{1/2'} H(\theta^*)'\Sigma^{1/2} W(\tau)$$

Proof. We note that quadratic function is continuous. Thus, we can apply the continuous mapping theorem to translate the results of the previous theorem to show:

$$D(\hat{\theta}_t)T_t + \frac{1}{\sqrt{t}}T_t'H(\hat{\theta}_t)T_t \Rightarrow D(\bar{\theta})'\Sigma^{1/2} W(\tau)$$

where $\bar{\theta} \neq \theta^*$. If $\bar{\theta} = \theta^*$, then $D(\theta^*) = 0$. Therefore

$$T_t'H(\hat{\theta}_t)T_t \Rightarrow \frac{1}{2} W(\tau)'\Sigma^{1/2'} H(\theta^*)'\Sigma^{1/2} W(\tau)$$

By assumption, the distance between the objective function and its quadratic approximation has stochastic order $o_p(|\theta - \bar{\theta}|^2)$. Therefore, given that $\hat{\theta}_t = \bar{\theta} + O_p(1/\sqrt{t})$, the error will have stochastic order $o_p(1)$ in both first and second order expansions.

To obtain the last expression, we combine the previous result with $[\tau t]/t \to \tau$, as $t \to \infty$. ∎

As we demonstrated, the scaled objective function can be approximated by a continuous stochastic process. We now focus on the stochastic process that approximates $\sqrt{t}(L(\hat{\theta}_t) - L(\bar{\theta}))$. Denote this process $L(\tau)$ with $\tau \in [0, 1]$. Then we can write its expression in differential form using stochastic calculus. If $\bar{\theta} \neq \theta^*$,

$$dL(\tau) = D(\bar{\theta})'\Sigma^{1/2} \, dW(\tau) \tag{2}$$

In case when $\bar{\theta} = \theta^*$, this process can be written as

$$dL(\tau) = \frac{1}{\sqrt{1-\tau}} \left(\frac{1}{4} + \text{tr}(\Sigma^{1/2'} H(\theta^*)'\Sigma^{1/2}) \, d\tau + W(\tau)'\Sigma^{1/2'} H(\theta^*)'\Sigma^{1/2} \, dW(\tau) \right) \tag{3}$$

Note that both expressions (2) and (3) are represented by diffusion processes. However, in the first case the diffusion term is pre-multiplied by a constant and in the second case it is pre-multiplied by a function that decays as $1/\sqrt{1-\tau}$ in expectation. In the next section, we use the notion of stochastic stability to distinguish between these two types of behavior.

STOCHASTIC STABILITY OF DIFFUSION PROCESSES

General Results

Consider a general diffusion-driven dynamic stochastic process $L(\tau)$, with the dynamics given by

$$d\,L(\tau) = f(\tau, L(\tau)) \, d\tau + G(\tau, \, L(\tau)) \, dw(\tau) \tag{4}$$

where $\tau \geqslant 0$, $L(\tau)$ is $k \times 1$, and $f(L(\tau))$ and $G(\tau, L(\tau))$ are a drift and diffusion coefficients respectively.

We note that we were able to characterize the limiting process corresponding to the behavior of the objective function along the simulated Markov chain in terms. In particular, in case where the maximum of the objective function does not coincide with the limit of the LTE estimator, then

$$f(\cdot, \cdot) \equiv 0, \ G(\tau, L(\tau)) = D(\bar{\theta})' \Sigma^{1/2}$$

If the maximum of the objective function coinsides with the LTE estimator, then

$$f(\tau, L(\tau)) = \frac{1}{\sqrt{1-\tau}} \left(\frac{1}{4} + \text{tr}(\Sigma^{1/2'} H(\theta^*) \Sigma^{1/2}) \right)$$

$$G(\tau, L(\tau)) = \frac{1}{\sqrt{1-\tau}} W(\tau)' \Sigma^{1/2'} H(\theta^*) \Sigma^{1/2}$$

In the latter case we consider the behavior of the de-trended LTE objective function

$$\tilde{L}(\tau) = L(\tau) - \int_0^\tau \frac{1}{\sqrt{1-u}} \left(\frac{1}{4} + \text{tr}(\Sigma^{1/2'} H(\theta^*) \Sigma^{1/2}) \right) du$$

We will abuse notation and denote the objective function $L(\tau)$ in both cases indicating which particular case we are considering.

We will restrict our analysis to the case when the solution to Eq. (4) is unique in the family of non-anticipating stochastic processes on [0,1]. Uniqueness is guaranteed by the following set of assumptions:

Assumption 2. Assume that

• L^* is an equilibrium of an unperturbed System (4), i.e.,

$$f(\tau, L^*) = 0$$

• $f(\tau, L)$ is bounded and Lipschitz continuous in $(\tau, L) \in [0, 1]l \times \mathbb{R}$;
• $G(\tau, L)$ is Lipschitz continuous in L with a Lipschitz constant $\mathscr{L} \geqslant 0$;
• For all $L \in \mathbb{R}$ and $\tau \in [0, 1]$ there exists a constant $K > 0$ such that

$$\| G(\tau, L) \| \leqslant K(1 + \| L \|);$$

• $L(0)$, the starting value of the process described by (4) is a second-order random vector independent of the family of σ-algebras $\mathscr{F}_t$ generated by the Brownian motion $W(\tau)$ for $\tau \in [0, 1]$.

We note that the first condition is trivially satisfied by the limiting process of the LTE objective function. By de-trending the process, we guarantee that the diffusion term will move in the vicinity of the origin. We also note that

$\sup_{\tau \to 1} \|\tilde{L}(\tau) - L(\tau)\| = 0$. In other words, asymptotically, the de-trended process in case where the LTE estimate indeed converges to the maximum of the objective function, is a good uniform approximation for the original process. To express our results in the spirit of the original results from the theory of stochastic stability, we make the change of variables $t = (1 - \tau)^{-1}$ so that the asymptotic results will be expressed for the variable $t \geqslant 1$ and $t \to +\infty$ as $\tau \to 1$. The following definition formalizes different concepts of stochastic stability from the literature on stochastic diffusion processes.[4]

Definition 1. Assume that L^* in $\mathbb{R}$ is a unique equilibrium of (4), and $L(t)$ for $t \geq 1$ is the stochastic process that satisfies (4). Then,

1. L^* is a stochastically stable equilibrium, if for all $\varepsilon > 0$

$$P_{\mathscr{F}_t} \left\{ \sup_{t \in \mathbb{R}_+} |L(t) - L^*| \geqslant \varepsilon |L(1)| \right\} \xrightarrow{p} 0$$

for all $L(1) \xrightarrow{p} L^*$. Otherwise, the equilibrium is stochastically unstable.

2. L^* is a locally asymptotically stochastically stable equilibrium, if it is stochastically stable and

$$P_{\mathscr{F}_t} \left\{ \lim_{t \to +\infty} |L(t) - L^*| = 0 |L(1)| \right\} \xrightarrow{p} 1$$

for all $L(1) \xrightarrow{p} L^*$.

3. L^* is a globally stochastically asymptotically stable equilibrium relative to set $\bar{\mathbb{R}} \ni L^*$, if it is asymptotically stochastically stable and

$$P_{\mathscr{F}_t} \left\{ \lim_{t \to +\infty} |L(t) - L^*| = 0 | L(1)| \right\} = 1$$

for all $L(1) \in \mathbb{L} \subset \mathbb{R}$.

Local stability of equilibrium implies that for all processes with starting points approaching the equilibrium L^*, the probability that the stochastic process leaves an arbitrary small neighborhood of equilibrium approaches zero. The definition of asymptotic stability strengthens the notion of stochastic stability by imposing further that a locally stable stochastic process approach the equilibrium with probability tending to one, when a starting point is tending to L^*. The requirement for a stochastic process (4) to be globally asymptotically stable is that besides being stable, all processes described by the system (4) find themselves in equilibrium with probability 1, when a starting point belongs to some set $\mathbb{L}$. Global stability is defined relative to a subset of starting values, which means that while a stochastic process may be globally unstable for some starting values, it may still be considered globally stable relative to another set of starting values.

Because ultimately we are interested in convergence from different starting points, the concept of global stochastic stability is the most relevant for this chapter. Theorem 4 provides the sufficient conditions for the global stability of the equilibrium for the process that satisfies Eq. (4).

Theorem 4. *Suppose the process described by system* (4) *satisfies assumption* 2, *and there exists a positive definite in Lyapunov's sense[5] function* $v(t, L) : [1, +\infty) \times \mathbb{R} \to \mathbb{R}$, *which is twice continuously differentiable with respect to* L, *and once continuously differentiable with respect to* t *everywhere except possibly at the equilibrium point* L^*, *such that*

$$\mathscr{L}v = \frac{\partial v(t, L)}{\partial t} + f(t, L)\frac{\partial v(t, L)}{\partial L} + \frac{1}{2}G(t, L)G(t, L)'\frac{\partial^2 v(t, L)}{\partial L^2} < 0 \qquad (5)$$

for all $(t, L) \in [1, +\infty) \times \mathbb{L}$; *moreover,* $v(t, L)$ *has an infinitesimal upper limit, i.e.,*

$$\lim_{\substack{L \to L^* \\ t > 1}} \sup v(t, L) = 0$$

and be radially unbounded, i.e.,

$$\lim_{\substack{|L| \to \infty \\ t > 1}} \inf v(t, L) = \infty$$

Then the equilibrium point L^* *is globally asymptotically stochastically stable relative to set* $\mathbb{L}$.

The proof of this theorem can be found in Gikhman and Skorokhod (2004). As follows from this theorem, the equilibrium of the process (4) is stochastically stable if a Lyapunov function $v(t, L)$ satisfying the conditions in Theorem 4 can be found such that the inequality in Eq. (5) holds.

A Stability-Based Convergence Criterion

The process approximating the normalized objective function L_t can be presented in the following form:

$$dL(\tau) = f(\tau, L(\tau))\, d\tau + G(\tau, L(\tau))\, dW(\tau)$$

where $W(\cdot)$ is independent p-dimensional Brownian motion, $G(\tau, L) = D(\bar{\theta})\Sigma^{1/2}$ in the unstable case and $G(\tau, L) = \frac{1}{\sqrt{1-\tau}} W(\tau)'\Sigma^{1/2'} H(\bar{\theta})\Sigma^{1/2}$ in the stable case. Suppose that the objective function is appropriately scaled, i.e., $\Sigma^{-1} = -H(\bar{\theta})$. Note that inlight of our change of variables $t = (1 - \tau)^{-1}$, we can express the coefficients for the diffusion term $G(t, L) = D(\bar{\theta})\Sigma^{1/2}$ and $G(t, L) = \sqrt{t}W(t)'\Sigma^{1/2'} H(\bar{\theta})\Sigma^{1/2}$. We then select the Lyapounov function to be

$$v(t, L) = -\exp(-|L - L(\bar{\theta})|/t) \tag{6}$$

Then in case where the LTE estimate function does not converge to the maximum of the objective function, the stability criterion almost everywhere leads to

$$\mathscr{L}v = \frac{1}{t}\exp(-|L - L(\bar{\theta})|/t) - \frac{1}{t^2}D(\bar{\theta})\Sigma D(\bar{\theta})' \exp(-|L - L(\bar{\theta})|/t) \to 0$$

Thus, $\lim_{t\to\infty} \mathscr{L}v = 0$. Therefore, the limiting process is not asymptotically stable. On the other hand, in case where the LTE estimate converges to the maximum, then

$$\mathscr{L}v = \frac{1}{t}\exp(-|L - L(\bar{\theta})|/t) - \frac{1}{t}W(t)'W(t)\exp(-|L - L(\bar{\theta})|/t) < 0$$

Thus, the limiting process is globally asymptotically stable. The limiting behavior will be deterimed by the product of two Brownian motions: $-\mathscr{L}v \to \frac{1}{t}W(t)'W(t) \sim \chi_p^2$.

The sufficient condition for the stability of this diffusion process from Theorem 4 can now be used to formulate the null hypotheses (which implies that the LTE converges to the maximum of the o):

$$H_0 : L_t \text{ is globally stochastically stable for (6):} \tag{7}$$

Assuming the continuous-time stochastic process is a good approximation for the empirical process of the cumulative average of the posterior Markov chain, we apply the stability test to the cumulative mean of the posterior draws. The simplest form for the test statistic can be constructed directly from the behavior of $-\mathscr{L}v$, which has asymptotic χ^2 distribution in case where the LTE converges to the maximum of the objective function. In this case,

$$-t(L(\hat{\theta}_t) - L(\bar{\theta})) \xrightarrow{d} \chi_p^2 \tag{8}$$

If the information matrix equality does not hold, the limit will be a mixture of χ^2 random variables. When the Lyapunov function is quadratic, the stability criterion for the driftless process is $G(\tau, W)G(\tau, W) < 0$. This means that test (8) corresponds to the test for model stability with quadratic Lyapunov function. Thus, the criterion in our case consists in calculating statistics CT_t

$$CT_t = -t(L(\hat{\theta}_t) - L(\bar{\theta})) \tag{9}$$

and comparing it with the corresponding quantile of the χ^2-distribution. If

$$CT_t > \chi_p^2(1 - q)$$

one can reject the null hypothesis $\bar{\theta} = \theta^*$.

Example

The following simple example illustrates the behavior of the objective function when the convergence to the maximum does and doesn't occur. Suppose the objective function to be maximized is a simple quadratic function $L(\theta) = -\theta^2/2$ and the parameter space is the interval $\theta \in [-1, 1]$. Then the distribution that will be associated with this exponentiated objective function is the standard normal distribution truncated to $[-1, 1]$: $f(\theta) = \varphi(\theta)\mathbf{1}\{\theta \in [-1, 1]\}/(1 - 2\Phi(-1))$. The maximum of this objective function coincides with the mean and it is equal to zero, $\theta^* = \bar{\theta} = 0$. Thus, given the sample of draws from density $f(\cdot)$, the normalized objective function is $L_t = -\sqrt{t}\,\hat{\theta}_t^2/2$ will collapse toward zero, while $-t\,\hat{\theta}_t^2/2$ will approach the χ^2-distributed random variable as $t \to \infty$.

Now consider an alternative quadratic objective, $\tilde{L}(\theta) = -(\theta - \frac{1}{2})^2/2$, defined over the same parameter space $[-1, 1]$. The corresponding quasi-posterior distribution associated with this objective function is the normal distribution truncated to $[-1, 1]$: $\tilde{f}(\theta) = \varphi(\theta - \frac{1}{2})\mathbf{1}\{\theta \in [-1, 1]\}/(1 - \Phi(-\frac{3}{2}) - \Phi(-\frac{1}{2}))$. While the maximum of the corresponding objective function is $\theta^* = \frac{1}{2}$, the mean of the corresponding distribution is

$$\bar{\theta} = \frac{1}{2} - \frac{e^{-\frac{1}{8}} - e^{-\frac{9}{8}}}{\sqrt{2\pi}(1 - \Phi(-\frac{3}{2}) - \Phi(-\frac{1}{2}))} < \frac{1}{2}$$

The normalized objective is

$$\tilde{L}_t = -\frac{\sqrt{t}}{2}\left(\left(\hat{\theta}_t - \frac{1}{2}\right)^2 - \left(\bar{\theta} - \frac{1}{2}\right)^2\right)$$

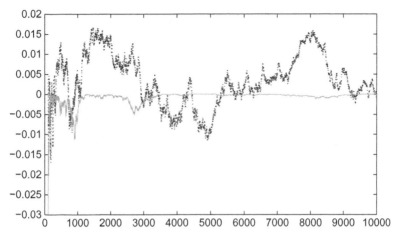

Fig. 1. Example. The Behavior of the Objective Function when the Stochastic Algorithm Does and Does Not Converge to the True Maximum.
Note: The solid line shows the normalized objective in case $\bar{\theta} = \theta^*$, while the dashed dotted line corresponds to the case when $\bar{\theta} \neq \theta^*$.

For both objective functions $L(\theta)$ and $\tilde{L}(\theta)$, we generate sequences $\{\theta_t\}_{t=1}^{T}$, where $T = 10^6$ by randomly sampling from distributions $f(\theta)$ and $\tilde{f}(\theta)$. Fig. 1 shows the trajectories of the normalized objectives L_t and $\tilde{L}_t$ in the two scenarios. The solid green line corresponds to the first case when $\bar{\theta} = \theta^*$, and the dotted blue line denotes the second scenario with $\bar{\theta} \neq \theta^*$. Consistent with the theory, the figure reveals that the statistics L_t stabilizes around 0 in the first scenario, while $\tilde{L}_t$ fails to converge to 0.

EMPIRICAL APPLICATION

We use a version of the dynamics stochastic general equilibrium (DSGE) model popular in the empirical macroeconomics (see Christiano et al., 2005 and Smets & Wouters, 2007). The model is summarized by a dynamic system of aggregate variables, such as output, consumption, employment, etc. The choice of the model is motivated by the fact that the DSGE models, although often enhanced with a number of features to facilitate the fit of the model to the data, are still simpler in terms of dynamics and less computationally intensive than models from the microeconometric literature. The use of a simpler model makes our argument stronger.

We choose to work with an artificial dataset to mitigate the problem of model misspecification. The objective function is the distance function that matches impulse responses between the model and the data. Using the model-generated samples, we estimate the structural vector autoregression (SVAR) model and obtain impulse responses from this model, following a common approach in the literature. Although this empirical model is misspecified by definition, it is widely used in the literature, and we find that the resulting bias is not significant.

In the remaining part of the chapter, we first describe the general structure of the model. We proceed by explaining how the model was calibrated, and how data samples were generated. Then, we explain the strategy to estimate model parameters. Finally, we present the results of the empirical exercise.

Model

The model is a version of the DSGE model studied in Christiano et al. (2005). We introduce real and nominal rigidities, such as variable investment costs and habit formation, and nominal rigidities by assuming Calvo-Yun style price and wage stickiness.[6] For simplicity, we abstract from modeling money, and focus on a cashless economy.

A representative infinitely lived household maximizes the expected lifetime utility

$$\mathscr{E}_0 \sum_{t=0}^{\infty} \beta^t u(c_t - bc_{t-1}, 1 - l_t)$$

where $\beta \in [0,1]$ is the discount factor, and $\mathscr{E}_0$ denotes expectation conditional on information in period $t = 0$. The logarithmic intratemporal utility is defined over consumption and leisure

$$u(c_t, 1 - l_t) = d_t \varphi \log(c_t - bc_{t-1}) + (1 - \varphi) \log(1 - l_t)$$

where $c_t - bc_{t-1}$ is the adjusted for habit consumption, $b \in [0,1]$ is the habits parameter, l_t represents hours of work, and d_t is the stochastic preference shock process evolving as follows

$$\log(d_{t+1}) = \rho_d \log(d_t) + \varepsilon_t^d \tag{10}$$

where $\rho_d \in [0,1)$ is parameter, $\varepsilon_t^d \sim$ i.i.d$(0, \sigma_d^2)$, and standard deviation $\sigma_d > 0$.

Each household supplies a continuum of differentiated labor types to the labor market in a monopolistically competitive fashion. These labor types are aggregated into homogenous labor by a competitive labor packer firm using a Dixit–Stiglitz aggregating technology where η_p is the intratemporal elasticity of substitution between different labor types. The homogeneous labor is then supplied to intermediate producers to use in the intermediate goods production. In each period, with probability $1 - \alpha_w$ households can freely change the wage rate for differentiated labor supplies. With probability α_w, the wage rate may not be changed freely; however it is allowed to partially adjust to the previous period inflation π_{t-1} according to the formula

$$W_t^j = W_{t-1}^j \pi_{t-1}^{\chi_w}$$

where $\chi_w \in [0, 1]$ is the parameter of partial wage indexation.

Households invest to accumulate capital, and then rent it to firms. Capital is produced from consumption goods using a linear technology, according to which, in every period t, 1 unit of consumption good makes Y_t units of new capital. The technology process Y_t is stochastic, and evolves according to

$$\log(Y_{t+1}) = \rho_Y \log(Y_t) + \varepsilon_t^Y \tag{11}$$

where $\rho_Y \in [0, 1)$ is parameter, $\varepsilon_t^Y \sim$ i.i.d.$(0, \sigma_Y^2)$, and $\sigma_Y > 0$. Capital depreciates at a rate δ, and any adjustment to the level of investment relative to the previous period level is associated with the capital loss. Following Christiano et al. (2005), we assume that the loss per unit of investment is

$$\Phi\left(\frac{i_t}{i_{t-1}}\right) = \frac{\kappa}{2}\left(\frac{i_t}{i_{t-1}} - 1\right)^2$$

where i_t denotes investment and $\kappa > 0$ is a parameter determining the convexity of the investment cost function.

Besides wage and rental income, households may receive dividends from ownership in firms, and net lump-sum transfers from government.

A continuum of intermediate firms of measure 1 produce differentiated goods according to the Cobb–Douglas technology

$$y_{i,t} \leq z_t k_{i,t}^{1-\theta} h_{i,t}^\theta$$

where $k_{i,t}$ denotes capital, $h_{i,t}$ is homogeneous labor factor, $\theta \in [0, 1]$ is the parameter determining the share of labor in production, and z_t is the exogenous stochastic technology process that evolves according to

$$\log(z_{t+1}) = \rho_z \log(z_t) + \varepsilon_t^z \tag{12}$$

where $\rho_z \in [0, 1)$ is the autocorrelation parameter, and ε_t^z is an i.i.d.$(0, \sigma_z^2)$ stochastic process, with $\sigma_z > 0$.

The intermediate goods are the inputs to the production of the final homogenous good y_t by competitive firms using a Dixit–Stiglitz aggregating technology, with parameter $\eta_p > 1$ determining the intratemporal elasticity of substitution between differentiated inputs. According to the Calvo–Yun price rigidity setting, in every period a firm can reset the price for its product with probability $1 - \alpha_p$. However, with probability α_p the firm cannot choose its price freely, but is allowed to partially adjust it for the previous period inflation π_{t-1} according to the formula

$$P_t^i = P_{t-1}^i \pi_{t-1}^{\chi_p}$$

where $\chi_p \in [0, 1]$ is the parameter of partial indexation for prices.

Monetary policy follows a simple Taylor type interest rate rule

$$\log\left(\frac{R_t}{R}\right) = \alpha_R \log\left(\frac{R_{t-1}}{R}\right) + \alpha_\pi \log\left(\frac{\pi_t}{\pi}\right) + \alpha_y \log\left(\frac{y_t}{y_{t-1}}\right) + \log(\mu_t^r)$$

where α_R, α_π, and α_y are parameters, and μ_t^r is the stochastic preference shock process evolving as follows

$$\log(\mu_{t+1}^r) = \rho_r \log(\mu_t^r) + \varepsilon_t^r \tag{13}$$

where $\rho_r \in [0, 1)$ is parameter, $\varepsilon_t^r \sim$ i.i.d.$(0, \sigma_r^2)$, and $\sigma_r > 0$.

Finally, the fiscal policy is very simple. The government spending g_t is exogenous and financed by lump-sum taxes, which implies that the following government budget constraint is satisfied in every period. The stochastic process for government spending is

$$\log(g_{t+1}) = \rho_g \log(g_t) + \varepsilon_t^g \tag{14}$$

where $\varepsilon_t^g \sim$ i.i.d.$(0, \sigma_g^2)$, and $\sigma_g > 0$.

As is standard in the literature, we focus on a symmetric equilibrium, where all firms with an opportunity to change prices will set them at the same level. By analogy, all wages that can be changed will be set by households at the same level for each labor type. The model equilibrium is then determined as a nonlinear dynamic system of 14 variables that, given shock processes in Eqs. (10)–(14), evolve over time according to the following system of 14 difference equations:

$$k_{t+1} = (1 - \delta)k_t + \Upsilon_t i_t \left(1 - \Phi\left(\frac{i_t}{i_{t-1}}\right)\right) \tag{15}$$

$$\frac{y_t}{s_t^p} = c_t + g_t + i_t \tag{16}$$

$$\lambda_t = u_1(c_t - bc_{t-1}, 1 - l_t) + \beta u_1(c_{t+1} - bc_t, 1 - l_{t+1}) \tag{17}$$

$$\lambda_t q_t = \beta \lambda_{t+1}(mc_{t+1} z_{t+1} \surd f_1(k_{t+1}, h_{t+1}) + q_{t+1}(1 - \delta)) \tag{18}$$

$$\lambda_t = q_t Y_t \Phi_{i_t}\left(\frac{i_t}{i_{t-1}}\right) + \beta \lambda_{t+1} q_{t+1} Y_{t+1} \Phi_{i_t}(i_{t+1}, i_t) \tag{19}$$

$$\lambda_t = b\beta r_t \frac{\lambda_{t+1}}{\pi_{t+1}} \tag{20}$$

$$s_{t+1}^p = (1 - \alpha_p)\tilde{p}_t^{-\eta_p} + \alpha_p \left(\frac{\pi_t}{\pi_{t-1}^{\chi_p}}\right)^{\eta_p} s_t \tag{21}$$

$$s_{t+1}^w = (1 - \alpha_w)\left(\frac{\tilde{w}_t}{w_t}\right)^{-\eta_w} + \alpha_w \left(\frac{w_{t-1}}{w_t}\right)^{-\eta_w} \left(\frac{\pi_t}{\pi_{t-1}^{\chi_w}}\right)^{\eta_w} s_t^w \tag{22}$$

$$\mathscr{F}_t = \frac{\eta_w - 1}{\eta_w} \tilde{w}_t \lambda_t \left(\frac{\tilde{w}_t}{w_t}\right)^{-\eta_w} h_t + \alpha_w \beta \left(\frac{\pi_{t+1}}{\pi_t^{\chi_w}}\right)^{\eta_w - 1} \left(\frac{\tilde{w}_{t+1}}{\tilde{w}_t}\right)^{\eta_w - 1} \mathscr{F}_{t+1} \tag{23}$$

$$\mathscr{F}_t = u_2(c_t, 1 - l_t) \left(\frac{\tilde{w}_t}{w_t}\right)^{-\eta_w} h_t + \alpha_w \beta \left(\frac{\pi_{t+1}}{\pi_t^{\chi_w}}\right)^{\eta_w} \left(\frac{\tilde{w}_{t+1}}{\tilde{w}_t}\right)^{\eta_w} \mathscr{F}_{t+1} \tag{24}$$

$$\mathscr{X}_t = y_t mc_t \tilde{p}^{-\eta_p - 1} + \alpha_p \beta \frac{\lambda_{t+1}}{\lambda_t} \left(\frac{\tilde{p}_{t+1}}{\tilde{p}_t}\right)^{\eta_p + 1} \left(\frac{\pi_{t+1}}{\pi_t^{\chi_p}}\right)^{\eta_p} \mathscr{X}_{t+1} \tag{25}$$

$$\mathscr{X}_t = \frac{\eta_p - 1}{\eta_p} y_t \tilde{p}_t^{-\eta_p} + \alpha_p \beta \frac{\lambda_{t+1}}{\lambda_t} \left(\frac{\tilde{p}_{t+1}}{\tilde{p}_t}\right)^{\eta_p} \left(\frac{\pi_{t+1}}{\pi_t^{\chi_p}}\right)^{\eta_p - 1} \mathscr{X}_{t+1} \tag{26}$$

$$\log\left(\frac{R_t}{R}\right) = \alpha_R \log\left(\frac{R_{t-1}}{R}\right) + \alpha_\pi \log\left(\frac{\pi_t}{\pi}\right) + \alpha_y \log\left(\frac{y_t}{y_{t-1}}\right) \tag{27}$$

where all the variables in Eqs. (15)–(27) are defined in Tables A1 and A2, and

$$w_t = mc_t z_t \theta \left(\frac{k_t}{h_t}\right)^{1-\theta}$$

$$y_t = \frac{z_t k_t^{1-\theta} h_t^\theta - \psi}{s_{t+1}^p}$$

$$l_t = s_t^w h_t$$

$$\tilde{p}_t = \left(\frac{1 - \alpha \left(\frac{\pi_t}{\pi_{t-1}^\chi} \right)^{\eta_p - 1}}{1 - \alpha} \right)^{-1/(\eta_p - 1)}$$

and

$$\tilde{w}_t = \left(\frac{w_t^{1 - \eta_w} - \alpha_w w_{t-1}^{1 - \eta_w} \left(\frac{\pi_t}{\pi_{t-1}^{\chi_w}} \right)^{1 - \eta_w}}{(1 - \alpha_w)} \right)^{1/(1 - \eta_w)}$$

are the real wage rate, final good output, labor supply, relative optimal price by firms, and relative optimal wage by households respectively.

The 14 endogenous variables that constitute the equilibrium dynamics of the model are: mc_t, q_t, i_t, h_t, c_t, λ_t, π_t, $\mathcal{F}_t$, $\mathcal{X}_t$, R_t, s_t^p, s_t^w, k_t, and y_t.

Data Generating Process

To generate the data, we calibrate the model as follows. We set the intertemporal discount factor $\beta = 0.9902$, which corresponds to a steady state annualized real interest rate of approximately 4 percent. Depreciation rate δ is set at a conventional value of 2.5 percent. The investment adjustment costs κ is 3, and habits parameter is calibrated at 0.6. The technology parameter θ that reflects the share of labor in output is set at 0.7, implying the capital share of 0.3. Calvo parameters for price (α_p) and wage (α_w) rigidities are 0.6 and 0.8 respectively, which implies that on average prices are set for a period of 2.5 quarter, and wages change every 5 quarters. Both wages and prices are subject to partial indexation, with χ_p and χ_w set at 0.5. The elasticities of substitution between different labor types and differentiated intermediate goods, η_w and η_p, are both set equal to 6 to imply steady state markups of 20 percent. Monetary policy rule coefficients α_R, α_π, and α_y are set at 0.7, $0.3 \times 1.5 = 0.45$ and $0.5 \times 0.3 = 0.15$ correspondingly, to imply that the rule is inertial, and satisfies the generalized Taylor principle. The steady state inflation is $\pi = 1$, steady state labor is $h = 0.3$, and the steady state shadow price of capital is fixed at $q = 1$. The steady state government consumption is 20 percent of GDP. Finally, the steady state technology is $z = 1$, the autocorrelations of all stochastic processes ρ_z, ρ_g, ρ_d, ρ_Y, ρ_r, are assumed 0.8, the standard deviations σ_z, σ_Y, σ_d, σ_g, are 0.03, and $\sigma_r = 0.01$. Table A2 and column 3 in Table A3 summarize the calibration of model parameters.

In the empirical exercise, we focus on matching theoretical responses to impulse responses obtained from the structural VAR (SVAR) model widely used in the empirical literature, where Cholesky factorization is used to identify shocks. Cholesky factorization implicitly assumes that some endogenous variables cannot respond contemporaneously to some shocks.[7] To avoid discrepancy between model and empirical impulse response functions, we incorporate timing constraints into the model in the same way as is done in Christiano et al. (2005). We solve the model using the perturbation method outlined in Kormilitsina (2012), which incorporates timing constraints in the solution. The solution to the model is given by a dynamic system of all model variables.

To obtain the artificial dataset, we generate samples for the following seven variables: GDP, consumption, investment, hours, the real wage rate, inflation, and the interest rate. Each sample is generated by feeding realizations of the stochastic processes in Eqs. (10)–(14) into the dynamic system describing the equilibrium of the model for $N = 200$ quarters. To avoid the problem of stochastic singularity as pointed out by Ireland (2004), we add measurement errors to the data, so that observations z_t^{obs} are related to the underlying model generated data z_t^{model} as follows

$$z_t^{\text{obs}} = z_t^{\text{model}}(1 + err_t)$$

where err_t is a multivariate (7×1) i.i.d. random variable with mean zero and the standard deviation of 0.1.

We use the sample z_t^{obs} to obtain data impulse responses following a commonly approach used in the literature. In particular, we estimate a vector autoregression model with two lags (VAR(2)) in the way an empirical economist would do. We place the productivity variable, $\log(\text{GDP}_t/H_t)$ first in the VAR. This variable identifies the neutral technology shock. Following the standards of the empirical literature, we order the interest rate last in the VAR. The interest rate represents the reaction of monetary policy to observed information about the current state of the economy. The variables with ordering from 2 to 6 are inflation, and the logs of labor, wages, consumption, and investment, correspondingly. We use this VAR model to obtain impulse response functions $\hat{X}_N$ of the seven variables of interest. These sample impulse responses are then used in an IRF matching exercise described in the next subsection.

By construction, the data impulse responses are misspecified because they are obtained from the misspecified VAR model, which includes only a finite number of lags. We follow this route because it is the most common strategy in estimation by matching impulse responses. We also estimate the model using true impulse responses as data. These responses can be thought of as data impulse responses obtained with a data set of infinite length, where the effect of misspecification is completely eliminated.

Estimation

We use the Laplace type estimator by Chernozhukov and Hong (2003) to estimate the vector of 10 parameters

$$\theta = \{b, \ \kappa, \ \alpha_p, \ \alpha_w, \ \chi_p, \ \chi_w \ \rho_z, \ \sigma_z, \ \rho_r, \ \sigma_r\}$$

The distance function $L_N(\theta)$ is the weighted average of the difference between theoretical and empirical impulse response functions:

$$L^N(\theta) = (X(\theta) - \hat{X}_N)' \hat{V}_N (X(\theta) - \hat{X}_N) \tag{28}$$

where $X(\theta)$ denotes impulse responses generated by the model, and $\hat{X}_N$ denotes impulse responses predicted by an empirical model with N data observations. $\hat{V}_N$ is the weighting matrix.[8] Following Christiano et al. (2005), we use the diagonal weighting matrix with inverse of variances of impulse responses along the diagonal.

The estimates are obtained by generating a Markov chain of 1 million draws using the random-walk Hastings – Metropolis algorithm. We assume that the prior distribution $\pi(\theta)$ is uniform over the parameter space. Some parameters (b, α_p, α_w, χ_p, χ_w, ρ_z, ρ_r) are restricted by a unit interval [0, 1], while others are assumed to be greater than 0 (κ, σ_z, σ_r). The transition kernel is $q(x|y) = f(|x - y|)$, where f is a multivariate 10×1 zero-mean normal distribution with variance $V = \sigma D$, where D is the inverse of the negative numerical hessian of the distance function, $D = -H^{-1}$, $H = \partial^2 L^N(\theta)/\partial\theta\partial\theta'$, and σ is a scaling parameter. The hessian is evaluated in a starting point for the Markov chain, ξ^0, and D is induced to be symmetric by deriving D from the following transformation:

$$D = V \Lambda V$$

where V is the matrix of eigenvectors of D, and Λ is the diagonal matrix with absolute values of eigenvalues of D along the diagonal. The scaling parameter σ is adjusted to achieve the acceptance rate of the algorithm between 30 and 40 percent.

Results

Table A3 presents the estimates and standard deviations of parameters obtained as means and standard deviations of the MCMC chains. Columns 1 and 2 provide list and describe the estimated parameters. Column 3 shows parameter values used to obtain the data, while Columns 4 and 5 list the estimates for the two cases, when data impulse responses are derived from the SVAR model with data set of length 200, and when $\hat{X}_N$ are the true impulse responses.

The estimates for the case $N = 200$ are quite close to the true parameters of the data generating process. The bias in estimates is the combination of the small sample, misspecification, and the possible estimation bias. Not surprisingly, the bias is much smaller for the case when true impulse responses are used as data. Interestingly, the parameters of nominal rigidities α_p, α_w, χ_p, and χ_w are estimated quite precisely for both cases. Canova and Sala (2009) state these parameters may be subject to identification issues and provide an example of a simple dynamic model without endogenous

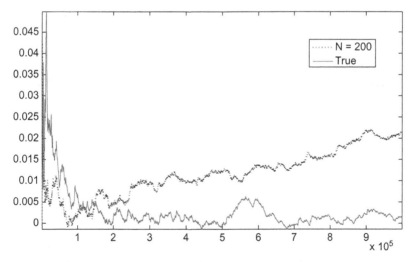

Fig. 2. Empirical Application: Normalized Distance Function.
Note: The figure shows the normalized distance L_t^N in empirical application. The dotted line represents the case when impulse responses are derived from the sample of data $N = 200$, and the solid line shows L_t^N when empirical impulse responses are given by the true model responses.

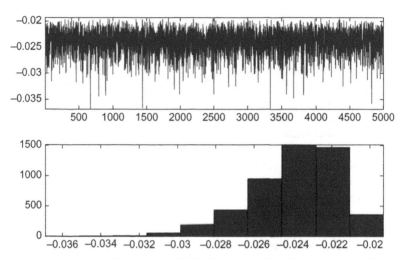

Fig. 3. Empirical Application: MCMC Chain and Distribution of the Distance Function, $N = 200$.
Note: The figure shows the MCMC chain and the histogram for the distance function $L^N(\theta_t)$.

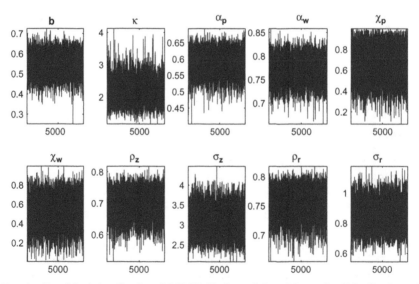

Fig. 4. Empirical Application: MCMC Chain and Quasi-Posterior Distribution of the Parameters, $N = 200$.

states where these parameters cannot be identified. However, identification does not seem to be an issue in our model because it has many features that give rise to multiple endogenous state variables, such as habits formation, investment costs, and inertial monetary policy. Moreover, we reduced the set of estimated parameters by excluding the coefficients of the monetary policy rule from estimation.[9] The lack of identification usually makes it problematic to obtain parameter estimates, because of the failure to achieve stationarity of Markov chains. Figs. 3–5 report the MCMC chains and posterior distributions for the objective function and parameters. These graphs visually verify that there are no obvious problems with estimation.[10] In particular, the MCMC chains mix well, and converge to a stationary distribution suggesting that all estimated parameters in the model are identified.

To apply our theory, we check whether the mean estimate $\bar{\theta}$ is a good estimator of the quasi-likelihood maximizer for both cases. To apply the test in Eq. (7), we rely on a two-step procedure. First, we generate an MCMC

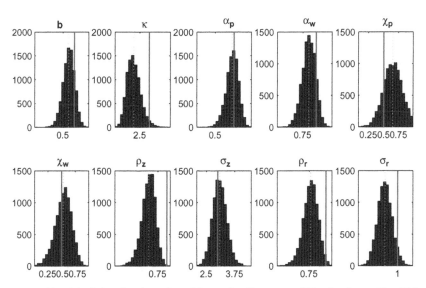

Fig. 5. Empirical Application: Quasi-Posterior Parameter Distributions, $N = 200$.
Note: The figure shows the histograms of estimated posterior parameter distributions for the empirical application with sample size $N = 200$. The vertical solid red line is the true value, and the vertical black dashed line is the mean of the quasi-posterior distribution.

chain to obtain the estimates for $\bar{\theta}$. Then, another MCMC chain is used to compute the normalized objective L_t^N.[11]

Fig. 2 plots the processes L_t^N for each 100th element of the Markov chain. The blue dotted line in the graph corresponds to $N = 200$ iterations, and the red solid line shows the statistics L_t^{True}. The graphs reveal that the process L_t^{200} does not concentrate around 0, especially in comparison with the process L_t^{True}. This happens because the running estimate $\hat{\theta}_t$ does not converge at the right speed for $N = 200$. At $t = 10^6$, L_t^{200} exceeds 0.02, and the test statistics in Eq. (9) calculates at the last iteration is $CT_t = 21.34$. This is greater than the critical value $\chi_{10}^2(0.95) = 18.3$, therefore the null hypothesis $\bar{\theta} = \theta^*$ is rejected. At the same time, L_t^{True} is close to zero for larger values of t. The implied test statistics is $CT_t = 1.4$, which is much smaller than the critical value $\chi_{10}^2(0.95)$. This allows to conclude that the null hypothesis $\bar{\theta} = \theta^*$ cannot be rejected in this case.

CONCLUSION

In this chapter, we investigate how well the Laplace-type estimator is able to match the extremum of the sample objective function. We show that the LTE may be arbitrarily far from the extremum, even if the distribution of simulation draws constructed from the objective function have converged to the quasi-posterior distribution. We emphasize that the LTE cannot be interpreted as an alternative way to compute the maximum of the sample objective function.

To obtain our results, we treat estimation as a stochastic process. We introduce the so-called normalized objective function, which is evaluated at the running estimate of the parameter of interest. We then show that the LTE can be approximated by a stable continuous time stochastic process when the LTE converges to the true maximum. Otherwise, it follows an unstable stochastic process. As a result, we suggest a simple test to verify if the LTE is close enough to the extremum of the sample objective function. We illustrate the performance of our test for a prototype simple DSGE model using artificial datasets of different length. We conclude that convergence of the LTE to the maximum of the objective function may be more problematic in smaller samples.

NOTES

1. Note that this function is evaluated at the running approximate maximum $\hat{\theta}_t = \frac{1}{t}\sum_{i=1}^t \theta_i$ rather than the tth MCMC draw θ_t.

2. Here we assume for simplicity that the objective function is smooth. However, the results can be extended to consider non-smooth discontinuous functions.

3. This result holds under the continuity of the first-order derivative, $\partial L(\bar{\theta})/\partial\theta$, and $\hat{\theta}_t \xrightarrow{a.s.} \bar{\theta}$.

4. These definitions can be found in Hasminskii (1980).

5. A function $v(t, L)$ is said to be positive definite in Lyapunov sense in a neighborhood of $L = L^*$, if $v(t, L^*) = 0$, and in this neighborhood $v(t, L) > w(L)$, where $w(L) > 0$, for $L \neq L^*$.

6. See Calvo (1983) and Yun (1996).

7. It is common to also impose long-run identifying restrictions to identify the neutral technology shock. However, there is no rationale for using long-run identification restrictions, because the dataset is obtained from the model without steady state growth. Using this identification strategy in our model would create additional specification bias that we would like to avoid.

8. In estimation, we use impulse responses for 20 steps of each variable, which gives rise to 140 points to match. Thus, $X(\theta)$ and $\hat{X}_N$ are vectors 140×1, and $\hat{V}_N$ is 140×140.

9. These parameters are often reported difficult to estimate in IRF matching problems.

10. We also use other means of diagnostics such as plots of autocorrelations and running means of MCMC chains, and the separated partial means test suggested by Geweke (2005).

11. At the second step, we run the algorithm with $\bar{\theta}$ as a starting value for the total of 1 million iterations. We record every 100th iteration to obtain the chain of 10,000 elements.

ACKNOWLEDGMENT

We would like to thank Han Hong and an anonymous referee for valuable comments.

REFERENCES

Altig, D., Christiano, L., Eichenbaum, M., & Lindé, J. (2011). Firm-specific capital, nominal rigidities and the business cycle. *Review of Economic Dynamics, 14*(2), 225–247.

Auerbach, A. J., & Gorodnichenko, Y. (2012). Measuring the output responses to fiscal policy. *American Economic Journal: Economic Policy, 4*(2), 1–27.

Auerbach, A. J., & Gorodnichenko, Y. (2012). Measuring the output responses to fiscal policy.

Calvo, G. (1983). Staggered prices in a utility-maximizing framework. *Journal of Economic Literature, 12*, 1383–1398.

Canova, F., & Sala, L. (2009). Back to square one: Identification issues in DSGE models. *Journal of Monetary Economics, 56*(4), 431–449.

Chernozhukov, V., & Hong, H. (2003). An MCMC approach to classical estimation. *Journal of Econometrics, 115*, 293–346.

Christiano, L. J., Eichenbaum, M., & Evans, C. A. (2005). Nominal rigidities and the dynamic effects of a shock to monetary policy. *Journal of Political Economy, 113*(1), 1–45.

Christiano, L. J., Ilut, C., Motto, R., & Rostagno, M. (2008, October). *Monetary policy and stock market boom-bust cycles.* Working Paper Series No. 955. European Central Bank, Germany.

Christiano, L. J., Trabandt, M., & Walentin, K. (2010, chap. 7). DSGE models for monetary policy analysis. In B. M. Friedman & M. Woodford (Eds.), *Handbook of monetary economics* (Vol. 3, pp. 285–367). North Holland: Elsevier.

Coibion, O. (2010). Testing the sticky information Phillips curve. *The Review of Economics and Statistics, 92*(1), 87–101.

DiCecio, R. (2009). Sticky wages and sectoral labor comovement. *Journal of Economic Dynamics and Control, 33*(3), 538–553.

Gelfand, S., & Mitter, S. (1993). Metropolis-type annealing algorithms for global optimization in R! d. *SIAM Journal on Control and Optimization, 31*, 111.

Geweke, J. (2005). *Contemporary Bayesian econometrics and statistics.* Wiley Series in Probability and Statistics. Hoboken, NJ: Wiley.

Gikhman, I. I., & Skorokhod, A. V. (2004). *The theory of stochastic processes II.* Berlin Heidelberg New York: Springer.

Hasminskii, R. Z. (1980). *Stochastic stability of differential equations.* Alphen aan den Rijn, The Netherlands: Sijthoff and Noordhoff.

Ireland, P. (2004). A method for taking models to the data. *Journal of Economic Dynamics and Control, 28*(6), 1205–1226.

Kormilitsina, A. (forthcoming). Solving rational expectations models with informational subperiods: A perturbation approach. *Computational Economics*, 1–31.

Kormilitsina, A. (2011). Oil price shocks and the optimality of monetary policy. *Review of Economic Dynamics, 14*(1), 199–223.

Kormilitsina, A. (2012). Solving rational expectations models with informational subperiods: A perturbation approach. *Computational Economics.*

Roberts, G., Gelman, A., & Gilks, W. (1997). Weak convergence and optimal scaling of random walk metropolis algorithms. *The Annals of Applied Probability, 7*, 110–120.

Roberts, G., & Rosenthal, J. (2007). Coupling and ergodicity of adaptive Markov chain Monte Carlo algorithms. *Journal of Applied Probability, 44*(2), 458.

Roberts, G., & Tweedie, R. (1996). Geometric convergence and central limit theorems for multidimensional Hastings and Metropolis algorithms. *Biometrika, 83*(1), 95–110.

Schmitt-Grohé, S., & Uribe, M. (2011). Business cycles with a common trend in neutral and investment-specific productivity. *Review of Economic Dynamics, 14*(1), 122–135.

Smets, F., & Wouters, R. (2007). Shocks and frictions in US business cycles: A Bayesian DSGE approach. *American Economic Review, 97*(3), 586–606.

Stock, J. (1994). Unit roots, structural breaks and trends. *Handbook of Econometrics, 4*, 2739–2841.

Yun, T. (1996). Nominal price rigidity, money supply endogeneity, and business cycles. *Journal of Monetary Economics, 37*(2), 345–370.

APPENDIX

Table A1. Model Variables.

Parameter	Description
k	Capital
y	Production
c	Consumption
g	Government spending
i	Investment
s^p	Price dispersion
s^w	Wage dispersion
λ	Marginal utility of habit-adjusted consumption
l	Labor supply
h	Labor demand
mc	Marginal cost
w	Wage rate
r	Real interest rate
R	Nominal interest rate
$\tilde{w}$	The wage rate of wage optimizing labor types relative to w
$\tilde{p}$	The relative price of optimizing firms
$\mathscr{F}$	Auxilary variable
$\mathscr{X}$	Auxilary variable

Table A2. Calibration of Model Parameters.

Parameter	Description	Value
δ	Depreciation rate	0.025
η_p	Dixit–Stiglitz aggregator, output	6
η_w	Dixit–Stiglitz aggregator, labor	6
β	Discount factor	$1.04^{-0.25}$
θ	Labor share	0.7
π	Inflation target	1
h	Labor	0.3
q	Shadow price of capital	1
SG	Government consumption share	0.2
ρ_Y	Steady state technology	0.8
σ_Y	Steady state technology	0.03
ρ_g	Autocorr., g shock	0.8
σ_g	SD, g shock	0.03
ρ_d	Autocorr., preference shock	0.8
σ_d	SD, preference shock	0.03
α_R	Monetary policy parameter	0.7
α_π	Monetary policy parameter	0.45
α_Y	Monetary policy parameter	0.15

Table A3.   Estimates of Model Parameters.

Parameter	Description	Parameter Value	$N = 200$	True Responses
b	Consumption habit	0.6	0.5503	0.5960
			(0.0510)	(0.0318)
κ	Investment cost	3	2.1815	2.9858
			(0.3652)	(0.2739)
α_p	Price rigidity	0.6	0.5909	0.5952
			(0.0334)	(0.0259)
α_w	Wage rigidity	0.8	0.7720	0.7981
			(0.0250)	(0.0146)
χ_p	Price indexation	0.5	0.6531	0.4867
			(0.1540)	(0.1006)
χ_w	Wage indexation	0.5000	0.5321	0.4794
			(0.1506)	(0.0875)
ρ_z	Autocorr., technology	0.8	0.6988	0.8001
			(0.0377)	(0.0095)
$\sigma_z \times 100$	SD, technology	3	3.0870	3.0041
			(0.3131)	(0.1829)
ρ_r	Autocorr., m. policy	0.8	0.7540	0.7955
			(0.0223)	(0.0168)
$\sigma_r \times 100$	SD, m. policy	1	0.8507	1.0167
			(0.0853)	(0.1007)

Note: The table provides parameter estimates for the empirical application. Column 3 shows parameter values used for the data generating process. Column 4 reports the estimates for the case when sample of size $N = 200$ is generated to obtain impulse responses. Column 5 presents the estimates for the case when the estimation procedure matches true impulse responses.

FREQUENCY DOMAIN ANALYSIS OF MEDIUM SCALE DSGE MODELS WITH APPLICATION TO SMETS AND WOUTERS (2007)

Denis Tkachenko and Zhongjun Qu

ABSTRACT

The chapter considers parameter identification, estimation, and model diagnostics in medium scale DSGE models from a frequency domain perspective using the framework developed in Qu and Tkachenko (2012). The analysis uses Smets and Wouters (2007) as an illustrative example, motivated by the fact that it has become a workhorse model in the DSGE literature. For identification, in addition to checking parameter identifiability, we derive the non-identification curve to depict parameter values that yield observational equivalence, revealing which and how many parameters need to be fixed to achieve local identification. For estimation and inference, we contrast estimates obtained using the full spectrum with those using only the business cycle frequencies to find notably different parameter values and impulse response functions. A further comparison between the nonparametrically estimated and model implied spectra suggests that the business cycle based method delivers better estimates of the features that the model is intended to capture. Overall, the results

DSGE Models in Macroeconomics: Estimation, Evaluation, and New Developments
Advances in Econometrics, Volume 28, 319–385
ISSN: 0731-9053/doi:10.1108/S0731-9053(2012)0000028011

suggest that the frequency domain based approach, in part due to its ability to handle subsets of frequencies, constitutes a flexible framework for studying medium scale DSGE models.

Keywords: Dynamic stochastic general equilibrium models; frequency domain; identification; MCMC; model diagnostics; spectrum

JEL classification: C11; C13; C32; E1

INTRODUCTION

Dynamic Stochastic General Equilibrium (DSGE) models have become a widely applied instrument for analyzing business cycles, understanding monetary policy, and for forecasting. Some medium scale DSGE models, such as that of Smets and Wouters (2007) (henceforth SW (2007)), are considered both within academia and by central banks. These models typically feature various frictions, often involving a relatively large number of equations and parameters with complex cross-equation restrictions. Although such sophistication holds promise for delivering rich and empirically relevant results, it also poses substantial challenges for identification, estimation, and inference. This chapter shows how these issues can be tackled from a frequency domain perspective, using the framework recently developed by Qu and Tkachenko (2012). We use SW (2007) as the working example throughout the chapter, motivated by the fact that it has become a workhorse model in the DSGE literature. The analysis of other medium scale DSGE models can be conducted in a similar manner.

The identification of DSGE models is important for both model calibration and formal statistical analysis, although the relevant literature has lagged behind relative to that concerning estimation until quite recently. Canova and Sala (2009) mark an important turning point by convincingly documenting the types of identification issues that can surface when analyzing a DSGE model. Iskrev (2010) gives sufficient conditions for the local identification of structural parameters based on the mean and a set of autocovariances. Komunjer and Ng (2011) and Qu and Tkachenko (2012) are the first to provide necessary and sufficient conditions for local identification. Qu and Tkachenko (2012) show that taking a frequency domain perspective can deliver simple identification conditions applicable to both singular and nonsingular DSGE systems without relying on a particular (say, the minimum state) representation.

In this chapter, we show that the methods in Qu and Tkachenko (2012) can be applied in a straightforward manner to SW (2007) to deliver informative results. We structure our identification analysis into the following steps: (1) Identification based on the second order properties. This shows whether the parameters can be identified based solely on the dynamic properties of the system. (2) Identification based on the first (i.e., the mean) and the second order properties. This reveals whether the information from the steady state restrictions can help identification. (3) Identification based on a subset of frequencies. This is motivated by the fact that DSGE models are often designed to model business cycle movements, not very long or very short term fluctuations. Upon completing the above three steps, we find that the parameters in SW (2007) are unidentified without further restrictions. (4) To obtain further insights, we derive the non-identification curves to depict parameter values that yield observational equivalence. The curves immediately reveal which and how many parameters need to be fixed to yield local identification. Note that the results from steps (1) and (2) are in accordance with Iskrev (2010) and Komunjer and Ng (2011, the web appendix). Although these two findings are not new, the analysis is, and it also illustrates the flexibility and simplicity of taking a frequency domain approach. Issues in steps (3) and (4) have not been previously considered for medium scale DSGE models.

Next, we consider estimating SW (2007) from a frequency domain perspective using the methodology developed in Qu and Tkachenko (2012). The method has two features. First, it allows for estimation and inference using a subset of frequencies, something that is outside the scope of conventional time domain methods. This is important because DSGE models are designed for medium term economic fluctuations, not very short or long term fluctuations. Second, it is straightforward to conduct Bayesian inference and the computation involved is similar to the time domain approach. Although Qu and Tkachenko (2012) analyzed the statistical properties of this method, they did not provide an application. This chapter is the first that applies the method to a medium scale DSGE model.

Specifically, we follow SW (2007) in specifying the priors and An and Schorfheide (2007) in obtaining the posterior mode and Hessian for the proposal distribution. A Random Walk Metropolis algorithm is used to obtain the posterior draws. We start with inference using the mean and the spectrum, then the full spectrum only, and finally consider inference using only business cycle frequencies. The same priors are used throughout. For the first two cases, we obtain estimates that are very similar to those of

SW (2007). This reflects the close linkage between the time and frequency domain likelihood. However, for the third case, we obtain noticeably different estimates of the parameters governing the exogenous disturbances. At the same time, the parameters governing contemporaneous interactions of the observables remain similar with only a few exceptions. The impulse response functions are noticeably different. To our knowledge, this is the first time such a finding is documented in the DSGE literature.

Then, we contrast the model implied spectrum and absolute coherency with that observed in the data. The analysis is motivated by Watson's (1993) suggestion of plotting the model and data spectra as one of the most informative diagnostics. It is also related to King and Watson (1996), who compared the spectra of the three quantitative rational expectations models with that of the data. Both the business cycle and the full spectrum based estimates do a reasonable job in matching these two key features. The business cycle based estimates achieve a better fit at the intended frequencies. However, they both underestimate the absolute coherency of the interest rate and other four variables (consumption growth, investment growth, output growth, and labor hours). The latter finding suggests a dimension along which the model can be further improved. To our knowledge, this is the first time such analysis is applied to medium scale DSGE models.

The results in the chapter suggest that the frequency domain perspective affords substantial depth and flexibility in identification analysis and in estimating the parameters of the model, while remaining simple in application and comparable in terms of computational burden relative to the conventional time domain methods. In practice, we suggest to carry out both the business cycle and the full spectrum based analysis jointly. This allows us to assess to what extent the results are driven by the very low frequency contaminants, which is a hard task to tackle using a time domain framework.

The remainder of the chapter is structured as follows. The second section includes a brief description of the SW (2007) model to make the chapter self-contained. The third section carries out identification analysis and reports non-identification curves. The fourth section presents estimation results. The fifth section conducts model diagnostics from a frequency domain perspective. The sixth section concludes. A brief summary of the model equations not included in the text is provided in the appendix. MATLAB code replicating the analysis is provided in an online supplement. (Code replicating the analysis is available for download at http://people.bu.edu/qu/dsge3/FD_DSGE_Code.zip.)

THE DSGE MODEL OF SW (2007)

SW (2007) has become a workhorse model in the DSGE literature and many medium scale DSGE models consist of modifications or extensions of this model. It is an extended version of the standard New Keynesian real business cycle model, featuring a number of frictions and real rigidities. To make this chapter self-contained, we subsequently briefly describe the structure of the model economy. Note that the discussion is meant to highlight the key elements in the model. For a more detailed description of the model equations, variables, and parameters, one should consult SW (2007).

The model has seven observable endogenous variables with seven exogenous shocks. In equilibrium, the model has a balanced growth path driven by deterministic labor-augmenting technological progress. We focus on the log-linearized system as in the original article. The annotated list of structural parameters can be found in Table 5.

The Aggregate Resource Constraint

The aggregate resource constraint is given by

$$y_t = c_y c_t + i_y i_t + z_y z_t + \varepsilon_t^g$$

Output (y_t) is composed of consumption (c_t), investment (i_t), capital utilization costs as a function of the capital utilization rate (z_t), and exogenous spending (ε_t^g). The latter is assumed to follow a first-order autoregressive model with an i.i.d. Normal error term (η_t^g), and is also affected by the fundamental productivity shock (η_t^a) as follows:

$$\varepsilon_t^g = \rho_g \varepsilon_{t-1}^g + \rho_{ga} \eta_t^a + \eta_t^g$$

The coefficients c_y, i_y, and z_y are functions of the steady state spending-output ratio (g_y), steady state output growth rate (γ), capital depreciation rate (δ), household discount factor (β), intertemporal elasticity of substitution (σ_c), fixed costs in production (φ_p), and share of capital in production (α) as follows: $i_y = (\gamma - 1 + \delta)k_y$, $c_y = 1 - g_y - i_y$, and $z_y = R_*^k k_y$. Here k_y is the steady state capital-output ratio, and R_*^k is the steady state rental rate of capital (see the appendix to SW (2007)):

$$k_y = \varphi_p \left(\frac{L_*}{k_*}\right)^{\alpha-1} = \varphi_p \left[\left(\frac{1-\alpha}{\alpha}\right)\left(\frac{R_*^k}{w_*}\right)\right]^{\alpha-1}$$

with

$$w_* = \left(\frac{\alpha^\alpha (1 - \alpha)^{(1-\alpha)}}{\varphi_p (R_*^k)^\alpha} \right)^{\frac{1}{(1-\alpha)}}$$

and

$$R_*^k = \beta^{-1} \gamma^{\sigma_c} - (1 - \delta)$$

Households

Households maximize a nonseparable utility function with two arguments (consumption and labor effort) over an infinite life horizon. Consumption appears in the utility function relative to a time varying external habit variable. The dynamics of consumption follow from the consumption Euler equation

$$c_t = c_1 c_{t-1} + (1 - c_1) E_t c_{t+1} + c_2 (l_t - E_t l_{t+1}) - c_3 (r_t - E_t \pi_{t+1}) - \varepsilon_t^b$$

where l_t is hours worked, r_t is the nominal interest rate, and π_t is inflation. The disturbance term ε_t^b can be interpreted as a risk premium that households require to hold a one period bond. It follows the stochastic process

$$\varepsilon_t^b = \rho_b \varepsilon_{t-1}^b + \eta_t^b$$

The relationship of the coefficients in the consumption equation to the habit persistence (λ), steady state labor market mark-up (φ_w), and other basic parameters highlighted above is

$$c_1 = \frac{\frac{\lambda}{\gamma}}{1 + \frac{\lambda}{\gamma}}, \quad c_2 = \frac{(\sigma_c - 1) \left(\frac{w_*^h L_*}{c_*} \right)}{\sigma_c \left(1 + \frac{\lambda}{\gamma} \right)}, \quad c_3 = \frac{1 - \frac{\lambda}{\gamma}}{\left(1 + \frac{\lambda}{\gamma} \right) \sigma_c}$$

where $w_*^h L_* / c_*$ is related to the steady state and is given by

$$\frac{w_*^h L_*}{c_*} = \frac{1}{\varphi_w} \frac{1 - \alpha}{\alpha} R_*^k k_y \frac{1}{c_y}$$

where R_*^k and k_y are defined as above, and $c_y = 1 - g_y - (\gamma - 1 + \delta) k_y$.

Households also choose investment given the capital adjustment cost they face. The dynamics of investment are given by

$$i_t = i_1 i_{t-1} + (1 - i_1) E_t i_{t+1} + i_2 q_t + \varepsilon_t^i$$

where ε_t^i is a disturbance to the investment specific technology process, given by

$$\varepsilon_t^i = \rho_i \varepsilon_{t-1}^i + \eta_t^i$$

The coefficients are functions of the investment adjustment cost elasticity (ϕ) and other structural parameters:

$$i_1 = \frac{1}{1 + \beta\gamma^{(1-\sigma_c)}}, \quad i_2 = \frac{1}{(1 + \beta\gamma^{(1-\sigma_c)})\gamma^2\phi}$$

The corresponding arbitrage equation for the value of capital is given by

$$q_t = q_1 E_t q_{t+1} + (1 - q_1)E_t r_{t+1}^k - (r_t - \pi_{t+1}) - \frac{1}{c_3}\varepsilon_t^b \tag{1}$$

with

$$q_1 = \beta\gamma^{-\sigma_c}(1 - \delta) = \frac{1 - \delta}{R_*^k + 1 - \delta}$$

Final and Intermediate Goods Market

The model has a perfectly competitive final goods market and a monopolistic competitive intermediate goods market. It features a symmetric equilibrium where all firms make identical decisions. At such an equilibrium, the aggregate production function is

$$y_t = \varphi_p(\alpha k_t^s + (1 - \alpha)l_t + \varepsilon_t^a)$$

where α captures the share of capital in production, and the parameter φ_p is one plus the fixed costs in production. Total factor productivity follows the AR(1) process

$$\varepsilon_t^a = \rho_a \varepsilon_{t-1}^a + \eta_t^a$$

The current capital service use (k_t^s) is a function of capital installed in the previous period (k_{t-1}) and the degree of capital utilization (z_t):

$$k_t^s = k_{t-1} + z_t$$

Furthermore, the capital utilization is a positive fraction of the rental rate of capital (r_t^k):

$$z_t = z_1 r_t^k$$

where

$$z_1 = \frac{1 - \psi}{\psi}$$

and ψ is the elasticity of the adjustment cost of capital utilization. The accumulation of installed capital (k_t) is given by

$$k_t = k_1 k_{t-1} + (1 - k_1)i_t + k_2 \varepsilon_t^i$$

where ε_t^i is the investment specific technology process as defined before, and k_1 and k_2 are given by

$$k_1 = \frac{1 - \delta}{\gamma}$$

$$k_2 = \left(1 - \frac{1 - \delta}{\gamma}\right)(1 + \beta\gamma^{(1-\sigma_c)})\gamma^2\phi$$

The price mark-up, defined as the difference between the average price and the nominal marginal cost, satisfies

$$\mu_t^p = \alpha(k_t^s - l_t) + \varepsilon_t^a - w_t$$

where w_t is the real wage. The firms set prices according to the Calvo model, leading to the following New Keynesian Phillips curve

$$\pi_t = \pi_1 \pi_{t-1} + \pi_2 E_t \pi_{t+1} - \pi_3 \mu_t^p + \varepsilon_t^p$$

where ε_t^p is a disturbance to the price mark-up, following the ARMA(1,1) process given by

$$\varepsilon_t^p = \rho_p \varepsilon_{t-1}^p + \eta_t^p - \mu_p \eta_{t-1}^p$$

The MA(1) term is intended to pick up some of the high frequency fluctuations in prices. The Phillips curve coefficients depend on price indexation (ι_p) and stickiness (ξ_p), the curvature of the goods market Kimball aggregator (ε_p), and other structural parameters:

$$\pi_1 = \frac{\iota_p}{1 + \beta\gamma^{(1-\sigma_c)}\iota_p}$$

$$\pi_2 = \frac{\beta\gamma^{(1-\sigma_c)}}{1 + \beta\gamma^{(1-\sigma_c)}\iota_p}$$

$$\pi_3 = \frac{1}{1 + \beta\gamma^{(1-\sigma_c)}\iota_p} \frac{(1 - \beta\gamma^{(1-\sigma_c)}\xi_p)(1 - \xi_p)}{\xi_p((\varphi_p - 1)\varepsilon_p + 1)}$$

Finally, cost minimization by firms implies that the rental rate of capital satisfies[1]

$$r_t^k = -(k_t^s - l_t) + w_t$$

Labor Market

Households supply their homogeneous labor to an intermediate labor union, which differentiates labor services and sets wages according to a Calvo scheme. The union then sells these services to intermediate labor packers, who in turn offer the differentiated labor package to the intermediate good producers. The wage mark-up is

$$\mu_t^w = w_t - \left(\sigma_l l_t + \frac{1}{1-\lambda}(c_t - \lambda c_{t-1}) \right)$$

where σ_l is the elasticity of labor supply with respect to real wage. Real wage w_t adjusts slowly due to the rigidity

$$w_t = w_1 w_{t-1} + (1 - w_1)(E_t w_{t+1} + E_t \pi_{t+1}) - w_2 \pi_t + w_3 \pi_{t-1} - w_4 \mu_t^w + \varepsilon_t^w$$

where the coefficients $w_1 - w_4$ are functions of wage indexation (ι_w) and stickiness (ξ_w) parameters, and the curvature of the labor market Kimball aggregator (ϵ_w):

$$w_1 = \frac{1}{1 + \beta \gamma^{(1-\sigma_c)}}$$

$$w_2 = \frac{1 + \beta \gamma^{(1-\sigma_c)} \iota_w}{1 + \beta \gamma^{(1-\sigma_c)}}$$

$$w_3 = \frac{\iota_w}{1 + \beta \gamma^{(1-\sigma_c)}}$$

$$w_4 = \frac{1}{1 + \beta \gamma^{(1-\sigma_c)}} \frac{(1 - \beta \gamma^{(1-\sigma_c)} \xi_w)(1 - \xi_w)}{\xi_w((\varphi_w - 1)\varepsilon_w + 1)}$$

The wage mark-up disturbance is assumed to follow an ARMA(1,1) process:

$$\varepsilon_t^w = \rho_w \varepsilon_{t-1}^w + \eta_t^w - \mu_w \eta_{t-1}^w$$

Government Policies

The empirical monetary policy reaction function is

$$r_t = \rho r_{t-1} + (1 - \rho)(r_\pi \pi_t + r_Y(y_t - y_t^*)) + r_{\Delta y}[(y_t - y_t^*) - (y_{t-1} - y_{t-1}^*)] + \varepsilon_t^r$$

The monetary shock ε_t^r follows an AR(1) process:

$$\varepsilon_t^r = \rho_r \varepsilon_{t-1}^r + \eta_t^r$$

The variable y_t^* stands for a time-varying optimal output level that is the result of a flexible price-wage economy. More generally, we use superscript star to denote variables in this economy. Such an economy needs to be solved along with the sticky price-wage economy for the purposes of identification and estimation. Since the equations for the flexible price-wage economy are essentially the same as above, but with the variables μ_t^p and μ_t^w set to zero, we place them in the appendix.

The Model Solution

Our analysis requires computing the spectral density matrix of the observed endogenous variables. This is straightforward to obtain using the GENSYS algorithm of Sims (2002), although other methods (e.g., Uhlig, 1999) can also be used.

The GENSYS algorithm requires representing the state variables in the following form:

$$\Gamma_0 S_t = \Gamma_1 S_{t-1} + \Psi Z_t + \Pi \zeta_t$$

where S_t is a vector of model variables that includes the endogenous variables, the conditional expectation terms, and the serially correlated exogenous shock processes, Z_t are serially uncorrelated structural disturbances, and ζ_t are expectation errors. For SW (2007) (note that the ordering of variables and parameters corresponds to our MATLAB code),

$$S_t = [\eta_t^w, \eta_t^p, z_t^*, r_t^{k*}, k_t^{s*}, q_t^*, c_t^*, i_t^*, y_t^*, l_t^*, w_t^*, r_t^*, k_t^*, \mu_t^w, z_t, r_t^k, k_t^s, q_t, c_t, i_t, y_t, l_t,$$
$$\pi_t, w_t, r_t, \varepsilon_t^a, \varepsilon_t^b, \varepsilon_t^g, \varepsilon_t^i, \varepsilon_t^r, \varepsilon_t^p, \varepsilon_t^w, k_t, E(i_{t+1}^*), E(c_{t+1}^*), E(r_{t+1}^{k*}), E(q_{t+1}^*),$$
$$E(l_{t+1}^*), E(i_{t+1}), E(c_{t+1}), E(r_{t+1}^k), E(q_{t+1}), E(l_{t+1}), E(\pi_{t+1}), E(w_{t+1})]'$$

where the elements 18 to 24 of S_t correspond to the observables used for identification analysis and estimation, which are (here lower cases denote log deviations from the steady state) output (y_t), consumption (c_t), investment (i_t), wage (w_t), labor hours (l_t), inflation (π_t), and the interest rate (r_t). The other elements correspond to model variables in both sticky and flexible price-wage economies, 7 shock processes, and 12 expectation terms. The vector of structural shocks is given by

$$Z_t = (\eta_t^a, \eta_t^b, \eta_t^g, \eta_t^i, \eta_t^r, \eta_t^p, \eta_t^w)'$$

where, as discussed above, η_t^a is a technology shock, η_t^b is a risk premium shock, η_t^g is an exogenous spending shock, η_t^i is an investment shock, η_t^r is a monetary policy shock, η_t^p and η_t^w are price and wage mark-up shocks respectively. The elements of ζ_t are all zero except the last 12 entries that correspond to the one period ahead expectation errors of the last 12 terms of S_t. This implies that Π, which is of dimension 45×12, is an identity matrix for the last 12 rows, and zero otherwise. The coefficient matrices Γ_0, Γ_1, and Ψ are functions of the structural dynamic parameters θ, with the latter consisting of

$$\theta = (\rho_{ga}, \mu_w, \mu_p, \alpha, \psi, \phi, \sigma_c, \lambda, \varphi_p, l_w, \xi_w, l_p, \xi_p, \sigma_l, r_\pi, r_{\Delta y}, r_y, \rho, \rho_a, \rho_b, \rho_g,$$
$$\rho_i, \rho_r, \rho_p, \rho_w, \sigma_a, \sigma_b, \sigma_g, \sigma_i, \sigma_r, \sigma_p, \sigma_w, \gamma, \beta, \delta, g_y, \varphi_w, \varepsilon_p, \varepsilon_w)$$

Under conditions that ensure the existence and uniqueness of the solution (Sims, 2002, p. 12), the system can be represented as

$$S_t = \Theta_1 S_{t-1} + \Theta_0 Z_t$$

where Θ_1 and Θ_0 are functions of θ,[2] which further implies

$$S_t = (I - \Theta_1 L)^{-1} \Theta_0 Z_t \tag{2}$$

Using the above vector moving average representation it is straightforward to obtain the representation for the observable endogenous variables. To see this, suppose that the observable Y_t, up to an unknown mean vector, is given by

$$(c_t - c_{t-1}, i_t - i_{t-1}, y_t - y_{t-1}, l_t, \pi_t, w_t - w_{t-1}, r_t) \tag{3}$$

To map this to the solution (2), we simply let $A(L)$ be a matrix of finite order lag polynomials that specifies the observables, then we compute

$$A(L)S_t = A(L)(I - \Theta_1 L)^{-1} \Theta_0 Z_t \tag{4}$$

with

$$
A(L) \atop 7\times45 =
\begin{bmatrix}
(1,1) & & (1,18) & (1,19) & (1,20) & (1,21) & (1,22) & (1,23) & (1,24) & & (1,45) \\
0 & \cdots & 1-L & 0 & 0 & 0 & 0 & 0 & 0 & \cdots & 0 \\
\vdots & \cdots & 0 & 1-L & 0 & 0 & 0 & 0 & 0 & \cdots & \vdots \\
\vdots & \cdots & 0 & 0 & 1-L & 0 & 0 & 0 & 0 & \cdots & \vdots \\
\vdots & \cdots & 0 & 0 & 0 & 1 & 0 & 0 & 0 & \cdots & \vdots \\
\vdots & \cdots & 0 & 0 & 0 & 0 & 1 & 0 & 0 & \cdots & \vdots \\
\vdots & \cdots & 0 & 0 & 0 & 0 & 0 & 1-L & 0 & \cdots & \vdots \\
0 & \cdots & 0 & 0 & 0 & 0 & 0 & 0 & 1 & \cdots & 0
\end{bmatrix}
$$

Remark 1. The vector moving average representation (4) plays a central role in our analysis. First, it enables straightforward computation of the spectrum of Y_t:

$$
f_\theta(\omega) = \frac{1}{2\pi} H(\exp(-i\omega); \theta) \Sigma(\theta) H(\exp(-i\omega); \theta)^* \tag{5}
$$

where * denotes the conjugate transpose,

$$
H(L; \theta) = A(L)(I - \Theta_1 L)^{-1} \Theta_0
$$

and $\Sigma(\theta)$ is the variance covariance matrix of Z_t^3. Second, we can easily compute the impulse response functions and the variance decomposition. Third, the choice of $A(L)$ offers substantial flexibility as we can vary it to study estimation and inference based on different combinations of variables.

For identification and inference based on the spectrum, there is no need to specify the steady state. However, it is also straightforward to incorporate the mean into the analysis. To see this, define an augmented parameter vector $\bar{\theta}$ that includes θ and parameters affecting only the steady state. Then, notice that for log-linearized DSGE models the observables Y_t can typically be related to the log deviations ($Y_t^d(\theta)$) and the steady states ($\mu(\bar{\theta})$) via

$$
Y_t = \mu(\bar{\theta}) + Y_t^d(\theta)
$$

The specification in SW (2007) corresponds to $Y_t^d(\theta)$ given by Eq. (2) and $\mu(\bar{\theta}) = (\bar{\gamma}, \bar{\gamma}, \bar{\gamma}, \bar{l}, \bar{\pi}, \bar{\gamma}, \bar{r})'$. The parameters $\bar{\gamma}$, $\bar{\pi}$ and $\bar{r}$ are functions of structural parameters and $\bar{l}$ is a new steady state parameter. The detailed discussion is presented in the section "Analysis of SW (2007) Based on the First and the Second Order Properties" below.

IDENTIFICATION ANALYSIS

In this section we perform identification analysis based on the (first and) second order properties of the model. We also consider identification from a subset of frequencies (business cycle frequencies) and implement a robustness check for the results. The value of θ_0 is set to the posterior mean from Table 1A in SW (2007):

$$\theta_0 = (0.52, 0.88, 0.74, 0.19, 0.54, 5.48, 1.39, 0.71, 1.61, 0.59, 0.73, 0.22, 0.65,$$
$$1.92, 2.03, 0.22, 0.08, 0.81, 0.95, 0.18, 0.97, 0.71, 0.12, 0.90, 0.97, 0.45,$$
$$0.24, 0.52, 0.45, 0.24, 0.14, 0.24, 1.0043, 0.9984, 0.025, 0.18, 1.5, 10, 10)$$

The above parameter values are used for illustration purposes. In practice, the same analysis can be carried out with other parameter values using the same methodology.

The Identification Framework

For the sake of expositional completeness, we briefly review the results in Qu and Tkachenko (2012) that are used in this section. The spectral density $f_\theta(\omega)$ plays a central role in the analysis. It can be computed using Eq. (5).

The first result concerns local identification based on the second order properties of the process. Specifically, the dynamic parameter vector θ is said to be locally identifiable from the second order properties of $\{Y_t\}$ at a point θ_0 if there exists an open neighborhood of θ_0 in which $\theta_1 \neq \theta_0$ implies $f_{\theta_1}(\omega) \neq f_{\theta_0}(\omega)$ for some $\omega \in [-\pi, \pi]$. Theorem 1 in Qu and Tkachenko (2012) establishes that a necessary and sufficient condition for local identification is that the following matrix is nonsingular:

$$G(\theta_0) = \int_{-\pi}^{\pi} \left(\frac{\partial \text{vec} f_{\theta_0}(\omega)}{\partial \theta'} \right)^* \left(\frac{\partial \text{vec} f_{\theta_0}(\omega)}{\partial \theta'} \right) d\omega$$

where * stands for the conjugate transpose and the vec operator vectorizes a matrix by stacking its columns. Although the identification condition is formulated in the spectral domain, it has a time domain interpretation as well. Specifically, under some regularity condition that ensures a one-to-one mapping between the spectral density matrix and the autocovariance functions, the condition is also necessary and sufficient for local identification through the complete set of autocovariances. In practice, verifying the rank of $G(\theta)$ amounts to using an algorithm for eigenvalue decomposition and counting the number of its nonzero eigenvalues. Such a decomposition always exists because $G(\theta)$ is real, symmetric, and positive semidefinite by construction. Note that $G(\theta)$ is relatively straightforward to compute in practice. First, the (j,k)-th element of $G(\theta)$ can be computed as

$$G_{jk}(\theta) = \int_{-\pi}^{\pi} \text{tr}\left\{\frac{\partial f_\theta(\omega)}{\partial \theta_j}\frac{\partial f_\theta(\omega)}{\partial \theta_k}\right\} d\omega$$

The remaining computational work is to obtain the derivatives and approximate the integral. This can be achieved using simple numerical methods. To compute the derivatives, we first divide the interval $[-\pi, \pi]$ into N subintervals to obtain $(N + 1)$ frequency indices. Let ω_s denote the s-th frequency in the partition. Then one can compute $\partial f_{\theta_0}(\omega_s)/\partial \theta_j$ numerically using a simple two-point method (a refined method can also be applied to further improve precision):

$$\frac{f_{\theta_0+e_j h_j}(\omega_s) - f_{\theta_0}(\omega_s)}{h_j} \quad (j = 1, \ldots, N+1)$$

where e_j is a $q \times 1$ unit vector with the j-th element equal to 1, h_j is a step size that can be parameter dependent. In practice, to obtain the above quantity we only need to solve the DSGE model twice, once using $\theta = \theta_0$, and once with $\theta = \theta_0 + e_j h_j$. After this is repeated for all parameters in θ, we can approximate the integral in $G_{jk}(\theta_0)$ using

$$\frac{2\pi}{N+1}\sum_{s=1}^{N+1}\text{tr}\left\{\frac{\partial f_\theta(\omega_s)}{\partial \theta_j}\frac{\partial f_\theta(\omega_s)}{\partial \theta_k}\right\}$$

Note that no simulation is needed in this process.

The identification condition can be extended to incorporate the mean (steady state properties) into the analysis. Define $\bar{\theta} = (\theta, \varkappa)'$, where the parameter vector $\varkappa$ affects only the steady state. Then, as stated in Theorem 2 of Qu and Tkachenko (2012), $\bar{\theta}$ is locally identifiable from the first and second order properties of $\{Y_t\}$ at a point $\bar{\theta}_0$ if and only if $\bar{G}(\bar{\theta}_0)$ is nonsingular, where

$$\bar{G}(\bar{\theta}) = \int_{-\pi}^{\pi}\left(\frac{\partial \text{vec} f_\theta(\omega)}{\partial \bar{\theta}'}\right)^* \left(\frac{\partial \text{vec} f_\theta(\omega)}{\partial \bar{\theta}'}\right) d\omega + \frac{\partial \mu(\bar{\theta})'}{\partial \bar{\theta}}\frac{\partial \mu(\bar{\theta})}{\partial \bar{\theta}'}$$

In practice, the term $\mu(\bar{\theta})$ often has a simple structure and hence the derivative can be evaluated analytically, e.g., using a symbolic algebra package such as MuPAD, which is true for the SW (2007) model as will be shown later.

Qu and Tkachenko (2012) also contains two corollaries that will be useful in our analysis. First, Corollary 2 of Qu and Tkachenko (2012) provides a necessary and sufficient condition for local identification from a subset of frequencies. Specifically, let $W(\omega)$ denote an indicator function defined on $[-\pi, \pi]$ that is symmetric around zero and equal to one over a finite number of closed intervals. Also, extend the definition of $W(\omega)$ to $\omega \in [\pi, 2\pi]$ by using $W(\omega) = W(2\pi - \omega)$. Then, θ is locally identifiable from the second order properties of $\{Y_t\}$ through the frequencies specified by $W(\omega)$ at a point θ_0 if and only if the following matrix is nonsingular:

$$G^W(\theta_0) = \left\{ \int_{-\pi}^{\pi} W(\omega) \left(\frac{\partial \mathrm{vec} f_{\theta_0}(\omega)}{\partial \theta'} \right)^* \left(\frac{\partial \mathrm{vec} f_{\theta_0}(\omega)}{\partial \theta'} \right) d\omega \right\}$$

The result for identification of $\bar{\theta}$ is analogous. Second, Corollary 4 of Qu and Tkachenko (2012) provides a necessary and sufficient condition for conditional identification, that is, identification of a subset of parameters keeping the others fixed. Specifically, let θ^s be an s-element subset of θ, then θ^s is conditionally locally identifiable from the second order properties of $\{Y_t\}$ at a point θ_0 if and only if

$$G(\theta_0)^s = \int_{-\pi}^{\pi} \left(\frac{\partial \mathrm{vec} f_{\theta_0}(\omega)}{\partial \theta^{s\prime}} \right)^* \left(\frac{\partial \mathrm{vec} f_{\theta_0}(\omega)}{\partial \theta^{s\prime}} \right) d\omega$$

is nonsingular. Again, the result is formulated in the same way for $\bar{\theta}^s$ using $\bar{G}(\bar{\theta}_0)^s$. It is important to note that the application of Corollary 4 does not require any additional computation once the original matrix $G(\theta_0)$ or $\bar{G}(\bar{\theta}_0)$ has been obtained. The matrices $G(\theta)^s$ or $\bar{G}(\bar{\theta}_0)^s$ for any subvector can be obtained by simply picking out the relevant elements of $G(\theta)$. Specifically, suppose we are interested in a particular k-element subvector of θ. If we number parameters inside θ, and let Φ be a set of parameter numbers of interest (i.e., if we want to vary only parameters 1, 2, and 5, then $\Phi = \{1, 2, 5\}$), then the (i, j)-th element of $G(\theta)^s$ is given by

$$G(\theta)_{i,j}^s = G(\theta)_{\Phi_i, \Phi_j}, \quad i = 1, 2, \dots, k; \ j = 1, 2, \dots, k$$

Also note that in case of Theorem 2, the same logic applies to the term

$$\frac{\partial \mu(\bar{\theta}_0)'}{\partial \bar{\theta}^s} \frac{\partial \mu(\bar{\theta}_0)}{\partial \bar{\theta}^{s'}}$$

Finally, we will use the procedure Qu and Tkachenko (2012) provided to trace out non-identification curves when lack of identification is detected. The subsequent discussion focuses on θ, but the procedure works the same way for $\bar{\theta}$. Suppose $G(\theta_0)$ has only one zero eigenvalue and let $c(\theta_0)$ be the corresponding real orthonormal eigenvector. Then, $c(\theta_0)$ is unique up to multiplication by -1, and thus can be made unique by restricting its first nonzero element to be positive. Let $\delta(\theta_0)$ be an open neighborhood of θ_0. Then we can define a non-identification curve χ using the function $\theta(v)$ that solves the differential equation:

$$\frac{\partial \theta(v)}{\partial v} = c(\theta)$$

$$\theta(0) = \theta_0$$

where v is a scalar that varies in a neighborhood of 0. Then, along χ, θ is not identified at θ_0 because

$$\frac{\partial \text{vecf}_{\theta(v)}(\omega)}{\partial v} = \frac{\partial \text{vecf}_{\theta(v)}(\omega)}{\partial \theta(v)'} c(\theta) = 0, \quad \forall \, \omega \in [-\pi, \pi]$$

Qu and Tkachenko (2012) shows that this curve is continuous and locally unique (see their Corollary 6). The curve can be evaluated numerically using any available method for solving differential equations. The simple Euler method, which amounts to recursively computing

$$\theta(v_{j+1}) \approx \theta(v_j) + c(\theta(v_j))(v_{j+1} - v_j), \quad v_{j+1} \geqslant v_j \geqslant 0, \quad j = 0, 1, \ldots$$
$$\theta(v_{j-1}) \approx \theta(v_j) + c(\theta(v_j))(v_{j-1} - v_j), \quad v_{j-1} \leqslant v_j \leqslant 0, \quad j = 0, -1, \ldots \quad (6)$$

works well in practice when setting the step size $|v_{j+1} - v_j|$ to some small number as specified below.

In cases where $G(\theta_0)$ has multiple zero eigenvalues, the following algorithm can be applied.

- Step 1. Apply the identification condition to verify whether all parameters in the model are locally identified. Proceed to Step 2 if lack of identification is detected.

- Step 2. Apply the conditional identification condition to each individual parameter. If a zero eigenvalue of $G(\theta_0)^s$ is found, then it implies that the corresponding parameter is not locally conditionally identified. Apply the procedure outlined in Eq. (6) to obtain a non-identification curve (changing only this element and fixing the value of the others at θ_0). Repeat this for all parameters to obtain a finite number of curves each being a scalar valued function of v.
- Step 3. Increase the number of parameters in the considered subsets of θ_0 by one at a time. Single out the subsets with the following two properties: (1) it does not include the subset detected in previous steps as a proper subset, and (2) when applying the conditional identification check, it reports only one zero eigenvalue. Repeat the procedure outlined above for all such subsets to obtain non-identification curves. Note that if the subset has k elements, then the associated curve is a k-by-1 vector valued function of v.
- Step 4. Continue Step 3 until all subsets are considered. Solve the model using parameter values from the curves to determine the appropriate domain for v. Truncate the curves obtained in Steps 1–4 to exclude parameter values contradicting economic theory or when discrepancies between $f_{\theta(v)}(\omega)$ and $f_{\theta_0}(\omega)$ are observed at some ω.

Remark 2. The procedure above delivers two types of useful information: (1) which parameter subsets are responsible for non-identification; (2) the curve for each subset that shows in what way the parameters in this subset need to simultaneously change in order to generate observational equivalence. Considering the curves is insightful, since it allows one to go beyond traditional zero-one identification analysis and get an idea about the neighborhood of non-identification. Very small non-identified neighborhoods may not present a serious problem, but if such neighborhood spans a large portion of the parameter space including empirically relevant parameter values, then it becomes a serious issue. Such information is useful for both building a model and for estimation and inference.

Analysis of SW (2007) Based on the Second Order Properties

To compute $G(\theta_0)$, the integral in $G(\theta_0)$ is approximated numerically by averaging over 10,000 Fourier frequencies from $-4,999\pi/5,000$ to $4,999\pi/5,000$ and multiplying by 2π. The step size for the numerical differentiation is set to $10^{-7} \times \theta_0$. The MATLAB default tolerance level tol = max (size(G)eps($\|G\|$)) is used to decide whether an eigenvalue is zero, where *eps* is the floating point precision of G. We obtain

$$\text{Rank}(G(\theta_0)) = 36$$

Since the dimension of θ_0 is 39, this implies that θ is unidentified at θ_0. Additionally, this result suggests that a minimum of three parameters needs to be fixed to achieve identification.

Since the model is not identified, we proceed to search for the non-identified subsets of parameters. Carrying out Step 2, no such one-element subset of θ is detected. Implementing Step 3, we find two subvectors for which $G(\theta_0)^s$ has exactly one zero eigenvalue:

$$(\xi_w, \varepsilon_w)$$

and

$$(\xi_p, \varepsilon_p)$$

This finding is unsurprising, as the parameters in each subset play very similar roles in the model after linearization (they determine the speed of adjustment of prices and wages through the Calvo probability, or curvature of demand, respectively). They enter only jointly and thus are separately unidentifiable. Iskrev (2010) reaches the same result by applying his condition. We do not report the non-identification curves for these subsets, as they are trivial and are highlighted here for illustrative purposes.

We then exclude all three-parameter subvectors that contain either of the two non-identification sets identified above as proper subsets and continue the analysis. We find no three- or four-element non-identification subsets. However, we pinpoint one five-element subvector that yields one zero eigenvalue:

$$(\phi, \lambda, \gamma, \beta, \delta)$$

where ϕ is the adjustment cost parameter, λ (denoted as h in SW (2007)) is the habit parameter, γ governs the steady state growth rate, β is the discount factor, and δ is the depreciation rate. This result is also in accordance with Iskrev (2010). After excluding all subvectors containing the non-identification sets highlighted above, we find no further sources of non-identification in this model. Therefore, our findings imply that fixing one parameter out of each of $(\phi, \lambda, \gamma, \beta, \delta)$, (ξ_w, ε_w), and (ξ_p, ε_p) is necessary and sufficient for identification from the second order properties.

We then evaluate the non-identification curve using the Euler method with step size $h = 10^{-4} \times \theta_0$ in a small neighborhood around θ_0. The result is presented in Fig. 1. It demonstrates how, for each of $\phi, \lambda, \gamma, \beta$, and δ, the parameters have to change simultaneously in order to generate non-identification. The curve is extended using Eq. (6) in the two directions starting from θ_0 (corresponding to $v = 0$ on the x-axis of the graphs), which are marked by the dotted (Direction 1) and bold (Direction 2) lines respectively. The curve is a five dimensional object. It is therefore broken down into five subplots, each corresponding to one parameter. Along Direction 1, the figure shows that increasing (ϕ, δ) and decreasing (λ, γ, β),

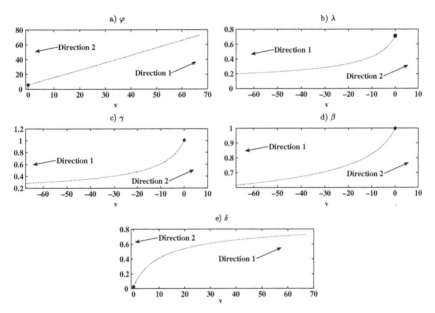

Fig. 1. The Non-Identification Curve $(\phi, \lambda, \gamma, \beta, \alpha)$.
Note: The non-identification curve is given by $\partial\theta(v)/\partial v = c(\theta), \theta(0) = \theta_0$, where $c(\theta)$ is the eigenvector corresponding to the only zero eigenvalue of $G(\theta)$. The approximation is computed recursively using the Euler method, so that $\partial(v_{j+1}) = \theta(v_j) + c(\theta(v_j))h$, where h is the step size, fixed at 1e-04. $(\phi, \lambda, \gamma, \beta, \alpha)$ change simultaneously along the curve in the indicated directions. Directions 1 and 2 are obtained by restricting the first element of $c(\theta)$ to be positive or negative respectively. Since a discount rate greater than 1 contradicts economic theory, Direction 2 is truncated at the last point where β is below 1. The curve is extended for 670,000 steps in Direction 1. Since there are only 472 steps in Direction 2, the respective curve appears as a bold dot on the graphs.

while keeping the rest of the parameters fixed at their θ_0 values results in equivalent spectral densities. The values along Direction 2 can be interpreted similarly. It should be noted that β is increasing along Direction 2. Because it represents the discount factor, it should not exceed 1. Therefore, we truncate the curve before β reaches 1. This leaves us with only 472 steps in Direction 2. This, compared to 670,000 steps computed for Direction 1, is very small. Hence, in Fig. 1, values corresponding to Direction 2 look like a bold dot rather than a line. Given the number of steps computed along Direction 1, we did not reach the point where natural bounds on parameters are violated, but it is clear that we would truncate it at a point where β reaches zero, λ reaches zero, or δ reaches 1, whichever happens first.

To give a further illustration of the parameter values on the curve, we report 10 points taken from it at equally spaced intervals in each direction. The results are summarized in Table 1. We also compute the smallest and the second smallest eigenvalues of $G(\theta_0)^s$. The results, also reported in Table 1, show that its rank stays constant along the curve.

To verify that the points on the curve indeed result in identical spectral densities, we compute the following three measures of discrepancies between $f_\theta(\omega)$ and $f_{\theta_0}(\omega)$ as in Qu and Tkachenko (2012):

$$\text{Maximum absolute deviation:} \quad \max_{\omega_j \in \Omega} |f_{\theta hl}(\omega_j) - f_{\theta_0 hl}(\omega_j)|$$

$$\text{Maximum absolute deviation in relative form:} \quad \frac{\max_{\omega_j \in \Omega} |f_{\theta hl}(\omega_j) - f_{\theta_0 hl}(\omega_j)|}{|f_{\theta_0 hl}(\omega_j)|}$$

$$\text{Maximum relative deviation:} \quad \max_{\omega_j \in \Omega} \frac{|f_{\theta hl}(\omega_j) - f_{\theta_0 hl}(\omega_j)|}{|f_{\theta_0 hl}(\omega_j)|}$$

where $f_{\theta hl}(\omega)$ denotes the (h, l)-th element of the spectral density matrix with parameter θ, and Ω includes the 5,000 frequencies between 0 and π.[4] The discrepancies are summarized in Tables 2 and 3. There, the rows correspond to the parameter values reported in Table 1. The columns contain the 10 largest deviations occurring across all 49 elements of $G(\theta)^s$ in descending order. The values show that even the largest deviations are very small. Given that there are numerical errors involved in the application of GENSYS and the computation of the $G(\theta)^s$ matrix, and that the Euler method involves a cumulative approximation error of the same order as the step size (10^{-4} in our case), we can conclude that the spectrum stays the same along the curve.

Table 1. Parameter Values and the Corresponding Two Smallest Eigenvalues Along the Non-Identification Curve.

	ϕ	λ	γ	β	δ	λ_1	λ_2
θ_0	5.740000	0.710000	1.004300	0.998400	0.025000	1.80E-10	0.392865
Panel (a): Direction 1							
θ_1	12.417476	0.482721	0.682812	0.862248	0.337109	1.96E-14	0.808082
θ_2	19.113813	0.389080	0.550356	0.794406	0.465700	4.57E-14	1.210705
θ_3	25.812574	0.334809	0.473589	0.750327	0.540228	3.01E-14	1.599268
θ_4	32.512006	0.298325	0.42198	0.718141	0.590328	5.53E-15	1.975594
θ_5	39.211698	0.271647	0.384246	0.693026	0.626964	3.26E-15	2.341212
θ_6	45.911511	0.25105	0.35511	0.672563	0.655256	8.58E-15	2.697239
θ_7	52.611389	0.234516	0.331724	0.655380	0.677954	1.04E-14	3.044732
θ_8	59.311305	0.220873	0.312427	0.640622	0.696688	4.10E-15	3.384357
θ_9	66.011244	0.209364	0.296147	0.627727	0.712493	5.40E-15	3.716722
θ_{10}	72.711198	0.199485	0.282174	0.616303	0.726059	9.96E-16	4.042423
Panel (b): Direction 2							
θ_{-1}	5.735346	0.710288	1.004707	0.998556	0.024605	5.27E-12	0.392485
θ_{-2}	5.730692	0.710576	1.005115	0.998711	0.024209	3.00E-12	0.392186
θ_{-3}	5.726038	0.710865	1.005523	0.998865	0.023812	2.95E-11	0.391895
θ_{-4}	5.721384	0.711154	1.005933	0.999019	0.023415	3.93E-11	0.391616
θ_{-5}	5.716730	0.711444	1.006342	0.999173	0.023018	9.91E-11	0.391323
θ_{-6}	5.712077	0.711732	1.006752	0.999328	0.022620	1.12E-10	0.391078
θ_{-7}	5.707423	0.712023	1.007162	0.999483	0.022221	8.78E-11	0.390749
θ_8	5.702770	0.712314	1.007573	0.999638	0.021823	8.39E-11	0.390467
θ_{-9}	5.698117	0.712605	1.007984	0.999793	0.021423	1.97E-10	0.390278
θ_{-10}	5.693464	0.712896	1.008396	0.999948	0.021024	1.13E-10	0.389814

Note: θ_j represent equally spaced points taken from the non-identification curve extended from θ_0 for 670,000 steps in Direction 1, and for 472 steps in Direction 2. λ_1 and λ_2 represent the smallest and the second smallest eigenvalues of $G(\theta_i)^s$. The step size for computing the curve is 10^{-4}. Along Direction 1, the curve is truncated at the point where β is closest to 1, as it is the discount factor. Results are rounded to the nearest sixth digit to the right of decimal.

Analysis of SW (2007) Based on the First and the Second Order Properties

This subsection incorporates the steady state of the model into the analysis. The measurement equations that relate the observables to the means and the log deviations are as follows (see SW (2007)):

$$dlCONS_t = \bar{\gamma} + c_t - c_{t-1}$$

Table 2. Deviations of Spectra Across Frequencies (Direction 1).

	1	2	3	4	5	6	7	8	9	10
	\multicolumn{10}{c}{10 Largest Deviations Across Frequencies and Elements Ordered in Descending Order}									

	1	2	3	4	5	6	7	8	9	10
				Maximum absolute deviations across frequencies						
θ_1	8.99E-05	2.98E-05	1.24E-05	1.24E-05	1.09E-05	1.09E-05	9.24E-06	9.24E-06	5.97E-06	5.97E-06
θ_2	1.17E-04	3.88E-05	1.61E-05	1.61E-05	1.42E-05	1.42E-05	1.20E-05	1.20E-05	7.77E-06	7.77E-06
θ_3	1.31E-04	4.31E-05	1.79E-05	1.79E-05	1.59E-05	1.59E-05	1.33E-05	1.33E-05	8.65E-06	8.65E-06
θ_4	1.38E-04	4.57E-05	1.90E-05	1.90E-05	1.68E-05	1.68E-05	1.41E-05	1.41E-05	9.16E-06	9.16E-06
θ_5	1.43E-04	4.74E-05	1.97E-05	1.97E-05	1.78E-05	1.74E-05	1.46E-05	1.46E-05	9.50E-06	9.50E-06
θ_6	1.47E-04	4.85E-05	2.02E-05	2.02E-05	1.78E-05	1.74E-05	1.50E-05	1.50E-05	9.72E-06	9.72E-06
θ_7	1.49E-04	4.94E-05	2.05E-05	2.05E-05	1.81E-05	1.81E-05	1.53E-05	1.53E-05	9.89E-06	9.89E-06
θ_8	1.51E-04	5.01E-05	2.08E-05	2.08E-05	1.83E-05	1.83E-05	1.55E-05	1.55E-05	1.00E-05	1.00E-05
θ_9	1.52E-04	5.06E-05	2.10E-05	2.10E-05	1.84E-05	1.84E-05	1.56E-05	1.56E-05	1.01E-05	1.01E-05
θ_{10}	1.53E-04	5.10E-05	2.12E-05	2.12E-05	1.86E-05	1.86E-05	1.58E-05	1.58E-05	1.02E-05	1.02E-05
				Maximum absolute deviations across frequencies in relative form						
θ_1	7.81E-06	5.33E-06	4.60E-06	4.34E-06	4.19E-06	3.73E-06	3.73E-06	3.34E-06	3.34E-06	2.91E-06
θ_2	1.02E-05	6.93E-06	5.98E-06	5.66E-06	5.47E-06	4.86E-06	4.86E-06	4.39E-06	4.34E-06	3.80E-06
θ_3	1.13E-05	7.73E-06	6.70E-06	6.32E-06	6.13E-06	5.41E-06	5.41E-06	4.89E-06	4.84E-06	4.23E-06

θ_4	1.20E-05	8.18E-06	7.07E-06	6.69E-06	6.49E-06	5.73E-06	5.73E-06	5.18E-06	5.13E-06	4.48E-06
θ_5	1.24E-05	8.48E-06	7.31E-06	6.93E-06	6.71E-06	5.93E-06	5.93E-06	5.37E-06	5.31E-06	4.64E-06
θ_6	1.27E-05	8.68E-06	7.50E-06	7.09E-06	6.86E-06	6.07E-06	6.07E-06	5.50E-06	5.43E-06	4.75E-06
θ_7	1.29E-05	8.82E-06	7.63E-06	7.21E-06	6.96E-06	6.18E-06	6.18E-06	5.59E-06	5.52E-06	4.84E-06
θ_8	1.31E-05	8.91E-06	7.71E-06	7.28E-06	7.07E-06	6.25E-06	6.25E-06	5.61E-06	5.60E-06	4.90E-06
θ_9	1.33E-05	8.98E-06	7.79E-06	7.34E-06	7.12E-06	6.31E-06	6.31E-06	5.66E-06	5.65E-06	4.95E-06
θ_{10}	1.34E-05	9.05E-06	7.85E-06	7.40E-06	7.18E-06	6.36E-06	6.36E-06	5.71E-06	5.70E-06	4.99E-06

Maximum relative deviations across frequencies

θ_1	5.94E-05	5.94E-05	2.67E-05	2.67E-05	1.52E-05	1.52E-05	1.37E-05	1.37E-05	8.46E-06	7.25E-06
θ_2	7.75E-05	7.75E-05	3.49E-05	3.49E-05	1.99E-05	1.99E-05	1.79E-05	1.79E-05	1.10E-05	9.43E-06
θ_3	8.65E-05	8.65E-05	3.91E-05	3.91E-05	2.23E-05	2.23E-05	2.00E-05	2.00E-05	1.22E-05	1.05E-05
θ_4	9.16E-05	9.16E-05	4.14E-05	4.14E-05	2.36E-05	2.36E-05	2.12E-05	2.12E-05	1.30E-05	1.11E-05
θ_5	9.48E-05	9.48E-05	4.28E-05	4.28E-05	2.44E-05	2.44E-05	2.20E-05	2.20E-05	1.34E-05	1.15E-05
θ_6	9.71E-05	9.71E-05	4.38E-05	4.38E-05	2.49E-05	2.49E-05	2.24E-05	2.24E-05	1.38E-05	1.18E-05
θ_7	9.88E-05	9.88E-05	4.45E-05	4.45E-05	2.53E-05	2.53E-05	2.28E-05	2.28E-05	1.40E-05	1.20E-05
θ_8	9.99E-05	9.99E-05	4.49E-05	4.49E-05	2.55E-05	2.55E-05	2.30E-05	2.30E-05	1.42E-05	1.21E-05
θ_9	1.01E-04	1.01E-04	4.54E-05	4.54E-05	2.56E-05	2.56E-05	2.32E-05	2.32E-05	1.44E-05	1.23E-05
θ_{10}	1.02E-04	1.02E-04	4.58E-05	4.58E-05	2.58E-05	2.58E-05	2.34E-05	2.34E-05	1.45E-05	1.24E-05

Note: θ_1 to θ_{10} are as defined in Table 1. We report 10 largest deviations across 49 elements of each $G(\theta_i)^s$ computed at 5,000 frequencies to conserve space.

DENIS TKACHENKO AND ZHONGJUN QU

Table 3. Deviations of Spectra Across Frequencies (Direction 2).

	1	2	3	4	5	6	7	8	9	10
	10 Largest Deviations Across Frequencies and Elements Ordered in Descending Order									
	Maximum absolute deviations across frequencies									
θ_{-1}	1.59E-07	3.14E-08	3.14E-08	3.09E-08	1.77E-08	1.77E-08	1.65E-08	1.65E-08	1.09E-08	1.09E-08
θ_{-2}	2.38E-07	6.50E-08	4.93E-08	4.93E-08	2.33E-08	2.33E-08	2.27E-08	2.27E-08	2.22E-08	2.22E-08
θ_{-3}	3.54E-07	1.14E-07	5.52E-08	5.52E-08	3.80E-08	3.80E-08	2.59E-08	2.59E-08	2.19E-08	2.19E-08
θ_{-4}	5.88E-07	1.68E-07	8.09E-08	8.09E-08	7.20E-08	7.20E-08	5.26E-08	5.26E-08	3.75E-08	3.75E-08
θ_{-5}	8.55E-07	2.42E-07	1.12E-07	1.12E-07	1.07E-07	1.07E-07	8.22E-08	8.22E-08	5.54E-08	5.54E-08
θ_{-6}	1.08E-06	3.11E-07	1.34E-07	1.34E-07	1.24E-07	1.24E-07	8.90E-08	8.90E-08	6.83E-08	6.83E-08
θ_{-7}	1.32E-06	3.76E-07	1.82E-07	1.82E-07	1.54E-07	1.54E-07	1.39E-07	1.39E-07	8.60E-08	8.60E-08
θ_{-8}	1.40E-06	4.11E-07	1.83E-07	1.83E-07	1.62E-07	1.62E-07	1.30E-07	1.30E-07	9.02E-08	9.02E-08
θ_{-9}	1.44E-06	4.42E-07	1.80E-07	1.80E-07	1.62E-07	1.62E-07	1.18E-07	1.18E-07	9.18E-08	9.18E-08
θ_{-10}	1.47E-06	4.57E-07	1.80E-07	1.80E-07	1.71E-07	1.71E-07	1.17E-07	1.17E-07	9.35E-08	9.35E-08
	Maximum absolute deviations across frequencies in relative form									
θ_{-1}	2.24E-08	1.54E-08	1.36E-08	1.16E-08	1.07E-08	9.44E-09	7.97E-09	7.78E-09	6.30E-09	6.30E-09
θ_{-2}	4.52E-08	3.14E-08	2.63E-08	1.82E-08	1.65E-08	1.56E-08	1.51E-08	1.51E-08	1.50E-08	1.30E-08
θ_{-3}	4.03E-08	2.96E-08	2.82E-08	2.75E-08	1.81E-08	1.48E-08	1.45E-08	1.45E-08	1.44E-08	1.34E-08

θ_{-4}	4.37E-08	4.35E-08	3.55E-08	3.55E-08	3.00E-08	2.52E-08	2.30E-08	2.30E-08	2.13E-08	2.12E-08
θ_{-5}	1.07E-07	6.35E-08	4.97E-08	4.44E-08	3.98E-08	3.56E-08	3.56E-08	3.09E-08	3.04E-08	2.86E-08
θ_{-6}	1.50E-07	8.22E-08	5.96E-08	5.90E-08	5.21E-08	4.62E-08	4.62E-08	4.11E-08	3.85E-08	3.68E-08
θ_{-7}	1.69E-07	9.95E-08	7.35E-08	7.21E-08	5.73E-08	5.73E-08	5.08E-08	4.82E-08	4.70E-08	4.55E-08
θ_{-8}	1.81E-07	1.08E-07	7.71E-08	7.59E-08	6.21E-08	6.02E-08	6.02E-08	5.22E-08	5.05E-08	4.74E-08
θ_{-9}	1.87E-07	1.17E-07	7.91E-08	7.73E-08	7.12E-08	6.13E-08	6.13E-08	5.62E-08	5.16E-08	4.85E-08
θ_{-10}	1.91E-07	1.20E-07	8.17E-08	7.94E-08	7.69E-08	6.10E-08	6.10E-08	5.76E-08	5.35E-08	5.29E-08

Maximum relative deviations across frequencies

θ_{-1}	8.38E-08	8.38E-08	6.39E-08	6.39E-08	5.12E-08	5.12E-08	3.22E-08	3.22E-08	2.21E-08	2.21E-08
θ_{-2}	2.51E-07	2.51E-07	1.38E-07	1.38E-07	1.23E-07	1.23E-07	5.72E-08	5.72E-08	4.92E-08	4.92E-08
θ_{-3}	3.32E-07	3.32E-07	1.68E-07	1.68E-07	1.12E-07	1.12E-07	7.00E-08	7.00E-08	3.72E-08	3.72E-08
θ_{-4}	3.76E-07	3.76E-07	1.89E-07	1.89E-07	1.39E-07	1.39E-07	1.02E-07	1.02E-07	5.18E-08	5.18E-08
θ_{-5}	4.58E-07	4.58E-07	2.23E-07	2.23E-07	1.64E-07	1.64E-07	1.42E-07	1.42E-07	7.58E-08	7.58E-08
θ_{-6}	6.72E-07	6.72E-07	3.34E-07	3.34E-07	2.28E-07	2.28E-07	1.93E-07	1.93E-07	1.21E-07	1.21E-07
θ_{-7}	6.52E-07	6.52E-07	3.07E-07	3.07E-07	2.63E-07	2.63E-07	2.14E-07	2.14E-07	1.82E-07	1.82E-07
θ_{-8}	8.18E-07	8.18E-07	3.95E-07	3.95E-07	2.78E-07	2.78E-07	2.38E-07	2.38E-07	1.63E-07	1.63E-07
θ_{-9}	9.84E-07	9.84E-07	4.79E-07	4.79E-07	2.88E-07	2.88E-07	2.55E-07	2.55E-07	1.41E-07	1.41E-07
θ_{-10}	1.06E-06	1.06E-06	5.19E-07	5.19E-07	2.97E-07	2.97E-07	2.62E-07	2.62E-07	1.30E-07	1.30E-07

Note: θ_{-1} to θ_{-10} are as defined in Table 1. We report 10 largest deviations across 49 elements of each $G(\theta_i)^s$ computed at 5,000 frequencies to conserve space.

$$dlINV_t = \bar{\gamma} + i_t - i_{t-1}$$
$$dlGDP_t = \bar{\gamma} + y_t - y_{t-1}$$
$$lHOURS_t = \bar{l} + l_t$$
$$dlP_t = \bar{\pi} + \pi_t$$
$$dlWAG_t = \bar{\gamma} + w_t - w_{t-1}$$
$$FEDFUNDS_t = \bar{r} + r_t$$

where l and dl stand for 100 times log and log difference, respectively; $\bar{\gamma} = 100(\gamma - 1)$, $\bar{\pi} = 100(\Pi_* - 1)$, and $\bar{r} = 100(\beta^{-1}\gamma^{\sigma_c}\Pi_* - 1) = \beta^{-1}\gamma^{\sigma_c}\bar{\pi} + 100(\beta^{-1}\gamma^{\sigma_c} - 1)$. Among the means, $\bar{\gamma}$ is a function of the dynamic parameter γ, $\bar{\pi}$ and $\bar{r}$ depend on the common steady parameter inflation rate Π_*, and $\bar{l}$ is a new parameter. Hence, we have

$$\bar{\theta} = (\theta, \bar{\pi}, \bar{l})$$

There are 41 parameters in total and $\mu(\bar{\theta})$ is given by

$$\mu(\bar{\theta}) = (\bar{\gamma}, \bar{\gamma}, \bar{\gamma}, \bar{l}, \bar{\pi}, \bar{\gamma}, \bar{r})'$$

We set $\bar{\pi}_0 = 0.78$ and $\bar{l}_0 = 0.53$ as in Table 1A in SW (2007). $\mu(\bar{\theta})$ can be differentiated analytically, e.g., using MATLAB's symbolic math toolbox.

Applying Theorem 2 yields

$$\text{Rank}(G(\bar{\theta}_0)) = 39$$

Since now $q = 41$, $\bar{\theta}$ is unidentified at $\bar{\theta}_0$ from the first and the second order properties of the observables. Furthermore, two parameters need to be fixed to achieve identification. The sources of non-identification in this case are the two subsets we have detected in the previous subsection, namely (ξ_w, ε_w) and (ξ_p, ε_p). This result is, again, not surprising and should be expected as discussed in the previous subsection. We no longer detect the $(\phi, \lambda, \gamma, \beta, \delta)$ subset. This is because γ determines the steady state growth rate $\bar{\gamma}$ and hence can be identified from the mean. Once γ is identified, the rest of the four parameters are uniquely determined. Iskrev (2010) reaches the same conclusion. Thus, fixing one parameter from each of (ξ_w, ε_w) and (ξ_p, ε_p) is necessary and sufficient for identification based on the mean and spectrum.

Analysis of SW (2007) Using a Subset of Frequencies

This subsection illustrates identification using a subset of frequencies. Without loss of generality, we focus on the business cycle frequencies (i.e., fluctuations with periods between 6 and 32 quarters as in King & Watson, 1996). We obtain

$$\text{Rank}(G^W(\theta_0)) = 36$$

and

$$\text{Rank}(\bar{G}^W(\bar{\theta}_0)) = 39$$

which coincide with the results when all frequencies are included. All results and conclusions are the same as in the previous two subsections. This shows that for this model, business cycle frequencies have the same local identifying power at θ_0 and $\bar{\theta}_0$ as the full spectrum.

Robustness Checks Using Non-Identification Curves

We first examine the sensitivity of $G(\theta_0)$ to a range of numerical differentiation steps (from $10^{-2} \times \theta_0$ to $10^{-9} \times \theta_0$) and tolerance levels (from $10^{-3} \times \theta_0$ to $10^{-10} \times \theta_0$). The results are reported in Table 4. The findings for the matrices $\bar{G}(\bar{\theta}_0), G^W(\theta_0)$, and $\bar{G}^W(\bar{\theta}_0)$ are similar and thus omitted.

Table 4. Rank Sensitivity Analysis.

	Differentiation Step Size $\times \theta_0$							
	1E-02	1E-03	1E-04	1E-05	1E-06	1E-07	1E-08	1E-09
TOL				Rank of $G(\theta_0)$				
1E-03	37	36	36	36	36	36	36	36
1E-04	37	37	37	36	36	36	36	36
1E-05	37	37	37	36	36	36	36	36
1E-06	37	37	37	36	36	36	36	36
1E-07	38	37	37	37	36	36	36	37
1E-08	39	37	37	37	36	36	37	37
1E-09	39	38	38	37	37	36	37	37
1E-10	39	39	39	37	37	37	37	39
Default	39	38	37	37	37	36	37	37

Note: TOL refers to the tolerance level used to determine the rank. Default refers to the MATLAB default tolerance level.

Table 4 shows that different choices of step sizes and tolerance levels can affect the rank decision. Specifically, the estimated rank changes if the step size is too large or too small, and when the tolerance level is more stringent. This is quite intuitive, as when the step size is too large, the numerical differentiation will induce a substantial error, since the estimation error for the two-point method is of the same order as the step size. When the step size is too small, the numerical error from solving the model using GENSYS will be large relative to the step size, therefore the rank will also be estimated imprecisely. In this example, the step size $10^{-7} \times \theta_0$ and the MATLAB default tolerance level seem to produce good balance between precision and robustness.

The dependence of the results on the step size and the tolerance level is certainly undesirable. To address this issue, Qu and Tkachenko (2012) suggest that the non-identification curve analysis be embedded into the following two-step procedure to reduce the reliance on step size and tolerance level:

- Step 1. Compute the ranks of $G(\theta_0)$ using a wide range of step sizes and tolerance levels. Locate the outcomes with the smallest rank.
- Step 2. Derive the non-identification curves conditioning on the smallest rank reported. Compute the discrepancies in spectral densities using values on the curve to verify observational equivalence. If the discrepancies are large, proceed to the outcome with the next smallest rank and repeat the analysis. Continue until spectral densities on the curve are identical or full local identification is established.

In applications, it often suffices to compute as few as 10 points on the non-identification curve to establish whether spectral densities are identical or not, as in the latter case the deviations often become quite large only a few steps away from θ_0, so the computational burden involved is not large. Applying this procedure using the step sizes and tolerance levels in Table 4 leads to the same conclusion as stated in the previous sections. This is simply because 36 is the smallest rank in the Table (Step 1) and the discrepancies between $f_\theta(\omega)$ and $f_{\theta_0}(\omega)$ along the curves are negligible (Step 2). In summary, this example demonstrates another reason why non-identification curves can be a useful tool for identification analysis.

ESTIMATION AND INFERENCE

This section considers estimation of SW (2007) from a frequency domain perspective. We start with briefly summarizing the quasi-Bayesian estimation procedure proposed in Qu and Tkachenko (2012).

The Basic Framework

Under the assumption that the DSGE system is nonsingular, the generalized frequency domain log-likelihood function of θ based on the sample $Y_1, \ldots, Y_T$ is given by

$$L_T(\theta) = -\sum_{j=1}^{T-1} W(\omega_j)[\log \det(f_\theta(\omega_j) + \text{tr}\{f_\theta^{-1}(\omega_j)I_T(\omega_j)\}]$$

where

$$\omega_j = 2\pi j/T \quad (j = 1, 2, \ldots T - 1)$$

denote the Fourier frequencies, $I_T(\omega_j)$ is the periodogram

$$I_T(\omega_j) = w_T(\omega_j)w_T^*(\omega_j)$$

with $w_T(\omega_j)$ being the discrete Fourier transform

$$w_T(\omega_j) = \frac{1}{\sqrt{2\pi T}} \sum_{t=1}^{T} Y_t \exp(-i\omega_j t)$$

and $W(\omega_j)$ is the indicator function to select frequencies for estimation and inference, as defined in the identification section.

Remark 3. The objective function $L_T(\theta)$ allows us to estimate the dynamic parameters using the spectrum of $\{Y_t\}$ without any reference to the parameters that affect only the steady state. Also, unlike for the time domain QML, the estimates can be obtained without demeaning the data, because the values of $w_T(\omega_j)$ at the Fourier frequencies are not affected by replacing Y_t with $Y_t - \mu(\bar{\theta})$.

The extension to the joint estimation of the dynamic and steady state parameters is straightforward. Define

$$w_{\bar{\theta},T}(0) = \frac{1}{\sqrt{2\pi T}} \sum_{t=1}^{T} (Y_t - \mu(\bar{\theta}))$$

and

$$I_{\bar{\theta},T}(0) = w_{\bar{\theta},T}(0)w_{\bar{\theta},T}(0)'$$

The log-likelihood function of $\bar{\theta}$ then takes the form

$$\bar{L}_T(\bar{\theta}) = L_T(\theta) - \left[\log \det(f_\theta(0)) + \text{tr}\left\{f_\theta^{-1}(0)I_{\bar{\theta},T}(0)\right\}\right]$$

The direct application of maximum likelihood methods to DSGE models is plagued by the problem that the parameter estimates are often at odds with economic theory, possibly due to the high dimensionality of the parameter vector and potential model misspecification. It has become common practice to introduce information not contained in the observed sample via the form of priors (see An and Schorfheide (2007) for discussion). Such an idea can be easily incorporated into the current framework.

Specifically, for the dynamic parameter only case, we consider

$$p_T(\theta) = \frac{\pi(\theta) \exp(L_T(\theta))}{\int_\Theta \pi(\theta) \exp(L_T(\theta)) d\theta}$$

where $\pi(\theta)$ can be a proper prior density or, more generally, a weight function that is strictly positive and continuous over the parameter space. The function $p_T(\theta)$ is termed quasi-posterior in Chernozhukov and Hong (2003), because, while being a proper distribution density over the parameters, it is in general not a true posterior in the Bayesian sense, as $\exp(L_T(\theta))$ is a more general criterion function than the likelihood due to the selection of the frequencies.

The estimate for θ_0 can be taken to be the quasi-posterior mean:

$$\hat{\theta}_T = \int_\Theta \theta p_T(\theta) d\theta$$

To compute the estimator, we can use Markov chain Monte Carlo (MCMC) methods, such as the Metropolis–Hastings algorithm, to draw a Markov chain

$$S = \left(\theta^{(1)}, \theta^{(2)}, \dots \theta^{(B)}\right)$$

and obtain

$$\hat{\theta}_T = \frac{1}{B} \sum_{j=1}^{B} \theta^{(j)} \tag{7}$$

Meanwhile, for a given continuously differentiable function $g: \Theta \to \mathbb{R}$ (e.g., an impulse response at a given horizon), its estimate can be obtained using

$$\hat{g}_T = \frac{1}{B} \sum_{j=1}^{B} g(\theta^{(j)}) \tag{8}$$

Details on Computation

In this chapter, we use the Random Walk Metropolis (RWM) algorithm to generate draws from $p_T(\theta)$. It belongs to the more general class of Metropolis–Hastings algorithms, the first version of which was proposed by Metropolis, Rosenbluth, Rosenbluth, Teller, and Teller (1953) and later generalized by Hastings (1970). Schorfheide (2000) and Otrok (2001) were the seminal contributions in using this algorithm for Bayesian estimation of DSGE models. We use the version of the algorithm implemented in Schorfheide (2000). The main steps involved and some discussion on their practical implementation are presented below.

- Step 1. Use a numerical optimization procedure to maximize $L_T(\theta) + \log(\pi(\theta))$ to find the posterior mode, denoted $\tilde{\theta}$.
- Step 2. Compute the inverse of the Hessian matrix evaluated at the posterior mode, denoted $\tilde{\Sigma}$.
- Step 3. Draw a starting value $\theta^{(0)}$ from $N(\tilde{\theta}, c^2\tilde{\Sigma})$, where c is a scaling parameter.
- Step 4. For $s = 1, 2, \ldots, B$, draw ϑ from the proposal distribution $N(\theta^{(s-1)}, c^2\tilde{\Sigma})$. Accept the draw $(\theta^{(s)} = \vartheta)$ with probability

$$\min\{1, \alpha(\theta^{(s-1)}, \vartheta \mid Y)\}$$

with

$$\alpha(\theta^{(s-1)}, \vartheta \mid Y) = \frac{\exp(L_T(\vartheta))\pi(\vartheta)}{\exp(L_T(\theta^{(s-1)}))\pi(\theta^{(s-1)})}$$

If it is rejected, then set $\theta^{(s)} = \theta^{(s-1)}$.
- Step 5. Compute the posterior mean as in Eqs. (7) and (8).

In Step 1, one of the practical problems is that the solution for the DSGE model may be non-unique or may not exist at some parameter values. To circumvent these issues, we use the csminwel optimization routine written by Chris Sims (see Leeper & Sims, 1994), which randomly perturbs the search direction if it reaches a cliff caused by indeterminacy or nonexistence. Regarding the prior, we use the same $\pi(\theta)$ as in Table 1A in SW (2007).

In Step 2, the Hessian matrix, computed assuming Normality, has its (j, l)-th element given by

$$\frac{1}{4\pi} \int_{-\pi}^{\pi} W(\omega) \mathrm{tr}\left[f_{\bar{\theta}}(\omega) \frac{\partial f_{\bar{\theta}}^{-1}(\omega)}{\partial \theta_j} f_{\bar{\theta}}(\omega) \frac{\partial f_{\bar{\theta}}^{-1}(\omega)}{\partial \theta_l} \right] d\omega$$

which can be estimated by replacing the integral with an average over the Fourier frequencies.

In Step 4, the choice of the scaling parameter c is determined by calibrating the acceptance rate of the Markov chain. Roberts, Gelman, and Gilks (1997) suggested tuning the proposal distributions so that the acceptance rate is close to 25% for models of dimension higher than two under the assumption that both the target and the proposal distribution are Normal. Since this assumption is not satisfied in our case, we follow the literature by running several independent chains and choosing c such that the acceptance rates fall between 20% and 40%. In our experience, for a given c, computing the acceptance rate of a chain of 1,000–5,000 draws gives a good idea about what to expect from a much longer chain.

The parameter draws from the proposal distribution $N(\theta^{(s-1)}, c^2\tilde{\Sigma})$ may yield indeterminacy or nonexistence of the DSGE solution, or fall outside of the specified bounds (our bounds are as in the Dynare code of SW (2007)). In such cases, we set $L_T(\theta) + \log(\pi(\theta))$ to a very large negative number (10^{-10}) so that such draws are always rejected.

Below, we first estimate $\bar{\theta}$ using both the mean and the full spectrum of observables, as this closely mirrors the analysis of SW (2007) conducted from a time domain perspective. In order to enhance comparability of results, we fix five parameters as in SW (2007), at the following values

$$\varepsilon_p = \varepsilon_w = 10, \quad \delta = 0.025, \quad g_y = 0.18, \quad \lambda_w = 1.5$$

Estimation Based on the Mean and the Full Spectrum

We use the dataset from SW (2007) and consider the same sample period as in their Dynare code, namely 1965.1–2004.4. The prior distribution is the same as in SW (2007) and is presented in Table 5. A sample of 250,000 draws from the posterior distribution is generated, and the first 50,000 are discarded. The scaling factor c is set to $\sqrt{0.15}$, which yields a rejection rate of 24%.[5] It should also be noted that the spectral density at frequency zero is singular, because the observables contain first differences of stationary variables. Computationally, we deal with this problem by using

Table 5. Prior Distributions of the Parameters.

	Parameter Interpretation	Distribution	Mean	St. Dev.
ρ_{ga}	Cross-corr.: tech. and exog. spending shocks	Normal	0.50	0.25
μ_w	Wage mark-up shock MA	Beta	0.50	0.20
μ_p	Price mark-up shock MA	Beta	0.50	0.20
α	Share of capital in production	Normal	0.30	0.05
ψ	Elasticity of capital utilization adjustment cost	Beta	0.50	0.15
ϕ	Investment adjustment cost	Normal	4.00	1.50
σ_c	Elasticity of inertemporal substitution	Normal	1.50	0.38
λ	Habit persistence	Beta	0.70	0.10
φ_p	Fixed costs in production	Normal	1.25	0.13
ι_w	Wage indexation	Beta	0.50	0.15
ζ_w	Wage stickiness	Beta	0.50	0.10
ι_p	Price indexation	Beta	0.50	0.15
ζ_p	Price stickiness	Beta	0.50	0.10
σ_l	Labor supply elasticity	Normal	2.00	0.75
r_π	Taylor rule: inflation weight	Normal	1.50	0.25
$r_{\Delta y}$	Taylor rule: feedback from output gap change	Normal	0.13	0.05
r_y	Taylor rule: output gap weight	Normal	0.13	0.05
ρ	Taylor rule: interest rate smoothing	Beta	0.75	0.10
ρ_a	Productivity shock AR	Beta	0.50	0.20
ρ_b	Risk premium shock AR	Beta	0.50	0.20
ρ_g	Exogenous spending shock AR	Beta	0.50	0.20
ρ_i	Interest rate shock AR	Beta	0.50	0.20
ρ_r	Monetary policy shock AR	Beta	0.50	0.20
ρ_p	Price mark-up shock AR	Beta	0.50	0.20
ρ_w	Wage mark-up shock AR	Beta	0.50	0.20
σ_a	Productivity shock std. dev.	Invgamma	0.10	2.00
σ_b	Risk premium shock std. dev.	Invgamma	0.10	2.00
σ_g	Exogenous spending shock std. dev.	Invgamma	0.10	2.00
σ_i	Interest rate shock std. dev.	Invgamma	0.10	2.00
σ_r	Monetary policy shock std. dev.	Invgamma	0.10	2.00
σ_p	Price mark-up shock std. dev.	Invgamma	0.10	2.00
σ_w	Wage mark-up shock std. dev.	Invgamma	0.10	2.00
$\bar{\gamma}$	Trend growth rate: real GDP, Infl., Wages	Normal	0.40	0.10
$100(\beta^{-1}-1)$	Discount rate	Gamma	0.25	0.10
$\bar{\pi}$	Steady state inflation rate	Gamma	0.62	0.10
$\bar{l}$	Steady state hours worked	Normal	0.00	2.00
δ	Capital depreciation rate	Fixed	0.025	
φ_w	Steady state labor market mark-up	Fixed	1.50	
g_y	Steady state exog. spending-output ratio	Fixed	0.18	
ε_p	Curvature of Kimball goods market aggregator	Fixed	10.00	
ε_w	Curvature of Kimball labor market aggregator	Fixed	10.00	

Note: Prior distributions are taken from SW (2007) Dynare code.

the generalized inverse to calculate $f_\theta^{-1}(0)$ and the product of nonzero eigenvalues of $f_\theta(0)$ to obtain $\det(f_\theta(0))$.

Table 6 presents the estimates and their 90% probability intervals. The results obtained in SW (2007) are also included for ease of comparison. Overall, the parameter estimates are very similar to their counterparts in SW (2007). In particular, the posterior means and modes are close and the 90% probability intervals overlap for 38 out of the 41 parameters. For the latter, the two exceptions are that our estimate of the technology shock persistence (ρ_a) is higher (0.98 compared to 0.95 in SW (2007)), while the estimated persistence parameter of the exogenous spending shock (ρ_g) is lower (0.92 v. 0.97). For these two parameters the corresponding 90% probability intervals are disjoint. We can also single out a somewhat higher estimate of the elasticity of consumption σ_c (1.81 compared to 1.38), although there is still slight overlap in the 90% intervals, and a lower estimate of the trend growth rate ($\bar{\gamma}$) of 0.27 versus 0.43 in SW (2007).

Estimation Based on the Full Spectrum

We now consider the estimation of θ based on the full spectrum. We use the same data set, prior, and MCMC algorithm, except we use $c = 0.4$, which produces an acceptance rate of 23%. The results are reported in Table 7.

Overall, the parameter estimates are very similar to those based on the mean and the full spectrum. The estimated trend growth rate is back in line with the results of SW (2007), but the estimated mean discount rate goes up from 0.76% to 1.04% on an annual basis. The rest of the estimates obtained using the full spectrum are virtually the same as those in Table 6. Consequently, overall the results using the full spectrum are very close to those obtained by SW (2007) using time domain methods.

Estimation Using Business Cycle Frequencies

DSGE models are constructed to explain business cycle movements. Schorfheide (2011) emphasized that "many time series exhibit low frequency behavior that is difficult, if not impossible, to reconcile with the model being estimated. This low frequency misspecification contaminates the estimation of shocks and thereby inference about the sources of business cycle."

Table 6. Posterior Distributions of the Parameters.

	Full Spectrum and Mean				SW (2007) Tables 1 A,B			
	Mode	Mean	5%	95%	Mode	Mean	5%	95%
ρ_{ga}	0.48	0.48	0.38	0.58	0.52	0.52	0.37	0.66
μ_w	0.94	0.92	0.88	0.96	0.88	0.84	0.75	0.93
μ_p	0.68	0.66	0.51	0.78	0.74	0.69	0.54	0.85
α	0.20	0.20	0.18	0.22	0.19	0.19	0.16	0.21
ψ	0.72	0.70	0.56	0.83	0.54	0.54	0.36	0.72
ϕ	5.47	5.72	4.26	7.41	5.48	5.74	3.97	7.42
σ_c	1.83	1.81	1.56	2.08	1.39	1.38	1.16	1.59
λ	0.64	0.65	0.59	0.71	0.71	0.71	0.64	0.78
φ_p	1.60	1.61	1.50	1.71	1.61	1.60	1.48	1.73
ι_w	0.55	0.54	0.37	0.72	0.59	0.58	0.38	0.78
ξ_w	0.84	0.82	0.76	0.87	0.73	0.70	0.60	0.81
ι_p	0.19	0.21	0.10	0.33	0.22	0.24	0.10	0.38
ξ_p	0.66	0.66	0.60	0.72	0.65	0.66	0.56	0.74
σ_l	2.16	2.05	1.22	2.98	1.92	1.83	0.91	2.78
r_π	2.18	2.20	1.95	2.47	2.03	2.04	1.74	2.33
$r_{\Delta y}$	0.24	0.25	0.21	0.28	0.22	0.22	0.18	0.27
r_y	0.13	0.13	0.10	0.17	0.08	0.08	0.05	0.12
ρ	0.85	0.85	0.82	0.87	0.81	0.81	0.77	0.85
ρ_a	0.98	0.98	0.98	0.99	0.95	0.95	0.94	0.97
ρ_b	0.19	0.21	0.11	0.31	0.18	0.22	0.07	0.36
ρ_g	0.93	0.92	0.89	0.95	0.97	0.97	0.96	0.99
ρ_i	0.71	0.71	0.64	0.78	0.71	0.71	0.61	0.80
ρ_r	0.08	0.10	0.03	0.17	0.12	0.15	0.04	0.24
ρ_p	0.86	0.85	0.78	0.91	0.90	0.89	0.80	0.96
ρ_w	0.97	0.96	0.94	0.98	0.97	0.96	0.94	0.99
σ_a	0.47	0.48	0.44	0.51	0.45	0.45	0.41	0.50
σ_b	0.24	0.24	0.21	0.27	0.24	0.23	0.19	0.27
σ_g	0.50	0.51	0.47	0.54	0.52	0.53	0.48	0.58
σ_i	0.47	0.47	0.42	0.53	0.45	0.45	0.37	0.53
σ_r	0.23	0.24	0.22	0.25	0.24	0.24	0.22	0.27
σ_p	0.14	0.14	0.12	0.17	0.14	0.14	0.11	0.16
σ_w	0.25	0.25	0.22	0.27	0.24	0.24	0.20	0.28
$\bar{\gamma}$	0.27	0.27	0.17	0.36	0.43	0.43	0.40	0.45
$100(\beta^{-1}-1)$	0.17	0.19	0.09	0.32	0.16	0.16	0.07	0.26
$\bar{\pi}$	0.71	0.73	0.56	0.91	0.81	0.78	0.61	0.96
$\bar{l}$	0.52	0.41	−0.90	1.76	−0.1	0.53	−1.3	2.32

Note: 5% and 95% columns refer to the 5th and 95th percentiles of the distribution of RWM draws.

Table 7. Posterior Distribution of the Dynamic Parameters.

	Full Spectrum				Business Cycle			
	Mode	Mean	5%	95%	Mode	Mean	5%	95%
ρ_{ga}	0.48	0.47	0.38	0.57	0.24	0.24	0.11	0.37
μ_w	0.94	0.92	0.88	0.96	0.28	0.32	0.11	0.58
μ_p	0.68	0.67	0.53	0.78	0.65	0.55	0.24	0.77
α	0.21	0.21	0.18	0.23	0.18	0.19	0.16	0.21
ψ	0.70	0.68	0.54	0.82	0.52	0.56	0.34	0.77
ϕ	5.52	5.76	4.32	7.39	2.55	3.03	2.15	4.37
σ_c	1.90	1.88	1.61	2.16	1.31	1.50	1.18	1.95
λ	0.64	0.64	0.58	0.70	0.58	0.55	0.45	0.66
φ_p	1.61	1.61	1.51	1.72	1.43	1.46	1.34	1.59
ι_w	0.55	0.55	0.37	0.72	0.58	0.56	0.33	0.79
ξ_w	0.84	0.82	0.76	0.87	0.81	0.80	0.73	0.86
ι_p	0.19	0.21	0.10	0.33	0.66	0.61	0.35	0.83
ξ_p	0.66	0.66	0.60	0.71	0.70	0.69	0.62	0.76
σ_l	2.05	1.97	1.14	2.88	2.66	2.51	1.53	3.53
r_π	2.18	2.20	1.95	2.46	2.11	2.10	1.82	2.40
$r_{\Delta y}$	0.24	0.25	0.21	0.28	0.21	0.22	0.18	0.26
r_y	0.13	0.13	0.10	0.17	0.15	0.15	0.10	0.20
ρ	0.85	0.85	0.82	0.87	0.77	0.76	0.71	0.81
ρ_a	0.98	0.98	0.97	0.99	0.82	0.84	0.70	0.94
ρ_b	0.19	0.21	0.11	0.31	0.81	0.75	0.60	0.87
ρ_g	0.92	0.92	0.89	0.95	0.90	0.89	0.83	0.95
ρ_i	0.72	0.72	0.65	0.79	0.70	0.67	0.53	0.79
ρ_r	0.08	0.09	0.03	0.17	0.35	0.34	0.13	0.55
ρ_p	0.86	0.86	0.79	0.91	0.80	0.75	0.48	0.91
ρ_w	0.97	0.96	0.93	0.98	0.57	0.56	0.37	0.73
σ_a	0.47	0.48	0.44	0.51	0.47	0.48	0.42	0.55
σ_b	0.24	0.24	0.21	0.27	0.07	0.08	0.06	0.11
σ_g	0.50	0.51	0.47	0.54	0.35	0.36	0.32	0.41
σ_i	0.47	0.47	0.42	0.52	0.33	0.38	0.27	0.53
σ_r	0.23	0.24	0.22	0.25	0.12	0.13	0.10	0.16
σ_p	0.14	0.14	0.12	0.17	0.08	0.08	0.06	0.12
σ_w	0.25	0.25	0.23	0.27	0.16	0.19	0.12	0.29
$\bar{\gamma}$	0.40	0.41	0.25	0.57	0.39	0.40	0.23	0.56
$100(\beta^{-1}-1)$	0.22	0.26	0.12	0.44	0.23	0.28	0.13	0.47

Note: 5% and 95% columns refer to the 5th and 95th percentiles of the distribution of the RWM draws.

Therefore, it is instructive to examine how the parameters change when they are estimated using only business cycles frequencies. Our procedure allows for such an investigation. We use the same methodology as the previous section, but selecting only the frequencies corresponding to periods of 6–32 quarters. The scaling factor is set to $c = \sqrt{0.13}$, which gives an acceptance rate of 23%.

The results are reported in the right panel of Table 7. A number of parameter estimates differ substantially from the full spectrum case. The most notable differences pertain to the parameters governing the exogenous shocks. Specifically, the AR coefficient of the total factor productivity process, ρ_a, drops from 0.98 to 0.84 while the standard deviation of its shock remains unchanged. The parameter governing the impact of productivity shocks on exogenous spending, ρ_{ga}, is almost halved from 0.47 to 0.24. Additionally, the AR coefficient of the wage mark-up process ρ_w comes down from 0.96 to 0.56 and its MA coefficient μ_w drops from 0.92 to 0.32. The standard deviation of its shock decreases but the two posterior intervals overlap. On the other hand, the AR coefficients for risk premium (ρ_b) and monetary policy (ρ_r) shocks rise from 0.21 to 0.75, and from 0.09 to 0.34 respectively. The standard deviations of the respective shocks decrease from 0.24 and 0.24 to 0.08 and 0.13, respectively. The parameter differences outlined above are significant in the sense that their 90% probability intervals do not overlap. For the remaining three shock processes, exogenous spending, monetary policy, and price mark-up, the magnitudes of the AR and MA coefficients either remain the same or show a small decrease, while the standard deviations of these shocks become smaller. Other notable differences in estimated parameters include the adjustment cost elasticity (ϕ), which goes down to 3.03 from 5.76, the degree of price indexation (ι_p), which increases from 0.21 to 0.61, and the coefficient on the lagged interest rate (ρ), which goes down from 0.85 to 0.76. These results imply that the model estimated using business cycle frequencies will potentially deliver different impulse responses from those obtained using the full spectrum. We explore this issue in the next section.

IMPULSE RESPONSE ANALYSIS

Motivated by the differences found between parameter estimates obtained using the full spectrum and business cycle frequencies, we estimate the

impulse response functions of the seven observables to the shocks for
the two cases. Figs. 2(a) through 2(g) report the posterior means, along with
the 90% posterior intervals for horizons of up to 20 quarters. Each figure
contains the response of a single observable to the seven shocks.

One notable difference between the responses of nearly all of the variables
to a risk premium shock is that the impulse responses obtained using
business cycle frequencies display a hump shaped dynamic, as opposed to an
almost monotonic decay of those obtained using the full spectrum, as well as
those in SW (2007). One exception is wage, where the impulse response in

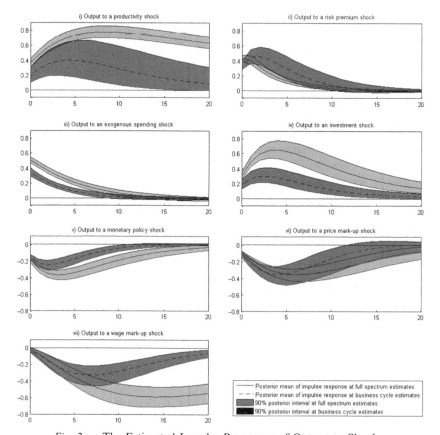

Fig. 2a.   The Estimated Impulse Responses of Output to Shocks.

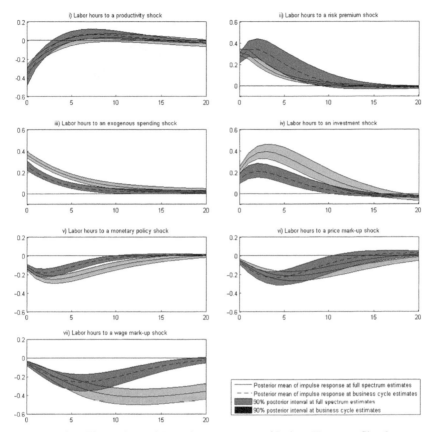

Fig. 2b. The Estimated Impulse Responses of Labor Hours to Shocks.

the full spectrum case is itself hump shaped, but still the pattern is much more pronounced in the business cycle frequency case.

The effects of both exogenous spending and investment shocks are significantly less pronounced when business cycle frequencies are used for estimation, with the exception of an investment shock to inflation and an exogenous spending shock to consumption and wage, for which the differences are not as clear cut.

The effect of a wage mark-up shock dies out faster for all variables if estimated using business cycle frequencies. Its effects are also significantly

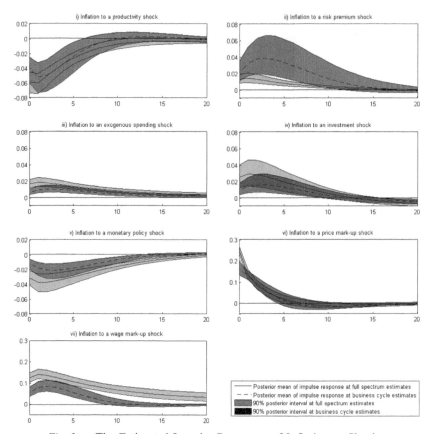

Fig. 2c. The Estimated Impulse Responses of Inflation to Shocks.

less pronounced after about 5 quarters for consumption and wage, after 10 quarters for output and labor hours, and for the whole 20 quarters for inflation and interest rate. It is interesting to note that in the business cycle case, the impulse response of investment to the wage mark-up shock is more pronounced initially for about 5 quarters, but then goes to zero faster after about 14 quarters.

The monetary policy shock also has a smaller impact and goes to zero faster in the business cycle case. Little difference can be observed when considering the responses to the price mark-up shock, as the two posterior

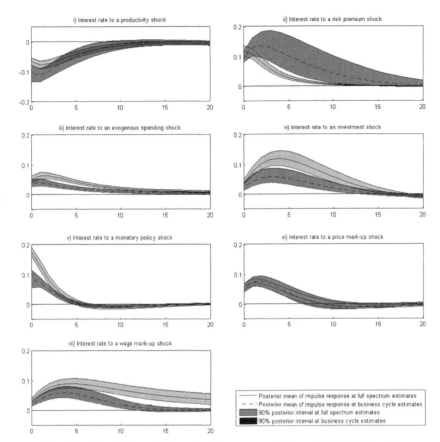

Fig. 2d. The Estimated Impulse Responses of Interest Rate to Shocks.

intervals mostly overlap for the whole 20 quarters. However, responses become less pronounced and decay faster for consumption after roughly 10 quarters, and for output and labor hours after 15 quarters. The responses to the productivity shock are also very similar in the two cases, except for output, consumption, and wage, for which the response is lower and decaying faster with business cycle frequencies.

It is important to ask whether the above difference is due to the impact of the prior, which has a greater effect in the business cycle frequency case as some information from the data is discarded. We address this as follows.

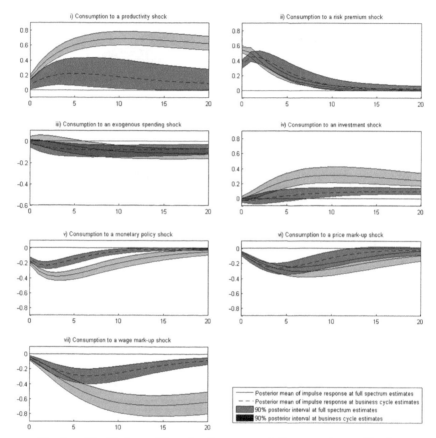

Fig. 2e.   The Estimated Impulse Responses of Consumption to Shocks.

First, we construct the log-likelihood using the business cycle frequencies, but evaluate it at the parameter values estimated from the full spectrum. Second, we construct the same likelihood function and evaluate it at the estimates from business cycle frequencies. The results are reported in Table 8. If the difference in the parameter estimates were entirely driven by the prior, then the likelihood in the second case would be smaller or of similar magnitude as the first case. The result suggests otherwise. Similarly, we construct the log-likelihood function using the full spectrum and evaluate it at both the business cycle and full spectrum based estimates. The difference is even more pronounced. Overall, the result suggests that

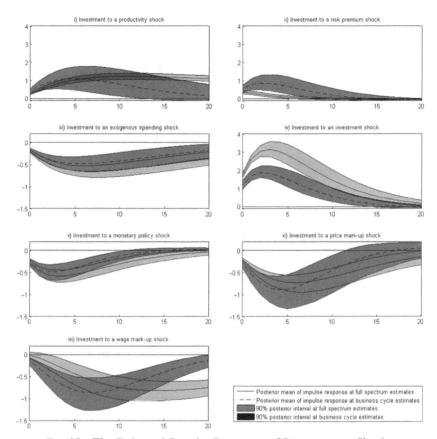

Fig. 2f. The Estimated Impulse Responses of Investment to Shocks.

business cycle based estimates achieve a better fit at such frequencies, but are at odds with other frequencies, in this case the very low frequencies as made clear below.

Since the above analysis omits frequencies from both sides of the business cycle frequency band, it leaves unclear which components are driving the difference. To investigate this, we first consider estimation omitting only frequencies below the business cycle band. Figs. 3(a)–3(g) contain the impulse responses for this case. The estimates from the full spectrum case are also included so that one can contrast Figs. 3(a)–3(g) with Figs. 2(a)–2(g). The figures show that the impulse responses computed omitting the low

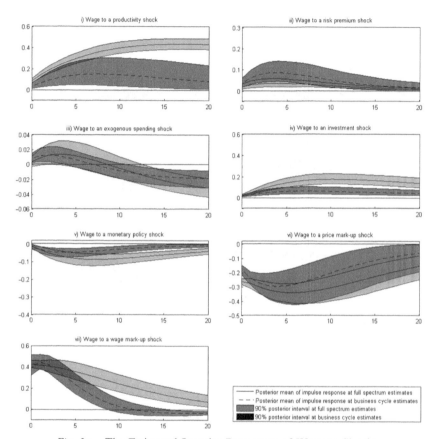

Fig. 2g.   The Estimated Impulse Responses of Wage to Shocks.

frequencies are overall similar to those using only business cycle frequencies. There are a few deviations from this pattern. The hump shaped responses of all seven variables to the risk premium shock observed in business cycle results are no longer present. The same can be noted about the initial few quarters of responses of inflation to the productivity and the price mark-up shocks, as well as of wage to the price mark-up shock.

Next, we consider estimation omitting frequencies above the business cycle band. The results are reported in Figs. 4(a)–4(g), where again the full spectrum based estimates are included as the benchmark. Interestingly, the responses with high frequencies omitted are nearly identical to those

Table 8. Log-Likelihood and Log-Posterior Values at Posterior Modes.

| | Posterior Mode | | | |
	SW (2007)	Full Spectrum	Full Spectrum and Mean	BC Frequencies
Log-likelihood				
Full spectrum	2390.46	**2440.24**	2440.18	1150.83
Full spectrum and mean	2351.66	n/a	**2388.28**	n/a
BC frequencies	511.74	523.42	523.71	**577.72**
Log-posterior				
Full spectrum	2375.75	**2418.07**	2416.88	1153.54
Full spectrum and mean	2368.27	n/a	**2412.28**	n/a
BC frequencies	497.03	501.25	500.40	**580.43**

Note: Entries in the table correspond to the log-likelihoods/log-posteriors, as specified by row labels, evaluated at different posterior modes, which were computed by maximizing the log-posterior specified by column labels. For example, the upper left corner gives the value of the log-likelihood constructed using Fourier frequencies between $2\pi/T$ and $2\pi(T-1)/T$ with the parameter value set to the posterior mode of SW (2007).
The bold numbers correspond to the values of log-likelihoods or log-posteriors evaluated at their corresponding posterior modes.

estimated using the full spectrum. The few exceptions are that in the former case we observe the hump shaped response to the risk premium shock, a somewhat lower initial response to exogenous spending, investment, and productivity shocks of some variables, as well as lower initial responses of inflation and interest rate to the price mark-up and monetary policy shocks.

In summary, most of the differences observed between the impulse responses computed using the full spectrum estimates and those using business cycle frequencies can be attributed to the omission of the frequencies below the business cycle band.

MODEL DIAGNOSTICS FROM A FREQUENCY DOMAIN PERSPECTIVE

King and Watson (1996) compared the spectra of three quantitative rational expectations models with that of the data. The models were calibrated and of small scale. Below, we carry out similar analysis for the medium scale

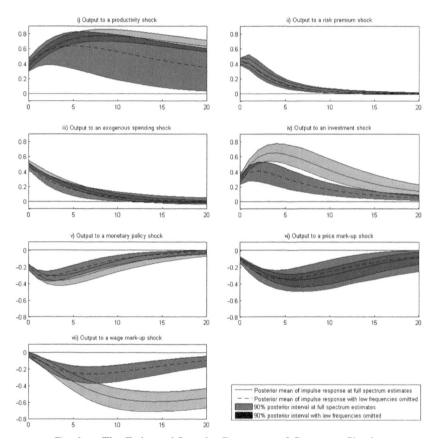

Fig. 3a. The Estimated Impulse Responses of Output to Shocks.

DSGE model considered here. The goal of the analysis is twofold. First, we examine whether the model captures the variability of and the comovements between relevant macroeconomic variables. Second, we compare the model spectrum estimated using all frequencies with that using only business cycle frequencies. The latter will highlight the potential value from using a subset of frequencies in estimation.

We obtain a nonparametric estimate of the spectral density by smoothing the periodograms using demeaned data. Suppose Y_t contains only one variable. Then, the estimator is given by

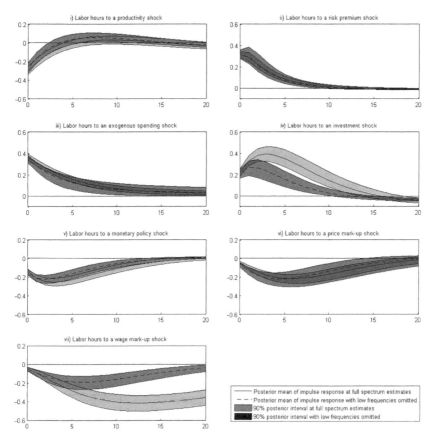

Fig. 3b. The Estimated Impulse Responses of Labor Hours to Shocks.

$$\hat{f}(\omega_j) = \sum_{|k| \leqslant m} \mathscr{W}_T(k) I_T(\omega_{j+k}) \quad \text{for } j \geqslant 1$$

and

$$\hat{f}(0) = \mathscr{W}_T(0) I_T(\omega_1) + 2 \sum_{k=1}^{m} \mathscr{W}_T(k) I_T(\omega_{j+k})$$

where m is a positive integer, $\mathscr{W}_T(k)$ is a weight function satisfying $\mathscr{W}_T(k) = \mathscr{W}_T(-k), \mathscr{W}_T(k) \geqslant 0 \; \forall \; k, \sum_{|k| \leqslant m} \mathscr{W}_T(k) = 1$, and $I_T(\omega_j)$ is the

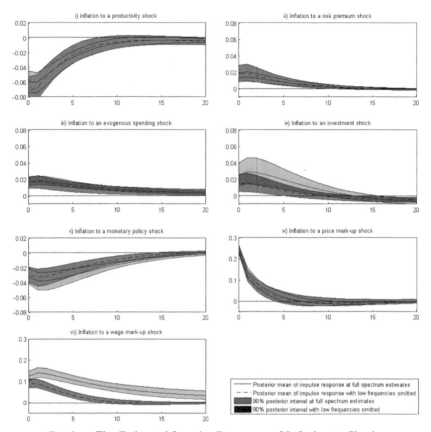

Fig. 3c.   The Estimated Impulse Responses of Inflation to Shocks.

periodogram. The estimator is consistent under mild conditions (see Brockwell & Davis, 1991, for a rigorous treatment) and the asymptotic 95% confidence intervals for the log of the spectral density are given by

$$\log(\hat{f}(\omega_j)) \pm 1.96 \left(\sum_{|k| \leq m} \mathscr{W}_T(k)^2 \right)^{1/2}$$

We apply the same type of estimator to obtain absolute coherency between pairs of variables. Let Y_t be a bivariate demeaned time series. The spectral density matrix is estimated in the same way as above but with

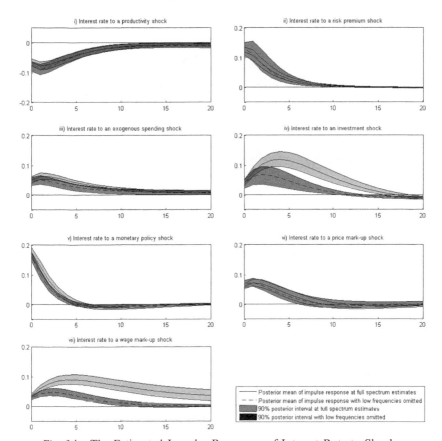

Fig. 3d.   The Estimated Impulse Responses of Interest Rate to Shocks.

$I_T(\omega_{j+k})$ being a 2×2 matrix. Let $\hat{f}_{hk}(\omega_j)$ denote the (h, k)-th element of $\hat{f}(\omega)$, then the absolute coherency estimate ($|\hat{\Re}_{12}(\omega_j)|$) between Y_{1t} and Y_{2t} is

$$|\hat{\Re}_{12}(\omega_j)| = \frac{[\hat{c}_{12}^2(\omega_j) + \hat{q}_{12}^2(\omega_j)]^{1/2}}{[\hat{f}_{11}(\omega_j)\hat{f}_{22}(\omega_j)]^{1/2}}$$

where

$$\hat{c}_{12}(\omega_j) = \frac{[\hat{f}_{12}(\omega_j) + \hat{f}_{21}(\omega_j)]}{2}$$

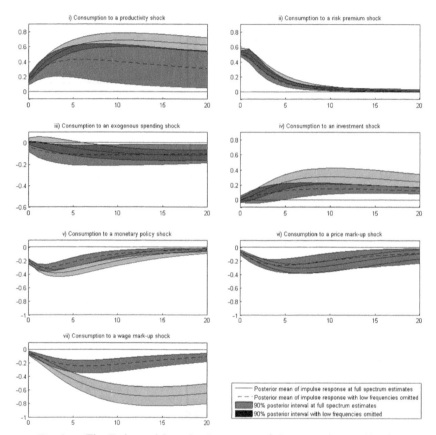

Fig. 3e. The Estimated Impulse Responses of Consumption to Shocks.

$$\hat{q}_{12}(\omega_j) = \frac{i[\hat{f}_{12}(\omega_j) - \hat{f}_{21}(\omega_j)]}{2}$$

The 95% confidence intervals can be computed as

$$|\hat{\Re}_{12}(\omega_j)| \pm \frac{1.96(1 - |\hat{\Re}_{12}(\omega_j)|^2)\left(\sum_{|k| \leqslant m} \mathcal{W}_T(k)^2\right)^{1/2}}{\sqrt{2}}$$

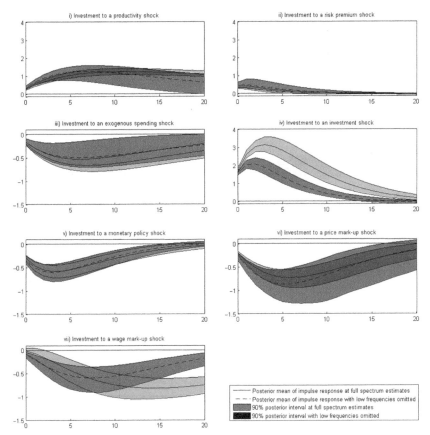

Fig. 3f. The Estimated Impulse Responses of Investment to Shocks.

In applications, the choice of $\mathcal{W}_T(k)$ depends on the characteristics of the data series at hand. It is possible and sometimes advantageous to use different weighting functions for estimation of different elements of the spectral density matrix due to potentially different features of the time series (see Chapter 9 in Priestley (1981) for a discussion). In our case, we apply the same weight function in all estimations, with $m = 4$ and the weights given by $\{\frac{1}{21}, \frac{2}{21}, \frac{3}{21}, \frac{3}{21}, \frac{3}{21}, \frac{3}{21}, \frac{3}{21}, \frac{2}{21}, \frac{1}{21}\}$, which is obtained by the successive application of two Daniell filters with weights given by $\{\frac{1}{3}, \frac{1}{3}, \frac{1}{3}\}$ and $\{\frac{1}{7}, \frac{1}{7}, \frac{1}{7}, \frac{1}{7}, \frac{1}{7}, \frac{1}{7}, \frac{1}{7}\}$. This choice of $\mathcal{W}_T(k)$ produces spectra

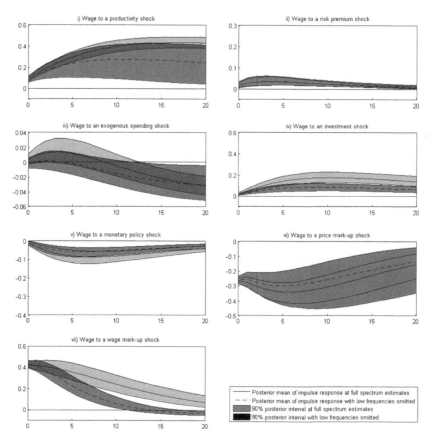

Fig. 3g. The Estimated Impulse Responses of Wage to Shocks.

estimates that are not as rough as the raw periodogram, and in the meantime do not appear oversmoothed.

Fig. 5 plots the log spectra of the seven variables. Three results are reported in each sub-figure. First, we report the nonparametric estimates of the spectrum of the demeaned data series along with the pointwise 95% confidence intervals. They are used as a benchmark to assess the model's ability in capturing these key features. The solid curve is the spectrum implied by the model with parameters estimated using the full spectrum. The dashed line is the same object but with business cycle

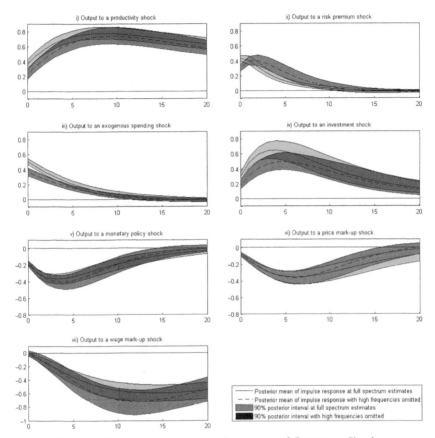

Fig. 4a. The Estimated Impulse Responses of Output to Shocks.

based estimates. Two patterns emerge. First, the solid curve captures the overall shape of the data spectrum, although there are noticeable departures which often occur inside of the business cycle frequencies. It should be noted that for the growth series (sub-figures i–iii,vi), the model implies that their spectral density at frequency zero is zero (as the figure reports log spectra, the frequency zero is omitted from the figures). This is inconsistent with the data spectra, which are positive at the origin. When frequencies very near zero are included in the estimation, the model will try to reduce such a departure by having very persistent

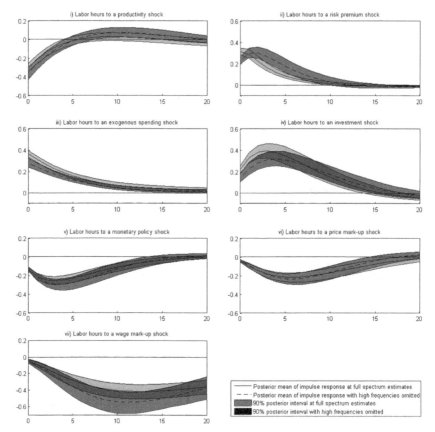

Fig. 4b.   The Estimated Impulse Responses of Labor Hours to Shocks.

estimates. This potentially affects the other frequencies, which partly explains why the full spectrum based estimates do not capture the slope of the spectrum very well inside of the business cycle frequencies. When using only business cycle frequencies for estimation, such a tension is absent and the estimates do a better job at matching variations at these frequencies. The lines never fall substantially outside of the confidence bands based on the nonparametric estimates. However, the departures from the data spectrum can be substantial outside of the business cycle frequencies. In practice, this offers the researcher a choice. If one firmly

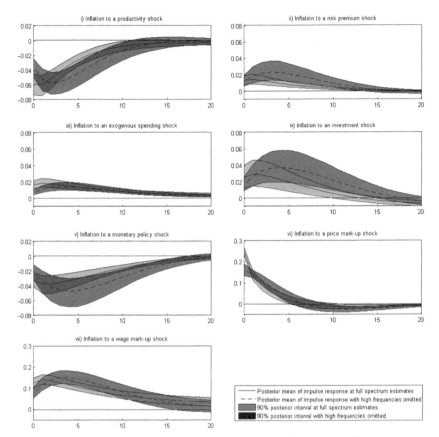

Fig. 4c. The Estimated Impulse Responses of Inflation to Shocks.

believes that the DSGE model is well specified at all frequencies, then, they should all enter the estimation and the estimates will be more efficient. If one suspects that the modeling of the trend, or, more generally, of the very low frequency behavior in the model is inconsistent with the data (e.g., the data has a broken trend while the model has a linear trend), then the subset based approach may be a more robust choice.

Figs. 6(a)–6(c) report the absolute coherency between the seven variables. Notice that their values can be interpreted as a measure of strength of

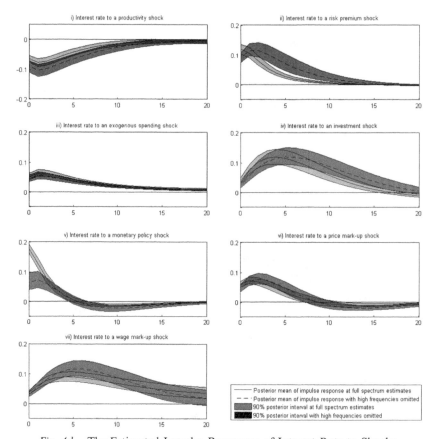

Fig. 4d. The Estimated Impulse Responses of Interest Rate to Shocks.

correlation at a particular frequency. Both the business cycle and the full spectrum based estimates achieve something at capturing their overall magnitudes, with the exception of the comovements between interest rate and other four variables (consumption growth, investment growth, output growth, and labor hours). In the latter case, the two estimates are close and are consistently below the nonparametric estimates. This unanimous finding suggests a dimension along which the model can be further improved. For the other cases, the business cycle based estimates typically do a better job at the intended frequencies. They largely stay within

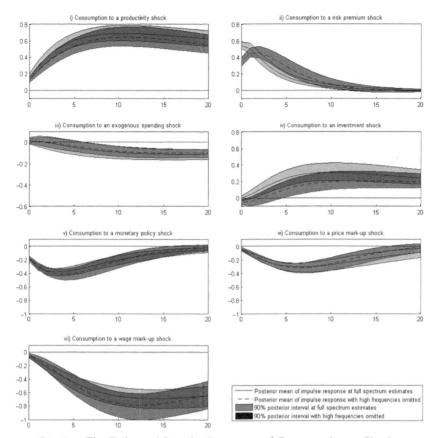

Fig. 4e. The Estimated Impulse Responses of Consumption to Shocks.

the confidence intervals, and are better at capturing the peaks of the coherency, while the full spectrum based estimates miss them in the majority of cases.

In summary, the SW (2007) model does a reasonable job at matching the spectra of individual time series and the absolute coherency implied by the data. The business cycle based estimates offer the flexibility to focus on a particular frequency band and to achieve a better fit at such frequencies. In practice, both analyses can be carried out, allowing us to assess to what extent the results are driven by some particular frequencies.

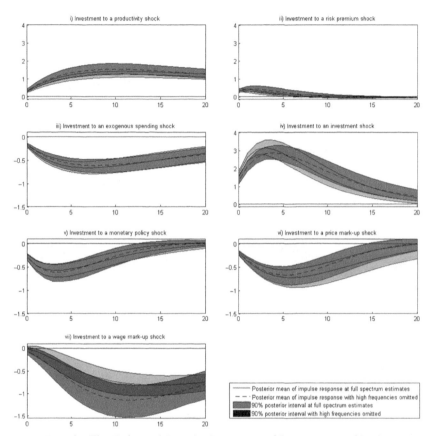

Fig. 4f.   The Estimated Impulse Responses of Investment to Shocks.

CONCLUSION AND DISCUSSION

The chapter has considered identification, estimation, and inference in medium scale DSGE models using SW (2007) as an illustrative example. A key element in the analysis is that we can focus on part of the spectrum.

For identification, we derived the non-identification curve to reveal which and how many parameters need to be fixed to achieve local identification. For estimation and inference, we compared estimates obtained using the full spectrum with those using only business cycle frequencies and reported

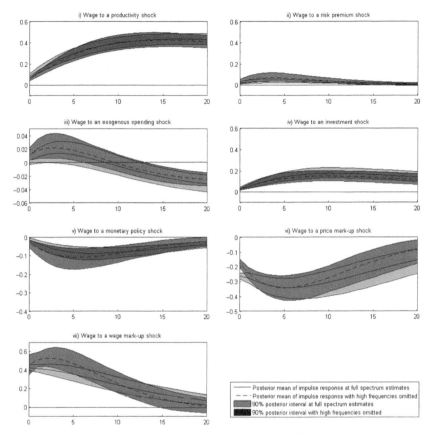

Fig. 4g. The Estimated Impulse Responses of Wage to Shocks.

notably different parameter values and impulse response functions. Further analysis shows that the differences are mainly due to the frequencies below the business cycle frequency band. We have also considered model diagnostics by contrasting the model based and the nonparametrically estimated spectra as well as examining the absolute coherency. The result suggests that SW (2007) does a reasonable job at matching these two features observed in the data, with the exception of the comovements between interest rate and other four variables (consumption growth, investment growth, output growth, and labor hours). The business cycle

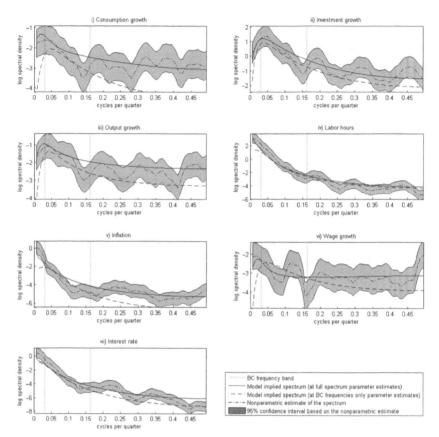

Fig. 5. Model Implied and Nonparametrically Estimated Log Spectra of Observables.

based estimate, due to its ability to focus on a particular frequency band, achieves a better fit at such frequencies.

From a methodological perspective, the results contribute to the relatively sparse literature that exploits the advantage of model estimation and diagnostics using a subset of frequencies. Engle (1974) is a seminal contribution. It proposed band spectrum regression as a way to allow for frequency specific misspecification, seasonality and measurement errors, and to obtain better understanding of some common time domain procedures, such as applying a moving average filter. Sims (1993) and Hansen and Sargent (1993) considered the effect of removing or downweighting seasonal

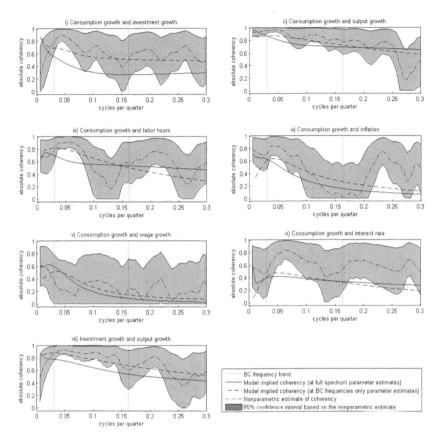

Fig. 6a. Model Implied and Nonparametrically Estimated Coherency Between Observables.

frequencies on estimating rational expectations models. Diebold, Ohanian, and Berkowitz (1998) discussed a general framework for loss function based estimation and model evaluation. In a different context, McCloskey (2010) considered parameter estimation in ARMA, GARCH, and stochastic volatility models robust to low frequency contamination caused by a changing mean or misspecified trend. Qu and Tkachenko (2012) provided a comprehensive treatment of the theoretical and computational aspects of the frequency domain quasi-likelihood applied to DSGE models. By working through a concrete example, this chapter demonstrates that such an approach is applicable to medium scale DSGE models and that it offers

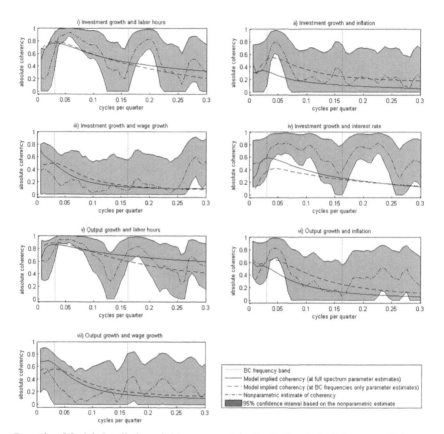

Fig. 6b. Model Implied and Nonparametrically Estimated Coherency Between Observables.

substantial depth and flexibility when compared with time domain methods. We intend to apply the methodology to a relatively broad class of DSGE models and hope to report results in the near future.

NOTES

1. In the original paper k_t instead of k_t^s shows up. In their Dynare code, SW (2007) have k_t^s.

2. Therefore, a complete notation should be $\Theta_0(\theta)$ and $\Theta_1(\theta)$. We omit such a dependence for simplicity.

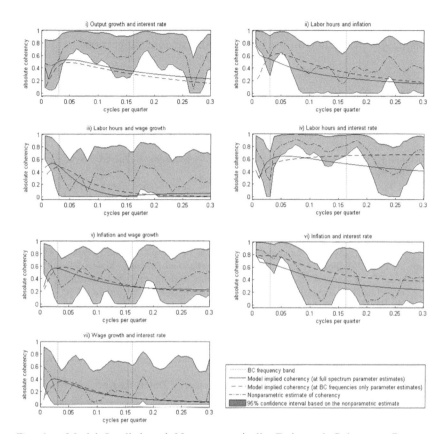

Fig. 6c. Model Implied and Nonparametrically Estimated Coherency Between Observables.

3. Note that in the code $\Sigma(\theta)$ is a 7×7 identity matrix, as the shock standard deviations are incorporated into Ψ when setting up the dynamic system.

4. There is no need to consider $\omega \in [-\pi, 0]$ because $f_\theta(\omega)$ is equal to the conjugate of $f_\theta(-\omega)$.

5. Here and below we used several scaling factors yielding the acceptance rates between 20% and 40%, and found that the results are not sensitive to these changes.

ACKNOWLEDGMENT

We thank participants at the 10th Annual Advances in Econometrics Conference: DSGE Models in Macroeconomics – Estimation, Evaluation, and New Developments (November 4–6, 2011), Ivan Jeliazkov, Fabio Milani, and Pierre Perron for useful comments and suggestions.

REFERENCES

An, S., & Schorfheide, F. (2007). Bayesian analysis of DSGE models. *Econometric Reviews, 26*, 113–172.

Brockwell, P., & Davis, R. (1991). *Time series: Theory and methods* (2nd ed.). New York, NY: Springer-Verlag.

Canova, F., & Sala, L. (2009). Back to square one: Identification issues in DSGE models. *Journal of Monetary Economics, 56*, 431–449.

Chernozhukov, V., & Hong, H. (2003). An MCMC approach to classical estimation. *Journal of Econometrics, 115*, 293–346.

Diebold, F. X., Ohanian, L. E., & Berkowitz, J. (1998). Dynamic equilibrium economies: A framework for comparing models and data. *The Review of Economic Studies, 65*, 433–451.

Engle, R. F. (1974). Band spectrum regression. *International Economic Review, 15*, 1–11.

Hansen, L. P., & Sargent, T. J. (1993). Seasonality and approximation errors in rational expectations models. *Journal of Econometrics, 55*, 21–55.

Hastings, W. K. (1970). Monte Carlo sampling methods using Markov chains and their applications. *Biometrika, 57*, 97–109.

Iskrev, N. (2010). Local identification in DSGE models. *Journal of Monetary Economics, 57*, 189–202.

King, R. G., & Watson, M. W. (1996). Money, prices, interest rates and the business cycle. *The Review of Economics and Statistics, 78*, 35–53.

Komunjer, I., & Ng, S. (2011). Dynamic identification of DSGE models. *Econometrica, 79*, 1995–2032.

Leeper, E. M., & Sims, C. A. (1994). Toward a modern macroeconomic model usable for policy analysis. In F. Stanley & J. J. Rotemberg (Eds.), *NBER Macroeconomics Annual* (pp. 81–118). Cambridge, MA: MIT Press.

McCloskey, A. (2010). *Parameter estimation robust to low-frequency contamination with applications to ARMA, GARCH and stochastic volatility models*. Working Paper, Boston University, Boston, MA.

Metropolis, N., Rosenbluth, A. W., Rosenbluth, M. N., Teller, A. H., & Teller, E. (1953). Equation of state calculations by fast computing machines. *Journal of Chemical Physics, 21*, 1087–1092.

Otrok, C. (2001). On measuring the welfare cost of business cycles. *Journal of Monetary Economics, 47*, 61–92.

Priestley, M. B. (1981). *Spectral analysis and time series* (Vol. 1). New York, NY: Academic Press.

Qu, Z., & Tkachenko, D. (2012). Identification and frequency domain QML estimation of linearized DSGE models. *Quantitative Economics, 3*, 95–132.

Roberts, G., Gelman, A., & Gilks, W. (1997). Weak convergence and optimal scaling of random walk Metropolis algorithms. *Annals of Applied Probability, 7*, 110–120.

Schorfheide, F. (2000). Loss function-based evaluation of DSGE models. *Journal of Applied Econometrics, 15*, 645–670.

Schorfheide, F. (2011). *Estimation and evaluation of DSGE models: Progress and challenges.* NBER Working Paper No. 16781. NBER, Cambridge, MA.

Sims, C. A. (1993). Rational expectations modeling with seasonally adjusted data. *Journal of Econometrics, 55,* 9–19.

Sims, C. A. (2002). Solving linear rational expectations models. *Computational Economics, 20,* 1–20.

Smets, F., & Wouters, R. (2007). Shocks and frictions in US business cycles: A Bayesian DSGE approach. *The American Economic Review, 97,* 586–606.

Uhlig, H. (1999). A toolkit for analyzing nonlinear dynamic stochastic models easily. In R. Marimon & A. Scott (Eds.), *Computational methods for the study of dynamic economies.* Oxford and New York: Oxford University Press.

Watson, M. W. (1993). Measures of fit for calibrated models. *Journal of Political Economy, 101,* 1011–1041.

APPENDIX: EQUATIONS AND VARIABLES IN THE FLEXIBLE PRICE-WAGE ECONOMY

The equations are similar to those in the sticky price-wage economy, but with the variables μ_t^p and μ_t^w set to zero. Stars are used to denote variables from this economy. Because the shock processes are identical to those in the sticky price-wage economy, we do not repeat them here.

1. The resource constraint:

$$y_t^* = c_y c_t^* + i_y i_t^* + z_y z_t^* + \varepsilon_t^g$$

2. The dynamics of consumption follow from the consumption Euler equation

$$c_t^* = c_1 c_{t-1}^* + (1 - c_1) E_t c_{t+1}^* + c_2 (l_t^* - E_t l_{t+1}^*) - c_3 (r_t^* - 0) - \varepsilon_t^b$$

   Note that the expected inflation is zero because the price adjusts instantaneously.

3. The dynamics of investment come from the investment Euler equation

$$i_t^* = i_1 i_{t-1}^* + (1 - i_1) E_t i_{t+1}^* + i_2 q_t^* + \varepsilon_t^i$$

4. The corresponding arbitrage equation for the value of capital is given by

$$q_t^* = q_1 E_t q_{t+1}^* + (1 - q_1) E_t r_{t+1}^{*k} - (r_t^* - 0) - \frac{1}{c_3} \varepsilon_t^b$$

   The expected inflation is zero for the same reason as above.

5. The aggregate production function is

$$y_t^* = \varphi_p \left(\alpha k_t^{*s} + (1 - \alpha) l_t^* + \varepsilon_t^a \right)$$

6. Current capital service use is a function of capital installed in the previous period and the degree of capital utilization

$$k_t^{*s} = k_{t-1}^* + z_t^*$$

7. The degree of capital utilization is a positive fraction of the rental rate of capital

$$z_t^* = z_1 r_t^{*k}$$

8. The accumulation of installed capital is

$$k_t^* = k_1 k_{t-1}^* + (1 - k_1) i_t^* + k_2 \varepsilon_t^i$$

9. Because $\mu_t^p = 0$ and the relationship with rigidity is:

$$\mu_t^p = \alpha(k_t^s - l_t) + \varepsilon_t^a - w_t$$

we have

$$0 = \alpha(k_t^s - l_t) + \varepsilon_t^a - w_t$$

or, equivalently,

$$\alpha r_t^{*k} + (1 - \alpha) w_t^* = \varepsilon_t^a$$

There is no New Keynesian Phillips curve as price adjusts instantaneously.

10. The rental rate of capital is

$$r_t^{*k} = -(k_t^{*s} - l_t^*) + w_t^*$$

11. The wage mark-up is now $\mu_t^w = 0$. Therefore,

$$0 = w_t^* - \left(\sigma_l l_t^* + \frac{1}{1 - \lambda} (c_t^* - \lambda c_{t-1}^*) \right)$$

or

$$w_t^* = \left(\sigma_l l_t^* + \frac{1}{1 - \lambda} (c_t^* - \lambda c_{t-1}^*) \right)$$

ON THE ESTIMATION OF DYNAMIC STOCHASTIC GENERAL EQUILIBRIUM MODELS: AN EMPIRICAL LIKELIHOOD APPROACH

Sara Riscado

ABSTRACT

In this chapter we approach the estimation of dynamic stochastic general equilibrium models through a moments-based estimator, the empirical likelihood. We attempt to show that this inference process can be a valid alternative to maximum likelihood, which has been one of the preferred choices of the related literature to estimate these models. The empirical likelihood estimator is characterized by a simple setup and only requires knowledge about the moments of the data generating process of the model. In this context, we exploit the fact that these economies can be formulated as a set of moment conditions to infer on their parameters through this technique. For illustrational purposes, we consider a standard real business cycle model with a constant relative risk averse utility function and indivisible labor, driven by a normal technology shock.

DSGE Models in Macroeconomics: Estimation, Evaluation, and New Developments
Advances in Econometrics, Volume 28, 387–419
ISSN: 0731-9053/doi:10.1108/S0731-9053(2012)0000028012

388 SARA RISCADO

Keywords: Moment conditions; empirical likelihood

JEL classification: C14; E27

INTRODUCTION

Dynamic stochastic general equilibrium (DSGE) models are widely used as
the standard tool of macroeconomic analysis. In a nutshell, a DSGE
model represents the economy as constrained optimization problem(s),
subject to the definition of preferences and technology, the laws of motion
of the economic variables, and the resource constraints of both the whole
economy and the agents. Furthermore, it is possible to introduce a variety
of uncertainty sources, such as productivity, preferences and/or policy
shocks. In this way, it is possible to simulate the economy's equilibrium
path under uncertain conditions and compare it with what is observed in
the real world (taking the model to the data). It is also possible to shock
the economy, and observe its behavior as it converges to its steady state
through a impulse response analysis (which is very useful from the policy-
making point-of-view). As Ruge-Murcia (2003) well explains, "DSGE
models are attractive because they specify explicitly the objectives and
constraints faced by households and firms, and then determine the prices
and allocations that result from their market interaction in an uncertain
environment."

From an econometric perspective DSGE models are interesting in two
main ways.

First, as Sargent (1989) showed, one can always write a likelihood
function from a DSGE model and, in this way, it is possible to estimate its
structural parameters. Sargent (1989) proposed to linearize the equilibrium
conditions of the economy around the steady state or, alternatively to
generate a quadratic approximation to the utility function of the economic
agents. From here, one would be able to obtain approximated policy
functions of the model (i.e., the optimal choices of the economic agents, at
each period of time), upon which the likelihood function would be written.
Sargent's seminal work originated a very extensive literature on the
maximum likelihood estimation of DSGE models, from which we outline
the recent studies of Fernandez-Villaverde and Rubio-Ramirez (2004, 2005,
2007). However, the implementation of maximum likelihood is analytically and computationally demanding, due to the two issues that have to
be addressed in order to reach the estimation stage. These two steps are

(i) writing down the likelihood function and (ii) evaluating the likelihood function.

Writing down the likelihood function requires solving the DSGE model in order to obtain its policy functions. The specific analytical structure of the system of equilibrium conditions of these models, which is generally a nonlinear system of difference equations, yields closed form solutions only in very few settings. Therefore, for the vast majority of DSGE models it is only possible to obtain approximated policy functions. The standard procedure in the literature to obtain these approximated policy functions has been to (log)linearize the system of equilibrium conditions around the steady state, and then solving the resulting system through one of the available linear methods. The resulting policy functions will be linear on the states of the economy. As an alternative to the linear option, there is also a set of numerical nonlinear methods to compute approximations to the policy functions (see, for instance, Aruoba, Fernandez-Villaverde, & Rubio-Ramirez, 2003, for a survey, classification, and comparison of numerical nonlinear methods).

The next step is to evaluate the likelihood and this depends crucially on the solution method choosen. If one chooses the linear path, one has to apply the Kalman filter to evaluate the likelihood function. Moreover, one has to assume that the stochastic component of the model follows a normal distribution. This imposes a strong assumption on the shocks hitting the economy. If one chooses the nonlinear paths, one has to apply nonlinear filters, such as the Sequential Monte Carlo filter proposed by Fernandez-Villaverde and Rubio-Ramirez (2004).

Then, the maximization of the likelihood function follows. At this stage, one can choose between the classical inference and the Bayesian estimation. The classical inference consists in maximizing the likelihood function with respect to the parameters and computing their asymptotic variance–covariance matrix. The Bayesian inference, instead, implies obtaining a posterior distribution for the parameters proportional to the observables' likelihood function times the priors on the parameters.

The choice of the solution method, and consequently of the filter applied on the estimation, has generated discussion on the accuracy, implementation and computation costs of each of the methods. Fernandez-Villaverde and Rubio-Ramirez (2005) address this question, by comparing linear with nonlinear likelihood based inference in a DSGE framework. They argue that eliminating the nonlinearities of the economy may not deliver sufficiently accurate policy functions, specially if we are far from the steady state of the model and if the nonlinearities are important features of the economy. Their results prove that the nonlinear choice is more suitable to take the model to the data, even when considering a relatively linear model. The discussion about the accuracy of the solution and evaluation methods has led to a more subtle thread, which is the problem of performing inference with an approximated likelihood function instead of the exact one. Fernandez-Villaverde, Rubio-Ramirez, and Santos (2006) are concerned with the possibility of having nonnegligible biases on estimates, if they use an approximated likelihood function instead of the true one. Ackerberg, Geweke, and Hahn (2009) investigate this same question and prove that *"second order approximation errors in the policy function* have at most *second order effects on parameter inference"*[1] meaning that the impact of the approximation error may not cause important biases in the estimates. Nonetheless, these authors note that these are asymptotic results, so the level of accuracy of estimates is the same as the level of accuracy of the approximated likelihood function (i.e., how close the approximated likelihood function is to the true one). In this way, the researcher should carefully choose the method that can deliver the most accurate policy functions.

Second, a DSGE model can also be represented by a set of moment conditions. This set of moments can be derived from the optimality conditions of the economic agents, and from the assumptions on the economy itself, such as the laws of motion of the economic variables and the moments of the stochastic shocks considered. This fact implies that it is also possible to estimate the structural parameters of DSGE models through the general method of moments and other moments-based family of estimators. The general method of moments is a less demanding estimation method in terms of distributional assumptions than the maximum likelihood estimation. In the context of the estimation of DSGE models this proves to be of great benefit. In the DSGE literature it is commonly assumed that shocks are normally distributed, which is very convenient when coming to write their likelihood function. However, authors like Geweke (1993) and, more recently, Justiniano and Primiceri (2005) and Fernandez-Villaverde and Rubio-Ramirez (2006) argue that this is an extremely strong assumption and that, very often, the observed data show "fat tails" and could be better described by other distributions. These authors show that the fit of an ARMA process to US output data improves substantially when the errors are distributed as a student-t distribution instead of a normal one. Kim and Nelson (1999), McConnel and Perez-Quirós (2000), and Stock and Watson (2002) seem to confirm this argument, showing that shocks in DSGE models may have a richer structure than normal innovations.

In this chapter, we also exploit the moment conditions of a DSGE model to estimate the structural parameters of the economy, but in a different framework. We approach the estimation of DSGE models with the empirical likelihood estimator. The empirical likelihood is also a moments-based estimator, which was first introduced by Owen (1988) as a likelihood ratio test, but it was soon found that it could be used to perform inference in a great variety of contexts, as explained by Qin and Lawless (1994). Briefly, the empirical likelihood estimator consists in a nested optimization of an empirical likelihood function, subject to a set of moment conditions. This optimization problem is solved by first optimizing with respect to the weights assigned to each element of the sample, provided that the moment conditions are satisfied, and then to the parameters embodied in the moments. As in the case of the general method of moments, the empirical likelihood estimator only requires knowledge on the moments of the data generating process of the model and not on the distribution function itself. In addition, it accomodates all types of uncertainty and respects the nonlinear struture of the economy considered. Furthermore, it is a maximum-likelihood type of optimization problem, which implies good high order asymptotic properties (confirmed by Schennach (2007)). Moreover, we can skip the cumbersome and discretionary steps of finding the most accurate policy functions and of evaluating the likelihood, which we have described above.

Hence, we will attempt to prove that the empirical likelihood estimator can be a valid way to perform inference with DSGE models. For that purpose, we will estimate the parameters of the standard business cycle model with a constant relative risk aversion utility function and indivisible labor, driven by a normal technology shock, using the empirical likelihood estimator.

In this exercise, we face two main problems. One is to find the adequate set of moment conditions, since our model will not deliver enough original moment conditions to estimate all the parameters. The other is to tackle the singularity problem arising from having less shocks than control variables.

The rest of this chapter is organized as follows. In the second section we describe the empirical likelihood estimator and discuss the definition of moments in the DSGE context. In the third section we present the economy which will illustrate the estimation process. In the fourth section we describe the estimation strategy followed and present some preliminary results. The fifth section concludes.

THE EMPIRICAL LIKELIHOOD FRAMEWORK

We present the empirical likelihood estimator, explain how it adapts to our estimation problem, and discuss the definition and selection of the moment conditions in a DSGE model's context.

The Empirical Likelihood Estimator

Setup. Let $x_1, \ldots, x_m$ be identically independently distributed random variables drawn from an unknown distribution F, and $\omega(F)$ a q-dimensional vector of parameters, associated with the distribution F. Assume also that there is available information about ω and F in the form of r independent functions $g_j(x_i, \omega), j = 1, \ldots, r$, with $r \geqslant q$, such that $E\{g_i(x_i, \omega)\} = 0, \forall j$, under F. We can summarize the required setting in the following vector form:

$$g(x_i, \omega) = (g_1(x_i, \omega), \ldots, g_r(x_i, \omega))' \qquad (1)$$

where

$$E_F\{g(x_i, \omega)\} = 0 \qquad (2)$$

Condition (2) delivers a set of general estimating equations, which will be imposed on the sample. In this setting, we define the empirical likelihood function as follows:

$$L_{EL}(\omega, p) = \left\{ \prod_{i=1}^{m} p_i | p_i > 0, \sum_{i=1}^{m} p_i = 1, \sum_{i=1}^{m} [p_i \cdot g(x_i, \omega)] = 0 \right\} \qquad (3)$$

where p is the vector of the weights assigned to the sample elements.

The empirical likelihood function described in Eq. (3) is simply the product of the probabilities assigned to the sample elements, which satisfies three restrictions. The weights, or probabilities, p_i assigned to the sample elements have to be strictly positive and have to sum to one. Also, the sample counterparts of the distribution moments defined by Eq. (2), computed with the probabilities p_i, have to be satisfied.

Optimization problem. The maximum empirical likelihood estimator of $\{\omega, p\}$ is given by:

$$\{\hat{\omega}, \hat{p}\} = \arg \max_{\omega, p} L_{EL}(\omega, p) \qquad (4)$$

The optimization problem defined by Eq. (4) is a reweighting problem, since we optimize with respect to the vector of weights p. Note that this is a nested optimization problem, and not a two step estimator. Hence, once we obtain an estimate of p we use it to estimate ω, which is then substituted again into the problem and we reoptimize with respect to p. The optimization proceeds in this way until we find the pair $(\hat{\omega}, \hat{p})$ that maximizes the objective function given by Eq. (3). The main idea underlying the empirical likelihood inference is to use optimally all the information embodied in the moments and in the sample in order to estimate the parameters in vector ω and the distribution F (see Section A.4 for details on the solution of this problem). As pointed out by Schennach (2005), the empirical likelihood estimation "seeks to reweight the sample so that it satisfies the moment conditions exactly, while maximizing the likelihood function of a multinomial supported on the sample." In other words, unlike what happens with the general method of moments, we impose that the sample moments coincide exactly with the theoretical ones, and we choose the proper weights of the sample elements that deliver exactly that result.

It is also possible to make a parallel between the empirical likelihood function and the bootstrap technique. As Kitamura (1997) explains "both are based in nonparametric likelihood," but "while the bootstrap assigns $1/N$ probability mass to each observation, the empirical likelihood 'chooses' probability mass under linear constraints."

Exponential Tilting Empirical Likelihood

This is an important extension of the empirical likelihood estimator and can be especially useful in our DSGE setup, because of possible misspecification problems. Schennach (2007) shows that, in the presence of model misspecification, the good high-order properties exhibited by the empirical likelihood estimator, are no longer verified. Schennach (2007) proposes to tilt the empirical likelihood with an exponential functional form to tackle the problem. In comparison with the simple empirical likelihood setting described by Eq. (3), the setting of the exponential tilted empirical likelihood is modified as follows:

$$\hat{\theta} = \arg\min_{\theta} \left(\frac{1}{n} \sum_{i=1}^{n} \tilde{h}(\hat{p}_i(\theta)) \right) \tag{5}$$

where $\hat{p}_i(\theta)$ is the solution to

$$\min_{p_i} \left\{ \frac{1}{n} \sum_{i=1}^{n} h(p_i) \mid \sum_{i=1}^{n} p_i = 1; \sum_{i=1}^{n} [p_i g(x_i, \theta)] = 0 \right\} \tag{6}$$

with $\tilde{h}(p_i) = -\log(np_i)$ and $h(p_i) = np_i \log(np_i)$. The idea underlying this problem is to use the exponential tilted likelihood to find $\hat{p}_i(\theta)$ and use the empirical likelihood function to obtain the estimate of θ. In this way, the empirical likelihood function is combined with the entropy of the exponential tilted to estimate θ.

In the estimation part of this work, we will assume that there is a a high probability that our model is misspecified, that is, $\inf_{\theta \in \Theta} \| E[g(x_i, \theta)] \| \neq 0$. In this way, we will use the exponential tilted empirical likelihood estimator to obtain the estimates of our parameters.

General Estimation Equations in the DSGE Models Context

The definition of a set of "good" moment conditions is crucial in the empirical likelihood framework. DSGE models can be formulated as a set of moments. The stylized nature of DSGE models results in the impossibility of having a sufficient number of moment conditions to estimate all the parameters of interest. Therefore, in most settings, we have to build more independent estimating equations. This is, very much, an arbitrary task. Hence, we should be careful when choosing the criteria to follow when constructing these "artificial" moments. Furthermore, even the selection of original moments, which derive directly from the equilibrium conditions of the economy, is not straighforward. We stress the fact that the moments' function is actually a hybrid object, since it accumulates economic and statistical characteristics. The moment conditions should represent the economy under study and, consequently, we should be able to interpret them at the light of the theory underlying our model. At the same time, they should comply with some statistical requirements such as low cross correlation and high sensibility to "false" values of the parameters. Therefore, each moment condition has to combine the economic interpretation with the desirable statistical features. Hence, the main difficulty arising when defining the set of moment conditions, whether they are original or not, is to combine the statistic requirements with the economic interpretation.

In this preliminary analysis we will consider two sets of moment conditions: one constructed with instruments Canova (2007); and the other chosen according to the low correlation criteria.

AN ILLUSTRATION

We illustrate our analysis with the standard stochastic neoclassical model with indivisible labor, assuming a constant relative risk aversion utility function, a constant returns to scale Cobb–Douglas production function, and a technology shock. In this section, we describe the economy in more detail, define and solve the representative household problem, and write down the competitive equilibrium of the economy. We choose this economy because it is simple and general enough, so that the estimation process can be adapted to other models with a similar structure, but different specifications of utillity and production functions, laws of motion, and more types of shocks.

Description of the Economy

Preferences. The instantaneous utility function describing households' preferences is defined as:

$$U(c_t, n_t) = \frac{[c_t^\theta (1 - n_t)^{1-\theta}]^{1-\tau}}{1 - \tau} \tag{7}$$

Eq. (7) is a constant relative risk aversion (or constant elasticity of intertemporal substitution) utility function with two arguments: consumption, c_t, and leisure time, l_t. We have normalized time endowment to 1, so that $l_t = 1 - n_t$, where n_t is labor hours supplied, and therefore household's total time endowment is allocated between leisure and hours worked. The parameter $\theta \in [0, 1]$ weights the relative importance of leisure and consumption in the bundle of the representative household. The curvature parameter or coefficient of relative risk aversion, $\tau \geq 0$, measures how averse to risk the representative household is. The representative household is less willing to change her pattern of consumption the higher is τ.

Production. We assume that output, y_t, is produced combining capital, k_t, and labor, n_t, and for an exogenous level of productivity, z_t, through the following Cobb–Douglas production function:

$$y_t = f(k_t, n_t) = e^{z_t} k_t^\alpha n_t^{1-\alpha} \tag{8}$$

Eq. (8) satisfies the usual neoclassical properties, namely decreasing marginal factor productivities and the Inada conditions. The parameter $\alpha \in (0, 1)$ measures the elasticity of output with respect to capital.

Laws of motion. We assume that the capital stock and technology evolve according to the following laws of motion:

$$k_{t+1} = i_t + (1 - \delta)k_t \tag{9}$$

$$z_t = \rho z_{t-1} + \varepsilon_t, \varepsilon_t \sim N(0, \sigma_\varepsilon^2) \tag{10}$$

Eq. (9) describes how capital evolves over time when the economy invests i_t and capital depreciates by a fraction $\delta \in [0, 1]$. Eq. (10) describes the technology or productivity process of the economy. In each period t, technology depends on two components: the persistence of past shocks, measured by ρ, and a normally distributed technology shock, ε_t. Note that we assume $\rho \in (-1, 1)$, which implies a stationary technology process.

Feasibility. The feasibility condition of this economy is simply:

$$y_t = c_t + i_t \tag{11}$$

Representative Household's Problem

The representative household solves the following maximization problem:

$$\max_{\{c_t, n_t, k_{t+1}\}_{t=0}^{+\infty}} E_t \sum_{t=0}^{\infty} \beta^t \frac{\left[c_t^\theta (1 - n_t)_t^{1-\theta}\right]^{1-\tau}}{1 - \tau}$$

subject to

$$y_t = e^{z_t} k_t^\alpha n_t^{1-\alpha}$$
$$k_{t+1} = i_t + (1 - \delta)k_t$$
$$z_t = \rho z_{t-1} + \varepsilon_t$$
$$y_t = c_t + i_t$$

and k_0, z_0 are known, and where β is the household's subjective discount factor, which reflects the households' rate of time preference, that is, households' valuation of future consumption and leisure, relatively to today's consumption and leisure. It is assumed that households are "impatient," and therefore the utility derived from future consumption and leisure is valued less the later it is obtained, so $\beta \in (0, 1)$.

Optimality conditions. From the optimization problem, the representative household derives the following first order conditions:

$$\frac{[c_t^\theta (1 - n_t)^{1-\theta}]^{1-\tau}}{c_t} = \beta E_t \left[\frac{[c_{t+1}^\theta (1-n_{t+1})^{1-\theta}]^{1-\tau}}{c_{t+1}} \times \left(1 - \delta + \alpha \frac{y_{t+1}}{k_{t+1}}\right) \right] \tag{12}$$

$$\frac{1 - \theta}{\theta} \times \frac{c_t}{1 - n_t} = (1 - \alpha)\frac{y_t}{n_t} \tag{13}$$

The optimality conditions (12) and (13) represent the intertemporal and intratemporal choices of the representative consumer. The Euler equation,

(12), represents the trade-off between consuming today and postponing consumption into the future. This depends on the marginal rate of substitution between consumption today and tomorrow and on the marginal productivity of capital, since postponing consumption means investing more today and consuming more tomorrow. The intratemporal condition, (13), equates the marginal rate of substitution between consumption and leisure to the marginal productivity of labor. Note that the stochastic shock that drives this economy is incorporated into both the optimality conditions of the representative agent through the production function, y_t.

Competitive Equilibrium

The competitive equilibrium of the economy consists in a sequence of real allocations $\{c_t, n_t, i_t, k_{t+1}, y_t\}_{t=0}^{\infty}$ that maximize consumer's utility and firm's profit, and clear the markets. Hence, the competitive equilibrium of the economy is described by Eqs. (8)–(13).

ESTIMATION STRATEGY

We define the set of moment conditions that will be considered in the estimation procedure. We also describe the estimation steps followed, as well as the problems faced in the procedure. Finally we present the preliminary results.

The Moment Conditions

Consider the competitive equilibrium defined by Eqs. (8)–(13), and notice that our economy is parameterized by the vector $\omega = \{\beta, \theta, \tau, \delta, \alpha, \rho, \sigma_\varepsilon\}$. According to the framework described by Eqs. (1) and (2), it is required that we formulate our economy as a set of moment conditions, that is, we need to define our general estimating equations $g(x_i, \omega) = (g_1(x_i, \omega), \ldots, g_r(x_i, \omega))'$ such that $E\{g_j(x_i, \omega)\} = 0, \forall j = 1, \ldots, r \geqslant 7$. We require at least seven equations to solve the system for the seven unknowns, the parameters of our economy. However, our economy will not generate enough moments so we will not have sufficient general estimating equations to retrieve the estimates of our seven parameters (i.e., enough information to identify the parameters). We can write at least five initial (we call them "original") moment conditions picking equations Eqs. (9), (10), (12), and (13) from the competitive equilibrium described above. These "original" moment conditions are:

$$E\left[\beta\left(\frac{c_{t+1}^{\theta}(1-n_{t+1})^{1-\theta}}{c_t^{\theta}(1-n_t)^{1-\theta}}\right)^{1-\tau}\left(\frac{c_t}{c_{t+1}}\right)\left(1-\delta+\alpha\frac{y_{t+1}}{k_{t+1}}\right)-1\right]=0 \quad (14)$$

$$E\left[\frac{1-\theta}{\theta}\frac{c_t}{1-n_t}-(1-\alpha)\frac{y_t}{n_t}\right]=0 \quad (15)$$

$$E\left[\delta-1+\frac{k_{t+1}}{k_t}-\frac{i_t}{k_t}\right]=0 \quad (16)$$

$$E[z_t-\rho z_{t-1}]=0 \quad (17)$$

$$E[(z_t-\rho z_{t-1})^2-\sigma_{\varepsilon}^2]=0 \quad (18)$$

The moment condition given by Eq. (14) results from the only expectational equation that arises in our economy, the Euler equation, (12). Condition (15) is obtained by applying the expectation operator to the intratemporal condition, Eq. (13). In a similar way, condition (16) is obtained by applying the expectation operator to the law of motion of capital, Eq. (9). Moment conditions (17) and (18) are obtained from Eq. (10), by exploiting the assumption $\varepsilon_t \sim N(0,\sigma_{\varepsilon}^2)$. Then we can write:

$$E_t[\varepsilon_t]=0 \Leftrightarrow E(z_t-\rho z_{t-1})=0$$

and also

$$E[(\varepsilon_t^2-E(\varepsilon_t)^2)]=\sigma_{\varepsilon}^2 \Leftrightarrow$$
$$\Leftrightarrow E(\varepsilon_t^2)=\sigma_{\varepsilon}^2 \Leftrightarrow E(z_t-\rho z_{t-1})^2=\sigma_{\varepsilon}^2 \Leftrightarrow$$
$$\Leftrightarrow E[(z_t-\rho z_{t-1})^2-\sigma_{\varepsilon}^2]=0$$

Since the technology process is not observable in the real data we can use the production function to write moments (17) and (18) in terms of observables. From the production function, Eq. (8), we can write the technology level, z_t, as follows:

$$z_t=\ln y_t-\alpha\ln k_t-(1-\alpha)\ln n_t$$

and the moments (17) and (18) can be redefined as:

$$E\left[\begin{array}{l}(\ln y_t-\rho\ln y_{t-1})-\alpha(\ln k_t-\rho\ln k_{t-1})\\ \quad -(1-\alpha)(\ln n_t-\rho\ln n_{t-1})\end{array}\right]=0 \quad (19)$$

$$E\left[\left(\begin{array}{c}(\ln y_t - \rho \ln y_{t-1}) - \alpha(\ln k_t - \rho \ln k_{t-1}) \\ -(1-\alpha)(\ln n_t - \rho \ln n_{t-1})\end{array}\right)^2 - \sigma_\varepsilon^2\right] = 0 \qquad (20)$$

Hence, we can define a starting $g_{\text{original}}(x_i, \omega)$ vector as follows:

$$g_{\text{original}}(x_i, \omega) = \left(g_1(x_i, \omega), \ldots, g_5(x_i, \omega)\right)'$$

$$= \begin{bmatrix} \beta\left(\frac{c_{t+1}^\theta (1-n_{t+1})^{1-\theta}}{c_t^\theta (1-n_t)^{1-\theta}}\right)^{1-\tau}\left(\frac{c_t}{c_{t+1}}\right)\left(1 - \delta + \alpha\frac{y_{t+1}}{k_{t+1}}\right) - 1 \\[2ex] \frac{1-\theta}{\theta}\frac{c_t}{1-n_t} - (1-\alpha)\frac{y_t}{n_t} \\[2ex] \delta - 1 + \frac{k_{t+1}}{k_t} - \frac{i_t}{k_t} \\[2ex] \left[\begin{array}{c}(\ln y_t - \rho \ln y_{t-1}) - \alpha(\ln k_t - \rho \ln k_{t-1})+ \\ -(1-\alpha)(\ln n_t - \rho \ln n_{t-1})\end{array}\right] \\[3ex] \left[\left(\begin{array}{c}(\ln y_t - \rho \ln y_{t-1}) - \alpha(\ln k_t - \rho \ln k_{t-1})+ \\ -(1-\alpha)(\ln n_t - \rho \ln n_{t-1})\end{array}\right)^2 - \sigma_\varepsilon^2\right] \end{bmatrix}$$

where the random variable $x_i's$ is a multivariate random vector including the economic variables of our economy, as well as their lags and leads. Therefore, the function $g_{\text{original}}(x_i, \omega)$ gathers all the essential information of the economy: the optimal choices of the representative household, the endogenous evolution of the capital stock, the autoregressive technology process, and the statistics of the exogenous technology shock hitting the economy every period.

In this setting, we have to identify seven parameters. From condition (16) it is possible to identify δ. Moments (19) and (20) allow the identification of the persistence parameter, ρ, and of the standard deviation of the technology shock, σ_ε. From conditions (14) and (15) we need to identify four parameters: $\beta, \theta, \tau, \alpha$. This can be done by constructing at least two additional moment conditions from the original moments (14) and (15). Hence, in order to have a just identified system of moment conditions, we have to write down two more moment conditions from conditions (14)–(16), (19), and (20).

We are forced to build at least two more moment conditions, in order to have a just identified system of moments. These two "artificial" moments should be preferably theory driven and satisfying the statistical property of low correlation. According to the related literature on the definition of moment conditions (check, for instance, Canova (2007)), one can use instruments to define more moment conditions, that is, one can use lagged values of the variables of interest. Thus, let us define the following moments, based on lagged values of the series of consumption, hours, and of the neutral technology process (written from the production function):

$$g^1_{\text{artificial}}(x_i, \omega) = \big(g_6(x_i, \omega), g_7(x_i, \omega)\big)' =$$

$$= \begin{bmatrix} g_1(x_i, \omega) \cdot \left(\frac{c_{t-2}}{n_{t-2}}\right) \\ g_4(x_i, \omega) \cdot (\ln y_{t-2} - \alpha \ln k_{t-2} - (1 - \alpha) \ln n_{t-2}) \end{bmatrix}$$

However, when we compute the matrix of correlations of the set of moment conditions $(g_{\text{original}}(x_i, \omega), g^1_{\text{artificial}}(x_i, \omega))$ to control for the "low correlation" criterium we obtain the results as shown in Table 1.

We observe that the first and sixth moments are almost perfectly correlated. This is expected since the sixth moment is constructed by multiplying the Euler equation by the lagged ratio of consumption and hours. This may be a problem for our inference process, since the sixth moment may not deliver the information needed so that our system of moments is just identified. In this way we will also define another set of "artificial" moment conditions $E[g^2_{\text{artificial}}(x_i, \omega)] = 0$, in order to obtain an overidentified system.

Hence, our second approach to the definition of moment conditions was based solely on the "low correlation" criterium. We have considered different nonlinear combinations between the moments and computed their

Table 1. Moments Correlation Matrix.

	g_1	g_2	g_3	g_4	g_5	g_6	g_7
g_1	1.000						
g_2	−0.001	1.000					
g_3	−0.006	−0.035	1.000				
g_4	0.032	−0.045	0.025	1.000			
g_5	−0.055	−0.110	−0.078	−0.033	1.000		
g_6	−0.999	−0.001	−0.005	−0.031	−0.056	1.000	
g_7	−0.031	0.102	−0.419	−0.176	−0.053	−0.029	1.000

correlation matrix (including also the correlation with the original moments). Then, we suggest the following "artificial" functions:

$$g^2_{\text{artificial}}(x_i, \omega) = (g_6(x_i, \omega), \ldots, g_{10}(x_i, \omega))'$$

$$= \begin{bmatrix} (g_1(x_i, \omega))^2 \cdot g_2(x_i, \omega) \\ (g_2(x_i, \omega))^2 \cdot g_1(x_i, \omega) \\ (g_1(x_i, \omega))^2 \cdot g_3(x_i, \omega) \\ (g_3(x_i, \omega))^2 \cdot g_1(x_i, \omega) \\ g_4(x_i, \omega) \cdot (\ln y_{t-1} - \alpha \ln k_{t-1} - (1 - \alpha)\ln n_{t-1}) \end{bmatrix}$$

to which corresponds the correlation matrix as shown in Table 2.

We still find some relatively high correlation values between the "artificial" and the "original" moments, and between the "artificial" moments themselves. The "original" moments are not very much correlated. We note that function $g_{10}(x_i, \omega)$ actually derives from the assumption of no autocorrelation in the technology shock of the economy, that is, $E(\varepsilon_t \varepsilon_{t-1}) = 0, \forall t$. However, we acknowledge that it will also be necessary to explain the economic reasoning behind all the other functions, and also that we might have moments that are not equal to zero. In this last case, we have a misspecified model, and it is advised to use the exponential tilting empirical likelihood estimator instead of the empirical likelihood one.

The general estimating equations that will be considered in our estimation problem are given by:

$$g^1(x_i, \omega) = \left(g'_{\text{original}}, g^{1'}_{\text{artificial}}\right)' \tag{21}$$

Table 2. Moments Correlation Matrix.

	g_1	g_2	g_3	g_4	g_5	g_6	g_7	g_8	g_9
g_1	1.000								
g_2	−0.001	1.000							
g_3	−0.006	−0.035	1.000						
g_4	0.032	−0.045	0.025	1.000					
g_5	−0.055	−0.110	−0.078	− 0.033	1.000				
g_6	−0.006	0.618	−0.007	−0.001	0.032	1.000			
g_7	0.400	−0.041	−0.004	0.017	−0.070	−0.162	1.000		
g_8	−0.067	−0.055	0.534	0.072	−0.115	−0.142	−0.043	1.000	
g_9	0.390	−0.009	0.082	0.028	−0.051	−0.003	0.167	0.097	1.000
g_{10}	−0.031	0.102	−0.419	− 0.176	−0.053	0.022	0.003	−0.283	−0.162

$$g^2(x_i, \omega) = \left(g'_{\text{original}}, g^{2\prime}_{\text{artificial}}\right)' \tag{22}$$

such that

$$E\{g^s(x_i, \omega)\} = 0 \Leftrightarrow E(g'_{\text{original}}, g^{s\prime}_{\text{artificial}})' = 0, \quad s = 1, 2 \tag{23}$$

Given the two sets of moment conditions defined by Eq. (23), we can proceed to the estimation process itself.

Estimation Procedure

Data generating process. We choose to perform our estimation experiment with quarterly "artificial data," generated from our economy. The final objective of this exercise is to obtain estimates on the parameters of our model and compare them with their "true" values. In this way, we can control the accuracy of the estimates obtained. In order to compute the policy functions and simulate the data, we assign values to the set $\{\beta, \theta, \tau, \delta, \alpha, \rho, \sigma\}$, which we will assume as "true" values. Since we wish to assume reasonable "true" values, we follow the suggestions of Aruoba et al. (2003), since they consider a similar economy. The parameter values proposed by Aruoba et al. (2003) are summarized in Table 3 (more details about these values can be found in Section A.3).

Table 3. "True" Parameter Values.

Parameter	β	θ	τ	δ	α	ρ	σ_ϵ
Value	0.9896	0.375	2	0.0196	0.4	0.95	0.007

Hence, given the above values, we obtain the decision rules of our economy by loglinearizing the competitive equilibrium conditions, Eqs. (8)–(13), and then applying the Blanchard and Kahn linear algorithm (see Sections A.1 and A.2 for details about these two steps).

The approximated policy functions computed are of the form:

$$\begin{bmatrix} \hat{k}_{t+1} \\ z_t \end{bmatrix} = S(\omega) \begin{bmatrix} \hat{k}_t \\ z_{t-1} \end{bmatrix} + \begin{bmatrix} 0 \\ 1 \end{bmatrix} \varepsilon_t \tag{24}$$

$$
\begin{bmatrix} \hat{y}_t \\ \hat{i}_t \\ \hat{n}_t \\ \hat{c}_t \end{bmatrix} = C(\omega) \begin{bmatrix} \hat{k}_t \\ \hat{z}_t \end{bmatrix}
\tag{25}
$$

where $S(\omega)$ and $C(\omega)$ are the solution matrices resulting from the Blanchard and Khan algorithm, whose elements depend on the parameters of our economy. Notice that at this point the variables are still measured in terms of log deviations from the steady state, as a result of the loglinearization procedure (we will take their exponential in order to evaluate $g(x_i, \omega)$, where they are considered in levels).

Notice that the decision rules (24) and (25) are linear on the states of our economy and that all the stochasticity is induced by just one source, the technology shock, ε_t. Since the number of sources of uncertainty is less than the number of endogenous variables (output, investment, hours, and consumption), the variables $y_t, n_t, i_t,$ and c_t are, in fact, linear combinations of the states, k_t and z_t. This is not enough to avoid deterministic relations between the endogenous variables of our economy, that is, "there are linear combinations of these variables that are predicted without noise," as Ruge-Murcia (2003) explains. Therefore, we face a singularity problem, which is usually tackled in the literature by introducing measurement errors in the policy functions. In this way, we define the following measurement errors $v_1 \sim N(0, \sigma_1^2), v_2 \sim N(0, \sigma_2^2), v_3 \sim N(0, \sigma_3^2)$ and introduce them linearly in the policy functions of output, investment, and hours worked:

$$
\begin{bmatrix} \hat{y}_t \\ \hat{i}_t \\ \hat{n}_t \\ \hat{c}_t \end{bmatrix} = C(\omega) \begin{bmatrix} \hat{k}_t \\ \hat{z}_t \end{bmatrix} + \begin{bmatrix} v_{1,t} \\ v_{2,t} \\ v_{3,t} \\ 0 \end{bmatrix}
\tag{26}
$$

Note that we do not introduce a measurement error in the policy function of the consumption since the feasibility condition of the economy has to be satisfied. Now, we have to assign values to the standard deviations of the measurement errors. Again, we wish to assign reasonable values to the measurement errors standard deviations. Here we follow the suggestions of Fernandez-Villaverde and Rubio-Ramirez (2005) summarized in Table 4 (the standard deviations are a proportion of the steady state values of output, investment, and hours worked, based on the relative importance of

Table 4. Measurement Errors Standard Deviations.

Parameter	σ_1	σ_2	σ_3
Value	$y \times 0.0001$	$i \times 0.002$	$n \times 0.0035$

these measurement errors in the National Income and Product Accounts (NIPA) of the United States):

The introduction of measurement errors will not imply any further assumption or restriction on our model. However, we acknowledge that it lacks a theoretical explanation and may capture instead misspecification errors.

The simulated series for our economic variables, $y_t, n_t, c_t, k_t,$ and i_t will be generated by Eqs. (24) and (26), for 500 periods.

Optimization. At this stage we should put together the two essential elements of this estimation procedure: the "artificial" data we generated and the moment conditions we defined. Therefore, we should evaluate function $g(x_i, \omega)$, given by Eq. (21), with the simulated series of our economic variables for starting values of the parameters in ω. Then the optimization algorithm associated with the empirical likelihood problem stated in Eq. (4) would deliver the estimates of the parameters of our economy. Note that this algorithm requires that we set starting values for our parameters. The inference would proceed then with the repetition of the optimization algorithm in a Monte Carlo way, and with the computation of means and relevant statistics of the estimates.

Findings

We show some very preliminary results associated with the estimator proposed.

We start by naively estimating our model, that is, we abstract from the fact that we had to add measurement errors to our policy functions, in order to tackle the singularity problem. Moreover, we are aware that maybe our two sets of moment conditions may not be exactly satisfied. This may be due to the fact that we are generating our data from approximated policy functions, but it may also be that the moment conditions, in particular, the "artificial" ones are not well specified. To minimize the misspecification problem, we will estimate our model using the exponential tilting empirical likelihood setup, proposed by Schennach (2007) that was described above.

As we have mentioned the objective function of this estimator is the entropy function. We will then compare the results of the exponential tilting empirical likelihood estimation with the ones obtained with the simple general method of moments estimator (see Section A.5, for a brief description of the general method of moments setting). We believe that estimating our problem through the standard method of moments can give us some insights on what we can expect from the empirical likelihood case. We assign starting values to ω which are close to their "true" values. Then, we replicate the inference procedure 100 times.[2] The results from the general method of moments (GMM) obtained are summarized in Tables A.6.1 and A.6.2. The exponential tilting empirical likelihood (ETEL) estimates are summarized in Tables A.6.3 and A.6.4 showed in Section A.6.

Comparing the "true" values of the parameters and their estimated means, we conclude that, for both methods, we obtain relatively precise estimates of β, δ, α, and σ_{ε}. However, we were not able to identify the parameters θ and τ. We observe that the optimization process didn't move far from the starting values of the parameters, even if these where set very close to the "true" values. We believe that this result is probably linked to the "quality" of the moments that allow us to identify θ and τ. Recall that we had to build additional moments because it was not possible to identify these two parameters from the original moment conditions. Also, note that the relatively high correlation between the "artificial" moments and the "original" ones may indicate that the explanatory power of the "artificial" moments is low. This is a worrying result since the estimation of curvature parameters, θ and τ, is extremely important in the context of the estimation of DSGE models. These two parameters characterize the utility function of the representative household and are responsible for most of the nonlinear features of our economy.

Comparing now the ETEL estimates with the GMM ones, we observe that one obtains more precise estimates with the general method of moments: the bias is, in general, smaller for all the parameters, and the same happens for standard deviations.[3] However, we know that the ETEL estimates take into account possible missepecification problems of our model, which is an advantage over the general method of moments.

CONCLUDING REMARKS: LIMITATIONS

This chapter is a preliminary attempt to present empirical likelihood as a valid inference method to estimate DSGE models. We have concluded that, compared with the general method of moments, empirical likelihood (or, more precisely, the exponential tilting empirical likelihood) estimates are not so close to the "true" values of the parameters and have higher standard deviations. However, both estimations share the difficulty in identifying the curvature parameters, that is, the coefficient of relative risk aversion and the relative weight of leisure in the utility function.

We stress the fact that the empirical likelihood setup, and in particular the exponential tilting empirical likelihood, presents some important advantages, so it is worth to invest in further research on the topic. As we have pointed out the empirical likelihood framework does not require that we compute the policy functions of the economy. Instead, we can work directly with the equilibrium conditions that describe our model. Moreover, we do not need to assume that the stochastic processes of our economy are normally distributed. Finally, we should note that the empirical likelihood estimation setup preserves the nonlinear structure of the equilibrium conditions of the economy.

For further research, we have to address the question of the definition and selection of the moment conditions. This is a common difficulty shared with the general moments estimator: the definition of "artificial" moments is, to a great extent, an arbitrary task. The difficulty of selecting "good" moments is reflected on the results obtained from the estimation with either the general method of moments and the exponential tilting empirical likelihood estimator. In particular, we experience difficulties when it comes to identifying the relative weight of consumption and leisure in the household's bundle and of the coefficient of risk aversion in empirical likelihood framework. Hence, we conclude that more work is needed in order to select "good artificial moments." In fact, we have presented a naive estimation of our example economy, since our analysis lacks still a complete time series analysis of the set of moment conditions (for instance, we haven't made any remark about the existence of unit roots or cointegrated relations of our series). So far we have studied the moments in terms of their correlation, in order to define the additional moments required for identifying all the parameters of our economy. Another problem that might be related with the difficulty of obtaining the plain empirical likelihood estimates of the parameters of interest is the data generated from a loglinearized economy, that is, from approximated policy functions (and we share this problem with the maximum likelihood estimation). The fact that the generated series are not quite the ones that solve the original nonlinear equilibrium system might also create difficulties to the empirical likelihood estimators. Moreover, it may be the case that the artificial moment conditions are not well specified. In order to tackle these problems, we follow Schennach (2007) and use as an objective function of the empirical likelihood setup the entropy function, that is, we use the exponential tilting empirical likelihood estimator. This allowed us to obtain the preliminary estimates we have presented above.

To summarize, the main limitations of this analysis are (i) the issue of the definition of "artificial" moment condition for identification purposes; (ii) the data generation process based upon approximated policy functions.

Finally, together with the two issues that should be addressed in further research, it would be interesting to find estimates using real economic data.

NOTES

1. Authors' emphasis in their original text.
2. We are aware that 100 replications are too few in the Monte Carlo simulation context, however, we just wanted to have some preliminary estimates.
3. Since the GMM alternative seemed to be better than the ETEL one, we also show in Section A.6 a the estimates resulting from 1,000 replications for GMM, considering an overidentified model in Table A.6.5.

REFERENCES

Ackerberg, A., Geweke, J., & Hahn, J. (2009). Comments on "convergence properties of the likelihood of computed dynamic models". *Econometrica, 77*(6), 2009–2017.

Aruoba, S., Fernandez-Villaverde, J., & Rubio-Ramirez, J. (2003). Comparing solution methods for dynamic equilibrium economies. Federal Reserve of Atlanta Working Paper No. 2003-27. Federal Reserve of Atlanta, Atlanta, United States.

Blanchard, O., & Kahn, C. (1980). The solution of linear difference models under rational expectations. *Econometrica, 48*(5), 1305–1312.

Canova, F. (2007). *Methods for applied macroeconomic research*. Princeton, NJ: Princeton University.

Fernandez-Villaverde, J., & Rubio-Ramirez, J. (2004). *Estimating nonlinear dynamic equilibrium economies: A likelihood approach*. Mimeo, University of Pennsylvania.

Fernandez-Villaverde, J., & Rubio-Ramirez, J. (2005). Estimating dynamic equilibrium economies: Linear versus nonlinear likelihood. *Journal of Applied Econometrics, 20*, 891–910.

Fernandez-Villaverde, J., & Rubio-Ramirez, J. (2006). The research agenda: Jesus Fernandez-Villaverde and Juan F Rubio-Ramirez on estimating DSGE models. *Economic Dynamics Newsletter, 8*, 6.

Fernandez-Villaverde, J., & Rubio-Ramrez, J. (2007). On the solution of the growth model with investment-specific technological change. *Applied Economic Letters, 14*, 549–553.

Fernandez-Villaverde, J., Rubio-Ramirez, J., & Santos, M. (2006). Convergence properties of the likelihood of computed dynamic models. *Econometrica, 74*(1), 93–119.

Geweke, J. (1993). Bayesian treatment of the independent student-t linear model. *Journal of Applied Econometrics, 8*, S19–S40.

Justiniano, A., & Primiceri, G. (2005). *The time varying volatility of macroeconomics fluctuations.* Mimeo, Northwestern.

Kim, C., & Nelson, C. (1999). Has the US economy become more stable? Bayesian approach based on a Markov-switching model of business cycle. *Review of Economics and Statistics, 81*, 608–616.

Kitamura, Y. (1997). Empirical likelihood methods with weakly dependent processes. *Annals of Statistics, 25*(5), 2084–2105.

McConnel, M., & Perez-Quiros, G. (2000). Output fluctuations in the United States: What has changed since the early 1980s? *American Economic Review, 90*, 1464–1476.

Owen, A. (1988). Empirical likelihood ratio confidence intervals for a single functional. *Biometrika, 75*(2), 237–249.

Qin, J., & Lawless, J. (1994). Empirical likelihood and general estimating equations. *The Annals of Statistics, 22*(1), 300–325.

Ruge-Murcia, F. (2003). *Methods to estimate dynamic stochastic general equilibrium models.* Cahier de recherche No. 17-2003, CIREQ, Canada.

Sargent, T. (1989). Two models of measurement and the investment accelerator. *The Journal of Political Economy, 97*(2), 251–287.

Schennach, S. (2005). Bayesian exponentially tilted empirical likelihood. *Biometrika, 92*(1), 31–46.

Schennach, S. (2007). Point estimation with exponential tilted empirical likelihood. *The Annals of Statistics, 35*(2), 654–672.

Stock, J., & Watson, M. (2002). *Has the business cycle changed, and why?* NBER Working Paper No. 9127.

APPENDIX A

A.1   Loglinearized Competitive Equilibrium and Steady State Values

In this section we present the loglinearized competitive equilibrium of the economy, obtained from Eqs. (8) to (13), and the nonstochastic steady state values of our variables ($\varepsilon_t = 0$).

The loglinearization process consists of taking the logs of each equation, and then writing a first order Taylor approximation around the steady state of each variable for each equation of the competitive equilibrium.

$$\frac{1}{\beta}\eta E_t\hat{c}_{t+1} + \frac{1}{\beta}\phi E_t\hat{n}_{t+1} = \frac{1}{\beta}\eta\hat{c}_t + \frac{1}{\beta}\phi\hat{n}_t + \gamma E_t\hat{y}_{t+1} - \gamma\hat{k}_{t+1} \qquad \text{(A.1.1)}$$

$$\hat{y}_t = \hat{c}_t + \varphi\hat{n}_t \qquad \text{(A.1.2)}$$

$$\hat{y}_t = \alpha\hat{k}_t + (1 - \alpha)\hat{n}_t + z_t \qquad \text{(A.1.3)}$$

$$\hat{k}_{t+1} = (1 - \delta)\hat{k}_t + \delta\hat{\imath}_t \qquad \text{(A.1.4)}$$

$$z_t = \rho z_{t-1} + \varepsilon_t \qquad \text{(A.1.5)}$$

$$\gamma\hat{y}_t = (\gamma - \alpha\delta)\hat{c}_t + \alpha\delta\hat{\imath}_t \qquad \text{(A.1.6)}$$

where $\gamma = (1/\beta) - 1 + \delta$, $\eta = 1 - (1 - \tau)\theta$, $\phi = (\theta\gamma(1 - \tau)(1 - \alpha))/\gamma - \alpha\delta$ and $\varphi = 1 + (\phi/(1 - \theta)(1 - \tau))$. The circumflex represents percentage deviations from the steady state value of each variable. Eqs. (A.1.1), (A.1.2), (A.1.3), (A.1.4), and (A.1.6) are the loglinearized version of Eqs. (12), (13), (8), (9) and (11), respectively. Note that Eq. (A.1.5) is exactly the same as Eq. (10). In the loglinerization process we also made use of the steady state values of the model variables: $z = 0$, $k = \frac{\alpha}{\gamma}y$, $i = \frac{\alpha\delta}{\gamma}y$, $c = (1 - \frac{\alpha\delta}{\gamma})y$, $n = [\frac{1-\theta}{\theta(1-\alpha)}(1 - \frac{\alpha\delta}{\gamma}) + 1]^{-1}$, $y = (\frac{\alpha}{\gamma})^{\frac{\alpha}{1-\alpha}}[\frac{1-\theta}{\theta(1-\alpha)}(1 - \frac{\alpha\delta}{\gamma}) + 1]^{-1}$.

A.2   Application of Blanchard and Kahn Algorithm

Given the loglinearized competitive equilibrium defined by Eqs. (A.1.1)–(A.1.6), we can find the policy functions of this economy by applying a linear algorithm, like the Blanchard and Kahn one (actually, if we had used any other linear algorithm, the solution would be the same). In order to apply the Blanchard and Kahn method let us define the following vectors: $u_t^0 = [\hat{k}_t\ \hat{c}_t]'$ and $v_t^0 = [\hat{y}_t\ \hat{\imath}_t\ \hat{n}_t]'$. The vector u_t^0 contains the model's dynamic predetermined and nonpredetermined endogenous variables and the vector v_t^0 contains the model's static nonpredetermined variables.

We can write Eqs. (A.1.1)–(A.1.6) into the following matrix form:

$$DE_t u_{t+1}^0 + FE_t v_{t+1}^0 = Gu_t^0 + Hv_t^0 \tag{A.2.1}$$

$$Iv_t^0 = Ju_t^0 + Kz_t \tag{A.2.2}$$

$$z_{t+1} = \rho z_t + \varepsilon_{t+1} \tag{A.2.3}$$

where

$$D = \begin{bmatrix} 1 & 0 \\ 0 & \frac{\eta}{\beta} \end{bmatrix}; F = \begin{bmatrix} 0 & 0 & 0 \\ -\gamma & 0 & \frac{\phi}{\beta} \end{bmatrix}; \quad G = \begin{bmatrix} 1-\delta & 0 \\ 0 & \frac{\eta}{\beta} \end{bmatrix}; \quad H = \begin{bmatrix} 0 & \delta & 0 \\ 0 & 0 & \frac{\phi}{\beta} \end{bmatrix}$$

and

$$I = \begin{bmatrix} 1 & 0 & \alpha-1 \\ \gamma & -\delta\alpha & 0 \\ 1 & 0 & -\varphi \end{bmatrix}; \quad J = \begin{bmatrix} \alpha & 0 \\ 0 & \gamma-\delta\alpha \\ 0 & 1 \end{bmatrix}; \quad K = \begin{bmatrix} 1 \\ 0 \\ 0 \end{bmatrix}$$

We focus on the autoregressive process for the technology shock. Eq. (A.1.5) can be solved "forward," in the following way. Take expectations on both sides of Eq. (A.1.5) to have:

$$z_t = \frac{1}{\rho} E_t z_{t+1} - \frac{1}{\rho} E_t \varepsilon_{t+1} \tag{A.2.4}$$

Then we iterate Eq. (A.2.4) one period into the future:

$$z_{t+1} = \frac{1}{\rho} E_{t+1} z_{t+2} - \frac{1}{\rho} E_{t+1} \varepsilon_{t+2} \tag{A.2.5}$$

We substitute Eq. (A.2.5) into Eq. (A.2.4). We also use the law of iterated expectations, and the fact that $\varepsilon_t \sim N(0, \sigma^2)$ to write z_t as follows:

$$z_t = \frac{1}{\rho^2} E_t z_{t+2} \tag{A.2.6}$$

If we keep iterating and repeatedly substituting on Eq. (A.2.6) we end up with:

$$E_t z_{t+j} = \rho^j z_t \tag{A.2.7}$$

Then we can substitute the autoregressive process of the technology shock in Eq. (A.2.3) by Eq. (A.2.7).

Assuming that $\exists I^{-1}$, we obtain from Eq. (A.2.2)

$$v_t^0 = I^{-1}Ju_t^0 + I^{-1}Kz_t$$

and recalling that $E_t z_{t+j} = \rho^j z_t$, we can write Eq. (A.2.1) as follows:

$$DE_t u_{t+1}^0 + FE_t(I^{-1}Ju_{t+1}^0 + I^{-1}Kz_{t+1}) = Gu_t^0 + H(I^{-1}Ju_t^0 + I^{-1}K\hat{z}_t)$$

$$(D + FI^{-1}J)E_t u_{t+1}^0 = (G + HI^{-1}J)u_t^0 + (HI^{-1}K - FI^{-1}K\rho)z_t$$

Assuming that $\exists(D + FI^{-1}J)^{-1}$ and defining:

$$A = (D + FI^{-1}J)^{-1}(G + HI^{-1}J)$$

$$B = (D + FI^{-1}J)^{-1}(HI^{-1}K - FI^{-1}K\rho)$$

we obtain the required Blanchard and Kahn setup:

$$E_t u_{t+1}^0 = Au_t^0 + B\hat{z}_t \Leftrightarrow$$

$$\Leftrightarrow \begin{bmatrix} \hat{k}_{t+1} \\ E_t\hat{c}_{t+1} \end{bmatrix} = A\begin{bmatrix} \hat{k}_t \\ \hat{c}_t \end{bmatrix} + Bz_t \qquad (A.2.8)$$

The solution of Eq. (A.2.8) is derived through the Jordan canonical form of matrix $A = M^{-1}\Lambda M$, where Λ is a diagonal matrix whose nonzero elements are the eigenvalues of A, λ_1, and λ_2, ordered by increasing absolute value, and M^{-1} is a (2×2) matrix whose colunms contain the associated eigenvectors of A. That is:

$$\Lambda = \begin{bmatrix} \lambda_1 & 0 \\ 0 & \lambda_2 \end{bmatrix}; \quad M = \begin{bmatrix} m_{11} & m_{12} \\ m_{21} & m_{22} \end{bmatrix}$$

Also, we let

$$B = \begin{bmatrix} b_1 \\ b_2 \end{bmatrix}$$

Hence, we can rewrite the Blanchard and Kahn system of difference equations as:

$$\begin{bmatrix} \hat{k}_{t+1} \\ E_t\hat{c}_{t+1} \end{bmatrix} = M^{-1}\Lambda M \begin{bmatrix} \hat{k}_t \\ \hat{c}_t \end{bmatrix} + Bz_t$$

$$M \begin{bmatrix} \hat{k}_{t+1} \\ E_t\hat{c}_{t+1} \end{bmatrix} = \Lambda M \begin{bmatrix} \hat{k}_t \\ \hat{c}_t \end{bmatrix} + MBz_t$$

$$\begin{bmatrix} m_{11} & m_{12} \\ m_{21} & m_{22} \end{bmatrix} \begin{bmatrix} \hat{k}_{t+1} \\ E_t\hat{c}_{t+1} \end{bmatrix} = \begin{bmatrix} \lambda_1 & 0 \\ 0 & \lambda_2 \end{bmatrix} \begin{bmatrix} m_{11} & m_{12} \\ m_{21} & m_{22} \end{bmatrix} \begin{bmatrix} \hat{k}_t \\ \hat{c}_t \end{bmatrix}$$

$$+ \begin{bmatrix} m_{11} & m_{12} \\ m_{21} & m_{22} \end{bmatrix} \begin{bmatrix} b_1 \\ b_2 \end{bmatrix} z_t$$

$$\Leftrightarrow \begin{cases} E_t u^1_{1t+1} = \lambda_1 u^1_{1t} + q_1 z_t \\ E_t u^1_{2t+1} = \lambda_2 u^1_{2t} + q_2 z_t \end{cases} \tag{A.2.9}$$

with

$$u^1_{1t} = m_{11}\hat{k}_t + m_{12}\hat{c}_t$$
$$q_1 = m_{11}b_1 + m_{12}b_2$$
$$u^1_{2t} = m_{21}\hat{k}_t + m_{22}\hat{c}_t$$
$$q_2 = m_{21}b_1 + m_{22}b_2$$

Assuming that λ_2 lies outside the unit circle, $E_t u^1_{2t+1} = \lambda_2 u^1_{2t} + q_2 \hat{z}_t$ can be solved "forward." Solving the equation for u^1_{2t} yields:

$$u^1_{2t} = \frac{1}{\lambda_2} E_t u^1_{2t+1} - \frac{q_2}{\lambda_2} z_t \tag{A.2.10}$$

Iterating on Eq. (A.2.10) one period forward gives:

$$u^1_{2t+1} = \frac{1}{\lambda_2} E_{t+1} u^1_{2t+2} - \frac{q_2}{\lambda_2} z_{t+1} \tag{A.2.11}$$

We then substitute Eq. (A.2.11) into Eq. (A.2.10) and obtain:

$$u^1_{2t} = \frac{1}{\lambda_2^2} E_t u^1_{2t+2} - \frac{q_2}{\lambda_2} \left(\frac{1}{\lambda_2} E_t z_{t+1} + z_t \right)$$

Successive forward substitution yields the following general expression:

$$u_{2t}^1 = -\frac{q_2}{\lambda_2} \sum_{j=0}^{\infty} \left(\frac{1}{\lambda_2}\right)^j E_t z_{t+j} \Leftrightarrow$$

$$\Leftrightarrow u_{2t}^1 = \frac{q_2}{\rho - \lambda_2} z_t \qquad (A.2.12)$$

At this point we are very close to the final solution, since:

$$u_{2t}^1 = m_{21}\hat{k}_t + m_{22}\hat{c}_t \Leftrightarrow$$

$$\Leftrightarrow \hat{c}_t = -\frac{m_{21}}{m_{22}}\hat{k}_t + \frac{1}{m_{22}}\frac{q_2}{\rho - \lambda_2} z_t$$

or

$$\hat{c}_t = \varphi_{ck}\hat{k}_t + \varphi_{cz}z_t \qquad (A.2.13)$$

where $\varphi_{ck} = -\frac{m_{21}}{m_{22}}$ and $\varphi_{cz} = \frac{1}{m_{22}}\frac{q_2}{\rho - \lambda_2}$.

Notice that φ_{ck} and φ_{cz} are nonlinear combinations of the eigenvectors and eigenvalues of A and also of the model parameters.

It is easy to obtain the solution for $\hat{k}_{t+1}$ given that:

$$u_{1t}^1 = m_{11}\hat{k}_t + m_{12}\hat{c}_t \Leftrightarrow$$

$$\Leftrightarrow u_{1t}^1 = m_{11}\hat{k}_t + m_{12}\left(\varphi_{ck}\hat{k}_t + \varphi_{cz}\hat{z}_t\right) \qquad (A.2.14)$$

Thus:

$$E_t u_{1t+1}^1 = \lambda_1 u_{1t}^1 + q_1 \hat{z}_t$$

$$E_t\left[m_{11}\hat{k}_{t+1} + m_{12}\left(\varphi_{ck}\hat{k}_{t+1} + \varphi_{cz}\hat{z}_{t+1}\right)\right] = \lambda_1\left[m_{11}\hat{k}_t + m_{12}\left(\varphi_{ck}\hat{k}_t + \varphi_{cz}\hat{z}_t\right)\right] + q_1\hat{z}_t$$

$$\hat{k}_{t+1} = \lambda_1\hat{k}_t + \left(m_{11} + m_{12}\varphi_{ck}\right)^{-1} \times$$

$$\times \left(q_1 + \lambda_1 m_{12}\varphi_{ck} - m_{12}\varphi_{cz}\rho\right)\hat{z}_t$$

or

$$\hat{k}_{t+1} = \varphi_{kk}\hat{k}_t + \varphi_{kz}\hat{z}_t \qquad (A.2.15)$$

where $\varphi_{kk} = \lambda_1$ and $\varphi_{kz} = (m_{11} + m_{12}\varphi_{ck})^{-1}(q_1 + \lambda_1 m_{12}\varphi_{cz} - m_{12}\varphi_{cz}\rho)$.

Therefore, the linear decision rules derived for this economy are given by Eqs. (A.2.13) and (A.2.15).

Furthermore, it is also possible to write a system where the endogenous variables $\hat{y}_t$, $\hat{\imath}_t$, and $\hat{n}_t$ are predicted by the predetermined level of capital and the technology shock. That is, we can also obtain the decision rules for $\{\hat{y}_t, \hat{i}_t, \hat{n}_t\}$. Recall that the vector of endogenous static nonpredetermined variables could be written as:

$$v_t^0 = I^{-1}Ju_t^0 + I^{-1}K\hat{z}_t$$

$$= I^{-1}J\begin{bmatrix} \hat{k}_t \\ \hat{c}_t \end{bmatrix} + I^{-1}K\hat{z}_t$$

$$= I^{-1}J\begin{bmatrix} \hat{k}_t \\ \varphi_{ck}\hat{k}_t + \varphi_{cz}\hat{z}_t \end{bmatrix} + I^{-1}K\hat{z}_t$$

$$= I^{-1}J\begin{bmatrix} 1 \\ \varphi_{ck} \end{bmatrix}\hat{k}_t + \left(I^{-1}K + I^{-1}J\begin{bmatrix} 0 \\ \varphi_{cz} \end{bmatrix} \right)\hat{z}_t$$

or

$$v_t^0 = \Phi_1\hat{k}_t + \Phi_2\hat{z}_t \tag{A.2.16}$$

with

$$\Phi_1 = I^{-1}J\begin{bmatrix} 1 \\ \varphi_{ck} \end{bmatrix}; \quad \Phi_2 = \left(I^{-1}K + I^{-1}J\begin{bmatrix} 0 \\ \varphi_{cz} \end{bmatrix} \right)$$

Finally, we can write the decision rules of all the nonpredetermined variables as a function of the predetermined and the exogenous variables as

$$\begin{bmatrix} v_t^0 \\ \hat{c}_t \end{bmatrix} = \begin{bmatrix} \Phi_1 & \Phi_2 \\ \varphi_{ck} & \varphi_{cz} \end{bmatrix}\begin{bmatrix} \hat{k}_t \\ \hat{z}_t \end{bmatrix} \Leftrightarrow$$

$$\Leftrightarrow \begin{bmatrix} \hat{y}_t \\ \hat{i}_t \\ \hat{n}_t \\ \hat{c}_t \end{bmatrix} = \begin{bmatrix} \varphi_{yc} & \varphi_{yz} \\ \varphi_{ik} & \varphi_{iz} \\ \varphi_{nk} & \varphi_{nz} \\ \varphi_{ck} & \varphi_{cz} \end{bmatrix}\begin{bmatrix} \hat{k}_t \\ \hat{z}_t \end{bmatrix} \Leftrightarrow$$

$$\Leftrightarrow \begin{bmatrix} \hat{y}_t \\ \hat{i}_t \\ \hat{n}_t \\ \hat{c}_t \end{bmatrix} = C\begin{bmatrix} \hat{k}_t \\ \hat{z}_t \end{bmatrix} \tag{A.2.17}$$

and for the endogenous states:

$$\begin{bmatrix} \hat{k}_{t+1} \\ z_t \end{bmatrix} = \begin{bmatrix} \varphi_{kk} & \varphi_{kz} \\ 0 & \rho \end{bmatrix} \begin{bmatrix} \hat{k}_{t+1} \\ z_{t-1} \end{bmatrix} + \begin{bmatrix} 0 \\ 1 \end{bmatrix} \varepsilon_t$$

$$\Leftrightarrow \begin{bmatrix} \hat{k}_{t+1} \\ z_t \end{bmatrix} = S \begin{bmatrix} \hat{k}_{t+1} \\ z_{t-1} \end{bmatrix} + \begin{bmatrix} 0 \\ 1 \end{bmatrix} \varepsilon_t \qquad (A.2.18)$$

where

$$C = \begin{bmatrix} \varphi_{yc} & \varphi_{yz} \\ \varphi_{ik} & \varphi_{iz} \\ \varphi_{nk} & \varphi_{nz} \\ \varphi_{ck} & \varphi_{cz} \end{bmatrix}; \quad S = \begin{bmatrix} \varphi_{kk} & \varphi_{kz} \\ 0 & \rho \end{bmatrix}$$

Matrices C and S are solution matrices. From them we obtain the approximated policy functions of the economy and we generate simulated data for our variables. We then use the simulated data to estimate our model.

A.3 Some Notes on the Calibration Proposed by Aruoba et al. (2003)

The calibration chosen by Aruoba et al. (2003) is justified by the authors in the following way. The subjective discount rate of the representative household, β, matches an annual interest rate of 4%. The relative weight of consumption and leisure in the household bundle, θ, is set so that labor supply amounts to 31% of the available time in the steady state. The value of the coefficient of risk aversion, τ, is a common choice in the literature. The depreciation rate, δ, sets the investment/capital ratio. The elasticity of output to capital, α, matches the labor share of US national income. The values of the persistence parameter, ρ, and of the standard deviation of the technology shock, σ_ε, were chosen so that they match the properties of the Solow residual for the US economy.

A.4 Solutions of the Empirical Likelihood Problem

In this section we explain analytically how to solve the empirical likelihood problem stated in Eq. (4).

First we apply logs to the empirical likelihood function given by Eq. (3) and rewrite the optimization problem as follows:

$$\max_{p_i}\left\{\sum_{i=1}^{m}\log p_i \Big| \sum_{i=1}^{m}p_i = 1; \sum_{i=1}^{m}[p_i \cdot g(x_i,\omega)] = 0\right\} \qquad (A.4.1)$$

The Lagrangean function associated with the optimization problem in Eq. (A.4.1) can be written as follows:

$$\mathcal{L} = \sum_{i=1}^{m}\log p_i - \xi\left(\sum_{i=1}^{m}p_i - 1\right) - \mu'\left(\sum_{i=1}^{m}[p_i \cdot g(x_i,\omega)]\right) \qquad (A.4.2)$$

where ξ and $\mu = (\mu_1,\ldots,\mu_r)'$ are the lagrangean multipliers associated with the constraints of the problem.

The first order condition derived from Eq. (A.4.2) with respect to p_i is:

$$\frac{1}{p_i} - \xi - \mu'g(x_i,\omega) = 0 \quad \forall i \qquad (A.4.3)$$

Summing condition (A.4.3) over all i's we obtain that $\xi = m$. We plug it back on Eq. (A.4.3) and find the expression for the optimal weight:

$$p_i^* = \frac{1}{m}\frac{1}{1 + \tilde{\mu}'g(x_i,\omega)} \qquad (A.4.4)$$

where $\tilde{\mu} = -\frac{1}{m}\mu$.

The empirical likelihood evaluated at the optimal weight is then:

$$L_{EL}(\omega,p) = \prod_{i=1}^{m}\frac{1}{m}\frac{1}{1 + \tilde{\mu}'g(x_i,\omega)}$$

and its log counterpart:

$$\log L_{EL}(\omega,p) = \sum_{i=1}^{m}\log\left(\frac{1}{m}\frac{1}{1 + \tilde{\mu}'g(x_i,\omega)}\right)$$
$$= -\sum_{i=1}^{m}\log m - \sum_{i=1}^{m}(1 + \tilde{\mu}'g(x_i,\omega)) \qquad (A.4.5)$$

The next step consists on maximizing Eq. (A.4.5) with respect to ω and also to $\tilde{\mu}$. This is equivalent to:

$$\min_{\omega,\tilde{\mu}}\left\{\sum_{i=1}^{m}(1 + \tilde{\mu}'g(x_i,\omega))\right\} \qquad (A.5.6)$$

The first order conditions of the problem in Eq. (A.4.6) are:

$$\omega : \sum_{i=1}^{m} \frac{1}{1 + \tilde{\mu}'g(x_i, \omega)} \left(\frac{\partial g(x_i, \omega)}{\partial \omega} \right)' \tilde{\mu} = 0 \qquad (A.4.7)$$

$$\tilde{\mu}' : \sum_{i=1}^{m} \frac{1}{1 + \tilde{\mu}'g(x_i, \omega)} g(x_i, \omega) = 0 \qquad (A.4.8)$$

Eqs. (A.4.7) and (A.4.8) form a system of two equations of two unknowns, and by solving this system we can obtain the expressions for the optimal ω and $\tilde{\mu}$.

A.5 General Method of Moments Formulation of the Problem

We consider the same setup as the one assumed in the empirical likelihood context, that is, we consider the framework given by Eqs. (1) and (2). However, we solve now the following optimization problem:

$$\min_{\omega} \frac{1}{m} \left[\sum_{i=1}^{m} g(x_i, \omega) \right]' W \left[\sum_{i=1}^{m} g(x_i, \omega) \right] \qquad (A.5.1)$$

where W is a positive definite weighting matrix.

A.6 Estimation Results

Table A.6.1. GMM Estimates for the First Set of Moments $g^1(x_i, \omega)$
(500 Periods; 100 Monte Carlo Replications).

Parameter	True	Start	Mean	Bias	SD
β	0.9896	0.9600	0.9892	0.000418	1.882×10^{-3}
θ	0.3750	0.4000	0.40198	−0.044984	1.654×10^{-4}
τ	2.0000	2.2000	2.20005	−0.020005	8.792×10^{-6}
δ	0.0196	0.0200	0.0197	−0.00005	1.245×10^{-5}
α	0.4000	0.5000	0.4061	−0.00614	0.0250
ρ	0.9500	0.9000	0.9912	−0.04118	2.746×10^{-3}
σ_ϵ	0.0070	0.0100	−0.0016	0.00859	6.993×10^{-3}

Table A.6.2. GMM Estimates for the Second Set of Moments $g^2(x_i, \omega)$ (500 Periods; 100 Monte Carlo Replications).

Parameter	True	Start	Mean	Bias	SD
β	0.9896	0.9600	0.9890	0.00057	1.803×10^{-3}
θ	0.3750	0.4000	0.4024	−0.04536	1.507×10^{-3}
τ	2.0000	2.2000	2.20008	−0.20008	1.289×10^{-5}
δ	0.0196	0.0200	0.01965	−0.00005	1.243×10^{-5}
α	0.4000	0.5000	0.4082	−0.00082	0.02419
ρ	0.9500	0.9000	0.9914	−0.04143	3.094×10^{-3}
σ_ϵ	0.0070	0.0100	0.00643	0.00057	3.143×10^{-3}

Table A.6.3. ETEL Estimates for the First Set of Moments $g^1(x_i, \omega)$ (500 Periods; 100 Monte Carlo Replications).

Parameter	True	Start	Mean	Bias	SD
β	0.9896	0.9600	0.9761	0.0135	0.0120
θ	0.3750	0.4000	0.4104	−0.0534	0.0853
τ	2.0000	2.2000	2.1816	−0.1816	0.8513
δ	0.0196	0.0200	0.0196	0.00003	0.00054
α	0.4000	0.5000	0.4712	−0.0712	0.0352
ρ	0.9500	0.9000	0.8856	0.0644	0.2771
σ_ϵ	0.0070	0.0100	0.020	−0.0139	0.0463

Table A.6.4. ETEL Estimates for the Second Set of Moments $g^2(x_i, \omega)$ (500 Periods; 100 Monte Carlo Replications).

Parameter	True	Start	Mean	Bias	SD
β	0.9896	0.9600	0.9798	0.0098	0.0117
θ	0.3750	0.4000	0.4459	−0.0889	0.1084
τ	2.0000	2.2000	2.2001	−0.200	0.0003
δ	0.0196	0.0200	0.1956	0.00004	0.0003
α	0.4000	0.5000	0.4588	−0.0588	0.0458
ρ	0.9500	0.9000	0.9166	0.0334	0.0201
σ_ϵ	0.0070	0.0100	0.0245	−0.0175	0.0229

Table A.6.5.   GMM Estimates for the Second Set of Moments $g^2(x_i, \omega)$
(500 Periods; 1000 Monte Carlo Replications).

Parameter	True	Start	Mean	Bias	SD
β	0.9896	0.9600	0.98890	0.00070	1.077×10^{-3}
θ	0.3750	0.4000	0.40235	−0.04535	1.626×10^{-3}
τ	2.0000	2.2000	2.20008	−0.20008	1.093×10^{-5}
δ	0.0196	0.0200	0.01965	−0.00005	1.220×10^{-5}
α	0.4000	0.5000	0.40994	−0.00994	1.460×10^{-2}
ρ	0.9500	0.9000	0.99129	−0.04129	3.114×10^{-3}
σ_ϵ	0.0070	0.0100	0.00670	0.00030	2.527×10^{-3}

STRUCTURAL ESTIMATION OF THE NEW-KEYNESIAN MODEL: A FORMAL TEST OF BACKWARD- AND FORWARD-LOOKING BEHAVIOR

Tae-Seok Jang

ABSTRACT

This chapter analyzes the empirical relationship between the pricesetting/ consumption behavior and the sources of persistence in inflation and output. First, a small-scale New-Keynesian model (NKM) is examined using the method of moment and maximum likelihood estimators with US data from 1960 to 2007. Then a formal test is used to compare the fit of two competing specifications in the New-Keynesian Phillips Curve (NKPC) and the IS equation, that is, backward- and forward-looking behavior. Accordingly, the inclusion of a lagged term in the NKPC and the IS equation improves the fit of the model while offsetting the influence of inherited and extrinsic persistence; it is shown that intrinsic persistence plays a major role in approximating inflation and output dynamics for the Great Inflation *period. However, the null hypothesis cannot be rejected at the 5% level for the* Great Moderation *period, that is, the NKM with*

DSGE Models in Macroeconomics: Estimation, Evaluation, and New Developments
Advances in Econometrics, Volume 28, 421–467
Copyright © 2012 by Emerald Group Publishing Limited
All rights of reproduction in any form reserved
ISSN: 0731-9053/doi:10.1108/S0731-9053(2012)0000028013

purely forward-looking behavior and its hybrid variant are equivalent. Monte Carlo experiments investigate the validity of chosen moment conditions and the finite sample properties of the chosen estimation methods. Finally, the empirical performance of the formal test is discussed along the lines of the Akaike's and the Bayesian information criterion.

Keywords: Backward- and forward-looking behavior; formal test; intrinsic persistence; maximum likelihood; method of moment; New-Keynesian

JEL classification: C12; C32; E12

INTRODUCTION

In the New-Keynesian model (NKM), some extensions such as habit formation and indexing behavior have gained popularity for the ability to fit the macro data well (see Christiano, Eichenbaum, & Evans, 2005; Rabanal & Rubio-Ramarez, 2005; Smets & Wouters, 2003, 2005, 2007). For example, the forward-looking behavior of price indexation has been challenged by macroeconomists over the last decade, because a hybrid variant of the model with backward-looking behavior provides a good approximation of inflation dynamics; see also Galí and Gertler (1999), Fuhrer (1997), Rudd and Whelan (2005, 2006). In the same way, inertial behavior in the dynamics of the output gap can be better explained by the presence of habit persistence in consumption rule (e.g., see Fuhrer, 2000). Accordingly, the lagged dynamics in the NKM influence the transmission of shocks to the economy; the backward-looking behavior in the pricesetting and consumption rules affects the degree of endogenous persistence in inflation and output. This also implies that a good approximation of the NKM to the data (e.g., the persistence of aggregate macro variables) can provide a potential explanation for the monetary transmission channel to inflation and output (see Amato & Laubach, 2003, 2004; Woodford, 2003, Chap. 3).

In a small-scale hybrid NKM, however, current inflation and output depend on its expected future and lagged values, which can give rise to a highly nonlinear mapping between structural parameters and the objective function during estimation. Because of this, we cannot easily overcome identification problems in the structural model; in other words, the minimization problem in extreme estimators often does not have a unique solution asymptotically (e.g., see Canova & Sala, 2009). The purpose of this chapter is to show to what extent classical estimation methods cope with structural parameter estimates and how these can be used to evaluate the model's empirical performance. Especially, we draw attention to an analytical solution of the model and conduct a structural econometric analysis to identify the effects of a lagged term in inflation and output.[1]

More generally, we apply the formal test of Hnatkovska, Marmer, and Tang (2012) (HMT henceforth) and examine the significant influence of the lagged term on the inflation and output dynamics. According to HMT, the Vuong-type χ^2 test evaluates the adequacy of a broad class of goodness-of-fit measures and allows for model misspecification; see also Linhart and Zucchini (1986) for model selection. Hence, the test statistic used in our study can simply indicate the goodness-of-fit of the model in hypothesis testing, which measures the discrepancy between the model-generated and empirical moments. For example, Vuong (1989) demonstrates how to use the likelihood ratio test for non-nested models. Rivers and Vuong (2002) generalize the hypothesis testing procedure to empirical application involving a wide range of estimation techniques. Their procedure extends to complex model selection situations where one or both models may be misspecified and the models may or may not be nested (see Golden, 2000, 2003).

The advantage of the formal test of HMT is that the model's empirical performance can be flexibly evaluated according to the chosen moment conditions. The flexibility is commonly associated with the transparency to the fit of the model when the moment conditions are directly binding for parameter estimation. Indeed, the limited information approach has been widely used to estimate parameters of a monetary DSGE model starting from Rotemberg and Woodford (1997). For example, one common approach to this problem is to use impulse responses that are most informative about the DSGE model; Dridi, Guay, and Renault (2007) and Hall, Inoue, Nason, and Rossi (2012) discuss the choice of binding functions – that is, a function which can connect the parameters of the model to the parameters of an auxiliary model – and information criteria for the selection of valid response. Especially, when the model misspecifications and complex structural system do not allow for efficient estimation, the adequacy of the model in fitting the data can be judged by using binding functions (see Gourieroux & Monfort, 1995). To conduct empirical analysis without the auxiliary model, Franke, Jang, and Sacht (2011) examine a small-scale DSGE model using analytical second moments of the sample auto- and cross-covariances up to lag 8 (two years) for estimation as well as model selection. While the empirical results using the moment matching approach are contrasted with the Bayesian estimation, however, the validity of their chosen moment conditions is not indicated by a statistical test.

In this study, we discuss the efficiency of the method of moments (MM) estimation and examine the validity of moment conditions along the lines of the maximum likelihood (ML) approach. To see this, first, we investigate the NKM's empirical performance by using the relationship between interest rate, inflation and output of US data. In particular, we attempt to assess the significance of the lagged dynamics in inflation and output. From the ML and MM estimations, we pinpoint an empirical link between the hybrid model structure and the persistence in inflation and output. Next, the empirical performances of the model with purely forward-looking behavior and its hybrid variant are evaluated using the model selection criterion. Accordingly, the inclusion of a lagged term in the New-Keynesian Phillips Curve (NKPC) and the IS equation improves the fit of the model while offsetting the influence of inherited and extrinsic persistence; it is shown that intrinsic persistence plays a major role in approximating inflation and output dynamics for the *Great Inflation* period. However, the null hypothesis cannot be rejected at the 5% level for the *Great Moderation* period, that is, the NKM with purely forward-looking behavior and its hybrid variant are equivalent. Finally, we carry out a Monte Carlo study to examine the statistical efficiency of the estimation methods.

This chapter is organized as follows: The second section reviews the standard New-Keynesian three-equations model and examines the importance of intrinsic persistence (or backward-looking behavior) for the co-movement between inflation and output. Estimation methodologies and model selection procedures are described in the third section. The fourth section presents the empirical results and the model comparison between the NKM with the forward-looking behavior and its hybrid variant. Moreover, the finite sample properties of the estimators are investigated using the Monte Carlo experiments in the fifth section. Finally, the sixth section concludes. All technical details are collected in the appendix.

EXPECTATION FORMATION IN A DSGE MODEL

In this section, we present the standard New-Keynesian model featuring aggregate supply, aggregate demand (IS), and monetary policy equations.[2] We explore the model specifications of the lagged dynamics in the NKPC and the IS equation, with a focus on the backward- and forward-looking behavior.

The New-Keynesian Three-Equations Model

Microfoundations of supply- and demand-side economy have been established as the key components of New-Keynesian model framework, for example, the behavior of optimizing economic agents. The monetary policy behavior is described by the Taylor rule where the lagged interest rate reflects the gradual adjustment of a central bank. Thus the model is a convenient tool for modeling systemic changes in the economy. Especially, in our current study, we attempt to examine to what extent the gaps of interest rate, inflation and output are related to each other and to what extent they affect the economy ($\hat{\pi}_t := \pi_t - \pi_t^*$, $\hat{r}_t := r_t - r_t^*$). The trend components of the quarterly data are estimated by using the Hodrick–Prescott (HP) filter with the smoothing parameter of $\lambda = 1,600$.[3] The standard model reads as follows:

$$\hat{\pi}_t = \frac{\beta}{1 + \alpha\beta} E_t \hat{\pi}_{t+1} + \frac{\alpha}{1 + \alpha\beta} \hat{\pi}_{t-1} + \kappa x_t + v_{\pi,t}$$

$$x_t = \frac{1}{1 + \chi} E_t x_{t+1} + \frac{\chi}{1 + \chi} x_{t-1} - \tau(\hat{r}_t - E_t \hat{\pi}_{t+1}) + v_{x,t}$$

$$\hat{r}_t = \varphi_r \hat{r}_{t-1} + (1 - \varphi_r)(\varphi_\pi \hat{\pi}_t + \varphi_x x_t) + \varepsilon_{r,t} \tag{1}$$

$$v_{\pi,t} = \rho_\pi v_{\pi,t-1} + \varepsilon_{\pi,t} \quad \text{(for indexing behavior)}$$

$$v_{x,t} = \rho_x v_{x,t-1} + \varepsilon_{x,t} \quad \text{(for consumption behavior)} \tag{2}$$

where the variable x_t is the output gap, $\hat{\pi}_t$ is the inflation gap and $\hat{r}_t$ is the interest rate gap. The discount factor and the slope coefficient of the Phillips curve are denoted by the parameters β and κ, respectively. The parameters α and χ measure the degree of price indexation in the NKPC ($0 \leqslant \alpha \leqslant 1$) and habit persistence of the household ($0 \leqslant \chi \leqslant 1$). And τ is a parameter that refers to the intertemporal elasticity of substitution of consumption ($\tau \geqslant 0$). In the Taylor rule, φ_r determines the degree of interest rate smoothing ($0 \leqslant \varphi_r \leqslant 1$). The other parameters φ_x and φ_π are the policy coefficients that measure the central bank's reactions to contemporaneous output and inflation ($\varphi_x, \varphi_\pi \geqslant 0$).

The shocks $\varepsilon_{z,t}$ are normally distributed with standard deviation σ_z (i.i.d. with $z = \pi, x, r$). Since $v_{\pi,t}$ and $v_{x,t}$ are autoregressive processes, the persistence of the cost-push and demand shocks are captured by the parameters ρ_π and ρ_x, respectively ($0 \leqslant \rho_\pi, \rho_x \leqslant 1$). In estimation, we do not take them together, but treat them as being an independent case in order to directly disentangle the sources of inflation and output persistence in the model.[4]

For the sake of simplicity, we present the above structural equations in canonical form. We denote by y_t and v_t the vector of three observable variables and the shocks respectively: $y_t = (\hat{\pi}_t, x_t, \hat{r}_t)'$, $v_t = (v_{\pi,t}, v_{x,t}, 0)'$.

$$AE_t y_{t+1} + By_t + Cy_{t-1} + v_t = 0$$
$$v_t = Nv_{t-1} + \varepsilon_t, \quad \varepsilon_t \sim N(0, \Sigma_\varepsilon) \tag{3}$$

where the matrices A, B, C, N are defined in Appendix B.

To solve the system, we can express the derivation of the solution as the recursive equation with matrices Ω and Φ. First, we use the method of undetermined coefficients to obtain the unique solution of the system under determinacy (i.e., $\varphi_\pi \geqslant 1$). Second, we apply the brute force iteration method of Binder and Pesaran (1995) to numerically evaluate the matrix Ω; see Appendix B for some intermediate steps.

$$y_t = \Omega y_{t-1} + \Phi v_t$$
$$v_t = Nv_{t-1} + \varepsilon_t \tag{4}$$

From the matrices Ω and Φ, it follows that the contemporaneous and lagged autocovariance process of the model can be computed recursively using the *Yule-Walker* equations (see Lütkepohl, 2005, Chap. 2). On the whole, we adjust the notation by changing the dating of the shocks and rewrite Eq. (4) as

$$\begin{bmatrix} y_t \\ v_{t+1} \end{bmatrix} = \begin{bmatrix} \Omega & \Phi \\ 0 & N \end{bmatrix} \begin{bmatrix} y_{t-1} \\ v_t \end{bmatrix} + \begin{bmatrix} 0 \\ I \end{bmatrix} \varepsilon_{t+1} \tag{5}$$

Moreover, we can transform Eq. (5) into the law of motion of $z_t = (y_t', v_{t+1}')'$. This can be more compactly written as

$$z_t = A_1 z_{t-1} + u_t, \quad u_t \sim N(0, \Sigma_u), \quad \Sigma_u = D\Sigma_\varepsilon D' \tag{6}$$

where the matrix A_1 and the covariance matrix Σ_u are functions of the parameter vector θ. The shocks are mapped into the vector of $u_t = D \cdot \varepsilon_{t+1}$ with $D = (0 \ I)'$. The estimation methodologies will be discussed later.

Sources of Persistence: Backward- and Forward-Looking Behavior

In the study of the model comparison, we put an emphasis on two polar cases of the behavior of economic agents. For example, when the price indexation parameter α is set to zero, it is assumed in the model that expectations are purely forward-looking. In this case, inflation persistence is exclusively driven by the exogenous shock process and inherited persistence from the

Table 1. Sources of Persistence in the NKPC and the IS Equation.

Persistence	Inflation	Output
Intrinsic	Indexing behavior (α)	Habit formation (χ)
Extrinsic	AR (1) of the shock (ρ_π)	AR (1) of the shock (ρ_x)
Inherited	Slope of Phillips curve (κ)	Intertemporal substitution (τ)

output gap (see Table 1). But allowing it to be a free parameter, we assume that agents in the market can choose naive expectations. As a result, the NKPC is affected by both expected future and lagged inflation. This allows the model to have a degree of inertia in the dynamics, which can provide structural insights on the comovement between inflation and output.

In the same vein, Table 1 shows that we can distinguish between the backward- and forward-looking behavior in the IS equation. As long as each household chooses consumption optimally (i.e., without habit formation $\chi = 0$), the output dynamics in the economy are only driven by the exogenous shock and the inherited persistence. The latter is implied by rational-expectations equilibrium in the intertemporal allocation of consumption. On the contrary, if habit persistence is present in the consumption rule (i.e., χ is now a free parameter), then the output dynamics is endogenously sustained by the optimizing behavior; the inclusion of habit formation in consumption can explain the dependence of the current expenditure on the past level of expenditure. As a result, the NKPC also depends on the lagged term in the IS equation.

In the current study, we aim to disentangle the sources of inflation and output persistence using classical estimation methods. Especially, we investigate the degree of endogenous dynamics in the model with the lagged term. In other words, it can be seen that the inclusion of the backward-looking behavior in the NKPC and the IS equation offsets the effects of the extrinsic and inherited persistence while strengthening the comovement between inflation and output. Note here that we pinpoint the sources of persistence by separately considering AR (1) of the shocks for the price indexing and consumption behavior.[5]

ESTIMATION METHODOLOGIES AND MODEL SELECTION

In this section, we explain our estimation methodologies, which must be based on the solution of the model: the method of moment and maximum likelihood estimation. And we present a formal testing procedure such that the empirical performance of the models can be compared.

Method of Moment and Model Comparison: HMT (2012)

From the law of motion in Eq. (6), it follows that a set of the second moments of z_t can be analytically computed. Thus the contemporaneous and lagged autocovariances of the first-order vector-autoregressive (VAR (1)) are given by:

$$\Gamma(h) := E(z_t z'_{t-h}) \in R^{K \times K}, \quad K = 2n, \quad h = 0, 1, 2, \ldots \quad (7)$$

where n is the dimension of the vector of observable variables y_t. Their computation proceeds in two steps. First, $\Gamma(0)$ is obtained from the equation $\Gamma(0) = A_1 \Gamma(0) A'_1 + \Sigma_u$, which yields

$$\text{vec}\Gamma(0) = (I_{K^2} - A_1 \otimes A_1)^{-1} \text{vec}\Sigma_u \quad (8)$$

where the symbol "$\otimes$" denotes the Kronecker product. The invertibility of the term $I_{K^2} - A_1 \otimes A_1$ is guaranteed, because A_1 is clearly a stable matrix, that is, $\varphi_\pi \geqslant 1$. Second, the *Yule-Walker* equations are employed, from which we can recursively obtain the lagged autocovariances as

$$\Gamma(h) = A_1 \Gamma(h-1) \quad (9)$$

This formula relates to a vector autoregressive process of the model. From Eq. (9), we can compute analytic second moments of the model, which will be used to match the empirical counterparts during the MM estimation.

For the purposes of comparison between two models (A and B), we must estimate the model parameters by minimizing a weighted objective function (the chosen goodness-of-fit measures):

$$J_I(\theta) \equiv \min_{\theta^I \in \Theta} T(\hat{m}_T - m^I(\theta^I))' W(\hat{m}_T - m^I(\theta^I)), \quad I = A, B \quad (10)$$

where m^I is a vector of moments, and $\hat{m}$ is a consistent and asymptotically normal estimator of true moments m_0.[6]

To examine the macroeconomic effects of the expected future and lagged term on the NKPC and the IS equation, we use auto- and cross-covariances at lag 1 (15 moments) from the interest rate gap ($\hat{r}_t$), the output gap (x_t), and the inflation rate gap ($\hat{\pi}_t$), (see also Appendix A). With reference to the alternative moment conditions, we present a case for the auto- and cross-covariances up to lag 4 (42 moments). The empirical results of moment estimates and their robustness will be discussed later. Note here that we use a set of the second moments to evaluate the model's empirical performance and apply a formal test to the model of purely forward-looking behavior and its hybrid variant.

In order to construct the objective function, we must estimate the weight matrix W. Here we simply use the Newey–West (1987) estimator:

$$\hat{\Sigma}_m = \hat{\Gamma}_T(0) + \sum_{k=1}^{5}(\hat{\Gamma}_T(k) + \hat{\Gamma}_T(k)') \tag{11}$$

where $\hat{\Gamma}_T(j)$ is $\frac{1}{T}\sum_{t=j+1}^{T}(m_t - \bar{m})(m_t - \bar{m})'$, and k is the number of lags.[7] In particular, we ignore off-diagonal elements of the weight matrix and compute the inverse of $\hat{\Sigma}_m$, that is, $W = 1/\hat{\Sigma}_{m,ii}$, $i = 1, \ldots, n_m$. The reason for this restriction is two-fold: (i) when the sample size is small, the correlation between the elements of the weight matrix and the second moments is likely to be high (e.g., see Altonji & Segal, 1996). (ii) If we consider a large set of the moment conditions up to lag of two or three years, the rows in the weight matrix are correlated to some extent. To avoid the dependence between the moments, we only use the diagonal components of the variance–covariance matrix.

Under the standard regularity conditions, the asymptotic distribution of the parameter estimates is given by:

$$\sqrt{T}(\hat{\theta}_T - \theta_0) \sim N(0, \Lambda) \tag{12}$$

where we can numerically compute the covariance matrix Λ using the first derivative of the moments at optimum, that is, $\Lambda = [(DWD')^{-1}] \times D'W\Sigma_m WD[(DWD')^{-1}]'$.[8] Note here that D is a gradient vector of moment functions evaluated at the estimated values:

$$\hat{D} = \left.\frac{\partial m(\theta; X_T)}{\partial \theta}\right|_{\theta=\hat{\theta}_T} \tag{13}$$

Next, we consider hypotheses comparing the goodness-of-fit of the competing models. The null hypothesis H_0 is that two non-nested models fit the data equally:

$$H_0 : \left\| W^{1/2}(\hat{m}_T - m^A(\theta^A)) \right\| - \left\| W^{1/2}(\hat{m}_T - m^B(\theta^B)) \right\| = 0 \tag{14}$$

The first alternative hypothesis is that model A performs better than model B when

$$H_1 : \left\| W^{1/2}(\hat{m}_T - m^A(\theta^A)) \right\| - \left\| W^{1/2}(\hat{m}_T - m^B(\theta^B)) \right\| < 0 \tag{15}$$

The second alternative hypothesis is that model B performs better than model A when

$$H_2 : \left\| W^{1/2}(\hat{m}_T - m^A(\theta^A)) \right\| - \left\| W^{1/2}(\hat{m}_T - m^B(\theta^B)) \right\| > 0 \qquad (16)$$

To carry out the model comparison, we define the quasi-likelihood-ratio (QLR) statistic as

$$\widehat{\mathrm{QLR}} = J^B(\hat{\theta}^B) - J^A(\hat{\theta}^A) \qquad (17)$$

According to HMT, the relationship between two models (A and B) can be defined in terms of the following terminologies: (i) nested, (ii) strictly non-nested, and (iii) overlapping models. Especially, if the two models share moment conditions for the data generating process and neither model is nested within the other, we assume that two models are overlapping; note here that the two models can not be identical, because they can still generate different moment conditions by using different numerical values for the parameters. Then we can conduct two sequential procedures of the hypothesis testing á la Vuong (1989). To begin, we compute critical values of the QLR distribution for the first step of the model comparison.[9] The simulated QLR distribution is defined as the following χ^2-type formula:

$$Z'\hat{\Sigma}_m^{1/2} W(V^B - V^A)W\hat{\Sigma}_m^{1/2}Z, \quad Z \sim N(0, E_{n_m}) \qquad (18)$$

where Σ is a positive definite covariance matrix of the moment estimates, and Z is drawn from the multivariate (n_m) normal distribution; Appendix E defines the n_θ^I by n_θ^I matrix V^I with $I = A$, B in Eq. (18). If $\widehat{\mathrm{QLR}}$ exceeds the critical value from a 95% confidence interval, then the null hypothesis is rejected. Next, the second step investigates whether or not the source of the rejection asymptotically comes from the same goodness-of-fit. The suggested test statistic has a standard normal distribution (z):

$$w_0 = 2 \cdot \sqrt{(m^B(\theta^B) - m^A(\theta^A))' W(m^B(\theta^B) - m^A(\theta^A))} \qquad (19)$$

The standard deviation w_0 measures the uncertainty of the $\widehat{\mathrm{QLR}}$ estimates of two models. Accordingly, the null of the equal fits can be rejected when $\sqrt{T} \cdot \mathrm{QLR}(\hat{\theta}^B, \hat{\theta}^A)/\hat{w}_0 > z_{1-0.05/2}$ in which case A is the preferred model, or $\sqrt{T} \cdot \mathrm{QLR}(\hat{\theta}^B, \hat{\theta}^A)/\hat{w}_0 < -z_{1-0.05/2}$ in which case B is preferred.

Maximum Likelihood and Model Selection

Likelihood inference has been widely used to estimate the parameters of DSGE models over the last decade (see Ireland, 2004; Lindé, 2005, and others). We briefly summarize the econometric steps for the ML estimation and model selection. From Eq. (4), we may write that:

$$
\begin{aligned}
y_t &= \Omega y_{t-1} + \Phi \cdot (N \cdot v_{t-1} + \varepsilon_t) \\
&= (\Omega + \Phi N \Phi^{-1}) y_{t-1} - \Phi N \Phi^{-1} \Omega y_{t-2} + \Phi \cdot \varepsilon_t
\end{aligned} \tag{20}
$$

where we define the variable $\Phi \cdot \varepsilon_t$ as η_t. Now we assume that η_t follows a multivariate normal distribution.

$$
\eta_t \sim N(0, \Sigma_\eta), \quad \Sigma_\eta \equiv \Phi \cdot \Sigma_\varepsilon \cdot \Phi' \tag{21}
$$

Hence, we can obtain the following conditional probability for the vector of observable variables y_t:

$$
y_t | y_{t-1}, y_{t-2} \sim N((\Omega + \Phi N \Phi^{-1}) y_{t-1} - \Phi N \Phi^{-1} \Omega y_{t-2}, \Sigma_\eta) \tag{22}
$$

Given the normality assumption of shocks and data set, the likelihood function can be constructed as:

$$
L(\theta) = -\frac{n \cdot T}{2} \ln(2\pi) - \frac{T}{2} \ln |\Sigma_\eta| - \frac{1}{2} \sum_{t=2}^{T} \eta_t' \cdot \Sigma_\eta^{-1} \cdot \eta_t \tag{23}
$$

where n is the dimension of y_t. Finally, we arrive at the ML estimates for the parameter θ by maximizing Eq. (23):

$$
\theta_{ml} = arg \max_{\theta \in \Theta} L(\theta) \tag{24}
$$

Under standard regularity conditions, the ML estimation is consistent and asymptotically normal:

$$
\sqrt{T}(\hat{\theta}_{ml} - \theta_0) \sim N(0, (\Upsilon/T)^{-1}) \tag{25}
$$

where $\Upsilon = E(\partial^2 L(\theta)/\partial\theta\partial\theta')$ is the information matrix. In our study, Υ is numerically computed using the Hessian matrix of the log likelihood function at optimum. For the purposes of the formal test, we use the well-known approach to model selection, the Akaike information criterion (AIC):

$$
\text{AIC} = -\frac{2}{T} \cdot \ln L(\theta) + \frac{2p}{T} \tag{26}
$$

where p is the dimension of the parameter θ. Then, we choose the model for which AIC is the smallest. As an alternative to the AIC, we also consider the Bayesian information criterion (BIC):

$$
\text{BIC} = -\frac{2}{T} \cdot \ln L(\theta) + \frac{p \cdot \ln T}{T} \tag{27}
$$

where the second term, $p \cdot \ln T$ penalizes the model with additional parameters.

EMPIRICAL APPLICATION

In this section, we present empirical results of the model using the US data. First, we attempt to disentangle the sources of persistence in inflation and output; we examine the empirical performance of the model using the formal test of HMT. Second, the similarities and dissimilarities between the MM and ML estimations are discussed. Finally, we investigate the validity of extra moment conditions based on the model's empirical performance.

Data

The data we use in this study comprise the GDP price deflator, the real GDP and the federal funds rate. The series are taken from the US model data sets by Ray C. Fair; http://fairmodel.econ.yale.edu/main3.htm. The trend rates underlying the gap formulation are treated as exogenously given. The trend from a HP filter is used with the smoothing parameter $\lambda = 1,600$. The data set covers the period 1960–2007. Due to the structural break beginning with the appointment of Paul Volcker as chairman of the U.S. Federal Reserve Board, we split data into two subsamples: the *Great Inflation* (GI, 1960:Q1-1979:Q2) and the *Great Moderation* (GM, 1982:Q4-2007:Q2). The data split in the US economy is standard in most existing empirical works.

Basic Results on Method of Moments Estimation and Model Comparison

In this section, we apply the MM estimation to the model and discuss the importance of the lagged dynamics for inflation and output persistence. Auto- and cross-covariances at lag 1 are used as chosen moment conditions. Next, the model comparison method, is used to provide a formal assessment of the performance of competing specifications.

Assessing the Fit of the Model to Inflation Persistence: 15 Moments
A set of second moment conditions is used to assess the performance of the two models to fit inflation persistence in the GI data. Table 2 shows the parameter estimates for the model with forward-looking behavior and its hybrid variant. As long as the profit maximizing rule without indexation to

Table 2. Parameter Estimates for Inflation Persistence with 15 Moments.

	GI		GM	
	Hybrid	Forward	Hybrid	Forward
α	**0.768**	0.0 (fixed)	**0.105**	0.0 (fixed)
	(0.007–1.000)	(–)	(0.000–1.000)	(–)
κ	**0.047**	0.123	0.052	0.058
	(0.009–0.084)	(0.000–0.318)	(0.000–0.136)	(0.008–0.107)
ρ_π	**0.000**	0.506	0.000	0.086
	(–)	(0.078–0.933)	(–)	(0.000–0.269)
σ_π	0.679	0.778	0.638	0.644
	(0.103–1.255)	(0.603–0.952)	(0.454–0.823)	(0.491–0.798)
χ	1.000	0.999	0.774	0.802
	(–)	(0.441–1.000)	(0.497–1.000)	(0.499–1.000)
τ	0.094	0.089	0.000	0.000
	(0.015–0.174)	(0.000–0.192)	(–)	(–)
ρ_x	0.0 (fixed)	0.0 (fixed)	0.0 (fixed)	0.0 (fixed)
	(–)	(–)	(–)	(–)
σ_x	0.727	0.662	0.404	0.369
	(0.547–0.907)	(0.416–0.909)	(0.118–0.691)	(0.068–0.671)
φ_π	1.659	1.744	1.798	1.943
	(1.000–2.334)	(1.084–2.404)	(1.000–4.039)	(1.000–4.465)
φ_x	0.378	0.181	0.729	0.652
	(0.026–0.731)	(0.000–0.452)	(0.226–1.231)	(0.087–1.217)
φ_r	0.544	0.463	0.841	0.849
	(0.323–0.765)	(0.248–0.678)	(0.698–0.984)	(0.707–0.991)
σ_r	0.786	0.662	0.391	0.384
	(0.382–1.190)	(0.155–1.169)	(0.099–0.684)	(0.080–0.688)
$J(\theta)$	1.30	3.24	2.26	2.44

Note: The discount factor parameter β is calibrated to 0.99. The 95% asymptotic confidence intervals are given in brackets.

past inflation (or purely forward-looking) determines the total amount of output in the economy, the inflation dynamics are primarily captured by inherited and extrinsic persistence. Indeed, from the model with purely forward-looking behavior, we obtain much higher estimated values for the parameters κ and ρ_π than its hybrid variant, that is, $\hat{\kappa} = 0.12$ (forward) > 0.05 (hybrid), $\hat{\rho}_\pi = 0.51$ (forward) > 0.0 (hybrid).

Turning to the formal test, we classify the two models into the nested case. Since the hybrid variant of the model can generate richer dynamics due to the lagged inflation with the price indexation parameter α, it nests the other model; the model with the forward-looking expectations does not allow for the effects of intrinsic persistence on the NKPC.

To test the null hypothesis that the two models have an equal fit to the data, we compare the estimated loss function values $(\hat{J}(\theta))$. We find QLR = 1.94. The simulated 1% and 5% critical values for the hypothesis testing are 2.42 and 1.31, respectively; see the left panel of Fig. F.1.1. Therefore we reject the null hypothesis at 5% level; the backward-looking behavior plays a significant role in approximating the inflation persistence of the GI.

This finding is summarized in Table 3. The results show that the hybrid variant of the model can approximate the inflation dynamics better than the other. The inclusion of the lagged term can almost provide perfect fit to the comovements between interest rate, inflation and output, for example, see $\text{Cov}(r_t, x_{t-k})$, $\text{Cov}(x_t, \pi_{t-k})$, $\text{Cov}(\pi_t, r_{t-k})$. However, this result does not indicate that the effects of the inherited and extrinsic persistence alone cannot explain the empirical regularities in the US economy. This point should be clear, since the evaluation of the fit of the nested model is not so bad; the estimated values of auto- and cross-covariances at lag 1 lie within the 95% confidence intervals of the empirical moments. According to the formal test, we can only say that there is a significant difference between model-generated moments of the two model, and the fit of the hybrid variant to the data is superior. Note here that we do not aim to match the auto- and cross-covariances up to higher lags; this will be discussed later.

Next, we consider the same steps for the model comparison using the GM data. However, most parameter estimates of the two models do not differ too much. For example, the estimated value for the price indexation is close to zero in the hybrid variant of the model, that is, $\hat{\alpha} = 0.105$. Accordingly, the result of the formal test shows that the two models fit the data equally well. We find that the estimated QLR statistic is small: QLR = 0.17. The simulated 1% and 5% criteria for the hypothesis testing are 0.51 and 0.27, respectively; see the right panel of Fig. F.1.1. Therefore the null hypothesis cannot be rejected.

To save space, we do not report the model-generated moments for GM. Indeed, when we compare trajectories of the model-generated moments (i.e., hybrid and forward), the model covariance profiles overlap each other. The two models provide a good fit to auto- and cross-covariances at the short lag. In other words, we conclude that the two models are not significantly different at 5% level. We discuss the evaluation of the fit of the model using alternative moment conditions later, because the model has

Table 3. Empirical and Model-Generated Moments for Inflation Persistence: 15 Moment Conditions.

Label	Emp.	95% CI	Hybrid	Forward	Label	Emp.	95% CI	Hybrid	Forward
$\mathrm{Var}(\hat{r}_t)$	3.296	1.297–5.296	3.400	3.524	$\mathrm{Cov}(x_t, x_{-1})$	2.523	1.356–3.690	2.365	2.495
$\mathrm{Cov}(\hat{r}_t, \hat{r}_{-1})$	2.886	1.142–4.629	**2.572**	2.388	**$\mathrm{Cov}(x_t, \hat{\pi}_t)$**	0.069	−0.415–0.552	**0.160**	0.236
$\mathrm{Cov}(\hat{r}_t, x_t)$	0.232	−0.611–1.075	**0.256**	0.270	**$\mathrm{Cov}(x_t, \hat{\pi}_{-1})$**	−0.350	−1.239–0.539	**−0.342**	−0.234
$\mathrm{Cov}(\hat{r}_t, x_{-1})$	0.991	0.235–1.746	**0.946**	0.782	**$\mathrm{Cov}(\hat{\pi}_t, \hat{r}_{-1})$**	1.288	−0.021–2.597	**1.067**	0.846
$\mathrm{Cov}(\hat{r}_t, \hat{\pi}_t)$	1.535	−0.026–3.097	**1.854**	2.155	**$\mathrm{Cov}(\hat{\pi}_t, x_{-1})$**	0.588	0.199–0.977	**0.527**	0.442
$\mathrm{Cov}(x_t, \hat{\pi}_{-1})$	1.401	0.038–2.765	1.731	1.714	$\mathrm{Var}(\hat{\pi}_t)$	1.989	0.615–3.364	1.713	1.921
$\mathrm{Cov}(x_t, \hat{r}_{-1})$	−0.450	−1.622–0.722	−0.490	−0.369	$\mathrm{Cov}(\hat{\pi}_t, \hat{\pi}_{-1})$	0.893	−0.216–2.001	1.033	0.789
$\mathrm{Var}(x_t)$	3.001	1.728–4.275	3.191	3.176					

Note: 95% CI means the 95% asymptotic confidence intervals for empirical moments. Bold face figures emphasize a better fit of the hybrid model to the empirical moments.

a bad fit to the sample autocovariances up to relatively large lags (two or three years).

Assessing the Fit of the Model to Output Persistence: 15 Moments
Turning to the output dynamics in the IS equation, we estimate the effects of habit persistence on the model. The estimated parameters for the model with or without a habit formation are presented in Table 4; in the purely forward-looking behavior χ is set to zero, whereas this parameter is subject to the estimation in the hybrid variant of the model. The MM

Table 4. Parameter Estimates for Output Persistence with 15 Moments.

	GI		GM	
	Hybrid	Forward	Hybrid	Forward
α	**0.517**	**0.740**	0.039	0.036
	(0.044–0.990)	(0.204–1.000)	(0.000–0.215)	(0.000–0.205)
κ	0.061	0.066	0.064	0.057
	(0.011–0.112)	(0.004–0.128)	(0.000–0.130)	(0.000–0.117)
ρ_π	0.0 (fixed)	0.0 (fixed)	0.0 (fixed)	0.0 (fixed)
	(–)	(–)	(–)	(–)
σ_π	0.876	0.715	0.684	0.687
	(0.576–1.175)	(0.447–0.983)	(0.545–0.824)	(0.547–0.826)
χ	**0.931**	0.0 (fixed)	**0.585**	0.0 (fixed)
	(0.000–1.000)	(–)	(0.000–1.000)	(–)
τ	0.441	0.422	0.480	0.506
	(0.000–0.943)	(0.000–0.995)	(0.000–1.223)	(0.000–1.315)
ρ_x	0.914	0.868	0.930	0.941
	(0.756–1.000)	(0.725–1.000)	(0.864–0.996)	(0.878–1.000)
σ_x	**0.214**	**0.445**	0.197	0.218
	(0.039–0.390)	(0.154–0.736)	(0.000–0.452)	(0.011–0.425)
ϕ_π	**1.857**	**2.256**	1.109	1.354
	(1.000–2.729)	(1.000–3.661)	(1.000–2.395)	(1.000–2.905)
φ_x	0.838	0.797	1.526	1.438
	(0.227–1.449)	(0.244–1.349)	(0.537–2.515)	(0.464–2.412)
φ_r	0.725	0.835	0.863	0.898
	(0.482–0.968)	(0.681–0.989)	(0.773–0.953)	(0.804–0.993)
σ_r	**0.695**	**0.240**	0.294	0.215
	(0.207–1.183)	(0.000–1.326)	(0.060–0.528)	(0.000–0.612)
$J(\theta)$	0.44	1.91	0.40	0.57

Note: The discount factor parameter β is calibrated to 0.99. The 95% asymptotic confidence intervals are given in brackets.

estimates of the two models have similar values except for the degree of the supply shock σ_x, monetary policy shock σ_r and the Taylor rule coefficient φ_π.

It can be seen from the GI data that the estimated demand shock is two times higher in an optimal consumption behavior without habit persistence than the other model ($\hat{\sigma}_x = 0.45$ (forward) > 0.21 (hybrid)). This result shows that the output dynamics are more or less driven by the high level of the demand shocks when a simple rule of thumb behavior is not allowed in the IS equation. As a result, the persistence from the demand shocks also affects inflation dynamics while offsetting the effects of inherited persistence. This is indicated by a relatively moderate degree of backward-looking behavior, that is, $\hat{\alpha} = 0.517$ (hybrid) and 0.740 (forward). Moreover, concerning the hybrid model specification, which allows a fraction of consumers to have a rule of thumb behavior, the estimation results indicate a low value for the monetary coefficients on inflation, that is, $\hat{\varphi}_\pi = 2.26$ (forward) > 1.86 (hybrid). Put differently, central banks react weakly to shocks due to the fact that the transmission of the shocks endogenously affects the output persistence; since the parameter estimates are poorly determined with a large confidence interval, however, we might raise doubts about appropriateness of this implication especially when the sample size is small. The reliability of the parameter estimates will be investigated later via a Monte Carlo study.

Now, we compute the loss function values to apply a formal test to the two specifications in the IS equation. In GI, these values are respectively 0.44 and 1.91 for the model with and without habit formation. The simulated 1% and 5% criteria for the hypothesis testing are 1.89 and 1.08, respectively; see the left panel of Fig. F.1.2. Since the estimated value for QLR exceeds the criterion at 5% level, we reject the null hypothesis that the two models are equivalent. This implies that the output dynamics are better approximated by the consumption behavior in a rule of thumb manner. This finding is shown in Table 5. For example, the hybrid variant of the model can almost provide perfect fit to the covariance profiles of (r_t, x_{t-k}), (x_t, x_{t-k}) and (π_t, π_{t-k}).

In the period of GM, the parameter estimates for the two models are found to be similar. The difference in the loss function values is small (i.e., QLR = 0.17). The simulated 1% and 5% criteria for the hypothesis testing are 7.58 and 12.37, respectively; see the right panel of Fig. F.1.2. We cannot reject the null hypothesis that the two models are equivalent. To save space, we do not report the model-generated moments for the GM period; the covariance profiles of the two models overlap each other.

Table 5. Empirical and Model-Generated Moments for Output Persistence: 15 Moment Conditions.

Label	Emp.	95% CI	Hybrid	Forward	Label	Emp.	95% CI	Hybrid	Forward
$\text{Var}(\hat{r}_t)$	3.296	1.297~5.296	3.305	3.196	$\mathbf{Cov(x_t, x_{-1})}$	2.523	1.356~3.690	**2.468**	2.187
$\mathbf{Cov(\hat{r}_t, \hat{r}_{-1})}$	2.886	1.142~4.629	**2.873**	3.041	$\text{Cov}(x_t, \hat{\pi}_t)$	0.069	−0.415~0.552	0.094	0.073
$\text{Cov}(\hat{r}_t, x_t)$	0.232	−0.611~1.075	0.164	0.342	$\text{Cov}(x_t, \hat{\pi}_{-1})$	−0.350	−1.239~0.539	−0.417	−0.368
$\mathbf{Cov(\hat{r}_t, x_{-1})}$	0.991	0.235~1.746	**0.984**	0.789	$\text{Cov}(\hat{\pi}_t, \hat{r}_{-1})$	1.288	−0.021~2.597	1.048	1.025
$\text{Cov}(\hat{r}_t, \hat{\pi}_t)$	1.535	−0.026~3.097	1.657	1.525	$\text{Cov}(\hat{\pi}_t, x_{-1})$	0.588	0.199~0.977	0.578	0.579
$\text{Cov}(x_t, \hat{\pi}_{-1})$	1.401	0.038~2.765	1.582	1.638	$\mathbf{Var(\hat{\pi}_t)}$	1.989	0.615~3.364	**1.907**	1.810
$\mathbf{Cov(x_t, \hat{r}_{-1})}$	−0.450	−1.622~0.722	**−0.252**	−0.073	$\mathbf{Cov(\hat{\pi}_t, \hat{\pi}_{-1})}$	0.893	−0.216~2.001	**0.934**	1.109
$\mathbf{Var(x_t)}$	3.001	1.728~4.275	**3.067**	3.331					

Note: 95% CI means the 95% asymptotic confidence intervals for empirical moments. Bold face figures emphasize a better fit of the hybrid model to the empirical moments.

Basic Results on Maximum Likelihood Estimation

For comparison purposes, we present the empirical results of the ML estimation of the NKM; it is known in empirical literature that likelihood inference has satisfactory asymptotic properties when the model is correctly specified. In addition, we will examine the large sample properties and statistical efficiency of the estimators in terms of our choice of moments via extensive Monte Carlo experiments later.

Table 6 shows that ML and MM give somewhat similar parameter estimates to the hybrid variant of the model for inflation persistence.[10] For example, the parameter estimates for the price indexation α are 0.45 and 0.16 for the GI and GM data, respectively. The likelihood inference also provides evidence of (moderate) intrinsic inflation persistence in the model. In other words, the backward-looking behavior in the pricesetting rule accounts for inflation persistence. Moreover, the ML estimation gives a very small value for the slope of the Phillips curve ($\hat{\kappa} = 0.0$ (GI) and 0.04 (GM)); individual firms are likely to be less responsive to changes in economic activity (i.e., the Phillips curve is flat). Hence, inflation dynamics in GI are primarily driven by intrinsic (moderate) and extrinsic (strong) persistence; i.e. $\hat{\alpha} = 0.446$, $\hat{\sigma}_{\pi} = 0.879$.

As far as the output persistence is concerned, we find a slight difference between the two estimators. For example, the comparison of the estimation results between ML and MM shows that the former gives a much lower value for the habit formation parameter ($\chi = 0.28$ and 0.25 for the GI and GM data). Further interesting observation from Table 6 is that the ML estimate for the intertemporal elasticity of substitution is found to be much lower ($\tau = 0.08$ and 0.03 for the GI and GM data). This implies that output persistence is not best captured by the substitution effects from the Fisher equation.

Overall, the slight difference in estimates can be attributed to the assumption of normality of the shocks; if the model is correctly specified, the ML estimation method is more accurate for estimating the NKM than the MM estimation. Since we consider that the model is possibly misspecified to capture the reality (or the true data generating process is not known), however, MM is likely to be a relevant choice for evaluating the model's goodness-of-fit to the data; the moment matching can provide a closer fit to the sample autocovariance. The statistical efficiency and consistency of the parameter estimation adopted in this study will be investigated via a Monte Carlo study later.

Table 6. ML Estimates for Inflation and Output Persistence.

	Inflation Persistence			Output Persistence	
	GI	GM		GI	GM
α	**0.446**	**0.157**	α	0.478	0.126
	(0.241–0.652)	(0.149–0.164)		(0.230–0.726)	(0.008–0.243)
κ	**0.000**	**0.036**	κ	0.018	0.046
	(–)	(0.034–0.037)		(0.000–0.099)	(0.015–0.077)
ρ_π	0.000	0.000	ρ_π	0.0 (fixed)	0.0 (fixed)
	(–)	(–)		(–)	(–)
σ_π	**0.879**	**0.654**	σ_π	0.869	0.663
	(0.740–1.019)	(0.649–0.660)		(0.737–1.002)	(0.597–0.729)
χ	1.000	0.998	χ	**0.281**	**0.254**
	(–)	(0.978–1.000)		(0.245–0.316)	(0.133–0.374)
τ	0.037	0.016	τ	**0.081**	**0.027**
	(0.001–0.073)	(0.014–0.019)		(0.038–0.125)	(0.014–0.040)
ρ_x	0.0 (fixed)	0.0 (fixed)	ρ_x	0.808	0.763
	(–)	(–)		(0.735–0.880)	(0.692–0.835)
σ_x	0.523	0.253	σ_x	0.211	0.098
	(0.442–0.604)	(0.252–0.255)		(0.174–0.248)	(0.093–0.104)
φ_π	1.353	1.001	φ_π	1.394	1.000
	(1.000–2.760)	(1.000–1.112)		(1.000–2.661)	(–)
φ_x	1.180	1.275	φ_x	1.352	1.456
	(0.295–2.064)	(1.225–1.324)		(0.710–1.995)	(1.135 -1.777)
φ_r	0.809	0.830	φ_r	0.803	0.843
	(0.690–0.927)	(0.827–0.833)		(0.754–0.852)	(0.828–0.857)
σ_r	0.734	0.477	σ_r	0.741	0.476
	(0.618–0.850)	(0.472–0.481)		(0.622–0.859)	(0.435–0.518)
$L(\theta)$	−308.86	−233.99	$L(\theta)$	−309.53	−231.84

Note: The discount factor parameter β is calibrated to 0.99. The 95% asymptotic confidence intervals are given in brackets.

Another important point is that the high dimension of the parameter space can give rise to multiple local optima in the likelihood function. However, in the current study, we have a strong confidence in the identification of the structural parameters, because the convergence of the optimization procedure is examined using different starting values. We found that our empirical results converge to a global optimum and are verified by using a set of different optimization such as iterative minimization, Nelder–Mead simplex, and random search method. In this respect, the structural estimation based on the analytic solution of the system is able to cope with the parameter identification problems in a small-scale hybrid NKM. To make a more systemic investigation on our choice of moments, the next section is devoted to examine the parameter estimation of the model using a large set of moment conditions.

Validity of Extra Moment Conditions

In this section, we examine the sensitivity of the MM estimation to the chosen moment conditions. From this investigation, we will find that alternative moment conditions do not induce qualitative changes in the parameter estimation. To make our choice of moment conditions more reliable, we make a case for the vector autoregressive (VAR) model with lag 4 as a reference model; see Appendix C for optimal lag selection criteria. Accordingly, we analyze the persistence of the macro data in the US economy using auto- and cross-covariances up to lag 4.

Assessing the Fit of the Model to Inflation Persistence: 42 Moments

With a focus on alternative moment conditions of auto- and cross-covariances up to lag 4 (42 moments), we now estimate two specifications of the NKM: forward-looking ($\alpha = 0$) and hybrid case (i.e., α is a free parameter). In Table 7, we find evidence of strong backward-looking behavior in the NKPC; $\hat{\alpha} = 1.0$. Moreover, the MM estimates with a small and large set of moments give qualitatively similar values except for the policy shock parameter ($\sigma_r = 0.0$).[11] For example, in the model with purely forward-looking behavior, the inherited and extrinsic persistence have a substantial influence on the system, compensating for the absence of intrinsic persistence in the NKPC: $\kappa = 0.155$ (forward) > 0.044 (hybrid), $\rho_\pi = 0.675$ (forward) > 0.0 (hybrid).

Next, we draw attention to the model comparison. In the GI data, we found that the price indexation parameter is a corner solution. Accordingly we treat α as being exogenously fixed at unity, because it is assumed in HMT that the estimated parameters are in the interior of the admissible region (see their assumption 2.5 (b)). Put differently, since we consider the price indexation parameter as being exogenously set to different values, it can be seen that two models are now equally accurate and identical in population. In this respect, we treat two models as being overlapping and apply a two step sequential test for model comparison. On the contrary, the value for the estimated price indexation parameter lies in the interior of the parameter space for fitting the GM data ($\alpha = 0.525$). In this case, the hybrid version of the model nests the one with the purely forward-looking expectations.

Table 7. Parameter Estimates for Inflation Persistence with
42 Moments.

	GI		GM	
	Hybrid	Forward	Hybrid	Forward
α	**1.0**	0.0 (fixed)	0.509	0.0 (fixed)
	(–)	(–)	(0.126–0.924)	(–)
κ	**0.044**	**0.155**	**0.037**	**0.102**
	(0.018–0.069)	(0.000–0.395)	(0.000–0.075)	(0.017–0.187)
ρ_π	**0.000**	**0.675**	**0.000**	**0.596**
	(–)	(0.387–0.964)	(0.000–0.813)	(0.367–0.825)
σ_π	0.470	0.518	0.364	0.231
	(0.000–1.686)	(0.233–0.790)	(0.048–0.680)	(0.093–0.369)
χ	1.0	1.0	0.770	0.915
	(–)	(–)	(0.515–1.000)	(0.518–1.000)
τ	0.092	0.063	0.020	0.027
	(0.045–0.140)	(0.008–0.118)	(0.000–0.055)	(0.000–0.074)
ρ_x	0.0 (fixed)	0.0 (fixed)	0.0 (fixed)	0.0 (fixed)
	(–)	(–)	(–)	(–)
σ_x	0.716	0.600	0.547	0.468
	(0.462–0.970)	(0.348–0.853)	(0.202–0.820)	(0.185–0.751)
φ_π	1.740	1.809	2.025	2.218
	(1.255–2.225)	(1.221–2.397)	(1.000–2.870)	(1.141–3.114)
φ_x	0.080	0.157	0.563	0.564
	(0.000–0.542)	(0.000–0.528)	(0.216–1.059)	(0.154–0.974)
φ_r	0.267	0.458	0.765	0.732
	(0.000–0.905)	(0.224–0.692)	(0.619–0.881)	(0.592–0.872)
σ_r	**0.000**	**0.000**	0.486	0.545
	(–)	(–)	(0.303–0.727)	(0.351–0.739)
$J(\theta)$	11.93	42.77	23.97	27.47

Note: The discount factor parameter β is calibrated to 0.99. The 95% asymptotic confidence intervals are given in brackets.

In the period of GI, the hybrid variant has a better goodness-of-fit to the data ($J = 11.93$) than the purely forward-looking version of the model ($J = 42.77$). As it is discussed above, the estimated AR (1) coefficient for the cost-push shock has no influence on the hybrid NKPC; $\hat{\rho}_\pi = 0.0$.[12] The results also show that inherited persistence has a smaller impact on the output dynamics in the hybrid variant of the model ($\hat{\kappa} = 0.044$). This implies that the persistence is best captured by the backward-looking behavior in the hybrid variant. As a result, we find almost perfect fit to the comovements between inflation and output from the hybrid NKM.

In order to examine the significant difference of the fit of the two models, we subtract the objective function value of purely forward-looking NKM from its hybrid variant; i.e. QLR = 30.83. According to the simulated test distribution, critical values for the 99% and 95% confidence intervals are 16.99 and 9.96, respectively (see the left panel of Fig. F.2.1). Since the test statistic exceeds the critical value at 5% level, we proceed to take the second step of the hypothesis testing, which asymptotically evaluates the estimated moments of two models from the empirical data.

In the second step of the formal test, we examine the uncertainty of the estimated difference between the two models for evaluating their fit to the data. We compute the plug-in estimate of $\hat{w}_0$ (2.54). Under the null hypothesis, the test static follows a standard normal distribution; i.e. $\sqrt{T} \cdot QLR(\theta^A, \theta^B) \sim N(0, w_0^2)$. The estimate of $\sqrt{T} \cdot QLR/\hat{w}$ is 1.37, which is smaller than a critical value at the 5% significance level of the two-tailed test. Therefore the results show that both models have the same goodness-of-fit to the profile of the empirical moments, and the null hypothesis cannot be rejected.[13] Fig. 1 depicts the model-generated moment conditions at three years for GI and contrasts them with the empirical counterparts of the VAR (4) model. Indeed, a visual inspection of this figure indicates that the two models have different moments, but their matching to the empirical counterparts is not significantly different.

In the period of GM (Table 7), it is shown that the hybrid variant fits the data better (23.97). The estimation results provide evidence of the (strong) inherited and extrinsic persistence in the model with purely forward-looking behavior, because these can offset the impact of inherited persistence on the output dynamics, that is, $\hat{\kappa} = 0.102$ (forward) > 0.037 (hybrid), $\hat{\rho}_\pi = 0.596$ (forward) > 0.0 (hybrid). However, the other parameter estimates are not different in both specifications.

These empirical findings seem to strengthen the relevance of backward-looking behavior for the GM data. However, the difference between the two models (3.49) does not exceed the critical value for the 95% confidence intervals in the formal test, that is, critical values for 99% and 95% confidence intervals are 38.39 and 21.46, respectively; also see the right panel of Fig. F.2.1. Put differently, the effects of intrinsic persistence on inflation can be adequately replaced by the inherited and extrinsic persistence. From this we cannot identify the sources of the persistence in the system. Therefore we do not proceed to take the second step of the model comparison method and conclude that the null hypothesis cannot be rejected. Fig. 2 depicts the model-generated moment conditions at three years for the GM data; the

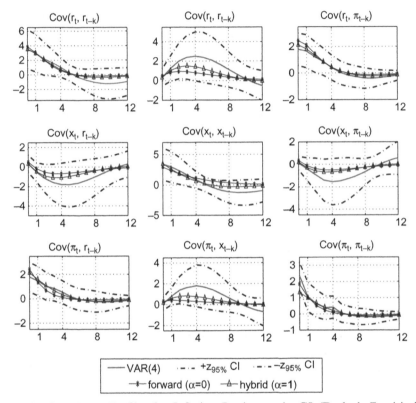

Fig. 1. Covariance Profiles for Inflation Persistence in GI (Dashed: Empirical, $\triangle$: Hybrid, *: Forward).
Note: The empirical auto- and cross-covariances are computed using an unrestricted fourth-order vector autoregression (VAR) model. The asymptotic 95% confidence bands are constructed following Coenen (2005).

comparison between the model-generated and empirical moments by a VAR (4) process is displayed here.

Assessing the Fit of the Model to Output Persistence: 42 Moments
Table 8 reports the MM estimation for the output persistence using alternative moment conditions. The results show that the output dynamics are strongly influenced by the inherited persistence. Indeed, in the case of the intertemporal elasticity of substitution, we obtain high estimated values for the two models: for example, in GI, $\hat{\tau} = 0.205$ (hybrid), 0.676 (forward).

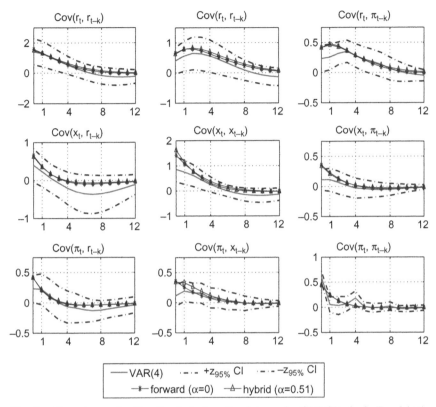

Fig. 2. Covariance Profiles for Inflation Persistence in GM (Dashed: Empirical, △: Hybrid, *: Forward).

Note: The empirical auto- and cross-covariances are computed using an unrestricted fourth-order vector autoregression (VAR) model. The asymptotic 95% confidence bands are constructed following Coenen (2005).

In addition, we find that all the estimated values for ρ_x exceed 0.7. Especially regarding the GI data, this value increases substantially in the model with purely forward-looking expectations, which can cover the absence of intrinsic persistence in the IS equation, that is, $\chi = 0.0$ (fixed), $\hat{\tau} = 0.676$.

Another point worthwhile mentioning here is that the estimation results of the purely forward-looking model indicate high monetary policy coefficients on interest rate, inflation and output in GI, that is, $\hat{\varphi}_\pi = 2.05$, $\hat{\varphi}_x = 1.10$, $\hat{\varphi}_r = 0.89$. Moreover, in the hybrid variant, the parameter χ is almost a corner solution for both the GI and GM data, which strengthens

Table 8. Parameter Estimates for Output Persistence with
42 Moments.

	GI		GM	
	Hybrid	Forward	Hybrid	Forward
α	1.0	0.998	0.186	0.203
	(–)	(–)	(0.000–0.396)	(0.000–0.441)
κ	0.054	0.037	0.086	0.088
	(0.005–0.102)	(0.010–0.065)	(0.037–0.134)	(0.027–0.149)
ρ_π	0.0 (fixed)	0.0 (fixed)	0.0 (fixed)	0.0 (fixed)
	(–)	(–)	(–)	(–)
σ_π	0.519	0.428	0.609	0.579
	(0.099–0.939)	(0.108–0.747)	(0.461–0.757)	(0.410–0.749)
χ	**1.0**	0.0 (fixed)	**0.991**	0.0 (fixed)
	(–)	(–)	(–)	(–)
τ	**0.205**	**0.676**	**0.237**	**0.236**
	(0.000–0.436)	(0.000–1.897)	(0.000–0.547)	(0.000–0.803)
ρ_x	**0.707**	**0.890**	**0.854**	**0.790**
	(0.290–1.000)	(0.743–1.000)	(0.686–1.000)	(0.583–0.997)
σ_x	0.213	0.519	0.140	0.340
	(0.016–0.410)	(0.169–0.869)	(0.000–0.298)	(0.037–0.642)
ϕ_π	**1.741**	**2.046**	2.133	2.224
	(1.154–2.327)	(1.000–3.134)	(1.000–3.279)	(1.000–3.764)
ϕ_x	**0.169**	**1.103**	0.762	0.588
	(0.000–0.584)	(0.275–1.931)	(0.189–1.335)	(0.000–1.202)
ϕ_r	**0.389**	**0.889**	0.770	0.783
	(0.000–0.853)	(0.753–1.026)	(0.640–0.900)	(0.648–0.917)
σ_r	0.012	0.016	0.447	0.448
	(–)	(–)	(0.248–0.645)	(0.212–0.685)
$J(\theta)$	10.54	31.64	20.79	23.85

Note: The discount factor parameter β is calibrated to 0.99. The 95% asymptotic confidence
intervals are given in brackets.

a rule of thumb behavior in consumption. In other words, the rule of thumb
behavior reinforces the degree of endogenous persistence in the output
dynamics. However, as long as the model predicts that the optimal behavior
of household is described by consumption without a simple rule of thumb
behavior ($\chi = 0$), the result indicates the strong degree of the demand
shocks; the estimated value is more than twice as high as the one of the
hybrid model, that is, $\hat{\sigma}_x = 0.519$ (forward) > 0.213 (hybrid) for GI, 0.340
(forward) > 0.140 (hybrid) for GM.

Turning to the model comparison by using the GI data, we treat the two
models as being overlapping, because the habit formation parameter is now
a corner solution. In the first step of the model comparison, we compare the

objective function values (QLR = 21.10). The simulated 5% and 1% criteria for the hypothesis testing are 19.63 and 34.59, respectively (see the left panel of Fig. F.2.2). Since the estimated QLR exceeds the 5% criterion for the model comparison, we support the hypothesis that two models have different moments. In the second step, we estimate $\sqrt{T} \cdot QLR/\hat{w}$ which is 1.02. However, this value does not exceed the criterion in the standard normal distribution. As a result, we conclude that there is no significant difference between two models in matching the empirical moments, that is, the two models have different moments, but an equivalent fit to the empirical moments. To save space, we do not provide the model covariance profiles for the output persistence. Note here that the result of the MM estimation with a large set of moments provides a closer fit to the sample auto- and cross-covariances up to large lags.

Now we draw attention to the model comparison by using the GM data. To begin, we treat the two models as being a nested case, since the estimated value for the habit formation parameter lies at an interior point. The model without habit persistence is nested within the other. Next, we compute the difference between the objective function values of the two models (QLR = 3.06). Then this value is used to evaluate the null hypothesis of the equal fit of the two models. Since the 5% and 1% criteria for the hypothesis testing are 18.52 and 29.05, respectively (see the right panel of Fig. F.2.2), the null hypothesis cannot be rejected. Therefore we conclude that two models have an equal fit to the empirical moments.

In sum, the MM estimation using a large set of moment conditions can provide a stronger evidence for the backward-looking behavior in the pricesetting and consumption rules compared to ML and MM with 15 moment conditions. This result is mainly attributed to the fact that the objective function to minimize is now the norm of additional sample second moments. However, the result of the model comparison becomes inconclusive, because the estimated values for the price indexation and habit persistence parameters were corner solutions; we used the two-step sequential hypothesis testing. We found that the null hypothesis cannot be rejected when the sample size is small. An elaborate analysis of model selection will be discussed in the next section.

ATTAINING EFFICIENCY FROM MOMENT CONDITIONS

In this section, first, we study the finite sample properties of the estimators for the NKM in addition, we investigate the effect of model misspecification on the parameter estimation. Second, we discuss the empirical performance of the formal test of HMT along the lines of the Akaike's and the Bayesian information criterion.

Monte Carlo Study

The Monte Carlo experiment attempts to clearly demonstrate the statistical efficiency of the estimation methods, which are used in the previous section. In this way, we aim to investigate the role of choice of moments and its influence on the parameter estimation. To begin, we consider the model specification of inflation persistence as the true date generating process; we simulate the artificial economy by using the parameters near to the results of the MM estimation with 15 moments (see Table 2): e.g. high degree of backward-looking behavior ($\alpha = 0.750$), moderate inherited persistence ($\kappa = 0.050$) and no extrinsic persistence ($\rho_\pi = 0.0$). Next, we generate 1,000 data sets each consisting of 550 observations. The first 50 observations are removed as a transient period. Three sample sizes are considered: 100, 200, and 500. We use the Matlab R2010a for this MC study. In optimization, we use the unconstrained minimization "fminicon" with the algorithm "interior-point"; maximum iteration and tolerance level are set to 500 and 10^{-6}, respectively.

We conduct the Monte Carlo experiments by considering two cases of model specification, that is, correctly specified and misspecified. In the former, we discuss the finite sample properties of the MM and ML estimation. Turning to the latter, we consider the model with purely forward-looking expectations and examine the degree of bias in the parameter estimates, that is, (1) to what extent the extrinsic persistence (ρ_π) is inflated due to the misspecification and (2) to what extent the model misspecification affects the estimates for the other structural parameters.

The main findings for the correctly specified case in Table 9 can be summarized as follows:

• The estimate of the price indexation parameter α is downward-biased, whereas the AR (1) coefficient of inflation shocks ρ_π is estimated to be positive. Especially, in ML, we found that the sum of the estimated values for the price indexation and extrinsic persistence parameters is close to the true value of α: i.e. $\alpha + \rho_\pi \approx 0.75$.
• ML has slightly poorer finite sample properties than MM. If the sample size is small, the conventional Gaussian asymptotic approximation to the sample distribution is not as much precise as MM.

Table 9. The Monte Carlo Results on the MM and ML Estimates, ( ): Root Mean Square Error, S.E: Mean of Standard Error.

	θ^0	ML			MM with 15 Moments			MM with 42 Moments		
		$T=100$	$T=200$	$T=500$	$T=100$	$T=200$	$T=500$	$T=100$	$T=200$	$T=500$
α	0.750	0.523 (0.375)	0.573 (0.322)	0.651 (0.228)	0.614 (0.256)	0.654 (0.196)	0.692 (0.121)	0.700 (0.245)	0.702 (0.205)	0.729 (0.118)
		S.E: 0.162	S.E: 0.170	S.E: 0.175	S.E: 0.319	S.E: 0.222	S.E: 0.138	S.E: 0.281	S.E: 0.190	S.E: 0.113
κ	0.050	0.074 (0.076)	0.066 (0.081)	0.056 (0.014)	0.083 (0.057)	0.068 (0.030)	0.058 (0.015)	0.093 (0.075)	0.073 (0.042)	0.058 (0.018)
		S.E: 0.054	S.E: 0.048	S.E: 0.041	S.E: 0.042	S.E: 0.025	S.E: 0.013	S.E: 0.050	S.E: 0.030	S.E: 0.014
ρ_π	0.000	0.218 (0.330)	0.172 (0.284)	0.097 (0.198)	0.175 (0.255)	0.129 (0.194)	0.082 (0.124)	0.194 (0.299)	0.147 (0.241)	0.078 (0.144)
		S.E: 0.112	S.E: 0.1000	S.E: 0.076	S.E: 0.327	S.E: 0.238	S.E: 0.152	S.E: 0.313	S.E: 0.230	S.E: 0.150
σ_π	0.675	0.602 (0.330)	0.619 (0.125)	0.640 (0.073)	0.613 (0.113)	0.624 (0.085)	0.639 (0.056)	0.564 (0.1778)	0.584 (0.136)	0.618 (0.088)
		S.E: 0.044	S.E: 0.047	S.E: 0.048	S.E: 0.143	S.E: 0.106	S.E: 0.068	S.E: 0.172	S.E: 0.130	S.E: 0.086
χ	1.000	0.935 (0.113)	0.949 (0.090)	0.967 (0.053)	0.932 (0.108)	0.948 (0.078)	0.962 (0.055)	0.941 (0.075)	0.956 (0.083)	0.966 (0.059)
		S.E: 0.159	S.E: 0.183	S.E: 0.201	S.E: 0.173	S.E: 0.126	S.E: 0.082	S.E: 0.207	S.E: 0.151	S.E: 0.098
τ	0.090	0.089 (0.031)	0.088 (0.023)	0.087 (0.014)	0.101 (0.039)	0.095 (0.026)	0.091 (0.016)	0.105 (0.044)	0.097 (0.030)	0.092 (0.018)
		S.E: 0.045	S.E: 0.047	S.E: 0.048	S.E: 0.040	S.E: 0.028	S.E: 0.017	S.E: 0.041	S.E: 0.029	S.E: 0.018
σ_x	0.700	0.695 (0.059)	0.697 (0.043)	0.699 (0.025)	0.743 (0.102)	0.735 (0.073)	0.724 (0.048)	0.738 (0.123)	0.729 (0.086)	0.721 (0.054)
		S.E: 0.050	S.E: 0.052	S.E: 0.053	S.E: 0.086	S.E: 0.062	S.E: 0.039	S.E: 0.121	S.E: 0.089	S.E: 0.057
φ_π	1.650	1.666 (0.183)	1.654 (0.118)	1.652 (0.074)	1.681 (0.194)	1.664 (0.123)	1.659 (0.076)	1.705 (0.229)	1.679 (0.145)	1.665 (0.088)
		S.E: 0.345	S.E: 0.316	S.E: 0.274	S.E: 0.210	S.E: 0.147	S.E: 0.093	S.E: 0.214	S.E: 0.151	S.E: 0.098
φ_x	0.375	0.362 (0.124)	0.361 (0.083)	0.366 (0.052)	0.337 (0.148)	0.343 (0.100)	0.352 (0.063)	0.294 (0.191)	0.317 (0.129)	0.344 (0.082)
		S.E: 0.227	S.E: 0.224	S.E: 0.228	S.E: 0.137	S.E: 0.097	S.E: 0.062	S.E: 0.156	S.E: 0.110	S.E: 0.071
φ_r	0.550	0.543 (0.048)	0.545 (0.034)	0.547 (0.021)	0.525 (0.063)	0.531 (0.045)	0.538 (0.027)	0.524 (0.080)	0.532 (0.056)	0.542 (0.034)
		S.E: 0.068	S.E: 0.070	S.E: 0.077	S.E: 0.074	S.E: 0.052	S.E: 0.033	S.E: 0.086	S.E: 0.061	S.E: 0.039
σ_r	0.750	0.738 (0.056)	0.743 (0.038)	0.748 (0.024)	0.723 (0.087)	0.736 (0.057)	0.746 (0.034)	0.617 (0.269)	0.672 (0.173)	0.721 (0.053)
		S.E: 0.053	S.E: 0.055	S.E: 0.056	S.E: 0.109	S.E: 0.076	S.E: 0.048	S.E: 1.407	S.E: 0.675	S.E: 0.087
$L(\theta)$ or $J(\theta)$		−385.76	−800.93	−2015.15	0.30	0.25	0.23	7.55	5.84	4.92

- The asymptotic efficiency of the ML estimation appears superior to MM, since the mean of standard errors over 1,000 estimations shows that the confidence intervals for the MM estimates are noticeably narrow. However, the large sample size remarkably improves the asymptotic efficiency of MM with 15 and 42 moments, for example, $T = 500$.
- It can be seen from the Monte Carlo results that the overall parameter uncertainty of MM with 42 moments is higher than ML and MM with 15 moments. However, in this case, MM with 42 moments can provide the most precise estimate on the price indexation parameter α. Note here that the accuracy of statistical inference for the behavior of economic agents (i.e., backward- or forward-looking) comes at the cost of allowing for large uncertainty in the estimates of other structural parameters; in other words, incorporating more second moments in the objective function improves the fit of the model to the persistence of inflation dynamics, but reduces efficiency in the other structural parameters.
- The results using MM with 42 moments show that we obtain the large asymptotic error for the policy shock parameter σ_r, that is, S.E $= 1.407$ for $T = 100$. This is attributed to the fact that the estimated values sometimes hit the boundary (i.e., $\sigma_r = 0.0$), which makes the numerical derivative of the moments unstable. This problem does not occur when the large sample size is used (e.g., $T = 500$).

Turning to the misspecified case, the results show that there is high correlation between the price indexation and AR (1) coefficient of the supply shocks (see Appendix G). Indeed, it is shown in Table G.1 that the AR (1) coefficient is strongly upward-biased for both MM and ML. The parameter estimates offset the effects of intrinsic persistence on the inflation dynamics, for example, $\rho_\pi = 0.616$ (ML), 0.632 (MM with 15 moments), 0.598 (MM with 42 moments) when the sample size is 100. The large sample size does not correct the bias of this parameter. Fortunately, the other structural parameters are not influenced by the model misspecification, that is, we obtain parameter estimates near to the true ones by using both MM and ML. They converge at some reasonable rate towards the true parameters as the sample size gets larger (consistency).

Similarly, the degree of the inflation shock σ_π is more or less downward-biased. In addition, the slope coefficient of the Phillips curve is upward-biased in ML, and the results of the MM estimation show very strong bias: $\hat{\kappa} = 0.096$ (ML), 0.176 (MM with 15 moments), 0.205 (MM with 42 moments) when $T = 100$. We can see that (strong) extrinsic and (moderate) inherited persistence offset the absence of intrinsic persistence from the model misspecification. When this result is contrasted by the correctly specified case, however, we obtain a relatively higher value for the estimated objective function: for example, $\hat{J} = 2.36$ (misspecifed) > 0.30 (correctly specified) for $T = 100$, MM with 15 moments. In other words, redirecting the intrinsic persistence to the inherited and extrinsic persistence is not satisfactory enough to provide a good approximation to the data. This is in line with our empirical findings in the previous section; the lagged terms in the NKPC and IS equation are empirically important.

Model Selection and Discussion

From the empirical investigation using MM with a large set of moments, we found that the statistical power of the model comparison test is weak and the result becomes inconclusive; in this case, we treat two models as being overlapping. Note here that we use the small sample to estimate the parameters of the NKM in which the asymptotic test of the model comparison is likely to make a Type II error, that is, we accept the null hypothesis when the equal fit of moments is false.[14]

To make the formal test more elaborate, we rank the model according to the well-known information criteria. For this purpose, we suppose that the parameter estimates using MM are to be a possible minimum point in the likelihood function. Tables 10 and 11 report the mean value for the log-likelihood and the model selection criterion: the cases of inflation and output persistence, respectively. Here we present MM with a small set of the moment conditions (auto- and cross-covariances at lag 1), because MM with alternative moments (auto- and cross-covariances at lag 4) yields the zero policy shock for the GI data.

According to AIC and BIC, by definition, we prefer the ML over the MM estimation with 15 moments for both GI and GM data. If the assumption of normality is not violated and the model is correctly specified, we can conclude that the ML estimation is the most efficient; this statistical inference is verified by the Monte Carlo study in the previous section. Nevertheless, the AIC and BIC of the MM estimation do not differ too much from the ML estimation; matching the auto- and cross-covariances at lag 1 can provide more or less the same efficiency as the likelihood inference. Also the statistical inference for the behavior of economic agents does not change, that is, the hybrid variant can approximate the dynamics in inflation and output better than the model with purely forward-looking behavior when fitting the GI data: for example, AIC $= 9.02$ (hybrid) < 9.90 (forward). On

Table 10.   Model Selection Using Information Criteria:
Inflation Persistence.

	GI ($T = 78$)			GM ($T = 99$)		
	ML	Hybrid	Forward	ML	Hybrid	Forward
$L(\theta)/T$	−3.96	−4.41	−4.82	−2.36	−2.69	−2.69
AIC	8.20	9.02	9.90	4.95	5.61	5.58
BIC	8.53	9.43	10.20	5.24	5.90	5.84
Ranking	1	2	3	1	3	2

Note: The backward- and forward-looking behaviors are examined using the MM estimation with auto- and cross-covariances at lag 1.

Table 11.   Model Selection Using Information Criteria:
Output Persistence.

	GI ($T = 78$)			GM ($T = 99$)		
	ML	Hybrid	Forward	ML	Hybrid	Forward
$L(\theta)/T$	−3.97	−4.62	−7.88	−2.34	−3.09	−4.22
AIC	8.22	9.51	16.01	4.91	6.41	8.64
BIC	8.55	9.85	16.31	5.19	6.69	8.90
Ranking	1	2	3	1	2	3

Note: The backward- and forward-looking behaviors are examined using the MM estimation with auto- and cross-covariances at lag 1.

the other hand, the inconclusive result using the GM data shows that the pricesetting rule without indexation to past inflation (or purely forward-looking) is preferred due to its parsimonious description of the data: that is, BIC = 5.90 (hybrid) > 5.84 (forward).

In Table 11, we have found essentially similar results for the output persistence; the results of the model comparison indicate that the backward-looking behavior in the IS equation is more appropriate for both GI and GM data. These exercises indicate that ML and MM have basically equivalent properties in statistical inference; they result in the same conclusion for the model comparison.[15] In other words, if the chosen moment conditions are efficient, we do not find significant difference between the ML and MM estimations. Nonetheless, the formal test of HMT serves as a convenient tool for evaluating the performance of the competing models;

since the data generating process is complex, we can attempt to find significant differences between two models along the lines of chosen moment conditions.

In addition, we can see from our empirical application that the moment-matching method achieves a high accuracy in taking the models to the data, but the parameter estimation becomes more uncertain than likelihood inference, that is, wide confidence intervals. Indeed, these empirical findings show the variations in the model selection for evaluating the effect of the lagged term on the NKPC and the IS equation. Moreover, in our empirical application, if we include additional second moments in the objective function, this improves the empirical performance of the two models, but will make the comparison between them inconclusive. The take-home message from this analysis is that the power of the test can decrease with a particular set of moment conditions.

CONCLUSION

This chapter considered the structural estimation of the NKM where we conducted a formal comparison of the model with purely forward-looking behavior and its hybrid variant. Especially, we examined the importance of the future expected and lagged values in the inflation and output dynamics using US data, that is, forward- and backward-looking behavior in the NKPC and the IS equation. The models are estimated by the classical estimation methods of MM and ML. In the former, we derived the analytic moments of the auto- and cross-covariances from a linear system of the NKM; we estimated the parameters by matching the model-generated moments with their empirical counterparts. These empirical findings are compared with the ML estimation while their sensitivity to the moment conditions is also examined.

According to the estimated loss function values obtained by MM, we evaluated two competing models using the formal test of HMT when they are overlapping or one model is nested within another. The empirical results show that the inclusion of a lagged term in the NKPC and the IS equation improves the model's empirical performance. In other words, the backward-looking behavior in the model plays an important role in approximating the persistence of inflation and output. This result suggests intrinsic persistence as the main source of the inflation and output dynamics in GI. However, in GM, we cannot reject the null hypothesis at 5% level, because the model with purely forward-looking expectations and its hybrid variant have an equal fit to the data. These empirical findings are verified using the Monte Carlo experiments; we investigated the statistical efficiency of the estimators and the implications for the model selection.

We close this chapter by pointing out that (analytic) moment conditions provide a relevant information about the data generating process, which can be used to estimate structural parameters in the model; from this, we can directly compare the competing specifications in the NKM using the formal test. Moreover, if the model does not have readily available expressions for moment conditions due to its nonlinear model structure, they can be replaced by an approximation based on simulations. For example, the model of De Grauwe (2011) connects the discrete choice theory to a monetary DSGE framework in which agents' belief can display endogenous waves of market optimism and pessimism. However, the nonlinear variant of the DSGE model does not have a simple closed-form expression for a VAR (q) process. If this is the case, the simulated method of moments can offer an empirical analysis of the model by approximating the nonlinearity in the moment conditions, for example, see Jang and Sacht (2012) regarding simulation based inference for the nonlinear group dynamics. Another example would be a DSGE model with recursive preference and stochastic volatility, see also Caldara Fernandez-Villaverde, Rubio-Ramirez, and Yao (2012) for the comparison of the solution methods. The nonlinearity from recursive preferences and stochastic volatility can be simply simulated and estimated via the moment conditions adopted in this chapter. We leave it to future research to empirically examine this kind of nonlinear models.

NOTES

1. Alternatively, the common and simple strategy to provide a quantitative assessment of inflation and output is to use a reduced form (or single equation) estimation, calibration, or simulation based inference (see also Gregory & Smith, 1991; Nason & Smith, 2008).

2. Smets and Wouters (2003, 2007) empirically examine a medium-scale version of the NKM. They estimate structural parameters and idiosyncratic shocks with the Bayesian techniques. In our study, however, we study a small-scale general equilibrium model and investigate the role of optimizing behavior in the dynamics of inflation and output.

3. Note here that we use the gaps instead of the levels for interest rate and inflation. Indeed, many empirical studies provide evidence for a time-varying trend in inflation and the natural rate of interest (see Castelnuovo, 2010; Cogley & Sbordone, 2008; Cogley, Primiceri, & Sargent, 2010). Moreover, the second moments are chosen to

match the data when we estimate the model parameters. As a result, if we would use the nonstationary data without making assumptions about the data generating process, it would cause substantial bias in parameter estimates of the structural model.

4. In the current study, we do not consider the presence of serially correlated shocks in the realizations of interest rate. It is assumed here that the shock persistence parameter of interest rate ρ_r is explained by its lagged term with the smoothing parameter φ_r. See also Carrillo, Féve, and Matheron (2007).

5. We also investigated the case where two extrinsic persistence are allowed in the model at the same time, that is, $\rho_\pi, \rho_x \neq 0$. But in this case we found unreliable parameter values, and the sources of persistence are not clearly identified. For example, in inflation persistence, the results of the model estimation indicate high degree of intrinsic persistence in the output dynamics ($\chi = 1.0$). This effect will enter into the Phillips curve, and eventually have influence on the inflation dynamics. If the model allows for extrinsic persistence in the supply shock ($\rho_x \neq 0$), then the effect of intrinsic persistence from the output will be offset by extrinsic persistence, and will affect the intrinsic persistence in inflation. These make it inherently difficult to provide a distinct analysis on the identification of the sources of persistence in the model. Therefore we decide to separately consider the AR (1) shocks in inflation and output.

6. The objective function in Eq. (10) is multiplied by the sample size T, since this gives an asymptotic χ^2 test statistic for testing the null hypothesis that the moment conditions hold, that is, the model misspecification.

7. The lag order is chosen following a simple rule of thumb for sample size ($\sim T^{1/4}$). For the GI and GM data, we have 78 and 99 quarterly observations respectively. Therefore k is set to 5.

8. If the weight matrix is chosen optimally ($\hat{W} = \Sigma_m^{-1}$), the estimated covariance matrix Λ becomes $(DWD')^{-1}$ (see Anatolyev & Gospodinov, 2011, Chap. 1), among others. However, in our study, the estimated confidence bands become wider, because the weighting scheme in the objective function is not optimal.

9. Appendix E presents intermediate steps for simulating the QLR distribution. The theoretical QLR distribution is derived from the mean value expansion to a binding function (or moment conditions).

10. We also investigated the likelihood ratio test between the model with purely forward-looking behavior and its hybrid variant. However, we found that its likelihood value does not differ too much, because the model with purely forward-looking behavior does not make a drastic change in the parameter estimates. In this case, the formal test based on the likelihood function is not effective. We do not report these results to save space.

11. Indeed, likelihood inference would avoid such an estimate provided that there is a stochastic singularity with zero policy shock (i.e., the likelihood value becomes negative infinity at this point).

12. The estimated value for the parameter σ_r hit the boundary. This makes the objective function ill-behaved and partial derivatives numerically unstable. We set it to zero and compute the numerical derivatives of the other parameters for the model comparison. See Appendix D for the matrix notation.

13. This statistical inference does not remain the same if the price indexation parameter is allowed to exceed unity. The constraint on habit formation parameter (χ) is also removed. See Franke et al. (2011) for details.

14. Marmer and Otsu (2012) discuss the general optimality of comparison of misspecified models and propose a feasible approximation to the optimal test, which is more powerful than Rivers and Vuong (2002).

15. However, remember that according to the formal test of HMT, the better fit of the hybrid variant is not significantly superior to the other model when the GM data is used. In this sense, the model comparison of HMT is more concerned with a direct comparison between the models rather than the accuracy of the approximation to the underlying data generating process.

16. We use the built-in procedures gradp and hessp in the GAUSS software package. The optimal step size for the gradient vector and the Hessian matrix is carefully adjusted, because difference approximations is likely to be imprecise provided that the first derivative is small. See Gill, Murray, and Wright (1981, Chap. 4, pp. 127–133) for the choice of the finite-difference interval.

ACKNOWLEDGMENTS

This chapter was presented at the seminars in CAU and the 10th Annual *Advances in Econometrics* Conference at SMU. I have benefited from discussions with Reiner Franke, Ivan Jeliazkov, Roman Liesenfeld, Thomas Lux, Vadim Marmer, Fabio Milani and Stephen Sacht. I also express my gratitude to all the participants for their active involvement in the conference. The support from the German Academic Exchange Service (DAAD) and the Möller fund from CAU is greatly acknowledged.

REFERENCES

Altonji, J., & Segal, L. (1996). Small-sample bias in GMM estimation of covariance structures. *Journal of Business and Economic Statistics, 14*, 353–366.

Amato, J. D., & Laubach, T. (2003). Rule-of-thumb behaviour and monetary policy. *European Economic Review, 47*(5), 791–831.

Amato, J. D., & Laubach, T. (2004). Implications of habit formation for optimal monetary policy. *Journal of Monetary Economics, 51*, 305–325.

Anatolyev, S., & Gospodinov, N. (2011). *Methods for estimation and inference in modern econometrics*. New York, NY: A Chapman and Hall Book.

Binder, M., & Pesaran, H. (1995). Multivariate rational expectations models and macroeconomic modeling: A review and some insights. In M. H. Pesaran & M. Wickens (Eds.), *Handbook of applied econometrics* (pp. 139–187). Oxford: Basil Blackwell.

Caldara, D., Fernandez-Villaverde, J., Rubio-Ramirez, J., & Yao, W. (2012). Computing DSGE models with recursive preferences and stochastic volatility. *Review of Economic Dynamics, 15*(2), 188–206.

Canova, F., & Sala, L. (2009). Back to square one: Identification issues in DSGE models. *Journal of Monetary Economics, 56*(4), 431–449.

Carrillo, J. A., Féve, P., & Matheron, J. (2007). Monetary policy inertia or persistent shocks: A DSGE analysis. *International Journal of Central Banking, 3*(2), 1–38.

Castelnuovo, E. (2010). Trend inflation and macroeconomic volatilities in the Post WWII U.S. economy. *North American Journal of Economics and Finance, 21,* 19–33.

Christiano, L., Eichenbaum, M., & Evans, C. (2005). Nominal rigidities and the dynamic effects of a shock to monetary policy. *Journal of Political Economy, 113*(1), 1–45.

Coenen, G. (2005). Asymptotic confidence bands for the estimated autocovariance and autocorrelation functions of vector autoregressive models. *Empirical Economics, 30*(1), 65–75.

Cogley, T., Primiceri, G. E., & Sargent, T. J. (2010). Inflation-gap persistence in the US. *American Economic Journal: Macroeconomics, 2*(1), 43–69.

Cogley, T., & Sbordone, A. (2008). Trend inflation, indexation, and inflation persistence in the New-Keynesian Phillips curve. *American Economic Review, 98*(5), 2101–2126.

De Grauwe, P. (2011). Animal spirits and monetary policy. *Economic Theory, 47,* 423–457.

Dridi, R., Guay, A., & Renault, E. (2007). Indirect inference and calibration of dynamic stochastic general equilibrium models. *Journal of Econometrics, 136*(2), 397–430.

Franke, R., Jang, T.-S., & Sacht, S. (2011). *Moment matching versus Bayesian estimation: backward-looking behaviour in the New-Keynesian three-equations model.* Economic Working Paper No. 2011-10, University of Kiel.

Fuhrer, J. C. (1997). The (un)importance of forward-looking behavior in price specifications. *Journal of Money, Credit and Banking, 29*(3), 338–350.

Fuhrer, J. C. (2000). Habit formation in consumption and its implications for monetary policy models. *American Economic Review, 90*(3), 367–390.

Galí, J., & Gertler, M. (1999). Inflation dynamics: A structural econometric analysis. *Journal of Monetary Economics, 44,* 195–222.

Gill, P., Murray, W., & Wright, M. (1981). *Practical optimization.* New York: Academic Press.

Golden, R. M. (2000). Statistical tests for comparing possibly misspecified and nonnested models. *Journal of Mathematical Psychology, 44,* 153–170.

Golden, R. M. (2003). Discrepancy risk model selection test theory for comparing possibly misspecified or nonnested models. *Psychometrika, 68*(2), 229–249.

Gourieroux, C., & Monfort, A. (1995). Testing, encompassing and simulating dynamic econometric models. *Econometric Theory, 11,* 195–228.

Gregory, A. W., & Smith, G. W. (1991). Calibration as testing: Inference in simulated macroeconomic models. *Journal of Business and Economic Statistics, 9*(3), 297–303.

Hall, A.R., Inoue, A., Nason, J. M., & Rossi, B. (2012). Information criteria for impulse response function matching estimation of DSGE models. *Journal of Econometrics, 170*(2), 499–518.

Hnatkovska, V., Marmer, V., & Tang, Y. (2012). Comparison of misspecified calibrated models: The minimum distance approach. *Journal of Econometrics, 169*(1), 131–138.

Ireland, P. N. (2004). A method for taking models to the data. *Journal of Economic Dynamics and Control, 28,* 1205–1226.

Jang, T.-S., & Sacht, S. (2012). *Identification of animal spirits in a bounded rationality model: An application to the Euro area.* MPRA Paper No. 37399. University Library of Munich, Germany.

Lindé, J. (2005). Estimating New-Keynesian Phillips curves: A full information maximum likelihood approach. *Journal of Monetary Economics, 52,* 1135–1149.

Linhart, H., & Zucchini, W. (1986). *Model selection.* New York, NY: Wiley.

Marmer, V., & Otsu, T. (2012). Optimal comparison of misspecified moment restriction models under a chosen measure of fit. *Journal of Econometrics*, *170*(2), 538–550.

Nason, J. M., & Smith, G. W. (2008). Identifying the New Keynesian Phillips curve. *Journal of Applied Econometrics*, *23*, 525–551.

Newey, W., & West, K. (1987). A simple positive semi-definite, heteroskedasticity and autocorrelation consistent covariance matrix. *Econometrica*, *55*, 703–708.

Rabanala, P., & Rubio-Ramirezb, J. F. (2005). Comparing New Keynesian models of the business cycle: A Bayesian approach. *Journal of Monetary Economics*, *52*(6), 1151–1166.

Rivers, D., & Vuong, Q. (2002). Model selection tests for nonlinear dynamic models. *Econometrics Journal*, *5*, 1–39.

Rotemberg, J., & Woodford, M. (1997). An optimization-based econometric framework for the evaluation of monetary policy. *NBER Macroeconomics Annual*, Cambridge, MA: MIT Press.

Rudd, J., & Whelan, K. (2005). New tests of the New-Keynesian Phillips curve. *Journal of Monetary Economics*, *52*, 1167–1181.

Rudd, J., & Whelan, K. (2006). Can rational expectations sticky-price models explain inflation dynamics. *American Economic Review*, *96*(1), 303–320.

Smets, F., & Wouters, R. (2003). An estimated stochastic dynamic general equilibrium model of the Euro area. *Journal of European Economic Association*, *1*(5), 1123–1175.

Smets, F., & Wouters, R. (2005). Comparing shocks and frictions in US and Euro area business cycles: A Bayesian DSGE approach. *Journal of Applied Econometrics*, *20*(2), 161–183.

Smets, F., & Wouters, R. (2007). Shocks and frictions in US business cycles: A Bayesian DSGE approach. *American Economic Review*, *97*(3), 586–606.

Vuong, Q. (1989). Likelihood ratio tests for model selection and non-nested hypotheses. *Econometrica*, *57*(2), 307–333.

Woodford, M. (2003). *Interest and prices: Foundations of a theory of monetary policy*. Princeton, NJ: Princeton University Press.

APPENDIX A: CHOICE OF MOMENTS

A.1 Auto- and Cross-Covariances at Lag 1 (One Quarter): 15 Moment Conditions

This section lists the moment conditions for the method of moment estimation. The auto- and cross-covariances at lag 1 include the following 15 moment conditions after removing double counting of the interest gap ($\hat{r}_t$), the output gap (x_t), and the inflation gap ($\hat{\pi}_t$).

1. m_1: Var ($\hat{r}_t$)
2. m_2: Cov ($\hat{r}_t$, $\hat{r}_{t-1}$)
3. m_3: Cov ($\hat{r}_t$, x_t)
4. m_4: Cov ($\hat{r}_t$, x_{t-1})
5. m_5: Cov ($\hat{r}_t$, $\hat{\pi}_t$)
6. m_6: Cov ($\hat{r}_t$, $\hat{\pi}_{t-1}$)
7. m_7: Cov (x_t, $\hat{r}_{t-1}$)
8. m_8: Var (x_t)
9. m_9: Cov (x_t, x_{t-1})
10. m_{10}: Cov (x_t, $\hat{\pi}_t$)
11. m_{11}: Cov (x_t, $\hat{\pi}_{t-1}$)
12. m_{12}: Cov ($\hat{\pi}_t$, x_{t-1})
13. m_{13}: Cov ($\hat{\pi}_t$, $\hat{r}_{t-1}$)
14. m_{14}: Var ($\hat{\pi}_t$)
15. m_{15}: Cov ($\hat{\pi}_t$, $\hat{\pi}_{t-1}$)

A.2 Auto- and Cross-Covariances at Lag 4 (One Year): 42 Moment Conditions

In the same vein, there are nine profiles of the sample covariance functions. Counting all the combination of three observable variables gives 42 moment conditions for the auto- and cross-covariances at lag 4. To save space, we abstract its list here by using the following notation:

$$\text{Cov}(u_t, v_{t-h}), \quad u\&v = \hat{r}_t, x_t, \hat{\pi}_t \qquad (A.1)$$

where h denotes the lag length used in the auto- and cross-covariances ($h = 0, 1, 2, 3, 4$).

APPENDIX B: REDUCED FORM OF MATRIX AND SOLUTION OF THE NKM

In this section we give a description of the matrix notation in Eq. (3) and the solution procedure for the system of the NKM. The matrices of A, B, C and N with $y_t = (\hat{\pi}_t, x_t, \hat{r}_t)'$ are defined as follows:

$$A = \begin{bmatrix} 0 & 0 & \dfrac{\beta}{1+\alpha\beta} \\ 0 & \dfrac{1}{1+\chi} & \tau \\ 0 & 0 & 0 \end{bmatrix}, \quad B = \begin{bmatrix} 0 & \kappa & -1 \\ -\tau & -1 & 0 \\ -1 & (1-\varphi_r)\varphi_x & (1-\varphi_r)\varphi_\pi \end{bmatrix}$$

$$C = \begin{bmatrix} 0 & 0 & \dfrac{\alpha}{1+\alpha\beta} \\ 0 & \dfrac{\chi}{1+\chi} & 0 \\ \varphi_r & 0 & 0 \end{bmatrix}, \quad N = \begin{bmatrix} 0 & 0 & \rho_\pi \\ 0 & \rho_x & 0 \\ 0 & 0 & 0 \end{bmatrix}$$

Using Eq. (4), we redefine the vector of observable variables y_t as terms of one-period-ahead.

$$\begin{aligned} y_{t+1} &= \Omega y_t + \Phi v_{t+1} \\ &= \Omega(\Omega y_{t-1} + \Phi v_t) + \Phi(N v_t + \varepsilon_{t+1}) \\ &= \Omega^2 y_{t-1} + (\Omega\Phi + \Phi N)v_t + \Phi\varepsilon_{t+1} \end{aligned} \tag{B.1}$$

Substitute Eqs. (B.1) and (4) into the canonical form of Eq. (3).

$$E_t[A\Omega^2 y_{t-1} + A(\Omega\Phi + \Phi N)v_t + A\Phi\varepsilon_{t+1} + B\Omega y_{t-1} + B\Phi v_t + Cy_{t-1} + v_t] = 0 \tag{B.2}$$

Drop the expectation and rearrange things.

$$(A\Omega^2 + B\Omega + C)y_{t-1} + (A\Omega\Phi + A\Phi N + B\Phi + I_n)v_t = 0, \quad \text{where } n = 3 \tag{B.3}$$

This implies that the following equations must hold for all y_{t-1} and v_t.

$$A\Omega^2 + B\Omega + C = 0$$
$$(A\Omega + B)\Phi + A\Phi N + I_n = 0 \tag{B.4}$$

An iterative method can provide the solution of the matrix Ω. The matrix Φ can be obtained by using some matrix algebra, that is, the solution of the Lyapunov equation.

APPENDIX C: VAR LAG ORDER SELECTION

In our study, a VAR (q) model describes the relationship between the empirical auto- and cross-covariances of interest rate, inflation and output. We employ the model of a K-dimensional multiple times series $y_t := (y_{1t}, \ldots, y_{Kt})'$ following Lütkepohl (2005):

$$y_t = v + A_1 y_{t-1} + \cdots + A_q y_{t-1} + u_t \qquad (C.1)$$

where v is a fixed $(K \times 1)$ vector of intercept, and u_t is a K-dimensional innovation process with $E(u_t) = 0$, $E(u_t u_t') = \Sigma_u$. The matrices A_i include fixed $(K \times K)$ coefficients. The following lag order selection criteria are considered in Table C1: final prediction error (FPE), Akaike information criterion (AIC), Hannan-Quinn information criterion (HQ), Bayesian information criterion (BIC). The chosen lag order for both periods is one year (VAR (4)).

Table C1. VAR Lag Order Selection Criteria.

	GI				GM			
Lag	FPE	AIC	HQ	BIC	FPE	AIC	HQ	BIC
0	14931.714	9.534	9.534	9.534	8926.601	9.036	9.036	9.036
1	194.525	5.309	5.302	5.466	205.437	5.554	5.558	5.699
2	106.200	4.822	4.805	5.137	112.227	4.843	4.851	5.136
3	24.202	3.462	3.435	3.936	26.806	3.505	3.515	3.945
4	1.136	0.522*	0.482*	1.156*	1.696	0.839*	0.851*	1.427*
5	1.058	0.569	0.515	1.365	1.759	0.970	0.983	1.708
6	0.944*	0.571	0.501	1.528	2.094	1.238	1.251	2.127
7	0.970	0.709	0.620	1.830	1.611	1.068	1.081	2.110
8	1.050	0.893	0.783	2.177	1.563*	1.129	1.139	2.324

Note: The star (*) indicates an optimal lag length.

APPENDIX D: MATRIX NOTATION

This section gives a matrix notation for the derivative of the moment conditions. This notation is used to implement the procedures for the model comparison of HMT; see Appendix E. Let $m(\theta)$ be a m_n by 1 vector. The parameter vector θ has a dimension of n_θ^I. The gradient matrix $\partial m(\theta)/\partial \theta'$ has dimension $m_{m_n} \times n_\theta^I$. The second derivative matrix $\partial/\partial \theta^{I'} \text{vec}(\partial m^I(\theta^I)/\partial \theta^{I'})$ has dimension $m_{m_n} \cdot n_\theta^I \times n_\theta^I$

$$\frac{\partial m(\theta)}{\partial \theta'} = \begin{bmatrix} \dfrac{\partial m_1}{\partial \theta_1} & \dfrac{\partial m_1}{\partial \theta_2} & \cdots & \dfrac{\partial m_1}{\partial \theta_{n_\theta^I}} \\[2ex] \dfrac{\partial m_2}{\partial \theta_1} & \dfrac{\partial m_2}{\partial \theta_2} & \cdots & \dfrac{\partial m_2}{\partial \theta_{n_\theta^I}} \\[2ex] \vdots & \vdots & \cdots & \vdots \\[2ex] \dfrac{\partial m_{m_n}}{\partial \theta_1} & \dfrac{\partial m_{m_n}}{\partial \theta_2} & \cdots & \dfrac{\partial m_{m_n}}{\partial \theta_{n_\theta^I}} \end{bmatrix}.$$

$$\frac{\partial}{\partial \theta^{I'}} \text{vec}\left(\frac{\partial m^I(\theta^I)}{\partial \theta^{I'}}\right) = \begin{bmatrix} \dfrac{\partial m_1}{\partial \theta_1 \partial \theta_1} & \dfrac{\partial m_1}{\partial \theta_1 \partial \theta_2} & \cdots & \dfrac{\partial m_1}{\partial \theta_1 \partial \theta_{n_\theta^I}} \\[2ex] \vdots & \vdots & \ddots & \vdots \\[2ex] \dfrac{\partial m_{m_n}}{\partial \theta_1 \partial \theta_1} & \dfrac{\partial m_{m_n}}{\partial \theta_1 \partial \theta_2} & \cdots & \dfrac{\partial m_{m_n}}{\partial \theta_1 \partial \theta_{n_\theta^I}} \\[2ex] \dfrac{\partial m_1}{\partial \theta_2 \partial \theta_1} & \dfrac{\partial m_1}{\partial \theta_2 \partial \theta_2} & \cdots & \dfrac{\partial m_1}{\partial \theta_2 \partial \theta_{n_\theta^I}} \\[2ex] \vdots & \vdots & \ddots & \vdots \\[2ex] \dfrac{\partial m_{m_n}}{\partial \theta_2 \partial \theta_1} & \dfrac{\partial m_{m_n}}{\partial \theta_2 \partial \theta_2} & \cdots & \dfrac{\partial m_{m_n}}{\partial \theta_2 \partial \theta_{n_\theta^I}} \\[2ex] \vdots & \vdots & \ddots & \vdots \\[2ex] \vdots & \vdots & \ddots & \vdots \\[2ex] \dfrac{\partial m_1}{\partial \theta_{n_\theta^I} \partial \theta_1} & \dfrac{\partial m_1}{\partial \theta_{n_\theta^I} \partial \theta_2} & \cdots & \dfrac{\partial m_1}{\partial \theta_{n_\theta^I} \partial \theta_{n_\theta^I}} \\[2ex] \vdots & \vdots & \ddots & \vdots \\[2ex] \dfrac{\partial m_{m_n}}{\partial \theta_{n_\theta^I} \partial \theta_1} & \dfrac{\partial m_{m_n}}{\partial \theta_{n_\theta^I} \partial \theta_2} & \cdots & \dfrac{\partial m_{m_n}}{\partial \theta_{n_\theta^I} \partial \theta_{n_\theta^I}} \end{bmatrix}.$$

APPENDIX E: TECHNICAL NOTE ON THE MODEL COMPARISON METHOD

This section recapitulates the equations for the model comparison method of HMT. Assume that model B is nested within model A. The quantitative goodness-of-fit of models to data is evaluated using the MM in section "Method of Moment and Model Comparison: HMT (2012)." The "full" model is tested against the "restricted" model.

Let m_T be a n_m vector of moments. $\hat{m}(\theta)$ is the consistent estimator of m_T. The uncertainty of moment estimates is assessed by estimating a Newey-West type weighted sum of autocovariance matrices ($\hat{\Sigma}_m$). Given the assumption of normality, we can consistently estimate the covariance matrix of moment conditions.

$$\sqrt{T}(m_T - \hat{m}(\theta)) \underset{d}{\to} N(0, \hat{\Sigma}_m) \tag{E.1}$$

The estimates $\hat{\theta}^I$ are obtained at the point where a weighted objective function is minimized:

$$J(\theta^I) \equiv \min_{\theta^I \in \Theta} T \parallel W^{1/2}(\hat{m}_T - m^I(\hat{\theta}^I)) \parallel^2, \quad I = A, B \tag{E.2}$$

$\parallel W^{1/2}(\hat{m}_T - m^I(\hat{\theta}^I)) \parallel$ is defined as $\sqrt{(\hat{m}_T - m^I(\hat{\theta}))' W(\hat{m}_T - m^I(\hat{\theta}))}$. The weight matrix W is set to the diagonal components of $1/\hat{\Sigma}_{m,ii}$ ($ii = 1, \ldots, n_m$). The quasi-likelihood ratio test statistic is constructed as the difference in fits between two models:

$$\text{QLR}(\hat{\theta}^B, \hat{\theta}^A) = J^B(\hat{\theta}^B) - J^A(\hat{\theta}^A) \tag{E.3}$$

J^I ($I = A, B$) is a minimum value of the objective function given parameter estimates from Eq. (E.2). It is assumed that the chosen moment functions in the models are twice continuously differentiable in neighborhoods of $\theta^I \subset \Theta^{n_\theta^I}$. Further, the matrix F and M are non-singular in neighborhoods of θ[16]:

$$F^I = \frac{\partial m^I(\theta^I)'}{\partial \theta^I} W \frac{\partial m^I(\theta^I)}{\partial \theta^{I'}} - M^I \tag{E.4}$$

$$M^I = (E_I \otimes (\hat{m}_T - m^I(\theta^I))' W) \frac{\partial}{\partial \theta^{I'}} \text{vec}\left(\frac{\partial m^I(\theta^I)}{\partial \theta^{I'}}\right) \quad I = A, B \tag{E.5}$$

E_I is the identity matrix of which dimension is $n_\theta^I \times n_\theta^I$. Note here that the dimensions of the matrices $\partial m^I(\theta^I)/\partial \theta^{I'}$ and $\partial/\partial \theta^{I'} \text{vec}(\partial m^I(\theta^I)/\partial \theta^{I'})$ are $n_m \times n_\theta^I$ and $n_m \cdot n_\theta^I \times n_\theta^I$. The dimension of F^I and M^I are n_θ^I by n_θ^I.

The theorem 3.1 in HMT states that the quasi-likelihood ratio test. QLR converges in distribution to Equation (18). The n_θ^I by n_θ^I matrix V^I is defined as $V^I = V_1^I - V_2^I - V_3^I$ with $I = A, B$:

$$V_1^I = \frac{\partial m^I(\theta^I)}{\partial \theta^{I\prime}}(F^{I\prime})^{-1}\frac{\partial m^I(\theta^I)\prime}{\partial \theta^I}W\frac{\partial m^I(\theta^I)}{\partial \theta^{I\prime}}(F^I)^{-1}\frac{\partial m^I(\theta^I)\prime}{\partial \theta^I}$$

$$V_2^I = \frac{\partial m^I(\theta^I)}{\partial \theta^{I\prime}}((F^{I\prime})^{-1} + (F^I)^{-1})\frac{\partial m^I(\theta^I)\prime}{\partial \theta^I}$$

$$V_3^I = \frac{\partial m^I(\theta^I)}{\partial \theta^{I\prime}}(F^{I\prime})^{-1}(M^{I\prime} + M^I)(F^I)^{-1}\frac{\partial m^I(\theta^I)\prime}{\partial \theta^I}$$

However, it is sometimes observed that the estimated $\hat{V}_B - \hat{V}_A$ is not a positive-definite matrix where some negative values are drawn in simulations. We should not discard the negative values of the test distribution when making statistical inference for the model comparison. The hypothesis test is assessed by critical values at the 1% and 5% confidence level (Q_{99}, Q_{95}) from the simulated asymptotic test distribution. When one model is nested within another, one rejects the null hypothesis at 5% level that two models are equivalent if $QLR(\hat{\theta}_A, \hat{\theta}_B) > Q_{95}$.

APPENDIX F: SIMULATED QLR DISTRIBUTION FOR MODEL COMPARISON

F.1 Auto- and Cross-Covariances at Lag 1: 15 Moment Conditions

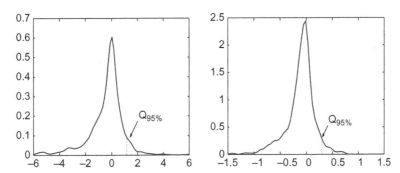

Fig. F.1.1. Test Distribution for Inflation Persistence: GI (left) and GM (right).

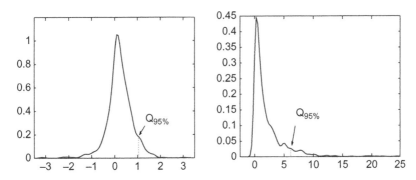

Fig. F.1.2. Test Distribution for Output Persistence: GI (left) and GM (right).

F.2 Auto- and Cross-Covariances at Lag 4: 42 Moment Conditions

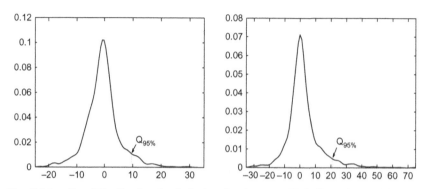

Fig. F.2.1.   Test Distribution for Inflation Persistence: GI (left) and GM (right).

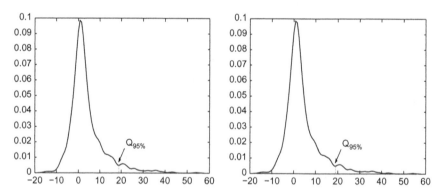

Fig. F.2.2.   Test Distribution for Output. Persistence: GI (left) and GM (right).

APPENDIX G: THE MONTE CARLO RESULT OF THE MISSPECIFIED CASE

Table G.1. Monte Carlo Results on the MM and ML Estimates of the Misspecified Model, ( ): Root Mean Square Error, S.E: Mean of Standard Errors.

	θ^0	ML			MM with 15 Moments			MM with 42 Moments		
		$T = 100$	$T = 200$	$T = 500$	$T = 100$	$T = 200$	$T = 500$	$T = 100$	$T = 200$	$T = 500$
κ	0.050	0.096 (0.186)	0.089 (0.212)	0.077 (0.031)	0.176 (0.140)	0.168 (0.125)	0.163 (0.118)	0.205 (0.175)	0.191 (0.152)	0.182 (0.136)
ρ_π	0.000	0.616 (0.621)	0.618 (0.620)	0.617 (0.618)	0.632 (0.635)	0.646 (0.647)	0.653 (0.654)	0.598 (0.604)	0.614 (0.617)	0.623 (0.624)
σ_π	0.675	0.491 (0.293)	0.487 (0.330)	0.474 (0.205)	0.560 (0.151)	0.543 (0.150)	0.531 (0.654)	0.661 (0.164)	0.633 (0.127)	0.612 (0.098)
χ	1.000	0.921 (0.132)	0.938 (0.100)	0.955 (0.066)	0.981 (0.053)	0.994 (0.020)	0.999 (0.015)	0.970 (0.083)	0.986 (0.047)	0.997 (0.014)
τ	0.090	0.085 (0.032)	0.085 (0.024)	0.085 (0.015)	0.089 (0.029)	0.086 (0.021)	0.084 (0.014)	0.088 (0.035)	0.083 (0.024)	0.080 (0.017)
σ_x	0.700	0.688 (0.064)	0.691 (0.046)	0.694 (0.026)	0.637 (0.123)	0.636 (0.103)	0.636 (0.082)	0.654 (0.132)	0.644 (0.106)	0.639 (0.083)
φ_π	1.650	1.667 (0.182)	1.657 (0.118)	1.657 (0.075)	1.691 (0.182)	1.681 (0.117)	1.679 (0.075)	1.848 (0.291)	1.783 (0.203)	1.775 (0.156)
φ_x	0.375	0.352 (0.127)	0.352 (0.085)	0.356 (0.054)	0.227 (0.211)	0.227 (0.203)	0.226 (0.164)	0.315 (0.282)	0.238 (0.197)	0.237 (0.166)
φ_r	0.550	0.540 (0.049)	0.541 (0.035)	0.356 (0.054)	0.488 (0.086)	0.487 (0.077)	0.489 (0.067)	0.527 (0.070)	0.524 (0.053)	0.525 (0.038)
σ_r	0.750	0.738 (0.056)	0.743 (0.039)	0.748 (0.024)	0.733 (0.101)	0.744 (0.069)	0.756 (0.043)	0.597 (0.313)	0.616 (0.244)	0.649 (0.164)
$L(\theta)$ or $J(\theta)$		−398.38	−805.68	−2026.45	2.36	3.46	6.95	24.22	29.36	49.73

Note: The misspecified model does not include the parameter α in the NKPC. To save space, we do not report the asymptotic standard errors for the parameter estimates, because these are not qualitatively different from the correctly specified case.